# DECISION MAKING AND THE THEORY OF THE FIRM

# DECISION MAKING AND THE THEORY OF THE FIRM

Ira Horowitz
Graduate School of Business, Indiana University



HOLT, RINEHART AND WINSTON, INC.

New York Chicago San Francisco Atlanta
Dallas Montreal Toronto London Sydney

Library of Congress Catalog Card Number: 70-94345
**SBN: 03-083034-6**
Printed in the United States of America
1 2 3 4 5 6 7 8 9

To Bob, Pat, and Nancy.

# PREFACE

This book has a good many pages of verbal text, mathematics, exercises, and footnotes. The verbal text attempts to discuss some of the decision-making tools that economics and operations research can offer management; the mathematics attempts to make microeconomic theory richer and to contribute to a better understanding of the scope, limitations, and level of sophistication of these decision-making tools; the exercises attempt to raise a few doubts and solidify comprehension of basic material; and, while a few of the footnotes attempt to qualify the text, the vast majority are intended to indicate the sources from which much of the above was "borrowed." The latter remark itself requires two qualifications. First, the name Robert L. Bishop appears quite often, but, as those others who have been privileged to have had access to Professor Bishop's famed manuscript will quickly recognize, not often enough. Second, the names of Professors David Baron and Gary Roodman do not appear at all. The omission was intentional, for their contributions to the manuscript were so great—both in terms of discussions which helped me to understand my own material and discussions which helped me to understand their research on uncertainty and the theory of the firm—that I could not bear to see mention of them buried and perhaps lost in a morass of unread references.

I am most grateful to Professor Albert J. Simone and Mr. Seibert Adams for originally suggesting, and ultimately convincing me to write, this book. Before that we were all friends. I am also grateful to Professors Maurice Desplas, Lawrence Jones, Edward Kane, Jerry Pogue, and particularly to my Indiana University colleagues—A. Victor Cabot, Ann R. Horowitz, and Robert L. Winkler—for reading, criticizing, and correcting earlier drafts. I alone am to blame for the resulting product (but if there is to be any credit, Ann R. has more than earned a share).

Bloomington, Indiana —I. H.
December 1969

# CONTENTS

# 1

# THE NATURE AND PURPOSES OF MICROECONOMIC MODELS

## 1.1 INTRODUCTION

There has been a traditional if narrowing gap between the body of thought comprising the neoclassical theory of the firm and the behavior of the modern corporation seeking to survive, grow, and prosper in the world in which most of us, eschewing the uncertainties of the alternatives, prefer to live. A partial explanation for this narrowing is that increasing numbers of economists are finding it respectable, if not profitable, to proffer solutions to the decision-making, as well as to the forecasting, problems facing the firm; and managers in increasing numbers are reciprocating by recognizing that economists may indeed have something to contribute in this direction. A second explanation for this narrowing stems from rapid developments in the areas of operations research, management science, and econometrics that have made it feasible to extend, expand, and give practical expression to a theory that for some serves mainly as a logical exercise and focal point for interesting academic debate.

This book explores some of the theory, extensions, and techniques that have helped to bridge the gap between neoclassical price theory and managerial decision making. The content is best classified as "managerial economics"—the study of economic decisions in the modern firm from a management science viewpoint.[1] The primary concern will therefore be the development of *quantitative* models and techniques for decision making and the analysis of decision making in the firm.

## 1.2 MODEL BUILDING IN GENERAL

A model is a representation of, or an abstraction from, reality. The globe on my desk is a physical model of the planet earth. The globe does not capture each and

[1] The scope of managerial economics is sufficiently broad and vague to admit the contents of a basic text in statistics, as well as the contents of an introductory text in economics of industry and econometrics with applications to problems of industry. The former is Robert Schlaifer's *Probability and Statistics for Business Decisions* (New York: McGraw-Hill, Inc., 1959), subtitled *An Introduction to Managerial Economics Under Uncertainty;* the latter is Milton Spencer's *Managerial Economics: Text, Problems, and Short Cases* (Homewood, Ill.: Richard D. Irwin, Inc., 1967).

every nuance of the earth's surface. Nonetheless, it does make it clear that by heading west from Barcelona an explorer will eventually encounter India. Similarly, suppose the economist is interested in exploring the monthly purchases of nationally advertised brands of frozen orange juice concentrate as opposed to purchases of nonadvertised brands. The economist's suspicion that the most important factor affecting relative purchases of concentrate brands is their relative prices may lead him to construct, and draw his inferences from, a chart presenting a history of relative prices and the associated purchases. Like many an explorer before him, he too will have placed his faith in a graphical model.

As a more sophisticated approach to the concentrate problem, the economist might proceed as follows. Denote by $Q_{1t}$ and $Q_{2t}$ the number of ounces of nationally advertised and nonadvertised concentrate sold in month $t$; further, let $P_{1t}$ and $P_{2t}$ denote the average price of the respective concentrates in cents per ounce in month $t$. Then, utilizing historical data in conjunction with special statistical techniques that will be introduced in later chapters, the equation

$$\frac{Q_{1t}}{Q_{2t}} = 17.4 \left(\frac{P_{1t}}{P_{2t}}\right)^{-1.6} P_{2t}^{-1.0} t^{-0.3}$$

illustrates an actual model that has been developed to help explain relative purchases of advertised to nonadvertised concentrates.[2] As in the case of the graph, this model undoubtedly overlooks factors such as quality and income that may influence the ratio, but the equation does point out the inverse relationship between the quantity and price ratios, and through the $t^{-0.3}$ factor points up the trend towards nonadvertised concentrate, given constant prices. That is, $Q_{1t}/Q_{2t}$ is lower the greater is $P_{1t}/P_{2t}$, or the greater is $t$, the other variables held constant.

A model does not attempt to represent reality in minute detail, for then we would have reality itself and not a model. Rather, the quest for knowledge about a system encourages one first to attempt a simplified verbal description of it. This, in turn, can lead to the construction of a physical analogue, such as a globe, or a mathematical statement, such as the concentrate equation, to provide an idealized representation capturing the heart of reality. Thus, building a model initially entails problem, system, or process formulation. Then, through a series of simplifying assumptions, one reformulates the situation so as to capture its essence and depict it within a tractable setting.

Model building can take place at several different levels of sophistication and with varying degrees of awareness and consideration of the institutional setting of the system being modeled. A model uses a set of hopefully well-chosen assumptions to strip a complex problem down to its barest essentials in order to simplify its resolution. The model can be *normative* and, based on a priori standards, indicate how a system *should* behave in an idealized world conforming to these standards, or it can be *descriptive* and indicate how a system under consideration actually *does* behave. If the model succeeds in capturing the essence of the system under scrutiny and the problem to be resolved, a careful analysis of it should yield prescriptions that will be applicable to the problem itself.

In effect all model building is initiated at the *verbal* level with a statement of the problem. Suppose the issue is the determination of the profit-maximizing output level

[2] Harold Demsetz, "The Effect of Consumer Experience on Brand Loyalty and the Structure of Market Demand," *Econometrica*, **30**:1 (Jan. 1962), 24–25.

of a single-product, single-production-process firm for the coming production period. The firm's decisions are made by a single entrepreneur, an owner-manager. The entrepreneur makes a considered judgment with respect to the price at which he can sell a given level of output during the period, as well as the cost of producing the various quantities. He prefers to behave as if his best judgments were certain to be realized. To maximize profit, then, the entrepreneur sets his output at a level such that he judges that any additional production will raise revenue to a lesser extent than costs, whereas any lesser production will reduce revenues by more than costs. The price reflects his judgment of what consumers are willing to pay for that particular quantity. This policy provides a *normative prescription* for how a particular firm in a particular situation should behave to achieve a particular goal, rather than a *description* of how entrepreneurs actually do behave.

Unfortunately, verbal models ordinarily lack the precision and rigor that a detailed analysis of a problem demands. The verbal statement that one can reach Bloomington, Indiana, from Indianapolis by driving 50 miles south on state highway 37 is quite accurate. Still, a map of the route indicating the hills, turns, quality of the road, and the yearly fatalities on this stretch would be much more useful to one wondering how much time to leave for the journey, or whether to forget the whole thing. Similarly, determining the *precise* effects on the employment of a particular factor of production by a firm, or the *precise* effects on the profit-maximizing price and output of an increase in the wage demanded by another factor of production, requires a quite detailed and comprehensive verbal description of the firm's operations. Given this detail, it is a rather small but significant and worthwhile step—though it must be taken through what many feel is an extremely treacherous morass of symbols and equations—to building a *mathematical* model. Indeed, the essential tasks will for the most part be completed in the verbal model. All that remains is the translation of the verbal statements and assumptions into the simpler and more precise and compact language of mathematics.

For example, let $P$ denote the price charged by the firm, $Q$ the quantity demanded, and $Y$ the level of per capita income. The firm might assume that the price commanded by its product will be a function of output and income. A more compact statement that translates this verbal model of demand into a mathematical model would be $P = D(Q, Y)$. If the firm's total costs, $C$, are assumed to be some function of the level of output, we can also write $C = c(Q)$. Profits, $\pi$, are then given by the accounting identity $\pi = PQ - c(Q)$. To maximize profit, $Q$ must be selected to maximize $\pi = PQ - c(Q) = D(Q, Y)Q - c(Q)$. Making the additional simplifying and most convenient assumption that $D$ and $c$ are continuous and differentiable functions, profit is maximized where

$$\frac{\partial \pi}{\partial Q} = \left(\frac{\partial D}{\partial Q}\right) Q + D - \frac{\partial c}{\partial Q} = 0 \quad \text{and} \quad \frac{\partial^2 \pi}{\partial Q^2} < 0.$$

The exact point at which this occurs will depend upon the actual demand and cost equations. Further, it is only when these are known that we can determine whether, at the output where $\partial \pi / \partial Q = 0$, the firm is earning a profit. It may well be that at this output the firm will succeed only in minimizing its loss. Under these circumstances, the preferred behavior for the profit maximizer might be to go out of business.

Unlike the previous concentrate model, the present model has time abstracted. It is a *static* model in which time does not play a direct and clearly definable role. We know, for example, that quantity demanded is meaningful only with respect to a specific period of time, and that a firm's decision to go out of business on the heels of a loss will ordinarily evolve only after some time has elapsed, or after a succession of accounting-period losses have been suffered. Yet, in a neoclassical microeconomic model such as the static model above, the exact timing of these events will commonly be ignored. This neglect of time is held by some economists to dilute much of the impact of microeconomic theory. The most important economic issues and the most useful economic models, they argue, are *dynamic* issues and *dynamic* models, such as the concentrate model, which explicitly recognize and feature the role of time as a variable. As we shall see, however, it is frequently necessary to solve a less complex static problem before tackling the more complex dynamic problem, and the resolution of the latter is often a small, if *significant*, step away.

Also, unlike the concentrate model, the present model does not provide specific functional forms. It is frequently unnecessary, however, for the theorist to be concerned with specific functional forms. For example, $(\partial D/\partial Q)Q + D$ measures the change in total revenue with respect to a small change in output; this is called marginal revenue. $\partial c/\partial Q$ measures the change in total cost with respect to a small change in output; this is called marginal cost. The previous static mathematical model therefore yields the conclusion that the single-product, single-process firm seeking to maximize profit produces the output that equates marginal revenue to marginal cost. It will do so as long as it does not thereby incur a loss that could be avoided by halting all operations.

Similarly, suppose one is interested in the effects on this firm when a sales tax is imposed on its product. Specifically, suppose one wishes to determine whether and how the price the firm receives, net of the tax, will differ from the pretax price. As we shall see, to determine this it would suffice to know that the demand curve is everywhere negatively sloped in the $PQ$ space, and whether the marginal cost function is increasing, constant, or decreasing at the current optimum output level. If, however, corporate management wishes to apply the theory in an actual decision-making context to determine the optimum pre- and posttax net price and output levels, the actual mathematical form of each function and the parameters to locate it must be specified. That is, it may be necessary to determine *both* the shape and position of each function of a theoretical model in order to apply the model to a practical problem.

Under some circumstances this determination would have to be quite precise. A corporation's profits could be very sensitive to comparatively minor swings in the economy, particularly changes in per capita income, because of the effects of the latter on demand. In this case the model $P = D(Q, Y)$ may not be adequate, nor will the particular functional form $P = AQ^{a_1}Y^{a_2}$ $(A > 0,\ a_1 < 0,\ a_2 > 0)$, even if the latter represents the best judgment as to the shape of the curve. Management could require explicit point estimates of the parameters $A$, $a_1$, and $a_2$. If the most appropriate value one can assign to $a_2$ is 5.3, but management operates on the assumption that $a_2 = 10.1$, the results could be catastrophic.

Alternatively, however, if widely disparate, but eminently sensible, estimates of the parameters, or differing, but quite justifiable, assumptions about the shapes and positions of the curves, all result in only minor discrepancies in the prescribed policies, a lower order of precision in determining the functions would be tolerable. Thus, if different hypotheses about the functions lead to a narrow range of optimal outputs, from a practical standpoint it might not matter which hypothesis is accepted as the basis for the decision.

In either event, however, the use of a mathematical model in a practical setting requires specific estimates of the relevant functions. In the main, this estimation will involve the employment of *econometrics*—that is, the application of certain statistical methods to the estimation of mathematical relationships built on an economic foundation.

In the earlier verbal model, the price the consumer would be willing to pay was assumed to be a function of output and per capita income. This verbal statement was readily translated into the mathematical model $P = D(Q, Y)$. Proceeding from the mathematical model, the econometrician will attempt to determine the most appropriate functional form for the demand curve in the institutional setting within which it is operative. He might take his clue to the *form* from theory, from perusal of a graph of the historical data for the variables involved, from preliminary statistical analysis, or more likely from some combination of the three. This first step will involve only partial or ad hoc use of the available data, the more extensive analysis being reserved for the final parameter estimation in the form suggested by the initial probes. The most appropriate form for the demand curve, based on the theoretical considerations and historical experience, might appear to be $P = \alpha Q^{\alpha_1} Y^{\alpha_2}$, where $\alpha$, $\alpha_1$, and $\alpha_2$ are parameters to be determined empirically. Statistical techniques such as multiple regression analysis will then be applied to the available historical data to obtain estimates of the parameters. One might suspect, a priori, that $\alpha > 0$, $-1 < \alpha_1 < 0$, and $\alpha_2 > 1$, in which case $P = \alpha Q^{\alpha_1} Y^{\alpha_2}$ becomes a *descriptive* model of the firm's demand curve. The best empirical estimate of the equation might be $P = 1.5Q^{-.4}Y^{5.3}$. This equation could be taken as a "given" to be incorporated into a larger *normative* model to determine the profit-maximizing price.

It is clear, then, that model building can take place at various levels of complexity and refinement and for a variety of theoretical and applied purposes. One need not build and obtain empirical estimates for an econometric model of demand in order to assess the direction in which price will change following an increase in per capita income. Vague judgments with respect to the shape of the demand curve or its parameters will often permit quite general statements as to the manner in which changes in per capita income will influence price. Still, a profit-oriented decision maker responsible for price policy in a real-life firm will want to know by *how much*, as well as in what direction, he should change price should consumer income change. The level of sophistication required in a model will depend on the purpose for which the exercise is undertaken—and the purposes may vary.

## 1.3 THE PURPOSES OF MODELS

The two most widely proclaimed purposes of models are *to predict* and *to explain behavior*. An econometric model of demand might be used by management to predict the effects on demand of a downturn in the economy that reduces per capita income; or a descriptive mathematical model of demand might suggest to the student of corporate behavior that an economic downturn will typically result in a firm's reducing its level of output. Alternatively, the purpose of a model could be to explain the extent of the decline in a particular firm's sales during an economic downturn, with specific reference to the income factor as isolated in the demand equation.

It must be borne in mind that, as an idealized representation of a system, a model cannot be expected to yield uniformly *perfect* predictions of reality. The model of demand, $P = D(Q, Y)$, is more appropriately written as $P = D(Q, Y, \epsilon)$, where $\epsilon$ is a random component reflecting the influence of "other" unspecified factors on price. The corresponding econometric model to be estimated empirically would be written as $P = \alpha Q^{\alpha_1} Y^{\alpha_2} \epsilon$. The influence of the "other" factors will ordinarily be irregular, for if there were any regularity we would be justified in incorporating such factors explicitly into the model. It is expected that these random influences will tend to cancel each other over many observations, and the model will pick up the systematic relationships. The importance of random factors will be reflected in how well or poorly the model predicts, based solely on those factors that are explicitly incorporated into the model.

It would not be uncommon, however, for a good predictive model to present an inaccurate explanation of *why* a system behaves as it does. For example, it might be the case that when per capita income rises, there is a slight tendency for consumers to shift away from the product in question to a product of superior quality. Yet, both per capita income and population size have tended to increase over time, and as the population increases, the total demand for the product increases. The positive effect of the increase in population far outweighs the negative effect of the higher incomes. Nevertheless, if one's a priori belief is that income and not population is exerting a regular influence on price, one's model may be in error, but from the estimation standpoint the coincidence between the income and population data is so close that it does not matter which variable is introduced into the model. A model incorporating either one or the other will yield equally good predictions. But, when the income data fulfill the role that is correctly assigned to the population data, the effects of population changes are incorrectly ascribed to income variations.

As an ideal, the model that is the best predictor for a system will also provide the most accurate explanation of the system's behavior. This ideal will not, however, necessarily be achieved. This is partially because the relationships prevailing historically may not remain unchanged in the future. Models are built by people and, like people, those that offer the best predictions do not necessarily offer the best explanations and vice versa.[3] In building a model it is necessary not only to recognize this fact but to take it into consideration. This may require modifying the model so as to better achieve the primary objective even to the neglect of the secondary objectives. Hence, what is a good model for one purpose may be unsatisfactory for another purpose.

A third purpose of model building, easily and frequently overlooked, is to help *generate new ideas*. Through the very process of constructing a model one frequently *obtains* new and interesting *insights* into particular facets of the problem being studied. The model, although in and of itself neither a very able predictor nor very illuminating, may *identify individual factors* of potentially unique importance or unimportance that should be incorporated into, or omitted from, refinements of the original version. It is useful to be able to eliminate variables from a model, for one seeks the optimum level of abstraction in model building. This suggests the desirability of limiting a model to the smallest number of variables compatible with retaining the model's ability, given its purpose, to give an accurate portrayal of reality.

[3] The offering of good arguments for why both one's predictions and explanations are in error is a skill that the model builder can ill afford not to acquire.

One means of determining those variables that may be omitted from a model, or those whose associated parameters must be estimated with the greatest care, is *sensitivity analysis*. Sensitivity analysis explores the implications of the model for a range of values taken on by particular parameters or for various functional representations of particular relationships. We literally test the sensitivity of the model to the assumptions or parameter assignments. In this way we may obtain clues as to which parameters must be estimated with great care and which may be neglected, or which functions must take particular forms and which may be more optional. If, for example, either the equation $P = 1.5Q^{-.4}Y^{5.3}$ or the equation $P = 2.0 - 1.3Q + 25.2Y$ will result in quite similar decisions, it will not necessarily matter which is used, though the former might be a more desirable form, given the structure of the other equations in the model. If, however, their use results in quite different decisions, it becomes important to determine which is the more appropriate of the two. Similarly, one might also determine whether more complex models are required because of the sensitivity of the model to changes in the assumed values of particular parameters. Moreover, the model may serve to *clarify* one's *information needs*. Thus, although itself endowed with little practical value, the model may indicate the sort of information that is needed before more valuable versions can be constructed. Admittedly, idea generation tends to lurk in the background, both when the model is being constructed and when its achievements are being evaluated. Still, if we were to classify all models as being either good or bad, useful or useless, we would fail to give appropriate due to models that serve mainly as stepping stones to models that successfully deal with the problems we hope to resolve.

It is particularly important to keep the multipurpose nature of models in mind when judging the economic models that will be presented here. It will be easy to exaggerate the value of some and to underestimate the worth of others. Before proceeding much further, then, the reader would do well to precondition both his perspective and his tolerance.

## 1.4 THE ROLE OF ASSUMPTIONS

The versatility of a model relates to its ability to perform a variety of tasks under a variety of circumstances. This will generally be a function of the assumptions that underlie it. A model is an abstraction from reality; it is not supposed to duplicate reality in every detail. This abstraction is achieved through a series of carefully selected assumptions, which may or may not be either very realistic or very restrictive. Assumptions can simplify the problem that the model is designed to help solve or simplify the model itself.

Assumptions allow us to construct a model of a system that we hope will be a useful abstraction. After the initial formulation, however, it may be necessary to introduce additional assumptions into the model in order to make it *manipulable* or *operational*. These terms are not synonomous. For example, at one level of abstraction one might assume that the demand curve facing the firm is known and that the demand relationship is $P = D(Q)$. To make the model manipulable we may need to assume only that the function is continuous and that its second- and third-order derivatives exist. To make the model operational, given the specification of the other functions in the model, it may next be necessary to assume a hyperbolic demand curve described by $P = AQ^{-a}$, $A$ and $a > 0$. This assumption in and of itself has a series of interesting implications that may or may not be valid. In particular, if $P = AQ^{-a}$, the firm's total revenue will be given by $R = PQ = AQ^{1-a}$. Hence, marginal revenue $= dR/dQ = (1 - a)AQ^{-a} = (1 - a)P$. It immediately follows that unless $a \leq 1$, the demand curve would imply that the greater the output sold by the firm, the less will be *total* revenue. The reason is that, with $a > 1$ and $P > 0$, $(1 - a)P$ or marginal revenue is negative. Thus, additions to output from *any* output level will result in a decline in total revenue. Moreover, as long as additional output always results in a higher *total* cost for the firm, marginal cost will be positive. It appears, then, that the earlier prescription that the profit-maximizing firm equate marginal revenue to marginal cost could not possibly be adhered to by a firm with the demand curve $P = AQ^{-a}$, unless the additional qualification is added that $1 > a > 0$ and $A > 0$. Hence the number and type of assumptions made will depend upon the motives for building the model and one's hopes for the model's accomplishments.

As suggested earlier, an analysis of the way in which the assumptions affect the inferences drawn from a model may also be of considerable interest. Just as a model's sensitivity to the level of particular parameters can be studied with profit, there can be great benefit in studying the model's sensitivity to particular assumptions. For example, for purposes of a particular model it may be necessary to assume that the demand curve is described by $P = D(Q)$ and is continuous, that its higher-order derivatives exist, and that the first derivative is always negative, but it may not be necessary to specify the sign of the second derivative. If one is concerned with the effects of an excise tax on the price charged by a profit-maximizing monopolist, however, it is fruitful to consider different assumptions about this second derivative, $d^2P/dQ^2$. One soon discovers that the effect of the tax will always be to increase the price paid by the consumer. Additionally, however, the increase will be greater the greater is the positivity of the second derivative, and lesser the greater is the negativity of the second derivative, relative to the case of a linear demand curve with $d^2P/dQ^2 = 0$. The assumption made about the sign of $d^2P/dQ^2$ will therefore be important in gauging the impact on the consumer of an excise tax.

It will generally be desirable to explore the manner in which particular assumptions influence the implications of a model. If omitting an assumption does not appreciably influence the model, one may wish to drop it in order to make the model less restrictive. If the assumption exerts an important influence on the conclusions, the assumption may itself warrant further intensive study. If the model suggests that an assumption is invalid even though it is normally taken for granted, this too will be a useful output of the model.

The necessity for precision in stating one's assumptions is illustrated by the subtle distinctions, and the ensuing differences in the implications, between different formulations of a model of demand. For example, an assumed demand relationship might be the implicit one $\bar{D}(P, Q) = 0$. The latter simply asserts, mathematically, that the prices consumers are willing to pay and the quantities they are willing to buy are linked according to the function $\bar{D}(P, Q) = 0$. As one alternative, it might be assumed that *price* is the *independent* variable and the *quantity* consumers are willing to purchase, at any given price, the *dependent* variable. Then, the relationship is $Q = \bar{\bar{D}}(P)$. As a second alternative, the *price* that consumers are willing to pay could be assumed to be the *dependent* variable related to the *independent* variable *quantity* according to the function $P = D(Q)$. As we shall see, the theoretical implications of these differing, if apparently similar, assumptions can be striking. Moreover, suppose we wish to estimate the demand curve empirically using the statistical technique of least squares.[4] Two econometric models that could be developed from the previous alternatives would be $P = \alpha Q^{-\alpha_1}\epsilon_1$ and $Q = \beta P^{-\beta_1}\epsilon_2$, where $\epsilon_1$ and $\epsilon_2$ are random-error terms. If there were no random errors and each equation precisely fitted the empirical data, the estimated curves would coincide. That is, the estimated equations would be $P = AQ^{-a}$ and $Q = BP^{-b}$, where $A$, $a$, $B$, and $b$ are estimates of the parameters. In this case, $A = B^{1/b}$ and $a = 1/b$. Such a perfect relationship will rarely exist, however, and there will almost always be some random error. When this is the case, $A \neq B^{1/b}$, $a \neq 1/b$, and the curves will not coincide. In general, then, at both the theoretical and the empirical level, assumptions are of interest both because they form the foundation upon which a model is built and because they themselves comprise an interesting package for further study.

## 1.5 TESTING THE MODEL

Even in an inflated economy models would be a dime a dozen. Most of the interesting economic problems have been modeled, and if there is a model gap—at least between economics and other major disciplines—economists will probably have to curtail their efforts if the gap is to be closed. The question arises, then, as to what characteristics a model should have to make it superior to an alternative designed to help elucidate the same problem.

The most distinguishing characteristic of a good model is how well it performs. Does the model do a better job than its competitors? The answer will depend upon the job for which the model is intended (which is not to say that a model intended for one purpose may not ultimately serve another). Criteria for evaluating a model's performance might be its validity as a predictor, or the reliability and consistency of its predictions. With respect to predictive *validity*, we are interested in determining whether the model predicts with sufficient accuracy to permit its employment in this capacity. With respect to predictive *reliability*, we are concerned with whether a model is a frequent and *consistently* accurate predictor, and whether it does well at crucial times or misses just when an accurate prediction is vital. For example, a model that predicted the quality and quantity of the annual tobacco crop would be a valuable planning aid for a tobacco company. It could be sufficiently accurate to lead the company to base their plans on its predictions. But the model might not be reliable, having the undetected defect that during the rare hard winters its performance tends to be haphazard.

An alternative criterion of performance is whether the model permits one to *deduce logical inferences* with respect to the behavior of the system. For example, one might assume a firm's weekly output $Q$ to be a function of the average number of men employed during the week, $L$, and the average employment of capital, $K$, including machines and raw materials. The function might be $Q = \alpha L^{\alpha_1}K^{\alpha_2}$, where $\alpha$, $\alpha_1$, and $\alpha_2$ are parameters. It is easy to see that if $\alpha_1 + \alpha_2 = 1$, changing both labor and capital by a factor of $\lambda$ will change $Q$ by a factor of $\lambda$, since $\alpha(\lambda L)^{\alpha_1}(\lambda K)^{\alpha_2} = \alpha\lambda^{(\alpha_1+\alpha_2)}L^{\alpha_1}K^{\alpha_2} = \lambda\alpha L^{\alpha_1}K^{\alpha_2} = \lambda Q$. Similarly, changing both labor and capital by a factor of $\lambda$ will change $Q$ by less than or more than a factor of $\lambda$ according as $\alpha_1 + \alpha_2 < 1$ or $\alpha_1 + \alpha_2 > 1$. Thus, the values that are assigned to the parameters will permit one to draw some interesting inferences with respect to the effects on output of changes in the *scale* of the firm's operations. If $\alpha_1 + \alpha_2 > 1$, on purely technological grounds increasing the scale of operations without bound is somewhat

[4] This will be discussed in Chapter 3.

appealing. Still, and even when it apparently intends to do so, a firm will not permit its operations to grow unceasingly. Through a larger model intended to explain the scale at which the firm operates, one can trace those factors that limit the size of the firm, and hence learn more about how an enterprise behaves and why.

The second distinguishing characteristic, and one that has been surrounded by great controversy, is the methodological issue as to the importance of the *validity* of the *assumptions* incorporated into the model. Some would maintain that if the model's assumptions are not valid, its value is greatly restricted, whereas others would maintain that as long as the model yields valid predictions or inferences about behavior that conform to reality, the model has passed its most important test.[5] This is not an issue to which one can give a definitive answer, and the beauty of a model will be in the eye of the beholder. The position taken here—a position that invites dissent—is that prediction and explanation are, as noted, but two purposes for which models may be constructed. If a model stimulates thought, generates ideas, and encourages the development of more sophisticated models which themselves may yield better predictions and explanations, then the model builder's time and effort have not gone for nought. Model building is an art, and the emergence of the slightest innuendo or the spark that flames a new idea may more than justify the effort.

There are several other features of interest in evaluating a model. One is whether or not the model is applicable to relevant issues. A model that provides predictions, inferences, and insights into irrelevant issues is not likely to merit or enjoy much attention. Similarly, a model dealing with the same issues dealt with by a series of predecessors must, at least in some regard, be demonstrably equal, and hopefully superior, to the former. If change for the sake of change were admitted as a criterion in the model builder's handbook, the plethora of models plaguing economics would soon become intolerable.

Finally, it is important that a model be accepted by its users, both actual and potential. A mathematical proof, for example, consists of a series of arguments that qualified mathematicians agree lead to the stated theorem. This does not imply that there cannot be disagreement among academicians, say, with respect to a model's theoretical virtues, or among corporate decision makers with respect to a model's applicability. There will not necessarily be unanimity among academicians in evaluating the validity, or the importance of the validity, of an assumption, nor need they agree on the possibility of generalizing a particular model's conclusions or even as to whether a model is overly simplified or too complex to be useful. Then, too, one corporate management could be having great success with, say, an econometric model as a forecasting device, whereas a second might have found econometric techniques a steady source of disillusionment. The "best" model will have a re-

[5] The views stretch from Milton Friedman's position that the merit of theory does not rest on the realism of its assumptions [*Essays in Positive Economics* (Chicago: University of Chicago Press, 1953)] to Paul Samuelson's position that we should not "relax our standards of scrutiny of the empirical validity that the propositions of economics do or do not possess" ["Discussion," *American Economic Review*, **LIII**:2 (May 1963), 236]. As an intermediate position, "Such an assumption is certainly not 'true,' but neither is it 'unreasonable.' The crucial question ... is whether it yields correct predictions" [Diran Bodenhorn, "A Note on the Theory of the Firm," *Journal of Business*, **XXXII**:2 (April 1959), 168]. Related issues are debated at some length in a series of papers in the May 1963 *American Economic Review*, pp. 204–236.

stricted usefulness if it fails to gain acceptance. Thus a further criterion on which to judge a model's value is that in some sense it should be convincing.[6]

Models, then, can be judged by a variety of criteria that can be accorded an infinite variety of weights. Thus there may be many rankings on the scale of wonderfulness for models, depending upon the tests that are used and the relative importance attached to each.

Perfectly good models can be built without the use of mathematics or statistics. Indeed, their virtues are as easy to overestimate as they are to overlook. In particular, we must not lose sight of the fact that mathematics is a language. Consequently a mathematical model is simply an analytical model that has been translated into a mathematical language. The virtue of this translation may merely be notational simplicity and condensation. A more prominent virtue is that one can manipulate the model by taking advantage of well-established mathematical principles or the wonders of a large-scale computer. This manipulation will frequently yield inferences that are obscured or unattainable until the verbal complexity of the model has been replaced by quantitative precision. The mathematics is not in and of itself an end; rather, it is a means to an end. Good mathematics cannot compensate for bad economics. It can, however, make good economics even better—and this is the purpose of economic model building.

Similarly, statistics enables one to extract the maximum benefits from a model. This may be accomplished in two ways. On the one hand, statistical *techniques* may be called upon to assist in the estimation of the parameters that are part and parcel of the mathematical model, since the values of these parameters may well be crucial for the inferences to be drawn from the model. And, like mathematics, statistics is often more abused than used. Mathematics and statistics are tools that can mislead and result in bad economics. On the other hand, statistical *principles* themselves, in particular the principles of probability theory (which in fact is a branch of mathematics), may be of vital importance to a model. This importance is highlighted once we recognize that the real world is beclouded by uncertainties and that probabilistic information can and should be accorded an integral role. Our study will therefore run a gamut from *deterministic* models, those yielding answers to problems that arise in a world free of risk, to *stochastic* models, those seeking better answers to problems that arise in an uncertain world.[7]

In extolling the virtues of mathematics, we must be careful not to slight the

[6] It has been called to my attention, and the point is well taken, that it is good for *good* models to be convincing, and they will be so in the long term. It is bad for *bad* models to be convincing in the short term.

[7] As Charles Hitch has commented, "There has been altogether too much obsession with optimizing on the part of operations researchers . . . . Most of our relations are so unpredictable that we do well to get the right sign and order of magnitude of first differentials. In most of our attempted optimizations we are kidding our customers or ourselves or both. If we can show our customer how to make a better decision than he would otherwise have made, we are doing well, and all that can reasonably be expected of us." ["Uncertainties in Operations Research," *Operations Research,* **8**:4 (July–August 1960), 445.]

It should also be noted that risk and uncertainty will be used interchangeably here, although traditionally the former implies the assignment of probabilities to the possible outcomes whereas the latter implies that probabilities have not been so assigned. This distinction goes back to Frank Knight, *Risk, Uncertainty and Profit* (Boston: Houghton Mifflin Company, 1921).

importance of behavioral considerations. Mathematics and statistics may be used to describe, but what they describe is the behavior of individuals, the organizations in which these individuals work, and the societies in which these individuals live. Moreover, people do not necessarily behave with the high degree of rationality and precision that our quantitative tools tend to ascribe to them. It is therefore important that, at every step of the way, we be prepared to qualify and modify models and their results to conform with the foibles of the people making up the system being modeled.

## 1.6 WHERE THE BOOK WILL JOURNEY

The models with which this book will be concerned are those of microeconomic theory—that is, those relating to the behavior of the individual economic unit. We shall be especially and almost exclusively concerned with the firm and its problems. One of the firm's problems is, of course, the consumer. Another comprises the factors of production that are employed. We shall therefore devote some attention to the theory of the individual consumer and the theory of product demand as well as to the theory of production and factor demand. The major purpose of the book is not to exposit the neoclassical theory of the firm and the theory of consumer behavior; nevertheless, an understanding of neoclassical theory is required before one can build a theory of the firm relevant to decision making in the modern business world. In effect, microeconomic theory will provide the starting point from which more advanced models can be developed that will be helpful in managerial decision making.

In order to secure the full benefits of what economic theory has to offer, the firm of the real world cannot be satisfied with general functions, principles, tendencies, and inclinations. The real-world decision maker is concerned with specifics: solving specific problems in a specific setting, for which he requires specific functions with specific parameters, and the historical information necessary for their estimation. Employing a quantitative tool kit consisting of a variety of mathematical and statistical techniques is, therefore, not merely a frill that makes a model more elegant, convincing, or salable, but a necessary prerequisite enabling the model to achieve the quantitative precision and numerical accuracy demanded of decision-making techniques in the modern world of the large-scale computer.

Similarly, decision making in the real world is not undertaken by a firm such as that considered in the neoclassical theory of the firm. The latter produces a single product by a single process. It is managed by a single owner seeking solely to maximize profits, who treats his world *as if* it were one of certainty. He behaves as *economic* man: that is, he is a rational decision maker who, in choosing among alternative courses of action, seeks to maximize his economic gains by using the best analytical tools at his disposal. The real business world, however, is populated by complex organizations responsible for the production of many products by many processes—organizations in which ownership and management may be separated. These highly individual organizations may have to reconcile a variety of preferences and attitudes; moreover, they operate under constant risk, uncertainty, and the human fallibility and potential for irrationality of *administrative* man seeking that alternative "which leads to the greatest accomplishment of administrative objectives."[8] If, then, the models we discuss are to play an integral role in managerial

[8] Herbert A. Simon, *Administrative Behavior* (New York: The Macmillan Company, 1958), pp. 38–39.

decision making, or if we are to learn something about the firm's decision-making processes from them, we must investigate these issues directly and not simply assume them away without prior empirical analysis or merely note them en passant to be a minor irritant.

This is not to say that all of the major problems of managerial decision making can be solved in this book. Not only are they too numerous and varied to deal with in any single volume, but those for which the answers are known would make up an embarrassingly small list and the omissions would be glaring—despite widespread and continuing efforts to resolve these problems and to improve our decision-making models. Nonetheless, the potential of these models remains largely untapped, and the relevance for decision making of this field of application is unquestioned.

Since this book will be concerned primarily with *economic* issues, it will accept as givens the reconciliation of many important problems. Some of these problems will have greater impact upon some firms than the economic issues into which they are injected, but their resolution more appropriately falls within the purview of other disciplines.[9]

In the light of these considerations, the book will outline the basic principles of neoclassical economic theory. In the process, it will introduce some of the mathematical and statistical techniques necessary to make the theory operational. With the basic microeconomic and quantitative principles well in hand, the theory will be extended towards the development of models, principles, and techniques to aid managerial decision making in the uncertain, computerized business world of the present and future.

[9] In her classic work, *Economics of Imperfect Competition* (London: Macmillan and Co., Ltd., 1950), Joan Robinson hits at the heart of the matter: "If individuals act in an erratic way, only statistical methods will serve to discover the laws of economics, and if individuals act in a predictable way, but from a large number of complicated motives, the economist must resign his task to the psychologist" (p. 6). And again: "The study of human decisions involves a study of human psychology, but the background of psychology which economics requires is a purely behaviorist psychology. When the technique of economic analysis is sufficiently advanced to analyze the results of neuroses and confused thinking, it will study them only insofar as they produce statistically measurable effects" (p. 16). One can also take the somewhat narrow position that the purpose of the economist "should be to understand better the way in which the pricing mechanism operates to allocate the economy's resources, not to understand how a firm best achieves its own particular goals" [Almarin Phillips, "Operations Research and the Theory of the Firm," *Southern Economic Journal*, **XXVIII**:4 (April 1962), 358].

# 2

# THE INDIVIDUAL CONSUMER

## 2.1 INTRODUCTION

The U.S. economy houses a motley assortment of firms. These firms come in a wide variety of shapes and sizes and owe their existence to diverse economic endeavors. There is not a one-to-one correspondence between an insurance company's problems and those of a large automobile manufacturer, nor between those of the corner grocer and those of the steel fabricator. Therefore no universally applicable models or techniques can be developed to handle all the problems that arise in business. But, as Baumol has remarked, it is often "absolutely essential to use the techniques of marginal analysis as it occurs in the theory of the firm, the theory of production, and in welfare economics . . . not the theorems but the methods of analysis and derivation . . . ." And, "every firm and every managerial situation requires a model which is more or less unique . . . . It will be necessary, in effect, to derive special theorems which enable one to deal with that specific situation."[1]

In this spirit, our guiding purpose will be to develop models, techniques, and principles to serve as basic theories amenable to such variations as may be appropriate to particular situations. In essence, we shall be creating some framework for economic decision making in general, and developing some of the mathematical and statistical tools necessary to make operative the particular mechanism housed within that framework. Thus, the management of a supermarket chain seeking an optimal location or stocking policy is not going to find the "right equation" in this book. What it will find are models and solutions for related, and generally more abstract, problems, intended to generate *ideas* for the resolution of specific, less abstract, problems and to indicate *how* some of the complexities of mathematical and statistical estimation can be handled within an actual business setting.

The *major* thrust of the models will be toward the problems faced by the manufacturer selling to the individual household or consumer, rather than those encountered by, say, the wholesaler or financial enterprise. Any number of the problems

[1] William J. Baumol, "What Can Economic Theory Contribute to Managerial Economics?" *American Economic Review*, **LI**:2 (May 1961), 145.

faced by this firm, irrespective of management's objectives and the methods used in an effort to attain them, will directly or indirectly require some consideration of consumer preferences. The manufacturer will want to know something about the wants and needs of consumers and their willingness to pay to have them satisfied; he will want to know how, and how far, these preferences can be influenced; and he will want to know how the consumer's demand for his product(s) will be affected by factors over which the manufacturer has no control, such as the prices of other products and the consumer's income level. The latter are singled out as *economic* variables of general interest to economists as well as of particular interest to the firm.

The firm would, in effect, like to learn all there is to know about the demand for its product(s). The firm's primary interest will lie with demand in the aggregate as opposed to each individual consumer's particular set of preferences. But an aggregate is the sum of its individual components. In order to *fully* appreciate why demand in the aggregate behaves as it does, we must first understand the behavior of the individual consumer. We therefore begin our study with the theory of consumer behavior.[2] An important by-product of the analysis will be the opportunity to acquire familiarity with the mathematical procedure for maximizing or minimizing a continuous function of several variables, where the variables are subject to one or more side relations expressible as equalities. The procedure involves the introduction of the so-called Lagrange multipliers and will be employed throughout the book.

## 2.2 THE THEORY OF CONSUMER BEHAVIOR: THE CONSUMER'S PROBLEM

One often thinks of the consumer as desiring to "get the most for his money." This applies both to any one product and to the total basket of goods he buys. Because of the nonmonetary costs involved in searching for the "best buys," his disdain for haggling over price, the possible convenience of failing to take the steps required to achieve the aforementioned goal, or simply the fact that this goal ranks too low in his goal hierarchy, the consumer will not necessarily either seek or attain the optimum allocation of his resources. He will, nonetheless, allocate these resources among *some* package of savings, securities, and commodities. The consumer may also be able to add to his expenditures through borrowing. In the analysis that follows, however, we shall neglect direct consideration of this aspect and simply restrict consumer purchases to a total expenditure of $I$ dollars of income, including borrowing.

Since a single consumer is one of many buyers, his purchases may be assumed to be relatively insignificant, so that he can secure as much as he desires of any good

[2] A good starting place for the reader who wishes to study the theory of consumer behavior in greater depth than herein is Book III of Alfred Marshall's *Principles of Economics* (New York: The Macmillan Company, 1948), pp. 83–137. Proceeding from there, head for Part I and its Appendices in J. R. Hicks' *Value and Capital* (Oxford: The Clarendon Press, 1946), pp. 11–52, 305–314; then go to Paul A. Samuelson's *Foundations of Economic Analysis* (Cambridge, Mass.: Harvard University Press, 1961), pp. 90–202. If along the way you do not meet E. E. Slutsky's "On the Theory of the Budget of the Consumer," reprinted in the American Economic Association's *Readings in Price Theory* (Homewood, Ill.: Richard D. Irwin, Inc., 1952), pp. 27–56, retrace your steps.

without affecting its going price. Suppose he is to choose among $n$ different goods. These goods are listed in a systematic manner, permitting us to write the price of the first good, say butter, as $P_1$ and the consumer's total purchases of butter as $q_1$; or, more generally, $P_i$ and $q_i$ will denote the price and quantity purchased of the $i$th good on the list, where $i$ takes on all values from 1 to $n$, or simply $i = 1, 2, \ldots, n$.[3] The consumer's total expenditure will be given by

$$E = \sum_{i=1}^{n} P_i q_i.$$

When such "purchases" as savings (including new cash balances) are included in the basket of goods that his income buys, $E = I$.

To facilitate the analysis, let us assume that each of the $q_i$ is infinitely divisible. That is, with $q_1$ infinitely divisible the consumer can purchase one pound of butter, half a pound of butter, an ounce of butter, or $1/\sqrt{2}$ ounces of butter if he so desires. Further, there will be a myriad of alternative combinations of the $q_i$ among which the consumer could choose, if he had the necessary funds. Suppose that $\mathbf{q}'$ and $\mathbf{q}''$ are two such combinations, where $\mathbf{q}' = (q_1', q_2', \ldots, q_n')$ and $\mathbf{q}'' = (q_1'', q_2'', \ldots, q_n'')$. We endow our consumer with sufficient sensitivity to permit him to say whether (1) he prefers $\mathbf{q}'$ to $\mathbf{q}''$ ($\mathbf{q}' \succ \mathbf{q}''$), (2) he prefers $\mathbf{q}''$ to $\mathbf{q}'$ ($\mathbf{q}'' \succ \mathbf{q}'$), or (3) he is *indifferent* between the two combinations ($\mathbf{q}' \sim \mathbf{q}''$). The consumer would reveal his indifference by permitting any second party to select the combination that he is to receive, cost considerations aside. That is, suppose that

$$\sum_{i=1}^{n} P_i q_i' = \sum_{i=1}^{n} P_i q_i''$$

and that the consumer *must* choose between purchasing $\mathbf{q}'$ or $\mathbf{q}''$. If he is willing to abrogate his decision-making authority to permit *any* other person to make the choice for him, then he must be indifferent between $\mathbf{q}'$ and $\mathbf{q}''$. If one combination were preferred to the other, the consumer would not permit all second parties to choose for him, lest he be given the least preferred basket. Similarly, so long as

$$\sum_{i=1}^{n} P_i q_i' \leq \sum_{i=1}^{n} P_i q_i''$$

and the consumer elects to purchase $\mathbf{q}''$, we can infer that $\mathbf{q}'' \succ \mathbf{q}'$. For at the present set of prices $\mathbf{q}''$ is more costly than $\mathbf{q}'$, but the consumer still chooses $\mathbf{q}''$, and so he must prefer it to $\mathbf{q}'$.[4]

[3] The small $q$ is used here to denote the individual consumer's purchases, as the large $Q$ will be used later to denote total purchases. The indexing, $i = 1, 2, \ldots, n$, permits us to deal with an indeterminate array of goods, thereby maintaining the generality of the analysis.

[4] The reader interested in revealed-preference theory, whereby an individual's indifference space is inferred from his behavior, should read Paul A. Samuelson's "Consumption Theory in Terms of Revealed Preference," *Economica*, N.S. **XV**:60 (Nov. 1948), 243–253, and H. S. Houthakker's "Revealed Preference and the Utility Function," *Economica*, N.S. **XVII**:66 (May 1950), 159–174.

Since the $q_i$ are infinitely divisible, there will also be a myriad of combinations $\mathbf{q}^t$ such that $\mathbf{q}' \sim \mathbf{q}^t$. All such combinations to which the consumer is indifferent are said to lie on the same *indifference surface.* Where there are but two goods to choose between, the indifference surface becomes an *indifference curve,* such as that of Figure 2.1. All combinations of $q_1$ and $q_2$ falling on this indifference curve are equally

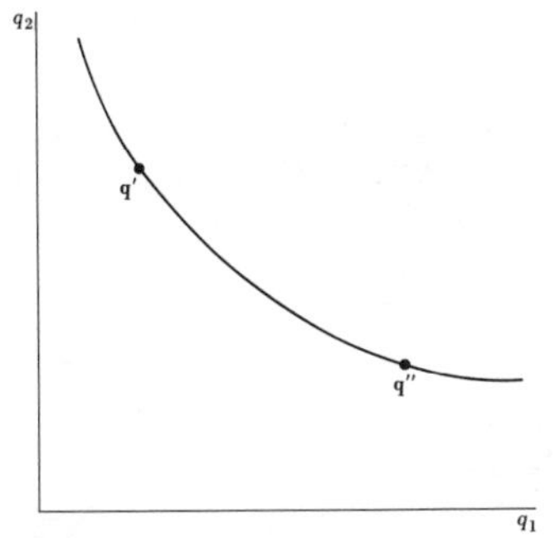


Fig. 2.1

preferred by the consumer. The points $\mathbf{q}' = (q_1', q_2')$ and $\mathbf{q}'' = (q_1'', q_2'')$ are two particular baskets of goods between which the consumer is indifferent. Moreover, it has been assumed that the consumer can express preference as well as indifference between baskets of goods. We shall speak of all baskets to which he is indifferent as having equal *utility;* if one combination is preferred to another, we shall say that it has greater utility for that *particular* consumer at that *particular* time. In referring to the greater or lesser utility of one particular combination relative to another, we shall be alluding to *one* person's *ordinal preference ranking* of the two combinations. There is no implication as to "the degree" to which the combination with the higher utility is preferred above the other. It should also be emphasized that one combination has a higher utility than another when it is preferred. The reverse is not true; that is, one combination is not preferred to another *because* it has the higher utility, although once we know it has the higher utility, we also know that it is preferred. The personalized nature of utility as an ordinal, not a cardinal, ranking of preference also means that the utility of individuals cannot be compared in any meaningful sense. For example, if two persons each assert that $\mathbf{q}'$ has a higher utility for them than $\mathbf{q}''$, we can only infer that $\mathbf{q}' \succ \mathbf{q}''$ for each. We cannot infer anything about the extent to which each prefers $\mathbf{q}'$ over $\mathbf{q}''$, nor about which has the higher *relative* degree of preference for $\mathbf{q}'$ over $\mathbf{q}''$.

Preference is assumed to be a *transitive* relationship. Transitivity in this sense means that if a consumer finds one basket of goods $\mathbf{q}'$ to be at *least* as desirable as a second basket $\mathbf{q}''$, that is if $\mathbf{q}' \succeq \mathbf{q}''$, and if $\mathbf{q}''$ is at least as desirable as a third basket $\mathbf{q}'''$, or $\mathbf{q}'' \succeq \mathbf{q}'''$, then $\mathbf{q}' \succeq \mathbf{q}'''$, or $\mathbf{q}'$ will be at least as desirable to him as $\mathbf{q}'''$. Although transitivity is assumed, in actuality the chap who expresses a preference for an apple over an orange, and a preference for an orange over a pear, may also express a preference for a pear when asked to choose between it and an apple—but this doesn't seem like a very reasonable thing to do; and reasonableness and rationality in behavior are qualities that we shall generally build into our models. A whim of the moment could yield a choice that would be rejected upon reflection.

From the analytical standpoint, however, it will be useful to assume that the consumer does behave in a rational manner[5] and that his preferences are transitive. Thus, if $\mathbf{q}'' \sim \mathbf{q}^s$ and $\mathbf{q}^t \succ \mathbf{q}''$, it follows that $\mathbf{q}^t \succ \mathbf{q}^s$ for all $t$ and all $s$. The $\mathbf{q}^s$ are then said to lie on a lower indifference surface than the $\mathbf{q}^t$. These surfaces cannot touch, of course, since if they did there would be at least one $\mathbf{q}^s$, call it $\mathbf{q}^{s'}$, such that $\mathbf{q}^{s'} \sim \mathbf{q}^t \succ \mathbf{q}^s \sim \mathbf{q}^{s'}$ for $s \neq s'$, and this is not possible by the transitivity assumption. Moreover, there are an infinite number of these indifference surfaces, which together form an *indifference space.*

Returning to the case of two goods, and recalling that in this case the indifference surfaces are indifference curves, the consumer's indifference space will consist of a set of indifference curves such as those of Figure 2.2(a). The lowest curve $U_s$

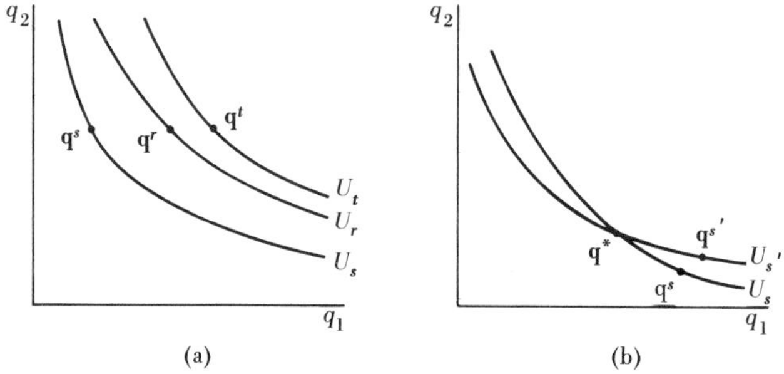


Fig. 2.2

describes each combination $\mathbf{q}^s = (q_1^s, q_2^s)$ and the highest curve $U_t$ describes each combination $\mathbf{q}^t = (q_1^t, q_2^t)$ such that $\mathbf{q}^t \succ \mathbf{q}^s$. If the indifference curves $U_s$ and $U_{s'}$ were to intersect, as in Figure 2.2(b), then the point of intersection, $\mathbf{q}^*$, would lie on both curves so that $\mathbf{q}^* \sim \mathbf{q}^s$ on $U_s$ and $\mathbf{q}^* \sim \mathbf{q}^{s'}$ on $U_{s'}$ for all $\mathbf{q}^s = (q_1^s, q_2^s)$ and all $\mathbf{q}^{s'} = (q_1^{s'}, q_2^{s'})$. From the transitivity assumption, we then require that $\mathbf{q}^s \sim \mathbf{q}^{s'}$, so that $U_s$ and $U_{s'}$ must coincide (that is, they are the same curve) but cannot intersect.

Now, although utility is an ordinal rather than a cardinal concept, we can assign an index to measure it. In particular, we are free to select any index or scale of measurement such that the consumer's utility or preference for any combination of goods will be a function of the $q_i$, or $U = u(q_1, q_2, \ldots, q_n)$. His utility for any of the combinations $\mathbf{q}^t$ or $\mathbf{q}^s$ will be, respectively, $U^t = u(\mathbf{q}^t)$ and $U^s = u(\mathbf{q}^s)$. Because of the ordinality of the index, however, we know only that $U^t > U^s$, since $\mathbf{q}^t \succ \mathbf{q}^s$. The preference relation $\succ$ commands the ordinal relation $>$. As previously noted, we cannot ascribe any cardinal significance to this difference in preference, such as the assertion that $\mathbf{q}^t$ is enjoyed "twice as much" as $\mathbf{q}^s$. We content ourselves with saying that $\mathbf{q}^t$ is preferred to $\mathbf{q}^s$. We might *wish* to go a bit further and say that the increase in utility in going from, say, $\mathbf{q}^s$ to $\mathbf{q}^r$, exceeds the increase achieved in going from $\mathbf{q}^r$ to $\mathbf{q}^t$. In the strict ordinal sense, however, we would be reluctant to be as specific as that. To understand this reluctance, suppose that the utility associated with

[5] In this connection, it is well to bear in mind Mrs. Robinson's comments quoted in footnote 9 of Chapter 1.

each combination on the curves $U_s$, $U_r$, and $U_t$ of Figure 2.2(a) is $U^s < U^r < U^t$, respectively. Assuming the consumer always prefers more of a good to less of it,[6] the higher indifference curves necessarily have the higher utility associated with them. This is so since, for any given level of one good, the higher the indifference curve the greater the quantity of the second good contained in the basket, and thus the greater the utility of the basket. Since we have a utility index, we can then determine whether the increase in utility in going from $U_s$ to $U_r$ exceeds the increase in utility in going from $U_r$ to $U_t$. But any numbers that we get will reflect the utility index that is assigned.

The *ordering* among indifference surfaces will be constant from one index to another, whereas the *changes* will depend upon the index. If one index is a *linear transformation* of the other, then under the second index we would have for $U_s$, $U_r$, and $U_t$, respectively, utility measures of $aU^s + A$, $aU^r + A$, and $aU^t + A$. Thus, either $U^r - U^s$, or $(aU^r + A) - (aU^s + A) = a(U^r - U^s)$, will measure the change in utility in going from $U_r$ to $U_s$ under each index. For all changes, the one index will yield a constant multiple of the other. This, however, will only be the case for linear transformations. In general, the relative magnitudes of the changes will depend upon the choice of index. Thus, in the strictly ordinal sense, we confine our statements about $U_r$, $U_s$, and $U_t$ solely to the *ordering* of $U^r$, $U^s$, and $U^t$, and to the fact that holding all $q_i$ save for $q_j$ fixed, while increasing $q_j$, will increase utility. Assuming the utility function to be differentiable, this implies that $\partial U/\partial q_j > 0$ $(j = 1, 2, \ldots, n)$. It will sometimes be *convenient* to refer to $\partial U/\partial q_j = u_j$ as the *marginal utility* of good $j$. Though this nomenclature suggests a *cardinal* utility measure, such is neither intended nor required; indeed, we shall be able to get along quite well without directly employing $u_j$ or making reference to its naughty name.

Note also that each of the indifference curves in Figures 2.1 and 2.2 has been drawn with a negative slope. This is by assumption, asserting for indifference surfaces in general that $(\partial q_j/\partial q_k)_{U=\bar{U}} < 0$ $(j \neq k; j, k = 1, 2, \ldots, n)$. In this notation, the $\partial q_j/\partial q_k$ expression is the ordinary partial derivative, and the $U = \bar{U}$ merely indicates that the differentiation is being performed along that particular indifference surface for which $U = \bar{U}$. Hence the implication of the assumption is that if we reduce $q_j$ by an appropriate amount while simultaneously increasing $q_k$, the consumer's utility can be held fixed and he can be kept on the same indifference surface. The expression $-(\partial q_j/\partial q_k)_{U=\bar{U}}$ reflects the extent to which the $k$th good can substitute for the $j$th while leaving utility unaltered; it is called the *rate of commodity substitution* of the $k$th good for the $j$th. As noted below, it is also commonly assumed that as more and more of the $k$th good is substituted for the $j$th, the consumer becomes increasingly reluctant to further reduce his declining quantity of the $j$th good. Mathematically, this means that $(\partial^2 q_j/\partial q_k^2)_{U=\bar{U}} > 0$, and this accounts for the *shape* of the indifference curves in Figures 2.1 and 2.2. It must be recognized, however, that the negative slope of the indifference curves arises because both items are *goods*. An indifference curve relating work and consumption, or one describing the tradeoffs that an investor is willing to accept between risk and return, is virtually certain to have positive slope.

The consumer's problem of "getting the most for his total expenditure" of

[6] "Commodities" that the consumer might not prefer more of, such as manual labor, can be readily incorporated into the analysis by redefining them as negative goods $i^*$ such that $q_{i^*} = -q_i$.

$I = E = \sum_{i=1}^{n} P_i q_i$ may now be translated into the following terms: the consumer wishes to select a basket of goods, $\mathbf{q} = (q_1, q_2, \ldots, q_n)$, to maximize his utility, subject to his limited income or *budget constraint.* In our notation, his problem is written

$$\text{Maximize} \quad U = u(q_1, q_2, \ldots, q_n) \tag{2.1}$$

$$\text{subject to} \quad E = I = \sum_{i=1}^{n} P_i q_i, \quad \text{or} \quad \sum_{i=1}^{n} P_i q_i - I = 0. \tag{2.2}$$

$U$ is the *criterion* or *objective function* and the $q_i$ are the *decision variables* whose levels must be determined to optimize the value of the objective function. This optimization is to take place subject to a single *constraint,* the consumer's budget, specified as an *equality* to which one or more of the variables are bound. The problem of Equations (2.1) and (2.2) is a special case of the more general problem in which an objective function is to be maximized or minimized subject to a single constraint, an equality. Constrained maximization problems occur quite frequently in the models of business and economics. It will therefore be useful to indicate how the general case of a single equality constraint is solved, for we shall come across such problems repeatedly in the course of the book. This will also ease our path into the still more general problem of optimizing an objective function subject to a *set* of constraints, equalities *and* inequalities.

## 2.3 MATHEMATICAL DIGRESSION: CONSTRAINED MAXIMIZATION, SINGLE EQUALITY CONSTRAINT

The general case of the previous problem would involve determining a set of decision variables, $x_i$, to maximize (or minimize) an objective function, $Z = f(x_1, \ldots, x_n)$, subject to a single constraint, $g(x_1, \ldots, x_n) = 0$.[7] One approach would be to *directly* incorporate the constraint into the objective function by solving $g(x_1, \ldots, x_n) = 0$ explicitly for one of the $x_i$, say $x_j$, in terms of the others. We would thereby obtain a solution, $x_j = x(x_1, \ldots, x_i \neq x_j, \ldots, x_n)$, to be substituted for $x_j$ in $f(x_1, \ldots, x_n)$. For example, consider the problem: Maximize $Z = 2x_1x_2$, subject to $x_1 + 4x_2 - 3 = 0$. To solve this problem, we might solve the constraint for $x_1 = 3 - 4x_2$. Substituting into the objective function, we obtain

$$Z = 2(3 - 4x_2)x_2 = 6x_2 - 8x_2^2.$$

To maximize $Z$ we set $dZ/dx_2 = 6 - 16x_2 = 0$, and solve for $x_2 = \frac{3}{8}$. For $Z$ as a function of the single variable $x_2$, this solution yields a maximum, since $d^2Z/dx^2 = -16 < 0$. Further, $x_1 = 3 - 4x_2 = 3 - 4(\frac{3}{8}) = \frac{3}{2}$. The maximum $Z$ is thus $Z^* = \frac{9}{8}$.

Unfortunately, if the constraint becomes more complex, say $x_1^2 + (x_1 + x_2)^2 = 0$ in the previous illustration, the task of explicitly solving for one decision variable and then substituting in the objective function can be overwhelming. We therefore introduce a mathematically equivalent procedure employing the so-called *Lagrange multipliers.* The Lagrange multiplier is a new variable, $\lambda$, that we shall introduce

[7] We assume that the functions are continuous and twice differentiable, and we shall make the continuity and differentiability assumptions throughout the book unless otherwise noted.

into the problem. There is one constraint and we introduce one Lagrange multiplier; with additional constraints we would have additional multipliers.

With the new variable $\lambda$, we can define a new objective function $L = L(x_1, \ldots, x_n, \lambda)$ called a *Lagrangian function*, such that $L = L(x_1, \ldots, x_n, \lambda) = f(x_1, \ldots, x_n) - \lambda g(x_1, \ldots, x_n)$. Since $g = 0$, $L = Z$ for *all* $\lambda$. Thus, we attempt to determine a set of $x_i$ $(i = 1, \ldots, n)$ *and* $\lambda$ to maximize $L$. This maximization takes place with $g = 0$ for *all* $\lambda$ so that these $x_i$ will also maximize $Z$ in the original problem.

To maximize a function of $n + 1$ variables, we first seek a stationary point such that each of the $n + 1$ first-order partial derivatives equals zero. Hence to maximize $L$ we need $\partial L/\partial x_i = 0$ $(i = 1, \ldots, n)$ and $\partial L/\partial \lambda = 0$. We therefore require that

$$\frac{\partial f}{\partial x_i} - \lambda \frac{\partial g}{\partial x_i} = 0, \qquad i = 1, \ldots, n,$$
$$g(x_1, \ldots, x_n) = 0.$$

It should be noted that the requirement $\partial L/\partial \lambda = 0$ will *always* yield the constraint back again as a restriction on the variables. We *always* require that the constraint be respected.

There are $n + 1$ equations and $n + 1$ unknowns. If solutions to these simultaneous, but not necessarily linear, equations can be found, they will occur at stationary points—points at which all first derivatives of the objective function $L$ equal zero. We must next determine whether any stationary point yields a maximum. For notational simplicity denote $\partial f/\partial x_i = f_i$ and $\partial g/\partial x_i = g_i$; we shall also require $\partial^2 f/\partial x_i^2 = f_{ii}$, $\partial^2 f/\partial x_i\, \partial x_j = \partial^2 f/\partial x_j\, \partial x_i = f_{ij} = f_{ji}$; and $\partial^2 g/\partial x_i^2 = g_{ii}$, $\partial^2 g/\partial x_i\, \partial x_j = \partial^2 g/\partial x_j \partial x_i = g_{ij} = g_{ji}$.

To determine whether a stationary point is a relative minimum or a relative maximum, or neither,[8] first form the matrix

$$\mathbf{M} = \begin{bmatrix} 0 & g_1 & g_2 & \cdots & g_n \\ g_1 & f_{11} - \lambda g_{11} & f_{12} - \lambda g_{12} & \cdots & f_{1n} - \lambda g_{1n} \\ g_2 & f_{21} - \lambda g_{21} & f_{22} - \lambda g_{22} & \cdots & f_{2n} - \lambda g_{2n} \\ \cdot & & & & \\ \cdot & & & & \\ \cdot & & & & \\ g_n & f_{n1} - \lambda g_{n1} & f_{n2} - \lambda g_{n2} & \cdots & f_{nn} - \lambda g_{nn} \end{bmatrix}.$$

The determinants formed from squared arrays of order $k$ taken along the principal diagonal of $\mathbf{M}$ are called the *principal minors* of $\mathbf{M}$. In particular,

$$M_1 = |0| = 0; \qquad M_2 = \begin{vmatrix} 0 & g_1 \\ g_1 & f_{11} - \lambda g_{11} \end{vmatrix} = -g_1^2;$$

$$M_3 = \begin{vmatrix} 0 & g_1 & g_2 \\ g_1 & f_{11} - \lambda g_{11} & f_{12} - \lambda g_{12} \\ g_2 & f_{21} - \lambda g_{21} & f_{22} - \lambda g_{22} \end{vmatrix}; \quad \ldots; \quad M_{n+1} = |\mathbf{M}|.$$

It can be shown[9] that the function has a relative minimum at the stationary point

[8] That is, it is a minimum (maximum) in the "neighborhood" of the point in the sense that there are points immediately to either side of the point that give higher (lower) values to the function. It might also be a saddle point or flex point, or simply a conglomeration requiring more specific inspection.

[9] See Samuelson, *Foundations of Economic Analysis*, pp. 362–378.

if $M_3 < 0, M_4 < 0, M_5 < 0, \ldots, M_{n+1} < 0$; it has a relative maximum at the stationary point if $M_3 > 0$, $M_4 < 0$, $M_5 > 0, \ldots,$ alternating sign. Other situations are more ambiguous.

To see better why the previous conditions hold, consider the curves in Figures 2.3(a) and 2.3(b). The former portray *convex* functions and the latter, *concave* functions. A function $W = w(\mathbf{y})$ is said to be convex if given (1) any two points $\mathbf{y}'$ and $\mathbf{y}''$, where $\mathbf{y} = (y_1, \ldots, y_n)$ and (2) a constant $\theta$, $0 \leq \theta \leq 1$, then $w(\theta\mathbf{y}' + (1 - \theta)\mathbf{y}'') \leq \theta w(\mathbf{y}') + (1 - \theta)w(\mathbf{y}'')$; if the inequality is reversed, the function is concave. If the equality signs may be eliminated, then the function is either *strictly* convex or *strictly* concave. In effect, a function is convex in an interval between two points if the weighted average of the function evaluated anywhere between these two points is greater than or equal to the value of the function at the same weighted average of the two points. Concave functions are interpreted analogously, with the inequality reversed. If $W = w(y_1)$ is a function of a single variable, $y_1$, the function can be portrayed in a two-dimensional graph as in Figure 2.3.

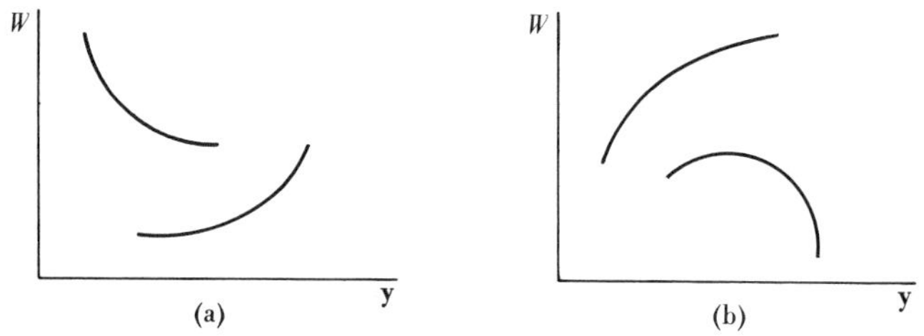


Fig. 2.3

An easy way to see whether the function is concave or convex is as follows. The function is concave (convex) if the straight line joining any two points on the curve falls on or below (above) the curve. The indifference curves of Figure 2.2 are convex. If $W = w(y_1, y_2)$ is a function of two variables, the function would be shown in three dimensions, and would be concave (convex) if a line passing through any two points lay on or below (above) the surface; similarly for functions of $n > 2$ variables—which are, unfortunately, more difficult to graph. Straight lines can be considered to be either concave or convex.

The vital importance of an objective function's convexity for optimization problems is shown by Figure 2.3. Clearly—and this is generalizable to $n$-dimensional functions—a strictly convex (concave) function will take on its global minimum (maximum) either at a boundary (if it is bounded) or at a stationary point. If the function is unbounded, the stationary point or the point at which the function has zero slope will be a global maximum point if the function is strictly concave and a minimum point if the function is strictly convex. The maximum (minimum) of a convex (concave) function will occur at a boundary, or will be unlimited. In terms of the matrix $\mathbf{M}$, the condition that $M_k < 0$ $(k = 3, \ldots, n + 1)$ is a sufficient condition for the *convexity* of $L$; the condition that $M_3 > 0$ with the signs of the subsequent $M_k$ $(k = 4, \ldots, n + 1)$ alternating is a sufficient condition for the *concavity* of $L$. Thus, when the first condition is fulfilled, $L$ is convex and minimized at the stationary point; when the second condition is fulfilled, $L$ is concave and maximized at the stationary point.

In terms of the illustrative example, the constraint $x_1 + 4x_2 - 3 = 0$ defines the *feasible set* of solutions. That is, any point, and *only* a point, falling on the line $x_1 + 4x_2 - 3 = 0$, shown in Figure 2.4(a), is admissible as a solution to this prob-

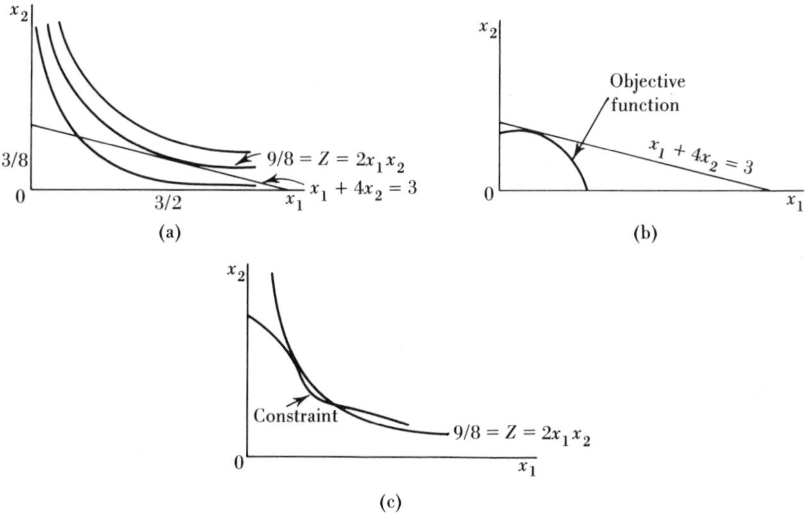


Fig. 2.4

lem. The objective function $Z = 2x_1x_2$ defines a set of rectangular hyperbolas with center at the origin. The segments of three of these hyperbolas lying in the positive quadrant are also shown in the figure. As $Z$ gets bigger, the hyperbolas shift to the northeast. The problem, then, is to get to that hyperbola lying furthest to the northeast, at least one point of which, the optimal solution, is contained in the set of feasible solutions. This hyperbola is the one for $Z = \frac{9}{8}$, and is just *tangent* to the constraint. In the first-order conditions, then, we are demanding *both* that the solution be a point contained in the feasible set and that the constraint and objective function be tangent at that point. In the second-order conditions we are requiring that the objective function look unlike that of Figure 2.4(b), and that the constraint look unlike that of Figure 2.4(c), for in neither instance will a point of tangency necessarily yield a global maximum; and the portraits painted by the latter figures are but a pair of the many possibilities that the second-order conditions guard against. To solve optimization problems such as those discussed in this section, then, the second-order conditions or the convexity requirements are at least as important as the first-order conditions or the requirements for a stationary point.

## 2.4 CONSUMER BEHAVIOR

### a. First-Order Conditions

From Equations (2.1) and (2.2) the *consumer's* Lagrangian function, $L = L(q_1, \ldots, q_n, \lambda) = L(\mathbf{q}, \lambda)$, may now be formed. His problem is to determine $\mathbf{q}$ and $\lambda$ so as to

$$\text{Maximize} \qquad L = u(q_1, q_2, \ldots, q_n) - \lambda\left[\sum_{i=1}^{n} P_iq_i - I\right]. \tag{2.3}$$

The *first-order* conditions, those for a stationary point, follow immediately. They are

$$\frac{\partial L}{\partial q_i} = u_i - \lambda P_i = 0, \qquad i = 1, \ldots, n; \tag{2.4a}$$

$$\frac{\partial L}{\partial \lambda} = I - \sum_{i=1}^{n} P_i q_i = 0, \tag{2.4b}$$

since $\dfrac{\partial}{\partial q_i}\left(\sum_{i=1}^{n} P_i q_i\right) = P_i$.

From (2.4a) it immediately follows that $\lambda = u_i/P_i$ for all $i = 1, \ldots, n$. Thus, at the stationary point,

$$\lambda = \frac{u_k}{P_k} = \frac{u_j}{P_j} \quad \text{or} \quad \frac{u_k}{u_j} = \frac{P_k}{P_j} \tag{2.5}$$

for all $j, k = 1, \ldots, n$. Therefore, *if* $L$ is a *concave* function, and since $u_i = \partial U/\partial q_i =$ the marginal utility of good $i$, we can infer from (2.5) that the consumer's utility will be maximized where the ratio of the marginal utilities of any two goods is equal to the ratio of their prices. Further, if the $m$th commodity is money with a unit money price of $P_m = 1$, then $\lambda = u_m/P_m = u_m =$ the marginal utility of money. In the next section, we consider the *assumptions* that we must make about the consumer's utility function for $L$ to be concave.

Recall, however, that the use of marginal utilities has the air of cardinality about it, an air that is offensive to many and that we need not introduce. To free the analysis of the explicit use of marginal utility, consider $U = u(q_1, \ldots, q_n)$. To effect a movement along a given indifference surface by changing the "mix" of the $q_i$ we calculate

$$dU = u_1\, dq_1 + u_2\, dq_2 + \cdots + u_n\, dq_n = \sum_{i=1}^{n} u_i\, dq_i = 0. \tag{2.6}$$

Let all $dq_i = 0$ with the exceptions of $dq_j$ and $dq_k$. We shall therefore be effecting a movement along an indifference curve with $U = U_0$ by altering only the purchases of the $j$th and $k$th commodities. Hence,

$$dU = 0 = u_j\, dq_j + u_k\, dq_k \quad \text{or} \quad -\left(\frac{dq_j}{dq_k}\right)_{U=U_0} = \frac{u_k}{u_j}.$$

That is, the rate of commodity substitution of the $k$th good for the $j$th on any indifference surface is equal to the ratio of their marginal utilities. Further, $-(dq_j/dq_k)_{U=U_0}$ is independent of the utility index; it describes only how much $k$ must be substituted for $j$ to leave the consumer's utility unchanged. Thus, condition (2.5) can be rewritten as

$$\frac{u_k}{u_j} = -\left(\frac{dq_j}{dq_k}\right)_{U=U_0} = \frac{P_k}{P_j} \tag{2.7}$$

for all $j, k = 1, \ldots, n$. It is useful to write the first-order conditions as (2.7) rather than (2.5), since the requirement that the rate of commodity substitution equal the price ratio for all commodities is independent of the choice of utility index, whereas a specific index is implicit in the use of marginal utility.

Additionally, since $I = \sum_{i=1}^{n} P_i q_i$, to alter purchases within a given income,

$$dI = P_1\,dq_1 + P_2\,dq_2 + \cdots + P_n\,dq_n = \sum_{i=1}^{n} P_i\,dq_i = 0. \tag{2.8}$$

Again varying only $q_j$ and $q_k$, we determine $dI = P_j\,dq_j + P_k\,dq_k = 0$; or for $I = I_0$, $-(dq_j/dq_k)_{I=I_0} = P_k/P_j$. That is, $-(dq_j/dq_k)_{I=I_0}$ is the *rate of exchange* of the $k$th good for the $j$th that can be achieved within a given income, and this rate of exchange is equal to the price ratio of the goods. Further, from (2.7),

$$-\left(\frac{dq_j}{dq_k}\right)_{U=U_0} = \frac{P_k}{P_j} = -\left(\frac{dq_j}{dq_k}\right)_{I=I_0}. \tag{2.9}$$

Equation (2.9) expresses the first-order conditions: the rate of commodity substitution between any two goods should equal their rate of exchange. This result is illustrated in Figure 2.5 for the case of two goods. Here $I = P_1q_1 + P_2q_2$ and $U =$

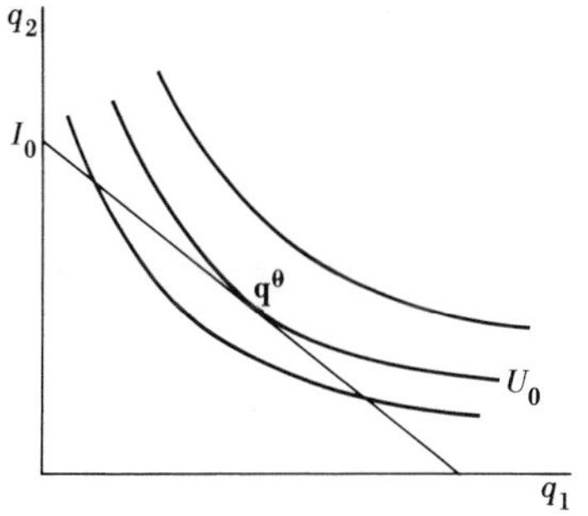


Fig. 2.5

$u(q_1, q_2)$. The consumer wishes to reach the highest indifference curve attainable, given his budget line labeled $I_0$. This indifference curve is labeled $U_0$, the curve that is just *tangent* to $I_0$ at $\mathbf{q}^0$. At this tangency point $\mathbf{q}^0$ the slope of the budget line equals the slope of the indifference curve; or equivalently the rate of exchange equals the rate of commodity substitution.

In the general $n$-good case we thus have shown that at the stationary point (1) the slope of the indifference curve in any two dimensions of commodity space is equal to the slope of the budget constraint in this subspace; (2) the negative of this slope, the rate of commodity substitution, is equal to both the ratio of the marginal utilities and the ratio of the prices of the two commodities; and (3) the slope of the indifference curve will be negative as long as the prices are positive, since $-dq_j/dq_k = P_k/P_j > 0$. We must now determine whether, and under what circumstances, the consumer's utility will be maximized at the stationary point. This requires inspection of the second-order conditions.

## b. Second-Order Conditions

To determine whether the second-order conditions hold at the stationary point we first develop the matrix comparable to **M** in Section 2.3. Recalling that the constraint is

$$g(q_1, \ldots, q_n) = \sum_{i=1}^{n} P_i q_i - I = 0,$$

we determine immediately that $g_i = \partial g/\partial q_i = P_i$ and $g_{ij} = \partial^2 g/\partial q_i \, \partial q_j = 0$ for $i$, $j = 1, \ldots, n$. If we let $\partial^2 u/\partial q_i \, \partial q_j = u_{ij}$ for $i, j = 1, \ldots, n$, the appropriate matrix will be

$$\mathbf{M} = \begin{bmatrix} 0 & P_1 & P_2 & \cdots & P_n \\ P_1 & u_{11} & u_{12} & \cdots & u_{1n} \\ P_2 & u_{21} & u_{22} & \cdots & u_{2n} \\ \cdot & & & & \\ \cdot & & & & \\ \cdot & & & & \\ P_n & u_{n1} & u_{n2} & \cdots & u_{nn} \end{bmatrix}.$$

$U$ will be maximized, subject to $I$, at the stationary point if $M_3 > 0$, $M_4 < 0$, . . . . Therefore let us consider

$$M_3 = \begin{vmatrix} 0 & P_1 & P_2 \\ P_1 & u_{11} & u_{12} \\ P_2 & u_{21} & u_{22} \end{vmatrix}.$$

Using the Laplace expansion and expanding along the first row, we obtain

$$\begin{aligned} M_3 &= 0 \begin{vmatrix} u_{11} & u_{12} \\ u_{21} & u_{22} \end{vmatrix} - P_1 \begin{vmatrix} P_1 & u_{12} \\ P_2 & u_{22} \end{vmatrix} + P_2 \begin{vmatrix} P_1 & u_{11} \\ P_2 & u_{21} \end{vmatrix} \\ &= -P_1(P_1 u_{22} - P_2 u_{12}) + P_2(P_1 u_{12} - P_2 u_{11}), \end{aligned}$$

since $u_{12} = u_{21}$; or

$$M_3 = -(P_1^2 u_{22} - 2P_1 P_2 u_{12} + P_2^2 u_{11}).$$

We are interested in determining whether $M_3$ is positive. Since $P_1$ and $P_2$ are positive, this will depend upon $u_{22}$, $u_{11}$, and $u_{12}$, and these in turn will reflect the shape of the indifference *curve* in the two-dimensional commodity space described by goods 1 and 2. To determine whether $M_3 > 0$, we must differentiate $(dq_2/dq_1)_{U=U_0} = -u_1/u_2$ with respect to $q_1$; or, for the general case of the indifference curve relating goods $j$ and $k$:

$$\frac{d^2 q_j}{dq_k^2} = \frac{\left[-u_{kk} - u_{kj}\left(\frac{dq_j}{dq_k}\right)\right] u_j - \left[u_{jk} + u_{jj}\left(\frac{dq_j}{dq_k}\right)\right][-u_k]}{u_j^2}$$

$$= \frac{\left[-u_{kk}u_j + u_{kj}\left(\frac{u_k}{u_j}u_j\right)\right] + u_{jk}u_k - u_k^2 u_{jj}\left(\frac{1}{u_j}\right)}{u_j^2} \left(\frac{u_j}{u_j}\right)$$

$$\frac{d^2 q_j}{dq_k^2} = \frac{-u_{kk}u_j^2 + 2u_{jk}u_k u_j - u_k^2 u_{jj}}{u_j^3}. \tag{2.10}$$

Letting $k = 1$ and $j = 2$, $d^2q_2/dq_1^2 = -[u_{22}u_1^2 - 2u_{21}u_1u_2 + u_{11}u_2^2]/u_2^3$. But, solving the first-order condition $u_1/u_2 = P_1/P_2$ for $u_1$ and substituting for $u_1$ in the preceding expression,

$$\frac{d^2q_2}{dq_1^2} = \frac{-[P_1^2u_{22} - 2P_1P_2u_{12} + P_2^2u_{11}]}{u_2P_2^2}, \qquad \text{with } u_{12} = u_{21}.$$

We see immediately that the numerator is $M_3$. Hence $d^2q_2/dq_1^2 = M_3/u_2P_2^2$. Recalling that, for the maximum we seek, we must have $M_3 > 0$, and that $u_2P_2^2$ is necessarily positive, it is clear that $M_3 > 0$ if and only if $d^2q_2/dq_1^2 > 0$. That is, $M_3 > 0$ requires that the slope of the indifference curve in the goods 1 and 2 commodity space be increasing. As is clear from Figure 2.3, when the slope of a curve is always increasing, the tangent to the curve at any point is turning counterclockwise and the curve will be convex. Therefore, the indifference curve *must be* convex for the stationary point and first-order conditions to assure a maximum. Moreover, since *any* two commodities may be selected as the first and second, the indifference curve in *any* two-commodity space *must be* convex to assure a maximum.

Still further, the alternating signs of $M_3 > 0$, $M_4 < 0$, ... imply that the indifference surface *must be* convex in $m$-commodity space ($m = 2, \ldots, n$) if the stationary point is to assure a maximum.[10] If the indifference surface is concave in $m$-space ($m = 2, \ldots, n$), that is if $M_3 < 0$, $M_4 < 0$, ..., then the stationary point yields a *minimum* rather than a maximum, and we want to move as far away from it as we can. If the surfaces are neither uniquely concave nor convex, the situation demands a more detailed examination.

Unless subsequent testing reveals it to be otherwise, a slice of the indifference space in two-commodity space will ordinarily be *assumed* to yield a negatively sloped *and* convex indifference curve. The curve will correspond to that in Figure 2.5 for $q_1$ and $q_2$. Given that all other $q_i$ ($i = 3, \ldots, n$) are determined so as to satisfy the first-order conditions, the consumer's utility will then be maximized for $I = I_0$ at $\mathbf{q}^0$, where $I_0$ is tangent to $U_0$, the highest indifference curve it touches. Were the indifference curves concave as in Figure 2.6, the consumer would maximize his utility "on the axis" at $\mathbf{q}^1$, rather than at the point of tangency $\mathbf{q}^0$. He prefers to consume only one good or the other. It would seem, however, that the former case is the more realistic. As consumers, we are ordinarily willing to sacrifice *some* of one desirable good, say steak, to get *more* of a second desirable good, say salad; and an exchange could be worked out whereby one's level of satisfaction would be unaltered. That is, $(dq_j/dq_k)_{U=U_0} < 0$, or the indifference curve is negatively sloped, with the slope the negative of the rate of commodity substitution. Further, as

[10] One must be careful to distinguish between the convexity of the indifference *surface* in $m$-commodity space ($m = 2, \ldots, n$) and the concavity of the indifference *space* in $(n + 1)$-space. The indifference space is of dimension $n$ (for the $n$ goods) plus 1 (for utility). For a global maximum at the stationary point, the Lagrangian function must be strictly *concave*. A function that is the sum of concave functions is concave. The budget constraint is linear, and therefore either concave or convex. Since $\lambda > 0$, if we consider the budget constraint to be convex, the $-\lambda\left[\sum_{i=1}^{n} P_iq_i - I\right]$ term in $L$ will be concave. Thus, for $L$ to be concave, $U = u(q_1, \ldots, q_n)$ must be concave. We therefore require a concave indifference space, slices of which will yield convex indifference surfaces.

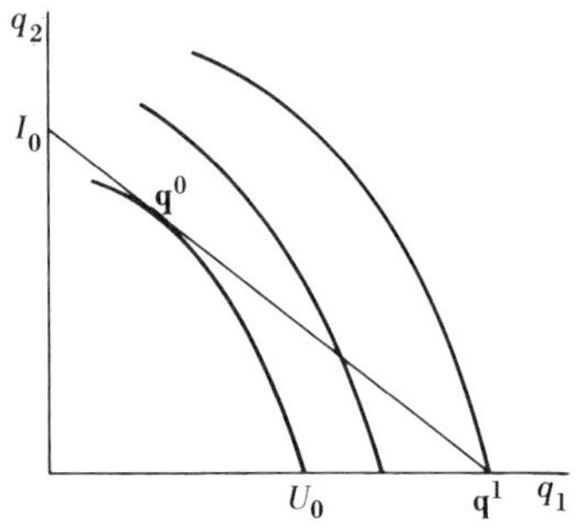


Fig. 2.6

consumers we will ordinarily be increasingly reluctant to permit the substitution of one desirable good, say salad, for a second desirable good, say steak, as the quantity of the first good increases and the quantity of the second good decreases. We will ordinarily require *increasing increments* of the first good before being willing to sacrifice additional fixed amounts of the second good. That is, $(d^2q_j/dq_k^2) > 0$, and the indifference curve is convex with a diminishing rate of commodity substitution. Thus the conditions

$$\frac{u_k}{u_j} = -\left(\frac{dq_j}{dq_k}\right)_{U=U_0} = \frac{P_k}{P_j} = -\left(\frac{dq_j}{dq_k}\right)_{I=I_0}$$

for $j, k = 1, \ldots, n$ will be the utility-maximizing conditions. It should, however, be reiterated that the second-order conditions here have been every bit as important as the first-order conditions and cannot be neglected. As will be seen later, second-order conditions are, in fact, occasionally more important in economic analysis than first-order conditions.

## 2.5 THE SLUTSKY EQUATION

### a. The Income Variation

The point at which utility is maximized in the previous analysis is called an *equilibrium point*, because once it is reached, the consumer has no inclination to deviate from it. He is distributing his resources among all feasible baskets of goods in an optimal manner in light of his preferences. It would be somewhat surprising to find all, or perhaps even any, consumers behaving with the sort of compulsive rationality that strict adherence to the utility-maximizing conditions demands. It would not, however, be unreasonable to expect that in their actual behavior, consumers will react to *changes* in the key parameters of prices and income in a fashion *similar* to that of the utility maximizer. That is, when the price of a particular good such as butter falls, all other prices and income remaining fixed, we might expect consumers to purchase more butter, less of some goods such as margarine, and more of other goods such as bread. *All* consumers will not necessarily have like reactions to such a change. Nevertheless, by analyzing the effects of *changes* in prices and income on the utility maximizer's equilibrium position, we will obtain some interesting and useful insights into actual consumer reactions to such changes.

Let us first consider how a change in income will affect the utility maximizer's equilibrium position, or the basket of goods that he purchases, all prices being held constant. We will want to determine the effects on each $q_i$ of a change in $I$, or $\partial q_i/\partial I$ $(i = 1, \ldots, n)$. The latter is called the *income variation* of the $i$th good. The use of the partial derivative reflects the fixity of all prices.

At the equilibrium position, $u_i = \lambda P_i$ $(i = 1, \ldots, n)$ and $\sum_{i=1}^{n} P_i q_i = I$. When we hold the $P_i$ fixed and vary $I$, the budget constraint yields

$$\sum_{i=1}^{n} P_i \frac{\partial q_i}{\partial I} = \frac{\partial I}{\partial I} = 1. \tag{2.11}$$

The first-order condition $u_i = \lambda P_i$ yields

$$\sum_{j=1}^{n} u_{ij} \frac{\partial q_j}{\partial I} = \frac{\partial \lambda}{\partial I} P_i, \qquad i = 1, \ldots, n, \tag{2.12}$$

since, for example,

$$\frac{\partial u_1}{\partial I} = \left(\frac{\partial u_1}{\partial q_1}\right)\left(\frac{\partial q_1}{\partial I}\right) + \left(\frac{\partial u_1}{\partial q_2}\right)\left(\frac{\partial q_2}{\partial I}\right) + \cdots + \left(\frac{\partial u_1}{\partial q_n}\right)\left(\frac{\partial q_n}{\partial I}\right) = \sum_{j=1}^{n} u_{1j} \frac{\partial q_j}{\partial I}.$$

Substituting $P_i = u_i/\lambda$, and rewriting (2.11) with a $0[-(1/\lambda)(\partial \lambda/\partial I)]$ term added for symmetry,

$$\sum_{i=1}^{n} u_i \left(\frac{\partial q_i}{\partial I}\right) + 0\left(-\frac{1}{\lambda}\frac{\partial \lambda}{\partial I}\right) = \lambda. \tag{2.11a}$$

Similarly, substituting $P_i = u_i/\lambda$ into (2.12) and rearranging terms,

$$\sum_{j=1}^{n} u_{ij} \left(\frac{\partial q_j}{\partial I}\right) + u_i\left(-\frac{1}{\lambda}\frac{\partial \lambda}{\partial I}\right) = 0, \qquad i = 1, \ldots, n. \tag{2.12a}$$

The effect of a shift in income on the purchase of the $i$th commodity will be given by $\partial q_i/\partial I$. Equations (2.11a) and (2.12a) comprise $n + 1$ *linear* equations with $n + 1$ unknowns, the $\partial q_i/\partial I$ $(i = 1, \ldots, n)$, and $[(-1/\lambda)(\partial \lambda/\partial I)]$. The equations are easily solved via Cramer's rule. Form the matrix of coefficients

$$\mathbf{D} = \begin{bmatrix} u_1 & u_2 & \cdots & u_n & 0 \\ u_{11} & u_{12} & \cdots & u_{1n} & u_1 \\ u_{21} & u_{22} & \cdots & u_{2n} & u_2 \\ \cdot & & & & \\ \cdot & & & & \\ \cdot & & & & \\ u_{n1} & u_{n2} & \cdots & u_{nn} & u_n \end{bmatrix}.$$

Then, from Cramer's rule, it immediately follows that

$$\partial q_i/\partial I = \frac{\begin{vmatrix} u_1 & u_2 & \cdots & \lambda & \cdots & u_n & 0 \\ u_{11} & u_{12} & \cdots & 0 & \cdots & u_{1n} & u_1 \\ \cdot & & & & & & \\ \cdot & & & & & & \\ \cdot & & & & & & \\ u_{i1} & u_{i2} & \cdots & 0 & \cdots & u_{in} & u_i \\ \cdot & & & & & & \\ \cdot & & & & & & \\ \cdot & & & & & & \\ u_{n1} & u_{n2} & \cdots & 0 & \cdots & u_{nn} & u_n \end{vmatrix}}{|\mathbf{D}|},$$

where the transpose of the row vector $(\lambda, 0, \ldots, 0)$ replaces the $i$th column of $\mathbf{D}$. The determinant in the numerator may be most easily evaluated by expanding it around the latter column, because all elements of the vector other than $\lambda$ equal zero. The numerator will therefore be given by $\lambda$ multiplied by its cofactor; and the cofactor of $\lambda$ is also the cofactor of $u_i$ in the matrix $\mathbf{D}$. Thus, the numerator of $\partial q_i/\partial I$ is equal to $\lambda D_i$, where $D_i$ is the cofactor of $u_i$, the $i$th element in the first row of $\mathbf{D}$. Hence, the income variation of the $i$th commodity is given by

$$\frac{\partial q_i}{\partial I} = \frac{\lambda D_i}{|\mathbf{D}|}, \qquad i = 1, \ldots, n, \tag{2.13a}$$

and

$$\frac{\partial \lambda}{\partial I} = \frac{-\lambda^2 D_{n+1}}{|\mathbf{D}|}. \tag{2.13b}$$

With $\lambda$ being given a cardinal interpretation as the marginal utility of income, $\partial\lambda/\partial I$ would be the rate of change in the marginal utility of income as income changes.

The effects of an income change on the consumer's equilibrium position are illustrated for the two-good case in Figures 2.7(a) and 2.7(b). Increases in income with

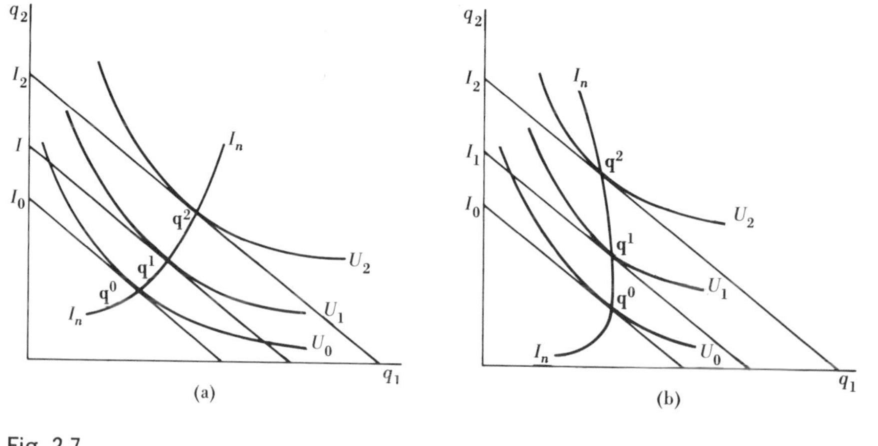


Fig. 2.7

prices in fixed ratio appear as a series of successively higher parallel lines. Moving from $I_0$ to $I_1$ and then $I_2$, we reach utility-maximizing equilibria of $\mathbf{q}^0$, $\mathbf{q}^1$, and $\mathbf{q}^2$ on $U_0$, $U_1$, and $U_2$. The locus of such equilibria traces out the consumer's *income-expansion curve*, labeled $I_n$-$I_n$.

It should be emphasized that $\partial q_i/\partial I$ will not necessarily be positive. That is, a consumer's purchases of a commodity will not necessarily be increased when his income increases, and might in fact be curtailed. For example, at higher income levels consumers *might* prefer to purchase bourbon rather than beer as they now "can afford it," whereas they "couldn't afford it" at lower income levels. The consistently positive slope of the income-expansion curve of Figure 2.7(a) illustrates a case where both $\partial q_1/\partial I$ and $\partial q_2/\partial I$ are positive. The backward-bending income-expansion curve of Figure 2.7(b) illustrates a case where $\partial q_2/\partial I$ is positive, but $\partial q_1/\partial I$ becomes negative. We define an *inferior good* as one for which $\partial q_i/\partial I < 0$: that is, one for which the demand decreases as income increases.

## b. The Substitution and Income Effects

In a similar manner, we may analyze the effects on the consumer's purchases of variations in the $P_i$ ($i = 1, \ldots, n$) while his resources remain fixed. This analysis is particularly interesting, because the consumer is affected by a price change in two ways. First, suppose the price of one good declines; then it has become cheaper relative to other goods, and the consumer may be expected to want more of it than prior to the decline. Indeed, he may be expected to shift many other purchases, both up and down. Second, the price decline in one good has the effect of giving the consumer more *real* income: he could still purchase his original basket and because of the price decrease in one good, have additional funds left over. Some of his purchases will increase as in response to the additional real income, while others may actually decline because the goods are inferior.

Suppose that $P_i$ is varied, income and all other prices remaining constant. From the budget constraint we obtain

$$\sum_{j=1}^{n} P_j \frac{\partial q_j}{\partial P_i} + q_i = \frac{\partial I}{\partial P_i} = 0. \tag{2.14}$$

From $u_i = \lambda P_i$ we obtain

$$\sum_{j=1}^{n} u_{ij} \frac{\partial q_j}{\partial P_i} = \lambda + P_i \frac{\partial \lambda}{\partial P_i}, \tag{2.15}$$

since

$$\begin{aligned} \frac{\partial u_i}{\partial P_i} &= \left(\frac{\partial u_i}{\partial q_1}\right)\left(\frac{\partial q_1}{\partial P_i}\right) + \left(\frac{\partial u_i}{\partial q_2}\right)\left(\frac{\partial q_2}{\partial P_i}\right) + \cdots + \left(\frac{\partial u_i}{\partial q_n}\right)\left(\frac{\partial q_n}{\partial P_i}\right) \\ &= \sum_{j=1}^{n} u_{ij} \frac{\partial q_j}{\partial P_i}. \end{aligned}$$

From $u_k = \lambda P_k$, $k \neq i$, however, we obtain

$$\sum_{j=1}^{n} u_{kj} \frac{\partial q_j}{\partial P_i} = P_k \frac{\partial \lambda}{\partial P_i}, \qquad k = 1, \ldots, n, \; k \neq i, \tag{2.16}$$

since $\partial P_k / \partial P_i = 0$ by assumption. As before, substituting $P_j = u_j/\lambda$ $(j = 1, \ldots, n)$ and rearranging terms, (2.14), (2.15), and (2.16) yield a set of $n + 1$ *linear* equations with $(n + 1)$ unknowns, the $\partial q_j/\partial P_i$ $(j = 1, \ldots, n)$ and $(-1/\lambda)(\partial \lambda/\partial P_i)$:

$$\sum_{j=1}^{n} u_j \left(\frac{\partial q_j}{\partial P_i}\right) + 0 \left(-\frac{1}{\lambda}\frac{\partial \lambda}{\partial P_i}\right) = -\lambda q_i, \tag{2.14a}$$

$$\sum_{j=1}^{n} u_{ij} \left(\frac{\partial q_j}{\partial P_i}\right) + u_i \left(-\frac{1}{\lambda}\frac{\partial \lambda}{\partial P_i}\right) = \lambda, \tag{2.15a}$$

$$\sum_{j=1}^{n} u_{kj} \left(\frac{\partial q_j}{\partial P_i}\right) + u_k \left(-\frac{1}{\lambda}\frac{\partial \lambda}{\partial P_i}\right) = 0, \qquad k = 1, \ldots, n, \; k \neq i. \tag{2.16a}$$

Except for the right-hand side, these are the same equations from which we derived the $\partial q_i/\partial I$ that are now replaced by $\partial q_j/\partial P_i$, while the $[-(1/\lambda)\ (\partial\lambda/\partial P_i)]$ term replaces the $[-(1/\lambda)\ (\partial\lambda/\partial I)]$ term. Placing Equation (2.15a) in the empty "$i$th" slot in the third set of equations, (2.16a), so that the vector on the right would be the transpose of $(-\lambda q_i, 0, \ldots, \lambda, \ldots, 0)$, and again using Cramer's rule, we derive

$$\frac{\partial q_j}{\partial P_i} = \frac{\begin{vmatrix} u_1 & u_2 & \cdots & -\lambda q_i & \cdots & u_n & 0 \\ u_{11} & u_{12} & \cdots & 0 & \cdots & u_{1n} & u_1 \\ \vdots & & & & & & \\ u_{i1} & u_{i2} & \cdots & \lambda & \cdots & u_{in} & u_i \\ \vdots & & & & & & \\ u_{n1} & u_{n2} & \cdots & 0 & \cdots & u_{nn} & u_n \end{vmatrix}}{|\mathbf{D}|}.$$

The $j$th column of $\mathbf{D}$ is replaced by the constant column vector to give the determinant in the numerator. Once again expanding on this $j$th column to take advantage of the $n - 1$ zeros appearing in it, the numerator of $\partial q_j/\partial P_i$ will be given by $-\lambda q_i$ multiplied by its cofactor, which is also the cofactor of $u_j$ in $\mathbf{D}$, plus $\lambda$ multiplied by its cofactor, which is the cofactor of $u_{ij}$ in $\mathbf{D}$. Thus, the numerator is equal to $-\lambda q_i D_j + \lambda D_{ij}$, where $D_j$ is the cofactor of $u_j$ and $D_{ij}$ is the cofactor of $u_{ij}$. The latter is the cofactor of the element in the $j$th column and $(i + 1)$th row of $\mathbf{D}$.

The term $(-1/\lambda)(\partial\lambda/\partial P_i)$ is of no special interest, and we concentrate on $\partial q_j/\partial P_i$, which is given by

$$\frac{\partial q_j}{\partial P_i} = \frac{-\lambda q_i D_j + \lambda D_{ij}}{|\mathbf{D}|}, \qquad j = 1, \ldots, n. \tag{2.17}$$

But from (2.13a), $\lambda D_j/|\mathbf{D}| = \partial q_j/\partial I$ is the income variation of the $j$th good. Letting $\lambda D_{ij}/|\mathbf{D}| = S_{ij}$, we may therefore write

$$\frac{\partial q_j}{\partial P_i} = -q_i \left(\frac{\partial q_j}{\partial I}\right) + S_{ij}, \qquad j = 1, \ldots, n. \tag{2.17a}$$

Equation (2.17a) is the Slutsky equation,[11] whereby the effect of a change in the price of the $i$th commodity on the purchases of the $j$th is analyzed as the sum of two components. The first component, $-q_i(\partial q_j/\partial I)$, is called the *income effect.* Since $q_i$ is necessarily positive, the income effect will be positive only if the *income variation* $\partial q_j/\partial I$ is negative. That is, the *income* effect on the $j$th good of a *fall* in the price of the $i$th good will act as an incentive for the consumer to *reduce* his purchases of the $j$th good when the latter is an inferior good. In other cases, the effect of giving the consumer more *real* income as a result of the price reduction will either be neutral or will encourage additional purchases of the $j$th good.

To interpret the $S_{ij}$ term we allow for the fact that a price change has the effect of changing the consumer's real income. If a price falls, the consumer can purchase the same basket of goods, *plus* an additional amount. The addition comes about because he need not spend as much money to acquire the same amount of the good that has fallen in price. Indeed, if the price of the $i$th good has changed by $dP_i$, the consumer can purchase exactly the same basket of goods if his total expenditures change by $dE = q_i\, dP_i$. We might therefore give (or take from) the consumer a *compensating variation* in income, $dI = dE = q_i\, dP_i$, so as to leave him with the *possibility* of purchasing exactly the same basket of goods he purchased before the price change. He will not, however, necessarily prefer this same basket, because the price change has altered the *relative* cost of each of the other goods to the $i$th good. Thus, if ham becomes less expensive relative to all other goods, even when one's income permits exactly the same purchases as before, one might *prefer* to purchase more ham and more eggs, but less corned beef and less cabbage.

In particular, the consumer will alter his purchases of the $j$th commodity by

$$dq_j = \frac{\partial q_j}{\partial P_i}\, dP_i + \frac{\partial q_j}{\partial I}\, dI = \frac{\partial q_j}{\partial P_i}\, dP_i + \frac{\partial q_j}{\partial I}\,(q_i\, dP_i),$$

since both $P_i$ and $I$ have been changed. Dividing both sides by $dP_i$,

$$\frac{dq_j}{dP_i} = \frac{\partial q_j}{\partial P_i} + \left(\frac{\partial q_j}{\partial I}\right) q_i.$$

The intuitive sense of the latter equation is that it expresses the *total* change in the consumer's purchase of the $j$th good when the $i$th price changes as the sum of two terms: the first term is the portion attributable to the change in *price* when all other prices *and* income are held fixed; the second term is the portion attributable to the compensating change in *income* when *all* prices are fixed. We obtain a *total* derivative as the sum of *partial* derivatives. Substituting for $\partial q_j/\partial P_i$ from the Slutsky

[11] See Slutsky, "On the Theory of the Budget of the Consumer."

equation (2.17a), we find

$$\frac{dq_j}{dP_i} = -q_i\left(\frac{\partial q_j}{\partial I}\right) + S_{ij} + q_i\left(\frac{\partial q_j}{\partial I}\right) = S_{ij}. \tag{2.18}$$

Hence, $dq_j/dP_i = S_{ij}$ is the variation in $q_j$ effected by a change in $P_i$ that is compensated for by an income change, or simply the *compensated variation*. This compensated variation $S_{ij}$ is called the *substitution effect* of a price change, for it isolates the *price* effects from the *income* effects of a price change. Thus $\partial q_j/\partial P_i$, the change in $q_j$ resulting from a change in $P_i$, all other prices and income held fixed, is given by the Slutsky equation as the sum of an income and substitution effect.

The effects of a price change are illustrated in Figure 2.8 for the two-good case. The curve labeled $P_r$-$P_r$ traces out the *price-expansion curve* showing the consumer's

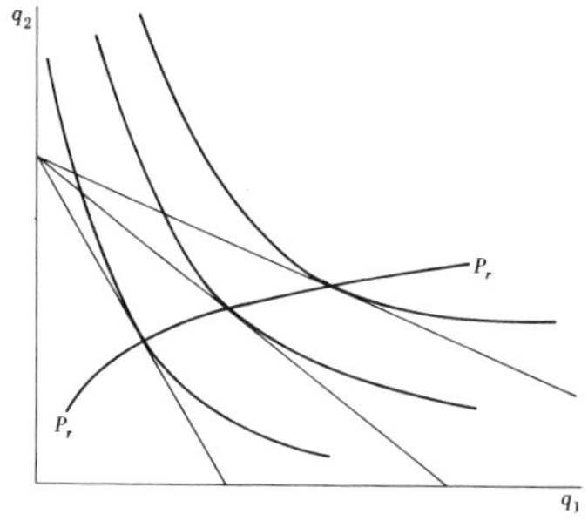


Fig. 2.8

preferred purchases as the ratio $P_2/P_1$ changes, or the change in consumer demand as $P_1$ changes, with other prices and income held fixed.

Figure 2.9 indicates how the substitution and income effects of a compensated price change may be analyzed. In Figure 2.9(a), $P_1$ falls, income and other prices remaining fixed. The effect is to move the consumer from $\mathbf{q}^0$ on $U_0$ to $\mathbf{q}^2$ on $U_2$. The consumer would also be on the indifference curve labeled $U_2$ with the price ratio un-

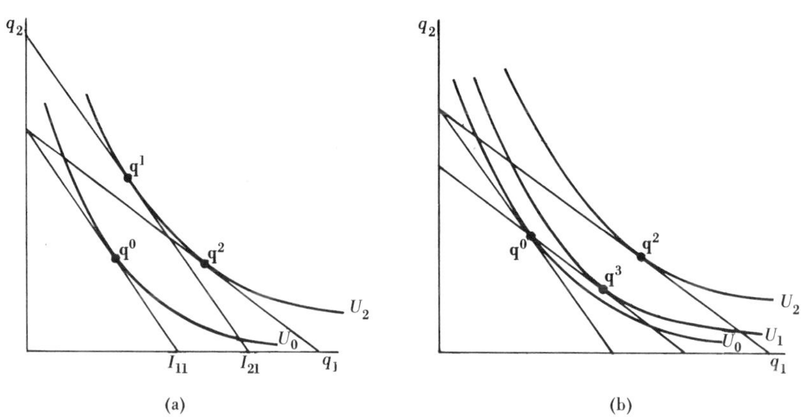


Fig. 2.9

altered and income raised from $I_{11}$ to $I_{21}$. Thus the move from $\mathbf{q}^0$ to $\mathbf{q}^2$ can be viewed as a move from $\mathbf{q}^0$ to $\mathbf{q}^1$ via the income effect and from $\mathbf{q}^1$ to the ultimate equilibrium of $\mathbf{q}^2$ through the substitution effect. Alternatively, the move from $\mathbf{q}^0$ to $\mathbf{q}^2$ might be viewed as depicted in Figure 2.9(b). Here, the consumer moves from $\mathbf{q}^0$ to $\mathbf{q}^3$ on a higher indifference curve $U_1$ via the substitution effect with the same (compensated) income but a different set of price ratios. He then moves from $\mathbf{q}^3$ to $\mathbf{q}^2$ via the higher income and the new price ratios. Neither of these two classic graphical interpretations of the Slutsky equation exactly conforms to the equation. Indeed, they differ slightly from each other. When, however, the price change is infinitesimal, as implied by the use of the derivative (that is, in the limit as $\Delta P_j \rightarrow 0$) the two approaches coincide.[12] The graphs are a useful way to depict the two effects.

### c. Substitutes and Complements

An elementary column operation makes $\mathbf{D}$ symmetric. Hence, $D_{ij} = D_{ji}$ and $S_{ij} = \lambda D_{ij}/|\mathbf{D}| = \lambda D_{ji}/|\mathbf{D}| = S_{ji}$. The substitution effect on the $j$th commodity of a price change in the $i$th is therefore the same as the substitution effect of a change in the price of the $j$th on the demand for the $i$th commodity. If $S_{ij} > 0$, the goods are called *substitutes*, since an increase (decrease) in the price of the $i$th commodity will increase (decrease) the quantity of the $j$th commodity demanded by the consumer; if $S_{ij} < 0$, the goods are called *complements*, since an increase (decrease) in the price of the $i$th commodity will decrease (increase) demand for the $j$th, income and other prices held constant. If $S_{ij} = 0$, the goods are independent.

The sense of this terminology follows on the heels of the fact that $S_{ii} = dq_i/dP_i$ can be shown to be negative when the indifference surface is, as it has been assumed to be, convex. Then a compensated price increase (decrease) will lead the consumer to demand less (more) of the good whose price has changed. If a second good "substitutes" for the good in question, the demand for it will increase (decrease); if the second good "complements" the good in question, the demand for it will also fall (rise). If the goods are independent, the second good will be unaffected. For a given consumer, for example, beer and bourbon might be substitutes, beer and pretzels might be complements, and beer and hand cream might be independent.

It is interesting to note that at least one pair of goods in a consumer's basket *must* be substitutes. Consider the expression

$$\sum_{i=1}^{n} \left(\frac{\partial q_j}{\partial P_i}\right) P_i.$$

From (2.17),

$$\sum_{i=1}^{n} \left(\frac{\partial q_j}{\partial P_i}\right) P_i = \sum_{i=1}^{n} \frac{-\lambda q_i D_j + \lambda D_{ij}}{|\mathbf{D}|} P_i$$

$$= \frac{1}{|\mathbf{D}|}\left(\sum_{i=1}^{n} \lambda D_{ij} P_i - \sum_{i=1}^{n} \lambda P_i q_i D_j\right).$$

But $\partial q_j/\partial I = \lambda D_j/|\mathbf{D}|$. Multiplying this expression by $I$ and adding it to the former

[12] See Hicks, *Value and Capital*, pp. 31–32 and 308–311. Also see J. L. Mosak, "On the Interpretation of the Fundamental Equation of Value Theory," in O. Lange, F. McIntyre, and T. O. Yntema, eds., *Studies in Mathematical Economics and Econometrics* (Chicago: University of Chicago Press, 1942), pp. 69–74.

expression gives

$$\sum_{i=1}^{n}\left(\frac{\partial q_j}{\partial P_i}\right)P_i + \frac{\lambda D_j I}{|\mathbf{D}|} = \frac{1}{|\mathbf{D}|}\left(\sum_{i=1}^{n}\lambda D_{ij}P_i - \sum_{i=1}^{n}\lambda P_i q_i D_j + \lambda D_j I\right)$$

$$= \frac{1}{|\mathbf{D}|}\left(\sum_{i=1}^{n}\lambda D_{ij}P_i + \lambda D_j\left[I - \sum_{i=1}^{n}P_i q_i\right]\right)$$

$$= \frac{1}{|\mathbf{D}|}\sum_{i=1}^{n}\lambda D_{ij}P_i = \frac{1}{|\mathbf{D}|}\sum_{i=1}^{n}\lambda D_{ij}\left(\frac{u_i}{\lambda}\right) = \frac{1}{|\mathbf{D}|}\sum_{i=1}^{n}D_{ij}u_i,$$

since $I - \sum_{i=1}^{n} P_i q_i = 0$ and $P_i = u_i/\lambda$ $(i = 1, \ldots, n)$ by the first-order conditions. But $\sum_{i=1}^{n} D_{ij}u_i$ is an expansion of $\mathbf{D}$ along the first row in terms of alien cofactors, those of the $j$th column and the $(i + 1)$th row. Such an expansion, it is well known, is necessarily 0. Hence

$$\frac{1}{|\mathbf{D}|}\sum_{i=1}^{n}\lambda D_{ij}P_i = 0 \quad \text{or} \quad \sum_{i=1}^{n}P_i S_{ij} = 0. \tag{2.19}$$

Since $S_{ii} < 0$, we must have at least one $S_{ij} > 0$, $i \neq j$. Therefore at least one pair of goods must, for a given consumer, be substitutes; they cannot all be complements or independent goods.

Moreover, since $\lambda$ and $q_i$ are necessarily positive, the sign of $\partial q_j/\partial P_i = -q_i(\partial q_j/\partial I) + S_{ij}$ will depend upon both the income and substitution effects. In particular, if $j = i$, since $S_{ii} < 0$, $\partial q_i/\partial P_i$ will be positive only if $q_i(\partial q_i/\partial I) < 0$ and of large enough absolute magnitude so that the first (positive) term in $\partial q_i/\partial P_i$ overcomes the second (negative) term. Hence a rise (fall) in price will cause the demand for the commodity to rise (fall), other prices and income constant, only (but not necessarily) if the good is an inferior good. Such a phenomenon, whereby a *reduction* in its price will have the paradoxical result of actually effecting a *decrease* in demand for a commodity, is referred to as *Giffen's Paradox*.[13]

[13] Alfred Marshall (*Principles of Economics*, p. 132), giving credit where credit was due, noted that "as Sir R. Giffen has pointed out, a rise in the price of bread makes so large a drain on the resources of the poorer labouring families and raises so much the marginal utility of money to them, that they are forced to curtail their consumption of meat and the more expensive farinaceous foods: and, bread being still the cheapest food which they can get and will take, they consume more, not less of it. But such cases are rare; when they are met with, each must be treated on its own merits." Had Marshall's *Principles* been written a century earlier (the first edition appeared in 1890), Marie Antoinette would probably have said "Let them eat farinaceous foods" and thereby captured the hearts of "the poorer labouring families."

## 2.6 THE CONSUMER'S DEMAND CURVE

### a. The Demand Curve

It is now clear that *if*—and it is a big *if*—(1) the consumer were as rational and unidirected as assumed here, and if (2) his demand for a product depended solely on his income and the prices of all products, we could derive his *demand curve* directly from our indifference surface-budget constraint analysis. That is, we could determine how much of each product the consumer would be willing to buy at any price, given his income and all other prices. In particular, once again consider the case of two goods as depicted in Figure 2.8. The levels of $q_1$ given by the series of points traced out by $P_r$-$P_r$ at various prices of $P_1$, with $P_2$ and $I$ fixed, could be plotted as in Figure 2.10. This curve, $D$-$D$, is the demand curve for good 1 with income held fixed.

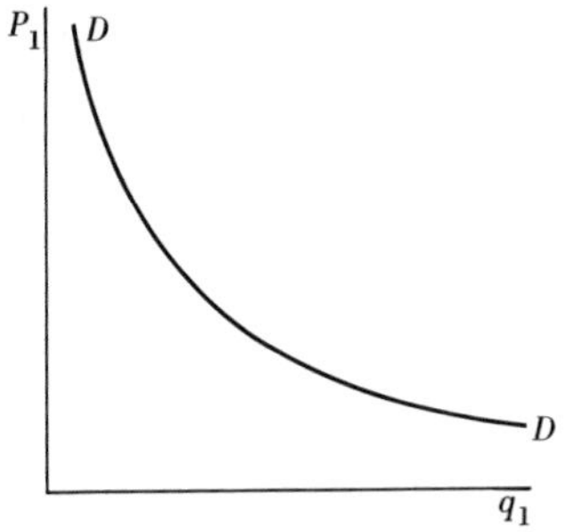


Fig. 2.10

The points on the curve $D$-$D$ correspond exactly to those on the curve $P_r$-$P_r$. From the previous assertion that $S_{11} = dq_1/dP_1 < 0$ *and the Slutsky equation*, it follows that the demand curve will be negatively sloped as long as the good is not an inferior good for which the conditions resulting in an instance of Giffen's Paradox apply. In the latter event, the price-expansion line $P_r$-$P_r$ would "bend backward" and the demand curve would have positive slope at some, if not all, prices. Reasoning from the Slutsky equation, then, we will be quite confident in drawing our individual demand curves with negative slope, on the grounds that Giffen's Paradox will be the exception rather than the rule. Moreover, when (as in later chapters) we are dealing with aggregates, and when in the aggregate we might expect individual Giffen effects to be overwhelmed, or at least their influence negated, by the behavior of non-Giffen consumers, the inferences we draw from the Slutsky equation will permit us to confidently draw our industry demand curves with negative slope—and this presumption will be of vital importance.

In general, depicting the demand curve in the two-dimensional price-quantity space is interesting, informative, and convenient. It can also be misleading, however, if one forgets that a host of other prices and factors will influence the consumer's preferences. Frequently we will find it useful to "hold these constant." This will, nonetheless, be a momentary neglect for the convenience of expositing a particular model and not a permanent and unjustifiable dismissal. The *theoretical* analysis of consumer behavior makes it abundantly clear that the consumer's demand curves will ordinarily not be only two dimensional. Furthermore, the theory can suggest circumstances under which an *empirical* analysis of demand might be expected, a priori, to yield particular signs and magnitudes for particular parameters. This could be the case when, for example, one had a sound basis for hypothesizing substitutability or complementarity between certain goods, or when a good was thought to be inferior. The theory of consumer behavior thus helps us to *anticipate how* the consumer might react to changes in the key economic variables of prices and income, as well as to *interpret why* he behaves as he does.

### b. Some Elasticity Concepts

It is frequently useful to know the relative change in, say, the demand (or supply) for the $j$th commodity that results from a small relative change in an influencing factor, say price or income. The ratios of these changes are called *elasticities*, for they measure the *responsiveness* of demand or supply to price or income changes. Thus the price *arc* elasticity of demand for the $j$th commodity *between* two points, $(q_{j1}, P_{j1})$ and $(q_{j2}, P_{j2})$, on the consumer's demand curve will be given by $\eta_a = (\Delta q_j/q_j)/(\Delta P_j/P_j)$. Unfortunately, the use of *arc* elasticity is somewhat ambiguous, for it is not clear whether the values for $q_j$ and $P_j$ should be $(q_{j1}, P_{j1})$ or $(q_{j2}, P_{j2})$ or an average of the two, and the answers will commonly differ depending upon the choice. With infinitely divisible $q_j$ and continuous demand curves, one can, however, speak of *point* elasticity, or the price elasticity of demand at *a* specific *point* $(q_j, P_j)$. This is defined as

$$\eta = \lim_{\Delta P_j \to 0} \left(\frac{\Delta q_j/q_j}{\Delta P_j/P_j}\right) = \left(\frac{\partial q_j}{\partial P_j}\right)\left(\frac{P_j}{q_j}\right).$$

As long as the demand curve is negatively sloped, $\partial q_j/\partial P_j < 0$ and the price elasticity will be nonpositive.[14]

A major advantage of describing demand in terms of its price elasticity is that $\eta$ is dimensionless. That is, when we compute $\eta$ we will always be evaluating $\eta =$ (quantity/price)(price/quantity) $=$ a scalar. Thus, the measure is independent of the arbitrary choice of units with which price and quantity are measured. Further, one can conveniently classify demand into the primary categories of perfectly elastic ($\eta = -\infty$), relatively elastic ($\eta < -1$), unit elastic ($\eta = -1$), relatively inelastic ($-1 < \eta < 0$), or perfectly inelastic ($\eta = 0$) and thereby compare the responsiveness of different commodity demands to price changes, even though one commodity is measured as tons of steel and the other as ounces of butter. Moreover, the price elasticity of demand will be of particular interest to a firm since, for example, if demand is price elastic at the given price, a price decrease will raise quantity proportionately more than the price decrease, so that total revenue $=$ (price)(quantity) will increase. With unit price elasticity total revenue will not change, and with inelastic demand it will decline when price is reduced. We shall frequently encounter elasticity concepts in our models to determine price and output in the firm, as the firm that is evaluating the impact of a price change, or the firm simply attempting to determine price, will have to assess the effects on its total revenue of various prices—in effect, it will have to assess the elasticity of demand.

Despite the temptation to do so, however, we should not equate elasticity and

[14] The price elasticity of demand is sometimes given as $|\eta|$ to eliminate the necessarily nonpositive posture that it takes. We will not so treat it unless explicity noted.

slope. The slope of the demand curve is only one aspect of demand. We must also beware of referring to *the* price elasticity of demand for a commodity. Ordinarily, the elasticity of demand will *vary* depending upon the *point* on the demand curve at which it is measured. In fact, since with a linear demand curve the slope is constant, $\eta$ will change as $P_j/q_j$ changes. As price falls, then, quantity increases and $\eta$ runs the gamut from $-\infty$ to 0 for nonnegative $P_j$ and $q_j$.

In a similar fashion, the *cross-elasticity* of demand for the $j$th commodity in terms of the $k$th price is given by $\eta_k = (\partial q_j/\partial P_k)(P_k/q_j)$. Also of interest is the *income elasticity*, analogously defined as $\eta_I = (\partial q_j/\partial I)(I/q_j)$. In each case, we have a dimensionless measure, unaffected by the arbitrary choice of units, to measure the responsiveness of demand to price and income changes. Similar measures are appropriate for descriptions of supply.

## EXERCISES

1. (a) Examine the following constrained functions for relative maxima and minima both by explicit substitution of the constraint into the objective function and by Lagrangian methods:

   (i) $f(x, y) = 2x - 3y^2$ subject to $g(x, y) = x^2 + y^2 - 1 = 0$.

   (ii) $f(x, y) = 3 + 4x^2 - 4x + 2y^2 - 2y$ subject to $x + y = 1$.

   (iii) $f(x_1, x_2, x_3) = x_1x_2^2x_3$ subject to $x_1 + x_2 + x_3 = 2$.

   (b) Illustrate the optimization for parts (a) and (b) via a graph.

2. Suppose one seeks the extreme point of a function $f(x_1, \ldots, x_n)$ subject to $m$ constraints $g_j(x_1, \ldots, x_n) = 0$ $(j = 1, \ldots, m)$. The Lagrangian becomes $L = f(x_1, \ldots, x_n) - \sum_{j=1}^{m} \lambda_j g_j(x_1, \ldots, x_n)$. The first-order necessary conditions for an extreme point are $\partial L/\partial x_i = 0$ $(i = 1, \ldots, n)$ and $\partial L/\partial \lambda_j = 0$ $(j = 1, \ldots, m)$. Let $\mathbf{0}$ be a zero matrix and define the following matrices:

$$\mathbf{R} = \left[\frac{\partial g_j}{\partial x_i}\right], \quad \mathbf{S} = \left[\frac{\partial^2 f}{\partial x_i\, \partial x_k} - \sum_{j=1}^{n} \lambda_j \frac{\partial^2 g_j}{\partial x_i\, \partial x_k}\right], \quad \mathbf{T} = \begin{bmatrix} \mathbf{0} & \mathbf{R} \\ \mathbf{R}' & \mathbf{S} \end{bmatrix}.$$

The second-order sufficient conditions for a local *minimum* are that the last $n - m$ principal minors of $\mathbf{T}$ be of sign $(-1)^m$. For a local *maximum* the last $n - m$ principal minors alternate in sign, the first being of sign $(-1)^{m+1}$.

Examine the following for maxima and minima:

   (a) $f(x, y, z) = x^2 + y^2 + z^2$ subject to $g_1(x, y, z) = z - xy - 5$ and $g_2(x, y, z) = x + y + z - 1$.

   (b) $f(x, y, z) = xyz/(2x + y + 3z)$ subject to $g_1(x, y, z) = 100 - xyz$ and $g_2(x, y, z) = 20 - x - z$.

3. An individual with a utility function given by $U = x_1^{1/2}x_2^{2/5}$ plans to spend his entire income of \$5000 on goods $x_1$ and $x_2$. The price of $x_1$ is \$2 and the price of $x_2$ is \$3.

   (a) How much of each good will he purchase to maximize his utility?

   (b) Graph the optimal indifference curve and the consumer's budget line.

   (c) Derive his demand curve for $x_1$ at his present income.

   (d) Derive the price elasticity of demand for $x_2$.

   (e) Derive the cross-elasticity of demand for $x_1$ in terms of the price of $x_2$.

   (f) Derive the income elasticity of $x_1$.

4. Suppose that the price of $x_1$ in the previous problem falls to \$1.75. Describe, in detail, the effects on the consumer's purchases of each of the two goods in terms of the substitution and income effects.

5. A cost-of-living index measures the percentage change in expenditures required to maintain a standard of living from one period to another. Develop *at least* two models for cost-of-living indexes and determine the change in the cost of living for the consumer of Exercise 3 as a result of the price decrease in $x_1$. By how much would the price of $x_2$ have to change under each index in order to leave the cost of living to this particular consumer unaltered? What does any of this have to do with indifference curves?

6. Sketch the indifference curves for two goods that are (a) perfect substitutes, (b) perfect complements, (c) independent. Define these concepts.

7. Demonstrate in a graph the phenomenon of Giffen's Paradox.

8. Show that the first-order conditions for utility maximization are invariant with respect to the choice of a utility index.

9. Show that changing all prices and income by a fixed factor $\theta$ will not alter the consumer's optimal basket of goods. Show that $S_{ii} < 0$.

10. Show that the income elasticity of a good for a particular consumer will be equal to the negative of the sum of the price elasticity of the good and the cross-elasticities of the good with respect to all other prices.

11. Derive the equation of a demand curve with constant price elasticity, given all other prices and income.

12. Prove that a local maximum of a concave function is a global maximum.

13. Consider an $n$-dimensional region $X$, and any two points from the region, $\mathbf{x}_1$ and $\mathbf{x}_2$. The *convex combination* of $\mathbf{x}_1$ and $\mathbf{x}_2$ is defined to be the point $\mathbf{x} = \theta\mathbf{x}_1 + (1 - \theta)\mathbf{x}_2$, $0 \leq \theta \leq 1$. $X$ is said to be *convex* whenever $\mathbf{x}$ is also contained in $X$, for all $\theta$. The $\mathbf{x}_i$ are then said to comprise a *convex set.*

(a) Give graphical interpretations in two and three dimensions of the concept of a convex set.

(b) Prove that if $W = w(\mathbf{y})$ is a convex function, the set of points $Y$ satisfying the constraint $w(\mathbf{y}) \leq 0$ is a convex set.

(c) Prove that the intersection of convex sets is also a convex set.

14. Consider the following problem: minimize $Z = 3x - 4y$ subject to (1) $y - 3x^2 - 2x - 3 \geq 0$; (2) $x \geq -1$; (3) $y - 20x + x^2 \leq 0$. The set of points satisfying all the (inequality) constraints is called the *feasible region.*

(a) Show that the set of points in the feasible region comprise a convex set.

(b) Solve the problem graphically.

(c) Suppose the third constraint were $y - 20x + x^2 \geq 0$. Would the set of points in the feasible region comprise a convex set? Would this problem seem to be more or less difficult to solve than the former problem?

(d) Based on the previous answers, make some suggestions as to the relationship between convex sets, feasible regions, and optimization problems in which there are inequality constraints.

# 3

# THE THEORY OF PRODUCT DEMAND: The Industry

## 3.1 INTRODUCTION

Few if any consumers are likely to budget their expenditures with the calculated precision that the equation of rates of commodity substitution and price ratios requires, and rare indeed is the opportunity to purchase alternative baskets of infinitely divisible commodities.[1] Yet the consumer's ability to satisfy various wants, desires, and needs *will* be restricted by his resources. With varying degrees of conscientiousness he *is* continually required to decide whether to purchase an additional unit of a commodity.

While most consumers are unlikely to react to price and income changes in as *systematic* a fashion as implied by the theory of consumer behavior, one can anticipate their *tendency* to behave along the *general lines* suggested by the model. When the price of a specific product in his list of fairly regularly purchased items undergoes a relatively small price increase, the average consumer is not necessarily going to *instantly* adjust his purchases in response to the slightly higher price. Within the price range involved, his demand for the product might, in fact, be perfectly inelastic. Or he may simply show a momentary inflexibility in adjusting to new information of comparatively minor importance. Perhaps his next purchases *will* be reduced to reflect the higher price and a reevaluation of how he prefers to spend his income.

At a given moment, consumers may underreact or overreact to new information about price. The consumer who threatens "never again" to buy a particular item, following an increase in the good's price, is likely to be somewhat overstating his position, and the credibility of a consumer who would "give anything" to own a particular piece of merchandise is somewhat in doubt. What does seem certain, however, is that the individual's demand for each product will commonly be related to its price. Unless the demand curve is perfectly inelastic in the price-quantity space, it

[1] This assumption could be abandoned without altering the conclusions. In practice, our observations would be limited to specific finite *points* and the consumer would choose from among these *points* so as to maximize his utility within his income. The fundamental principles used to make this choice would not change.

will ordinarily look something like that of Figure 2.10, even if it does have discontinuities as well as an apparent inconsistency or two. Figure 2.10 might describe how many pounds of steak a housewife would be willing to purchase on a particular Monday at various prices per pound, given a set of all other prices, the family's income, their tastes and preferences, whether the weather forecast indicates they will be able to take advantage of their outdoor grill, plans for entertaining, and so forth.

If a demand curve for a product could be obtained for each consumer, and if these curves were independent of one another, each consumer's willingness to purchase being independent of the desires of others, aggregate demand for the product could be obtained by summing up the individual demands at each price. The practical facts of empirical analysis are, however, that normally we do not gather the individual data but instead observe only the aggregated demands. Nevertheless, we do well to recognize the aggregate as the sum of individual components, and behavior in the aggregate as reflecting the combined behavior of diverse individuals, each of whom has his own unique set of preferences.

It should also be noted that the "product," the "industry," and the "market" to which a demand curve refers may be broadly or narrowly defined. Soft drinks may represent a product, and for certain purposes the demand for soft drinks in the United States may represent a meaningful concept. One can, however, distinguish between lemon-lime soft drinks and cola drinks. With equal relevance, one can refer to the demand for each of these products and consider the producers of each to comprise an analytically meaningful industry. Further, all firms do not necessarily sell their product in each and every submarket—that is, in each place where the product is sold. It is even clearer that not all buyers, and certainly not individual consumers, shop in each submarket. There are marketing areas, and "the market" may be composed of distinct and isolated submarkets or of overlapping and interrelated submarkets. Thus, one could be interested in the demand for cola drinks in Texas, the demand for lemon-lime drinks in New England, or the demand for soft drinks in the United States.[2]

Very frequently, the definitions of product and market will be arbitrary and dependent upon empirical needs. When, therefore, we note that the focus of this chapter will be the demand for the product of a particular industry, we might also note that in application this description would warrant considerably greater precision. For theoretical convenience, however, we shall by and large simply refer to the total demand for a homogeneous product (such that each and every consumer considers all varieties to be perfect substitutes), stripping away the homogeneity assumption only as the occasion demands.

## 3.2 THE INDUSTRY DEMAND CURVE

Assume, then, that there are $M$ consumers, each of whom has a demand for a homogeneous product $H$. The $j$th consumer's demand curve will be given by $q_{jH} = D_j(P, V)$, where $q_{jH}$ denotes the quantity of $H$ demanded by the $j$th consumer, $P$ denotes price, and for the moment $V$ encompasses "all other influential factors," including income. Ceteris paribus—that is, holding these other variables constant at $V = \bar{V}$—the industry demand curve in the price-quantity space, subject to a

[2] Determining the most relevant market is of particular interest in the application of antitrust laws. The latter are frequently concerned with the dominance of individual firms in specific markets, and particularly with the effects of mergers in these markets. The definition of the *relevant* market is, therefore, very often the heart of the issue.

qualification noted below, will be given by

$$Q = \sum_j D_j(P, \bar{V}) = D(P, \bar{V}).$$

Specifically, with price the ordinate and quantity the abscissa, the industry demand curve will be the horizontal sum of the individual demand curves, or the total demand at each price will be the sum of the individual demands.

Figure 3.1 illustrates this horizontal summation for two consumers with linear demand curves of $q_{1H} = 1000 - 100P$ and $q_{2H} = 1010 - 90P$. These curves are shown in Figure 3.1(a). The total demand of *these two* consumers is denoted by $Q_{1+2}$. Since consumer 1 will not pay more than 10 for the product (that is, $q_{1H} = 0$ when $P = 10$), total demand at prices of 10 or more but no greater than 11.22, where $q_{2H} = 0$, is given by

$$Q_{1+2} = q_{2H} = 1010 - 90P.$$

At prices no greater than 10,

$$Q_{1+2} = q_{1H} + q_{2H} = (1000 - 100P) + (1010 - 90P) = 2010 - 190P.$$

Where $P = 9$, for example,

$$q_{1H} = 1000 - 100(9) = 100, \qquad q_{2H} = 1010 - 90(9) = 200,$$

and

$$Q_{1+2} = 2010 - 190(9) = 300.$$

The total demand curve is therefore composed of the two linear segments, $Q_{1+2} = 1010 - 90P$ $(11.22 \geq P \geq 10)$ and $Q_{1+2} = 2010 - 190P$ $(10 \geq P \geq 0)$, shown in Figure 3.1(b). Note that a *horizontal* summation yields an aggregate demand curve whether quantity is written as a function of price, $q_{jH} = f_j(P, V)$, price as a function

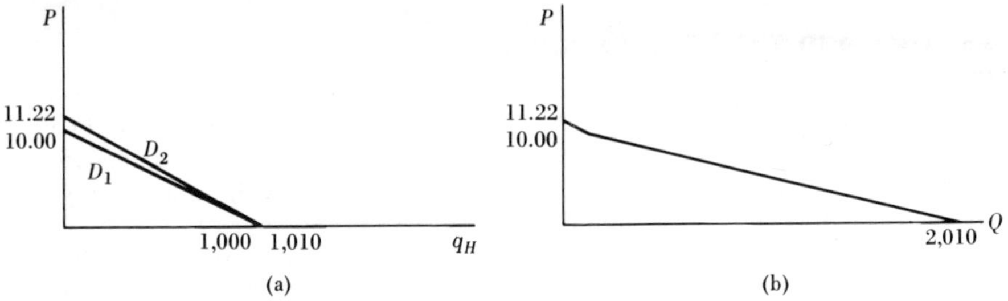


Fig. 3.1

of quantity, $P = g_j(q_{jH}, V)$, or whether it is not explicitly stated which is the independent and which the dependent variable. In this last case, demand would be given by the implicit function $h_j(P, q_{jH}, V) = 0$.

The previous example demonstrates that the industry demand curve will not necessarily be continuous even when the individual curves are. Discontinuities are caused by the fact that in summing the functions we only add those functions for which $q_{jH} \geq 0$ at the prices in question. If *all* $q_{jH}$ were nonnegative functions of $P$ for *all* $P \geq 0$, *then* the statement $Q = \sum_j q_{jH}$ would hold without qualification. As it is, discontinuities in the industry demand curve can arise, even when all consumers have continuous demand curves, at each price at which individual consumers leave the market. Nevertheless, as the number of consumers increases and $M \to \infty$, for all intents and purposes the industry demand curve can be assumed to be continuous; unless otherwise noted, we shall make this assumption. Industry demand will be given by $Q = D(P, V) = D(P, V_1, \ldots, V_s)$. The continuity assumption permits the use of the calculus, simplifies the analysis and exposition, and where invoked does not cause one's desire for realism undue stress. Hence, the industry price elasticity is written $\eta = (\partial Q/\partial P)(P/Q)$. The elasticity with respect to $V_k$ is $\eta_k = (\partial Q/\partial V_k) \cdot (V_k/Q)$, so long as $\partial Q/\partial V_k$ exists at the point at which the elasticity is desired.

The $V_k$ are potentially many and (as the $V$ suggests) varied. $V_1$ might be personal disposable income or $I$; $V_k$ $(k = 2, \ldots, n)$ might be the price of another commodity or $P_k$ $(k = 2, \ldots, n)$; $V_{n+1}$ might be consumer purchases at some previous time or $Q_{-1}$; $V_{n+2}$ might be a discontinuous *dummy variable* reflecting whether or not it has been a particularly cold season or $D_1$. Here "particularly cold season" might mean that the temperature averages less than 32°, so that $D_1 = 1$ if the temperature does average less than 32°, but $D_1 = 0$ otherwise. In this case, demand would not be a continuous function of $V_{n+2}$. In a situation in which the product in question is a durable good, the demand at any moment of time can be expected to be related to the stocks of the good held by prospective buyers, or $V_{n+3}$. This factor could become particularly crucial with respect to interindustry demand for machinery and raw materials, say, or any other products that may have investment or inventory potential. An especially attractive feature of such a "capital stock" variable is that it injects an important element of dynamism into what might otherwise erroneously appear to be a very static demand curve. Similar definitions would be applied to the remaining $s - n - 3$ variables. The point is that we might not refer to these other variables in much of the theoretical discussion, relegating them, via a ceteris paribus assumption, to the immediate background. Their relevance and existence are still recognized, however, and will necessarily be taken into consideration as our models become more general, applicable, and empirical in nature.

## 3.3 TIME AND THE DEMAND CURVE

Time is an important factor from which much of microeconomic theory is in effect protected. It is reasonable to expect the demand for color television sets to vary from one day to the next. The number of color television sets consumers will be willing to buy at an *average* price $P$ during any one year may differ between years; it will assuredly differ from the number they will be willing to purchase at that average price on a given day. The quantity demanded, like the quantity the firm produces, will be a *rate* per unit of that time period chosen as the base. The demand function could, therefore, be more explicitly written as

$$Q = Q_t = D(P_t, V_t) = D(P_t, V_{1t}, \ldots, V_{st}),$$

where, for example, $Q_t$ denotes the quantity demanded during time period $t$ of length $T$, and $V_{kt}$ denotes the level of variable $V_k$ during time period $t$. If the dependent variable $Q_t$ is hypothesized to be a function of time, then time as a *variable* could be *explicitly* incorporated into the previous demand function as variable $V_{(n+4)t}$. For example, the demand curve might be written $Q_t = AP_t^{a_1}I_t^{a_2}(a_3)^t$, where $A$, $a_1$, $a_2$, and $a_3$ are parameters, and price and income in period $t$ ($P_t$ and $I_t$) as well as $t$ are variables. If time is given in years between 1900 and 1970, then $t$ would take on all integer values from 1900 to 1970. Given this demand curve, it is clear that for time $t + 1$ we can write

$$Q_{t+1} = AP_{t+1}^{a_1}I_{t+1}^{a_2}a_3^{(t+1)}.$$

Thus, if neither price nor income changes from $t$ to $t + 1$, $P_t = P_{t+1}$ and $I_t = I_{t+1}$, and we would have a relative growth in demand of $Q_{t+1}/Q_t = a_3$. In the absence of price and income changes, the percentage rate of growth of demand would therefore be $r = a_3 - 1$. The latter growth rate might stem from a combination of population growth, technological improvements that make the product more desirable, changing tastes, and a host of other factors not explicitly identified and isolated by individual variables. In effect, the variable $t$ is used to *shift* the demand curve over time, raising or reducing the quantity demanded at any given price and income as time marches on.

Still further, the functional relationship itself, indeed the particular parameters themselves, might also be functions of the particular time period. The parameter $a_1$

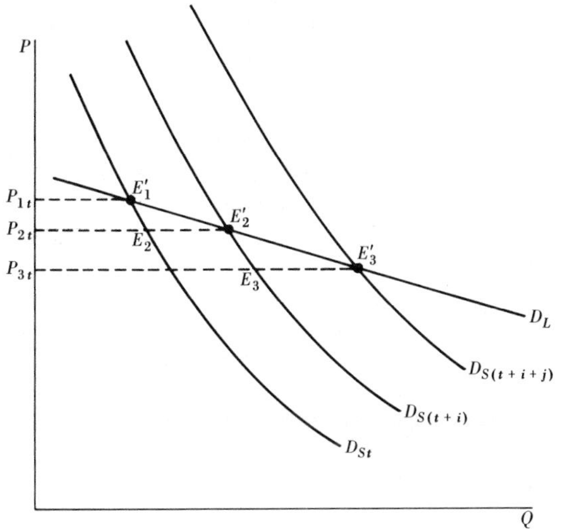


Fig. 3.2

in the previous demand curve might be written as $a_1 = b + b_1 t$, where $b$ and $b_1$ are constants. Then

$$Q_t = AP_t^{b+b_1 t} I_t^{a_2} (a_3)^t.$$

Since the price elasticity of demand at time $t$ will be given by $(\partial Q_t/\partial P_t)(P_t/Q_t) = b + b_1 t = a_1$, this hypothesis asserts that the price elasticity will be a linear function of time. The explicit use of time as a variable in the demand function therefore permits one to introduce *systematic* changes into the demand curve, *where such might be appropriate*, in lieu of specifically *redefining* the demand relationship for each time period.

When an unsubscripted $Q$ denotes quantity, the fact that we are referring to a rate during some specific, although unnoted, time interval will be understood. $Q$ will refer to quantity during the $t$th of these intervals. This use of time is distinct from its implications in the concepts of the short, intermediate, and long runs.

Suppose, for example, that the curve $D_{St}$ of Figure 3.2 represents the short-run demand curve in the price-quantity space for some commodity DURK during the

$t$th period of length $T$. The meaning of "short run" is that consumers (or firms) will not be inclined to vary purchases of some goods (or factor inputs) during an interval of length $T$ to the extent that they otherwise might, because they are prevented from varying their purchases of other goods (or inputs). For example, the consumer who chooses to live within a weekly budget might commit himself to dine out on a Friday evening. The restaurant meal becomes a good in his basket of goods. If the price of cameras falls, he might want to buy a camera. If he could extricate himself from his dining commitment he *would* buy the camera. He can't, so he doesn't—but he might well choose to purchase the camera rather than dine out *next* week. In essence, during any short enough interval of length $T$ certain purchases can ordinarily be assumed to be held at fixed levels, although they could be varied after a "sufficient" number of intervals of $T$ have passed. The short run refers to such an interval.

Consider DURK, a commodity requiring the use of electrical outlets. Assume that $T$ is sufficiently short so that the total available electrical outlets can be considered to be invariant. If at time $t$ the price of DURK is lowered from $P_{1t}$ to $P_{2t}$, consumers will demand more DURK by *moving along* the industry demand curve $D_{St}$ from the point $E_1'$ to $E_2$. With the passage of time, however, more electrical outlets can and will be installed, because DURK and electrical outlets are complements. The result is that the demand curve for DURK will *shift* from $D_{St}$ at time $t$ to $D_{S(t+i)}$ at time $t + i$. During an interval of length $T$, industry demand that *formerly* would have been at $E_2$ on $D_{St}$ is now at $E_2'$ on $D_{S(t+i)}$. A further drop in price to $P_{3t}$ would lead to further adjustments in the number of electrical outlets installed. Initially, consumers would *move along* $D_{S(t+i)}$ to $E_3$. Ultimately, once *all* expenditures have been varied and put in balance, the demand for DURK during an interval of $T$ will have shifted to its final resting place of $D_{S(t+i+j)}$. Here, at a price of $P_{3t}$ the preferred point will be $E_3'$. The locus of all points $E_1'$, $E_2'$, $E_3'$, . . . traces out $D_L$, the long-run demand curve for DURK during a time interval of length $T$. It is important to note that the interval $T$ has not changed from the short run to the long run; it is *consumers'* abilities to vary other factors that have changed.

Furthermore, since at any point lying on both the short- and long-run demand curves the ratio of price to quantity is fixed, any differences in the price elasticity of demand $\eta = (\partial Q/\partial P)(P/Q)$ between the short and long runs will depend solely upon the $\partial Q/\partial P$ term. The latter is *necessarily* smaller (greater absolutely) for the long-run curve than for that of the short run. A similar result, with similar curves, would follow if we were to inspect *partial* variations in other factors to determine any of the *intermediate-run* demand curves. That is, the shorter is the short run, the more inelastic is the demand curve at a given point, for the less flexible are quantity decisions.

Additionally, if it is assumed that $P_{2t}$ is "the" price that somehow has gotten itself established in the market, the analysis above says the following. If price should increase, cutbacks in quantity desired during an interval $T$ will in the long run be more substantial than short-run cutbacks. Similarly, should price fall below $P_{2t}$, the quantities purchased over $T$ will be greater in the long run than in the short.

Finally, note again the earlier remarks about the definitions of product and industry and possible ambiguities that could arise. It is important to keep these remarks in mind when discussing shifting demand curves, for there are a host of products whose *quality* varies over time. These quality variations may be real or imagined. When the quality or character of a product undergoes a particularly pro-

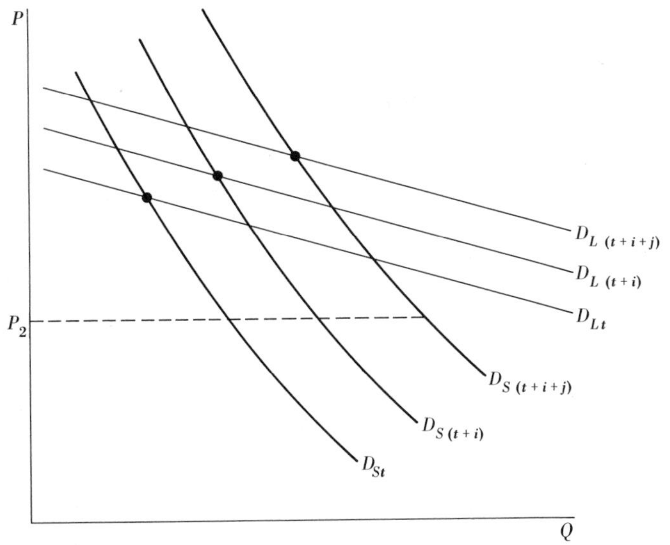


Fig. 3.3

nounced transformation, the different species of the product might meaningfully be classified into different products. Today's automobiles, for better or for worse, are not the same automobiles as those of the early 1900s, and could certainly be dealt with as separate products; lorgnettes, spectacles, and contact lenses may all be eyeglasses, but are not perfect substitutes. Disclaimers to the contrary, however, aspirin does not vary too much from one year to the next, give or take a little buffering. Often it is not clear exactly whether or when a DURK stops being a DURK and instead becomes a KNIF. Unless otherwise noted, any product variations that do occur will be wrapped up in the "other factors" such as $V_{n+5}$. If some index can be assigned to measure the particular variety of product on the market during the $t$th time period, it will be denoted by $V_{(n+5)t}$ and directly incorporated into the demand curve. The shifts from $D_{St}$ to $D_{S(t+i)}$ to $D_{S(t+i+j)}$ could be described as having occurred at a given price of $P_2 = P_{2t} = P_{2(t+i)} = P_{2(t+i+j)}$, and as having been stimulated by improvements in the DURK as reflected through $V_{(n+5)t}$. The long-run demand curve would also shift to the right as in Figure 3.3. There will be a given long-run demand curve for each set of short-run demand curves and each variety of product quality or each $V_{(n+5)t}$.

## 3.4 EMPIRICAL ESTIMATION OF INDUSTRY DEMAND

One may inquire how all the wonderful demand curves that have been assumed into existence would be determined empirically. Certainly they will not simply introduce themselves. Somehow, if *industry* demand as opposed to *firm* demand is itself of concern to management—and it should be—the industry demand curve will have to be *estimated* or *assessed*. These terms are not synonymous and their distinction will become clearer in the next and subsequent chapters. For the moment, however, we merely call attention to the basic distinguishing characteristic.

An assessment is subjective in nature and is *intimately* bound to one's personal judgment, whereas an estimate is not. The choice of an estimat*or*, the function used to estimate a parameter, may rest on personal judgment. Once chosen, however, the estimator will process observations in a completely objective and mechanistic fashion in generating the estimate. Certainly an assessment may be founded on the basis of quite objective information and criteria, but one's experience, intuition, and judgment will determine what and how much of the information is used in arriving at an overall assessment. As will be seen, this assessment might in turn be revised as new information is received, but the ultimate assessment will ordinarily reflect one's initial judgments unless the weight of new data simply overwhelms these. Estimates are not *based* on judgment. This is not to say that an estimate cannot take a judgment into *consideration;* but if it does, the judgment is quantified as an additional piece of historical information. Consider a knowledgable individual's assessment of the level of consumer spending on durable goods. This subjective assessment could be used as one of several variables to explain product demand via an objective estimation procedure.

The remainder of this chapter introduces the econometric approach to parameter *estimation.* We are led to this point by the initial desire to base estimates of industry demand exclusively on objective statistical techniques, in the absence of subjective judgments. The analysis can then be extended to include subjective judgments. Moreover, the econometric approach is applicable to the general problems of specification, empirical estimation, and testing of functional forms of relevance to economic issues. We shall therefore have repeated occasion to take advantage of this approach. Nonetheless, it must be recognized that what follows is only an *introduction* to econometrics. It will provide a foundation upon which to build and expand as model and estimation needs dictate. Much of the discussion will, however, be cursory and selective, although hopefully fruitful and enlightening.[3]

## a. Linear Regression

### i. THE PROBLEM

Assuming quantity demanded to be the dependent variable, let us write the demand curve as $Q_t = D(V_{1t}, \ldots, V_{mt})$. Here $Q_t$, the quantity demanded during the $t$th interval of length $T$, is an *endogenous* variable to be determined by the model. Each of the independent variables $V_{it}$ $(i = 1, \ldots, m)$ is for the present assumed to be *exogenous* or predetermined and given outside the model. The latter assumption will be modified in later chapters.

Assume, too, that the demand curve is thought to be linear. The problem, then, is to estimate a set of parameters $\alpha_i$ of the function

$$Q_t = \alpha_0 + \alpha_1 V_{1t} + \alpha_2 V_{2t} + \cdots + \alpha_m V_{mt} + \epsilon_t = \sum_{i=0}^{m} \alpha_i V_{it} + \epsilon_t, \tag{3.1}$$

where $V_{0t} = 1$ and $\epsilon_t$ is a *disturbance* or *error* term. The error term is included in (3.1) by virtue of the following facts: (a) the linear relationship between the independent variables and the dependent variable is, in actuality, unlikely to be exact;

[3] For more extensive treatments, see A. S. Goldberger, *Econometric Theory* (New York: John Wiley & Sons, Inc., 1964) and E. Malinvaud, *Statistical Methods of Econometrics* (Skokie, Ill.: Rand McNally & Company, 1966). At a less terrifying level try L. R. Klein, *An Introduction to Econometrics* (Englewood Cliffs, N.J.: Prentice-Hall, Inc., 1962). It is assumed that the reader is familiar with "basic" statistics and has an understanding, however imprecise, of such concepts as probability and density function. If this assumption is false, go directly to Hoel [Paul G. Hoel, *Introduction to Mathematical Statistics* (New York: John Wiley & Sons, Inc., 1964)], do not pass Goldberger and do not collect your $200.

(b) there will be occasional random disturbances occurring outside the model, such as a temporary income tax surcharge, a currency devaluation, or unusual climatic conditions, which may directly affect the dependent variable or affect the relationship between the dependent and one or more of the independent variables in an unidentifiable manner, thereby undermining exact empirical estimation; and (c) we may occasionally err in measuring the variables. Equation (3.1) states (1) that there will be a *systematic* linear relationship between the dependent and the independent variables, *and* (2) that the dependent variable will also be influenced by other factors whose effects we are unable to identify and explicitly incorporate into the model. In light of this inability, we assume these effects to be random.

The estimation of the $m + 1$ parameters of the *hyperplane* defined by (3.1) is to be based on a series of $N$ joint observations on the $V_{it}$ ($i = 1, \ldots, m$; $t = 1, \ldots, N$) and $Q_t$ ($t = 1, \ldots, N$). Each series of observations can be written in the form of a a vector:

$$\mathbf{Q} = \begin{pmatrix} Q_1 \\ Q_2 \\ \cdot \\ \cdot \\ \cdot \\ Q_N \end{pmatrix} \quad \text{and} \quad \mathbf{V}_i = \begin{pmatrix} V_{i1} \\ V_{i2} \\ \cdot \\ \cdot \\ \cdot \\ V_{iN} \end{pmatrix}.$$

Hence, we may modify and rewrite (3.1) in vector and matrix notation as

$$\mathbf{Q} = \mathbf{V}\boldsymbol{\alpha} + \boldsymbol{\varepsilon}, \tag{3.1a}$$

where, by assumption, $\mathbf{V} = (\mathbf{i}, \mathbf{V}_1, \ldots, \mathbf{V}_m)$ is an $N \times (1 + m)$ matrix and

$$\mathbf{i} = \begin{pmatrix} 1 \\ 1 \\ \cdot \\ \cdot \\ \cdot \\ 1 \end{pmatrix}, \quad \boldsymbol{\alpha} = \begin{pmatrix} \alpha_0 \\ \alpha_1 \\ \cdot \\ \cdot \\ \cdot \\ \alpha_m \end{pmatrix}, \quad \boldsymbol{\varepsilon} = \begin{pmatrix} \epsilon_1 \\ \epsilon_2 \\ \cdot \\ \cdot \\ \cdot \\ \epsilon_N \end{pmatrix}.$$

$\mathbf{V}$ is assumed to be of rank $m + 1$, which implies that the columns of $\mathbf{V}$ are linearly independent and $N > m$. The first condition demands that *no* two *exogenous variables* be linearly related; the second condition requires that the estimation be based upon at least as many observations as the numbers of parameters to be estimated.[4]

Equation (3.1) formulates a *stochastic* model of demand. In a stochastic model the variables are random variables for which a probabilistic process determines particular values with fixed probabilities. The process generating such values is

[4] The nature of this assumption is clarified below in Section 3.4c. There we will assume that the independent variables are *statistically* independent random variables. Specifically, the probability that $V_{it}$ takes on any value or set of values is not affected by the value or set of values taken on by any other $V_{jt}$. In the present illustration, the probability that $V_{it}$ is less than $V_j^*$ *and* that $V_{jt}$ will be less than $V_j^*$ in any joint observation on $V_{it}$ and $V_{jt}$ equals the product of the individual probabilities defined by the stochastic process (note the next paragraph in the text) generating the variables.

called a stochastic process. The formulation of a stochastic model is called the *specification* problem.

To obtain an estimate **a** of $\boldsymbol{\alpha}$ in our model, we first require a criterion function by which to evaluate the estimate. Let $\hat{Q}_t$ denote the value of the dependent variable $Q_t$ that would be estimated once **a** has been determined, given the levels of the independent variables $V_{it}$. In regression analysis we determine a "hyperplane of best fit,"

$$\hat{Q}_t = \sum_{i=0}^{m} a_i V_{it},$$

wherein the estimates of $\boldsymbol{\alpha}$ minimize

$$\sum_{t=1}^{N} (Q_t - \hat{Q}_t)^2 = \sum_{t=1}^{N} e_t^2,$$

the sum of the squared residuals between the actual and the estimated $Q_t$.[5] Notice that the *residual* $e_t$ is calculated directly as the difference between the actual value of the dependent variable and the value that would be determined by the estimated linear relationship, given the estimate **a** and the levels of the independent variables. Hence

$$Q_t = \sum_{i=0}^{m} a_i V_{it} + e_t,$$

but the residual $e_t$ is not the same as the disturbance $\epsilon_t$. The residual *can be calculated* once the model is estimated; the disturbance *is not observable*. The hyperplane determines a mean value for the dependent variable *conditional* upon the values of the independent variables. The process that performs this determination is called multiple *regression*. The hyperplane is called the regression hyperplane—or, with a single independent variable, the regression line; the parameters of the regression are called regression coefficients. Figure 3.4(a) illustrates possible conditional distributions of $Q_t$ given $V_{1t}$. Figure 3.4(b) is a scatter diagram showing a set of points $(V_{1t}, Q_t)$ and the estimated regression line $\hat{Q}_t = a_0 + a_1 V_{1t}$ of best fit.

## ii. THE METHOD OF LEAST SQUARES

Denoting the transpose by the "prime," we wish to determine a vector of estimates **a** for $\boldsymbol{\alpha}$ to minimize $\sum_{t=1}^{N} e_t^2 = \mathbf{e}'\mathbf{e}$. The problem, then, is to determine an estimator for **a** that will

$$\begin{aligned} \text{Minimize} \qquad \mathbf{e}'\mathbf{e} &= (\mathbf{Q} - \mathbf{Va})'(\mathbf{Q} - \mathbf{Va}) \\ &= \mathbf{Q}'\mathbf{Q} - \mathbf{a}'\mathbf{V}'\mathbf{Q} - \mathbf{Q}'\mathbf{Va} + \mathbf{a}'\mathbf{V}'\mathbf{Va} \\ &= \mathbf{Q}'\mathbf{Q} - 2\mathbf{a}'\mathbf{V}'\mathbf{Q} + \mathbf{a}'\mathbf{V}'\mathbf{Va} = \text{a scalar}, \end{aligned} \tag{3.2}$$

[5] This criterion is not the only possibility, but it has some exceedingly pleasant properties not available in analogous criteria. In particular, under certain conditions such estimators —called least-squares estimators—will also be maximum-likelihood estimators (see Goldberger, *Econometric Theory*, pp. 179–180), and they satisfy the very important Gauss-Markov theorem (see below, Section 3.4d).

since $\mathbf{a'V'Q} = \mathbf{Q'Va}$. The vector we seek will satisfy $\partial(\mathbf{e'e})/\partial\mathbf{a} = \mathbf{0}$ and second-order conditions involving $\partial^2(\mathbf{e'e})/\partial\mathbf{a}^2$.[6] The vector of least-squares estimates will thus be determined from

$$\frac{\partial(\mathbf{e'e})}{\partial\mathbf{a}} = -2\mathbf{V'Q} + 2\mathbf{V'Va} = \mathbf{0}. \tag{3.3}$$

The estimate of $\boldsymbol{\alpha}$ will therefore be

$$\mathbf{a} = (\mathbf{V'V})^{-1}\mathbf{V'Q}. \tag{3.4}$$

By previous assumption rank $\mathbf{V} = 1 + m$. Hence $(\mathbf{V'V})^{-1}$ exists and like $\mathbf{V'V}$ is positive definite. Since $\partial^2(\mathbf{e'e})/\partial\mathbf{a}^2 = 2\mathbf{V'V}$ the estimator does indeed minimize $\mathbf{e'e}$.[7]

The least-squares equation to estimate (3.1a) will be $\mathbf{Q} = \mathbf{Va} + \mathbf{e}$. The vector of estimates of the dependent variable will be given by $\hat{\mathbf{Q}} = \mathbf{Va}$, and $\mathbf{Q} - \hat{\mathbf{Q}} = \mathbf{e}$

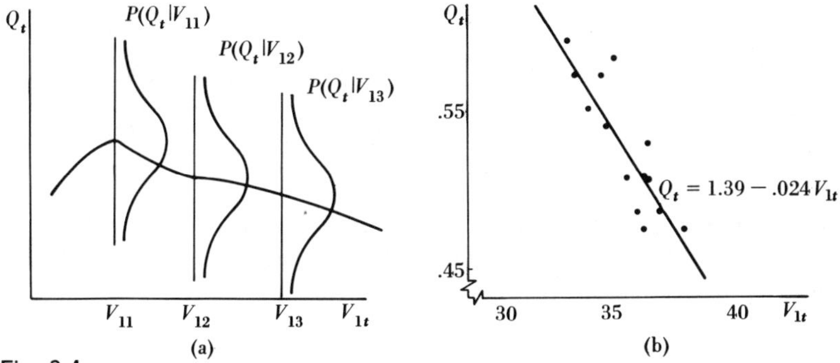


Fig. 3.4

is the vector of computed residuals. The minimized sum of squared residuals is given by

$$\mathbf{e'e} = (\mathbf{Q} - \hat{\mathbf{Q}})'\mathbf{e} = \mathbf{Q'e} - \hat{\mathbf{Q}}'\mathbf{e}.$$

Note, however, that

$$\begin{aligned}\hat{\mathbf{Q}}'\mathbf{e} &= \hat{\mathbf{Q}}'(\mathbf{Q} - \hat{\mathbf{Q}}) = \hat{\mathbf{Q}}'\mathbf{Q} - \hat{\mathbf{Q}}'\hat{\mathbf{Q}} \\ &= \mathbf{a'V'Q} - \mathbf{a'V'Va}.\end{aligned}$$

But, $\mathbf{a} = (\mathbf{V'V})^{-1}\mathbf{V'Q}$ by (3.4). Hence

$$\begin{aligned}\hat{\mathbf{Q}}'\mathbf{e} &= \mathbf{a'V'Q} - \mathbf{a'V'V}(\mathbf{V'V})^{-1}\mathbf{V'Q} \\ &= \mathbf{a'V'Q} - \mathbf{a'V'Q} = 0,\end{aligned} \tag{3.5}$$

[6] In general, when a function $f(\mathbf{x})$ is continuous and $\mathbf{x}' = (x_1, \ldots, x_n)$, then $\partial f(\mathbf{x})/\partial\mathbf{x}$ yields a *vector* $\nabla\mathbf{f}$ called the *gradient* vector, and $\nabla\mathbf{f} = (\partial f/\partial x_1, \ldots, \partial f/\partial x_n)'$. Further, $\partial^2 f/\partial\mathbf{x}^2$ yields a *matrix* $\mathbf{H}_f$ called the *Hessian* matrix, and $\mathbf{H}_f = [\partial^2 f/\partial x_i\, \partial x_j]$. In particular, if $f(\mathbf{x}) = \mathbf{x'Yy}$, where $\mathbf{x}'$ is a $1 \times n$ vector, $\mathbf{Y}$ is an $n \times k$ matrix, and $\mathbf{y}$ is a $k \times 1$ vector, $\partial f(\mathbf{x})/\partial\mathbf{x} = \partial(\mathbf{x'Yy})/\partial\mathbf{x} = \mathbf{Yy}$, an $n \times 1$ vector, by the ordinary rules of differentiation. Similarly, from the product rule of differentiation, if $f(\mathbf{x}) = \mathbf{x'YY'x}$, then $\partial f(\mathbf{x})/\partial\mathbf{x} = \mathbf{YY'x} + (\mathbf{x'YY'})' = 2\mathbf{YY'x}$, also an $n \times 1$ vector. Further, $\partial^2 f(\mathbf{x})/\partial\mathbf{x}^2 = \partial(2\mathbf{YY'x})/\partial\mathbf{x} = 2\mathbf{YY'}$, an $n \times n$ matrix.

[7] This holds since, if a symmetric matrix $\mathbf{A}$ is positive definite, then $\mathbf{A}^{-1}$ is also positive definite. $\mathbf{A}$ is positive definite if and only if $Z = \mathbf{y'Ay} > 0$ for all $\mathbf{y} \neq 0$, which implies that $Z$ is strictly convex. Then, a global minimum obtains where the first-order conditions hold. It can be shown that if rank $\mathbf{V}$ is $1 + m$, $\mathbf{V'V}$ is positive definite.

since $\mathbf{V'V(V'V)^{-1} = I}$, the identity matrix. Equation (3.5) reveals that the sum of the products of the values of the dependent variable estimated from the least-squares equation and the residuals is zero. When we substitute $\mathbf{\hat{Q}'e} = 0$ into the expression for $\mathbf{e'e}$, the minimized sum of squared residuals, denoted by $S^2$, is given by

$$S^2 = \mathbf{e'e} = \mathbf{Q'e} = \mathbf{Q'(Q - \hat{Q})} = \mathbf{Q'Q - Q'\hat{Q}}. \tag{3.6}$$

Further, let $\bar{Q}$ be the arithmetic mean of the $Q_t$, or

$$\bar{Q} = \frac{1}{N}\sum_{t=1}^{N} Q_t$$

with $\bar{\hat{Q}}$ similarly defined. As before, $\mathbf{i'} = (1, \ldots, 1)$ is the sum vector. Thus

$$\sum_{t=1}^{N} \hat{Q}_t = \mathbf{i'\hat{Q}} = \mathbf{i'Va} = \mathbf{i'Q}$$

by the first of the "normal" equations (3.3), since the first row of $\mathbf{V'}$ is $\mathbf{i'}$; or,

$$\sum_{t=1}^{N} \hat{Q}_t = \sum_{t=1}^{N} Q_t. \tag{3.7}$$

Consequently $\bar{\hat{Q}} = \bar{Q}$, or the mean of the observed values of the dependent variable will be equal to the mean of its least-squares estimates. Additionally, from (3.6) the mean of the squared residuals will be

$$\begin{aligned}\frac{S^2}{N} &= \left(\frac{1}{N}\right)\mathbf{Q'Q} - \left(\frac{1}{N}\right)\mathbf{Q'\hat{Q}} - \bar{Q}^2 + \bar{Q}^2 \\ &= \left(\frac{1}{N}\right)\mathbf{Q'Q} - \bar{Q}^2 - \left(\frac{1}{N}\right)\mathbf{Q'\hat{Q}} + \bar{\hat{Q}}^2,\end{aligned}$$

since $\bar{\hat{Q}} = \bar{Q}$. But, from (3.6),

$$\mathbf{e'e} = \mathbf{(Q - \hat{Q})'(Q - \hat{Q})} = \mathbf{Q'Q - Q'\hat{Q} - \hat{Q}'Q + \hat{Q}'\hat{Q}} = \mathbf{Q'Q - Q'\hat{Q}}.$$

Therefore, $\mathbf{-\hat{Q}'Q + \hat{Q}'\hat{Q}} = 0$ or $\mathbf{\hat{Q}'Q} = \mathbf{\hat{Q}'\hat{Q}}$; and hence

$$\frac{S^2}{N} = \left[\left(\frac{1}{N}\right)\sum_{t=1}^{N} Q_t^2 - \bar{Q}^2\right] - \left[\left(\frac{1}{N}\right)\sum_{t=1}^{N} \hat{Q}_t^2 - \bar{\hat{Q}}^2\right]. \tag{3.8}$$

The first bracketed term is the variance[8] of the sample $Q_t$'s used in the least-squares procedure. This variance is denoted by $s_Q^2$. The second bracketed term is the variance

[8] The variance is the mean of the sum of the squared deviations of the individual observations from the mean; or,

$$\begin{aligned}\frac{1}{N}\left[\sum_{t=1}^{N} (Q_t - \bar{Q})^2\right] &= \frac{1}{N}\left[\sum_{t=1}^{N} Q_t^2 - 2\sum_{t=1}^{N} Q_t\bar{Q} + \bar{Q}^2\right] \\ &= \frac{1}{N}\sum_{t=1}^{N} Q_t^2 - 2\bar{Q}\left[\frac{1}{N}\sum_{t=1}^{N} Q_t\right] + \bar{Q}^2 = \frac{1}{N}\sum_{t=1}^{N} Q_t^2 - 2\bar{Q}\bar{Q} + \bar{Q}^2 = \frac{1}{N}\sum_{t=1}^{N} Q_t^2 - \bar{Q}^2.\end{aligned}$$

of the sample estimated $\hat{Q}_t$'s denoted by $s^2_{\hat{Q}}$. Thus

$$\frac{S^2}{N} = s^2_Q - s^2_{\hat{Q}}, \tag{3.8a}$$

or the mean of the squared residuals is equal to the difference between the *variance* of the *actual* values of the dependent variable, quantity demanded, and the *variance* in the *estimated* values of the dependent variable.

One can also show that the *variance* of the *residuals* is given by $S^2/N$. We need only note that the mean of the residuals is

$$\bar{e} = \left(\frac{1}{N}\right)\mathbf{i}'\mathbf{e} = \left(\frac{1}{N}\right)\mathbf{i}'(\mathbf{Q} - \hat{\mathbf{Q}}) = 0, \tag{3.9}$$

by (3.7); or, the mean of the residuals is zero. Hence, the variance of the residuals is $(1/N)\mathbf{e}'\mathbf{e} - \bar{e}^2 = (1/N)\mathbf{e}'\mathbf{e} - 0 = S^2/N$. Equation (3.8a) may be rewritten as

$$s^2_Q = \frac{S^2}{N} + s^2_{\hat{Q}}, \tag{3.8b}$$

revealing the sample variance of the dependent variable to be equal to the sum of the variance in the sample estimates of the variable plus the variance of the residuals or "error" terms. $S^2/N$ and $s^2_{\hat{Q}}$ are frequently referred to as the unexplained and explained parts of the variance in the dependent variable. The former term computes the variance in the dependent variable "caused by" variance in the unobservable factors; the latter computes the variance "caused by" variance in the independent variables whose systematic relationship with the dependent variable is described by the least-squares equation.

We may further manipulate (3.8a) by dividing both sides by $s^2_Q$. This gives the proportion of the variance of the dependent variable that has not been accounted for by the observable factors included in the regression, or

$$\frac{S^2}{Ns^2_Q} = \frac{s^2_Q - s^2_{\hat{Q}}}{s^2_Q} = 1 - \frac{s^2_{\hat{Q}}}{s^2_Q}. \tag{3.8c}$$

To measure the "goodness of fit" of the least-squares equation, or how good an estimating job it does, we notice that (1) if $S^2/N = 0$ there are no residuals left "unexplained" by the equation; and (2) the maximum value that $s^2_{\hat{Q}}/s^2_Q$ can take on is 1, since $S^2/N \geq 0$ and $s^2_{\hat{Q}} \leq s^2_Q$. It is therefore useful to *define* the *coefficient of multiple determination* $R^2$:

$$R^2 = 1 - \frac{S^2}{Ns^2_Q} = 1 - \left[1 - \frac{s^2_{\hat{Q}}}{s^2_Q}\right] = \frac{s^2_{\hat{Q}}}{s^2_Q}, \tag{3.10}$$

where $0 \leq R^2 \leq 1$. The closer is $R^2$ to unity, the smaller is the proportion of the variance of the dependent variable that is not accounted for by the regression. When $R^2$ approaches zero, the proportion of the variance in the dependent variable that can be ascribed to random factors about which we have no knowledge approaches unity. The coefficient of multiple determination thus provides *one* piece of information for an analyst to consider in evaluating a single-equation stochastic model fitted to a set of sample observations via least squares. $R^2$ indicates how well the estimated model fits the data. There will be other considerations as well, some of which are indicated below, and not the least of which is whether the signs and/or magnitudes of the parameter estimates conform to prior beliefs. We want the model to fit the data, but it will also be nice if the results make sense.

## b. Simple Linear Regression

To help clarify the previous matrix manipulations, let us consider the simple regression case of two variables. In particular, suppose least-squares estimates are required for the parameters in the equation $Y_t = \alpha_0 + \alpha_1 X_t + \epsilon_t$, where $t = 1, \ldots, N$. We desire estimates $a_0$ and $a_1$ of $\alpha_0$ and $\alpha_1$ such that

$$\hat{Y}_t = a_0 + a_1 X_t \quad \text{and} \quad Y_t - \hat{Y}_t = e_t.$$

Using (3.4), we find the vector of estimates $\mathbf{a}' = (a_0, a_1)$ as

$$\mathbf{a} = (\mathbf{X}'\mathbf{X})^{-1}\mathbf{X}'\mathbf{Y},$$

where

$$\mathbf{X} = \begin{bmatrix} 1 & X_1 \\ \cdot & \cdot \\ \cdot & \cdot \\ \cdot & \cdot \\ 1 & X_N \end{bmatrix} \quad \text{and} \quad \mathbf{Y} = \begin{pmatrix} Y_1 \\ \cdot \\ \cdot \\ \cdot \\ Y_N \end{pmatrix}.$$

Written explicitly,

$$\begin{aligned} \mathbf{a} &= \begin{bmatrix} N & \Sigma\, X_t \\ \Sigma\, X_t & \Sigma\, X_t^2 \end{bmatrix}^{-1} \begin{bmatrix} \Sigma\, Y_t \\ \Sigma\, X_t Y_t \end{bmatrix} \\ &= \frac{1}{N\,\Sigma\, X_t^2 - (\Sigma\, X_t)^2} \begin{bmatrix} \Sigma\, X_t^2 & -\Sigma\, X_t \\ -\Sigma\, X_t & N \end{bmatrix} \begin{bmatrix} \Sigma\, Y_t \\ \Sigma\, X_t Y_t \end{bmatrix} \\ &= \frac{1}{N\,\Sigma\, X_t^2 - (\Sigma\, X_t)^2} \begin{bmatrix} \Sigma\, X_t^2\, \Sigma\, Y_t - \Sigma\, X_t\, \Sigma\, X_t Y_t \\ N\,\Sigma\, X_t Y_t - \Sigma\, X_t\, \Sigma\, Y_t \end{bmatrix}. \end{aligned} \qquad (3.11)$$

Denote the means and standard deviations of the observed $X_t$ and $Y_t$ by $\bar{X}$, $s_X$ and $\bar{Y}$, $s_Y$, respectively; denote the sample *covariance* between $X_t$ and $Y_t$ by $s_{XY} = (\Sigma\, X_t Y_t / N) - \bar{X}\bar{Y}$; and let $r = s_{XY}/s_X s_Y$. Expanding (3.11), it is then readily determined that

$$\mathbf{a}' = \left[\bar{Y} - r\left(\frac{s_Y}{s_X}\right)\bar{X},\, r\left(\frac{s_Y}{s_X}\right)\right].$$

Now, the variance in the estimates $\hat{Y}_t$ is simply the mean of the sum of the squared deviations of the individual estimates from the mean. But

$$\bar{\hat{Y}} = \frac{1}{N}\sum_{t=1}^{N} (a_0 + a_1 X_t) = a_0 + a_1 \bar{X}.$$

Hence,

$$s_{\hat{Y}}^2 = \frac{1}{N}\sum_{t=1}^{N}[(a_0 + a_1X_t) - (a_0 - a_1\bar{X})]^2$$

$$= \frac{1}{N}\sum_{t=1}^{N} a_1^2(X_t - \bar{X})^2 = \frac{1}{N}a_1^2\left[\sum X_t^2 - 2\bar{X}\sum X_t + N\bar{X}^2\right]$$

$$= r^2\left(\frac{s_Y^2}{s_X^2}\right)\left[\frac{\Sigma X_t^2}{N} - \bar{X}^2\right] = r^2\left(\frac{s_Y^2}{s_X^2}\right)s_X^2 = r^2 s_Y^2.$$

Recalling from (3.10) that $R^2 = s_{\hat{Y}}^2/s_Y^2$, it immediately follows by direct substitution that $R^2 = r^2s_Y^2/s_Y^2 = r^2$. Thus $-1 \leq r \leq 1$, and $r$, the *correlation coefficient*, indicates the extent to which the two variables, $X_t$ and $Y_t$, are *linearly* related. Since the regression coefficient $a_1 = rs_Y/s_X$, if $r = 0$ the *observed* $Y_t$ are not linearly related to the *observed* $X_t$. In this case, $a_1 = 0$ and the level of $X_t$ does not influence the least-squares estimate of $Y_t$. The estimate of $Y_t$ that minimizes the sum of the squared residuals becomes $a_0 = \bar{Y} - r(s_Y/s_X)\bar{X} = \bar{Y}$; here, all the variance in $Y_t$ is ascribed to random disturbances, and the best estimate of $Y_t$ in the least-squares sense is *always* the mean, irrespective of the level of $X_t$. If, however, $r = \pm 1$, then $S^2/N = 0$ and the least-squares line *exactly* fits each point; here, there is a perfect linear relationship between $X_t$ and $Y_t$. The square of the correlation between two variables thus indicates the extent to which the variance in one variable "is explained" by the variance in the other.

TABLE 3.1

| Year | Beer Price Index (Dollars per Barrel) | Per Capita Consumption (In Barrels) |
|---|---|---|
| 1946 | 34.94 | .58 |
| 1947 | 34.51 | .57 |
| 1948 | 33.16 | .59 |
| 1949 | 33.44 | .57 |
| 1950 | 34.04 | .55 |
| 1951 | 34.40 | .54 |
| 1952 | N/A | N/A |
| 1953 | 35.50 | .51 |
| 1954 | 36.31 | .53 |
| 1955 | 36.33 | .51 |
| 1956 | 36.20 | .51 |
| 1957 | 36.86 | .49 |
| 1958 | 36.16 | .48 |
| 1959 | 37.85 | .48 |
| 1960 | 36.05 | .49 |

Putting some numerical meat on the algebraic bones, consider the data in Table 3.1. These are the data shown in Figure 3.4(b). The $Q_t$'s are per capita consumption of beer, in barrels, in the United States between 1946 and 1960. The figures are placed on a per capita basis to allow for population changes. The $V_{1t}$'s represent the barrel price of beer corrected for changes in the consumer price index to allow for overall price appreciation during the period.[9] Let us assume that price is determined exogenously and that consumers can purchase as much beer, per capita, as they like at each price. The $Q_t$'s will then measure demand at each price, neglecting other factors such as income. Let us hypothesize that the demand for beer is a linear function of price and other unobservable factors. The demand equation we wish to estimate is $Q_t = \alpha_0 + \alpha_1 V_{1t} + \epsilon_t$. Given the observations in Table 3.1, $N = 14$,

$$\Sigma Q_t = 7.40, \qquad \Sigma Q_t^2 = 3.9306,$$
$$\Sigma V_{1t} = 495.75, \qquad \Sigma V_{1t}^2 = 17{,}579.0497,$$
$$\Sigma Q_t V_{1t} = 261.4494.$$

Hence, substituting into (3.11) with $X_t = V_{1t}$ and $Q_t = Y_t$,

$$\mathbf{a} = \frac{1}{338.6333}\begin{bmatrix} 471.4277 \\ -8.2584 \end{bmatrix} = \begin{bmatrix} 1.3921 \\ -.0244 \end{bmatrix}$$

and $r = -.81$. The least-squares line is thus $Q_t = 1.39 - .024V_{1t} + e_t$ with $r^2 = .6561$. One may infer from this that 66 percent of the variance in per capita demand can be attributed to variation in the price index for beer. It should be noted, however, that no attempt has been made to isolate factors such as income in the regression. Were this done, the inferences drawn from the analysis could change. The Appendix illustrates multiple regression calculations.

### c. Assumptions in Linear Regression

The estimates for $\boldsymbol{\alpha}$ and $\boldsymbol{\varepsilon}$ in (3.1a) will be based on sample observations. The sample will consist of $N$ joint observations of $Q_t$'s and $V_{1t}$'s taken from a population of such joint observations.[10] In order to analyze the properties of the estimators and subsequently draw inferences about the population from these sample estimates, we make the following assumptions:

(1) The $N$ sets of $V_{it}$ values are nonstochastically determined in sampling from a population in which $V_i$ and $V_j$ are independent (for all $i$ and $j$); $Q_t$ is drawn at random from a fixed distribution that is conditional upon the $V_{it}$; and $Q_t$ is a constant linear function of the $V_{it}$ and a disturbance term.
(2) The rank of $\mathbf{V}$ is $1 + m$ and $N \geq 1 + m$.
(3) The disturbance term $\epsilon_t$ in any period $t$ is independent of the disturbance in any other period, $\epsilon_v$ ($v = 1, \ldots, N$). Moreover, the disturbance is distributed independently of the exogenous variable $V_i$ ($i = 1, \ldots, m$); and each $\epsilon_t$ is drawn from a population of disturbances with zero mean and constant variance $\sigma^2$ over all $t$.

[9] This is in lieu of performing a multiple regression that would include, say, per capita income, the consumer price index, and a time variable. The index is on a 1957–1959 base. It might also be preferable to compute per capita consumption with regard solely to the population of beer-drinking age. The latter is sufficiently vague so that, for this illustration, everybody was given the benefit of the doubt.

[10] More generally, they are samples from a *universe* that includes the values that have occurred as well as those that *might* have occurred, but did not.

The first assumption implies that the disturbance term is the sole source of random variation in $Q_t$. The second assumption assures that $(\mathbf{V}'\mathbf{V})^{-1}$, an inverse of which we have made repeated use, exists. In particular, assuming $N \geq 1 + m$, the rank of $\mathbf{V}$ is $1 + m$, since $\mathbf{V}$ has $N$ rows and $1 + m$ columns that are linearly independent by the first assumption. $\mathbf{Q} = \mathbf{V}\boldsymbol{\alpha} + \boldsymbol{\varepsilon}$ would be solvable for a unique vector of coefficients, $\mathbf{a}$, when $N = 1 + m$; there would be an exact relationship. With $m + 1 = 2$ variables and $N = 2$ observations, for example, there is a unique line passing through both points. With $N < 1 + m$, $1 + m - N$ of the $\alpha_i$ would be determined from $\mathbf{Q} = \mathbf{V}\boldsymbol{\alpha} + \boldsymbol{\varepsilon}$ as linear functions of the $N$ remaining $\alpha_i$, and we could not determine a unique vector of estimates, $\mathbf{a}$.

To appreciate the third set of assumptions, note that with $X$ a random variable with density function $f(X)$, the $r$th moment about a point $b$ is given by the *mathematical expectation*

$$E[(X - b)^r] = \int (X - b)^r f(X)\, dX$$

(a summation replacing the integral in the discrete case). In particular, $E[(X - 0)^1] = E[X] = \bar{X} =$ the population mean; $E[(X - \bar{X})^1] = 0$; $E[(X - \bar{X})^2] = \sigma_X^2 =$ the population variance; and, given a second random variable $Y$ such that $X$ and $Y$ are subject to the joint density $f(X, Y)$, we define

$$E[(X - \bar{X})(Y - \bar{Y})] = \int (X - \bar{X})(Y - \bar{Y}) f(X, Y)\, dX\, dY = \sigma_{XY}$$

to be the population covariance between $X$ and $Y$. As above, the correlation in the population between $X$ and $Y$ or $\rho_{XY} = \sigma_{XY}/\sigma_X\sigma_Y$. The third set of assumptions therefore states that $E[\epsilon_t] = 0$, $E[(\epsilon_t - 0)(\epsilon_t - 0)] = E[\epsilon_t\epsilon_t] = \sigma^2$, and

$$E[(\epsilon_t - 0)(\epsilon_{t+k} - 0)] = 0.$$

Now, once it is recognized that the joint observations on the variables represent a sample, it is immediately clear that $\mathbf{a}$, the estimate of $\boldsymbol{\alpha}$, is a *sample* estimate. The mean of the distribution of possible values that $\mathbf{a}$ might have taken on is given by $E[\mathbf{a}] = E[(\mathbf{V}'\mathbf{V})^{-1}\mathbf{V}'\mathbf{Q}]$, from (3.4). But $\mathbf{Q} = \mathbf{V}\boldsymbol{\alpha} + \boldsymbol{\varepsilon}$ by (3.1a). Hence,

$$\begin{aligned} E[\mathbf{a}] &= E[(\mathbf{V}'\mathbf{V})^{-1}\mathbf{V}'\mathbf{V}\boldsymbol{\alpha} + (\mathbf{V}'\mathbf{V})^{-1}\mathbf{V}'\boldsymbol{\varepsilon}] \\ &= E[\boldsymbol{\alpha}] + (\mathbf{V}'\mathbf{V})^{-1}\mathbf{V}'E[\boldsymbol{\varepsilon}] = \boldsymbol{\alpha}, \end{aligned} \tag{3.12}$$

since (1) the expectation of a sum is the sum of the individual expectations; (2) the expectation of a constant times a random variable equals the constant times the expectation of the random variable, and $(\mathbf{V}'\mathbf{V})^{-1}\mathbf{V}'$ is nonstochastic; and (3), $E[\boldsymbol{\varepsilon}] = \mathbf{0}$ by the third assumption. With the mathematical expectation or *expected value* of $\mathbf{a}$ equal to the population mean of $\boldsymbol{\alpha}$, we say that $\mathbf{a}$ is an *unbiased estimate* of $\boldsymbol{\alpha}$. Moreover, since $\mathbf{a}$ is a sample estimate, there is a set of *sample* variances $\sigma_{a_i}^2$ and covariances $\sigma_{a_ia_j}$ associated with the $a_i$ that may be summarized in the variance-covariance *matrix* $\mathbf{Cov\ a} = E[(\mathbf{a} - \boldsymbol{\alpha})(\mathbf{a} - \boldsymbol{\alpha})']$, since $E[\mathbf{a}] = \boldsymbol{\alpha}$ by (3.12). But, substituting for $\mathbf{a}$ from (3.4),

$$E[(\mathbf{a} - \boldsymbol{\alpha})(\mathbf{a} - \boldsymbol{\alpha})'] = E[([\mathbf{V}'\mathbf{V}]^{-1}\mathbf{V}'\mathbf{Q} - \boldsymbol{\alpha})([\mathbf{V}'\mathbf{V}]^{-1}\mathbf{V}'\mathbf{Q} - \boldsymbol{\alpha})'];$$

and, since $(\mathbf{V}'\mathbf{V})^{-1}\mathbf{V}'\mathbf{Q} = (\mathbf{V}'\mathbf{V})^{-1}\mathbf{V}'(\mathbf{V}\boldsymbol{\alpha} + \boldsymbol{\varepsilon}) = \boldsymbol{\alpha} + (\mathbf{V}'\mathbf{V})^{-1}\mathbf{V}'\boldsymbol{\varepsilon}$,

$$\begin{aligned} \mathbf{Cov\ a} &= E[(\boldsymbol{\alpha} + (\mathbf{V}'\mathbf{V})^{-1}\mathbf{V}'\boldsymbol{\varepsilon} - \boldsymbol{\alpha})(\boldsymbol{\alpha} + (\mathbf{V}'\mathbf{V})^{-1}\mathbf{V}'\boldsymbol{\varepsilon} - \boldsymbol{\alpha})'] \\ &= E[([\mathbf{V}'\mathbf{V}]^{-1}\mathbf{V}'\boldsymbol{\varepsilon})([\mathbf{V}'\mathbf{V}]^{-1}\mathbf{V}'\boldsymbol{\varepsilon})'] \\ &= E[(\mathbf{V}'\mathbf{V})^{-1}\mathbf{V}'\boldsymbol{\varepsilon}\boldsymbol{\varepsilon}'\mathbf{V}(\mathbf{V}'\mathbf{V})^{-1}] \\ &= (\mathbf{V}'\mathbf{V})^{-1}\mathbf{V}'E[\boldsymbol{\varepsilon}\boldsymbol{\varepsilon}']\mathbf{V}(\mathbf{V}'\mathbf{V})^{-1} \end{aligned}$$

because of the assumption that **V** is nonstochastic. Therefore, with $E[\boldsymbol{\varepsilon\varepsilon}'] = \sigma^2\mathbf{I}$ by the third assumption,

$$\mathbf{Cov\ a} = \sigma^2(\mathbf{V}'\mathbf{V})^{-1}\mathbf{V}'\mathbf{V}(\mathbf{V}'\mathbf{V})^{-1} = \sigma^2(\mathbf{V}'\mathbf{V})^{-1}. \qquad (3.13)$$

The element in the $i$th row and $j$th column of **Cov a** gives the covariance term $\sigma_{a_ia_j}$, or $\mathbf{Cov\ a} = [\sigma_{a_ia_j}]$. In particular, the diagonal element $\sigma_{a_ia_i} = \sigma_{a_i}^2$. Its square root, $\sigma_{a_i}$, is called the *standard error* of $a_i$. We do not, of course, know $\sigma^2$, nor can we determine it, since the disturbances are not observable. We can, however, obtain an unbiased estimate of it from the *residuals* as $S^2/(N - m - 1) = S^2/N_c$.[11] Substituting $S^2/N_c$ in (3.13) gives an estimate $s_{a_ia_j}$ of $\sigma_{a_ia_j}$.

The argument can also be developed that with the disturbances normally distributed, and we shall so assume, $(a_i - \alpha_i)/s_{a_i}$ is distributed as $t_{N-m-1}$.[12] This is a $t$-distribution with $N - m - 1$ degrees of freedom. The beauty of the statistic $(a_i - \alpha_i)/s_{a_i}$ is that one so inclined can employ it in order to make probability statements with respect to the value of the *population* parameter, based solely upon its *small sample* estimate.[13] A classical application, for example, might test the hypothesis that $\alpha_i = \alpha_i^* = 0$. This would be done by computing $(a_i - 0)/s_{a_i} = a_i/s_{a_i}$, and from tables of the $t$-distribution determining the *probability* of obtaining this large a value for the test statistic if $\alpha_i$ were indeed zero. Such an application is illustrated in the Appendix.

## d. The Gauss-Markov Theorem

One of the most important theorems of regression analysis is the Gauss-Markov theorem. It is important because it assures that our least-squares estimator of $\boldsymbol{\alpha}$ will have two very desirable properties: (1) **a** will be a linear unbiased estimator; (2) **a** will have the minimum variance of all such estimators.

To prove the theorem, first recall from (3.4) that $\mathbf{a} = (\mathbf{V}'\mathbf{V})^{-1}\mathbf{V}'\mathbf{Q}$. By assumption (1) we may write $(\mathbf{V}'\mathbf{V})^{-1}\mathbf{V}' = \mathbf{V}^*$ and $\mathbf{a} = \mathbf{V}^*\mathbf{Q}$; or, **a** is a linear function of **Q**. We have already shown in (3.12) that $E[\mathbf{a}] = \boldsymbol{\alpha}$. Thus **a** is a *linear unbiased* estimator.

Further, consider any other estimator that is a linear unbiased function of **Q**, say $\hat{\mathbf{a}} = (\mathbf{V}^* + \mathbf{K})\mathbf{Q}$. For $\hat{\mathbf{a}}$ to be unbiased, we require that $E[\hat{\mathbf{a}}] = E[\mathbf{V}^*\mathbf{Q}] + E[\mathbf{KQ}] = \boldsymbol{\alpha}$. Since in the derivation of (3.12) it was shown that $E[\mathbf{V}^*\mathbf{Q}] = E[(\mathbf{V}'\mathbf{V})^{-1}\mathbf{V}'\mathbf{Q}] = \boldsymbol{\alpha}$, for $E[\hat{\mathbf{a}}] = \boldsymbol{\alpha}$ we require that $E[\mathbf{KQ}] = E[\mathbf{K}(\mathbf{V}\boldsymbol{\alpha}) + \mathbf{K}\boldsymbol{\varepsilon}] = \mathbf{KV}\boldsymbol{\alpha} + \mathbf{KE}[\boldsymbol{\varepsilon}] = \mathbf{0}$. But, $E[\boldsymbol{\varepsilon}] = \mathbf{0}$ by the third assumption. Consequently, if $\hat{\mathbf{a}}$ is to be unbiased for any $\boldsymbol{\alpha}$, we *require* $\mathbf{KV} = \bar{\mathbf{0}}$. Computing the variance-covariance matrix associated with $\hat{\mathbf{a}}$,

$$\begin{aligned}\mathbf{Cov\ \hat{a}} &= E[(\hat{\mathbf{a}} - \boldsymbol{\alpha})(\hat{\mathbf{a}} - \boldsymbol{\alpha})'] = E[(\mathbf{V}^*\mathbf{Q} + \mathbf{KQ} - \boldsymbol{\alpha})(\mathbf{V}^*\mathbf{Q} + \mathbf{KQ} - \boldsymbol{\alpha})'] \\ &= E[(\mathbf{V}^*\mathbf{V}\boldsymbol{\alpha} + \mathbf{V}^*\boldsymbol{\varepsilon} + \mathbf{KV}\boldsymbol{\alpha} + \mathbf{K}\boldsymbol{\varepsilon} - \boldsymbol{\alpha})(\mathbf{V}^*\mathbf{V}\boldsymbol{\alpha} + \mathbf{V}^*\boldsymbol{\varepsilon} + \mathbf{KV}\boldsymbol{\alpha} + \mathbf{K}\boldsymbol{\varepsilon} - \boldsymbol{\alpha})'] \\ &= E[(\mathbf{V}^*\boldsymbol{\varepsilon} + \mathbf{KV}\boldsymbol{\alpha} + \mathbf{K}\boldsymbol{\varepsilon})(\mathbf{V}^*\boldsymbol{\varepsilon} + \mathbf{KV}\boldsymbol{\alpha} + \mathbf{K}\boldsymbol{\varepsilon})']\end{aligned}$$

[11] See Goldberger, *Econometric Theory*, pp. 166–167. $N_c$ corrects for degrees of freedom.

[12] See Goldberger, *Econometric Theory*, pp. 113–115 and 178–179.

[13] Using our symbols for convenience, it is useful to bear in mind the following remarks: "It is comforting, of course, to have some measure of how much $a_i$ varies from sample to sample. What is upsetting is that the measure is itself a *guess*. True, it is better than nothing, but this is no consolation if by some quirk of fate we have picked a sample so atypical that it gives us not only a really wrong parameter estimate $a_i$, but also a really small $s_{a_i}^2$. The moral is: Don't be cocksure about the excellence of your guess of $\alpha_i$ just because you have guessed that its variance $\sigma_{a_i}^2$ is small." (Stefan Valavanis, *Econometrics*, New York: McGraw-Hill, Inc., 1959, p. 43.)

after substituting $\mathbf{V}\boldsymbol{\alpha} + \boldsymbol{\varepsilon}$ for $\mathbf{Q}$ and noting that $\mathbf{V}^*\mathbf{V}\boldsymbol{\alpha} = (\mathbf{V}'\mathbf{V})^{-1}\mathbf{V}'\mathbf{V}\boldsymbol{\alpha} = \boldsymbol{\alpha}$. Upon performing the appropriate matrix multiplications and recognizing that $\mathbf{K}$ and $\mathbf{V}$ are nonstochastic matrices, we may write the former equation as follows:

$$\begin{aligned}\mathbf{Cov}\ \hat{\mathbf{a}} = {} & \mathbf{V}^*E[\boldsymbol{\varepsilon\varepsilon}']\mathbf{V}^{*\prime} + \mathbf{V}^*E[\boldsymbol{\varepsilon\alpha}']\mathbf{V}'\mathbf{K}' + \mathbf{V}^*E[\boldsymbol{\varepsilon\varepsilon}']\mathbf{K}' \\ & + \mathbf{KV}E[\boldsymbol{\alpha\varepsilon}']\mathbf{V}^{*\prime} + \mathbf{KV}E[\boldsymbol{\alpha\alpha}']\mathbf{V}'\mathbf{K}' + \mathbf{KV}E[\boldsymbol{\alpha\varepsilon}']\mathbf{K}' \\ & + \mathbf{K}E[\boldsymbol{\varepsilon\varepsilon}']\mathbf{V}^{*\prime} + \mathbf{K}E[\boldsymbol{\varepsilon\alpha}']\mathbf{V}'\mathbf{K}' + \mathbf{K}E[\boldsymbol{\varepsilon\varepsilon}']\mathbf{K}'.\end{aligned}$$

We require, however, that $\mathbf{KV} = \bar{\mathbf{0}}$. Therefore $(\mathbf{KV})' = \mathbf{V}'\mathbf{K}' = \bar{\mathbf{0}}$, as do $\mathbf{V}^*\mathbf{K}' = (\mathbf{V}'\mathbf{V})^{-1}\mathbf{V}'\mathbf{K}'$ and $\mathbf{KV}^{*\prime} = \mathbf{KV}(\mathbf{V}'\mathbf{V})^{-1}$. Inasmuch as $\mathbf{E}[\boldsymbol{\varepsilon\varepsilon}'] = \sigma^2\mathbf{I}$, the previous expression reduces to

$$\begin{aligned}\mathbf{Cov}\ \hat{\mathbf{a}} &= \mathbf{V}^*E[\boldsymbol{\varepsilon\varepsilon}']\mathbf{V}^{*\prime} + \mathbf{K}E[\boldsymbol{\varepsilon\varepsilon}']\mathbf{K}' \\ &= \sigma^2(\mathbf{V}'\mathbf{V})^{-1} + \sigma^2\mathbf{KK}'. \end{aligned} \tag{3.14}$$

The diagonal terms of $\mathbf{Cov}\ \hat{\mathbf{a}}$ will be the variances of the $\hat{a}_i$. The diagonal terms of $\mathbf{KK}'$ will necessarily be nonnegative, as the elements will all be squared terms. Hence, to *minimize the variances* of the $a_i$, $\mathbf{K}$ must be a zero matrix, for if any elements of $\mathbf{K}$ are nonzero, $\mathbf{KK}'$ will contain some positive diagonal elements and some diagonal terms of $\mathbf{Cov}\ \hat{\mathbf{a}}$ will be greater than those of $\mathbf{Cov}\ \mathbf{a}$. Thus $\hat{\mathbf{a}} = (\mathbf{V}^* + \mathbf{K})\mathbf{Q} = \mathbf{V}^*\mathbf{Q} = \mathbf{a}$ is the linear unbiased estimator that has the minimum variance, often referred to as the best linear unbiased estimator (BLUE).

These two properties are summarized in the Gauss-Markov theorem: The estimator $\mathbf{a} = (\mathbf{V}'\mathbf{V})^{-1}\mathbf{V}'\mathbf{Q}$ with variance-covariance matrix $\mathbf{Cov}\ \mathbf{a} = \sigma^2(\mathbf{V}'\mathbf{V})^{-1}$ is the minimum variance linear unbiased estimator of $\boldsymbol{\alpha}$ in the linear regression $\mathbf{Q} = \mathbf{V}\boldsymbol{\alpha} + \boldsymbol{\varepsilon}$.

## e. Some Problem Areas

With the invaluable assistance of the computer and a stock of "canned" programs, classical linear regression is a technique that is easy to use and even easier to abuse. Anyone with enough assistants to gather and feed data into a computer can easily immerse himself in pages of output featuring all sorts of correlations and regression coefficients. Nevertheless, the appropriate application and interpretation of least squares and its results is not without complications, and one needs to proceed with great caution. We have made a number of assumptions, including the implicit one that economic data will be valid and we can use them to measure what we think we are measuring. Violations of these assumptions will be of varying importance. A detailed discussion of the problems and of when and how they might be handled would extend well beyond the scope of this presentation. At the very least we must, however, call attention to their existence and their potential effects.

The assumptions made in classical linear regression relate to the data and their statistical properties as well as to the validity of the model and its premises. Like other social scientists, the economist is forced to rely on data that may not accurately measure the variables of concern to him. The data may tend to under- or overestimate the "true" values of a particular variable. If we err in estimating the dependent variable, the random-error term may pick up the discrepancy. If, however, the data measuring an independent variable are biased in one direction, this bias will in turn be passed on to the associated parameter estimate.

Secondly, individual components from a joint observation may be missing from the data series for one variable or another, but not for all variables. Discarding the entire joint observation could involve discarding potentially useful information. In contrast, since the dependent variable is assumed to be a constant linear function of the independent variables for *all* joint observations, it might well be appropriate to either discard or in some manner make special allowances for certain joint observations whose blind inclusion in the analysis would distort the results. The former problem may require statistical adjustments; the latter may require adjustments in the model. A study of demand that included observations from 1935 through 1968 and that failed to recognize the distinctiveness of the period of World War II, the possibilities of rationing, price control, and black-market operations, could be in serious error. Occasionally data problems can be avoided; occasionally they can be satisfactorily resolved. Their pervasiveness should not be overlooked.

A variety of interesting statistical problems arise because economic data tend to violate our basic assumptions about them. For the economist, perhaps the most frequently recurring problem is that of *multicollinearity*. We have assumed that the exogenous variables in the regression equation will be independently distributed and hence uncorrelated. With economic data such as prices, income, population, and output this is scarcely likely to occur. Rather, the correlation among the exogenous variables, the multicollinearity, is likely to be a matter of degree. The situation can easily get out of hand, because in addition to pairwise correlation, one or more of the exogenous variables may be a linear function of several other exogenous variables. This issue will be reflected in the results in two ways. In the first place, although the estimated regression coefficients remain unbiased, their interpretation is open to considerable question. Because there is statistical dependence between the exogenous variables, their *individual effects* are difficult to isolate, for the variables tend to move together. Hence, even where multicollinearity appears, the least-squares equation may fit the data quite well, and the estimates or predictions it yields may be quite accurate, but the behavioral implications of the individual coefficients should probably be greeted with some skepticism.

In the second place, it must be recognized that we are, after all, merely *estimating* the standard errors of the regression coefficients. When multicollinearity runs rampant, our estimates will tend to be too high. We may readily see this by considering the matrix $\mathbf{V}'\mathbf{V}$. When there is multicollinearity, the columns of the matrix will no longer be completely independent. With perfect correlation between two exogenous variables, one column could be written as a linear function of "the first" and another column. In this case, $\mathbf{V}'\mathbf{V}$ would be singular, its inverse would not exist, and we could obtain neither the standard errors nor the regression coefficients. As the correlation between the exogenous variables approaches unity, the matrix $\mathbf{V}'\mathbf{V}$ approaches singularity and the elements of $(\mathbf{V}'\mathbf{V})^{-1}$ become larger and larger (and, incidentally, we lose more and more digits in the computational procedure). Since the covariance matrix is given by $\sigma^2(\mathbf{V}'\mathbf{V})^{-1}$, the elements of the inverse become larger and the estimated standard errors greater.

We have also assumed that the disturbances will be drawn from populations with constant variance (homoscedasticity) and will not be autocorrelated. We might expect, however, that these assumptions will be violated. In particular, heteroscedasticity (nonconstant variance) might be a concern where one would anticipate a relationship between the magnitude of the variance in the disturbances and the magnitude of one or more of the variables. For example, an extensive time series of income data might contain observations that are increasing over time fairly regularly. If income is the dependent variable in a linear regression, it might be suspected that the higher incomes are associated with disturbances drawn from populations with higher variances than is the case with the lower incomes. If this relationship is ignored, the regression coefficients will no longer be minimum variance estimators. Alternatively, if the disturbances are autocorrelated, the regression coefficients will be unbiased, but we will tend to underestimate their standard errors. Similarly, the explanatory variables and the disturbances may be correlated, and this too will lead to bias in the regression coefficients. And, similarly, the difficulty may be corrected if the relationship is known.

Although these have been considered to be data problems and statistical problems, some are, in a sense, model problems, for their resolution requires adjustments in the basic model. Additionally, our model may require adjustments when it contains errors of *specification*. That is, we simply have failed to include the appropriate form of equation in the analysis. A related difficulty might be that our analysis failed to recognize the *inter*relationships among the variables. Some independent variables, for example, may well be dependent upon the dependent variable as well as upon each other. In this case, the appropriate analysis may require more complex multi-equation models.

Experience suggests that these problems and others will commonly arise in economic analysis. Some will be considered in greater detail in later chapters. Each should be a source of constant concern. In as brief a treatment of econometrics as this has been, it seems especially appropriate to add the caution that when one's results are particularly attractive, one should be particularly suspicious.

## 3.5 LOSS FUNCTIONS AND LEAST-SQUARES ESTIMATORS

Later chapters will consider some of the problems confronting a decision maker who must select a course of action $A$ from among several options open to him. In a deterministic world (one in which there is no uncertainty), selecting the optimal act may be time-consuming and may require a good deal of thought and manipulation; and, as in the case of the consumer selecting a basket of goods to maximize utility under a budget constraint, the choice will depend upon the objective. But the problem is at least theoretically soluble. In a world of uncertainty, however, a decision maker's life is complicated by his lack of omniscience with respect to all factors that will determine the success, or lack thereof, of his selection.

In general, let $\theta$ denote a particular set of circumstances that *could* exist, or a particular *state* that these uncertain factors can take on. In order to measure the loss incurred by the decision maker through his choice of act $A$ when state $\theta$ obtains, we define the *opportunity loss function* $l(A; \theta)$. The latter is so called because it *assigns* values to reflect the losses the decision maker suffers when he fails to take the opportunity to select the optimal choice in light of the occurrence of $\theta$. The function $l(A; \theta)$ could be in terms of dollars, utility, and so on. The only restrictions we shall impose on $l(A; \theta)$ are that it be real-valued and nonnegative for all acts and all states, and that there be at least one $A$ for each $\theta$ such that $l(A; \theta) = 0$; that is, the function is defined over the set of nonnegative real numbers, and there is an optimal act for each possible state of the uncertain factors such that there is no loss when this act is chosen. For example, an individual may have to choose between the acts of taking ($A_1$) or not taking ($A_2$) an umbrella to work with him. There are two possible states: it will ($\theta_1$) or will not ($\theta_2$) rain. $A_1$ is optimal if $\theta_1$ obtains; $A_2$ is optimal if $\theta_2$ obtains. Hence $l(A_1; \theta_1) = l(A_2; \theta_2) = 0$, since what we judge to have been the optimal decision has been made. If, however, $A_1$ is chosen and $\theta_2$ obtains, or if $A_2$ is chosen and $\theta_1$ obtains, the decision maker will suffer some discomfort, so that $l(A_1; \theta_2) > 0$ and $l(A_2; \theta_1) > 0$. Each situation will not necessarily entail equal discomfort, and $l(A_1; \theta_2)$ will not necessarily equal $l(A_2; \theta_1)$. Moreover, it should be clear that it will be necessary for *each individual* to make some numerical assignment reflecting the loss *he* personally suffers under each circumstance. We shall require that this assignment be such as to provide a *ranking* of least regretted to most regretted opportunity lost. Thus, as a general matter, we neither expect nor require all individuals to greet all outcomes with a common tolerance.

Suppose now that the choice of $A$ is based upon a set of data, $x_1, \ldots, x_N$, in accordance with the *decision function* $A = d(x_1, \ldots, x_N)$. The loss associated with this decision function and the particular set of data will be $l(A; \theta) = l(d; \theta)$. Moreover, suppose that the data we observe depend to one degree or another upon the actual state $\theta$. If there were a perfect one-to-one correspondence there would be no problem, for given the data we would know the $\theta$; if there were absolutely no relationship, then there wouldn't be much point to basing a decision on the data. Rather, we can assume that each $x_i$ is a sample observation from a population, and that each $x_i$ has a *probability* of occurrence that depends upon $\theta$. Specifically, $\theta$ and $x_i$ are linked via the density $f(x_i; \theta)$. Then, the mean or *expected opportunity loss* associated with the decision rule $d$ will be given by

$$EL = E[l(A; \theta)] = \int \cdots \int l(A; \theta) f(x_1; \theta) \cdots f(x_N; \theta)\, dx_1 \cdots dx_N. \tag{3.15}$$

Expected opportunity loss will provide us with what we shall call a *certainty equivalent*. That is, it is a single number that summarizes an entire distribution of possibilities. We shall substitute the number for the distribution in our analysis and reach decisions on the basis of certainty equivalents. In Chapter 12, we shall provide theoretical justification for the intuitively appealing objective of selecting that decision rule which minimizes expected opportunity loss.

In the present context of least squares, the "actual state" $\theta$ with which we are concerned is the values taken on by the elements contained in the vector $\boldsymbol{\alpha}$. The action that we have to take is to choose a vector of estimates $\mathbf{a}$ based upon sample data and a decision rule. In making this choice, we have been implicitly concerned with the loss $l(\mathbf{a}; \boldsymbol{\alpha})$ that results when our subsequent behavior proceeds on the assumption that $\mathbf{a}$ and $\boldsymbol{\alpha}$ are in fact equal. In this instance the subsequent behavior is the basing of estimates of $\mathbf{Q}$ on the estimated $\hat{\mathbf{Q}} = \mathbf{Va}$. We have not, however, explicitly defined the form of the loss function. One form that is frequently encountered in decision problems is the *quadratic loss function*,

$$l(\mathbf{a}; \boldsymbol{\alpha}) = (\mathbf{a} - \boldsymbol{\alpha})'\mathbf{D}(\mathbf{a} - \boldsymbol{\alpha}). \tag{3.16}$$

In this equation, $\mathbf{D}$ is an arbitrarily selected positive definite matrix and $(\mathbf{a} - \boldsymbol{\alpha})$ is a column vector. Consequently $l(\mathbf{a}; \boldsymbol{\alpha})$ will be a nonnegative scalar whose value is a convex function of $(\mathbf{a} - \boldsymbol{\alpha})$. In the case where $\mathbf{a}$ and $\boldsymbol{\alpha}$ consist of single parameters, the quadratic loss function can be reduced to $l(\mathbf{a}; \boldsymbol{\alpha}) = D(a - \alpha)^2$, where $D > 0$ is frequently chosen as some function of $\alpha$. In addition to being most tractable, this particular loss function has some very nice properties that conveniently tie in with the more general decision-making problem discussed in Chapter 12. Here we might simply note two: (1) $l(\mathbf{a}; \boldsymbol{\alpha}) = 0$ when the parameters and the estimates are equal (that is, when $\mathbf{a} = \boldsymbol{\alpha}$); and (2) the further $\mathbf{a}$ is from $\boldsymbol{\alpha}$, in either direction, the greater is the loss—and the loss mounts by a squared factor as more serious errors are accorded proportionately greater weight.

With this loss function, the expected loss from employing the decision function, or in this context the estimator, $\boldsymbol{d}_1$ to obtain an estimate $\mathbf{a}_1$ based on the $x_i$, given that $\boldsymbol{\alpha}$ obtains, will be

$$E[l(\mathbf{a}_1;\ \boldsymbol{\alpha})] = E[(\mathbf{a}_1 - \boldsymbol{\alpha})'\mathbf{D}(\mathbf{a}_1 - \boldsymbol{\alpha})].$$

Similarly, the expected loss from any other estimator $\boldsymbol{d}_2$ resulting in $\mathbf{a}_2$ will be

$$E[l(\mathbf{a}_2;\ \boldsymbol{\alpha})] = E[(\mathbf{a}_2 - \boldsymbol{\alpha})'\mathbf{D}(\mathbf{a}_2 - \boldsymbol{\alpha})].$$

The estimator $\boldsymbol{d}_1$ will entail a smaller expected loss than will $\boldsymbol{d}_2$ as long as $E[l(\mathbf{a}_1;\ \boldsymbol{\alpha})] < E[l(\mathbf{a}_2;\ \boldsymbol{\alpha})]$. Choosing $\mathbf{D} = \mathbf{I}$, for example, we see immediately that $E[(\mathbf{a} - \boldsymbol{\alpha})'\mathbf{I}(\mathbf{a} - \boldsymbol{\alpha})]$ is simply the sum of the variances of the individual estimates in $\mathbf{a}$. We seek the estimator that minimizes this sum; or, the expected loss computed via the quadratic loss function is at a minimum when our parameter estimates are minimum mean square error, or minimum variance, estimates. By the Gauss-Markov theorem, the least-squares estimates, in addition to being linear unbiased estimates, have this minimum variance property. This will be of some comfort to those who later reconsider the least-squares approach, and the decision rule $\mathbf{a} = (\mathbf{V}'\mathbf{V})^{-1}\mathbf{V}'\mathbf{Q}$, in light of the discussion of expected loss in Chapter 12, and the so-called Bayesian tack that we introduce in the next chapter. It should be noted, however, that in general the choice of a "best" estimator in the opportunity loss sense will depend upon how the estimator is to be used. One is unlikely to encounter very many universally "best" estimators; and the estimator that is deemed "best" in any one instance may depend upon the statement of the problem. The square of an unbiased estimate of the standard deviation, for example, will not be an unbiased estimate of the variance. The point is, then, that the choice of an optimal act, a decision rule, or an estimator will depend upon the *conditions* surrounding the choice and the *objectives* of the individual decision maker.

# Appendix to Chapter 3

## 3A.1 AN ILLUSTRATION OF MULTIPLE REGRESSION

As a second illustration, suppose that the quantities of DURK sold in each year from 1946–1965 are as given in Table 3.2. Suppose also that *long-run* demand in year $t$, $Q_{tL}$, is thought to be a *multiplicative* function of price in year $t$, $P_t$, and personal disposable income in year $t$, $I_t$. Both price and income are considered to be exogenous variables—that is, they are established outside of the model. These data are also given in Table 3.2. In effect it is assumed that consumers are able to purchase all the DURK they want without affecting its price. Here, then, purchases and demand are synonymous. The model of long-run demand is thus written

TABLE 3.2

| **Year** | $Q_t$ | $P_t$ | $I_t$ |
|---|---|---|---|
| 1946 | 7000 | 101 | 160 |
| 1947 | 7100 | 102 | 170 |
| 1948 | 7100 | 100 | 189 |
| 1949 | 7050 | 100 | 189 |
| 1950 | 7100 | 100 | 207 |
| 1951 | 7100 | 105 | 227 |
| 1952 | 7150 | 107 | 238 |
| 1953 | 7300 | 106 | 253 |
| 1954 | 7300 | 107 | 257 |
| 1955 | 7400 | 107 | 275 |
| 1956 | 7700 | 106 | 293 |
| 1957 | 7850 | 109 | 309 |
| 1958 | 7900 | 107 | 319 |
| 1959 | 7950 | 110 | 337 |
| 1960 | 8000 | 110 | 350 |
| 1961 | 8050 | 112 | 364 |
| 1962 | 8100 | 115 | 385 |
| 1963 | 8200 | 115 | 405 |
| 1964 | 8400 | 115 | 437 |
| 1965 | 8500 | 118 | 469 |

$$Q_{tL} = \beta_0 P_t^{\beta_1} I_t^{\beta_2} \epsilon_t. \qquad (3.17)$$

We do not, however, *observe* the actual values of $Q_{tL}$. Rather we observe $Q_{tS}$, the short-run quantities demanded. Nonetheless it might be assumed that the ratio $(Q_{tL}/Q_{tS})$ will be closer to unity than will the ratio $(Q_{tL}/Q_{t-1,S})$ because there will tend to be greater coincidence between short- and long-run demand in year $t$ than between short- and long-run demand in successive years. This implies that[14]

$$\frac{Q_{tL}}{Q_{tS}} = \left(\frac{Q_{tL}}{Q_{t-1,S}}\right)^{\lambda}, \qquad 0 < \lambda < 1. \tag{3.18}$$

By substitution into (3.17), and rearranging (3.18),

$$Q_{tL} = \left(\frac{Q_{tS}}{Q_{t-1,S}^{\lambda}}\right)^{1/(1-\lambda)} = \beta_0 P_t^{\beta_1} I_t^{\beta_2} \epsilon_t;$$

hence

$$Q_{tS} = \beta_0^{(1-\lambda)} P_t^{\beta_1(1-\lambda)} I_t^{\beta_2(1-\lambda)} Q_{t-1,S}^{\lambda} \epsilon_t^{(1-\lambda)}. \tag{3.19}$$

This equation describes the *short-run* demand curve.

Let $\log Q_{tS} = Q_t$, $\log P_t = V_{1t}$, $\log I_t = V_{2t}$, $\log Q_{t-1,S} = V_{3t}$, and $(1 - \lambda) \log \epsilon_t = \epsilon_t^*$; also write $(1 - \lambda) \log \beta_0 = \alpha_0$, $(1 - \lambda)\beta_1 = \alpha_1$, $(1 - \lambda)\beta_2 = \alpha_2$ and $\lambda = \alpha_3$. Upon taking logarithms on both sides of Equation (3.19), the latter may be written

$$Q_t = \alpha_0 + \alpha_1 V_{1t} + \alpha_2 V_{2t} + \alpha_3 V_{3t} + \epsilon_t^*, \tag{3.20}$$

which is precisely the form of (3.1). Hence we may obtain estimates $a_i$ of the $\alpha_i$ from (3.4). It is apparent, then, that it is not necessary to restrict the functions to be estimated by least squares to linear equations as long as they can be *transformed* into linear equations.

Suppose it is also known that the quantity of DURK sold in 1945 was 7000. We would, then, have $N = 20$ joint observations on $Q_t$, $V_{1t}$, $V_{2t}$, and $V_{3t}$. Equation (3.3) can be written as $\mathbf{V'Q} = \mathbf{V'Va}$, where

$$\mathbf{Q}' = (\log 7000, \log 7100, \ldots, \log 8500),$$

$$\mathbf{V} = \begin{bmatrix} 1 & \log 101 & \log 160 & \log 7000 \\ 1 & \log 102 & \log 170 & \log 7000 \\ \cdot & \cdot & \cdot & \cdot \\ \cdot & \cdot & \cdot & \cdot \\ \cdot & \cdot & \cdot & \cdot \\ 1 & \log 118 & \log 469 & \log 8400 \end{bmatrix}.$$

Hence (3.3) becomes

$$\begin{bmatrix} \Sigma Q_t \\ \Sigma Q_t V_{1t} \\ \Sigma Q_t V_{2t} \\ \Sigma Q_t V_{3t} \end{bmatrix} = \begin{bmatrix} N & \Sigma V_{1t} & \Sigma V_{2t} & \Sigma V_{3t} \\ \Sigma V_{1t} & \Sigma V_{1t}^2 & \Sigma V_{1t}V_{2t} & \Sigma V_{1t}V_{3t} \\ \Sigma V_{2t} & \Sigma V_{1t}V_{2t} & \Sigma V_{2t}^2 & \Sigma V_{2t}V_{3t} \\ \Sigma V_{3t} & \Sigma V_{1t}V_{3t} & \Sigma V_{2t}V_{3t} & \Sigma V_{3t}^2 \end{bmatrix} \begin{bmatrix} a_0 \\ a_1 \\ a_2 \\ a_3 \end{bmatrix} \tag{3.21a}$$

or

$$\begin{aligned} \Sigma Q_t &= N\alpha_0 + \Sigma V_{1t}\alpha_1 + \Sigma V_{2t}\alpha_2 + \Sigma V_{3t}\alpha_3, \\ \Sigma Q_t V_{1t} &= \Sigma V_{1t}\alpha_0 + \Sigma V_{1t}^2\alpha_1 + \Sigma V_{1t}V_{2t}\alpha_2 + \Sigma V_{1t}V_{3t}\alpha_3, \\ \Sigma Q_t V_{2t} &= \Sigma V_{2t}\alpha_0 + \Sigma V_{1t}V_{2t}\alpha_1 + \Sigma V_{2t}^2\alpha_2 + \Sigma V_{2t}V_{3t}\alpha_3, \\ \Sigma Q_t V_{3t} &= \Sigma V_{3t}\alpha_0 + \Sigma V_{1t}V_{3t}\alpha_1 + \Sigma V_{2t}V_{3t}\alpha_2 + \Sigma V_{3t}^2\alpha_3, \end{aligned} \tag{3.21b}$$

[14] This approach harks back to Marc Nerlove and William Addison, "Statistical Estimation of Long-run Elasticities of Supply and Demand," *Journal of Farm Economics*, **XL**:4 (Nov. 1958), 861–880. For an alternative formulation of which we are particularly fond, see Ira Horowitz, "An Econometric Analysis of Supply and Demand in the Synthetic Rubber Industry," *International Economic Review*, **4**:3 (Sept. 1963), 325–345.

which are popularly known as the "normal" equations. In the present example, (3.21a) becomes

$$\begin{bmatrix} 77.61274 \\ 157.66439 \\ 189.78282 \\ 300.87413 \end{bmatrix} = \begin{bmatrix} 20 & 40.62566 & 48.88644 & 77.52842 \\ 40.62566 & 82.53140 & 99.35729 & 157.49253 \\ 48.88644 & 99.35729 & 119.85888 & 189.57230 \\ 77.52842 & 157.49253 & 189.57230 & 300.54673 \end{bmatrix} \begin{bmatrix} a_0 \\ a_1 \\ a_2 \\ a_3 \end{bmatrix}.$$

Similarly, the solution is given by (3.4) as $\mathbf{a} = (\mathbf{V'V})^{-1}\mathbf{V'Q}$, which becomes

$$\begin{bmatrix} a_0 \\ a_1 \\ a_2 \\ a_3 \end{bmatrix} = \begin{bmatrix} N & \Sigma V_{1t} & \Sigma V_{2t} & \Sigma V_{3t} \\ \Sigma V_{1t} & \Sigma V_{1t}^2 & \Sigma V_{1t}V_{2t} & \Sigma V_{1t}V_{3t} \\ \Sigma V_{2t} & \Sigma V_{1t}V_{2t} & \Sigma V_{2t}^2 & \Sigma V_{2t}V_{3t} \\ \Sigma V_{3t} & \Sigma V_{1t}V_{3t} & \Sigma V_{2t}V_{3t} & \Sigma V_{3t}^2 \end{bmatrix}^{-1} \begin{bmatrix} \Sigma Q_t \\ \Sigma Q_tV_{1t} \\ \Sigma Q_tV_{2t} \\ \Sigma Q_tV_{3t} \end{bmatrix}. \tag{3.22}$$

In the present example, (3.22) becomes

$$\begin{bmatrix} a_0 \\ a_1 \\ a_2 \\ a_3 \end{bmatrix} = \begin{bmatrix} 11{,}193.47967 & -1596.74199 & 698.20142 & -2491.11846 \\ -1596.74199 & 1171.27562 & -157.92009 & -102.27029 \\ 698.20142 & -157.92009 & 50.66960 & -129.31357 \\ -2491.11846 & -102.27029 & -129.31357 & 777.76443 \end{bmatrix} \begin{bmatrix} 77.61274 \\ 157.66439 \\ 189.78282 \\ 300.87413 \end{bmatrix}$$

$$= \begin{bmatrix} .81052 \\ -.06931 \\ .06075 \\ .79001 \end{bmatrix}.$$

Given **a**, the estimate of $\lambda$ is determined as $\hat{\lambda} = a_3 = .79001$. Indeed, $0 < \hat{\lambda} = .79001 < 1$. Further, $b_0$, $b_1$, and $b_2$, the estimates of the $\beta_i$, are given by $b_0$ = antilog $(.81052/.20999) = 7241.667$; $b_1 = (-.06931/.20999) = -.33006$; $b_2 = (.06075/.20999) = .28929$. Hence the short-run demand curve (3.19) is estimated by

$$Q_{tS} = 6.464P_t^{-.06931}I_t^{.06075}Q_{t-1,S}^{.79001}e_t^{.20999};$$

the long-run demand curve (3.17) is estimated by

$$Q_{tL} = 7241.667P_t^{-.33006}I_t^{.28929}e_t.$$

It is also calculated that $S^2/N_c = .0000175$. Therefore the variance-covariance matrix is estimated by

$$\textbf{Cov a} = (S^2/N_c)[\mathbf{V'V}]^{-1} = \begin{bmatrix} .19589 & -.02794 & .01222 & -.04359 \\ -.02794 & .02050 & -.00276 & -.00179 \\ .01222 & -.00276 & .00089 & -.00226 \\ -.04359 & -.00179 & -.00226 & .01361 \end{bmatrix}.$$

Suppose now that one wishes to make a probability statement with respect to $\alpha_i$, based exclusively upon the sample data. One of the classical applications is to test the hypothesis that $\alpha_i$ is "significantly different" from zero. As indicated earlier, to perform this test we first compute the ratio of the sample estimates $a_i/s_{a_i}$. With specific regard to $\alpha_1$, the *t-ratio* is $a_1/s_{a_1} = -.48$. Tables of the cumulative *t*-distribution with $N - m - 1 = 20 - 3 - 1 = 16$ degrees of freedom show that when in fact $\alpha_1$ does equal zero, the probability of getting a $t$-ratio of this magnitude exceeds .30. Thus we would not be very confident about rejecting the hypothesis that $\alpha_1 = 0$. Alternatively, suppose we want to consider the possibility that $\alpha_1 = -1$. Calculating $t = (a_1 - [-1])/s_{a_1} = 6.50$, the probability of a $t$-ratio of this magnitude is less than .0005. We can therefore say with great confidence that short-run demand is price-inelastic, since, as was shown earlier, with this form of demand curve $a_1$ *is* the estimated price elasticity of demand, and it is most unlikely that $\alpha_1 = -1$.

In similar fashion, and with respect to $\alpha_2$, since $a_2/s_{a_2} = 2.04$, the probability is less than .05 of obtaining a $t$-ratio of this magnitude if $\alpha_2 = 0$; and since $(a_2 - 1)/s_{a_2} = -31.31$, it is just about inconceivable that a $t$-ratio such as the latter would be obtained with $\alpha_2 = 1$. Therefore $\alpha_2$, which is easily seen to be the income elasticity, appears to be positive and below unity; or, it seems quite likely that $0 < \alpha_2 < 1$.

It might also be mentioned that if $Y = f(X_1, \ldots, X_m)$,

$$s_Y^2 = \sum_{i=1}^{m} \sum_{j=1}^{m} \left(\frac{\partial f}{\partial X_i}\right)\left(\frac{\partial f}{\partial X_j}\right) s_{X_iX_j},$$

where the derivatives are evaluated at the sample means. To estimate the standard error of $b_1$, then, with $b_1 = a_1/(1 - \hat{\lambda})$, we require the square root of

$$\begin{aligned} s_{b_1}^2 &= \left(\frac{1}{1-\hat{\lambda}}\right)^2 s_{a_1}^2 + \left(\frac{-a_1}{(1-\hat{\lambda})^2}\right)^2 s_{1-\hat{\lambda}}^2 - 2\left(\frac{a_1}{(1-\hat{\lambda})^3}\right) s_{a_1(1-\lambda)}. \\ &= \left(\frac{1}{.20999}\right)^2 (.02050) + \left(\frac{.06931}{.04410}\right)^2 (.01361) - 2\left(\frac{-.06931}{.00926}\right)(.00179) \\ &= (4.76192)(.02050) + (2.47010)(.01361) + (14.97138)(.00179) \\ &= .15804; \end{aligned}$$

or $s_{b_1} = .39754$. As was true of the estimate of the short-run price elasticity of demand, the long-run price elasticity estimate has an estimated standard error that is larger than the coefficient itself. Based on the sample observations, then, the value of the population parameter $\beta_1$ is open to considerable doubt.

Finally, we note that the regression on (3.19) gives an $R^2 = .978$. Unhappily, a high $R^2$ does not guarantee against model error. Note also that high $R^2$'s are quite easy to generate when one can select and manipulate the data.

## EXERCISES

1. Remember the consumer of Exercise 3 in Chapter 2? Well, he has an independently wealthy wife with an income of 10,000 dollars that she spends on $x_1$ and $x_2$. Her utility function is given by $U = x_1^{2/5}x_2^{1/2}$. Derive and graph this husband *and* wife's demand curve for $x_1$. Does their demand curve shift after the fall in the price of $x_1$ as in Exercise 4, Chapter 2? Explain!

2. Suppose there are 349 additional families with demand curves for $x_2$ like that of the couple in the previous problem. Nobody else can stand $x_2$. Derive an expression for the elasticity of demand of $x_2$.

3. "In the long run we're all dead." Comment.

4. *Prove* that the first four sentences of footnote 7 are true.

5. Discuss the possibilities of the hyperplane that minimizes $\sum_{t=1}^{N} e_t$. What about the one that minimizes $\sum_{t=1}^{N} e_t^3$? Reassess footnote 5 with some thoughts along these lines.

6. The likelihood function of random variables $x_1, \ldots, x_n$ is the joint density of those variables, $L(\theta) = f(x_1, \ldots, x_n; \theta)$, as a function of $\theta$. If $\hat{\theta}$ is an estimate of $\theta$ such that $\hat{\theta} = g(x_1, \ldots, x_n)$, then the function $g(x_1, \ldots, x_n)$ that maximizes $L(\theta)$ is the *maximum-likelihood* estimator of $\theta$. Show that if the disturbance terms in (3.1) are assumed to be normally distributed with zero mean, zero covariances, and constant variance, the maximum-likelihood estimates of $\boldsymbol{\alpha}$ coincide with the least-squares estimates.

7. Show that if two random variables are statistically independent, they will be uncorrelated. If in a random sample two variables are uncorrelated, can we conclude the variables are statistically independent? Why?

8. Suppose one hypothesized that the regression equation fitted to the data for Table 3.1 should have the price index as the dependent variable and per capita consumption as the independent variable.
   (a) Without peeking, which regression would yield the higher $R^2$? Why?
   (b) Compute this second least-squares equation.

9. The 1946–1960 population figures (in millions) are as follows:

| Year | Population | Year | Population | Year | Population |
|---|---|---|---|---|---|
| 1946 | 142 | 1951 | 155 | 1956 | 169 |
| 1947 | 145 | 1952 | 158 | 1957 | 172 |
| 1948 | 147 | 1953 | 160 | 1958 | 175 |
| 1949 | 150 | 1954 | 163 | 1959 | 178 |
| 1950 | 152 | 1955 | 166 | 1960 | 181 |

The figures on personal disposable income for 1946–1960 are given in Table 3.2. Obtain least-squares estimates for the $\alpha_i$ in the regression equation

$$Q_t = \alpha_0 + \alpha_1 V_{1t} + \alpha_2 V_{2t} + \epsilon_t,$$

where $Q_t$ is per capita beer consumption, $V_{1t}$ is the beer price index, and $V_{2t}$ is per capita disposable income. Based on these results, would you conclude that beer is an inferior good?

10. Using the data of the previous exercise, compute the least-squares estimates for the equation

$$Q_t = \alpha_0 V_{1t}^{\alpha_1} V_{2t}^{\alpha_2} \epsilon_t.$$

11. Compare and assess the results in the previous two least-squares equations. Which results do you feel give a more valid impression of consumer preferences? On which would you prefer to base pricing decisions? Why?

12. Given your results in Exercise 10, comment (statistically and otherwise) on the following statements:
   (a) The demand for beer is price inelastic.
   (b) Beer is an inferior good.

13. Suppose an omniscient economist told you that, without doubt, $\alpha_1$ in Exercise 10 is equal to $-.8$. Derive the least-squares estimates for $\alpha_0$ and $\alpha_2$.

14. Discuss the extent to which the assumptions of Section 3.4c are violated in Exercises 9 and 10.

15. One is often interested in the correlation that would obtain between two variables if other, related variables could be held constant. In a sample of observations on three variables, for example, this correlation, the *partial correlation*, between variables 1 and 2 with 3 held constant, is defined to be

$$r_{12.3} = \frac{r_{12} - r_{13}r_{23}}{[(1 - r_{13}^2)(1 - r_{23}^2)]^{1/2}}.$$

With reference to the data in Table 3.2, compute and analyze the partial correlations between $P_t$ and $Q_t$ ($I_t$ held constant) and between $I_t$ and $Q_t$ ($P_t$ held constant). Do these results seem to have any connection with the multiple regression results? Should they? Discuss in detail!

# 4

# THE THEORY OF PRODUCT DEMAND: The Firm

## 4.1 INTRODUCTION

Industry demand will be a function of many variables. If all variables except price are held constant, the industry demand curve is expected to be negatively sloped in the price-quantity space. This is also true of the firm's demand curve. The firm's demand curve will, however, be much more complex than the industry's. Industry demand will depend on the prices charged for substitutes and complements. In addition, the firm's demand will depend upon the prices charged for the same or "only slightly" differentiated products produced by other firms to which potential buyers have access.

This interdependence among firms has delineated several classical forms of market structure within which we undertake the discussion of the shape of the firm's demand curve in the price-quantity space. With respect to a homogeneous product the following structures are distinguished: (1) monopoly, a single seller having the power to establish price in the market; (2) oligopoly, a few firms, each of which *influences* market price, special cases being duopoly (two firms), triopoly (three firms), and the like; and (3) polypoly, or pure competition, where none of the numerous firms individually has a perceptible influence on price.[1] Additionally, we may explicitly analyze the interrelationships between firms producing slightly differentiated products. Here each may be looked upon as if it were, in a sense, the sole producer in a distinct market. Still, each firm is forced to give special consideration to its interdependence with other firms producing similar, though not necessarily homogeneous, products. Thus each firm could have some, though not complete,

[1] The term polypoly blends nicely with the previous terms but is not precisely synonomous with pure competition. The pure competitor perceives himself as having a negligible influence on market price. He is the extreme case of the polypolist, "a seller who is unconcerned about rivals' reactions because he has too many competitors (or colleagues) to consider any one of them as his rival." See Fritz Machlup, *The Economics of Sellers' Competition* (Baltimore: The Johns Hopkins Press, 1952), p. 86 in particular, and pp. 79–132 in general.

discretion over price, depending upon how many others produced a like product.[2] There may be few or many firms in such *monopolistically competitive* markets, so called because they combine elements of monopoly and competition.[3]

Given the firm's demand curve, traditional microeconomic theory has had as a central concern the determination of price and quantity in the market, and by the profit-maximizing firm. Both the short and long runs are discussed, where the long and short of things is now determined by the *firm's* ability to vary its factors of production. The process by which *equilibrium* prices and quantities are established is also a focal point. As noted earlier, an equilibrium position is one from which there is no tendency to deviate once it has been reached. But the equilibrium will not necessarily be stable, in the sense that once it has been disturbed there may be a tendency to resist returning to it. The analysis of equilibria and the movements whereby they are attained is of considerable interest, but it will be advantageous to delay our discussion of these issues until later chapters. For the present, where it is necessary to raise the matter, we shall simply assume that the price and quantity decisions have somehow gotten themselves resolved and that it makes sense to refer to "the price in the market." We shall also push the time element into the background. The firm's demand schedule will summarize quantities demanded at various prices per unit in an unspecified time period, and the discussion will be independent of short- vs. long-run considerations.

The discussion will, however, recognize and embrace the impact that uncertainty has on the firm and especially its demand curve. As will be argued, it is necessary to incorporate uncertainty directly and *explicitly* into microeconomic theory. This provides a broader, yet more precise framework for describing the firm's demand curve than is permitted by the more traditional approach. First, however, it will be helpful to consider the firm's demand curve within the classical industry classification schemes. In these, the firm behaves *as if* it is faced with a known demand schedule that summarizes the *exact* quantities it is *certain* to be able to sell at various prices.

## 4.2 TRADITIONAL VIEWS

### a. Pure Competition

A purely competitive *market* exists when there are enough noncolluding buyers and sellers so that no single buyer or seller exercises a perceptible influence on price. If, in addition, there is free entry into and exit from the industry, free and perfect

[2] Although it is tempting to try to structure such markets in terms of the cross-elasticity of demand, say by evaluating the effects on the $j$th seller's quantity of a change in the $i$th seller's price, this involves two major pitfalls. First, this cross-elasticity depends upon the degree of homogeneity of the differentiated products. Second, it depends upon the number of sellers in the market. For a discussion see R. L. Bishop, "Elasticities, Cross-Elasticities, and Market Relationships," *American Economic Review*, **XLII**:5 (Dec. 1952), 779–803.

*Potential* competition will also be important, and "differences between substitute products, in cost of production and service value, are nowadays often no more serious than similar differences between different varieties of what we think of as the 'same' product." See J. M. Clark, "Toward a Concept of Workable Competition," *American Economic Review*, **XXX**:2 (June 1940), 241–256 and 247 in particular.

[3] See Edward H. Chamberlin, *The Theory of Monopolistic Competition* (Cambridge, Mass.: Harvard University Press, 1960), particularly pp. 73–74.

knowledge of all factors of concern to the industry, and complete certainty, the pure becomes perfect.[4]

We confine our discussion to the firm's demand curve in the price-quantity space with price the ordinate.[5] As before, the industry demand curve is written $Q = D(P, V)$. With many buyers and sellers having free access to one another, and with firms producing a standardized product, consumers will not purchase from the seller whose price exceeds the market price. As will be seen, this price is such that the profit-maximizing firm bearing the brunt of the succeeding discussion has no incentive to undercut it. The result is that in equilibrium all firms charge the same price for the standardized product and one can readily determine the firm's demand curve from the industry curve.

This determination will depend upon the assumptions made with respect to the nature of *supply* conditions in the industry. Some alternatives are considered in Chapter 7. In general, however, it makes good intuitive sense that any one firm's demand will depend upon the number of competitors it has and hence on the number of alternatives the buyers have, as well as the ability of its competitors to satisfy the buyer's demands.

To indicate how *supply* conditions can influence the determination of the individual firm's *demand* curve, it is useful to consider the following highly specialized case. Suppose there are $n$ like firms in an industry and that for the period under consideration the number of firms is invariant. Further, irrespective of the price and quantity determined in the market, the firms will secure equal market shares. This assumption is unnecessary for the analysis of the purely competitive industry where firms may enter and leave as industry price and output vary, but it will be convenient for the moment, without being misleading. At each price the $i$th firm will sell a quantity of $Q_i = Q/n = D(P, V)/n$. For a given $Q$, as the number of firms increases, $\lim_{n \to \infty} Q_i \to 0$. That is, the individual firm's sales—though *not* the industry's sales, which are being held constant—approaches zero. The slope of the industry demand curve with only $V$ fixed is given by $\partial P/\partial Q = 1/[\partial Q/\partial P] = 1/D'$; the elasticity of demand is given by $(\partial Q/\partial P)(P/Q) = D'(P/Q)$. The slope of the firm's demand curve is given by $n/D'$ and the elasticity of demand is given by $(D'/n)(P/Q_i) = (D'/n)(nP/Q) = D'(P/Q)$. With $D'$ negative, although the industry and firm price elasticities are equal at every price, the slope of the firm's demand curve is more negative than that for the industry by a factor of $n$. This always holds for fixed and equal market *shares* because then we note that $\partial P/\partial Q_i = (\partial P/\partial Q)(dQ/dQ_i)$ and $dQ/Q_i = n$. Indeed, as $n$ approaches infinity the slope of the firm's demand curve approaches negative infinity. But, under the particular assumptions, firm and industry demand *elasticity* will be equal at *all* prices.

As an illustration, consider the industry demand curve $Q = AP^{-a}$ with $A$ and $a$ greater than zero. This is a rectangular hyperbola and would have the shape of the curve $D_I$ in Figure 4.1(a). The slope of the curve is $dP/dQ = 1/[dQ/dP] = 1/[-aAP^{-(a+1)}] = (-1/aA)P^{a+1}$.[6] The elasticity of demand is then calculated as $-a$.

[4] For a discussion see George J. Stigler, "Perfect Competition, Historically Contemplated," *Journal of Political Economy*, **LXV**:1 (Feb. 1957), 1–17.

[5] As a final reminder, this policy will be adhered to whether price or quantity is chosen as the dependent variable, or whether their functional relationship is an implicit one.

[6] The total derivative rather than the partial is used here because this is the special case of a single independent variable.

The $i$th firm's demand curve, $i = 1, \ldots, n$, based on the previous assumption of fixed and equal market shares at every price, is given by $Q_i = (A/n)P^{-a}$. This curve, too, has a constant elasticity of demand of $-a$. The slope, however, is $dP/dQ_i = (dP/dQ)(dQ/dQ_i) = (-n/aA)P^{a+1}$. If we change the scale of the abscissa in Figure 4.1(b) so that $Q_i = Q/n$, the curve $D_n$ represents the firm's demand curve. The curve $D_m$ represents the firm's demand curve, where $m = 2n$ firms yield the same industry price and quantity combination as in the $n$-firm case. These curves have a steeper slope than the industry demand curve at each and every *price* by constant factors of $n$ and $2n$, respectively. It is only the difference in scale of the abscissa that makes it *appear* otherwise. As $n$ increases, Figure 4.1(b) clearly reveals that the firm's demand curve becomes steeper. The horizontal sum of the individual firm's demand curves yields the industry demand curve. These particular curves have been graphed for $A = 10{,}000$, $a = 2$, and $n = 500$, and $m = 1000$.

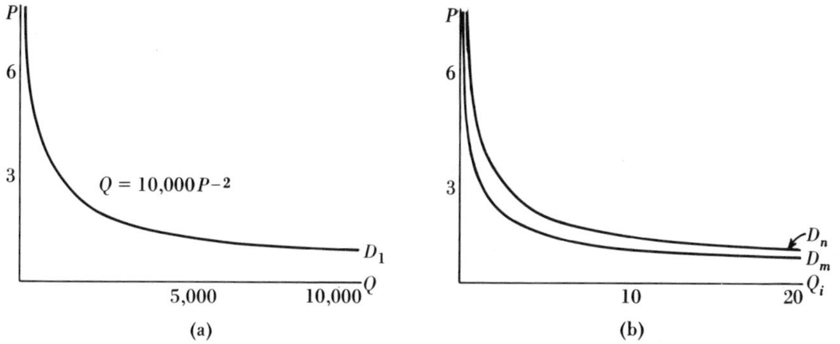


Fig. 4.1

These steep demand curves facing the individual firm bear scant resemblance to the *horizontal* demand curves that one commonly encounters upon first exposure to the purely competitive firm and industry. One reason, as we shall see in later chapters, is that the number of firms in the purely competitive industry is *not* invariant with industry output, nor is any firm's market share going to be a fixed percent of industry output. As we shall also see, however, the firm's demand curve *will* have a downward slope. The precise slope will depend upon the extent to which the firm's presence in the market and level of output influence industry price and output. Under pure competition it is *assumed* that each firm's output is a comparatively minor proportion of the industry total, and each firm's scale of operation is too small to have it be otherwise. Thus it is *assumed* that each firm's influence on price is negligible. This influence will not, however, necessarily be nonexistent, and $dP/dQ_i$ will not necessarily be zero. Within the very narrow price range that any *one* firm's presence or absence from the market can possibly effect, a *graph* of the demand curve will *appear* to have zero slope. Indeed, for all intents and purposes we may so draw it and so treat it. We thereby *assume* that the pure competitor will be a *price-taker*. He accepts the price that is determined in the market. In effect his *perception* of his demand curve is that he will be able to sell as much as he wishes at the going price, and his demand curve will be infinitely elastic.

## b. Monopoly

The monopolist's demand curve is also the industry demand curve. In the framework above, $n = 1$. When we analyze the monopolist's position, however, we tend to develop a greater awareness of the importance of the "other factors" that we hold constant than when we consider the purely competitive industry. In particular, we explicitly recognize that the quantity the monopolist can sell at a given price depends upon the prices charged by other firms or industries. The same will, of course, hold for the purely competitive industry with respect to other industries. Similarly, the quantities sold and prices that obtain in one industry will in turn affect prices and quantities elsewhere. This network of interrelationships suggests that demand curves for the competitive industry *or* the monopolist can be depicted either (1) with all other prices and quantities held constant or (2) after other prices have been permitted to vary in response to price movements in the industry under consideration. The curve $D_2$ of Figure 4.2 would be a demand curve of the latter

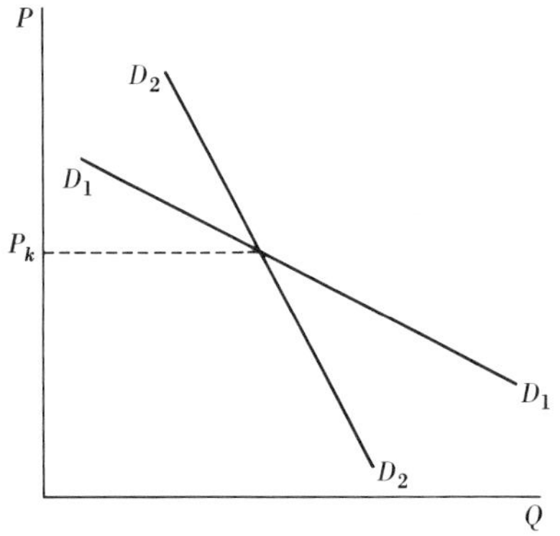


Fig. 4.2

type. In terms of the derivative, the slope of the former curve $D_1$ is given by the partial derivative $\partial P/\partial Q$, whereas the slope of the latter curve is given by the total derivative $dP/dQ$. In the specific case of the demand curve $Q = D(P, V_1, \ldots, V_s)$, we would calculate the slope either by computing $\partial Q/\partial P$ or by computing

$$\frac{dQ}{dP} = \left(\frac{\partial D}{\partial P}\right) + \left(\frac{\partial D}{\partial V_1}\right)\left(\frac{dV_1}{dP}\right) + \cdots + \left(\frac{\partial D}{\partial V_s}\right)\left(\frac{dV_s}{dP}\right) = \left(\frac{\partial D}{\partial P}\right) + \sum_i \left(\frac{\partial D}{\partial V_i}\right)\left(\frac{dV_i}{dP}\right).$$

Suppose that a price of $P_k$ obtained in the market. The flatter curve, $D_1$, recognizes that if the firm (industry) reduced price below $P_k$ there would be a greater impact on demand if the prices charged by others were held constant than if they were also reduced. In contrast, if prices rose above $P_k$, the drop in quantity demanded would be much greater if other prices held the line than if they too were to drift upward. Thus the firm with the power to set price might labor under the illusion that its price changes will not incur a response from other firms and that $D_1$ is its demand curve. Its price changes will, however, be rewarded with quantity responses according to the demand schedule $D_2$, for others may indeed respond to these price changes.

From the standpoint of decision making, the relevant demand curve is the one on which management bases its pricing and production decisions. This need not be the actual demand curve. From the decision-making standpoint it suffices that management behaves *as if* it were the demand curve.[7] Presumably, as more and more experience with pricing decisions is obtained, the firm improves its understanding of the actual demand curve. Thus, a management with some modicum of ability will soon recognize how others might react to the prices that it charges. In essence, this is Mrs. Robinson's view of the demand curve. It has embodied into it the price reactions of others.[8] Professor Chamberlin recognized the existence of this demand curve, $D_2$, but contended that entrepreneurial *action* may be guided by the perceived demand curve, $D_1$. The firm may operate under the continuing illusion that price cuts, say, will not be met by the counteraction of others. When firms are few enough, however, the mutuality of interests is more readily recognized and firms are not as inclined to hold to initial illusions. In any case, *results* of the entrepreneurial action will be determined by $D_2$.[9]

In the present discussion the firm will harbor no illusions as to the actions, or lack of actions, of other firms. When referring to *the* demand curve facing the firm, we shall mean the curve $D_2$, which recognizes the prices charged by other firms at given prices charged by the firm under consideration.

In Mrs. Robinson's *imperfect* competition, then, the monopolistic firm has the power to establish price and is a price-*setter*, whereas in *perfect* competition the firm does not have this power and is a price-*taker*. The firm cannot, however, ignore the price policies of other firms when setting price. It must be particularly alert to the prices charged by firms producing similar products. Indeed, it is sufficiently alert to incorporate their likely actions into its own demand curve. Professor Chamberlin's *monopolistic* competition suggests that *all* firms may have *some* power to set price. There will be a finite number of firms, and each firm's demand curve will to some degree be downward sloping. Each firm may have to consider the price reactions of many firms or few firms to its own behavior. As indicated later, however, the Chamberlinian monopolistic competitor does so with more than his share of naiveté.

## c. Oligopoly

Oligopoly presents a situation in which *several* firms produce a *standardized* product. Where all buyers have access to all sellers, and where all sellers have a capacity to satisfy total demand at the market price, *all* buyers will purchase from the seller charging the lower price. This need not be the case where the sellers cannot satisfy total demand at a particular price.

[7] In Weintraub's words, "The demand curve whose image spurs entrepreneurial action will be referred to indiscriminately as the subjective, or imagined, or anticipated demand curve. It may even be called the ex ante demand curve. The market curve which finally confronts the entrepreneur, whether or not he ever becomes aware of its full course, will be referred to as such, or as the objective or real or actual demand curve . . . . The ex ante curve tells us nothing except the producer's actual price and output policy. It reflects only the motives or forces stirring entrepreneurial behavior, but not the ultimate consequences." Sidney Weintraub, "Monopoly Equilibrium and Anticipated Demand," *Journal of Political Economy*, L:3 (June 1942), 428–429 and 431.

[8] Joan Robinson, *The Economics of Imperfect Competition* (London: Macmillan and Co., Ltd., 1950), pp. 20–21.

[9] Chamberlin, *The Theory of Monopolistic Competition*, pp. 70–116.

The oligopoly situation is particularly interesting because the firms are few enough that each is able, indeed forced, to give detailed consideration to the behavior of each of the other firms producing the product and to recognize their mutual dependence. In constructing its demand curve, the firm of oligopoly theory specifically incorporates into it a behavior postulate about the other producers. Some of the classical suggestions, such as the assumption that a competitor will not vary his price or will hold his quantity fixed during a succeeding production period, will be considered in Chapter 7.

As an illustration of the sort of assumption that one might make, consider the curves $D_1$ and $D_2$ of Figure 4.2. Suppose that the market price has in fact settled at $P_k$. The firm might assume that any price cuts on its part will be met by other oligopolists, but that price increases will not. It might then *perceive* its demand curve to be the *kinked* curve consisting of the portion of $D_1$ that lies above $P_k$ and the portion of $D_2$ that lies below $P_k$.[10]

## 4.3 TIME, CETERIS PARIBUS, AND UNCERTAINTY

Most of the models in this book concerned with pricing decisions require that a decision maker determine a price based upon a particular demand schedule for an unspecified time period. This is hardly the way of the real world. Current managerial decisions will ordinarily affect future options, and in the modern corporate conglomerate a decision in one area of the firm can have repercussions at an ostensibly unrelated appendage. Decision making *throughout* the managerial hierarchy of the modern firm therefore involves *policies* and *strategies*, a planned *series* of decisions, and not isolated choices within unrelated sets of alternatives.

Nevertheless, much of the ensuing discussion will narrow its focus to the need to resolve specific questions at particular times. The *indirect* consequences of a decision will not be entirely neglected; they will lurk in the background and be absorbed into the problem through the simple expedient of momentarily defining them away. Thus, suppose a current decision will in fact affect profitability in the future. Our analysis might not *explicitly* mention this future profit effect, but *implicitly* it will be built into our model. This will be done through definitions that make such future effects part of, say, the firm's *current* costs or its *current* revenues. Such an expedient is justified by the fact that the broader problem cannot be handled until we have successfully dealt with the less complex issue. In this spirit the firm's pricing decisions will be made with an eye on the firm's demand curve, and the latter will deal only with the quantity that the firm can sell at any given price during a particular time period, as perceived by the firm.[11] If there are aftereffects, such as the possi-

[10] See Paul M. Sweezy, "Demand Under Conditions of Oligopoly," *Journal of Political Economy*, **XLVII**:4 (Aug. 1939), 568–573. Also, M. Brofenbrenner, "Applications of the Discontinuous Oligopoly Demand Curve," *Journal of Political Economy*, **XLVIII**:3 (June 1940), 420–427, and George J. Stigler, "The Kinky Oligopoly Demand Curve and Rigid Prices," *Journal of Political Economy*, **LV**:5 (Oct. 1947), 432–449.

The curves of Figure 4.2 have been drawn for differentiated products. As the products approach homogeneity, the kink approaches a right angle with a horizontal and vertical segment. The implication is that as the products become more standardized, increases over the market price result in sharper cutbacks in sales, while price decreases will be met immediately, thereby forestalling volume increases.

[11] Such a procedure has long been a sore point. For example, "The fact that demand in the future depends upon present as well as future price, which makes it impossible to derive

bility that a "low" current price will call forth "high" current volume but reduce future sales, we shall assume that these reactions have already been allowed for and built into the demand curve.[12]

Additionally, much of the theoretical analysis will proceed ceteris paribus. We shall generally write the demand curve that has been stressed to be $Q = D(P, V)$ simply as $Q = D(P)$, abstracting from the other variables. We shall *not* be holding the prices of the "same or similar" products constant, though for the most part such factors as income and technology *will* be held constant. Nevertheless, we shall *implicitly* build into the function the reactions of others. Hence the $Q$ in $Q = D(P)$ will be the actual quantity that the firm can sell at a price of $P$, given the prices that will be charged by other firms.

We shall not necessarily assume certainty. In describing the traditional theory we *shall* assume that the firm behaves *as if* it knew with certainty that $Q = D(P)$ is its demand curve. Analysis of price and quantity determination under this assumption will prove to be most enlightening and useful. Still, once this assumption is dropped, the analysis undergoes considerable alteration, and it is of interest to consider the differences in the results yielded by the two approaches.

In the real world uncertainty is the norm. We must therefore understand how a formal description of uncertainty can be incorporated into an analytical framework. In particular, we describe how uncertainty can be explicitly introduced into the description of the firm's demand curve, and how it subsequently enters into the traditional formulation.[13]

---

marginal revenue from any single demand curve, is usually dismissed, if it is considered at all, with a brief reference to 'maintaining goodwill' or 'spoiling the market,' " in the classic article by R. L. Hall and C. J. Hitch, "Price Theory and Business Behavior," *Oxford Economic Papers*, no. 2 (May 1939), p. 15. Or, again, "In making his price decision, the businessman is more concerned with the fact of uncertainty regarding future shifts in demand than with the shape of the demand curve at any particular moment" [R. A. Gordon, "Short-Period Price Determination in Theory and Practice," *American Economic Review*, **XXXVIII**:3 (June 1948), 277]. Despite these compelling thoughts, we shall bravely go forward, and we shall attempt to justify this headstrong behavior in the course of the book.

[12] For a general defense of this approach, see Fritz Machlup, "Marginal Analysis and Empirical Research," *American Economic Review*, **XXXVI**:4 (Sept. 1946), 518–554. E. A. G. Robinson offers a rather succinct rejoinder to the "footnote 11" position: "Clearly the effects of present actions on the levels and elasticities of future demand curves have to be taken into account. Whether one prefers to do this by including these considerations, appropriately discounted into the present, in the actual demand or cost curves, or whether one prefers to use purely short-term curves and add these considerations as an extra ingredient into the final decision is a matter of convenience." ["The Pricing of Manufactured Products and the Case Against Imperfect Competition: A Rejoinder," *Economic Journal*, **LXI**:242 (June 1951), p. 430.]

[13] Despite the Hall and Hitch conviction that "Producers cannot know their demand or marginal revenue curves, and this for two reasons: (a) they do not know consumer's preferences; (b) most producers are oligopolists, and do not know what the reactions of their competitors would be to a change in price" ("Price Theory and Business Behavior," p. 22).

## 4.4 UNCERTAINTY AND THE DEMAND CURVE

### a. Probability

It is somewhat like putting the cart before the horse to discuss probability *after* discussing least squares. We have assumed that the reader has had *some* previous exposure to probability and probability densities. He may merely be aware that a probability is a number between zero and one describing the relative likelihood that an event will have a particular outcome; such an awareness would suffice for the previous discussion. There are, however, some fundamental issues underlying the *assignment* of probabilities and hence the interpretation of the concept of "a probability." If we are to be forced to put up with the uncertainties of the real world, and if probabilistic information is to be of any value in arriving at real-world decisions, then somehow we must be able to obtain the numbers that are to "describe the relative likelihood" of an outcome. It is with this issue that we shall now be concerned.

As we have hinted, students of probability theory can, have, do, and will continue to disagree as to the exact nature of probability. The position taken here is that a *probability* is a number between zero and one that reflects an individual's *degree of belief* about the likelihood of occurrence of a particular outcome. When quoting odds or assigning probabilities, one is quantifying his personal judgments based upon his experience and knowledge, insight and information. Such personal or subjective probabilities may be well thought-out or ill-conceived, but they should not be labeled either "correct" or "incorrect."[14] Different people might, and quite frequently will, arrive at different probability judgments. Clearly some people exercise better judgment than others. After the test of time has been graded, some will prove to have made more reliable probability assignments than others—assignments that a

[14] This position invites dissent, and the invitation has been accepted by those who look upon probabilities as logical relations between propositions or statements. For example, J. M. Keynes [*A Treatise on Probability* (London: Macmillan and Co., Ltd., 1921)] argued that "The Theory of Probability is logical, therefore, because it is concerned with the degree of belief which it is *rational* to entertain in given conditions and not merely with the actual beliefs of particular individuals, which may or may not be rational (p. 4) .... Between two sets of propositions, therefore, there exists a relation, in virtue of which, if we know the first, we can attach to the latter some degree of rational belief. This relation is the subject matter of the logic of probability (p. 6)." Jefferys asserts: "Probability theory is more complicated than deductive logic, and even in pure mathematics we must often be content with approximations .... The theory is in fact the system of thought of an ideal man that entered the world knowing nothing, and always worked out his inferences completely, just as pure mathematics is part of the system of thought of an ideal man who always gets his arithmetic right. But that is no reason why the actual man should not do his best to approximate to it." [Harold Jefferys, *The Theory of Probability* (Oxford: Clarendon Press, 1939), p. 37.] Or, to dissent to the point of uncivil disobedience, "It cannot, of course, be denied that there is also a subjective, psychological concept for which the term 'probability' may be used and sometimes is used. This is the concept of the degree of actual, as distinguished from rational, belief: 'the person $X$ at the time $t$ believes in $h$ to the degree $r$.' This concept is of importance for the theory of human behavior, hence for psychology, sociology, economics, etc. But it cannot serve as a basis for inductive logic or a calculus of probability applicable as a general tool of science." [Rudolf Carnap, *Logical Foundations of Probability* (Chicago: University of Chicago Press, 1950), p. 51.]

betting man would have found more rewarding. Still, these assignments will be neither correct nor incorrect. Some will merely *appear to be* more appropriate than others, or will be judged "better" on the basis of a prespecified criterion function.

Certainly one cannot simply randomly assign numbers between zero and one to outcomes and have these numbers be perfectly respectable probabilities. Instead, the individual is presumed to assign probabilities in accordance with his *best considered* judgment. The probabilities that he assigns must be *consistent* and *coherent.*[15] To be consistent, one should have the strongest degree of belief in the likelihood of the outcome that the evidence suggests is most likely and assign to it the highest probability—and so on down the line. If there are two possible outcomes, A and B, and the individual infers from the evidence that A is the more likely to occur, then he would be inconsistent in assigning a higher probability to B.

To be coherent, one's probability assignments should preclude the construction of a bet that one is bound to lose.[16] Suppose one is forced to put one's money where one's mouth is, and still one assigns probabilities of $\frac{1}{3}$ to heads and $\frac{1}{3}$ to "anything but heads" on a single toss of a coin. The $\frac{1}{3}$ assigned to the probability of heads may be likened to a willingness on the individual's part to give 2-to-1 odds against heads; the $\frac{1}{3}$ assigned to "anything but heads" may be likened to a willingness to give 2-to-1 odds against "anything but heads." If $1 is invested against this individual in each bet, then when heads comes up $2 is won in the first bet and $1 is lost in the second bet; and when "anything but heads" comes up, $1 is lost in the first bet and $2 is won in the second bet. Thus $1 is won from this person no matter what the outcome of the toss. In similar fashion the probabilities of particular outcomes should conform to those assigned to combinations of these outcomes. Suppose, for example, a probability of $\frac{1}{3}$ is assigned to outcome A and a probability of $\frac{1}{3}$ is assigned to outcome B. If either A or B but not both can occur, the probability assigned to the outcome A or B should be $\frac{2}{3}$.

Probability assignments must therefore be made such that if there are $i = 1, \ldots, N$ mutually exclusive and exhaustive outcomes $E_i$, the probability of the $i$th outcome, $P(E_i)$, must be assigned in such a way that $P(E_i) \geq 0$ and $\sum_i P(E_i) = 1$. This states that probabilities are nonnegative and that it is a certainty, probability of one, that one of the $N$ outcomes will obtain.

Historically, discussions of probability have placed the greater stress on the relative-frequency interpretation as opposed to the subjectivist stance taken here. In the frequentist approach, probabilities are assigned exclusively to the outcomes of *repetitive* events. This is done as follows: (1) a priori, if an event can occur in $N$ mutually exclusive and equally likely ways, and if $n$ of these ways result in the outcome $E_i$, then $P(E_i) = n/N$; (2) a posteriori, if one *has observed* a series of $N$ outcomes and if $n$ of these were the outcome $E_i$, then $P(E_i) \approx n/N$. Given the same information as the frequentist, the subjectivist *may* make the same probability

[15] For a discussion of these concepts in subjective probability see Henry E. Kyburg, Jr., and Howard E. Smokler, eds., *Studies in Subjective Probability* (New York: John Wiley & Sons, Inc., 1964), pp. 7–12. With particular regard to coherence and its importance, see Bruno DeFinetti, "Foresight: Its Logical Laws, Its Subjective Sources," reprinted in *Studies in Subjective Probability,* pp. 103–104. The latter article, in its entirety, is a "must" for the interested reader, and it wouldn't hurt the disinterested reader to have a look at it.

[16] This is *weak* coherence. *Strict* coherence obtains if the bettor cannot win and might lose.

assignments. When asked for the probability of a six on any one toss of an evenly balanced die, each will assert this probability to be $\frac{1}{6}$; when informed that *a* die has been rolled 90,000,004 times and that a randomly occurring 45,000,002 sixes were recorded, each is likely to assign a probability of $\frac{1}{2}$ to the outcome "a six" on the next toss of the die.

When, however, the frequentist is asked for the probability that U.S. Soughto will raise the price of its Soughtos for the coming year, he is at something of a disadvantage relative to the subjectivist. He might determine the relative frequency of past price increases; he might determine a relative frequency of past price increases under conditions approximating those of the period in question. Still, and although these data could be suggestive, the price charged by U.S. Soughto in the coming year may well be considered a *unique* event occurring under *unique* circumstances. The lengthy series of past observations on similar events required by the frequentist just is not available. The available data are informative but not definitive. These data should not be neglected, however, for they may well be suggestive.

The frequentist refuses to assign probabilities to unique events. The subjectivist glories in assigning probabilities to unique events *as well as* to repetitive events. These probability assignments reflect his degree of belief or what he would consider to be "fair" betting odds. Thus, the subjectivist might assign a probability of .8 to U.S. Soughto's raising its price; in effect he asserts that by taking odds of 8:2 or 4:1 one has a "fair bet" against a price increase. The sense in which this is a "fair bet" is discussed below, but for the moment one's intuitive understanding will suffice.

Accepting the subjectivist view gives probability theory a much wider range of application. For one concerned with economic problems this enlarged scope is important, since many economic problems in fact embody unique or infrequently recurring issues, requiring solutions in the absence of extensive historical information. Where the problems deal with repetitive events, the subjectivist and the frequentist *may* ultimately make the same probability assignments; but, as we shall see, the subjectivist approach lets us take advantage of the decision maker's judgments and experience *in conjunction with* the historical data. The subjectivist posture therefore does not waste valuable decision-making assets.

Further, the familiar axioms of probability may be required of subjective probabilities just as they are of the classical variety. In particular, $P(E_iE_j)$, the *joint* probability of outcomes $E_i$ *and* $E_j$, is given by

$$P(E_iE_j) = P(E_i \mid E_j)P(E_j) = P(E_j \mid E_i)P(E_i),$$

where $P(E_i \mid E_j)$ is the *conditional* probability of $E_i$ occurring, given that $E_j$ has occurred. If the occurrence of $E_i$ precludes the occurrence of $E_j$, and vice versa, $E_i$ and $E_j$ are said to be *mutually exclusive*. In this case, $P(E_i \mid E_j) = 0$ and $P(E_iE_j) = 0$. If the occurrence of $E_i$ in no way influences the likelihood of occurrence of $E_j$, and vice versa, $E_i$ and $E_j$ are *independent*. In this case, $P(E_i \mid E_j) = P(E_i)$ and $P(E_iE_j) = P(E_i)P(E_j)$. The probability of $E_i$ *or* $E_j$ occurring is given by $P(E_i \text{ or } E_j) = P(E_i) + P(E_j) - P(E_iE_j)$. If $E_i$ and $E_j$ are mutually exclusive outcomes, then $P(E_iE_j) = 0$ and $P(E_i \text{ or } E_j) = P(E_i) + P(E_j)$.

### b. Bayes' Rule

Now, if $P(E_kE_i) = P(E_k \mid E_i)P(E_i) = P(E_i \mid E_k)P(E_k)$, then when $P(E_k) \neq 0$ it follows that $P(E_i \mid E_k) = P(E_k \mid E_i)P(E_i)/P(E_k)$. This formulation of the conditional probability $P(E_i \mid E_k)$ is Bayes' rule.[17] Although at first glance this rule might seem to be but a harmless algebraic manipulation, the Bayesian formulation will prove to be of great value in the analysis of problems under uncertainty. To help reveal its potential, note first that $P(E_k)$ is a *marginal* probability. The term marginal signals the fact that we are only concerned with the relative likelihood of $E_k$ rather than the relative likelihood of the *joint* occurrence of $E_k$ and any other outcome(s). In this case,

$$\begin{aligned} P(E_k) &= P(E_k \mid E_1)P(E_1) + P(E_k \mid E_2)P(E_2) + \cdots + P(E_k \mid E_N)P(E_N) \\ &= \sum_i P(E_k \mid E_i)P(E_i). \end{aligned}$$

Therefore, Bayes' rule may be written as

$$P(E_i \mid E_k) = \frac{P(E_k \mid E_i)P(E_i)}{\sum_i P(E_k \mid E_i)P(E_i)}. \tag{4.1}$$

To understand the use of Bayes' rule and its potential importance to the firm's decision making, consider the following problem. General Soughto, one of several oligopolists producing Soughtos, is preparing a price list for publication. Firms in the industry make it a policy not to deviate from published price lists. Each firm must, therefore, make some assessment of its rivals' intentions in setting its own price. General Soughto is particularly concerned with the price that U.S. Soughto will establish. It is well known that U.S. Soughto's price changes are always 1 percent of current price.

General Soughto's management assesses current business conditions and U.S. Soughto's past policies and arrives at the judgment that the probability that U.S. Soughto's price will remain fixed is $P(F) = .05$. Management also assigns probabilities of $P(D) = .15$ and $P(I) = .80$ to the outcomes "price decrease" and "price increase."

Like any other group of intelligent noncolluding oligopolists, the Soughto producers exchange imprecise and very often misleading information in a variety of ways. One interesting approach is to hint at future price policy in *Wall Street Journal* interviews. Tracing these interviews back for almost half a century, the General Soughto analysts have determined that half the time that U.S. Soughto holds the price line their officials suggest that they will do so in prior interviews. On 60 percent of the occasions in which they ultimately raised price (always by 1 percent) and on 10 percent of the occasions in which they dropped price (also by 1 percent) they also indicated that they would hold the price line. Management feels justified in using these past relative frequencies to approximate probabilities $P(H \mid F) = .50$, $P(H \mid D) = .10$, and $P(H \mid I) = .60$, the conditional probabilities that a hold-the-line price policy will be hinted at when prices will be held fixed, decreased, or increased, respectively.

[17] Named after the Reverend Thomas Bayes, an eighteenth-century clergyman credited with discovering the rule. Having been suitably impressed with the power of the rule, he took it to the grave with him and his discovery was published posthumously. In a speech at Indiana University in the spring of 1967, Dr. M. G. Kendall suggested that the neo-Bayesians (that is, the subjectivists) might do well to do likewise.

By a happy coincidence, General Soughto's president happens to be perusing the *Wall Street Journal* and notices that, in an exclusive interview, U.S. Soughto's president is quoted as intending to try to maintain prices at current levels in the coming period. The General Soughto problem is to determine the probability that he will actually do so.

This probability is *not* $P(H \mid F)$, the probability that a no-price-change policy will be hinted at, given that prices are to be held fixed. The desired probability is $P(F \mid H)$, the probability that prices will be held fixed, *given* the announced intention of holding them fixed. To determine the latter probability we make use of *both* management's initial probability assessment with respect to the probability that U.S. Soughto's price will not change, $P(F) = .05$, *and* the information provided by the past interviews. The latter is quantified in the probabilities $P(H \mid F) = .50$, $P(H \mid D) = .10$, and $P(H \mid I) = .60$, which have been based on historical data. Substituting these probabilities into Bayes' rule, the initial assessment of $P(F) = .05$ will be revised to obtain $P(F \mid H)$, the probability of no price change given the outcome of the interview. Specifically,

$$P(F \mid H) = \frac{P(H \mid F)P(F)}{P(H \mid F)P(F) + P(H \mid D)P(D) + P(H \mid I)P(I)}$$
$$= \frac{(.50)(.05)}{(.50)(.05) + (.10)(.15) + (.60)(.80)} = \frac{.025}{.520} = .048.$$

In like manner it is determined that $P(D \mid H) = .015/.520 = .029$ and $P(I \mid H) = .480/.520 = .923$. The sum $.048 + .029 + .923$ is necessarily equal to 1. More generally, $\sum_i P(E_i \mid E_k) = 1$, since, given any piece of new information, irrespective of what that information suggests, one of the $N$ outcomes *must* obtain. Note, however, that $\sum_i P(E_k \mid E_i) \neq 1$, generally. In the present example, $.50 + .10 + .60 \neq 1$. What *would* be true is that $\sum_k P(E_k \mid E_i) = 1$. That is, irrespective of the price policy that has been followed, *some* policy would have been hinted at. Note also that the denominator in the expression for Bayes' rule, $\sum_i P(E_k \mid E_i)P(E_i) = P(E_k)$, gives the probability that $E_k$ will be the outcome observed or information that is obtained. In the Soughto example, this probability is $(.50)(.05) + (.10)(.15) + (.60)(.80) = .520$. Hence .520 is the probability that U.S. Soughto will hint at a no-price-change policy—given General Soughto's assessments of their probable action.

Bayes' rule therefore enables us to use a priori probabilities $P(E_i)$, probabilities that have been assigned on the basis of information, experience, and personal judgment, before consideration of new information. The latter is referred to as *sample* information, because it is just one of the possible observations that might have evolved from the information search. Once this new information is obtained, the a priori assessments are systematically revised via Bayes' rule into *posterior* probabilities. The term posterior is used to reflect the fact that an initial assessment has been made and subsequently revised via Bayes' rule on the basis of new information. As additional information is obtained, the *posterior* probabilities will be revised by another application of Bayes' rule. In this second application, the posterior probabilities are now inserted as the prior probabilities in the equation. Note that we obtain the same final answer as we would if we combined *all* the information and revised the initial prior probabilities once via Bayes' rule. It should also be noted that the conditional probabilities, $P(E_k|E_i)$, as well as the marginal probabilities, $P(E_i)$, may be subjective probabilities.

Now, different individuals with similar experience who are required to make probability assignments based on the same information may well disagree in their assessments. This possibility may make some people uncomfortable about the subjectivist view. When we are going to base decisions upon numbers, most of us would like to be able to agree on the numbers to be used. It is therefore comforting to note that (1) unless one has a *dogmatic prior* (which even *sounds* like a bad thing to have!)—that is, unless one assesses a probability of 1 or 0 to the $P(E_i)$ term in (4.1)—then, (2) as more and more sample information is received, and (3) if there is a specific framework for evaluating the information and incorporating it into Bayes' rule, different parties will tend to reach accord in their *final* probability judgments. If one has a dogmatic prior, then *no* information can alter the assessment—that is why the prior is called dogmatic. In situations akin to coin tossing where the event is repetitive, as more and more outcomes are observed and when the different priors are not dogmatic, these priors will ultimately be revised by Bayes' rule so that they tend to come together. The probability values that they approach will be the observed relative frequencies of the relevant outcomes in the sample of observations.[18]

Further, a particular *function* might be used to generate probability assessments in lieu of giving an individual assessment for each outcome. Thus one might judge that the random variable $X$ is distributed by $f(X)$. If the probability distribution of sample information $S$ conditional upon $X$ is given by $h(S \mid X)$, Bayes' rule states that the posterior distribution of $X$, conditional upon information $S$, is given by the following: (1) $f(X \mid S) = f(X)h(S \mid X)/\sum_X h(S \mid X)f(X)$ if $X$ is discrete; or (2) $f(X \mid S) = f(X)h(S \mid X)/\int h(S \mid X)f(X)\,dX$ if $X$ is continuous.

Of particular interest is a situation such as the following. Suppose that General Soughto's management is interested in sales during the *next* accounting period, should prices not change. Management judges that these sales will act approximately as a random variable, $s$, distributed as the continuous gamma distribution with parameters $R$ and $T$. Formally

$$P(s) = T\,\frac{e^{-sT}(sT)^{R-1}}{(R-1)!} = P_\gamma(s; T, R). \tag{4.2}$$

Suppose, too, that the distribution of sales during a *current* time interval $t$, denoted by $r$, is thought to be expressible in terms of sales during the next accounting period. Specifically, the probability of $r$ conditional upon $s$ is assessed as the discrete Poisson distribution. Formally

$$P(r \mid s) = \frac{e^{-st}(st)^r}{r!}. \tag{4.3}$$

[18] See DeFinetti, "Foresight," pp. 118–152.

Substituting (4.2) and (4.3) into Bayes' rule,

$$P(s \mid r) = \frac{\left[T \dfrac{e^{-sT}(sT)^{R-1}}{(R-1)!}\right]\left[\dfrac{e^{-st}(st)^r}{r!}\right]}{\displaystyle\int_s \left[T \dfrac{e^{-sT}(sT)^{R-1}}{(R-1)!}\right]\left[\dfrac{e^{-st}(st)^r}{r!}\right] ds}. \tag{4.4}$$

But the product of the bracketed terms is

$$\frac{e^{-s(T+t)}s^{R+r-1}T^Rt^r}{(R-1)!r!} = \left[\frac{(T+t)e^{-s(T+t)}(s[T+t])^{R+r-1}}{(R+r-1)!}\right]\cdot\left[\frac{T^Rt^r(R+r-1)!}{(T+t)^{R+r}(R-1)!r!}\right]$$
$$= \left[\frac{T^Rt^r(R+r-1)!}{(T+t)^{R+r}(R-1)!r!}\right] P_\gamma(s; T+t, R+r).$$

Hence, (4.4) becomes

$$P(s \mid r) = \frac{\dfrac{T^Rt^r(R+r-1)!}{(T+t)^{R+r}(R-1)!r!} P_\gamma(s; T+t, R+r)}{\dfrac{T^Rt^r(R+r-1)!}{(T+t)^{R+r}(R-1)!r!} \displaystyle\int_s P_\gamma(s; T+t, R+r)\, ds}$$
$$= P_\gamma(s; T+t, R+r), \tag{4.5}$$

since $\int_s P_\gamma(s; T+t, R+r)\, ds = 1$, because the total area under any probability density function is unity.

Equation (4.5) shows that, in this case, the posterior probability *distribution* of $s$ and its prior probability *distribution* are of precisely the same form, a gamma distribution. The sole alteration is in the two parameters necessary to completely describe the distribution. When prior and posterior distributions are of the same form, the prior is called the *natural conjugate* of the conditional distribution. The natural conjugate relationship exists between many of the more familiar probability distributions.[19] The obvious computational advantages yielded by the natural conjugate relationship encourage us to express probability assessments in terms of natural conjugates, if such is at all feasible.

Moreover, dealing with continuous distributions need not trouble us, although ordinarily it will entail the use of integral calculus. For any *particular* value of a continuous random variable the probability is, of course, zero. Nonetheless, one can use integral calculus to determine probabilities for the variable falling *between* specified values. The midpoint of these values could then be assigned the probability weight of the entire area between the limits. The closer together are the limits, the better will be the approximation.

## c. Expected Value

Recall that the mathematical expectation of a random variable $X$ subject to the probability distribution $f(X)$ is given by $E(X) = \int Xf(X)\, dX$ if the variable is continuous, or $E(X_i) = \sum_i X_i f(X_i)$ if the variable is discrete. In the present context, suppose the event $\pi$ has discrete outcomes $E_i$ occurring with probabilities

[19] For a discussion of such relationships see Howard Raiffa and Robert Schlaifer, *Applied Statistical Decision Theory* (Cambridge, Mass.: The M.I.T. Press, 1968), pp. 43–58.

$P(E_i)$. Each $E_i$ has the numerical result or payoff $\pi_i$. Then, the mathematical expectation $E(\pi) = \sum \pi_i P(E_i)$ is called the *expected value* of the event $\pi$. In the continuous case $\int$ would replace $\Sigma$. In effect, then, an expected value is a weighted average, with the probabilities being the weights. That is, the probability weighted average of the $\pi_i$ is

$$\frac{\sum_i \pi_i P(E_i)}{\sum_i P(E_i)} = \sum_i \pi_i P(E_i),$$

since $\sum_i P(E_i) = 1$. If $\pi$ were a repetitive event having outcomes occurring in accordance with an assigned probability distribution, the expected value would be the average payoff of an extended series of trials. If the event is a game or bet with an expected value of zero, the game is called *fair*—that is, on average nothing would be won or lost.

In the Soughto example, U.S. Soughto's expected price change, as determined a priori by General Soughto, is

$$EC_1 = .05(0) + .15(-1) + .80(1) = .65 \text{ percent.}$$

The .05, .15, and .80 figures are the prior probabilities assigned to the outcomes no price change ($E_1$), price decrease ($E_2$), and price increase ($E_3$). The 0, −1, and 1 figures are the previously assumed price-change possibilities, $\pi_1$, $\pi_2$, and $\pi_3$, respectively. After the sample information contained in the interview is analyzed and the probabilities are revised, the expected change is

$$EC_2 = .048(0) + .029(-1) + .923(1) = .894 \text{ percent.}$$

Note that the expected change can be calculated even though we are referring to a unique event. Further, in the present instance the actual and the expected change *necessarily* differ. In general it might not be possible to realize the expected change on any single trial of an experiment. Expected value provides information about the distribution of potential payoffs from a set of outcomes in the same way that any average provides information about the distribution from which the average is derived; but the information often will be misleading and of little value.

In addition, the variance in the $\pi_i$ is given by

$$V(\pi) = \sum_i P(E_i)[\pi_i - E(\pi)]^2$$

with $\int$ replacing $\Sigma$ in the continuous case. The variance associated with $EC_1$ is

$$VC_1 = .05(-.65)^2 + .15(-1.65)^2 + .80(.35)^2 = .5275 \text{ percent;}$$

and the variance associated with $EC_2$ is

$$VC_2 = .048(-.894)^2 + .029(-1.894)^2 + .923(.106)^2 = .152764 \text{ percent.}$$

The variance provides information about the dispersion in the possible payoffs, after giving weight to the probability of their occurrence. Section 10.5 illustrates the use of expected value and variance in a decision-making problem set in a probabilistic context. In that situation, since it reflects the probability weighted dispersion in the payoffs, the variance is used as a surrogate to measure "risk," while the expected value is used to measure "return." In the present context, before General Soughto's president reads the *Wall Street Journal*, the expected price change is less than the postinterview evaluation; but the variance has been reduced following the reassessment, reflecting greater certainty in the anticipated result. Similarly, the inverse of the variance is called the *precision* of a probabilistic process or of a distribution of a random variable, because it helps to reflect the accuracy that one associates to one's point estimates.

In the case of the regression parameter estimates, for example, the precision is estimated by $h_i = (1/s_{a_i}^2)$. Thus, the greater is the standard error associated with a parameter, the lower is the precision, and the lesser is our confidence that the estimate is an accurate estimate of the "true" value of the parameter. If one had a completely diffuse prior distribution with respect to a parameter value—that is, if the variance in one's prior assessment is $\infty$—then the *prior precision* is 0; if, then, sample information should lead one to a dogmatic posterior distribution with respect to the parameter (if the variance in the posterior assessment is 0), then the *posterior precision* is $\infty$. Note, however, that the variance *could* get larger, and the precision get smaller, as new information is obtained. The effects of new information on the precision will depend upon how this information affects the probability assignments—in effect, upon whether this information increases or decreases one's relative "dogmatism" and degree of uncertainty.

## d. Risk, Uncertainty, and Least-Squares Estimation

The term "risk" has traditionally described situations whose outcomes could be described through known probability distributions. If the probability distribution were not known, the situation would be described as one of uncertainty.[20] If we accept the view that one can *always* assign probabilities based upon personal judgment, the distinction between risk and uncertainty becomes unnecessary. Here, therefore, the terms will be used interchangeably.

It is particularly important to stress the relationship between uncertainty and the least-squares coefficients. It is all too easy to overlook the fact that the least-squares coefficients are only point *estimates* and ordinarily not actual values known with certainty. Specifically, the industry short-run demand curve estimated in the Appendix to Chapter 3 was

$$Q_{tS} = 6.464P_t^{-.06931}I_t^{.06075}Q_{t-1,S}^{.79001}e_t^{.20999}.$$

But, as indicated in the previous chapter, under certain assumptions each of the $a_i$ is itself the mean or expected value of normally distributed possible values. The estimated variance of the distribution is $s_{a_i}^2$. Thus any decisions based on this demand curve are decisions made under risk or uncertainty, even if the parameters have been estimated to the fifth decimal place.

Recall that, in general, the equation to be estimated, (3.1a), is $\mathbf{Q} = \mathbf{V}\boldsymbol{\alpha} + \boldsymbol{\varepsilon}$. Consider a single joint observation on $\mathbf{V}$, $\mathbf{V}_p = (1, V_{1p}, V_{2p}, \ldots, V_{mp})$. This observa-

[20] The distinction, as noted in Chapter 1, goes back to Frank H. Knight, *Risk, Uncertainty and Profit* (Boston: Houghton Mifflin Company, 1921).

tion yields a forecast or estimate of $Q$, $\hat{Q}_p = \mathbf{V}_p\mathbf{a}$. The variance of the estimate is given by

$$E[(\hat{Q}_p - Q_p)(\hat{Q}_p - Q_p)'] = E[(\mathbf{V}_p\mathbf{a} - \mathbf{V}_p\boldsymbol{\alpha})(\mathbf{V}_p\mathbf{a} - \mathbf{V}_p\boldsymbol{\alpha})'] = E[\mathbf{V}_p(\mathbf{a} - \boldsymbol{\alpha})(\mathbf{a} - \boldsymbol{\alpha})'\mathbf{V}_p'] \\ = \mathbf{V}_p E[(\mathbf{a} - \boldsymbol{\alpha})(\mathbf{a} - \boldsymbol{\alpha})']\mathbf{V}_p' = \mathbf{V}_p\sigma^2(\mathbf{V}'\mathbf{V})^{-1}\mathbf{V}_p'$$

by Equation (3.13). Hence the variance of an individual estimate for a particular observation $\mathbf{V}_p$ is given by

$$\sigma^2_{\hat{Q}_p} = \mathbf{V}_p\,(\mathbf{Cov\ a})\mathbf{V}_p'. \tag{4.6}$$

Referring to the example in the Appendix to Chapter 3, consider the observation $P_t = 100$, $I_t = 400$, $Q_{t-1,S} = 8000$. Equation (3.19) is estimated with the variables in logarithms. Converting the present observation to logs, $\mathbf{V}_p$ becomes the vector $\mathbf{V}_p = (1, V_{1p}, V_{2p}, V_{3p}) = (1, 2, 2.60206, 3.90309)$. The estimate of $Q_t = \log Q_{tS}$ is

$$\hat{Q}_p = \mathbf{V}_p\mathbf{a} = (1, 2, 2.60206, 3.90309)\begin{pmatrix} .81052 \\ -.06931 \\ .06075 \\ .79001 \end{pmatrix} = 3.91346.$$

Hence $\hat{Q}_{pS} = \text{antilog}\ (3.91346) = 8193$. The variance of the estimate, $\sigma^2_{\hat{Q}_p}$, is then *estimated* from the *estimated* **Cov a** as follows:

$$s^2_{\hat{Q}_p} = (1, 2, 2.60206, 3.90309)\begin{bmatrix} .19589 & -.02794 & .01222 & -.04359 \\ -.02794 & .02050 & -.00276 & -.00179 \\ .01222 & -.00276 & .00089 & -.00226 \\ -.04359 & -.00179 & -.00226 & .01361 \end{bmatrix}\begin{pmatrix} 1 \\ 2 \\ 2.60206 \\ 3.90309 \end{pmatrix}$$

$$= .0002176.$$

Now, the actual value of $Q_p$, conditional upon $\mathbf{V}_p$, has an expectation of $Q_p^* = E(Q_p/\mathbf{V}_p)$. It can be shown that under certain commonly made assumptions, $(\hat{Q}_p - Q_p^*)/s_{\hat{Q}_p}$ is distributed as $t_{N-M-1}$.[21] Thus, even in this case when the estimated equation fits the data to the rather pleasant tune of $R^2 = .978$, for a specific observation on the independent variables the estimate of the dependent variable should be presented together with some probabilistic statement or statements reflecting the likelihood that alternative values of particular interest may obtain for the dependent variable. We are quite literally certain to be in error in our estimate; what we want to know, from the standpoint of the decision maker who is forced to act upon the basis of the estimate, is the probability of making an error of a particular magnitude.

Suppose, for example, one is concerned with the possibility that for the specific observation $\mathbf{V}_p$, $Q_{pS}^*$ will be 8300 rather than the estimated 8193. Finding $Q_p^* = \log Q_{pS}^* = 3.91908$, we calculate the associated $t$-ratio as $t = (3.91346 - 3.91908)/.01475 = -.381$. Since there are three independent variables and twenty observations, there are $20 - 3 - 1 = 16$ degrees of freedom. The probability of obtaining a $t$-ratio of this magnitude if the actual value of $Q_{pS}^*$ happens to be 8300 is approximately .3. It would appear, then, that while the hypothesis that $Q_{pS}^* = 8300$ does not seem to be an odds-on favorite, it certainly cannot be rejected out of hand.

[21] See Arthur S. Goldberger, *Econometric Theory* (New York: John Wiley & Sons, Inc., 1964), pp. 108–113, 172–173, 178–179.

This analysis suggests that any discussion of the relevant functions can and *should* take place in the context of uncertainty when we rely on econometric methods to *estimate* the functions, as well as when we rely on managerial judgment to *assess* them. Moreover, one is not necessarily betraying the subjectivist cause by evincing a willingness to assign certain probabilities on the basis of classical estimation methods. Indeed, *if* one accepts the underlying assumptions necessary to justify the inferences drawn from the $t$-ratios, *then* it would be inconsistent *not to* base probability assignments upon them. When one's prior convictions as to the parameter values in a regression are sufficiently vague that he is happy to accept the least-squares assumptions, estimates, and assorted $t$-ratios, he can do so with a clear conscience. When, however, one does have sufficient prior knowledge of parameter values to justify a *modification* of the least-squares assumptions, it is appropriate that they be so modified.

## e. Subjectivist Thought and Least Squares—A Brief Digression

The previous discussion of econometric estimation assumed that the regression coefficients will be estimated solely on the basis of the sample observations. Introducing the notion of subjective probability suggests that perhaps judgment should also play an even greater role than it does in regression analysis. Judgment and experience do, of course, help to guide model specification. Additionally, we may well want to incorporate into the analysis prior judgments—that is, prior to observing the sample—about the parameters themselves. A detailed treatment of this complex subject goes beyond our present scope, although the subject will be broached in Section 14.7. To illustrate the possibilities, however, suppose one is virtually certain that the values of the parameters $\alpha_{k+1}, \ldots, \alpha_m$ in the vector $\boldsymbol{\alpha}$ of (3.1a) are given by $\alpha^*_{k+1}, \ldots, \alpha^*_m$. Note that by the very act of specifying the model we are asserting that $\alpha_{m+j} = \alpha^*_{m+j} = 0$ $(j = 1, \ldots, \infty)$ for the infinite variety of exogenous variables that might have systematic causal linkage with the dependent variable, but which we are judging a priori to have none. Now we are broadening our perspective so that in assessing $\alpha_i$ we can use numbers other than 0, for there is indeed quite a handsome selection of alternatives.

Let us write the matrix $\mathbf{V}$ of Equation (3.1a) as $\mathbf{V} = (\mathbf{W}_1, \mathbf{W}_2)$, where $\mathbf{W}_1 = (\mathbf{i}, \mathbf{V}_1, \ldots, \mathbf{V}_k)$ and $\mathbf{W}_2 = (\mathbf{V}_{k+1}, \ldots, \mathbf{V}_m)$. Thus $\mathbf{W}_1$ is a matrix containing the sample values of those variables whose associated parameters are to be determined exclusively on the basis of the sample data. $\mathbf{W}_2$ is a matrix containing the sample values of those variables whose associated parameters are thought to be known. In similar fashion the vector $\boldsymbol{\alpha}'$ will be written as $\boldsymbol{\alpha}' = (\boldsymbol{\gamma}_1', \boldsymbol{\gamma}_2')$, where $\boldsymbol{\gamma}_1' = (\alpha_0, \ldots, \alpha_k)$ and $\boldsymbol{\gamma}_2' = (\alpha_{k+1}, \ldots, \alpha_m)$. Equation (3.1a) may now be rewritten as

$$\mathbf{Q} = \mathbf{W}_1\boldsymbol{\gamma}_1 + \mathbf{W}_2\boldsymbol{\gamma}_2 + \boldsymbol{\varepsilon}. \tag{4.7}$$

The vector $\boldsymbol{\gamma}_2$ is assumed to be known. Retaining as the estimation criterion the minimization of the sum of squared residuals, we therefore seek an estimate of $\boldsymbol{\gamma}_1$, denoted by $\mathbf{a}_c = (a_0, \ldots, a_k)$, such as to

$$\begin{aligned}
\text{Minimize}\quad \mathbf{e}'\mathbf{e} &= (\mathbf{Q} - \mathbf{W}_1\mathbf{a}_c - \mathbf{W}_2\boldsymbol{\gamma}_2)'(\mathbf{Q} - \mathbf{W}_1\mathbf{a}_c - \mathbf{W}_2\boldsymbol{\gamma}_2) \\
&= \mathbf{Q}'\mathbf{Q} - 2\mathbf{a}_c'\mathbf{W}_1'\mathbf{Q} - 2\boldsymbol{\gamma}_2'\mathbf{W}_2'\mathbf{Q} + (\mathbf{W}_1\mathbf{a}_c)'\mathbf{W}_1\mathbf{a}_c + 2(\mathbf{W}_1\mathbf{a}_c)'\mathbf{W}_2\boldsymbol{\gamma}_2 \\
&\qquad + (\mathbf{W}_2\boldsymbol{\gamma}_2)'(\mathbf{W}_2\boldsymbol{\gamma}_2) \\
&= \mathbf{Q}'\mathbf{Q} - 2\mathbf{a}_c'\mathbf{W}_1'\mathbf{Q} - 2\boldsymbol{\gamma}_2'\mathbf{W}_2'\boldsymbol{\gamma}_2 + 2\mathbf{a}_c'\mathbf{W}_1'\mathbf{W}_2\boldsymbol{\gamma}_2 + \mathbf{a}_c'\mathbf{W}_1'\mathbf{W}_1\mathbf{a}_c \\
&\qquad + \boldsymbol{\gamma}_2'\mathbf{W}_2'\mathbf{W}_2\boldsymbol{\gamma}_2.
\end{aligned}$$

To minimize this expression, we seek an estimate of $\gamma_1$ such that

$$\frac{\partial(\mathbf{e}'\mathbf{e})}{\partial \mathbf{a}_c} = -2\mathbf{W}_1'\mathbf{Q} + 2\mathbf{W}_1'\mathbf{W}_2\gamma_2 + 2\mathbf{W}_1'\mathbf{W}_1\mathbf{a}_c = \mathbf{0}.$$

Premultiplying by $(\mathbf{W}_1'\mathbf{W}_1)^{-1}$, canceling the 2's in each term, and rearranging terms, we derive

$$\mathbf{a}_c = (\mathbf{W}_1'\mathbf{W}_1)^{-1}\mathbf{W}_1'\mathbf{Q} - (\mathbf{W}_1'\mathbf{W}_1)^{-1}\mathbf{W}_1'\mathbf{W}_2\gamma_2 \tag{4.8}$$

as the constrained minimum variance estimator of $\gamma_1$ (since, as before, we also have $\partial^2(\mathbf{e}'\mathbf{e})/\partial\mathbf{a}_c^2 = 2\mathbf{W}_1'\mathbf{W}_1$, a positive definite matrix).

For example, consider again the problem in the Appendix to Chapter 3. Suppose that the years have been both kind and informative, and experience leads one to be quite certain that the short-run demand curve is unit elastic with respect to price. One might therefore set $\alpha_1^* = \gamma_2 = -1$. $\mathbf{W}_1 = [\mathbf{i}, \mathbf{V}_2, \mathbf{V}_3]$ and $\mathbf{W}_2 = \mathbf{V}_1$. Hence, we extract from the earlier results

$$\mathbf{W}_1'\mathbf{Q} = \begin{bmatrix} 77.61274 \\ 189.78282 \\ 300.87413 \end{bmatrix}, \qquad \mathbf{W}_1'\mathbf{W}_2 = \begin{bmatrix} 40.62566 \\ 99.35729 \\ 157.49253 \end{bmatrix},$$

$$(\mathbf{W}_1'\mathbf{W}_1)^{-1} = \begin{bmatrix} 20 & 48.88644 & 77.52842 \\ 48.88644 & 119.85888 & 189.57230 \\ 77.52842 & 189.57230 & 300.54673 \end{bmatrix}^{-1}$$

$$= \begin{bmatrix} 9016.72048 & 482.91678 & -2630.53848 \\ 482.91678 & 29.37764 & -143.10241 \\ -2630.53848 & -143.10241 & 768.83467 \end{bmatrix}.$$

Therefore,

$$\mathbf{a}_c = \begin{bmatrix} 9016.72048 & 482.91678 & -2630.53848 \\ 482.91678 & 29.37764 & -143.10241 \\ -2630.53848 & -143.10241 & 768.83467 \end{bmatrix} \begin{bmatrix} 77.61274 \\ 189.78282 \\ 300.87413 \end{bmatrix}$$

$$+ \begin{bmatrix} 9016.72048 & 482.91678 & -2630.53848 \\ 482.91678 & 29.37764 & -143.10241 \\ -2630.53848 & -143.10241 & 768.83467 \end{bmatrix} \begin{bmatrix} 40.62566 \\ 99.35729 \\ 157.49253 \end{bmatrix}$$

$$= (2.07661, .18775, .87377)'.$$

The short-run demand curve is reestimated as

$$Q_{tS} = 11.929 P_t^{-1.00000} I_t^{.18775} Q_{t-1,S}^{.87377} e_t^{.12623}.$$

The associated $R^2$ is now .821. The reduction in $R^2$ from the former .978 occurs because a restriction has been imposed on the estimates, and the unrestricted regression maximizes $R^2$. Here, however, we are concerned with determining the most appropriate equation as opposed to the equation yielding the greatest $R^2$. The discrepancy between the two philosophies may arise because the $R^2$ is based on a specific *sample*, whereas the preferred estimates may consider extraneous information not included in the sample. Indeed, if the judgment about price elasticity is valid, the new equation will tend to be a better predictor for the *population* in the future than the former equation, even though it is an inferior fit to the *sample*. Prediction error, with respect to the sample, is taking a backseat to model error.

When restrictions are in the form of inequalities, the problem can take on greater complexity. We touch on this issue in Section 9.8.

## f. Demand Under Uncertainty

The clear implication of the foregoing is that management in the real world will rarely have certain knowledge of the firm's demand curve. It will not be able to assert that, with probability of 1, $Q = D(V_1, \ldots, V_m)$. It will, however, ordinarily be able to assign a probability to the outcome "a quantity $Q$ will be sold," conditional upon the factors $V_1, \ldots, V_m$. This assignment may be a subjective assessment, it may be derived from some statistical technique such as regression analysis, or it may result from a combination of these. Nonetheless, the point is that such an assignment can be made.

Suppose, then, that a decision maker judges that the quantity $Q$ demanded of the firm during $t$ will depend upon the price $P$ the firm charges, the prices $P_i$ charged for comparable products by other firms ($i = 1, \ldots, k$), and "other factors" $V$. Suppose, too, that our decision maker assigns a probability $f(P; Q \mid P_1, \ldots, P_k; V)$ to the demand relationship between price and quantity, given the levels of other prices and variables. In much of the discussion the firm will be considered to set a price, with the quantity demanded being a function of that price. The preceding probability would in this case more appropriately be written as $f(Q \mid P, P_1, \ldots, P_k; V)$. For greater generality, and to avoid the need to specify an independent variable, we shall adhere throughout to the former notation.

The decision maker can also assign (1) probabilities $p(P_i)$ to express his feelings about the likelihood that the $i$th firm will charge a price of $P_i$ during $t$, as well as (2) a probability $p(V)$ that the "other factors" will be at level $V$ during $t$. We can therefore write

$$p(P_1, \ldots, P_k; V) = \prod_{i=1}^{k} p(P_i)p(V)$$

to represent the probability that the vector of other prices and factors will be the vector $(P_1, \ldots, P_k; V)$. Although the specific expression assumes that the $P_i$ and $V$ are statistically independent, and are independent of both $P$ and $Q$, the assumption is unnecessary and readily relaxed through a minor notational change.

The question of time is handled in the following manner. The level of $Q$ is that quantity which will be sold during the time period $t$ beginning immediately following the firm's *conscious decision* to charge a price of $P$ and the implementation of this price, and ending when the firm makes another *conscious* price decision. This second decision may, of course, be the decision to leave price unaltered. A time period is thus defined by the length of time between consideration of pricing decisions. For convenience, the latter are assumed to be immediately implemented. The vector $(P_1, \ldots, P_k; V)$ need not be assumed fixed during $t$, though for the moment it is notationally convenient to assume it so. Again, the simplification does not alter the succeeding analysis.

The probability that the firm can sell a quantity $Q$ at a price of $P$, or that buyers are willing to pay a price of $P$ for a quantity $Q$ is therefore given by

$$f(P; Q) = \int_{P_1} \cdots \int_{P_k} \int_V f(P; Q \mid P_1, \ldots, P_k; V) p(P_1, \ldots, P_k; V)\, dP_1 \cdots dP_k\, dV, \tag{4.9}$$

with a $\Sigma$ replacing the $\int$ when the probability distributions are discrete. The *expected quantity* that will be demanded at a price of $P = P^*$ is given by

$$Q^* = \int_Q Qf(P^*; Q)\, dQ = \int_Q Qf\, dQ. \tag{4.10}$$

Indeed, the demand curve that was previously written as $Q = D(P)$ could now be written as $Q^* = D(P^*)$, the average or expected demand curve, given the decision maker's judgments. The elasticity of demand, explicitly recognizing the probabilistic features, becomes an expectation

$$\eta = \left(\frac{dQ^*}{dP^*}\right)\left(\frac{P^*}{Q^*}\right) = \frac{d\left[\int_Q Qf\, dQ\right]}{dP^*} \frac{P^*}{\int_Q Qf\, dQ}. \tag{4.11}$$

## 4.5 DEMAND UNDER UNCERTAINTY AND THE CLASSICAL APPROACH

We have rather scrupulously avoided mentioning that the firm's various decision makers may hold discordant views of the probabilities that should be assigned. Somehow all these views are going to have to be reconciled, by fiat if necessary. This reconciliation may be no small problem. But it is not a problem of economics and need not concern us here, though from a practical standpoint we must remain conscious of it. The point is that some probability judgments will be reached and subsequently accepted by management as a guide to understanding its demand curve.

What should concern us here, however, is whether the various machinations with probabilities are worth the bother. Might it not make sense to simply start the analysis of the firm's price-quantity determination with the demand curve $Q^* = D(P^*)$ as opposed to, say, the estimated curve $Q = D(P) + e$ and the probabilistic information that goes along with it?

Classical economists have not ignored uncertainty in describing demand. The firm's demand curve has been described at various levels of sophistication as being a best guess, something learned by hunt and peck, or some average such as the mode or an expected value.[22] It is then suggested that the firm behaves *as if* this best guess or expected value *is* the actual demand curve. Such a suggestion suffers from several defects absent in the present approach.

First, as we shall see, the strongest impact of uncertainty on decision making is not necessarily that it imposes the need to assign probabilities and to think in probabilistic terms. Rather, it is that decision making under uncertainty forces the

[22] For example, Oskar Lange, "A Note on Innovations" in the American Economic Association's *Readings in Income Distribution* (New York: McGraw-Hill, Inc., Blakiston Division, 1946), p. 181; William Fellner, "Average-Cost Pricing and the Theory of Uncertainty," *Journal of Political Economy*, **LVI**:3 (June 1948), 250; F. E. Balderston, "Scale of Output of Internal Organization of the Firm," *Quarterly Journal of Economics*, **LXIX**:1 (Feb. 1955), pp. 51–52; and R. M. Cyert, W. R. Hill, and J. G. March, "The Role of Expectations in Business Decision Making," *Administrative Science Quarterly*, **3**:3 (Dec. 1958), 309.

decision maker to incorporate into his decision-making calculus his attitude towards risk. In particular, the firm that views sales of 1,000,000 or 500,000 units as being equally likely when price is set at \$10, will not necessarily behave in the same way as the firm that is certain of selling the mathematical expectation of $(\frac{1}{2})(1{,}000{,}000) + (\frac{1}{2})(500{,}000) = 750{,}000$ units at a price of \$10. This is akin to the fact that not every man is willing to make a fair bet, one with an expected return of zero, whereas some men are willing to bet in Las Vegas with a one-armed bandit offering them a negative expected return.

Second, the present approach is actually simpler and more general in that it encompasses *all* market structure situations. It *explicitly* details and quantifies conjectures about the policies to be followed by other firms. Thus, an analysis of decision making based upon the present approach need not be compartmentalized into discussions of monopoly vs. pure competition, monopolistic vs. imperfect competition, or oligopoly vs. monopoly. We need merely talk about a firm reaching a particular set of probability judgments. These *judgments* will, of course, be influenced by consideration of market structure. The *effects* of the judgments will be influenced by market structure. But the decision-making calculus and subsequent behavior need not be so influenced.

Third, as will be seen, the explicit treatment of uncertainty makes it clear that different decision makers, acting on the basis of precisely the same information and reaching precisely the same probability judgments, can rationally prefer different decisions. Except by defining the problem away within the basic functions, this is not possible under the neoclassical approach. Yet, as anyone who has ever attended a faculty meeting knows, the world is marked by the penchant of intelligent men for not accepting the choices made by other intelligent men.

Finally, the present analysis will be seen to provide a decision-making procedure that management shows every tendency to be as unaware of as it is of the classical framework. It will, however, present an *operational* framework that, given acceptance of the very reasonable underlying premises, will provide management with a means of reaching optimal decisions—that is, decisions that are more in accordance with management's attitudes, preferences, and judgments than would otherwise be the case.

## EXERCISES

1. "The firm of pure competition perceives its demand curve as a horizontal line intersecting the vertical (price) axis at the price determined in the market. This firm has no particular interest in what the industry demand curve looks like." Discuss.

2. The pure competitor can sell as much as he desires at the market price. In order to increase his sales, however, the monopolist must lower price. Shouldn't we consumers try to get pure competitors to merge into monopolists so that we can get these lower prices? Explain your answer.

3. Suppose a monopolist has a demand curve given by $Q = D(P)$. The monopoly is "broken up" by the courts into two firms. Each firm is now a duopolist. What will their demand curves look like and why? Suppose one of the two duopolists "breaks up" into two firms. We now have triopolists. What effects if any will this last split have on the "other" firm's demand curve? Why?

4. It is frequently suggested that in an industry in which the firms feature "kinked" demand curves for a homogeneous good, all kinks occurring at the price obtaining in the market, price will tend to be stable at the kink. Firms will eschew price cuts or price increases. Do you agree? Why?

5. What difficulties would you foresee in estimating a firm's demand curve using least squares?

6. (a) What do you judge the probability to be that you are a subjectivist?
   (b) What do you judge this probability to be in view of the information contained in your answer to the first part of this question?

7. Suppose you observe three dice and see only the six on each. One die is a fair die, another has all sixes, and the third has two each of the two, the four, and the six.
   (a) What is the probability the middle die is the fair die?
   (b) You role the middle die twice and observe a six on each roll (you can't see the die when it is being rolled). What is the probability the middle die is the fair die?
   (c) Before rolling the die you are offered the following bet. If a six comes up on a prearranged roll, you get $2; if any other even number comes up, you neither win nor lose; if an odd number comes up, you lose $3. Would you accept the bet? Why?
   (d) How have the two observations affected your decision on the bet? How do they affect the expected value and variance of the bet?
   (e) Would it be worth anything to you to see one more roll before deciding on the bet?

8. A beta distribution of the random variable $p$ with parameters $\alpha$ and $\beta$ is given by

$$P(p;\, \alpha,\, \beta) = \frac{(\beta - 1)!}{(\alpha - 1)!(\beta - \alpha - 1)!}\, p^{\alpha-1}(1 - p)^{\beta-\alpha-1}.$$

In a Bernoulli process, the number of successes, $s$, in $n$ trials is given by the conditional binomial distribution

$$P(s \mid p) = C_s^n p^s (1 - p)^{n-s}.$$

Show that the beta distribution bears a natural conjugate relationship to the binomial.

9. The Edley Corporation judges its management trainees' suitability for promotion on the basis of the number of correct decisions they reach. The firm believes that candidates for promotion should have a probability $p_1$ of reaching a decision judged to have been correct. These are the superior decision makers. Other decision makers have a probability $p_2 < p_1$ of reaching a correct decision. For simplicity, Edley assumes that all decision makers fall into these two classes and that $r$ percent of its trainees are superior.
   (a) If the only people promoted are those who never err, what is the probability of promoting a man who is not superior, based on three decisions?
   (b) What is the probability of failing to promote a superior man if six decisions are analyzed?
   (c) What will happen to the ratio of superior to nonsuperior men if five decisions are analyzed and the criterion for promotion is lowered from no incorrect decisions to no more than a single incorrect decision?
   (d) What difficulties would you expect to encounter in using this method of promotion in a modern firm.

10. In the problem of Section 4.4e, suppose we were to estimate $\alpha_1$ by least squares using $(Q_{tS} - P_t)$ as the dependent variable, and $I_t$ and $Q_{t-1,S}$ as the independent variables.
   (a) Derive an estimator for $\alpha_1$.
   (b) Using this estimator calculate $\mathbf{a}_c$.
   (c) What do you conclude from this fascinating experiment?

11. "I am absolutely certain that the demand for beer is not price elastic—and I drink enough of it to know." Using the data in Chapter 3, make use of this information to reestimate the demand for beer using least squares.

12. What do you judge the probability to be that personal disposable income has increased by less than 3 percent per year over the past two decades? less than 4 percent? more than 5 percent? Compare your assessments with the least-squares estimates derived after fitting the regression $I_t = G(g)^t$ to the data in Table 3.2.

# 5

# THE NEOCLASSICAL THEORY OF PRODUCT SUPPLY: The Theory of Production

## 5.1 INTRODUCTION

Economists tend to be incurable romantics. This romanticism reaches its peak when they discover an unrequited demand curve anxiously seeking a compatible supply curve for a mate. This chapter takes the first steps toward satisfying both the economists and the demand curves.

The industry supply curve in the price-quantity space shows the quantities that all firms in the industry are willing to supply at various prices, given the fixed set of circumstances obtaining for those variables, besides price, that will affect the firms' output decisions. Prominent among these are production technology and the supply conditions for the factors of production whose inputs will be converted into the firms' outputs. Just as the industry demand curve is the horizontal sum of the individual consumers' demand curves, so too the industry supply curve will be derived as the horizontal sum of the individual firms' supply curves. Moreover, just as the consumer's demand curves were obtained from an indifference space and a budget constraint, derivation of the firm's supply curve, as well as the curves describing the firm's demand for its factors of production, will require the analysis of a production space, summarizing a set of factor input-product output relationships, and a factor cost constraint.

The initial discussion is confined to the neoclassical derivation of the firm's cost and product curves; the derivation of the firm's demand curves for its factors of production is discussed in the next chapter. The neoclassical approach will ultimately provide the foundation for a more modern and managerial approach to these issues.

## 5.2 THE NEOCLASSICAL FIRM'S PRODUCTION PROBLEM

Consider a single-product firm. The firm's technical possibilities for converting factor inputs $F_i$ into a final product $Q$ are summarized in its *production function.* For a given technology and $i = 1, \ldots, m$ factors of production or inputs, the production function may be written

$$Q = q(F_1, \ldots, F_i, \ldots, F_m). \tag{5.1}$$

We shall initially assume that the factors and product are infinitely divisible and that the function $q$ is continuous and twice differentiable. There are, therefore, a myriad of alternative combinations of factors that will yield the same total output. The $Q$ of Equation (5.1) is the maximum output produced during a time period of length $T$ by the specific combination of factors employed during this time interval. All input combinations yielding $Q$ are said to lie on a particular production *isoquant*. The set of all isoquants makes up the production space.

Figure 5.1(a) illustrates several isoquants in the $F_1$-$F_2$ space. In appearance, these are depressingly similar to the indifference curves of Chapter 2. Whereas, however, the indifference curves were assumed to be strictly ordinal in nature, the isoquants are delightfully cardinal. Once a unit of measurement is selected, the difference between $Q_1 = 1000$ units of output and $Q_2 = 2000$ units of output is eminently clear—1000 units of output.

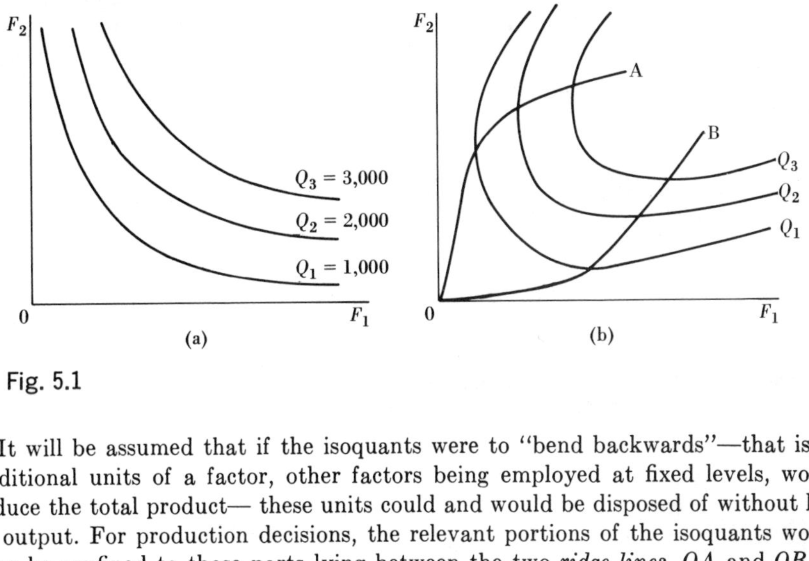


Fig. 5.1

It will be assumed that if the isoquants were to "bend backwards"—that is, if additional units of a factor, other factors being employed at fixed levels, would reduce the total product— these units could and would be disposed of without loss of output. For production decisions, the relevant portions of the isoquants would thus be confined to those parts lying between the two *ridge lines*, $OA$ and $OB$, of Figure 5.1(b). The ridge lines set off the maximum amount of factor 1 that would be used with a given amount of factor 2, and vice versa, at given levels of the other factors.

The cost per unit of factor $i$, which we shall call its wage, is given by $W_i$. It is assumed that unit factor costs or wages are a function of the number of units employed. We let $W_i = w_i(F_i)$ represent the supply curve for factor $i$ to the firm, since its inverse describes the number of units of factor $i$ that the firm can purchase at a wage of $W_i$. Any and all combinations of factors that could be employed for a cost of $C$ fall on a given *isocost* curve defined by

$$C = W_1F_1 + W_2F_2 + \cdots + W_iF_i + \cdots + W_mF_m = \sum_i W_iF_i. \qquad (5.2)$$

Although it is tempting to think of the isocost curve in the $F_1$-$F_2$ space as *looking* like the consumer's budget line, this need not be the case. For the consumer as a small buyer, the prices or $P_i$ were fixed; for the firm, however, the wages or $W_i$ may vary with the $F_i$. Thus, in the case of two factors, $i = 1, 2$, with $W_2 =$ a constant $= \bar{W}_2$, an isocost curve $C = W_1F_1 + \bar{W}_2F_2$ may look like either one of three curves $C_1$, $C_2$, or $C_3$ of Figure 5.2 according as $W_1$ is decreasing, constant, or increasing as $F_1$ increases.

The firm that is managed by economic man has as its production problem the determination of the combination of inputs to be employed for a cost of $C = C_0$ in order to maximize total output $Q$, given the factor supply and technology conditions. Formally, the problem is

$$\text{Maximize} \quad Q = q(F_1, \ldots, F_i, \ldots, F_m) \tag{5.3a}$$

$$\text{subject to} \quad C_0 = \sum_i W_iF_i. \tag{5.4a}$$

Alternatively, this could be stated as a cost-minimization problem in which the firm seeks the least-cost combination of factors with which an output of $Q = Q_0$ can be produced; or

$$\text{Minimize} \quad C = \sum_i W_iF_i \tag{5.3b}$$

$$\text{subject to} \quad Q_0 = q(F_1, \cdots, F_i, \cdots, F_m). \tag{5.4b}$$

It is easy to show that these formulations lead to equivalent solutions. We shall deal only with the formulation of (5.3a) and (5.4a). This problem is easily seen to be

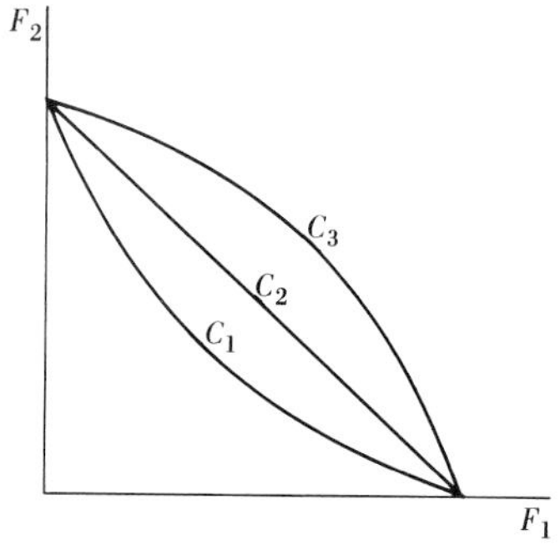


Fig. 5.2

completely analogous in mathematical form to the consumer's probem of (2.1) and (2.2). Here, the production function $q$ plays the same role as the utility function $u$ did in the theory of consumer behavior. The isoquant is analogous to the indifference surface and the cost constraint is analogous to the budget constraint. Now, however, it is not assumed that the $W_i$, like the $P_i$, are constant. Therefore the cost constraint will not necessarily be linear.

### a. First-Order Conditions

As in the theory of consumer behavior, the problem of (5.3a) and (5.4a) can be handled using Lagrangian methods. In particular, with $\lambda$ the Lagrangian multiplier, we may reformulate the firm's production problem as

$$\text{Maximize} \quad L(F_1, \ldots, F_m, \lambda) = q(F_1, \ldots, F_m) - \lambda\left[\sum_{i=1}^{m} W_iF_i - C_0\right] \tag{5.5}$$

by the appropriate choice of $F_i$ $(i = 1, \ldots, m)$ and $\lambda$. The first-order conditions for a maximum are

$$\frac{\partial L}{\partial F_i} = \frac{\partial q}{\partial F_i} - \lambda\left[W_i + \frac{\partial w_i}{\partial F_i}F_i\right] = 0, \qquad i = 1, \ldots, m, \tag{5.6a}$$

$$\frac{\partial L}{\partial \lambda} = \sum_{i=1}^{m} W_iF_i - C_0 = 0, \tag{5.6b}$$

since $\partial[W_iF_i]/\partial F_i = \partial[w_i(F_i)F_i]/\partial F_i = [w_i(F_i) + (\partial w_i/\partial F_i)F_i] = [W_i + (\partial w_i/\partial F_i)F_i]$.

Condition (5.6b) demands that the cost constraint be respected. Condition (5.6a) determines the necessary conditions for a maximum as

$$\lambda = \frac{\dfrac{\partial q}{\partial F_i}}{W_i + \left(\dfrac{\partial w_i}{\partial F_i}\right)F_i}, \qquad i = 1, \ldots, m. \tag{5.7}$$

$\partial q/\partial F_i$ is the slope of the production surface in the quantity-factor $i$ space at given levels of the other factors; it indicates the change in total product resulting from an infinitesimal change in the level of factor $i$, all other factors remaining constant. This is called the *marginal physical product* of factor $i$, or $MPP_i$. Since it is assumed that additional units of a factor are employed only within the ridge lines where they necessarily result in increased total product, $MPP_i > 0$. In general, suppose we hold $m - 1$ of the factors of production fixed at $\bar{F}_j$ $(j \neq i)$ and permit only the $i$th factor to vary. The levels of $Q$ for *all* values of $F_i$ can be computed from the production function with $Q = q(\bar{F}_1, \ldots, F_i, \ldots, \bar{F}_m)$. The latter is the *total product* for the $i$th factor, given the $\bar{F}_j$, or $TP_i$. The average product per unit of factor $i$, called the *average physical product* of factor $i$ or $APP_i$, is defined as $Q/F_i$. The $i$th factor's marginal physical product, or $MPP_i$, is given by $\partial Q/\partial F_i = \partial q/\partial F_i = q_i$. Clearly, each factor could have associated with it a myriad of product curves, since these depend upon the levels at which the other factors are fixed. A particular set of such curves—particular with respect to the levels at which the $F_j$ $(j \neq i)$ have been fixed—is illustrated in Figure 5.3(a). In general, changing the level of any $F_j$ $(j \neq i)$ will yield a new set of product curves.

Similarly, $W_iF_i$ gives the *total cost of factor* $i$, and this may be illustrated as in Figure 5.3(b). The *average factor cost* per unit of factor $i$ employed is given by $W_iF_i/F_i = W_i$, or simply the factor's wage. The change in total cost resulting from an infinitesimal change in factor $i$, or $\partial C/\partial F_i$, is equal to $\partial(W_iF_i)/\partial F_i$. This is called the *marginal cost of factor* $i$, or $MC_i$. It will be assumed that $MC_i > 0$. That is, the total costs of employing a factor increase as more of the factor is employed. $MC_i$ is thus given by $\partial C/\partial F_i = [W_i + (\partial w_i/\partial F_i)F_i]$. The first-order conditions (5.7) may therefore be rewritten as

$$\lambda = \frac{MPP_j}{MC_j} = \frac{MPP_k}{MC_k}, \qquad j, k = 1, \ldots, m. \tag{5.8}$$

That is, if the stationary point is indeed the sought-after maximum, then at this point the ratio of marginal physical product to marginal factor cost is equal for all factors and equal to $\lambda$. Also, $\lambda > 0$, since $MPP_i, MC_i > 0$.

Note that if a factor supply curve, say that for factor $k$, is horizontal, the firm can purchase as much of factor $k$ as it desires at a wage of $\bar{W}_k$. Then, $\partial w_k/\partial F_k = 0$ and $MC_k = \bar{W}_k$. This will be the case under pure competition in the factor market where there are innumerable sellers and where the firm is an insignificant one of many employers of the factor. In this situation, to all intents and purposes the firm

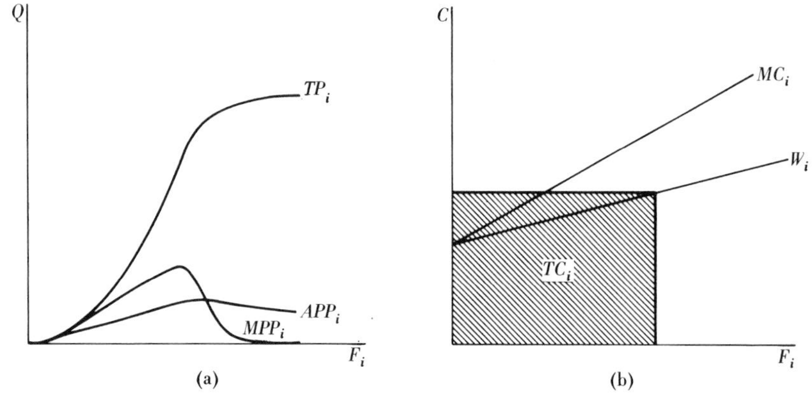


Fig. 5.3

*can* purchase as much of the factor as it desires without having a perceptible influence on the wage. If this holds for *all* factors, condition (5.8) becomes

$$\lambda = \frac{MPP_j}{\bar{W}_j} = \frac{MPP_k}{\bar{W}_k}, \qquad j, k = 1, \ldots, m, \tag{5.8a}$$

which may be rewritten as

$$\frac{MPP_j}{MPP_k} = \frac{\bar{W}_j}{\bar{W}_k}, \qquad j, k = 1, \ldots, m. \tag{5.8b}$$

In a purely competitive economy, then, the first-order condition for production is that the ratio of marginal physical products of any two factors is equal to the ratio of their prices or wages.

Moreover, note that $dC = \sum_i (\partial C/\partial F_i)\, dF_i$. Holding total cost fixed at $C = C_0$ and permitting factors $j$ and $k$ to vary, we determine that

$$dC = \left(\frac{\partial C}{\partial F_j}\right) dF_j + \left(\frac{\partial C}{\partial F_k}\right) dF_k = 0;$$

or

$$-\left(\frac{dF_j}{dF_k}\right)_{C=C_0} = \frac{\partial C/\partial F_k}{\partial C/\partial F_j} = \frac{MC_k}{MC_j}. \tag{5.9a}$$

That is, the negative of the slope of the isocost constraint in the $F_j$-$F_k$ space is equal to the ratio of the marginal factor costs. Similarly, $dQ = \sum_i (\partial q/\partial F_i)\, dF_i$. Thus, on any given isoquant in the $F_j$-$F_k$ space with $Q = Q_0$, when we permit factors $j$ and $k$ to vary we find that

$$dQ = \left(\frac{\partial q}{\partial F_j}\right) dF_j + \left(\frac{\partial q}{\partial F_k}\right) dF_k = 0;$$

or

$$-\left(\frac{dF_j}{dF_k}\right)_{Q=Q_0} = \frac{\partial q/\partial F_k}{\partial q/\partial F_j} = \frac{MPP_k}{MPP_j}. \tag{5.9b}$$

That is, the negative of the slope of the isoquant is equal to the ratio of the factors' marginal physical products. Since $-(dF_j/dF_k)_{Q=Q_0}$ shows the change in factor $j$ that is required when factor $k$ changes in order to leave total product unaltered, it is called the *rate of substitution* of factor $k$ for factor $j$.

Combining (5.9a), (5.9b), and (5.8), and rearranging terms, we find the necessary conditions to be

$$-\left(\frac{dF_j}{dF_k}\right)_{C=C_0} = \frac{MC_k}{MC_j} = \frac{MPP_k}{MPP_j} = -\left(\frac{dF_j}{dF_k}\right)_{Q=Q_0}, \qquad j, k = 1, \ldots, m. \tag{5.9c}$$

The equalities of (5.9c) describe the first-order conditions for a production maximum as requiring the equality of the slopes of the isoquants and the slopes of the isocost curves with respect to any two factors. Then, the isocost curve in the $F_j$-$F_k$ space (for all $j$, $k$) is tangent to the isoquant in that space, and the rates of factor substitution are equal to the ratios of marginal factor costs for all pairs of factors. This is illustrated in Figure 5.4.

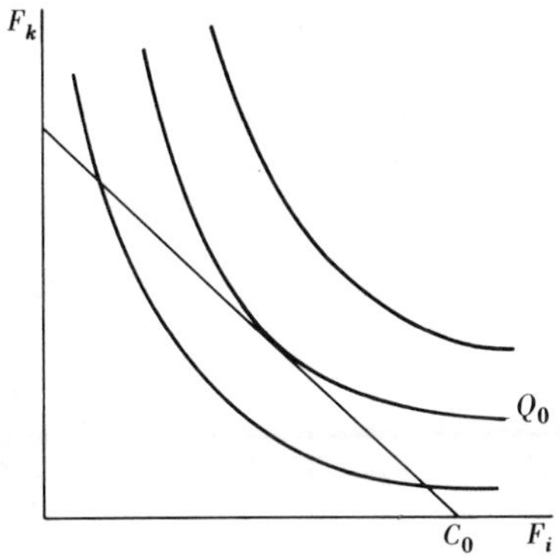


Fig. 5.4

### b. Second-Order Conditions

To determine whether the stationary point is in fact a maximum, we test the sufficiency conditions of Section 2.3. These require that we determine the matrix

$$\mathbf{M} = \begin{bmatrix} 0 & C_1 & C_2 & \cdots & C_m \\ C_1 & q_{11} - \lambda C_{11} & q_{12} - \lambda C_{12} & \cdots & q_{1m} - \lambda C_{1m} \\ C_2 & q_{21} - \lambda C_{21} & q_{22} - \lambda C_{22} & \cdots & q_{2m} - \lambda C_{2m} \\ \cdot & & & & \\ \cdot & & & & \\ \cdot & & & & \\ C_m & q_{m1} - \lambda C_{m1} & q_{m2} - \lambda C_{m2} & \cdots & q_{mm} - \lambda C_{mm} \end{bmatrix},$$

where $C_i = \partial\left[\sum_i W_i F_i - C_0\right] / \partial F_i = MC_i$, $C_{ij} = \partial^2\left[\sum_i W_i F_i - C_0\right] / \partial F_i \, \partial F_j = \partial MC_i/\partial F_j = MC'_i$ for $i = j$ and 0 otherwise (since the supply curve of any factor is assumed independent of other factors), and $q_{ij} = \partial^2 q/\partial F_i \, \partial F_j = MPP_{ij}$. Thus, $\mathbf{M}$ may be written

$$\mathbf{M} = \begin{bmatrix} 0 & MC_1 & MC_2 & \cdots & MC_m \\ MC_1 & MPP_{11} - \lambda MC'_1 & MPP_{12} & \cdots & MPP_{1m} \\ MC_2 & MPP_{21} & MPP_{22} - \lambda MC'_2 & \cdots & MPP_{2m} \\ \cdot & & & & \\ \cdot & & & & \\ \cdot & & & & \\ MC_m & MPP_{m1} & MPP_{m2} & \cdots & MPP_{mm} - \lambda MC'_m \end{bmatrix}.$$

For a maximum at the stationary point, we require $M_3 > 0$, $M_4 < 0$, $\ldots$, where $M_r$ is the $r$th order determinant along the principal diagonal.

In particular, it is readily determined that with

$$M_3 = \begin{vmatrix} 0 & MC_1 & MC_2 \\ MC_1 & MPP_{11} - \lambda MC'_1 & MPP_{12} \\ MC_2 & MPP_{21} & MPP_{22} - \lambda MC'_2 \end{vmatrix},$$

$$M_3 = -[C_1^2 q_{22} - 2C_1 C_2 q_{12} + C_2^2 q_{11}] + \lambda[C_1^2 C_{22} + C_2^2 C_{11}]. \tag{5.10}$$

As in Section 2.4(b), to establish whether $M_3 > 0$, we must establish the negativity or positivity of the bracketed terms (with $\lambda > 0$). This will depend upon the convexity of the isoquant and isocost curve in the $F_1$-$F_2$ space.

With respect to the isoquant, in general, with $-(dF_j/dF_k)_{Q=Q_0} = (\partial q/\partial F_k)/(\partial q/\partial F_j)$, we determine that

$$\left(\frac{d^2F_j}{dF_k^2}\right)_{Q=Q_0} = \frac{[-q_{kk}q_j^2 + 2q_{kj}q_j q_k - q_{jj}q_k^2]}{q_j^3} \tag{5.11}$$

with $q_i = \partial q/\partial F_i$. Equation (5.11) is derived in precisely the same fashion as (2.10) and its derivation is therefore not spelled out. Letting $k = 1$ and $j = 2$,

$$\left(\frac{d^2F_2}{dF_1^2}\right)_{Q=Q_0} = -\frac{[q_{11}q_2^2 - 2q_{12}q_2 q_1 + q_{22}q_1^2]}{q_2^3}.$$

But, from (5.9c), $MPP_1 = (MC_1/MC_2)MPP_2$ or $q_1 = (C_1/C_2)q_2$. Therefore, by substitution into the previous equation,

$$\left(\frac{d^2F_2}{dF_1^2}\right)_{Q=Q_0} = -\frac{\left[q_{11}q_2^2 - 2q_{12}\left(\frac{C_1}{C_2}\right)q_2^2 + q_{22}\left(\frac{C_1^2}{C_2^2}\right)q_2^2\right]}{q_2^3}$$

$$= -\frac{[C_2^2q_{11} - 2C_1C_2q_{12} + C_1^2q_{22}]}{C_2^2q_2}. \tag{5.11a}$$

Recall, moreover, that $-(dF_j/dF_k)_{C=C_0} = (\partial C/\partial F_k)/(\partial C/\partial F_j) = C_k/C_j$. Hence,

$$\left(\frac{d^2F_j}{dF_k^2}\right)_{C=C_0} = -\frac{\left[C_{kk}C_j + C_{jj}\left(\frac{dF_j}{dF_k}\right)_{C=C_0}(-C_k)\right]}{C_j^2}$$

$$= -\frac{[C_{kk}C_j^2 + C_{jj}C_k^2]}{C_j^3}. \tag{5.12}$$

In particular, for $k = 1$ and $j = 2$,

$$\left(\frac{d^2F_2}{dF_1^2}\right)_{C=C_0} = -\frac{[C_{11}C_2^2 + C_{22}C_1^2]}{C_2^3}. \tag{5.12a}$$

The bracketed terms in (5.11a) and (5.12a) are precisely the bracketed terms in (5.10). Substituting $C_2^2q_2(d^2F_2/dF_1^2)_{Q=Q_0}$ and $-C_2^3(d^2F_2/dF_1^2)_{C=C_0}$ for the equivalent terms in (5.10), we rewrite $M_3$ as

$$M_3 = C_2^2q_2\left(\frac{d^2F_2}{dF_1^2}\right)_{Q=Q_0} - \lambda C_2^3\left(\frac{d^2F_2}{dF_1^2}\right)_{C=C_0}$$

$$= C_2^3\left[\left(\frac{d^2F_2}{dF_1^2}\right)_{Q=Q_0}\left(\frac{q_2}{C_2}\right) - \lambda\left(\frac{d^2F_2}{dF_1^2}\right)_{C=C_0}\right].$$

But $q_2/C_2 = \lambda$. Therefore, factoring $\lambda$ out of both terms,

$$M_3 = C_2^3\lambda\left[\left(\frac{d^2F_2}{dF_1^2}\right)_{Q=Q_0} - \left(\frac{d^2F_2}{dF_1^2}\right)_{C=C_0}\right]$$

$$= MC_2^3\lambda\left[\left(\frac{d^2F_2}{dF_1^2}\right)_{Q=Q_0} - \left(\frac{d^2F_2}{dF_1^2}\right)_{C=C_0}\right], \tag{5.13}$$

since $C_2 = MC_2$.

Both $\lambda$ and $MC_2$ are positive. It therefore follows that $M_3$ will be positive so long as $(d^2F_2/dF_1^2)_{Q=Q_0} > (d^2F_2/dF_1^2)_{C=C_0}$. Note, however, that $(d^2F_2/dF_1^2)_{Q=Q_0}$ and $(d^2F_2/dF_1^2)_{C=C_0}$ measure the convexity of the isoquant and isocost curve, respectively, in the $F_1$-$F_2$ space. Thus, $M_3$ will be positive, as required to assure that the first-order conditions yield a maximum, only if the isoquant is more convex (or equivalently less concave) in the $F_1$-$F_2$ space than is the isocost curve. If the isoquant is less convex (or more concave), the stationary point will be a minimum rather than a maximum. Since the $F_j$ and $F_k$ were arbitrarily chosen as $F_1$ and $F_2$, this sufficiency condition must hold between *any* pair of factors, and indeed can be generalized for the isoquants and isocost constraints binding *any combination* of factors. Further, (1) $\lambda$ must be positive and (2) the Lagrangian of (5.5) is maximized where the first-order conditions hold, if $L(F_1, \ldots, F_m, \lambda)$ is a concave function. The Lagrangian will be concave as long as the production function is concave and the cost constraint is convex, or of a lesser degree of concavity than the production function.[1]

Note that the isoquants will ordinarily be *expected* to be *strictly* convex. In the case of two factors, if $(d^2F_j/dF_k^2)_{Q=Q_0} = 0$, the isoquant is linear. Then, within the ridge lines, a given number of units of $F_j$ can always be substituted for a unit of $F_k$ without changing total output. The *strict* convexity expectation is based on the assumption that substitution of one factor for another becomes progressively more difficult as less and less of the second factor is employed. Intuitively, this assumption would seem to make a good deal of technological sense.

Note also that (5.12) may be written

$$\left(\frac{d^2F_j}{dF_k^2}\right)_{C=C_0} = -\frac{[MC_k'(MC_j)^2 + MC_j'(MC_k)^2]}{MC_j^3}.$$

Thus, the isocost curve in the $F_j$-$F_k$ space is linear (convex *or* concave) if $MC_k' = MC_j' = 0$ (that is, if the factor supply curves for $F_j$ and $F_k$ are horizontal lines). It is strictly convex if $[MC_k'(MC_j)^2 + MC_j'(MC_k)^2] < 0$. In particular, it will be strictly convex as long as both factors have nonincreasing marginal costs and at least one factor has decreasing marginal costs. It will be strictly concave as long as both factors have nondecreasing marginal costs and at least one factor has increasing marginal costs. In mixed cases the particulars will decide the issue.

In sum, then, the single-product firm will maximize output for a given total cost, or minimize the total cost of producing a given output, by hiring its factors of production so as to equate for each pair the ratio of marginal physical product to marginal factor cost, so long as the production isoquants are more convex than the isocost curves for all factor combinations.

## 5.3 COST AND PRODUCT CURVES IN THE LONG RUN

In the theory of the firm the concept of the long run conveys the fact that the firm has the freedom to vary *all* of its factors of production. All factors, including such items as plant and equipment, are variable. In the short run in which the day-to-day decisions are made, the latter factors will ordinarily be considered to be fixed. In the long run, then, in determining a factor input combination to produce a quantity of $Q$ during a time period of $T$, the firm is free to choose the optimal input combination as described by the previously derived optimality conditions. In the short run, this freedom is restricted somewhat by the fixity of certain factors of production.

The locus of all points of tangency of the isoquants and the isocost surfaces traces out the firm's *expansion path*. The expansion path (or *scale line*) indicates the minimum cost, factor input combination for producing any given output. In particular, output $Q$ and the $m$ factor levels $F_i$ are $m + 1$ variables whose values will be determined through the production function, and the $m - 1$ nonredundant conditions of optimality. Together these equations, (5.1) and (5.8), provide $m$ simultaneous

[1] The interpretation of the Lagrangian multiplier, and the relationship between the convexity of the constraints and (1) the sign of the multiplier and (2) the convexity of the objective function are discussed in detail in Sections 9.3 and 9.7.

equations. Equations (5.8), $MPP_j/MC_j = MPP_k/MC_k$, are functions exclusively of the $F_i$. With $m$ equations and $m + 1$ unknowns, it is at least theoretically possible, if algebraically difficult for certain nonlinear equations, to determine any set of $m$ of these unknowns in terms of the $(m + 1)$st. Thus, it can be assumed that the optimality conditions and the production function will enable one to determine values of the $F_i$ in terms of $Q$ such that $F_i = f_i(Q)$. Substituting the latter functions into the cost constraint, we determine the scale line:

$$C = \sum_i W_i F_i = \sum_i w_i[f_i(Q)]f_i(Q) = c(Q). \tag{5.14}$$

This scale line describes the firm's long-run *total cost* curve, $C = c(Q)$. The total cost curve indicates the minimum total cost for which one could produce a given output.[2] The one-to-one correspondence between the scale line and the firm's total cost curve is illustrated in Figures 5.5(a) and (b).

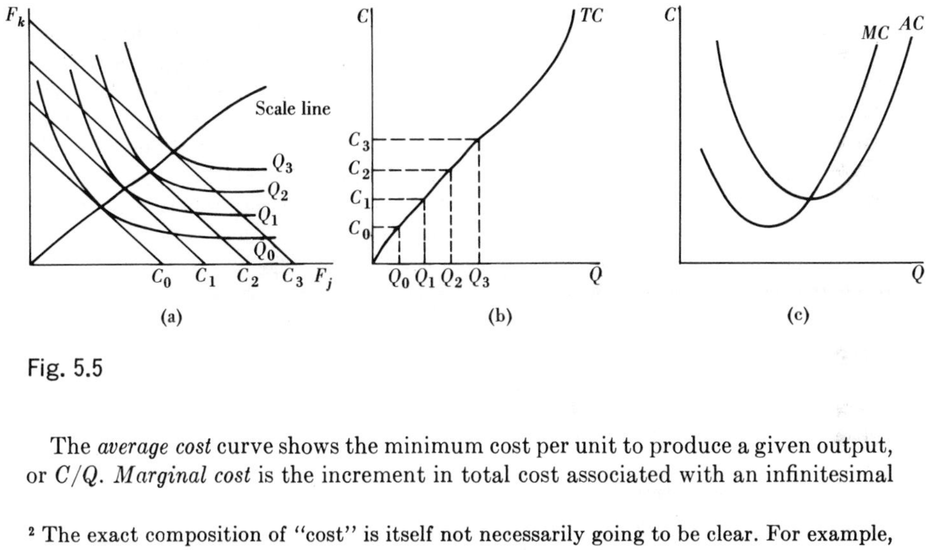


Fig. 5.5

The *average cost* curve shows the minimum cost per unit to produce a given output, or $C/Q$. *Marginal cost* is the increment in total cost associated with an infinitesimal

[2] The exact composition of "cost" is itself not necessarily going to be clear. For example, "The difficulties inherent in such a concept of cost (e.g., prime cost) are, in general, passed over, often by considering cost as consisting merely of payments to factors. It may, of course, be a considerably more complicated concept . . . . So prime cost must be measured in some way which will subtract from 'prime payments' the appreciation in the value of equipment due to them, in order to obtain a value representing the 'direct' cost of production, which can be compared with the receipts due to production." G. D. A. MacDougall, "The Definition of Prime and Supplementary Costs," *Economic Journal*, **XLVI**:183 (Sept. 1936), 449–450. As a more determinate standard that will suffice for the present discussion, "Cost of production includes all expenses which must be met in order to provide the commodity or service, transport it to the buyer, and put it into his hands ready to satisfy his wants . . . . A simple criterion is this: of all the costs incurred in the manufacture and sale of a given product, those which alter the demand curve for it are selling costs, and those which do not are costs of production." Edward H. Chamberlin, *The Theory of Monopolistic Competition* (Cambridge, Mass.: Harvard University Press, 1960), p. 123.

change in output, or $dC/dQ$. It is interesting to note that the slope of the average cost curve is given by

$$\frac{d\left(\frac{C}{Q}\right)}{dQ} = \frac{\left(\frac{dC}{dQ}\right)Q - C}{Q^2} = \frac{\left(\frac{dC}{dQ}\right) - \left(\frac{C}{Q}\right)}{Q}. \tag{5.15}$$

It is clear from (5.15) that average cost will be increasing with increasing output—that is, that $d(C/Q)/dQ$ will be positive—only when $dC/dQ > C/Q \geq 0$. That is, the average cost curve will be increasing only when marginal cost exceeds average cost. In the reverse case, when average cost exceeds marginal cost, the average cost curve will be declining. Additionally, if the average cost curve is *strictly* convex (that is, if $d^2(C/Q)/dQ^2 > 0$) average cost will be minimized where $d(C/Q)/dQ = 0$, or where $dC/dQ = C/Q$. Thus, if the average cost curve is U-shaped, as in Figure 5.5(c), marginal and average costs are equal at the point of minimum average cost. This relationship may be thought of as resulting from the fact that, on the one hand, when the production of an additional unit costs less than the average cost of producing all units, this average is pulled down when the additional unit is produced. On the other hand, when the additional or marginal unit costs more than the average, the average will increase with the production of another unit. Similarly, the average will neither rise nor fall when an additional unit is produced if marginal and average costs are equal. In the limit, for a continuous strictly convex function, this will occur at the point of minimum average cost. It might also be noted that while these average-marginal relationships will hold in general, when the average function is strictly concave the average and marginal curves will intersect at the *maximum* point on the average curve. This accounts for the shapes of the average and marginal physical product curves in Figure 5.3(a).

Given the total cost curve, marginal factor cost for the $i$th factor may now be determined as

$$\frac{\partial C}{\partial F_i} = \left[\frac{dC}{dQ}\right]\left[\frac{\partial Q}{\partial F_i}\right], \qquad i = 1, \ldots, m;$$

or, after rearranging terms,

$$\frac{dC}{dQ} = \frac{\left[\frac{\partial C}{\partial F_i}\right]}{\left[\frac{\partial Q}{\partial F_i}\right]} = \frac{1}{\lambda}, \qquad i = 1, \ldots, m. \tag{5.16}$$

Equation (5.16) shows, then, that the reciprocal of the Lagrangian multiplier is actually marginal cost, or that $\lambda = dQ/dC$. Thus in this case the Lagrangian multiplier measures the extent to which output would change with an infinitesimal change in input expenditures. In general, as will be seen, the value of the Lagrangian multiplier will be of more than passing interest.

It should also be emphasized that the product curves are *always* short run in nature, for any product curve is drawn for *fixed* levels of *all* other factors. In order to discuss these in the context of the long run, however, the product curves referred to will ordinarily be those which consider all other factors *fixed at their optimal levels* as dictated by the tangency conditions and the firm's yet-to-be-determined desired level of output.

## 5.4 THE LAWS OF FACTOR PROPORTIONS AND SCALE

The law of diminishing returns is one of the most famous tenets of economic theory. This "law" is actually an *assumption* that we make about the production function and may be stated in two forms. One form states that, holding $m - 1$ of the factors fixed at $F_j = \bar{F}_j (j = 1, \ldots, m; j \neq i)$, beyond a certain level of employment of the $i$th factor $(i = 1, \ldots, m)$, its *average* physical product will decline; the second form states that, beyond a certain level of employment, the *marginal* physical product of the $i$th factor will decline. Now, with $Q$ and $F_i > 0$ a declining average curve implies a lower marginal curve. If the average curve is strictly concave, the two curves will intersect at the maximum point on the average curve. Hence diminishing marginal physical product will necessarily occur "first" that is, at lower employment levels than diminishing average physical product, and the latter implies the former. Whenever referring to the law of diminishing returns, however, we shall mean the law in its marginal form, since the marginal physical product will prove to be the more important of the two concepts for decision making.

The law of diminishing returns contains a good deal of intuitive appeal. Its suggestion is that as we apply more and more of a single variable factor to a set of fixed factors, we may *initially* achieve *technological economies* in the sense that successive additions to total output increase, for equal increments of the variable factor. Beyond a certain point, however, even though it may still be possible to increase total product with further increments in the variable factor, *technological diseconomies* set in and the additions to total product get successively smaller for constant increments in any single variable factor.

The law of diminishing returns thus concentrates on technological economies as factor *proportions* change when a single factor varies. It is therefore essentially short run in nature. We can, however, also consider technological economies of *scale*. The latter refer to the effects on output as the levels of *all* factors change, but with their *proportions* fixed. These effects will therefore be essentially long run in nature. In particular, with $Q = q(F_1, \ldots, F_m)$ let $Q'$ represent the level of output when factor levels are at $F'_i$ $(i = 1, \ldots, m)$. If all factors are increased to $\theta F'_i$ $(\theta > 1)$, increasing returns to scale imply that the new output, $Q'' = f(\theta F'_1, \ldots, \theta F'_m)$, is greater than $\theta Q'$; with decreasing returns to scale $Q'' < \theta Q'$; with constant returns to scale $Q'' = \theta Q'$.

Though the idea of constant returns to scale may be quite appealing, it is unlikely that these can be maintained, particularly once we recognize that entrepreneurship and decision-making ability are themselves crucial factors of production. These factors are especially susceptible to disproportionate variations in efficiency when their levels are varied, and they are especially difficult to measure. At "high" rates of input, however, when we double all inputs and double all decisions, it seems unlikely that a doubling of output will be achieved. Lengthening lines of communication within the firm, and the need to delegate more and more authority as the firm grows, inhibits efficient decision making. Although we assume them to be so, the factors of production will not necessarily be homogeneous. Yet, small differences between individual units when many such are being employed may not be too distortive. Entrepreneurship is a scarce quality, however, and homogeneity in this factor is a most heroic assumption. It would seem that, ultimately at least, the scarcity of entrepreneurship and its heterogeneous quality will necessarily limit the range of output within which economies of, or constant returns to, scale are secured.[3]

The distinction between proportions and scale is illustrated in Figure 5.6 for the two factor case. The returns to factor 2 may be measured from intersections of the vertical line with the isoquants at $F_1 = \bar{F}_1$. Since successively higher isoquants increase by the same *absolute* amount in the graph, namely 1000, where the isoquants are further apart at $\bar{F}_1$, there are diminishing returns to factor 2; increasing returns occur where, at $\bar{F}_1$, the isoquants are closer together. Similarly, the returns to factor 1 would be identified via a horizontal line at any particular level of $F_2 = \bar{F}_2$.

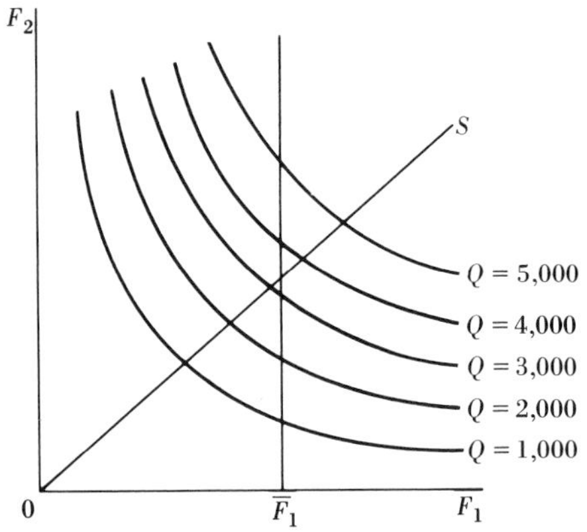


Fig. 5.6

Whereas the effects of varying proportions are seen by taking a vertical or horizontal "slice" of the production surface, the effects of varying scale are seen by taking a "slice" of the surface from the origin. If, along a linear cut from the origin, the surface is rising at an increasing (decreasing) rate, there are increasing (decreasing) returns to scale. If the surface is linear along a linear path from the origin, there

[3] From both the theoretical and institutional points of view the role of the decision-making unit in the production function has long been, and continues to be, a major sore point. See, for example, the following: N. Kaldor, "The Equilibrium of the Firm," *Economic Journal*, **XLIV**:173 (March 1934), 67–71; E. A. G. Robinson, "The Problem of Management and the Size of Firms," *Economic Journal*, **XLIV**:174 (June 1934), 242–257, particularly 249–251; J. R. Hicks, "The Theory of Monopoly," *Econometrica*, **3** (Jan. 1935), 19; R. H. Coase, "The Nature of the Firm," *Economica*, **IV**:4 (Nov. 1937), 386–405; K. E. Boulding, "The Incidence of a Profits Tax," *American Economic Review*, **XXXIV**:1 (Sept. 1944), 568; P. W. S. Andrews, *Manufacturing Business* (London: Macmillan and Co., Ltd., 1949), 127–131; Edith T. Penrose, *The Theory of the Growth of the Firm* (New York: John Wiley & Sons, Inc., 1959), p. 64; Richard B. Heflebower, "Observations on Decentralization in Large Enterprises," *Journal of Industrial Economics*, **IX**:1 (Nov. 1960), 7–8; Neil W. Chamberlain, *The Firm: Microeconomic Planning and Action* (New York: McGraw-Hill, Inc., 1962), p. 395; and K. George, "The Growth of Firms: An Empirical Study," *Australian Economic Papers*, **3**:1, 2 (June–Dec. 1964), 78.

are constant returns to scale. In Figure 5.6, line $OS$ is drawn with $F_1$ and $F_2$ in fixed proportion. Where the successive lengths between the isoquants get smaller (larger) along $OS$, there are increasing (decreasing) returns to scale. Where successive lengths are equal, there are constant returns to scale.

## 5.5 HOMOGENEOUS PRODUCTION FUNCTIONS

Of particular interest are production functions $Q = q(F_1, \ldots, F_m)$ having the property that

$$q(\theta F_1, \ldots, \theta F_i, \ldots, \theta F_m) = \theta^r q(F_1, \ldots, F_i, \ldots, F_m) = \theta^r Q. \tag{5.17}$$

Such functions are called homogeneous of degree $r$. When $r = 1$ we have the special case of a linear homogeneous production function and constant returns to scale. Setting $r = 1$ and $\theta = 1/F_i$, we rewrite Equation (5.17) as

$$\left(\frac{1}{F_i}\right) q(F_1, \ldots, F_i, \ldots, F_m) = q\left(\frac{F_1}{F_i}, \ldots, 1, \ldots, \frac{F_m}{F_i}\right).$$

It directly follows that the original production function may be written as

$$Q = F_i q\left(\frac{F_1}{F_i}, \ldots, \frac{F_m}{F_i}\right) = F_i q.$$

This is a particularly convenient form for deriving Euler's theorem.[4] The theorem states that when the production function is linear homogeneous, the sum of the products of the factor levels and the respective marginal physical products of the factors at these levels equals the total product. This is of particular interest in distribution theory, for it states that if the factors of production are rewarded for their efforts by being paid their marginal physical products as their unit wages, with a linear homogeneous production function the total product will be exactly exhausted.

In order to prove the theorem, we shall first compute the marginal physical products, $\partial Q/\partial F_k$, and then compute the sum of $F_k(\partial Q/\partial F_k)$ over all $k = 1, \ldots, m$.

Calculating $\partial Q/\partial F_j$ $(j \neq i)$,

$$\begin{aligned}\frac{\partial Q}{\partial F_j} &= \left[\frac{\partial Q}{\partial(F_j/F_i)}\right]\left[\frac{\partial(F_j/F_i)}{\partial F_j}\right] \\ &= [F_i q_j']\left[\frac{1}{F_i}\right] = q_j', \qquad \text{where } q_j' = \frac{\partial q}{\partial(F_j/F_i)}.\end{aligned}$$

Further,

$$\begin{aligned}\frac{\partial Q}{\partial F_i} &= \sum_{j \neq i}\left[\frac{\partial q}{\partial(F_j/F_i)}\right]\left[\frac{\partial(F_j/F_i)}{\partial F_i}\right]F_i + q = \sum_{j \neq i} q_j'\left[-\frac{F_j}{F_i^2}\right]F_i + q \\ &= -\sum_{j \neq i} q_j'\left(\frac{F_j}{F_i}\right) + q.\end{aligned}$$

[4] Named for its discoverer, Leonard Euler (1707–1783), a Swiss mathematician.

Therefore,

$$\begin{aligned}\sum_{k=1}^{m} F_k\left(\frac{\partial Q}{\partial F_k}\right) &= F_i\left(\frac{\partial Q}{\partial F_i}\right) + \sum_{j\neq i} F_j\left(\frac{\partial Q}{\partial F_j}\right)\\ &= F_i\left[-\sum_{j\neq i} q_j'\left(\frac{F_j}{F_i}\right) + q\right] + \sum_{j\neq i} F_j q_j'\\ &= -\sum_{j\neq i} q_j' F_j + F_i q + \sum_{j\neq i} F_j q_j';\end{aligned}$$

$$\sum_{k=1}^{m} F_k\left(\frac{\partial Q}{\partial F_k}\right) = F_i q = Q. \tag{5.18}$$

Equation (5.18) is the mathematical statement of Euler's Theorem. It is a useful and interesting theorem to be aware of, because of its inherent suggestions about how the production pie might be distributed amongst the factors of production so as to leave no residuals: namely, reward each factor with a wage equal to its marginal physical product. It must be borne in mind, however, that the theorem is satisfied only when the production function is linear homogeneous, exhibiting constant returns to scale.

The case of *fixed technological coefficients* is also of singular interest as a special case of constant returns to scale. Fixed technological coefficients mean that the factors are most efficiently combined in a specific proportion irrespective of their relative costs. In the two-factor case of Figure 5.7(a), each isoquant consists of a

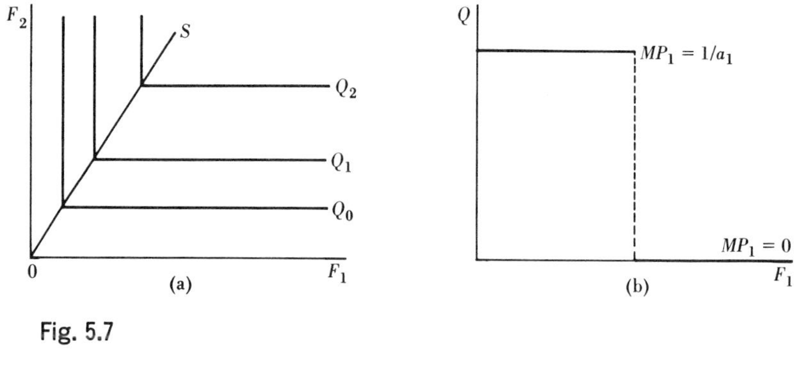


Fig. 5.7

horizontal and vertical segment joining in a right angle at the optimal factor combina tion for that level of output. In effect, the ridge lines converge into a single line. Formally, $F_i/Q = a_i$, a constant, for all $i = 1, \ldots, m$.

Note that with fixed technological coefficients the marginal physical product curves are discontinuous. Formally, output cannot be larger than the smallest of the $F_i/a_i$. With all factors except factor $j$ fixed at $\bar{F}_i$ $(i \neq j)$, we have $Q \leq \min_i [\bar{F}_i/a_i]$. Hence, $MPP_j = \partial Q/\partial F_j = 1/a_j$ for $F_j \leq \min_i [\bar{F}_i/a_i]a_j$ $(i \neq j)$ and $MPP_j = 0$ otherwise. This is depicted in Figure 5.7(b) for the isoquants of Figure 5.7(a) and $F_1$.

Now, suppose that $\min_i [F_i/a_i] = \bar{F}_k/a_k$. If the level of employment of the $k$th factor rises, then, at the point of the discontinuity, $MPP_j$ will increase from 0 to $1/a_j$. This is because at these levels of employment, and given the other factors, $j$ and $k$ *complement* one another.

In general, if $\partial(\partial Q/\partial F_j)/\partial F_k = \partial^2 Q/\partial F_j\,\partial F_k > 0$, the factors are called *complements*; if $\partial^2 Q/\partial F_j\,\partial F_k < 0$, they are *rivals;* if $\partial^2 Q/\partial F_j\,\partial F_k = 0$, they are neutral. Thus we *define* complementarity and rivalry of factors in terms of their effects on the other's marginal physical products. Pecuniary considerations do not enter into the definitions at all. Further, since $\partial^2 Q/\partial F_j\,\partial F_k = \partial^2 Q/\partial F_k\,\partial F_j$, the relationship is symmetrical.[5] It should be noted that rivalry differs from substitutability. Except for cases of fixed coefficients and other isolated instances, one can commonly "substitute" one factor for another, albeit with difficulty.[6] Further, if the isoquants are continuous, $dF_j/dF_k$ will be negative and $-(dF_j/dF_k)_{Q=Q_0}$ will measure the rate of *substitution*. If, however, the two factors are *rivals*, then the addition of one reduces the contribution of the other—that is, it lowers the other's marginal physical product.

## 5.6 SHORT-RUN CONSIDERATIONS

There is no "the" short run for the firm. Instead, there are *hosts* of possible short runs, each of which we effect by considering certain factors of production, or combinations of factors, to be fixed. The shift from the long run to the short is thus accomplished by fixing the levels of various factors of production. In particular, let us designate the factors so as to permit only the first $k$ factors to be variable. The last $m - k$ factors will be considered fixed in "the" short run. The production function may now be written

$$Q = q(F_1, \ldots, F_k, F_{k+1}, \ldots, F_m) = q(F_1, \ldots, F_k; \bar{F}_{k+1}, \ldots, \bar{F}_m)$$

with $F_i$ fixed at $\bar{F}_i$ $(i = k + 1, \ldots, m)$. Moreover, since the various product curves for factor $i$ require that *all* other factors remain fixed, these will be constructed precisely as in the long run. Now, however, from the short-run decision-making standpoint, interest will center on the product curves for the variable factors 1 through $k$, given the specific short-run levels of factors $k + 1$ through $m$, which the firm can do nothing about.

In the short run, then, the firm's production problem can be written

$$\text{Maximize} \quad Q = q(F_1, \ldots, F_k; \bar{F}_{k+1}, \ldots, \bar{F}_m)$$

$$\text{subject to} \quad C_S = C_0 = \sum_{i=1}^{k} W_i F_i + \sum_{i=k+1}^{m} W_i \bar{F}_i = \sum_{i=1}^{k} W_i F_i + K. \qquad (5.4a')$$

[5] See Robert L. Bishop, "A Firm's Short-Run and Long-Run Demands for a Factor," *Western Economic Journal*, V:2 (March 1967), 132–133. Also, see J. R. Hicks, *Value and Capital* (Oxford: Clarendon Press, 1946), pp. 89–98. The term "complements" is also referred to as "cooperants." See A. C. Pigou, *The Economics of Welfare* (London: Macmillan and Co., Ltd., 1962), 659–662.

[6] With respect to "substitution," by analogy with demand elasticities, "it appears appropriate to call the proportionate change in the ratio of the amounts of the factors employed divided by the proportionate change in the ratio of their prices to which it is due, the elasticity of substitution." Joan Robinson, *The Economics of Imperfect Competition* (London: Macmillan and Co., Ltd., 1950), p. 256. Mrs. Robinson suggests (p. 330) replacing prices with marginal physical products, in the absence of pure competition.

Here $C_S$ is short-run total cost, and $K = \sum_{i=k+1}^{m} W_i\bar{F}_i$ is *total fixed cost*—the outlay to which the firm is committed for the fixed factors of production. The firm's short-run production problem can be formulated as a Lagrangian problem:

$$\begin{aligned}\text{Maximize} \quad L_S &= L_S(F_1, \ldots, F_k, \gamma) \\ &= q(F_1, \ldots, F_k, \bar{F}_{k+1}, \ldots, \bar{F}_m) - \gamma\left[\sum_{i=1}^{k} W_iF_i + K - C_0\right]. \qquad (5.5')\end{aligned}$$

The problem could also have been formulated by introducing the additional *constraints* $F_i - \bar{F}_i = 0$ $(i = k + 1, \ldots, m)$ into the earlier long-run problem (5.5). Then, (5.5′) would be written

$$\begin{aligned}\text{Maximize} \quad L_S = q(F_1, \ldots, F_k, F_{k+1}, \ldots, F_m) - \gamma\left[\sum_{i=1}^{m} W_iF_i - C_0\right] \\ - \sum_{i=k+1}^{m} \gamma_i[F_i - \bar{F}_i]. \qquad (5.5'')\end{aligned}$$

Equations (5.5′) and (5.5″) yield identical solutions. The former merely incorporates the additional constraints directly into the production and cost functions. The previous analysis is then duplicated to reveal that, in the short run, the *variable* factors should be employed so as to equate for each pair the ratios of marginal physical products to marginal factor costs. Clearly, max $L_S \leq$ max $L$. That is, if the firm is free to vary *all* factors, it can get at least as much output for a given cost as it can get when it is only free to vary *some* factors. The maximum $Q$ obtainable for a given $C_0$ has previously been found in the solution to (5.5). It might be *possible*, however, to do just as well here, depending upon the levels chosen for the fixed factors; they would have to be fixed at their long-run optima.

As before, the $k - 1$ equations $MPP_i/MC_i = MPP_j/MC_j$ $(i, j = 1, \ldots, k)$ and the production function can be solved for the variable $F_i$ in terms of $Q$ to obtain $F_i = f_{iS}(Q)$. The firm's short-run total cost curve shows the minimum cost for which a given quantity can be produced, given the fixed factor levels. This is now given by

$$C_S = \sum_{i=1}^{k} W_i[f_{iS}(Q)] + K = c_S(Q) + K. \qquad (5.19)$$

Moreover, just as the long-run total cost curve holds a one-to-one correspondence with the firm's expansion path, the short-run total cost curve has a one-to-one correspondence with a short-run scale line. Given the other $m - 2$ factor levels and holding fixed at $F_j = \bar{F}_j$ the factor plotted on the horizontal axis in the $j$–$k$ space, the short-run scale line consists of the intersections of the vertical line at $\bar{F}_j$ with the isoquants. The quantity is determined by the isoquant, and the total variable cost by the isocost curve passing through the intersection. This is illustrated in Figures 5.8(a) and 5.8(b).

As in the long run, average cost is given by $C_S/Q = c_S(Q)/Q + K/Q$, where $c_S(Q)/Q$ is average variable cost and $K/Q$ is average fixed cost. In the long run, with *all* factors variable, the fixed cost term does not appear, since $K = 0$. Short-run marginal cost is given by $dC_S/dQ = dc_S(Q)/dQ = d[c_S(Q)Q/Q]/dQ = d$ (total variable cost)$/dQ$. Thus the short-run marginal cost curve is the curve marginal to both the total *variable* cost curve and the total cost curve. The average-marginal relationships previously discussed hold between the marginal cost curve and *both* the average total cost *and* average variable cost curves. For a U-shaped average total cost curve, these would appear as in Figure 5.8(b).

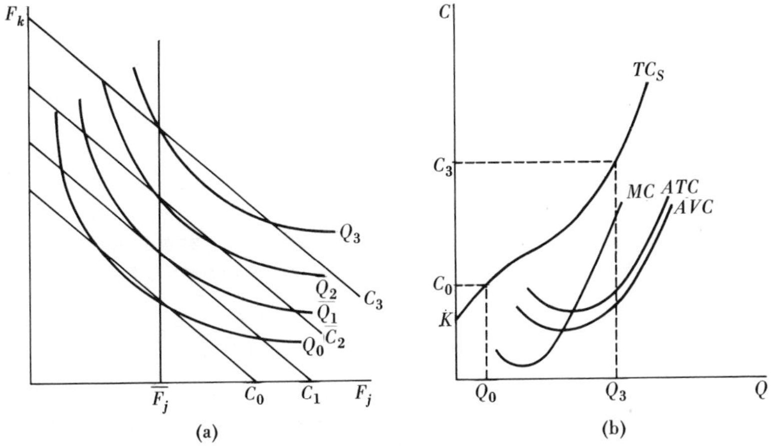


Fig. 5.8

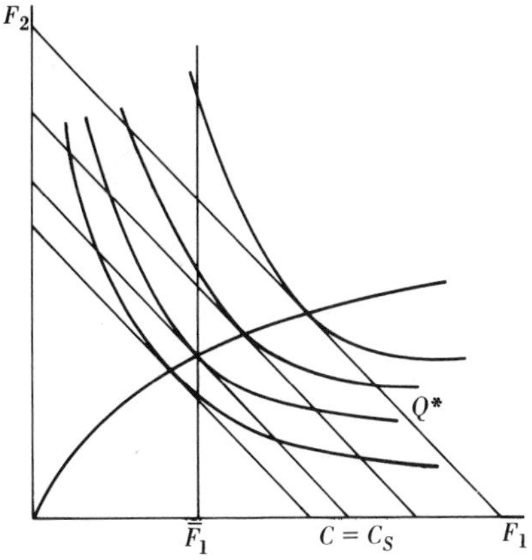


Fig. 5.9

## 5.7 THE LONG RUN AND THE SHORT: THE COST CURVES

The short- and long-run scale lines intersect at a single point on a particular isoquant, as illustrated in the two-factor case of Figure 5.9. It therefore follows that the short- and long-run *cost* curves will coincide at this quantity. At any other point at which an isoquant intersects the short-run scale line we are on an isocost surface higher than the isocost surface just tangent to that isoquant. Hence, the short-run total cost curve will necessarily lie above the long-run total cost curve, except for this particular quantity at which they will be tangent.

Indeed, where there are more than two factors, depending upon the choice of levels for the fixed factors, *a* short-run total cost curve could lie above the long-run total cost curve at *every* quantity. It will be assumed, however, that the levels of the fixed factors will have been chosen such that, for *some* $Q = Q^*$, at $F_i = \bar{F}_i$ $(i = k + 1, \ldots, m)$,

$$\frac{MPP_i}{MC_i} = \frac{MPP_j}{MC_j}, \qquad i, j = 1, \ldots, m.$$

At this point, long-run and short-run total costs are equal; or $C = C_S$ and hence $C/Q^* = C_S/Q^*$. That is, at this quantity short- and long-run *average* total costs are equal. At all other quantities factors $k + 1, \ldots, m$ will be varied in the long run though fixed in the short. Hence, long-run average cost will be *less than* short-run average cost except at $Q = Q^*$. Further, Equation (5.16) shows that we have $MC_i/MPP_i = dC/dQ$ $(i = 1, \ldots, m)$. Thus, at $Q^*$ short- and long-run *marginal* costs are equal. Since, however, $C < C_S$ for $Q > Q^*$, it follows that

$$\frac{dC_S}{dQ} > \frac{dC}{dQ} \text{ for } Q > Q^* \qquad \text{and} \qquad \frac{dC}{dQ} > \frac{dC_S}{dQ} \text{ for } Q < Q^*.$$

That is, the optimal factor arrangement obtains at $Q^*$, short run or long. To produce greater quantities requires *greater additional* costs when all factors cannot be varied than when they can. To produce smaller quantities results in a *lesser reduction* of cost when all factors cannot be varied than when they can. In the long run, greater variations in quantity can be accomplished with lesser variations in cost than is the case in the short run. Thus, the short- and long-run marginal cost curves *intersect* at quantities $Q^*$, where the short- and long-run average total cost and total cost curves are *tangent*. Further, the marginal curves intersect at quantities $Q^*$ at which the long- and short-run total cost curves have the same slope. The now familiar average-marginal relationship holds between each associated pair of curves. This is illustrated for U-shaped average cost curves in Figure 5.10.

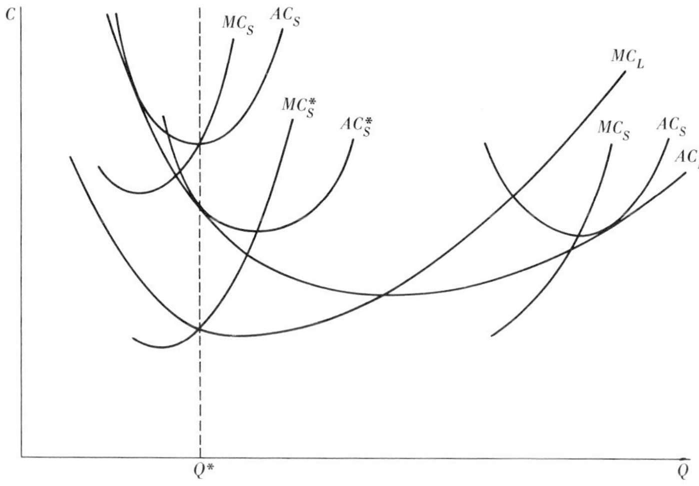


Fig. 5.10

In sum, then, the firm must make a decision as to a quantity $Q^*$ to produce in a series of time intervals of length $T$. When it is still free to vary all factors of production, the firm selects levels of factors $F_{k+1}$ through $F_m$ such that $MPP_i/MC_i = MPP_j/MC_j$ for all $m$ factors. The last $m - k$ factors must then be maintained at the previously selected levels through a series of intervals of length $T$. This is true even though the firm might at some time wish to vary the first $k$ factors because of a decision to change $Q^*$. Suppose plant and equipment, say, are the firm's only fixed factors in the short run. Thus, in terms of Figure 5.10, the judgment that over the long run $Q^*$ will be the optimal production level during $T$ will lead the firm to purchase plant and equipment such that the short-run average cost curve $AC_S^*$ will be the relevant average cost curve for short-run decision making.

Note that this will not necessarily, nor indeed ordinarily, be the short-run average cost curve for which, at $Q^*$, short-run average costs are minimized. The successive short-run average cost curves might be thought of as reflecting larger levels of plant and equipment as they move to the right. Suppose the long-run decision is to produce a smaller quantity than that which minimizes long-run average cost. In the present instance $Q^*$ can be produced at a lower cost with more plant and equipment than is contained in the operation for which $Q^*$ is the minimum total cost production level. Overcapacity in this sense would become the economically optimal outcome.[7]

## 5.8 ECONOMETRICS AND THE PRODUCTION FUNCTION

Econometricians have not overlooked the possibilities of applying their techniques to the empirical estimation of production functions, nor have they been unmindful of the accompanying difficulties.[8] In employing least squares to estimate some

[7] The question arises as to whether, in fact, firms typically tend to have excess capacity. This is of particular interest in considering possible violations of the antitrust laws, where the excess capacity might be a purposeful means of discouraging potential entrants into an industry. It has been suggested "that there is typically no definite 'optimum size,' but rather a wide optimum range of size, within which most plants fall; and that economies due to size are far from being such a vitally important factor as is suggested by the type of theoretical cost curve now in general use." J. M. Clark, "Toward a Concept of Workable Competition," *American Economic Review*, **XXX**:2 (June 1940), 249. An interesting aspect, not ordinarily incorporated into the analysis of capacity, is the question of timing. For example, "...competitive forces can result in *more* rather than less idle capacity in situations where the cost of waiting is very high. Some idle capacity can now be seen as evidence of efficient production in many cases, and 'excess capacity' which is often observed in economic analysis may sometimes, if not often, arise out of a seeking of efficiency rather than restriction. This will be true insofar as there are any rigidities (or what an economist might call indivisibilities with respect to time) in the economy which could give rise to a queueing process." A. B. Araoz and H. B. Malmgren, "Congestion and Idle Capacity in an Economy," *Review of Economic Studies*, **XXVIII**:77 (June 1961), 209.

[8] For excellent reviews of empirical analyses of production and cost functions see the following: A. A. Walters, "Production and Cost Functions: An Econometric Survey," *Econometrica*, **31**:1–2 (January–April 1963), 1–66; George H. Hildebrand and T. C. Liu, *Manufacturing Production Functions in the United States, 1957* (Ithaca, N.Y.: New York State School of Industrial and Labor Relations, 1965), pp. 19–43; and J. Johnston, *Statistical Cost Analysis* (New York: McGraw-Hill, Inc., 1960).

specific form of $Q = q(F_1, \ldots, F_m, \epsilon)$, one requires both some judgment as to the appropriate specification, as well as the requisite data. If $F_1$ is "capital," one might measure this variable by "gross book value of plant and equipment" available during the production period; or one might use the latter figure less depreciation and depletion; or, if the figure is obtainable, one might measure capital by the "number of available machines." Ordinarily, one simply has to "make do" with the data that are available and the best judgment that one can bring to bear on the problem. There are, however, some additional, quite interesting, general econometric issues that arise in the empirical estimation of production functions. In particular, we shall consider here the question of simultaneous-equations estimation.

For *expository* purposes, let us hypothesize a production function of the form

$$Q_t = \alpha_0 L_t^{\alpha_1} K_t^{\alpha_2} M_t^{\alpha_3} \epsilon_{1t}, \tag{5.20}$$

where $Q_t$ is output during period $t$, $L_t$, $K_t$, and $M_t$ are measures of nonmanagement labor, capital, and management employed during $t$, and $\epsilon_{1t}$ is a random-disturbance term. Also, suppose that the level of management is itself a function of output and nonmanagement labor and, like Topsy, grows with time. In particular,

$$M_t = \beta_0 Q_t^{\beta_1} L_t^{\beta_2} (\beta_3)^t \epsilon_{2t}, \tag{5.21}$$

with $\epsilon_{2t}$ a random-disturbance term. With the tilde denoting logarithm, the production model (5.20) and (5.21) may be rewritten as

$$\tilde{Q}_t = \tilde{\alpha}_0 + \alpha_1 \tilde{L}_t + \alpha_2 \tilde{K}_t + \alpha_3 \tilde{M}_t + \tilde{\epsilon}_{1t}, \tag{5.20a}$$
$$\tilde{M}_t = \tilde{\beta}_0 + \beta_1 \tilde{Q}_t + \beta_2 \tilde{L}_t + \tilde{\beta}_3 t + \tilde{\epsilon}_{2t}. \tag{5.21a}$$

There are two endogenous variables, $\tilde{Q}_t$ and $\tilde{M}_t$ to be determined from the model on the basis of three exogenous variables, $\tilde{L}_t$, $\tilde{K}_t$, and $t$, predetermined outside the model.[9] Although we make the usual least-squares assumptions regarding the disturbance terms and the exogenous variables—that is, assumptions 2 and 3 of Section 3.4c—there is, unhappily, some difficulty in estimating the parameters of (5.20a) and (5.21a) via ordinary least squares. The difficulty arises from the fact that, because each of the endogenous variables is itself a function of the other, neither $\tilde{M}_t$ in (5.20a) nor $\tilde{Q}_t$ in (5.21a) is independent of the disturbance terms in its equation. This is a violation of one of the basic assumptions of ordinary least squares.

To demonstrate that, for example, $\tilde{M}_t$ is not independent of $\tilde{\epsilon}_{1t}$, first substitute (5.20a) into (5.21a) to obtain

$$\tilde{M}_t = \left[\frac{\tilde{\beta}_0 + \tilde{\alpha}_0\beta_1}{1 - \alpha_3\beta_1}\right] + \left[\frac{\beta_2 + \alpha_1\beta_1}{1 - \alpha_3\beta_1}\right]\tilde{L}_t + \left[\frac{\alpha_2\beta_1}{1 - \alpha_3\beta_1}\right]\tilde{K}_t + \left[\frac{\tilde{\beta}_3}{1 - \alpha_3\beta_1}\right]t + \left[\frac{\tilde{\epsilon}_{2t} + \beta_1\tilde{\epsilon}_{1t}}{1 - \alpha_3\beta_1}\right]; \tag{5.21b}$$

[9] The need to worry about the simultaneity of several relationships in estimating the production function was first raised as a serious issue by J. Marschak and W. H. Andrews, "Random Simultaneous Equations and the Theory of Production," *Econometrica*, **12**:3–4 (July–Oct. 1944), 143–205. Their concern stemmed from a recognition of (1) an implicit tie between the levels of employment of the factors of production, and between

or, rewriting this so as to combine the parameters,

$$\tilde{M}_t = \gamma_{01} + \gamma_{11}\tilde{L}_t + \gamma_{21}\tilde{K}_t + \gamma_{31}t + \xi_{1t}. \tag{5.21c}$$

Taking the mathematical expectation of (5.21c),

$$E[\tilde{M}_t] = \gamma_{01} + \gamma_{11}\tilde{L}_t + \gamma_{21}\tilde{K}_t + \gamma_{31}t, \tag{5.21d}$$

since $\gamma_{i1}$ $(i = 0, \ldots, 3)$ is a population parameter and the variables on the right side are all exogenous, so that, for instance,

$$E[\gamma_{11}\tilde{L}_t] = \gamma_{11}E[\tilde{L}_t] = \gamma_{11}\tilde{L}_t;$$

and, by the third of the initial least-squares assumptions,

$$E[\tilde{\epsilon}_{1t}] = E[\tilde{\epsilon}_{2t}] = 0 \quad \text{so that} \quad E[\xi_{1t}] = 0.$$

Now, with $E[\tilde{\epsilon}_{1t}] = 0$ by assumption, the covariance between $\tilde{\epsilon}_{1t}$ and $\tilde{M}_t$ will be given by

$$E[(\tilde{\epsilon}_{1t} - E[\tilde{\epsilon}_{1t}])(\tilde{M}_t - E[\tilde{M}_t])] = E[\tilde{\epsilon}_{1t}(\tilde{M}_t - E[\tilde{M}_t])].$$

If $\tilde{\epsilon}_{1t}$ and $\tilde{M}_t$ are not independent, they will be correlated and their covariance will not be zero. To see whether this is the case, we therefore compute

$$\begin{aligned} E[\tilde{\epsilon}_{1t}(\tilde{M}_t - E[\tilde{M}_t])] &= E[\tilde{\epsilon}_{1t}(\tilde{M}_t) - \tilde{\epsilon}_{1t}E[\tilde{M}_t]] \\ &= \gamma_{01}E[{}_1\tilde{\epsilon}_t] + \gamma_{11}E[\tilde{\epsilon}_{1t}\tilde{L}_t] + \gamma_{21}E[\tilde{\epsilon}_{1t}\tilde{K}_t] + \gamma_{31}E[\tilde{\epsilon}_{1t}t] \\ &\qquad + E[\tilde{\epsilon}_{1t}\xi_{1t}] - E[\tilde{\epsilon}_{1t}]E[\tilde{M}_t]. \end{aligned}$$

Even assuming that the disturbance terms are independent of one another and of the exogenous variables, $\tilde{M}_t$ and $\tilde{\epsilon}_{1t}$ are necessarily correlated since (1) $E[\tilde{\epsilon}_{1t}] = 0$ and (2)

$$E[\tilde{\epsilon}_{1t}^2] = E[(\tilde{\epsilon}_{1t} - E[\tilde{\epsilon}_{1t}])^2] = \sigma_{\tilde{\epsilon}_{1t}}^2 \neq 0,$$

as a consequence of which the previous expression reduces to

$$E[\tilde{\epsilon}_{1t}(\tilde{M}_{1t} - E[\tilde{M}_t])] = E[\tilde{\epsilon}_{1t}\xi_{1t}] = \left[\frac{\beta_1}{1 - \alpha_3\beta_1}\right] E[\tilde{\epsilon}_{1t}^2] \neq 0.$$

Hence, the covariance between $\tilde{\epsilon}_{1t}$ and $\tilde{M}_t$ is nonzero, or the disturbance term in (5.20a) is not independent of one of the "independent" variables in the equation. This violates one of the initial least-squares assumptions and argues against the use of ordinary least squares to estimate (5.20a). A similar argument holds for (5.21a), leading one to infer that $\tilde{Q}_t$ and $\tilde{\epsilon}_{2t}$ are not independent.

Note, however, that just as (5.21b) was derived by solving for $\tilde{M}_t$ in terms of exogenous variables exclusively, (5.21a) can be substituted into (5.20a) to deter-

---

the factor levels and the output level, resulting from the first-order conditions for a production and a profit optimum; and (2) the likelihood that random disturbances would, under any circumstances, prevent the exact realization of these conditions. As a simplification, this tie has been ignored in the present discussion of estimation.

mine $\tilde{Q}_t$ solely in terms of exogenous variables. Specifically,

$$\tilde{Q}_t = \left[\frac{\tilde{\alpha}_0 + \alpha_3\tilde{\beta}_0}{1 - \alpha_3\beta_1}\right] + \left[\frac{\alpha_1 + \alpha_3\beta_2}{1 - \alpha_3\beta_1}\right]\tilde{L}_t + \left[\frac{\alpha_2}{1 - \alpha_3\beta_1}\right]\tilde{K}_t + \left[\frac{\alpha_3\tilde{\beta}_3}{1 - \alpha_3\beta_1}\right]t + \left[\frac{\alpha_3\tilde{\epsilon}_{2t} + \tilde{\epsilon}_{1t}}{1 - \alpha_3\beta_1}\right]; \tag{5.20b}$$

or, simplifying terms,

$$\tilde{Q}_t = \gamma_{00} + \gamma_{10}\tilde{L}_t + \gamma_{20}\tilde{K}_t + \gamma_{30}t + \xi_{0t}. \tag{5.20c}$$

Equations (5.20c) and (5.21c), which express the endogenous variables as functions of all and only the exogenous variables, are called *the reduced-form* equations of the simultaneous-equation model of (5.20) and (5.21). The latter are called *structural equations*—equations describing the model's initial specification. The parameters of the reduced-form equations can be estimated by applying ordinary least squares to each equation. If the only concern were to obtain estimates for the endogenous variables based solely on the set of exogenous variables, this procedure would suffice. If, however, there is the additional concern of estimating the parameters of the structural equations, the problem takes on additional complexity. In the present discussion two of several alternative procedures will be considered.[10]

## a. Indirect Least Squares and Identification

Applying ordinary least squares to (5.20c) and (5.21c), one would obtain least-squares estimates of the $\gamma_{ij}$. Call these $d_{ij}$. The estimated reduced-form equations would be

$$\tilde{Q}_t = d_{00} + d_{10}\tilde{L}_t + d_{20}\tilde{K}_t + d_{30}t + e_{0t}; \tag{5.20ĉ}$$
$$\tilde{M}_t = d_{01} + d_{11}\tilde{L}_t + d_{21}\tilde{K}_t + d_{31}t + e_{1t}. \tag{5.21ĉ}$$

If we denote the estimates of $\alpha_i$ and $\beta_i$ by $a_i$ and $b_i$, respectively, it is readily apparent that estimates of (5.20b) and (5.21b) may be solved for $a_i$ and $b_i$ in terms of the $d_{ij}$ of (5.20ĉ) and (5.21ĉ). For example, note from (5.21b) and (5.21c) that $\alpha_2\beta_1/(1 - \alpha_3\beta_1) = \gamma_{21}$; and, from (5.20b) and (5.20c), $\alpha_2/(1 - \alpha_3\beta_1) = \gamma_{20}$. Hence, $\beta_1 = \gamma_{21}/\gamma_{20}$ and, for the estimate, $b_1 = d_{21}/d_{20}$. In similar fashion, one can determine the following set of relationships:

$$b_2 = d_{11} - \frac{d_{21}}{d_{20}}d_{10}; \qquad \tilde{b}_3 = d_{31} - \frac{d_{21}}{d_{20}}d_{30};$$

$$\tilde{b}_0 = d_{01} - \frac{d_{21}}{d_{20}}d_{00}; \qquad \tilde{a}_0 = d_{00} - \frac{d_{30}}{d_{31}}d_{01};$$

$$a_1 = d_{10} - \frac{d_{30}}{d_{31}}d_{11}; \qquad a_2 = d_{20} - \frac{d_{30}}{d_{31}}d_{21};$$

$$a_3 = \frac{d_{30}}{d_{31}}.$$

[10] For more extensive discussions see H. Thiel, *Economic Forecasts and Policy* (Amsterdam: North-Holland, 1961), particularly pp. 204–240 and 334–355. Also, see Arthur S. Goldberger, *Econometric Theory* (New York: John Wiley & Sons, Inc., 1964), pp. 288–388.

The model of (5.20) and (5.21) is said to be *just identified,* as each of the structural parameters is *uniquely* determined from combinations of the reduced-form parameters. When this is the case, this is clearly a most fortuitous occurrence and the model builder has probably done his share to see that the breaks went his way. Suppose, however, that (5.21) had initially been specified as $M_t = \beta_0 Q_t^{\beta_1} L_t^{\beta_2} \epsilon_{2t}$, which is simply (5.21) with $\beta_3 = 1$ and $\tilde{\beta}_3 = 0 = d_{30} = d_{31} = 0$. In this case, the reduced form would lead to estimates of $b_1 = d_{21}/d_{20}$, $b_2 = d_{11} - (d_{21}/d_{20})d_{10}$, and $\tilde{b}_0 = d_{01} - (d_{21}/d_{20})d_{00}$. Unhappily, however, it is no longer possible to express the $a_i$ solely in terms of the $d_{ij}$. The $a_i$ and Equation (5.20) are thus said to be *under-identified.*

Moreover, suppose that both $\tilde{\beta}_3 = 0$ *and* $\beta_2 = 0$, so that (5.21) becomes $M_t = \beta_0 Q_t^{\beta_1} \epsilon_{2t}$. Then the reduced form would lead to either of *two* estimates of $\beta_1$. That is, the solution of the equations could yield *either* $b_1 = d_{11}/d_{10}$ *or* $b_1 = d_{21}/d_{20}$. In this case, (5.21) is said to be *overidentified.*

The procedure whereby estimates of the structural parameters in a simultaneous-equation model are obtained from the least-squares estimates of the reduced-form equations is called *indirect least squares.* In general, the structural equations of a simultaneous-equation model can be written

$$\begin{aligned} &\theta_{11} y_{1t} + \cdots + \theta_{N1} y_{Nt} + \phi_{11} x_{1t} + \cdots + \phi_{M1} x_{Mt} + \epsilon_{1t} = 0, \\ &\quad\vdots \\ &\theta_{1N} y_{1t} + \cdots + \theta_{NN} y_{Nt} + \phi_{1N} x_{1t} + \cdots + \phi_{MN} x_{Mt} + \epsilon_{Nt} = 0, \end{aligned} \tag{5.22}$$

for $t = 1, \ldots, T$. Here, there are $N$ endogenous variables, the $y_{it}$; there are $M$ exogenous variables, the $x_{jt}$; there are $N$ simultaneous equations (one for each endogenous variable), each containing a random-disturbance term, the $\epsilon_{it}$. The $i$th structural equation could also be written

$$y_{it} = -\theta_{1i} y_{1t} - \cdots - \theta_{Ni} y_{Nt} - \phi_{1i} x_{1t} - \cdots - \phi_{Mi} x_{Mt} - \epsilon_{it}. \tag{5.22i}$$

with $\theta_{ii} = 1$. Similarly, the $i$th reduced-form equation would be written

$$y_{it} = \gamma_{1i} x_{1t} + \cdots + \gamma_{Mi} x_{Mt} + \xi_{it}. \tag{5.22ia}$$

Note that if we let $x_{1t} = 1$ $(t = 1, \ldots, T)$, $\phi_{1i}$ and $\gamma_{1i}$ become the constant terms in their respective equations.

Writing

$$\mathbf{y}_i = \begin{pmatrix} y_{i1} \\ \cdot \\ \cdot \\ \cdot \\ y_{iT} \end{pmatrix} \quad \text{and} \quad \mathbf{x}_j = \begin{pmatrix} x_{j1} \\ \cdot \\ \cdot \\ \cdot \\ x_{jT} \end{pmatrix}$$

with $\mathbf{X} = (\mathbf{x}_1, \ldots, \mathbf{x}_M)$,

$$\boldsymbol{\gamma}_i = \begin{pmatrix} \gamma_{1i} \\ \cdot \\ \cdot \\ \cdot \\ \gamma_{Mi} \end{pmatrix} \quad \text{and} \quad \boldsymbol{\xi}_i = \begin{pmatrix} \xi_{i1} \\ \cdot \\ \cdot \\ \cdot \\ \xi_{iT} \end{pmatrix},$$

the initial estimation problem is to obtain estimates of the reduced-form parameters from

$$\mathbf{y}_i = \mathbf{X}\boldsymbol{\gamma}_i + \boldsymbol{\xi}_i. \tag{5.22ib}$$

The estimate of $\boldsymbol{\gamma}_i$ will be a vector $\mathbf{d}_i$, given by (3.4) as

$$\mathbf{d}_i = (\mathbf{X}'\mathbf{X})^{-1}\mathbf{X}'\mathbf{y}_i. \tag{5.23}$$

With $\mathbf{D} = (\mathbf{d}_1, \ldots, \mathbf{d}_M)$, the estimates of the $\phi_{ij}$ and the estimates of the $\theta_{ik}$ will be determined as unique functions of $\mathbf{D}$ when the system of equations is just identified. In general, a *necessary* condition for the identifiability of a structural equation is that the number of exogenous variables excluded from it must be *at least* as great as the number of endogenous variables included in the equation, less one. The exact equality is necessary for exact identification.[11] In the model of (5.20) and (5.21), each equation contains two endogenous and two exogenous variables. Hence, each excludes one exogenous variable, and this equals the number of endogenous variables (two) less one. With $\beta_3 = 1$, there are only two exogenous variables, so that (5.20) excludes zero exogenous variables and is not identified. With $\beta_3 = 1$ and $\beta_2 = 0$, (5.21) excludes two exogenous variables and no endogenous variables; $2 > (2 - 1) = 1$, and the equation is overidentified.

## b. Two-Stage Least Squares

The problem in estimating (5.20) and (5.21) using ordinary least squares stems from the fact that the endogenous variables and the disturbances are not independent, but are correlated. Note, however, that if the disturbance term $\xi_{1t}$ in (5.21c) is subtracted from $\tilde{M}_t$ to give a new variable, $\hat{\tilde{M}}_t = \tilde{M}_t - \xi_{1t}$, $\hat{\tilde{M}}_t$ and $\tilde{\epsilon}_{1t}$ will now be independent and uncorrelated. In general, then, let $\theta_{ii} = 1$, and let $\boldsymbol{\theta}_i' = (\theta_{1i}, \ldots, \theta_{ji}, \ldots, \theta_{Ni})$ for $j \neq i$ and $\boldsymbol{\phi}_i' = (\phi_{1i}, \ldots, \phi_{Mi})$. Also, let $\mathbf{Y} = (\mathbf{y}_1, \ldots, \mathbf{y}_j, \ldots, \mathbf{y}_N)$ for $j \neq i$ and $\boldsymbol{\varepsilon}_i' = (\epsilon_{i1}, \ldots, \epsilon_{iT})$. The $i$th structural equation of (5.22) to be estimated is written

$$\mathbf{y}_i = -\mathbf{Y}\boldsymbol{\theta}_i - \mathbf{X}\boldsymbol{\phi}_i - \boldsymbol{\varepsilon}_i. \tag{5.22ic}$$

But, from (5.22ib), $\mathbf{y}_j = \mathbf{X}\boldsymbol{\gamma}_j + \boldsymbol{\xi}_j$. Let $\boldsymbol{\xi}' = (\boldsymbol{\xi}_1, \ldots, \boldsymbol{\xi}_j, \ldots, \boldsymbol{\xi}_N)$ for $j \neq i$, and $\boldsymbol{\gamma}' = (\boldsymbol{\gamma}_1, \ldots, \boldsymbol{\gamma}_j, \ldots, \boldsymbol{\gamma}_N)$ for $j \neq i$. Then, let us rewrite (5.22ic) as follows:

$$\begin{aligned} \mathbf{y}_i &= -\mathbf{Y}\boldsymbol{\theta}_i - \mathbf{X}\boldsymbol{\phi}_i - \boldsymbol{\varepsilon}_i + \boldsymbol{\xi}'\boldsymbol{\theta}_i - \boldsymbol{\xi}'\boldsymbol{\theta}_i, \\ &= -(\mathbf{Y} - \boldsymbol{\xi}')\boldsymbol{\theta}_i - \mathbf{X}\boldsymbol{\phi}_i - (\boldsymbol{\varepsilon}_i + \boldsymbol{\xi}'\boldsymbol{\theta}_i). \end{aligned} \tag{5.22id}$$

Although $\boldsymbol{\xi}'$ is not known, it can be estimated by $\mathbf{e}' = (\mathbf{e}_1, \ldots, \mathbf{e}_j, \ldots, \mathbf{e}_N)$ for $j \neq i$, the least-squares *residuals* of the reduced-form equations for all but the $i$th endogenous variable. Then, least squares could once again be applied to

$$\mathbf{y}_i = -(\mathbf{Y} - \mathbf{e}')\boldsymbol{\theta}_i - \mathbf{X}\boldsymbol{\phi}_i - (\boldsymbol{\varepsilon}_i + \mathbf{e}'\boldsymbol{\theta}_i), \tag{5.22ie}$$

for now both $\mathbf{X}$ and $(\mathbf{Y} - \mathbf{e}')$ are independent of the disturbance term. Thus, let $\hat{\mathbf{Y}}$ be the estimate (from the reduced form) of $\mathbf{Y}$, and let $-\boldsymbol{\varepsilon}_{iW}$ denote the disturbance term $\boldsymbol{\varepsilon}_i + \mathbf{e}'\boldsymbol{\theta}_i$. Ordinary least squares could be applied to

$$\mathbf{y}_i = -\hat{\mathbf{Y}}\boldsymbol{\theta}_i - \mathbf{X}\boldsymbol{\phi}_i + \boldsymbol{\varepsilon}_{iW} \tag{5.22if}$$

[11] Goldberger, *Econometric Theory*, pp. 313–316.

or

$$\mathbf{y}_i = \hat{\mathbf{Y}}_W \boldsymbol{\theta}_{iW} + \mathbf{X}_W \boldsymbol{\phi}_{iW} + \boldsymbol{\varepsilon}_{iW}, \tag{5.22if$'$}$$

where $\hat{\mathbf{Y}}_W$ is the matrix of reduced-form least-squares estimates of the endogenous variables included in the $i$th structural equation and $\mathbf{X}_W$ is a matrix of observations on the exogeneous variables included in the $i$th structural equation; $\boldsymbol{\theta}_{iW}$ and $\boldsymbol{\phi}_{iW}$ contain the negative of the nonzero components of $\boldsymbol{\theta}_i$ and $\boldsymbol{\phi}_i$, respectively. The procedure is called *two-stage least squares,* because the estimates for the structural parameters are obtained in two successive applications of least squares. The vector of estimates will therefore be given by

$$\mathbf{G} = [(\hat{\mathbf{Y}}_W, \mathbf{X}_W)'(\hat{\mathbf{Y}}_W, \mathbf{X}_W)]^{-1}(\hat{\mathbf{Y}}_W, \mathbf{X}_W)'\mathbf{y}_i, \tag{5.24}$$

which can be determined so long as the structural equation is not underidentified. Indeed, it can be shown that if the structural equation is exactly identified, the two-stage least-squares estimates and indirect least-squares estimates will coincide. Two-stage least squares has an additional advantage over indirect least squares in permitting the estimation of standard errors for the structural parameters,[12] a useful luxury not offered by indirect least squares. The approaches are illustrated in the the Appendix that follows.

[12] Goldberger, *Econometric Theory,* p. 333.

# Appendix to Chapter 5

## 5A.1 AN ILLUSTRATION OF SIMULTANEOUS-EQUATION ESTIMATION

Consider the stochastic model

$$Q_t = \alpha_0 L_t^{\alpha_1} K_t^{\alpha_2} M_t^{\alpha_3} \epsilon_{1t}, \tag{5.20}$$
$$M_t = \beta_0 Q_t^{\beta_1} L_t^{\beta_2} (\beta_3)^t \epsilon_{2t}. \tag{5.21}$$

Suppose the data for $T = 20$ production periods are as shown in columns 2–5 of Table 5.1. Applying ordinary least squares to perform the regressions for (5.20) and (5.21) yields the estimates in Table 5.2. The figures in parentheses are the ratios of the parameters to their standard errors with the equations in logarithmic (linear) form.

The reduced-form equations for (5.20) and (5.21) as estimated by least squares are indicated in Table 5.2. Columns 6 and 7 of Table 5.1 contain the estimates of

**TABLE 5.1**

| (1) $t$ | (2) $L_t$ | (3) $K_t$ | (4) $M_t$ | (5) $Q_t$ | (6) $\hat{M}_t$ | (7) $\hat{Q}_t$ |
|---|---|---|---|---|---|---|
| 1 | 100 | 5 | 10 | 6400 | 9.685 | 6205.5 |
| 2 | 110 | 5 | 10 | 6460 | 10.422 | 6351.2 |
| 3 | 110 | 5 | 11 | 6480 | 10.577 | 6489.8 |
| 4 | 112 | 5 | 11 | 6500 | 10.855 | 6539.3 |
| 5 | 115 | 6 | 11 | 6770 | 11.217 | 6902.8 |
| 6 | 113 | 7 | 11 | 6850 | 11.279 | 7081.8 |
| 7 | 115 | 7 | 12 | 7080 | 11.572 | 7133.4 |
| 8 | 120 | 7 | 12 | 7250 | 12.053 | 7277.3 |
| 9 | 120 | 7 | 12 | 7255 | 12.238 | 7266.8 |
| 10 | 140 | 6 | 13 | 7600 | 13.632 | 7562.8 |
| 11 | 145 | 6 | 14 | 7775 | 14.132 | 7685.7 |
| 12 | 160 | 8 | 15 | 8710 | 15.284 | 8618.4 |
| 13 | 161 | 8 | 16 | 8725 | 15.572 | 8633.2 |
| 14 | 172 | 8 | 17 | 9110 | 16.460 | 8910.6 |
| 15 | 183 | 8 | 17 | 9150 | 17.354 | 9178.0 |
| 16 | 185 | 7 | 18 | 9120 | 17.710 | 8934.0 |
| 17 | 191 | 7 | 19 | 9245 | 18.330 | 9064.8 |
| 18 | 200 | 7 | 19 | 9350 | 19.133 | 9263.0 |
| 19 | 220 | 7 | 20 | 9450 | 20.595 | 9701.2 |
| 20 | 235 | 7 | 22 | 9700 | 21.767 | 10125.2 |

$Q_t$ and $M_t$ based on these reduced-form least-squares equations and the data in columns 1–3 of Table 5.1. Thus, the structural parameter $\beta_3$ would be estimated from $\tilde{b}_3 = d_{31} - (d_{21}/d_{20})d_{30}$. From the second reduced-form equation, $d_{31} = \log 1.01495 = .00645$ and $d_{21} = .00927$; from the first reduced-form equation, $d_{20} = .23200$ and

$d_{30} = \log .99860 = -.00061$. Hence,

$$\tilde{b}_3 = .00645 - \left(\frac{.00927}{.23200}\right)(-.00061) = .00645 - (.03996)(-.00061) = .00647.$$

Since the system of equations is just identified, this estimate, and all other estimates of the structural parameters by indirect least squares, exactly correspond to the two-stage least-squares estimates, so labeled in Table 5.2. (*Note:* log 1.01501 = .00647.) These equations would be estimated by regressing $Q_t$ and $M_t$, respectively,

**TABLE 5.2**

Single-Equation Least Squares (Structural Equations)

$$Q_t = 740.56 \underset{(2.33927)}{L_t^{.29017}} \underset{(5.77225)}{K_t^{.20386}} \underset{(1.48992)}{M_t^{.20202}} e_{1t} \qquad (R^2 = .9879)$$

$$M_t = .07258 \underset{(1.20154)}{Q_t^{.27557}} \underset{(3.95442)}{L_t^{.53666}} \underset{(1.77012)}{(1.01160)^t} e_{2t} \qquad (R^2 = .9889)$$

Single-Equation Least Squares (Reduced Form)

$$Q_t = 427.98 \underset{(5.15851)}{L_t^{.49990}} \underset{(5.12007)}{K_t^{.23200}} \underset{(-.28986)}{(.99860)^t} e_{0t} \qquad (R^2 = .9863)$$

$$M_t = .55595 \underset{(4.07477)}{L_t^{.61406}} \underset{(.13158)}{K_t^{.00927}} \underset{(1.96371)}{(1.01495)^t} e_{1t} \qquad (R^2 = .9879)$$

Two-Stage Least Squares (Structural Equations)

$$Q_t = 404.85 \underset{(1.88318)}{L_t^{.55812}} \underset{(4.9222)}{K_t^{.23287}} \underset{(-.28962)}{M_t^{-.09485}} e_{1t}$$

$$M_t = .54948 \underset{(.13150)}{Q_t^{.03994}} \underset{(3.99307)}{L_t^{.59509}} \underset{(2.04327)}{(1.01501)^t} e_{2t}$$

against the $L_t$, $K_t$, $\hat{M}_t$ or $\hat{Q}_t$ data, respectively, as given in Table 5.1. The data would, of course, first have to be converted into logarithms. It is both interesting and important to note that the ordinary least-squares estimates and the indirect (or two-stage) least-squares estimates are, in a couple of instances, quite different. In view of the fairly large estimates, relative to the parameters, of a couple of standard errors, for example $s_{b_1} = .30370$ and $b_1 = .03994$, and since the sign of a parameter such as $\alpha_3$ is estimated to be negative (though one with a lesser sense of humor would prefer it to be positive[13]), one might do well to investigate the possibilities of model error. In particular, one might wish to reestimate the model with $\beta_1 = \alpha_3 = 0$, and this would entail ordinary least squares, as the simultaneous links would thereby be eliminated.

## 5A.2 AN ILLUSTRATION OF A COST EQUATION ESTIMATE

Table 5.3 presents data for the average output, in thousands of barrels, per brewery in the United States between 1946 and 1960, denoted $Q_t$, as well as cost per barrel figures, deflated by the wholesale commodity price index, denoted $C_{At}$. A simple linear regression on these data yields the least-squares estimate

$$C_{At} = 25.92286 + \underset{(4.67897)}{.01952 Q_t} + e_t \qquad (R^2 = .6459).$$

[13] That is, as a prior expectation one might hypothesize a positive causal relationship between the level of management personnel and output.

In view of the U-shape of the average cost curves frequently postulated in the theory, there has been a fairly common practice of fitting parabolic average cost curves to average cost data. In the present case, without the linear term, we would obtain the equation

$$C_{At} = \underset{}{29.20563} + \underset{(4.70507)}{.00003Q_t^2} + e_t \qquad (R^2 = .6485);$$

and, with the linear term,

$$C_{At} = 27.93382 + \underset{(.22093)}{.00748Q_t} + \underset{(.35868)}{.00002Q_t^2} + e_t \qquad (R^2 = .6500).$$

The simple correlation between $Q_t$ and $Q_t^2$ is $r = .99178$. The low ratios of the parameters to their standard errors in the multiple regression is a reflection of this collinearity between the exogenous variables. The latter causes the effects of the

**TABLE 5.3**

| | Cost per Barrel (Deflated) | Barrels per Brewer |
|---|---|---|
| 1946 | 32.73 | 217 |
| 1947 | 29.58 | 221 |
| 1948 | 29.86 | 237 |
| 1949 | 30.47 | 330 |
| 1950 | 30.68 | 308 |
| 1951 | 29.93 | 320 |
| 1952 | N/A | N/A |
| 1953 | 33.20 | 327 |
| 1954 | 34.59 | 359 |
| 1955 | 34.08 | 379 |
| 1956 | 34.12 | 387 |
| 1957 | 34.72 | 422 |
| 1958 | 34.51 | 456 |
| 1959 | 35.79 | 478 |
| 1960 | 35.31 | 511 |

independent variables to be distributed among the variables and makes it difficult to isolate these effects. Also, collinearity causes the standard errors of the regression parameters to be biased upwards, thereby reducing the *t*-ratios. In any case, either of the simple regressions would seem to be as informative as the multiple regression, and both suggest a gently rising average cost curve. It is important to note, however, that the $Q_t$ figures are "averages." The regressions would, therefore, tell us little about the cost curve of "a firm," even one producing within the range of these figures, and less about the industry giants producing well above a million barrels a year. The "average" firm is unlikely to be very "representative." In interpreting the results of a regression analysis, it will usually be wise to know a little something about the data that have provided the inputs.

## EXERCISES

1. Consider the production function $Q = \alpha_0 F_1^{\alpha_1} F_2^{\alpha_2}$ and the cost curve $C = W_1F_1 + W_2F_2$, where the $\alpha_i$ and $W_i$ are constants.

(a) Determine conditions for the $\alpha_i$ under which the firm will hire the factors at the point where $MPP_1/MPP_2 = W_1/W_2$.

(b) Sketch the total cost curve for: (i) $\alpha_1 + \alpha_2 < 1$; (ii) $\alpha_1 + \alpha_2 = 1$; (iii) $2 > \alpha_1 + \alpha_2 > 1$.

2. Consider the production function $Q = 1000F_1^{.2}F_2^{.3}F_3^{.4}$ and the cost curve $C = 20F_1 + 5F_1^2 + 25F_2 + 100F_3$.

(a) Derive and sketch the following curves:

(i) $TPP_1$; $APP_1$; $MPP_1$ (long run).

(ii) $W_1$; $MC_1$.

(b) Derive and sketch the firm's long-run and short-run average and marginal cost curves.

3. (a) Show that the solution to (5.3b) and (5.4b) is the same as the solution to (5.3a) and (5.4a).

(b) Solving this second problem via Lagrangian methods, interpret the Lagrangian multiplier.

4. Discuss the possibilities of having a factor exhibit a tendency similar to Giffen's Paradox.

5. If all wages and the firm's total expenditure were to change by a factor $\theta$, would the firm's output change? What about its employment of factor $j$? Discuss in detail.

6. Suppose that, in Exercise 1, $F_2$ is a measure of entrepreneurial services. Discuss the sorts of values that you might anticipate for $\alpha_2$ and defend your suggestions.

7. Show that two-stage least-squares estimates cannot be obtained for the structural equations of an underidentified system. Also, show that when the system is just identified, the two-stage least-squares estimates of the structural parameters will coincide with the indirect least-squares estimates.

8. The residuals calculated from the single-equation least-squares estimates in Table 5.2, in *logarithms*, for the $Q_t$ and $M_t$ equations respectively are as follows:

| | | | | |
|---|---|---|---|---|
| $e_{1t}$: | .01178 ($t$ = 1) | −.01226 (6) | .00382 (11) | .00671 (16) |
| | .00382 (2) | −.00776 (7) | .00920 (12) | .00386 (17) |
| | −.00320 (3) | −.00282 (8) | .00350 (13) | .00296 (18) |
| | −.00413 (4) | −.00252 (9) | .00861 (14) | −.00893 (19) |
| | −.00593 (5) | .00485 (10) | −.00270 (15) | −.01426 (20) |

| | | | | |
|---|---|---|---|---|
| $e_{2t}$: | .01102 ($t$ = 1) | −.00914 (6) | −.00262 (11) | .00571 (16) |
| | −.01729 (2) | .01562 (7) | −.01418 (12) | .01513 (17) |
| | .01874 (3) | −.00213 (8) | .00721 (13) | −.00194 (18) |
| | .00918 (4) | −.00720 (9) | .00797 (14) | −.00814 (19) |
| | −.00684 (5) | −.01891 (10) | −.01199 (15) | .00977 (20) |

The two-stage least-squares residuals are:

| | | | | |
|---|---|---|---|---|
| $e_{1t}$: | .01341 ($t$ = 1) | −.01445 (6) | .00502 (11) | .00895 (16) |
| | −.00261 (2) | −.00330 (7) | .00459 (12) | .00854 (17) |
| | −.00066 (3) | −.00163 (8) | .00460 (13) | .00406 (18) |
| | −.00262 (4) | −.00072 (9) | .00961 (14) | −.01140 (19) |
| | −.00844 (5) | .00214 (10) | −.00133 (15) | −.01376 (20) |

| | | | | |
|---|---|---|---|---|
| $e_{2t}$: | .01392 ($t$ = 1) | −.01087 (6) | −.00425 (11) | .00707 (16) |
| | −.01794 (2) | .01579 (7) | −.00814 (12) | .01559 (17) |
| | .01700 (3) | −.00200 (8) | .01178 (13) | −.00314 (18) |
| | .00575 (4) | −.00845 (9) | .01403 (14) | −.01273 (19) |
| | −.00848 (5) | −.02063 (10) | −.00895 (15) | .00463 (20) |

Are the single-equation residuals uncorrelated with all the independent variables in their respective equations? What about the two-stage residuals? What would you infer from these results?

9. Suppose that the actual values of the reduced-form parameters in the production model are as follows:

$$\gamma_{00} = 400; \quad \gamma_{10} = .5000; \quad \gamma_{20} = .2500; \quad \gamma_{30} = 1.0100;$$
$$\gamma_{01} = .5000; \quad \gamma_{11} = .6000; \quad \gamma_{21} = .0200; \quad \gamma_{31} = 1.0200.$$

The values for $t$, $L_t$, and $K_t$ are as given in Table 5.1. The actual disturbances, however, are as follows (in logarithms):

| | | | | |
|---|---|---|---|---|
| $\epsilon_{0t}$: | .00505 ($t$ = 1) | .00958 (6) | −.01448 (11) | −.01143 (16) |
| | .00456 (2) | −.00160 (7) | .00857 (12) | −.00069 (17) |
| | .00217 (3) | −.00136 (8) | −.00847 (13) | −.00264 (18) |
| | .00463 (4) | −.00327 (9) | .00409 (14) | −.01379 (19) |
| | −.00075 (5) | .00892 (10) | −.00265 (15) | −.01344 (20) |

| | | | | |
|---|---|---|---|---|
| $\epsilon_{1t}$: | .00460 ($t$ = 1) | .01703 (6) | −.00898 (11) | −.00203 (16) |
| | .01395 (2) | .01556 (7) | −.01084 (12) | −.00817 (17) |
| | −.01276 (3) | .00578 (8) | .01400 (13) | −.00848 (18) |
| | −.01791 (4) | .00704 (9) | .01576 (14) | −.00423 (19) |
| | −.00317 (5) | −.00845 (10) | .01175 (15) | −.02060 (20) |

Determine $Q_t$ and $M_t$ and estimate $\alpha_i$ and $\beta_i$ anew using both two-stage and single-equation least squares. How good are the estimates relative to the known, actual, values? Does this problem suggest an approach for studying the merits of alternative estimation methods? Discuss in detail!

10. Derive estimators for the standard errors of the structural parameters determined via two-stage least squares.

# 6

# THE NEOCLASSICAL THEORY OF PRODUCT SUPPLY: Factor Demand

## 6.1 INTRODUCTION

It is tempting to carry the analogy between the theories of consumer behavior and production still further and to derive the firm's demand curves for its factors of production as we derived the consumer's demand curves for final commodities. Whereas, however, if its assumptions are accepted, the theory of consumer behavior provides a complete description of how the consumer can achieve his *primary* objective of utility maximization, the theory of production indicates only how the firm can achieve a *subsidiary* objective of output maximization or cost minimization. Achieving this subsidiary objective is a necessary precondition for achieving profit maximization, but it is not sufficient, and neoclassical theory assumes that profit maximization is the firm's primary goal.

For the present assume the firm's guiding principle *is* profit maximization. The firm is also assumed to produce a single product, and to make decisions *as if* it were operating in a world of certainty and were guided into the future by a set of specific functions about which specific judgments have been reached. In this setting, the firm's demand for its factors of production will depend upon (1) its desired level of output, (2) the prices of all factors, and (3) technological conditions. In turn, the desired level of output will depend upon the price for which the product can be sold and the cost for which it can be produced. Through this chain of interrelationships, factor demand becomes a *derived* demand influenced by technology, cost, and product demand considerations.

## 6.2 THE FIRM'S SECOND PROBLEM

The firm's production function is $Q = q(F_1, \ldots, F_m)$. Each factor is assumed to supply $F_i$ units at a wage of $W_i$, where $W_i = w_i(F_i)$. It will be assumed that all production during a given interval $T$ is sold at a net price of $P$ per unit, satisfying the specific demand schedule $P = D(Q, V)$. Producing $Q$ units will therefore generate a net total revenue of $R = PQ$. We let all costs be included as part of production costs.[1] As before, then, total costs will be given by $C = \sum_i W_i F_i$. Total profit will be given by $\pi = R - C$.

The firm's problem now is to select values for the $F_i$ such as to maximize profit, $\pi$. That is,

$$\text{Maximize} \quad \pi = R - C = PQ - \sum_i W_i F_i. \tag{6.1}$$

Let us first consider the long run, in which all factors are variable and continuous. All functions are assumed twice differentiable. For an entrepreneur who knows calculus, (6.1) is then an easy problem to solve. As first-order conditions, he seeks values for the $F_i$ such that $\partial\pi/\partial F_i = 0$ $(i = 1, \ldots, m)$:

$$\frac{\partial \pi}{\partial F_i} = \left(\frac{\partial D}{\partial Q}\right)\left(\frac{\partial Q}{\partial F_i}\right) Q + D\left(\frac{\partial Q}{\partial F_i}\right) - \left(\frac{\partial w_i}{\partial F_i}\right) F_i - W_i = 0, \qquad i = 1, \ldots, m. \tag{6.2}$$

Rearranging terms,

$$\left[\left(\frac{\partial D}{\partial Q}\right) Q + D\right]\left[\frac{\partial Q}{\partial F_i}\right] = \frac{\partial w_i}{\partial F_i} F_i + W_i, \qquad i = 1, \ldots, m. \tag{6.3}$$

Here, $\partial R/\partial Q = \partial(PQ)/\partial Q = (\partial D/\partial Q)Q + D$ gives the change in total revenue resulting from an infinitesimal change in quantity sold. In what by now is a presumably familiar fashion, this is called *marginal revenue* ($MR$). $[\partial Q/\partial F_i]$ and $[(\partial w_i/\partial F_i)F_i + W_i]$ were previously defined as the marginal physical product and marginal cost of factor $i$. Hence, the first-order necessary conditions for a profit maximum are that the firm should employ each of its factors at levels such that $[MR]\cdot[MPP_i] = MC_i$. Defining $[MR]\cdot[MPP_i] = MRP_i$ to be the *marginal revenue product* of factor $i$, the long-run profit-maximizing condition becomes the equating of marginal revenue product to marginal factor cost for each factor of production.

These equalities will be readily achieved, however, if the firm is carrying out production in accordance with the previously derived tangency conditions for least-cost production of a given output. Recall from the production optimality conditions that $[(\partial w_i/\partial F_i)F_i + W_i]/(\partial Q/\partial F_i) = 1/\lambda = \partial C/\partial Q$ $(i = 1, \ldots, m)$. Now, dividing both sides of (6.3) by $\partial Q/\partial F_i$, we obtain

$$\left(\frac{\partial D}{\partial Q}\right) Q + D = \frac{\left(\dfrac{\partial w_i}{\partial F_i}\right) F_i + W_i}{\dfrac{\partial Q}{\partial F_i}} = \frac{\partial C}{\partial Q}, \tag{6.4}$$

or marginal revenue ($MR$) equals marginal cost ($MC$). Thus the firm that follows the production optimality conditions *and* simultaneously equates marginal revenue product to marginal factor cost for any one factor will (1) automatically equate these for all factors and (2) maximize profit by equating marginal revenue to marginal cost.

It should be emphasized, however, that this will yield a profit *maximum* only if the second-order conditions are satisfied. That is, if the principal minors of the matrix

[1] As previously noted, costs such as advertising costs are not production costs. These could be included in an additional "fixed cost" term that at the present stage would add little to the analysis and would absorb a scarce resource—a Latin letter.

$[\partial^2\pi/\partial F_i\,\partial F_j]$ alternate in sign with $\partial^2\pi/\partial F_1^2 < 0$, $(\partial^2\pi/\partial F_1^2)(\partial^2\pi/\partial F_2^2) > (\partial^2\pi/\partial F_1\,\partial F_2)^2$, and so on, when evaluated at the point where $\partial\pi/\partial F_i = 0$. A particularly interesting implication of these second-order conditions is the requirement that

$$\frac{\partial^2\pi}{\partial F_i^2} = \frac{\partial[\partial R/\partial F_i]}{\partial F_i} - \frac{\partial^2 C}{\partial F_i^2} < 0,$$

or

$$\frac{\partial[\partial R/\partial F_i]}{\partial F_i} < \frac{\partial^2 C}{\partial F_i^2}, \qquad i = 1, \ldots, m. \tag{6.5}$$

The latter inequality states that, for each factor, the marginal factor cost curve must be increasing more rapidly than the marginal revenue product curve in the neighborhood of the point where the two curves intersect.[2]

Now, this is extremely important. Verbally, (6.3) and (6.5) assert that additional units of a factor of production will be hired by the profit-maximizing firm as long as these units effect additional production that adds more to total revenue than to total cost. In effect, the inequality (6.5) becomes more important than the equality (6.3). This will be particularly true when the relevant functions are afflicted with discontinuities. Then, absent a unique derivative at each of the points of discontinuity, it may not be possible to determine (6.3). Still, (6.5) tells us that if there is a discontinuity at $F_i = \bar{F}_i$, and if (1) $\partial C/\partial F_i > \partial R/\partial F_i$ at higher values of $F_i$ and (2) $\partial C/\partial F_i < \partial R/\partial F_i$ at lower values of $F_i$, then $\bar{F}_i$ is the optimum. This is so, for at $F_i > \bar{F}_i$ ($F_i < \bar{F}_i$) total cost increases more (decreases less) than does total revenue. If a point such as $\bar{F}_i$ exists, it will be called an equilibrium point, for once it is reached there is no basis for change unless something in the system is altered. As we shall see in greater detail in Section 6.2c, the inequality analysis is imperative with fixed technological coefficients where the isoquant has a discontinuity at the corner.[3]

[2] There may, of course, be more than one such point. The optimum would then be the maximum of these; or, if for all values of $F_i$ greater than a value at which (6.3) holds, the inequality in (6.5) were reversed, $F_i$ would be increased without bound. Having noted the multi-intersection possibility, we shall feel fewer qualms for neglecting it in the remaining discussion.

As Mrs. Robinson has noted, however, "no monopolist will hit upon the exact point at which his net revenue will be greatest unless he has an accurate and enlightened system of cost accounting and a good knowledge of the market conditions in which he has to sell .... As long as marginal revenue exceeds marginal cost, there will be a tendency for him to increase output, and as long as marginal revenue falls short of marginal cost, there will be a tendency for him to contract output, and he will be in equilibrium at the monopoly point .... It may happen, however, that there are several points of equilibrium and if he hits upon one of them there will be no tendency for him to move, even though a greater net revenue could be gained at some other point." Joan Robinson, *The Economics of Imperfect Competition* (London: Macmillan and Co., Ltd., 1950), pp. 56–57.

[3] The failure to appreciate the importance of the second-order conditions may lead one to the following sort of erroneous argument: " ... it is not surprising that most firms fail to think in marginal terms. Even in the cases where firms do calculate the probable effects of price variation, the change in price is usually of some appreciable size, and is associated with changes in marketing strategy, and sometimes with the technical conditions of production. While it is reasonable to accept profit maximization as the ruling motive in the business world, marginalism is unhelpful in the presence of discontinuities. And discontinuity is the rule rather than the exception." H. F. Lydall, "Conditions of New Entry and the Theory of Price," *Oxford Economic Papers*, **7**:2 (Oct. 1955), 310.

## a. Long-Run Factor Demand[4]

In the long run the firm will employ more of a factor of production as long as the additional cost of hiring an additional unit is less than the factor's marginal revenue product. The firm's total demand for factor $i$, at any given $MC_i$, will be determined by $MRP_i$. Hence, *if* the firm decides to employ the factor, the marginal revenue product curve represents the firm's demand curve for the factor of production. Moreover, since $MRP_i = [MR]\cdot[MPP_i]$, the following are clear: (1) depending as it does on marginal revenue, factor demand is a derived demand, intimately related to product demand; and (2) depending as it does on marginal physical product, factor demand will depend upon the production function *and* the levels at which *all other* factors are employed. The latter will in turn depend upon all factor costs.

As an illustration, consider Figure 6.1. The curves marked $MRP_i$, $MC_i$, and $W_i$ are as previously defined. $MRP_i = [MR]\cdot[MPP_i]$ is calculated at an $MPP_i$ deter-

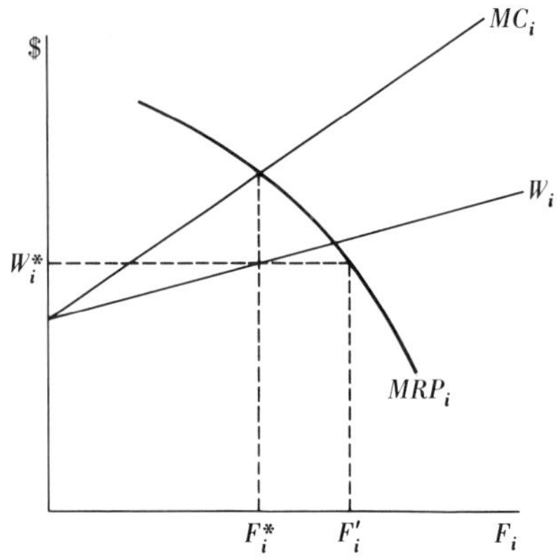


Fig. 6.1

mined by holding all other factors fixed at their long-run optimal levels in accordance with (6.3). Thus, (6.3) is solved to determine *all* $F_i$ ($i = 1, \ldots, m$). Then, with all other factors fixed at their optimal levels, it is possible to determine $MPP_i$ and consequently $MRP_i$. The graph indicates that the firm will hire $F_i^*$ units of factor $i$ since, at $F_i^*$, $MRP_i = MC_i$; and the inequality (6.5) holds in the neighborhood of $F_i^*$. Note that as far as the firm is concerned, there is no new information in this graph. $F_i^*$ would already have been determined together with the values for the other factors that were required in order to draw the graphs. Figure 6.1 merely depicts what the mathematics has already told us.

The firm pays each unit of the factor a wage of $W_i^*$ in accordance with the factor supply schedule. Of course, if *additional* quantities of the factor could be purchased for $W_i^*$, the firm *would like* to employ $F_i'$ units as indicated by $MRP_i$. At *that* wage, each additional unit of $i$ adds more to revenue than it does to cost. But, additional

[4] Although much of the subsequent analysis of factor demand has Robinsonian roots, the style and flavor are strictly Bishopian, as in Robert L. Bishop, "A Firm's Short-Run and Long-Run Demands for a Factor," *Western Economic Journal*, V:2 (March 1967), 122–140.

units of the factor cannot be purchased at this wage. The rising supply curve prevents this. Hence, at the wage rate $W_i^*$ that is paid, demand for the factor exceeds supply. Supply and demand will be equal, given that the $MRP_i$ curve is downward sloping at the equilibrium point, only if the factor supply curve is a horizontal line. If the supply curve is downward sloping at this point, it is readily demonstrated that, at the equilibrium wage, supply exceeds demand. In this case, however, because the factor's wage declines with increased employment, the units purchased beyond the supply-equals-demand point add less to cost than they contribute to revenue, and the firm permits itself the luxury of purchasing them.[5]

Moreover, the firm's total revenue is given by $R = R(F_i/F_i) = (R/F_i)F_i$. Define $R/F_i$, the total revenue per unit of factor $i$, to be the *average revenue product* of factor $i$ or $ARP_i$. Further, $R/F_i = [PQ/F_i] = P[Q/F_i]$ = average revenue (or price) multiplied by the average physical product of factor $i$. $VMP_i$, the *value of the marginal*

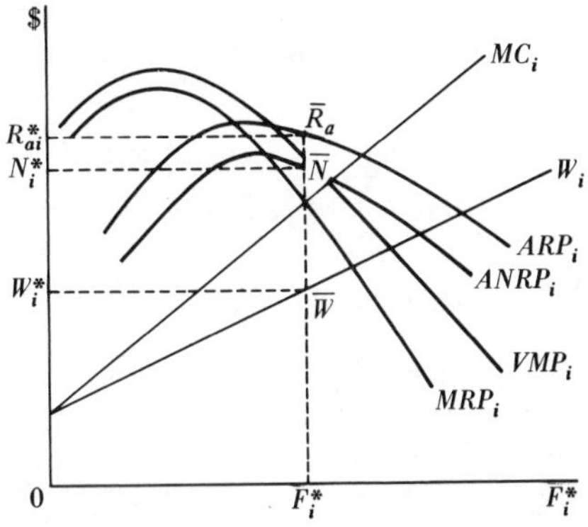


Fig. 6.2

*physical product*, is similarly defined as $P \cdot [MPP_i]$. With $MRP_i = MR \cdot [MPP_i]$, $VMP_i$ and $MRP_i$ will differ as marginal and average revenue differ. Further, if the demand curve is downward sloping, as it is commonly presumed to be, from the usual average-marginal relationship, marginal revenue will be less than average revenue. Consequently, $MRP_i$ will be below $VMP_i$. They will be equal only if the firm's demand curve is horizontal. Then, $P = MR$ and $VMP_i = MRP_i$. Thus, they will be equal with pure competition in the product market and a "large enough" number of sellers. Further, $[ARP_i] \cdot F_i = P[Q/F_i]F_i = R$ and $\partial R/\partial F_i = [\partial R/\partial Q] \cdot [\partial Q/\partial F_i] = MRP_i$. Thus, the $MRP_i$ curve is bound to the $ARP_i$ curve, with the usual average-marginal relationships holding between them. For this reason, in Figure 6.2, $MRP_i$ is drawn to intersect $ARP_i$ where $ARP_i$ is a maximum.

Now, at the profit-maximizing output level, the total cost of factor $i$ is given by $W_i^*F_i^*$, the area of the rectangle $OF_i^*\bar{W}W_i^*$ in Figure 6.2. The average revenue that accrues per unit of $F_i^*$ employed is $\bar{R}_a = R_{ai}^*$, the subscript $a$ implying an average revenue. *Total* revenue $R^*$ is equal to $R_{ai}^*F_i^*$, the area of the rectangle $OF_i^*\bar{R}_aR_{ai}^*$. The difference between the two areas, the rectangle $W_i^*\bar{W}\bar{R}_aR_{ai}^*$, is given by $R_{ai}^*F_i^* - W_i^*F_i^*$.

[5] Note that if the factor supply curve is downward sloping and $\partial[\partial R/\partial F_i]/\partial F_i > \partial^2 C/\partial F_i^2$, the situation is *unstable* in the sense that the firm will want to keep hiring additional units of the factor ad infinitum, or until its wage is driven to zero.

The latter determines the net revenue available to purchase factors *other than* factor $i$. If this net revenue exceeds the total cost of the other factors, given by $\sum_{j \neq i} W_j^* F_j^*$, the firm makes a profit; if the net revenue is below this total cost, the firm must suffer a loss; if they are equal, there is zero profit. In the long run all factors are variable, and it is assumed that the profit-maximizing firm will not abide losses. Hence, if

$$R_{ai}^* F_i^* - W_i^* F_i^* < \sum_{j \neq i} W_j^* F_j^*,$$

the firm will halt production. If we move $W_i^* F_i^*$ to the right-hand side of the inequality, the summation then holds over all $j = 1, \ldots, m$. The left-hand side is then simply $R_{ai}^* F_i^* = R^*$. Thus the inequality may be rewritten to indicate that

$$F_i = 0 \qquad \text{if} \qquad R^* < \sum_{j=1}^{m} W_j^* F_j^*.$$

That is, when total revenue is less than total cost, the firm will cease to operate.

We could, then, simply subtract $\sum_{j \neq i} W_j^* F_j^*$, the total cost of all other factors, from $R$ to get the *net total revenue product* of factor $i$, or $R - \sum_{j \neq i} W_j^* F_j^*$. Note that we subtract from $R$ rather than $R^*$. This is because we can compute a net total revenue product for *any* level at which we might employ factor $i$. It is only at $F_i = F_i^*$ that $R = R^*$, given the optimal employment of the other factors. In the customary manner

$$\frac{\left[R - \sum_{j \neq i} W_j^* F_j^*\right]}{F_i} = ANRP_i$$

gives the *average net revenue product* of factor $i$—that is, net of *all* other factor costs. The curve marginal to the net total revenue product curve is determined by

$$\frac{\partial \left[R - \sum_{j \neq i} W_j^* F_j^*\right]}{\partial F_i} = \frac{\partial R}{\partial F_i} = MRP_i.$$

Hence, $MRP_i$ and $ANRP_i$ will satisfy the usual average-marginal relationship and are so drawn in Figure 6.2. Total profit at the *optimal* employment level of factor $i$ is given by

$$\begin{aligned}
\pi^* = R^* - C^* &= \left(\frac{R^*}{F_i^*}\right) F_i^* - \sum_{i=1}^{m} W_i^* F_i^* \\
&= (ARP_i) F_i^* - W_i^* F_i^* - \sum_{j \neq i}^{m} W_j^* F_j^* \left(\frac{F_i^*}{F_i^*}\right) \\
&= \left[ARP_i - \sum_{j \neq i} W_j^* \frac{F_j^*}{F_i^*}\right] F_i^* - W_i^* F_i^* \\
\pi^* &= [ANRP_i - W_i^*] F_i^*.
\end{aligned}$$

Hence, in Figure 6.2, total profit is given by the area of the rectangle $W_i^* \bar{W}\bar{N}N_i^*$. Consequently, in the long run, as long as $W_i^* \leq ANRP_i$ the firm will make a profit or break even and continue to produce. Thus, the firm would be willing to purchase factor $i$ in accordance with the $MRP_i$ curve at all wages at or below the maximum of the $ANRP_i$ curve; at any wage above this point, the firm will cease to operate. Hence, we can represent the demand for factor $i$ by the $MRP_i$ curve at wages below or at the maximum $ANRP_i$, and by the vertical axis (that is, zero demand for factor $i$) at wages above the maximum.[6] The firm will never pay a wage to factor $i$ greater than the maximum of $ANRP_i$.

It should be emphasized, however, that the exact portion of $MRP_i$ that can be considered to correspond to a demand curve will depend upon the $ANRP_i$ curve, and the latter need not be as conveniently concave as it has been drawn in Figure 6.2. Further,

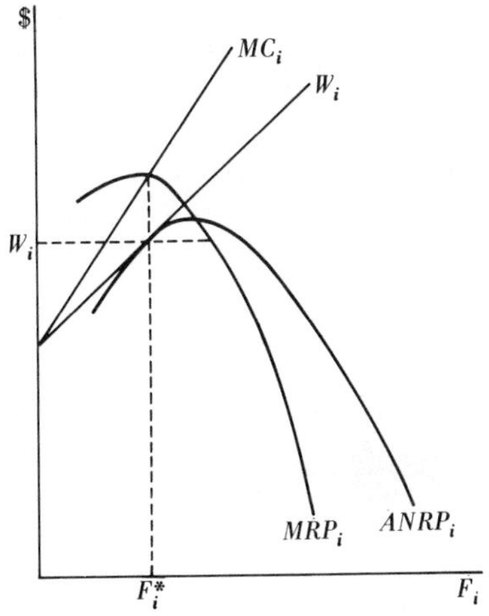


Fig. 6.3

suppose that $MRP_i = MC_i$ at a level of $F_i$ such that, at that level of employment, $MC_i > ANRP_i \geq W_i$. In this case, as illustrated in Figure 6.3 with $W_i = ANRP_i$, the amount of the factor that the firm *would like* to purchase at a wage of $W_i$ is given by the $MRP_i$ curve. The $MRP_i$ curve below the maximum $ANRP_i$ is still the demand curve for the factor, but a portion of this demand remains unsatisfied at the equilibrium wage.[7]

## b. Short-Run Factor Demand

The firm's short- and long-run factor demand schedules differ (or coincide) in a manner akin to the relationship between the consumer's short- and long-run demand schedules. Differences are effected by the fixity of certain factors in the

[6] There is actually a two-point indeterminacy at the maximum $ANRP_i$, since the firm is indifferent between producing and earning zero profit or not producing and earning zero profit. To avoid this indeterminacy the firm is assumed to produce at this point.
[7] This feature is bothersome only if one introduces into the analysis some preconceived prejudices about supply having to equal demand.

short run. In particular, with factors $k + 1$ through $m$ fixed at $\bar{F}_i$ ($i = k + 1, \ldots, m$) in the short run, the firm will incur a total fixed cost of

$$\sum_{i=k+1}^{m} W_i\bar{F}_i = K.$$

Short-run profit is given by

$$\pi_S = PQ - \sum_{i=1}^{k} W_iF_i - K \tag{6.6}$$

and maximized, with respect to the variable $F_i$, where

$$\frac{\partial \pi_S}{\partial F_i} = \left(\frac{\partial R}{\partial Q}\right)\left(\frac{\partial Q}{\partial F_i}\right) - \left(\frac{\partial w_i}{\partial F_i}\right)F_i - W_i = 0,$$

or

$$MRP_{iS} = MC_i; \qquad \frac{\partial(MRP_{iS})}{\partial F_i} < \frac{\partial(MC_i)}{\partial F_i}, \qquad i = 1, \ldots, k, \tag{6.7}$$

and $MRP_{iS}$ is the short-run marginal revenue product of factor $i$.

The firm's net total revenue—that is, net solely of fixed costs—will be given by $PQ - K$. With the levels of the $k - 1$ variable factors held constant at *their* optimal levels $F_j^*$ ($j = 1, \ldots, k, j \neq i$), and given associated wage levels $W_j^*$, short-run average net revenue product of factor $i$ is now given by

$$ANRP_{iS} = \left[PQ - K - \sum_{j\neq i} W_j^*F_j^*\right]\left(\frac{1}{F_i}\right).$$

When the wage of factor $i$ at $F_i^*$ is $W_i^*$, short-run profit is given by

$$\pi_S^* = PQ - K - \sum_{j\neq i}^{k} W_j^*F_j^* - W_i^*F_i^*.$$

If the firm were to halt operations, short-run profit would be given by $\bar{\pi}_S = -K$; that is, a loss equal to total fixed cost would be incurred. Hence, the firm will hire the variable factors as long as $\pi_S^* \geq \bar{\pi}_S$, or

$$PQ - \sum_{j=1}^{k} W_j^*F_j^* \geq 0;$$

that is, as long as total revenue exceeds total *variable* cost. Dividing both sides of the last inequality by $F_i^*$ reveals that the firm will pay factor $i$ a wage of $W_i^*$ as long as

$$\frac{PQ}{F_i^*} - W_i^* - \sum_{j\neq i}^{k} W_j^* \frac{F_j^*}{F_i^*} \geq 0$$

or equivalently

$$\frac{\left[PQ - \sum_{j\neq i}^{k} W_j^*F_j^*\right]}{F_i^*} \geq W_i^*.$$

The profit-maximizing firm in the short run will pay a variable factor a wage as high as but no higher than the factor's average net revenue product, net only of the other *variable* factors' total cost given their employment at optimal production levels. Denote this average net revenue product by $ANRP_{iVS}$. Clearly, $ANRP_{iVS} \geq ANRP_{iS}$, since they differ only in that the latter contains a $(-K/F_i)$ term not included in the former. The firm's short-run factor demand schedule is thus segmented into the short-run marginal revenue product curve, $MRP_{iS}$, at wages at or below the maximum $ANRP_{iVS}$, and the vertical axis at wages above this maximum (see footnote 6). With this as its demand curve for the factor, the firm might thereby suffer a loss in the short run, but as long as it covers its variable costs it will continue in production.

As a particularly illuminating illustration, suppose that *all* factors but factor $i$ are fixed in the short run. Then, $ANRP_{iVS} = ARP_i$. Figure 6.2 will once again suffice to depict this case. $ANRP_{iS}$ will be net of *all* other factor costs. Hence, the area of the rectangle $W_i^* \bar{W} \bar{N} N_i^*$ gives short-run profit, or

$$\left( \frac{\left[ PQ - \sum_{j \neq i}^{m} W_j \bar{F}_j \right]}{F_i^*} - W_i^* \right) F_i^* = R - C = \pi_S^*.$$

The area of the rectangle $OF_i^* \bar{R}_a \bar{R}_{ai}^*$ gives total revenue, or $(PQ/F_i^*)F_i^* = PQ = R$. The area of the rectangle $N_i^* \bar{N} \bar{R}_a R_{ai}^*$ gives total fixed cost, or

$$\left( \frac{PQ}{F_i^*} - \frac{\left[ PQ - \sum_{j \neq i}^{m} W_j \bar{F}_j \right]}{F_i^*} \right) F_i^* = \sum_{j \neq i}^{m} W_j \bar{F}_j.$$

It may also be seen that, short run or long, if the firm perceives its product demand curve as being infinitely elastic—that is, $\eta = (\partial Q/\partial P)(P/Q) = -\infty$ and $\partial P/\partial Q$ may to all intents and purposes be taken as zero—then $MR = (\partial P/\partial Q)Q + P = (0)Q + P = P$. In this case, $VMP_i = MRP_i$ and factor $i$ is employed at a level $F_i^{**}$ at which $MC_i = MRP_i = VMP_i$. Moreover, since it is assumed that $\partial P/\partial Q \leq 0$, the $MRP_i$ curve with infinitely elastic demand will be *above* the $MRP_i$ curve with finite elasticity at any given price. In effect, the $MRP_i$ curve is shifted *up* to coincide with the $VMP_i$ curve. Hence, $F_i^{**} > F_i^*$. Therefore the fact that the firm does have a downward-sloping demand curve and can exercise control over price in turn results in lower employment of the factors of production than would otherwise be the case.

### c. Discontinuities and Marginal Inequalities

Neither the $MRP_i$ curve nor the $MC_i$ curve will necessarily be continuous. All the cost functions will be discontinuous when, for example, the supply curve of a factor is a step function. In this case, the wage required by the factor will be $W_{ik}$ so long as $F_{ik} \leq F_i < F_{i(k+1)}$. Discontinuities in the $MC_i$ curve will exist at each of the steps $F_{ik}$. The revenue product functions will be discontinuous when, for example, the production function is discontinuous, owing say to fixed technological coefficients, or when the firm's demand curve has one or more kinks.

The importance of the second-order conditions and the marginal inequalities is highlighted when there are discontinuities in the functions employed in decision making. In particular, consider the case of fixed technological coefficients. In the long run, when all factors are variable, the firm will always want to employ its factors at a "corner" of an isoquant. This means that each factor $i$ will be employed in fixed proportion, $a_i$, to total output, or $F_i = a_iQ$. Therefore, total output as a function of factor $j$'s employment will be given by $Q = F_j/a_j$. Now, profit is given by

$$\pi = PQ - \sum_i W_iF_i = P\left(\frac{F_j}{a_j}\right) - \sum_i W_iF_i.$$

But $F_i = a_iQ = a_i(F_j/a_j) = (a_i/a_j)F_j$. We may therefore substitute for $F_i$ in the profit equation and write

$$\pi = \frac{PF_j}{a_j} - \sum_i W_i\left(\frac{a_i}{a_j}\right)F_j;$$

$$\frac{d\pi}{dF_j} = \left(\frac{\partial P}{\partial Q}\right)\left(\frac{1}{a_j}\right)\left(\frac{F_j}{a_j}\right) + \frac{P}{a_j} - \sum_{i=1}^{m}\left[\left(\frac{dW_i}{dF_i}\right)\left(\frac{a_i}{a_j}\right)^2 F_j + W_i\left(\frac{a_i}{a_j}\right)\right].$$

The total derivative $d\pi/dF_j$ is used rather than the partial derivative $\partial\pi/\partial F_j$ as *all other* factors are permitted to vary along with $F_j$ in order to maintain the fixed proportions among factors. Thus,

$$\begin{aligned}\frac{d\left[\sum_i W_i\left(\frac{a_i}{a_j}\right)F_j\right]}{dF_j} &= \sum_i \left(\frac{a_i}{a_j}\right)F_j\left[\frac{dW_i}{dF_j}\right] + \sum_i W_i\left(\frac{a_i}{a_j}\right)\left[\frac{dF_j}{dF_j}\right]\\ &= \sum_i \left(\frac{a_i}{a_j}\right)F_j\left[\left(\frac{\partial W_i}{\partial F_i}\right)\left(\frac{dF_i}{dF_j}\right)\right] + \sum_i W_i\left(\frac{a_i}{a_j}\right)\\ &= \sum_i \left(\frac{a_i}{a_j}\right)F_j\left[\frac{dW_i}{dF_i}\right]\left(\frac{a_i}{a_j}\right) + \sum_i W_i\left(\frac{a_i}{a_j}\right),\end{aligned}$$

since

$$\frac{\partial W_i}{\partial F_i} = \frac{dW_i}{dF_i} \quad \text{when } W_i = w_i(F_i) \quad \text{and} \quad \frac{d\left[F_i = \left(\frac{a_i}{a_j}\right)F_j\right]}{dF_j} = \left(\frac{a_i}{a_j}\right).$$

Letting $(a_i/a_j)F_j = F_i$ in the first term under the summation sign, and factoring out an $(a_i/a_j)$,

$$\begin{aligned}\sum_{i=1}^{m}\left[\left(\frac{dW_i}{dF_i}\right)\left(\frac{a_i}{a_j}\right)^2 F_j + W_i\left(\frac{a_i}{a_j}\right)\right] &= \sum_{i=1}^{m}\left(\frac{a_i}{a_j}\right)\left[\left(\frac{dw_i}{dF_i}\right)F_i + W_i\right]\\ &= \sum_{i=1}^{m}\left(\frac{a_i}{a_j}\right)MC_i.\end{aligned}$$

Furthermore, $(\partial P/\partial Q)(F_j/a_j) + P = MR$. We therefore require, as first-order conditions for profit maximization,

$$\frac{d\pi}{dF_j} = MR\left(\frac{1}{a_j}\right) - \sum_{i=1}^{m}\left(\frac{a_i}{a_j}\right) MC_i = 0$$

or

$$MR = \sum_{i=1}^{m} a_i MC_i. \tag{6.8}$$

To establish the second-order conditions, we compute

$$\frac{d^2\pi}{dF_j^2} = \frac{\partial\left(\dfrac{MR}{a_j}\right)}{\partial Q}\frac{dQ}{dF_j} - \left[\frac{d\left[\sum_i\left(\dfrac{a_i}{a_j}\right) MC_i\right]}{dF_i}\right]\frac{dF_i}{dF_j}$$

$$= \frac{\left[\dfrac{\partial(MR)}{\partial Q}\right]}{a_j^2} - \sum_i\left[\frac{d(MC_i)}{dF_i}\right]\left(\frac{a_i}{a_j}\right)^2.$$

The sufficiency condition $d^2\pi/dF_j^2 < 0$ becomes

$$\frac{\partial(MR)}{\partial Q} - \sum_i a_i^2\left[\frac{d(MC_i)}{dF_i}\right] < 0. \tag{6.9}$$

That is, profit is maximized at an output where (1) marginal revenue equals the weighted sum of marginal factor costs, weighted by the factors' respective technological coefficients, so long as at that output (2) marginal revenue is decreasing more rapidly than the weighted average of the marginal factor costs, with the *squares* of the respective technological coefficients being the weights.

With $Q$ thus determined, the $F_i$ are uniquely determined. We readily determine each factor's long-run demand curve by letting "it" be "factor $j$" and computing $MR \cdot MPP_j = MR/a_j = MRP_j$.

In the short run suppose all factors but factor $j$ are fixed. Then

$$Q \le \min_{i \ne j}\left[\frac{\bar{F}_i}{a_i}\right] = \frac{\bar{F}_k}{a_k}.$$

That is, output is restricted by the level of $F_k$. The short-run profit function will be written in the following manner:

$$\begin{cases} \pi_{1S} = PQ - W_jF_j - \sum_{i \ne j} W_i\bar{F}_i = PQ - W_jF_j - K, & \dfrac{F_j}{a_j} \le \dfrac{\bar{F}_k}{a_k}, \\ \pi_{2S} = P\left[\dfrac{\bar{F}_k}{a_k}\right] - W_jF_j - K, & \dfrac{F_j}{a_j} > \dfrac{\bar{F}_k}{a_k}. \end{cases} \tag{6.10}$$

Now, the firm initially seeks an $F_j$ such that

$$\begin{cases} \dfrac{\partial \pi_{1S}}{\partial F_j} = MR \cdot \left[\dfrac{1}{a_j}\right] - MC_j = 0, \qquad F_j \leq \left(\dfrac{a_j}{a_k}\right)\bar{F}_k, \\ \dfrac{\partial^2 \pi_{1S}}{\partial F_j^2} = \dfrac{\partial [MRP_j]}{\partial F_j} - \dfrac{\partial (MC_j)}{\partial F_j} < 0, \end{cases} \tag{6.11a}$$

and compares profit at that level of $F_j$ with profit at the level of $F_j$ at which

$$\begin{cases} \dfrac{\partial \pi_{2S}}{\partial F_j} = -MC_j = 0, \qquad F_j > \left(\dfrac{a_j}{a_k}\right)\bar{F}_k, \\ \dfrac{\partial^2 \pi_{2S}}{\partial F_j^2} = -\dfrac{\partial (MC_j)}{\partial F_j} < 0. \end{cases} \tag{6.11b}$$

$\partial^2\pi_{2S}/\partial F_j^2$ will be negative when $\pi_{2S}$ is a concave function of $F_j$. The slope of the function is necessarily nonpositive, and indeed is negative if we assume $MC_j > 0$; and $\partial\pi_{2S}/\partial F_j = -MC_j$. Hence, as noted in Chapter 2, (6.11b) shows that the function will be maximized either where $MC_j = 0$ or, if this point does not lie within the bounds of the function, at the *lower* bound of $F_j$. From (6.11a) there are two possibilities for a maximum, assuming that the second-order condition holds—that is, that the profit function is concave. Either an $F_j^*$ exists such that $\partial\pi_{1S}/\partial F_j = 0$ at $F_j^*$, or it does not. In any event, the possibility that $\partial\pi_{1S}/\partial F_j$ or $\partial\pi_{2S}/\partial F_j$ equals zero is contingent upon the specific demand and cost functions and need not distract us here. The second possibility, with $MRP_j > MC_j$, would indicate a maximum for a positively sloped concave function at the upper bound of $F_j$. Thus, although the $MRP_j$ curve is discontinuous at $F_j = (a_j/a_k)\bar{F}_k$, the second-order conditions imply a maximum at $F_j = (a_j/a_k)\bar{F}_k$—or, given the concavity of the profit function, at the point such that the marginal inequalities, $MRP_j > MC_j$ and $MC_j > MRP_j$, hold at immediately lower and higher levels, respectively, of $F_j$.

## d. The Long Run and the Short: The Factor Demand Curves

The relationship between the short- and long-run factor $ARP_i$, $ANRP_i$, and $MRP_i$ curves mirrors that between the short- and long-run average and marginal cost curves. In the previous chapter we saw that in the short run the neoclassical firm selects levels for its fixed factors in accordance with long-run quantity optima, $Q^*$. Given the levels of the fixed factors, the optimum levels of the variable factors, and consequently short-run costs, would be determined for all other output levels. Thus, for each $Q^*$ the firm fixes $F_i = \bar{F}_i$ $(i = k + 1, \ldots, m)$. The levels of the variable factors are then determined in accordance with $MRP_{iS} = MC_i$ $(i = 1, \ldots, k)$. With values $F_j = \bar{F}_j$ so determined $(j \neq i)$, we obtain an infinite set of short-run marginal revenue product curves for factor $i$. To avoid confusion and draftsman fatigue, only a few of these $MRP_{iS}$ curves are sketched in Figure 6.4.

Suppose that the long-run profit maximum is attained at a $Q^*$ such that the optimum employment of factor $i$ is at $F_i^*$ $(i = 1, \ldots, m)$. If the levels of the factors to be fixed in the short run are set at their long-run optimum values of $F_i^*$ $(i = k + 1, \ldots, m)$, then long- and short-run profit will be equal and maximized at $\pi^* = \pi_S^* = ANRP_i(F_i^*)$. Therefore, long- and short-run average net revenue product are equal at $F_i^*$. At any other value of $F_i \neq F_i^*$ long-run profit is necessarily greater than short-run profit. Consider a level $F_i^{**}$. In the long run $MRP_i = MC_i$ for $i = 1, \ldots, m$ at $F_i = F_i^*$. In the short run the equality will not necessarily be maintained. Indeed, in the short run the marginal equalities may hold only for the variable factors $F_i$ $(i = 1, \ldots, k)$. When they do not hold for the fixed factors as well, $\pi_S^{**} < \pi^{**}$, and long-run average net revenue product is greater than short-run average net revenue product at $F_i^{**}$. With $\pi^* = \pi_S^*$ and $\pi_S^{**} < \pi^{**}$, the short- and long-run total profit and $ANRP_i$ curves will be *tangent* at $F_i = F_i^*$, for the long-run curve will be higher than the short-run curve at all other values of $F_i = F_i^{**} \neq F_i^*$.

Similarly, long- and short-run $MRP_i$ are necessarily equal at $F_i^*$ and each equals $MC_i$. Suppose, however, that we consider $F_i^{**} > F_i^*$. At this higher level of employment, short-run profit is less than long-run profit. Since, for increases in $F_i$ above $F_i^*$, $\pi$ will decline by less than $\pi_S$, long-run $MRP_i$ will be declining less rapidly than short-run $MRP_i$. This is so, for each may be determined as the slope of the respec-

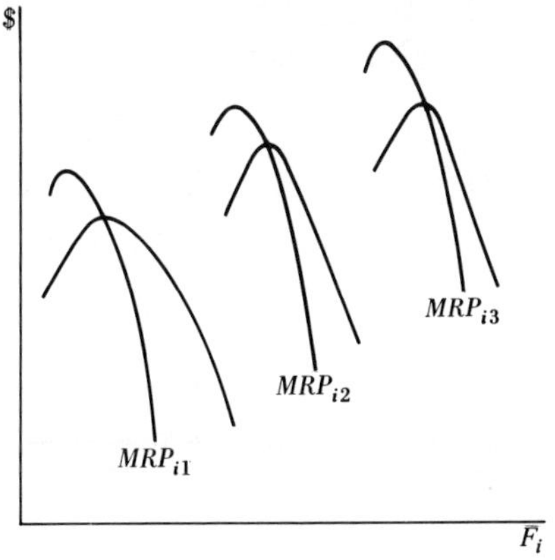


Fig. 6.4

tive profit curves. Similarly, for $F_i^{**} < F_i^*$ we also have $\pi_S^{**} < \pi^{**}$. Once again, then, at employment levels below $F_i^*$, short-run profit declines more rapidly than does long-run profit. This is so because in the long-run the other factors can also be adjusted to achieve a combination economically superior to that at which they have been set when $F_i = F_i^*$. The smaller change in profit means that long-run $MRP_i$ is less than short-run $MRP_{iS}$. Hence, the long- and short-run $MRP_i$ curves *intersect* at $F_i^*$, with the short-run curves the steeper of the two. Finally, the usual average-marginal relationships hold between the $ANRP_i$ and $ANRP_{iS}$ curves and the $MRP_i$ and $MRP_{iS}$ curves, respectively.

These relationships are depicted in Figure 6.5. The less steeply sloping long-run curves reflect the fact that in the long run the firm can adjust *all* factors of production. Therefore, a change in the conditions of supply for any one factor will tend to have a greater effect on the factor's employment in the long run than in the short. This holds because in the long run the other factors can also be employed at different levels to take advantage of the new cost conditions. Thus, suppose that factor $i$ is the only variable factor. If at all levels $F_i$ there is a sudden increase in $MC_i$, the firm will reduce the short-run employment of factor $i$ in order to maintain the equality $MR \cdot [MPP_{iS}] = MC_i$ (assuming that the factor is employed at a point on the declining portion of the $MPP_{iS}$ curve). In the long run, however, when the decrease in employment of factor $i$ raises (lowers) the marginal physical product of rival (complementary) factors, the firm will want to increase (decrease) their employment. Because of the symmetry of the rivalry and complementary relationships, the increased (decreased) employment of rivals (complements) will now lower the new $MPP_{iS}$ figure. To retain $MRP_{iS} = MC_i$ now will necessitate an additional reduction in $F_i$, beyond the original decrease. When the $MRP_{iS} = MC_i$ relationship has eventually been restored for all factors, the total reduction in $F_i$ will necessarily be greater in the long run than the short, because of the effects on rivals and comple-

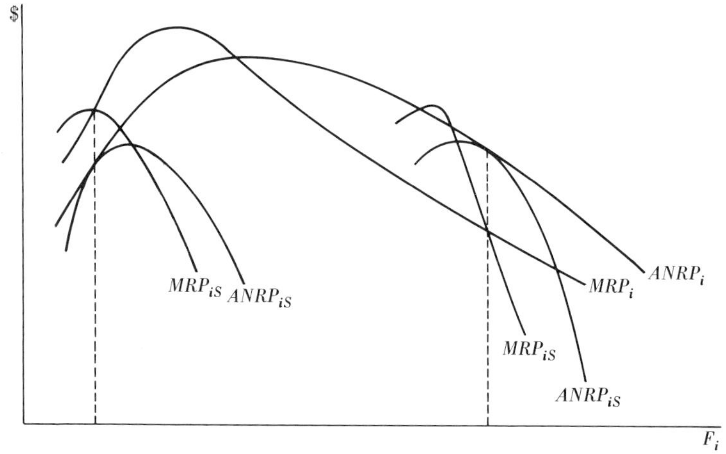


Fig. 6.5

ments of the changes in $F_i$. A similar argument holds for decreases in $MC_i$ calling forth larger increases in $F_i$ in the long run than the short.

## 6.3 THE FIRM'S SUPPLY CURVE

It has been seen that in both its long- and short-run planning the neoclassical firm employs its variable factors of production commensurate with a level of output at which marginal revenue equals marginal cost. As long as the relevant marginal cost curve is increasing more rapidly than the marginal revenue curve, profit will be maximized at this output. This policy expresses the firm's willingness to supply additional output as long as the cost incurred does not exceed the additional revenue that the sale of this output is expected to bring in. The $MC$ curve therefore describes how many units the firm would be willing to supply at any given price—as long as this price enables the firm to make a profit.

In the long run, the firm will be willing to operate as long as $ANRP_i - W_i^* \geq 0$ for $i = 1, \ldots, m$. Multiplying by $F_i^*/Q$ yields the equivalent expression

$$(ANRP_i - W_i^*)\frac{F_i^*}{Q} = \frac{PQ - \sum_{i=1}^{m} W_i^* F_i^*}{Q} = P - \frac{C}{Q} \geq 0.$$

That is, price must not be less than average cost. In the short run, the condition for production is stated only in terms of the variable factors, or

$$PQ - \sum_{i=1}^{k} W_i^* F_i^* \geq 0.$$

Equivalently, $P - C_v/Q \geq 0$, where $C_v$ represents total *variable* cost. That is, price must exceed or equal average *variable* cost. In the long-run *all* costs are variable. It can therefore be stated with perfect generality that at any given price the firm would *like* to supply output in accordance with its marginal cost curve, as long as that price is at least as great as average variable cost. If price is below average variable cost, the firm ceases to operate.

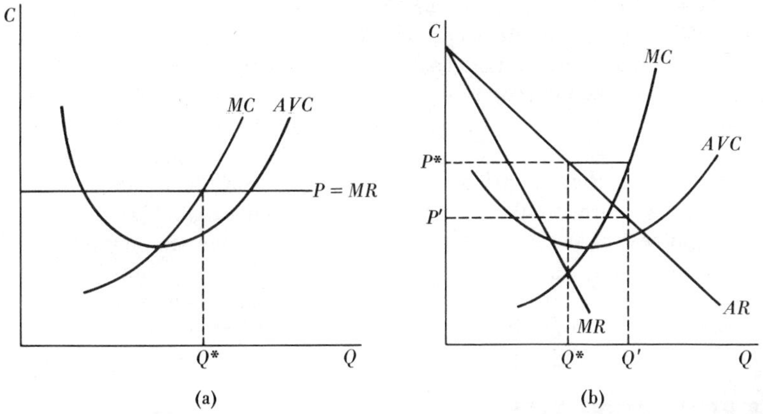


Fig. 6.6

When $MR = P$ and the firm's demand curve is infinitely elastic, it is easy to accept the portion of the marginal cost ($MC$) curve that lies at or above the average variable cost ($AVC$) curve as being one segment of the firm's discontinuous supply curve. The second segment, corresponding to $MC < AVC$, would be the vertical axis. The firm in the purely competitive industry is assumed to face such a horizontal demand curve. It equates $MR = P = MC \geq AVC$ and therefore *does* supply output in accordance with its marginal cost schedule. This is seen in Figure 6.6(a).

The actions of the firm facing a downward-sloping demand curve are, however, quite another matter. This firm operates where $P > MR = MC$ and $P \geq AVC$. It does not actually sell output in accordance with its $MC$ schedule. It is commonly remarked, therefore, that the supply curve for this firm does not exist.[8] It has, how-

[8] For example: "It is apparent that a monopoly has no supply curve—that there is no schedule of quantities forthcoming at various prices" [George J. Stigler, *The Theory of Price* (New York: The Macmillan Company, 1957), p. 212]. The supply-equals-demand fixation can also lead to some interesting semantic gyrations: "For a monopolistic firm the supply curve is not so easy to come by .... The equilibrium price then is that unique price associated with the profit-maximizing output by the average revenue curve, not one determined by the intersection of a supply curve and a demand curve. Notice, however, that in equilibrium the monopolist does supply a particular output and, moreover,

ever, already been noted that *any* firm's demand curve will commonly be downward sloping if quite gently so. The exception occurs in the purely competitive industry when the firm perceives its demand curve as being horizontal. Since there are few if any *purely* competitive industries, does it follow that individual firms' supply curves are few and far between?

The answer depends upon whether one has a fixation on the need for supply and demand to be *equated.* When the demand curve is downward sloping, price and quantity are set at $P^*$ and $Q^*$ respectively such that at $Q^*$, $MR = MC$. This is illustrated in Figure 6.6(b). With $P^* \geq AVC$, the firm would be both willing and anxious to supply the quantity of $Q'$ at which marginal cost equals $P^*$. Unfortunately for the firm, the demand curve is such that consumers will only pay $P' < P^*$ for a quantity of $Q'$. At $P^* < AVC$, the firm is not willing to supply anything.

As long as the term "supply curve" is used to reflect the quantities that firms are *willing* to supply at given prices, the discontinuous curve described by the vertical axis for $P < AVC$ and the marginal cost curve for $P \geq AVC$ will be the firm's supply curve. For nice, convex average cost curves, the supply curve would be the vertical axis at prices below minimum average variable cost, and the portion of the marginal cost curve at and above this minimum cost. The quantities that the profit-maximizing firm *actually* supplies at a given price will, however, fall short of what it would *like* to supply at that price. This is because of the consumers' unwillingness to purchase all that the firm would like to sell at the profit-maximizing price. The firm's *actual* output will be determined by the marginal revenue and marginal cost curves. As demonstrated in Figure 6.6(b), $MR = MC$ at $Q^*$, the price is set at $P^*$, and the excess of supply over demand, in the previous sense, is given by $Q' - Q^*$. At every price, then, units sold and supply will always be equal for the firm in *pure* competition, but this will not generally be true for the firm in *imperfect* competition.

## 6.4 JOINT PRODUCTION

Let us extend the previous analysis somewhat by relaxing the assumption that the firm produces a single product. Instead, it will be assumed that the firm has a *technological possibility function*, $f(x_1, \ldots, x_s) = 0$. This function is defined such that there are $m$ factors of production $F_v$ that combine to yield $n$ products $Q_u$. When $x_i < 0$, then $x_i = x_v$ is an input of $F_v$; when $x_i > 0$, then $x_i = x_u$ is an output of $Q_u$. If $x_i = 0$, this may be considered to be an intermediate material or service that never reaches the outside world. It will not restrict the analysis to assume that the latter do not exist, and that $x_i \neq 0$ $(i = 1, \ldots, s)$; hence, $n + m = s$. We shall also assume that the price (wage) for which each product (factor) can be sold (purchased) is a function of $x_i$ exclusively. That is, $P_u = \theta^u(x_u)$ and $W_v = \theta^v(x_v)$. The firm's profit will thus be given by

$$\pi = \sum_{i=1}^{s} \theta^i(x_i)x_i.$$

$\pi$ gives the firm's profit because when $x_i$ is positive it is a commodity that adds to revenue, and when $x_i$ is negative it is a factor that adds to cost.

---

he sets a price such that this quantity will just be purchased. Thus, even in monopolistic equilibrium, supply is equal to demand, although we are not able to utilize this fact alone in establishing where the equilibrium point will be." [Cliff Lloyd, *Microeconomic Analysis* (Homewood, Ill.: Richard D. Irwin, Inc., 1967), p. 186.]

The Lagrangian function is

$$L_\pi = \sum_{i=1}^{s} \theta^i(x_i)x_i - \lambda f.$$

The first-order conditions for a maximum are

$$\left(\frac{\partial \theta^i}{\partial x_i}\right) x_i + \theta^i - \lambda \frac{\partial f}{\partial x_i} = 0, \qquad i = 1, \ldots, s,$$
$$f(x_1, \ldots, x_s) = 0. \tag{6.12}$$

Rearranging terms and letting $\partial\theta^i/\partial x_i = \theta^i_i$ and $\partial f/\partial x_i = f_i$, the first $s$ conditions yield the following result:

$$\lambda = \frac{\theta^i_i x_i + \theta^i}{f_i} = \frac{\theta^j_j x_j + \theta^j}{f_j}, \qquad i, j = 1, \ldots, s. \tag{6.12a}$$

For the second-order conditions, we require $\partial\theta^i_i/\partial x_i = \theta^i_{ii}$ and $\partial^2 f/\partial x_i\, \partial x_j = f_{ij} = f_{ji}$. It is assumed that the price (wage) of product (factor) $x_i$ is independent of the level of $x_j$ $(j \neq i)$, so that $\partial\theta^i/\partial x_j = \theta^i_j = 0$.

As before, profits will be maximized at the stationary point if $M^*_3 > 0$, $M^*_4 < 0$, ..., where the $M^*_i$ are the successive principal minors of $\mathbf{M}^*$, which alternate in sign, for

$$\mathbf{M}^* = \begin{bmatrix} 0 & f_1 & f_2 & \cdots & f_s \\ f_1 & \theta^1_{11}x_1 + 2\theta^1_1 - \lambda f_{11} & -\lambda f_{12} & \cdots & -\lambda f_{1s} \\ f_2 & -\lambda f_{21} & \theta^2_{22}x_2 + 2\theta^2_2 - \lambda f_{22} & \cdots & -\lambda f_{2s} \\ \cdot & & & & \\ \cdot & & & & \\ \cdot & & & & \\ f_s & -\lambda f_{s1} & -\lambda f_{s2} & \cdots & \theta^s_{ss}x_s + 2\theta^s_s - \lambda f_{ss} \end{bmatrix}.$$

We shall presume that the functions have the appropriate convexity properties to assure that the second-order conditions are fulfilled and that we have a maximum at the stationary point. Now, repeating our earlier machinations,

$$df = \sum_{i=1}^{s} \left(\frac{\partial f}{\partial x_i}\right) dx_i;$$

and, with all $dx_i$ but $dx_j$ and $dx_k$ held at 0,

$$df = \left(\frac{\partial f}{\partial x_j}\right) dx_j + \left(\frac{\partial f}{\partial x_k}\right) dx_k = 0$$

gives

$$-\frac{dx_j}{dx_k} = \frac{f_k}{f_j}. \tag{6.13}$$

If $x_j$ is a product and $x_k$ is a factor, then $-dx_j/dx_k$ is the change in the output of product $j$ resulting from a small change in the employment of factor $k$. The latter expression, however, is simply the marginal physical product of factor $k$ with respect to product $j$, or $MPP_{kj}$. Moreover, in this case $\theta_j^j x_j + \theta^j = MR_j$ and $\theta_k^k x_k + \theta^k = MC_k$. The first-order optimality condition could thus be expressed as

$$\frac{MC_k}{MR_j} = MPP_{kj} \qquad \text{or} \qquad MC_k = MPP_{kj} MR_j. \tag{6.12b}$$

That is, the $k$th factor is employed such that its marginal factor cost is equal to its marginal revenue product, for all products. Similarly, where $j$ and $k$ are both inputs, $-dx_j/dx_k$ becomes the rate of factor substitution. Hence, (6.13) and (6.12a) combine to imply that to maximize profits,

$$-\frac{dx_j}{dx_k} = \frac{f_k}{f_j} = \frac{\theta_k^k x_k + \theta^k}{\theta_j^j x_j + \theta^j} = \frac{MC_k}{MC_j}. \tag{6.13a}$$

That is, the ratio of marginal factor costs equals the rate of factor substitution for all inputs. Analogously, where $j$ and $k$ are both outputs, $-dx_j/dx_k$ is called the rate of product transformation. The latter measures the amount by which the output of product $j$ will have to be altered if more of product $k$ is to be produced, and if all other factors and products are held at fixed levels. In this instance, then, (6.13) and (6.12a) yield, as the first-order conditions,

$$-\frac{dx_j}{dx_k} = \frac{MR_k}{MR_j}, \tag{6.13b}$$

or the rate of product transformation between any two products is to be equal to the ratio of their marginal revenues. Note that where the firm is a pure competitor having a negligible effect on prices of products and factors, price would replace marginal revenue, and wage would replace marginal factor cost, in each of the previous expressions.

Finally, $\lambda = (\partial\pi/\partial x_i)/(\partial f/\partial x_i) = \partial\pi/\partial f$. Thus $\lambda$ measures the marginal profit effected by a shift in the technological possibility function—either more output with the given inputs or fewer inputs producing the same outputs. The value of $\lambda$ thus reflects the opportunity cost to the firm associated with the given *technology*, measured at the point where the first-order conditions obtain.

Additionally, with pure competition $P_u = r_u = MR_u$ and $W_v = r_v = MC_v$. We then have $\lambda = r_i/f_i$ or $r_i = \lambda f_i$. Let us analyze the effects of a small change in $r_i$, all other $r_j$ constant $(j \neq i)$, on the level of all $x_j$ $(j = 1, \ldots, s)$. First, since $r_i = \lambda f_i$,

$$\frac{\partial r_i}{\partial r_i} = 1 = \left(\frac{\partial\lambda}{\partial r_i}\right) f_i + \lambda \sum_{j=1}^{s} \left(\frac{\partial f_i}{\partial x_j}\right)\left(\frac{\partial x_j}{\partial r_i}\right).$$

But, since $\partial f_i/\partial x_j = f_{ij}$, after dividing both sides by $\lambda$, this equation becomes

$$f_i\left(\frac{1}{\lambda}\right)\left(\frac{\partial\lambda}{\partial r_i}\right) + \sum_{j=1}^{s} f_{ij}\left(\frac{\partial x_j}{\partial r_i}\right) = \frac{1}{\lambda}. \tag{6.14a}$$

Further, for $r_k = \lambda f_k \; (k \neq i)$,

$$\frac{\partial r_k}{\partial r_i} = 0 = \left(\frac{\partial \lambda}{\partial r_i}\right) f_k + \lambda \sum_{j=1}^{s} \left(\frac{\partial f_k}{\partial x_j}\right)\left(\frac{\partial x_j}{\partial r_i}\right), \qquad k \neq i,$$

or

$$f_k \left(\frac{1}{\lambda}\right)\left(\frac{\partial \lambda}{\partial r_i}\right) + \sum_{j=1}^{s} f_{kj} \left(\frac{\partial x_j}{\partial r_i}\right) = 0, \qquad k \neq i. \tag{6.14b}$$

Finally, from the technological possibility function, $\partial f/\partial r_i = 0$ or

$$\sum_{j=1}^{s} f_j \left(\frac{\partial x_j}{\partial r_i}\right) = 0. \tag{6.14c}$$

A set of $s + 1$ simultaneous linear equations is formed by (6.14a), (6.14b), and (6.14c). There are, also, $s + 1$ unknowns: $\partial x_j/\partial r_i$ $(j = 1, \ldots, s)$ and $(1/\lambda)$ $(\partial \lambda/\partial r_i)$. We are particularly interested in $\partial x_j/\partial r_i$, for this measures the change in the level of the $j$th factor or product effected by a change in the $i$th factor or product's marginal cost or revenue. The latter change will be the subsequent result of a change in the factor's supply schedule or in the product's demand curve. We shall apply Cramer's rule to solve these simultaneous equations. Place (6.14a) in the empty $i$th position in the set (6.14b) and write (6.14c) as the first equation. Let

$$\mathbf{F} = \begin{bmatrix} 0 & f_1 & f_2 & \cdots & f_s \\ f_1 & f_{11} & f_{12} & \cdots & f_{1s} \\ f_2 & f_{21} & f_{22} & \cdots & f_{2s} \\ \cdot & & & & \\ \cdot & & & & \\ \cdot & & & & \\ f_s & f_{s1} & f_{s2} & \cdots & f_{ss} \end{bmatrix}$$

and $F_{ij}$ be the cofactor of $f_{ij}$. Then,

$$\left(\frac{\partial x_j}{\partial r_i}\right) = \frac{\begin{array}{r|cccccc|} & & & & \overset{j}{\downarrow} & & \\ & 0 & f_1 & \cdots & 0 & \cdots & f_s \\ & f_1 & f_{11} & \cdots & 0 & \cdots & f_{1s} \\ & \cdot & & & & & \\ & \cdot & & & & & \\ & \cdot & & & & & \\ i \rightarrow & f_i & f_{i1} & \cdots & 1/\lambda & \cdots & f_{is} \\ & \cdot & & & & & \\ & \cdot & & & & & \\ & \cdot & & & & & \\ & f_s & f_{s1} & \cdots & 0 & \cdots & f_{ss} \end{array}}{|\mathbf{F}|} = \frac{F_{ij}}{\lambda\,|\mathbf{F}|}. \tag{6.15}$$

The equation $(\partial x_j/\partial r_i) = (1/\lambda)(F_{ij}/|\mathbf{F}|)$ is analogous to the Slutsky equation (2.17) of consumer behavior. Now, however, the effects on $x_j$ of a change in $r_i$ would seem to depend solely on $S'_{ij} = (1/\lambda)(F_{ij}/|\mathbf{F}|)$, or a "substitution" term. There is no "income effect" added to the "substitution effect." In essence, the "income effect" term—or what would be more comparable for the firm, the "profit effect" term—is zero. That is, if profits should change with *all marginal* revenue to *marginal* factor cost ratios unaltered (which could occur even though factor supply and product demand curves shifted to effect the change in profits) and the technological possibility function fixed, the firm's optimal factor input and product output optima would not be affected.

The implications of whether $S'_{ij}$ is positive or negative, and the anticipated sign of $S'_{ij}$, depend upon whether factors or products are involved. If, for example, $i$ is a factor and $j$ is a product, one might expect that $S'_{ij}$ will be negative: that is, a rise in $W_i$ causes a decrease in output $Q_j$. Where both $i$ and $j$ are factors or products, the implications are more interesting, for the sign of $S'_{ij}$ will depend upon their complementarity as inputs or outputs. In particular, since $\sum_j f_j F_{kj}$ is an expansion of $|\mathbf{F}|$ via the first row using the cofactors of the $(1 + k)$th row and $j$th column, and since the expansion of a determinant by alien cofactors is zero,

$$\sum_j f_j F_{kj} = \frac{|\mathbf{F}|}{|\mathbf{F}|} \sum_j \left(\frac{r_j}{\lambda}\right) F_{kj} = |\mathbf{F}| \sum_j r_j \left(\frac{\partial x_j}{\partial r_k}\right) = 0. \qquad (6.16)$$

Further, given that $\partial x_k/\partial r_k = F_{kk}/\lambda\,|\mathbf{F}| > 0$ (that is, a ceteris paribus increase in $Q_k$'s marginal revenue, or a decrease in $F_k$'s marginal cost, will result in more of the product being produced or more of the factor being used), since $r_j \geq 0$ $(j = 1, \ldots, s)$, (6.16) shows that at least one $\partial x_j/\partial r_k < 0$ so long as $r_k > 0$. In particular, if $x_k$ is a product (factor), an upward shift in the marginal revenue (factor cost) curve will result in a reduction in output of at least one other product and/or the increased use of at least one other factor. In the purely competitive case, $r_k = P_k$ or $W_k$, as the case may be, leading to the simplified analysis.[9] Even then, however, as has been emphasized, the prime movers determining the $x_i$ are the *marginal* revenues and *marginal* factor costs. Under pure competition these simply happen to equal prices and wages.

## 6.5 UNCERTAINTY IN THE PRODUCTION FUNCTION

In order to gain some initial impressions of the potential impact of uncertainty on the firm's operations, again consider the single-product firm's operating decisions. Further, let us maintain the simplification that the demand and total cost curves

[9] See J. R. Hicks, *Value and Capital* (Oxford: Clarendon Press, 1946), pp. 89–98, 320–322. It might be noted that in the absence of an "income" effect in Equation (6.15), Giffen's Paradox with respect to a factor of production would seem to be ruled out for the profit-maximizing firm. This need not be the case, however, if the firm leans towards something other than profit maximization. See R. D. Portes, "Input Demand Functions for the Profit-Constrained Sales-Maximizer: Income Effects in the Theory of the Firm," *Economica*, **XXXV**:139 (Aug. 1968), 233–248.

are indeed known with certainty. It will be convenient to express the former as $P = D(Q)$; the latter is given by

$$C = \sum_{i=1}^{m} W_i F_i.$$

Uncertainty is introduced here via the production function. Specifically, we recognize the likelihood that *some* defective output will be produced, that there will be *some* human error, an *occasional* machine breakdown, and the like. The production function is now written $Q = q(u, F_1, \ldots, F_m)$, where $u$ is a random variable described by the density $g(u)$. The most simplified interpretation of the traditional approach would immediately integrate $u$ and uncertainty out of the picture by focusing on the expected value of $u$ as a certainty equivalent. Then, the production function could be written as $\tilde{Q} = q(E[u], F_1, \ldots, F_m)$, and the factors of production would be employed so as to maximize

$$\pi = D(\tilde{Q})\tilde{Q} - \sum_i W_i F_i.$$

The maximization requires the familiar $MRP_i = MC_i$ equality for all factors, where $MRP_i$ is computed with respect to $\tilde{Q}$.

In a somewhat more sophisticated version of the traditional approach, giving a bit more benefit of the doubt to the neoclassicists, the random variable $u$ would be "integrated out" of the problem by determining the *expected output* yielded by the specific combination $(F_1, \ldots, F_m)$. Profit becomes a function of the random variable $Q$, but the firm's decisions would be based solely on the expectation of this variable, $E[Q]$. In the decision-theoretic terminology of Section 3.5, $E[Q]$ is a certainty equivalent that summarizes all of the information about the *distribution* of the random variable output that is deemed relevant by the decision maker. Similarly, *expected* profit is the certainty equivalent that summarizes all the information that he considers relevant about the *distribution* of the random variable profit. Here, *expected* profit would be given by price multiplied by *expected* output less the actual cost of employing $(F_1, \ldots, F_m)$, or

$$E_1[\pi] = P(E[Q]) - C = D(E[Q])E[Q] - C. \tag{6.17a}$$

Let

$$\bar{Q} = E[Q] = \int_u q(u, F_1, \ldots, F_m)g(u)\, du$$
$$= \bar{q}(F_1, \ldots, F_m) = \text{expected output},$$

a function solely of the $F_i$. (6.17a) may be rewritten

$$E_1[\pi] = D(\bar{Q})\bar{Q} - \sum_i W_i F_i. \tag{6.17b}$$

To maximize long-run expected profit, the firm sets $\partial E_1[\pi]/\partial F_i = 0$, for $i = 1, \ldots, m$. Presuming that the second-order conditions hold, the maximization occurs as before where marginal revenue product equals marginal factor cost for each factor. Now, however, marginal revenue product is evaluated at the *expected* output. This will be called *marginal revenue* of *expected product* ($MREP$). In effect, then, the more sophisticated firm of neoclassical theory will have behaved *as if* it were certain that the factors of production would generate *precisely* their expected output.

Suppose, however, that the firm's objective, although still a profit-maximizing one, is now viewed as that of maximizing *expected* profit given by *expected revenue* less actual cost. This expectation differs from the previous one in that $P(E[Q]) \neq E[PQ]$. That is, the certainty equivalent with which the firm is concerned is expected revenue and not expected output. In this event, expected profit is given by

$$E_2[\pi] = E[PQ] - C = E[D(Q)Q] - \sum_i W_i F_i$$

or

$$E_2[\pi] = \int_u D(Q)Qg(u)\,du - \sum_i W_i F_i. \tag{6.18}$$

Since in general

$$\frac{\partial\left[\int_a^b f(x, y)\,dy\right]}{\partial x} = \int_a^b \left[\frac{\partial f(x, y)}{\partial x}\right] dy$$

for constant $a$ and $b$, and since

$$\frac{\partial[D(Q)Q]}{\partial F_i} = \left(\frac{\partial[D(Q)Q]}{\partial Q}\right)\left(\frac{\partial Q}{\partial F_i}\right),$$

the first-order conditions for a profit maximum are

$$\frac{\partial E_2[\pi]}{\partial F_i} = \int_u \left[\frac{\partial[D(Q)Q]}{\partial Q}\right]\left[\frac{\partial Q}{\partial F_i}\right] g(u)\,du - MC_i = 0 \qquad i = 1, \ldots, m.$$

These may be rewritten as

$$\int_u [MR]\cdot[MPP_i]g(u)\,du = MC_i, \qquad i = 1, \ldots, m. \tag{6.19}$$

Again presuming the appropriate second-order conditions are satisfied, expected profit is maximized where *expected marginal revenue product* (*EMRP*) equals marginal factor cost for each factor. Any difference between this and the previous solution stems from the differences between the $MREP_i$ and $EMRP_i$ for the $i = 1, \ldots, m$ factors of production. Given a vector $(F_1, \ldots, F_m)$ of factor employment, each of these marginal revenue products will be functions of the random variable $u$. Despite our inability to infer that one expression will *necessarily* be greater than the other, and therefore that the employment of factor $i$ will *necessarily* be greater under one mode of analysis than under the other, the situation can lead us to some interesting observations.

Recall that a function $h(y)$ defined in the interval $(a, b)$ is called convex if $h(\gamma y_1 + (1 - \gamma)y_2) \leq \gamma h(y_1) + (1 - \gamma)h(y_2)$ for $a < y_1,\ y_2 < b$ and $0 \leq \gamma \leq 1$. As a further generalization, we have Jensen's inequality, which may be expressed in the following convenient manner.[10] If $h(y)$ is a continuous convex function defined over

[10] For discussions, see G. H. Hardy, J. E. Littlewood, and G. Polya, *Inequalities* (London: Cambridge University Press, 1967), pp. 69–75, and Walter Rudin, *Real and Complex Analysis* (New York: McGraw-Hill, Inc., 1966), pp. 60–62.

$(a, b)$ and if $p(y)$ is a nonnegative continuous function such that $\int_a^b p(y)\,dy = 1$, then

$$h\left(\int_a^b yp(y)\,dy\right) \leq \int_a^b h(y)p(y)\,dy$$

or

$$h(E[y]) \leq E[h(y)]. \tag{6.20}$$

In the earlier discussion of convexity it was noted that a convex function in two-dimensional space is a curve shaped such that it always lies at or below the line segment joining any two points on the curve—that is, the function evaluated at some weighted average of two points will never be greater than this weighted average of the function evaluated at the two points. Equation (6.20) generalizes the statement to the weighted average of *any* number of points. In the discrete case, $\Sigma$ replaces $\int$.[11] The direction of the inequality would be reversed for concave functions. It should be borne in mind that $y$ may also be any $(n \geq 2)$-dimensional vector.

In the present context, suppose that $Q$ is a convex function of $u$. In the simplest "neoclassical" philosophy, one would evaluate $\tilde{Q} = q(E[u], F_1, \ldots, F_m)$ and reach decisions on this basis. A somewhat more explicit recognition of uncertainty would, however, evaluate the expected output of $\bar{Q} = E[q(u, F_1, \ldots, F_m)]$. In essence, we should be concerned with the average output as a certainty equivalent rather than the output generated with an average degree of randomness. Equation (6.20) shows that the two will not ordinarily be equivalent. Indeed, $q(E[u]\,F_1, \ldots, F_m) \leq E[q(u, F_1, \ldots, F_m)]$, so that the simplest neoclassical approach would consistently tend to *underestimate* the output generated by a set of factors; the reverse would be true if $Q$ were a concave function of $u$. Further, suppose it is a factor's *services* that introduce the randomness into production. In particular, suppose the *services* obtained when factor $i$ is employed at a level of $F_i$ are described by $F_i(u)$.[12] Then the production function might be written $Q = q(F_1, F_2, \ldots, F_i(u), \ldots, F_m)$. Suppose that *total* physical product of factor $i$ is a *concave* function of the services yielded by

[11] Rudin, *Real and Complex Analysis,* offers the following appealing illustration. Let $h(y_i) = e^{y_i}$ $(i = 1, \ldots, n)$ and let $p(y_i) = 1/n$. Then, from (6.20),

$$e^{y_1/n + y_2/n + \cdots + y_n/n} \leq e^{y_1}/n + \cdots + e^{y_n}/n,$$

because $e^y$ is a convex function of $y$. But the left-hand side of the inequality may be written as $e^{y_1/n}e^{y_2/n} \cdots e^{y_n/n}$. Letting $x_i = e^{y_i}$, we may rewrite the inequality as

$$x_1^{1/n} \cdots x_n^{1/n} \leq \frac{x_1}{n} + \cdots + \frac{x_n}{n}$$

or

$$(x_1 \cdots x_n)^{1/n} \leq \left(\frac{1}{n}\right)(x_1 + \cdots + x_n).$$

The latter is the well-known rule that the geometric mean of a series of $n$ positive numbers (positive since $e^y > 0$) is less than or equal to the arithmetic mean.

[12] This approach was suggested for fixed technological coefficients by A. A. Walters in his "Marginal Productivity and Probability Distributions of Factor Services," *Economic Journal,* **LXX** (June 1960), 325–330.

$F_i(u)$, as in Figure 6.7. The simplest "neoclassical" interpretation of $\tilde{Q} = q(F_1, F_2, \ldots, E[F_i(u)], \ldots, F_m)$ would lead the firm behaving *as if* its world were one of certainty to anticipate a *higher* output for a given level of factor employment than if it considered the *expected* output of $\bar{Q} = E[q(F_1, F_2, \ldots, F_i(u), \ldots, F_m)]$.

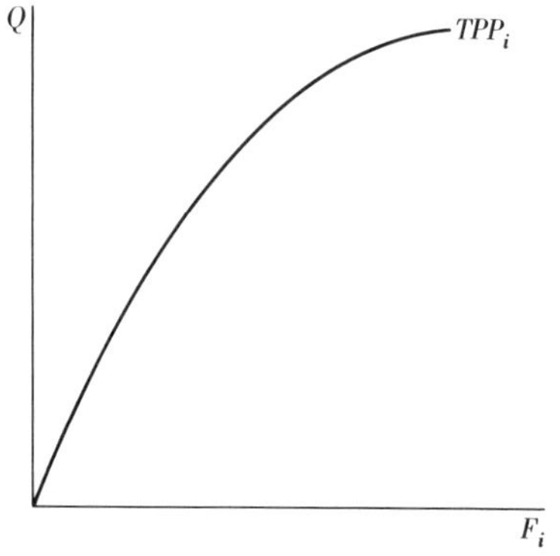


Fig. 6.7

As an additional point of note, suppose that $h(y)$ is a nonnegative continuous function defined for all $y$, where $0 \le y \le Y$. We may expand $h(y)$ by Taylor series[13] as follows:

$$h(y) = \sum_{j=0}^{N} h^{(j)}(a) \frac{(y-a)^j}{j!} + \frac{1}{N!} \int_a^y h^{(N+1)}(t)(y-t)^N \, dt.$$

Taking expectations on both sides of the equation,

$$E[h(y)] = E[h(a)] + E[(y-a)]h'(a) + E\left[\frac{(y-a)^2 h''(a)}{2!}\right] + \cdots. \tag{6.21}$$

Setting $a = E[y]$,

$$E[h(E[y])] = h(E[y]); \qquad E[(y - E[y])] = E[y] - E[y] = 0;$$

$$E\left[\frac{(y-a)^2 h''(a)}{2!}\right] = \frac{h''(E[y])\sigma_y^2}{2},$$

where $\sigma_y^2$ is the variance of $y$; similarly for the higher-order terms. Hence, (6.21) may be written

$$E[h(y)] = h(E[y]) + \frac{h''(E[y])\sigma_y^2}{2} + \phi, \tag{6.21'}$$

[13] This derivation is a variation on a theme by Kenneth Mullen in "A Note on the Ratio of Two Independent Random Variables," *American Statistician*, **21**:3 (June 1967), 30–31.

Taylor's theorem states that where $h(y)$ is a continuous function differentiable $N + 1$ times in a given interval containing $a$ and $y$, we may write

$$h(y) = h(a) + h'(a)(y-a) + \frac{h''(a)(y-a)^2}{2!} + \cdots + \frac{h^{(N)}(a)(y-a)^N}{N!} + \int_a^y \left[\frac{h^{(N+1)}(t)(y-t)^N}{N!}\right] dt.$$

where $\phi$ is the sum of the higher-order terms. From (6.20), however, $E[h(y)] \geq h(E[y])$ if $h(y)$ is convex. Thus, the term $h''(E[y])\sigma_y^2/2 + \phi \geq 0$. Now, suppose $y$ is a random variable distributed in accordance with a symmetric density function such as the normal density. For such a distribution the odd moments about the mean disappear and the even moments are functions of the variance. Thus for symmetric distributions the last inequality could be written $\sigma_y^2[h''(E[y])/2 + \xi] \geq 0$, where the bracketed term is necessarily positive when the function is convex. In *this* case, as depicted in Figure 6.8, the difference between $E[h(y)]$ and $h(E[y])$ will be greater, the greater is the variance of the random variable. The same argument holds, with the inequality reversed, for $h(y)$ concave.

Thus, if as seems likely, $Q$ is a *concave* function of factor $i$'s services (so that increases in the services lead to successively smaller increments in $Q$), and if randomness enters into production through the symmetrically random services of factor $i$,

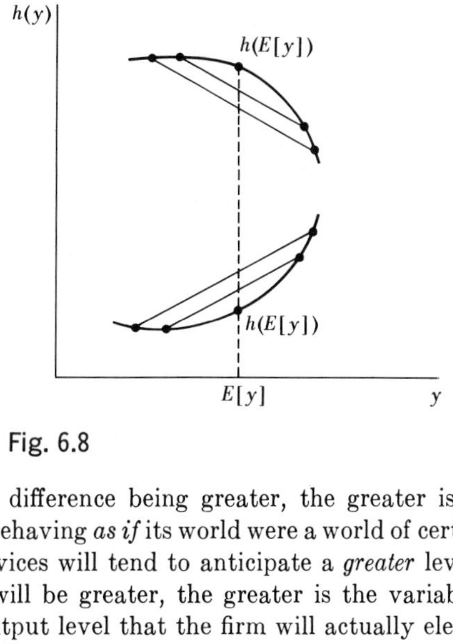


Fig. 6.8

then $\tilde{Q} > \bar{Q}$, with the difference being greater, the greater is the variance. This suggests that the firm behaving *as if* its world were a world of certainty at the average of a set of random services will tend to anticipate a *greater* level of output than it should; and its error will be greater, the greater is the variability of the service. With respect to the output level that the firm will actually elect, the most general suggestion would seem to be that the specific forms of the demand and cost curves, as well as the form of the production function, will determine which of the three concepts of marginal revenue product lead to the greater and lesser output levels. There is also the implicit suggestion, however, that *either* of the two neoclassical options will have been selected via an inappropriate decision rule.

Recognition of the impact of random factors may, therefore, alter the firm's chosen course of action. The decisions taken by the firm can be still further affected when explicit recognition is given to the entrepreneur's attitude towards risk or his gambling inclinations in a world of uncertainty. We shall touch on this aspect of the problem in Chapter 12, after the analytical concepts to deal with it have been introduced.

## 6.6 EMPIRICAL ESTIMATION AND PROFIT MAXIMIZATION

We noted in Chapter 5 that the production function itself is only one of *several* elements determining how much the firm produces of a product and the combination of factors it uses in production—a fact that we should recognize and allow for in empirical estimation of the production function. To illustrate this, we shall discuss one of four models developed and estimated for several industries in the United States by Hildebrand and Liu.[14]

In their analysis, Hildebrand and Liu use 1957 interstate data for a variety of U.S. industries. Theirs is thus a *cross-section*, as opposed to a *time-series*, study in that their data consist of observations at a given time for several components, rather than observations for a single component over several time periods. In "version III" of their model, the value of output of the $i$th firm is given by

$$V_i = P_i Q_i \tag{6.22}$$

where $P_i$ and $Q_i$ are, respectively, the price charged and quantity produced by the firm. A Cobb-Douglas production function[15] of the form

$$Q_i = \alpha L_i^{\beta} K_{i,-1}^{\gamma \log R_{i,-1}} \epsilon_i \tag{6.23}$$

is hypothesized, where $\alpha$, $\beta$, and $\gamma$ are constants and $\epsilon_i$ is a random-disturbance term. $L_i$ is labor, measured by the sum of production and nonproduction workers. In more complex versions of the model, these two classes of employees are treated separately. $K_{i,-1}$ is a measure of capital input (gross book value of plant and equipment at the beginning of the period). $R_{i,-1}$ is the ratio of net to gross capital at the beginning of the period. This is injected into the exponent of $K_{i,-1}$ to reflect the "efficiency"—the age and the use—of the $i$th firm's capital stock.

The demand function for output is

$$Q_i = d_i P_i^{-h}, \tag{6.24}$$

where $-h$ is the elasticity of demand. With $L_i^*$ the long-run "equilibrium" demand for labor, it is hypothesized that

$$\frac{L_i}{L_{i,-1}} = \left[\frac{L_i^*}{L_{i,-1}}\right]^{\lambda} \tag{6.25}$$

with $0 \leq \lambda < 1$. That is, (6.25) reflects the adjustment of the short-run actual demand for labor ($L_i$) towards its long-run equilibrium level ($L_i^*$).

The marginal physical product of labor is given by $\partial Q_i/\partial L_i$, or

$$\frac{\partial Q_i}{\partial L_i} = \beta \alpha L_i^{\beta-1} K_{i,-1}^{\gamma \log R_{i,-1}} \epsilon_i = \frac{\beta Q_i}{L_i}. \tag{6.26}$$

Marginal revenue is determined from the demand curve as $\partial(P_i Q_i)/\partial Q_i = [1 - (1/h)]P_i$. Hence, the marginal revenue product of labor is given by

$$MRP_{Li} = \left(\frac{\beta Q_i}{L_i}\right)\left(1 - \frac{1}{h}\right)P_i = \frac{\beta V_i \left(1 - \frac{1}{h}\right)}{L_i}, \tag{6.27}$$

since $V_i = P_i Q_i$. Stated in terms of the "equilibrium" demand for labor, $L_i^*$ replaces $L_i$ in (6.27).

[14] George H. Hildebrand and Ta-Chung Liu, *Manufacturing Production Functions in the United States, 1957* (Ithaca, N.Y.: The New York State School of Industrial and Labor Relations, 1965), pp. 44–70.

[15] C. W. Cobb and P. H. Douglas, "A Theory of Production," *American Economic Review*, **XVIII,** suppl. no. 2 (March 1928), 139–165.

If there is pure competition with the marginal cost of labor equal to its wage $W_i$, then we would have $MRP_i = W_i$. It is suggested, however, that there will be differences effected by the size of the producing unit, as measured by $V_i$, and by the wage rate itself, as well as discrepancies caused by random disturbances, $\xi_i$. It is then hypothesized that

$$\frac{\beta V_i(1 - 1/h)}{L_i^*} = W_i[\phi W_i^{-\theta} K V_i^{\tau} \xi_i]. \tag{6.28}$$

With (6.23), (6.24), (6.25), and (6.28) forming the heart of the model, and the substitution of value added for value of output (so that $V_i = VP_iQ_i$, where $V$ is a constant), the production function to be estimated is

$$\log V_i = \log (V\alpha P_i) + \beta \log L_i + \gamma \log R_{i,-1} \log K_{i,-1} + \log \epsilon_i, \tag{6.23a}$$

from (6.23). The demand-for-labor equation is to be estimated from

$$\log L_i = \lambda \log \left[\frac{\beta}{\phi K}\left(1 - \frac{1}{h}\right)\right] + (1 - \lambda) \log L_{i,-1} + (1 - \tau)\lambda \log V_i - (1 - \theta)\lambda \log W_i - \lambda \log \xi_i. \tag{6.28a}$$

This is derived by substituting (6.25) into (6.28) and taking logarithms. The exogenous variables are $\log R_{i,-1}$, $\log K_{i,-1}$, $\log L_{i,-1}$, and $\log W_i$. The endogenous variables are $\log V_i$ and $\log L_i$. Using two-stage least squares, Hildebrand and Liu obtain estimates for, say, rubber and plastic products of

$$\begin{aligned} \log V &= .851 \log L + .140 \log R \log K + e_1, \\ \log L &= .728 \log L_{-1} + .273 \log V - .434 \log W + e_2, \end{aligned}$$

where the $i$ subscript and constant terms have been deleted for notational convenience. It is of particular interest that, in order to estimate all functions in the model, we would need to make an assessment of $-h$, the elasticity of demand. From the estimates above, however, one can also draw some important inferences. For example, the estimate of $\beta$ is .851 and that of $\gamma$ is .140. These suggest that output of rubber and plastic products is more responsive to labor changes than to capital changes. Further, the estimate of $(1 - \lambda)$ is .728. Hence, the estimate of $\lambda$ would be .272, implying a rather large discrepancy between short-run employment and the long-run equilibrium level. The remaining coefficients would be analyzed in a similar manner.

The various Hildebrand and Liu models demonstrate that despite the static and vacuum-sealed world in which the neoclassical firm finds itself, its decision-making behavior suggests a pattern that one can and should incorporate in an empirical analysis of industrial operations. By applying liberal doses of imagination and insight, one can extend and enrich the neoclassical model and translate it into terms suitable for empirical study and practical application.

## EXERCISES

1. Consider a firm whose production function is given by $Q = \alpha_0 L^{\alpha_1} K^{\alpha_2}$, where $\alpha_i$ is a constant. The supply curves of the two factors $L$ and $K$ are given by $W_L = \gamma_0 L^{\gamma_1}$ and $W_K = k$, respectively, where $\gamma_0$, $\gamma_1$, and $k$ are positive constants. The firm's demand curve is given by $P = \eta_0 Q^{-\eta_1}$ ($\eta_0$ and $\eta_1$ positive constants).

(a) Determine expressions for the short-run average revenue product, marginal revenue product, average net revenue product, and value of the marginal product curves for $L$.
(b) What is the long-run profit-maximizing price and output for the firm?
(c) Will the answer to the last question be affected by whether there are increasing or decreasing returns to scale? Why or why not?
(d) How are the previous answers affected by changes in the elasticity of demand?
(e) Will the previous results be altered if $\gamma_1 = 0$? What if $\gamma_1 > 0$?
(f) Determine the elasticity of substitution of labor for capital. Are these factors rivals or complements?

2. Suppose that, in the previous question, $\alpha_0 = 1000$, $\alpha_1 = .4$, and $\alpha_2 = .5$. Also, suppose $\gamma_0 = 5$, $\gamma_1 = 0$, and $k = 3$.
(a) Determine expressions for the firm's short- and long-run demand curves for labor.
(b) Determine expressions for the firm's short- and long-run marginal cost curves.
(c) If the firm is one of 50,000 like firms in the industry, determine the long-run industry supply curve.
(d) Each firm considers its demand curve to be given by $P = \bar{P}$. Determine the long-run industry demand curve for labor.
(e) If each firm is in long-run equilibrium, determine the short-run industry demand curve for labor.
(f) Would this problem have been altered substantially by having $\gamma_1 = .6$? Why or why not?

3. Suppose the government sets a minimum wage for a factor of production for the purpose of maximizing that factor's employment in a neoclassical firm. How high should the minimum wage be set?

4. Discuss the possibility of having Giffen's Paradox arise with respect to the demand for a factor of production.

5. A. P. Lerner ["The Concept of Monopoly and the Measurement of Monopoly Power," *Review of Economic Studies*, **I** (1934), 157–175] has suggested the inverse of the absolute value of the elasticity of demand as a measure of monopoly power.
(a) Show that an equivalent measure is given by the expression $[VMP_i - MRP_i]/VMP_i$.
(b) If a firm is the single buyer of a factor, it is a *monopsonist*. Suggest an index of the firm's monopsony power analogous to Lerner's Index of monopoly power.

6. Suppose the firm of Exercise 2 faces a demand curve of $P = \eta_{00}Q^{-\eta_{10}}$ in one market and a demand curve of $P = \eta_{01}Q^{-\eta_{11}}$ in a second market geographically isolated from the first. The firm is able to charge one price in one market and another price in the second market: that is, it is a *discriminating monopoly* that can discriminate in price.
(a) Determine the firm's long-run demand curve for labor.
(b) How much will the firm sell in each market and at what price?
(c) How is the discriminating monopolist's price policy influenced by the elasticities of demand in the various markets in which he sells?

7. Suppose a product is made by combining two factors in fixed proportion such that $Q = \min\,[F_1/a_1,\ F_2/a_2]$. Discuss the implications for the marginal physical product of factor 1 if the *services* of factor 2 are generated by a random process.

8. Discuss the determination of factor wages and factor employment if (1) there are fixed technological coefficients of production and (2) the firm has a kinked demand curve.

9. Suppose that the neoclassical firm's advertising expenditures act so as to increase the number of units the firm can sell at any price.
(a) Determine an expression for the optimal level of advertising.
(b) How does this change the firm's demand for its factors of production?

10. Suppose the price of the product that was the subject of discussion in the Appendix to Chapter 5 was as follows:

| | | | |
|---|---|---|---|
| 75 ($t$ = 1) | 75 (6) | 72 (11) | 64 (16) |
| 75 (2) | 75 (7) | 70 (12) | 60 (17) |
| 75 (3) | 74 (8) | 68 (13) | 55 (18) |
| 77 (4) | 70 (9) | 68 (14) | 55 (19) |
| 77 (5) | 70 (10) | 65 (15) | 57 (20) |

There is the strong presumption on the part of management that demand is unit elastic. The wages of nonmanagement labor, management, and capital were constant at $5, $10, and $20 per unit, respectively, during the period in question. Assuming the firm's production function to be of the Cobb-Douglas type, develop a model to estimate the parameters of the production function, and then do the estimating.

# 7

# THE NEOCLASSICAL THEORY OF THE FIRM: Price-Quantity Determination

## 7.1 INTRODUCTION

We have seen that in its effort to maximize profit the neoclassical firm of microeconomic theory employs its factors of production so as to equate, for each factor, marginal revenue product to marginal factor cost. Simultaneously, the firm will be selecting that level of output at which marginal revenue equals marginal cost. The present chapter extends the previous analysis to analyze differences in output among like firms, as the structure of the industry housing them changes. Price-quantity determination for the industry as a whole also is discussed, and differences effected by differences in market structure are indicated. Particular attention is given to the cases of monopoly, monopolistic competition, and pure competition, as well as to certain classical oligopoly models. Chapter 8 considers some implications of shifts in the relevant functions.

The present discussion is confined to the neoclassical theory—a theory that has been subjected to more than its share of criticism and has been the beneficiary of extremely able and agile defenses. Much of the criticism centers on the assumptions upon which the theory is founded. The assumptions and the criticisms are discussed in some detail in Chapter 11. For the present, however, we shall simply note the major assumptions upon which the neoclassical model has been built.

## 7.2 THE BASIC ASSUMPTIONS OF THE NEOCLASSICAL THEORY

The firm of microeconomic theory is ordinarily assumed to produce a single product via a single process. The process is summarized in the firm's production function, at a given level of technology.

The firm's major decisions are made by an entrepreneur whose single goal for the firm is the maximization of profit. The entrepreneur has somehow resolved the firm's organization, production, personnel, and financial problems in an optimum manner—or at least these do not interfere with his relentless quest for a profit maximum.

The profit referred to is itself the subject of some debate.[1] Here, profit will be the difference between total revenue and total cost, where total cost includes an opportunity cost for the entrepreneur's entrepreneurial services. That is, the entrepreneur's decision-making talent is a factor of production that enters into the production function. The cost associated with providing this talent is an opportunity cost made up of the income sacrificed by the entrepreneur because of his decision not to sell his services elsewhere to the highest bidder. Thus, when profit is zero, the entrepreneur is perfectly happy to remain in business for he is earning as much as he could earn elsewhere—his normal profit. Any profit the firm earns above this norm also accrues to the entrepreneur, and will be called *abnormal* profit.

The entrepreneur is presumed to behave *as if* he knew his demand and cost curves with certainty. Sometimes he will err and be disappointed, and upon occasion pleasantly surprised, but he learns from his mistakes: he learns the relevant functions that he requires for his price-quantity determination decision. From the entrepreneur's standpoint, then, when he determines output he is also determining profit. He is free to select any output and profit combinations made feasible by the relevant functions. The combination that the neoclassical theory assumes he will choose is the combination compatible with profit maximization.

Specifically, the entrepreneur seeks to maximize profit over a given *time horizon*.[2] The time horizon may be a period of five years or a period of fifty. He seeks the greatest total profit, summed over the entire period, but allowing for the fact that a dollar received today is more valuable than a dollar received tomorrow.[3] The neo-

[1] Though the debate can frequently be resolved as a matter of definition. For example: "The firm's profit from any level of output is the difference between its costs of producing and marketing the output and its revenue from selling the output" [Cliff Lloyd, *Microeconomic Analysis* (Homewood, Ill.: Richard D. Irwin, Inc., 1967), p. 101], or, "[Profits] are the returns to productive services in excess of what they can earn in alternative employments" [George Stigler, *The Theory of Price* (New York: The Macmillan Company, 1952), p. 180]. Contrast these with the following: "There are three measures of profit which tend to be used (singly or collectively) to compare a firm's performance with its budget, with its past, and with other companies' records. These are the percentage profit return on sales, the percentage profit return on total assets, and the percentage profit return on net worth." [Neil W. Chamberlain, *The Firm: Micro-Economic Planning and Action* (New York: McGraw-Hill, Inc., 1962), p. 55.] Also, "The profit with which we are concerned is not the reported net profit but the real net profit. The two are not necessarily the same. There are a number of ways in which they may diverge, usually owing to management's desire to make a good showing." (Chamberlain, *The Firm*, p. 55.) Chapter 4 of Chamberlain's book contains a nice discussion of "profits" in this same general vein. The implications of uncertainty for definitions of profit are discussed by William Fellner in *Probability and Profit* (Homewood, Ill.: Richard D. Irwin., 1965), pp. 109–138.

[2] For some interesting comment in the neoclassical spirit on the role of time horizon in influencing current decisions see the following: J. M. Clark, "Toward a Concept of Workable Competition," *American Economic Review*, **XXX**: 2 (June 1940), 241–256 and particularly 248; Oscar Lange, "A Note on Innovations," *Review of Economics and Statistics*, **XXV**:1 (Feb. 1943), 19–25; Edward S. Mason, "Various Views on the Monopoly Problem," *Review of Economics and Statistics*, **XXXI**:2 (May 1949), 105. Also see P. Gutmann, "Intertemporal Profit Maximization and the Firm," *Western Economic Journal*, **5**:3 (June 1967), 271–275; and E. Zabel, "A Dynamic Model of the Competitive Firm," *International Economic Review*, **8**:2 (June 1967), 194–208.

[3] This will be discussed in Section 10.7.

classical theory is, however, basically a static theory in which a fifty-year period is made up of a number of like smaller periods. These are commonly assumed to be independent of one another. Hence, given the certainty of things, the optimum decision for any one period will be the optimum decision for each period throughout the entire time horizon. Any period may be short run or long, depending upon the firm's ability to vary its factors of production. The firm always sells all that it produces during the production period. Profit maximization therefore becomes an unambiguous goal, because each production decision may be viewed as essentially isolated from preceding or subsequent decisions. When the firm *is* free to vary all factors of production, it hires them so as to maximize *long-run* profit. In the process some factors may thereby become fixed. The firm subsequently makes production decisions so as to maximize *short-run* profit, until such time as the now fixed factors may once again be varied.[4]

If the firm cannot cover the cost of its variable factors, it will go out of business. If the firm is making abnormal profit, other firms may or may not be both willing and able to enter the industry, produce the same product at the same cost, cut price to wean away the profiteer's custom, and thereby erode his abnormal profit. Thus the firm's price-quantity decision will necessarily be tempered by the ability of potential producers to enter the industry, by the number and strength of other firms producing a like product, and by its own ability to leave the industry.[5] In discussing the behavior of the firm in the neoclassical theory, one must therefore make specific assumptions about the firm's actual and potential competition. These assumptions may be many and varied. Several will be specified and their implications developed as the discussion proceeds.

## 7.3 PRICE-QUANTITY DETERMINATION

For the moment it is not necessary to specify whether the firm is planning for the long run or the short. We require only that the firm derive its total cost function, $C = c(Q)$. This will be determined from the production function and factor supply curves so as to minimize the cost of producing a given output (or, equivalently, maximize the output produced for a given cost). For notational convenience, in *writing* the demand curve we shall omit all of the "other factors" to be held fixed.

[4] Some interesting *dynamic* issues are raised when, for example, technical change and the progressively worsening obsolescence of equipment encourages the firm to start thinking in terms of simply scrapping a fixed factor or its usage. Then the firm must weigh the advantages of operating in one short run with its given factors, or in another short run with the alternative technology and alternative sets of fixed factors.

[5] Joe S. Bain ["Pricing in Monopoly and Oligopoly," *American Economic Review*, **XXXIX**:2 (March 1949), 448–464] has commented: "Assuming correct appraisal of limit prices... by established sellers, we get three major possibilities: (1) pricing to maximize industry profit with no entry resulting; (2) pricing to forestall entry with industry profit not maximized but the profit of established sellers maximized; and (3) pricing to maximize industry profit but with resulting attraction of additional entry. The first two cases find industries already in long-run equilibrium; the third finds industries in process of dynamic change in structure" (p. 463). The particularly acute importance of potential competition in situations of rising, as opposed to stationary, demand is discussed in Carl Kaysen, "A Dynamic Aspect of the Monopoly Problem," *Review of Economics and Statistics*, **XXXI**:2 (May 1949), 109–113. Also, see P. W. S. Andrews, *On Competition in Economic Theory* (London: Macmillan and Co., Ltd., 1964).

Only price and quantity will appear. It will also be convenient to write the firm's demand curve as $P = D(Q)$, with quantity as the independent variable. The firm will therefore be called upon to fix a level of production, and price will be set via the demand curve so as to assure the sale of the total output during the production period.

For any one production period, then, profit is given by total revenue less total cost, or

$$\pi = PQ - c(Q) = D(Q)Q - c(Q). \tag{7.1}$$

The firm seeks to maximize profit. To do so it extends production to the point at which further increments in output would add more to total cost than they would add to total revenue. In terms of the calculus, the firm seeks an output $Q^*$ such that

$$\frac{d\pi}{dQ} = D'(Q^*)Q^* + D(Q^*) - c'(Q^*) = 0 \tag{7.2a}$$

and that

$$\frac{d^2\pi}{dQ^2} = D''(Q^*)Q^* + 2D'(Q^*) - c''(Q^*) < 0, \tag{7.2b}$$

where the prime indicates the derivative with respect to $Q$ and the double prime the second derivative with respect to $Q$. Rearranging terms, (7.2a) may be written

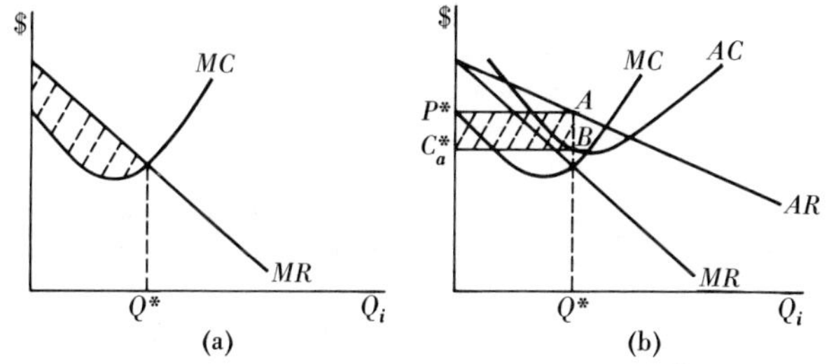


Fig. 7.1

$D'(Q^*)Q^* + D(Q^*) = c'(Q^*)$; or, as previously indicated, the first-order condition for a profit maximum is that production takes place where marginal revenue ($MR$) equals marginal cost ($MC$). Condition (7.2b) may be written $c''(Q^*) > D''(Q^*)Q^* + 2D'(Q^*)$. The second-order condition for a profit maximum is that, at the point where $MR = MC$, $MC$ must be increasing more rapidly, or decreasing less rapidly, than $MR$. This implies that producing where $MR = MC$ will maximize profit as long as the $MC$ curve intersects the $MR$ curve from below. There may, of course, be more than a single point of intersection. In this case the optimum production point will be the maximum of the individual or local maxima. It will, however, be assumed that profit as described by (7.1) is a strictly concave function of $Q$, and therefore any local maximum is a global maximum.

This is illustrated in Figure 7.1(a). The area underneath the marginal cost curve from the vertical axis to any $Q$ gives the total cost of producing that quantity. Mathematically, the area is given by

$$\int_0^Q c'(Q)\, dQ = c(Q).$$

In similar fashion, the area under the marginal revenue curve gives total revenue. Hence, the difference between the two areas, or the shaded area in Figure 7.1(a), gives the total profit at the optimal production rate of $Q^*$. In Figure 7.1(b) the $MR$ and $MC$ curves are reproduced together with the average revenue (that is, demand) and average cost curves. Here, the same maximum total profit, calculated at the output where $MR = MC$, is given by the area $ABC_a^*P^*$. Since $C_a^*$ is the average cost of the optimal output, this is the area of the rectangle with sides of length $Q^*$ and $P^* - C^*/Q^*$.

## 7.4 THE PURELY COMPETITIVE INDUSTRY

### a. The Short Run

The distinguishing characteristic of the short run is that resources have limited flexibility. This restriction is especially important in the analysis of the purely competitive industry, because it carries with it the presumption that, in the short run, the number of firms in the industry, as well as their scale of operation, is fixed.

Assume that there are $n$ firms producing a homogeneous product. Buyers have ready access to all firms and preference for none. Moreover, at comparatively low output levels each firm will be subject to technological and/or pecuniary diseconomies[6] and, consequently, rising marginal costs. "Comparatively low" output levels are relative to the output demanded of the industry as a whole at the price ultimately determined in the market. Implicit in the reference to *the* price is the assumption that, except for temporary aberrations, a single price for the good will obtain and all sellers will eventually come to accept it. The firms will thus behave as price-takers rather than price-setters. This assumption follows from the previous two assumptions. On the one hand, if buyers have access to all sellers and the latter produce what is for all buyers a homogeneous commodity, none will purchase from the seller who charges a price higher than that charged by any other single seller. On the other hand, if one seller charges a price lower than any other, he will not be willing, or perhaps able, to produce all that is demanded of him at that price because of the rapidly rising production costs. To extend output he will require a higher price. Simultaneously, to sell their outputs, the other sellers will have to accept a lower price.

In the last chapter we saw that the firm's marginal cost curve describes the quantities the firm would like to supply at all prices at or above average variable cost. The horizontal sum of the individual firms' marginal cost curves at or above average variable cost therefore represents the total industry supply at each price. With marginal cost below average variable cost, the vertical axis is the supply curve. For convenience it will be assumed that the supply curve has but these two segments and that the first segment is a continuous curve.

Let the industry demand curve be given by $P = D(Q)$ and the $i$th firm's total cost curve by $C_i = c_i(Q_i)$. The firm's marginal cost curve will be given by $C_i' = c_i'(Q_i)$.

[6] Technological diseconomies (or economies) are those which derive from the production function. With constant factor prices and decreasing returns to scale, long-run marginal cost will be steadily rising because of a technological restriction. Alternatively, with upward-sloping factor supply curves and constant returns to scale, long-run marginal cost will be steadily rising because the factors become progressively more expensive to employ as their usage increases.

The relevant portion of the industry supply curve will be given by $C' = c'(Q)$. The industry demand and supply curves are depicted in Figure 7.2(a). At prices above $P^* = D(Q^*) = c'(Q^*)$, sellers wish to supply more than buyers wish to purchase. A reduction in total output and price is required if total output is to be sold. At prices below $P^*$, buyers want to purchase more than sellers are willing to supply, so that both price and production are increased. At $P^*$, allegedly everybody is happy and the market is in equilibrium—there is no reason to change price from $P^*$ and output from $Q^*$. Nevertheless, we have previously witnessed each *firm's* desire to equate $MR$ to $MC$. We must, therefore, inquire into whether this too is being achieved.

At equilibrium, the $i$th firm's total profit will be given by

$$\pi_i = PQ_i - C_i = D(Q_i + \sum_{j \neq i} Q_j)Q_i - c_i(Q_i),$$

as *all* firms charge a price of $P$. To maximize profit, the firm requires that

$$MR_i = \left(\frac{dP}{dQ_i}\right) Q_i + P = \frac{dC_i}{dQ_i} = MC_i.$$

Note, however, that for the *industry* marginal cost equals price, for price is determined where the industry marginal cost or supply curve crosses the demand curve.

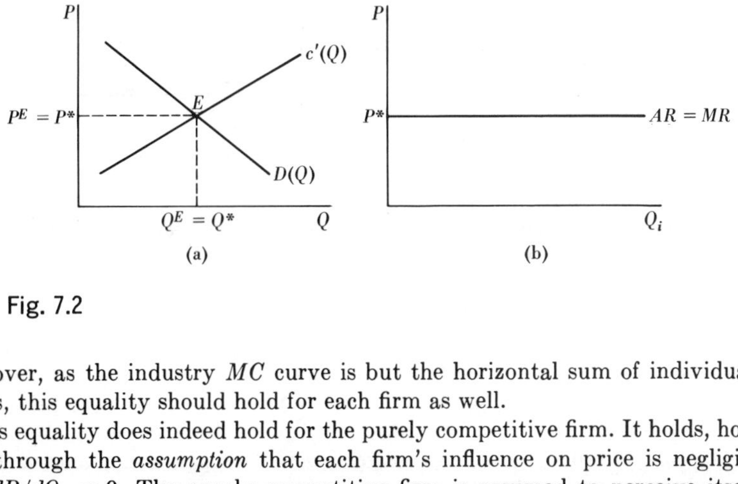


Fig. 7.2

Moreover, as the industry $MC$ curve is but the horizontal sum of individual $MC_i$ curves, this equality should hold for each firm as well.

This equality does indeed hold for the purely competitive firm. It holds, however, only through the *assumption* that each firm's influence on price is negligible, or that $dP/dQ_i \approx 0$. The purely competitive firm is assumed to perceive itself as a noninfluential factor in the determination of market price. For the sorts of quantity changes it contemplates, the firm feels that it will not affect price. Thus, the purely competitive firm is commonly *thought of* as being able to sell as much as it might wish at the market price, even if in fact it cannot. We thus *think of* the firm's demand curve as being horizontal at the market price of $P^*$, as in Figure 7.2(b). Here, it is in fact true that $(dP/dQ_i)Q_i + P = MR_i = P^* = MC_i$; or, marginal revenue equals average revenue (price) equals marginal cost, since $dP/dQ_i \approx 0$.

In practice, it will ordinarily not be true that $dP/dQ_i = 0$. As was seen in Chapter 4, the firm's demand curve and, consequently, its marginal revenue curve will depend upon the assumptions made with respect to $dP/dQ_i = (dP/dQ)(dQ/dQ_i)$.

If it is assumed that all other firms hold their outputs fixed when $Q_i$ changes, then $dQ/dQ_i = d(\Sigma Q_j)/dQ_i = 1$, and $dP/dQ_i = dP/dQ$. That is, the *slopes* of the firm and industry demand curves are equal. Since the firm and industry prices are each $P^*$, in this case the demand *elasticities* will differ. The firm's demand curve will be more elastic than that for the industry as $(dQ/dP)(P^*/Q_i^*) < (dQ/dP)(P^*/Q^*)$, because $Q_i^* < Q^*$ and both expressions are negative.

If all firms adjust output so as to produce equal quantities, then $dQ/dQ_i = d(nQ_i)/dQ_i = n$, and $dP/dQ_i = (dP/dQ)n$. That is, the firm's demand curve has $n$ times the *slope* of the industry curve. Now, however, the elasticities are equal, since

$$\left(\frac{dQ_i}{dP}\right)\left(\frac{P^*}{Q_i^*}\right) = \left(\frac{1}{n}\right)\left(\frac{dQ}{dP}\right)\left(\frac{P^*}{Q_i^*}\right) = \left(\frac{dQ}{dP}\right)\left(\frac{P^*}{Q^*}\right).$$

The assumption that $dP/dQ_i = 0$ is equivalent to assuming that $d(\Sigma Q_j)/dQ_i = 0$. This implies that when a single firm changes output, *total* output remains unchanged; other firms reduce output to compensate for the $i$th firm's increase, leaving price unaltered. This would seem to be somewhat magnanimous behavior on the part of a host of profit-maximizing firms. In point of fact, when the $i$th firm's production varies, this will ordinarily have *some* effect on price, given the output levels of the other firms. This price effect will in turn influence the output decisions of these other firms.

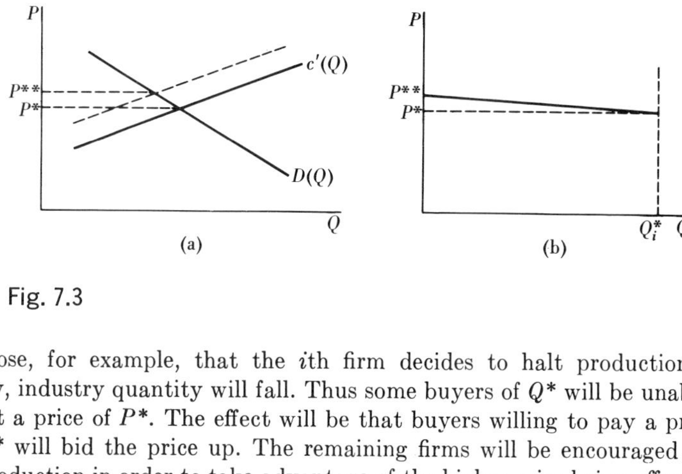


Fig. 7.3

Suppose, for example, that the $i$th firm decides to halt production entirely. Initially, industry quantity will fall. Thus some buyers of $Q^*$ will be unable to purchase at a price of $P^*$. The effect will be that buyers willing to pay a price higher than $P^*$ will bid the price up. The remaining firms will be encouraged to extend their production in order to take advantage of the higher price being offered. Recall, however, the assumption that firms very quickly run into diseconomies. Further, these diseconomies make it unprofitable for them to increase production, in total, to the extent that the disappearing firm reduced production. This is particularly true since, as each increases production, price must be reduced from the higher level to which it has been bid up, if the market is to be cleared. The result is that price finally settles at, say, $P^{**}$ in Figure 7.3(a). The $i$th firm's presence in the industry has, therefore, influenced price somewhat, and each and every unit that it sells will influence price, although the influence will be negligible. In particular, its demand curve will be the locus of points such as $P^{**}$ (when 0 units are produced) and $P^*$ (when $Q^*$ units are produced) and will appear as in Figure 7.3(b). Only because $Q_i$ will be small relative to $Q$ and $P^{**}$ will be close to $P^*$ is the pure competitor's demand curve drawn *as if* it is horizontal and the analysis advanced *as if* the curve had zero slope. This simplification, however, has as negligible an effect on the analysis as the pure competitor is assumed to have on industry price. Subject to the qualification that one is not being strictly accurate, one can feel quite comfortable in assuming that, for the pure competitor, $dP/dQ_i = 0$ and $MR = P$. Hence, each firm in the purely competitive industry is in fact equating marginal revenue to marginal cost at the market-clearing price of $MR_i^* = P^* = c'(Q^*) = c_i'(Q_i^*) = MC_i^*$.[7]

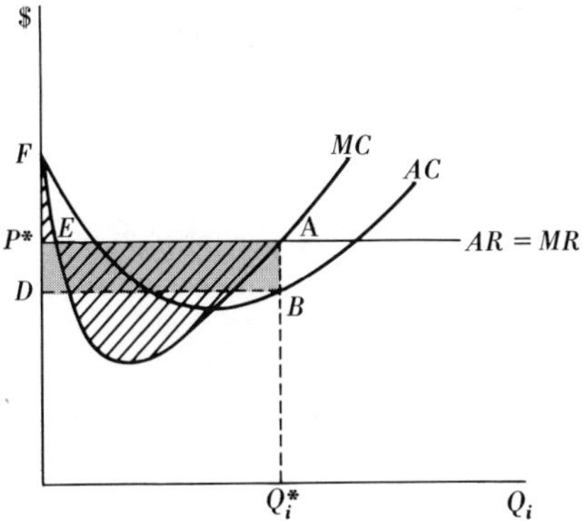


Fig. 7.4

The *i*th pure competitor will therefore make an abnormal profit of

$$\pi_i = \left[P^* - \frac{c_i(Q_i^*)}{Q_i^*}\right] Q_i^* = \int_0^{Q^*} P^*\, dQ_i - \int_0^{Q^*} c_i'(Q_i)\, dQ_i.$$

The first of these two expressions, price less average cost per unit, or profit per unit, multiplied by the total number of units, is the shaded rectangle $ABDP^*$ of Figure 7.4. The second expression for total revenue less total cost is determined from the crosshatched area in the figure between the marginal revenue and marginal cost curves. It is the area above the $MC$ curve to the line segment $EA$, *less* the area $FEP^*$.

[7] As will shortly be indicated, the profit-maximization assumption has come in for more than its share of abuse. Yet, consider Chamberlin's comment: "Competitive equilibrium is not only consistent with unqualified maximum profits for everyone; it involves them as a necessary condition" [Edward H. Chamberlin, *The Theory of Monopolistic Competition* (Cambridge, Mass.: Harvard University Press, 1960), p. 20]. Benjamin Higgins ["Elements of Indeterminacy in the Theory of Non-Perfect Competition," *American Economic Review,* **XXIX**:3 (Sept. 1939), 476] concurs in the view that "entrepreneurs under perfect competition maximize profits or disappear altogether." He goes on to note that "The same analysis applies to the 'tangency case' of monopolistic competition." (See below.) Note, however, that "It is normal profit that must exist *ex definitione* in a perfectly competitive situation—and normal profit is a purely subjective matter.... In the absence of knowledge concerning the objective of businessmen, it is impossible to determine that equilibrium position. We must say, as the older economists used to say, that the individual entrepreneur will attempt to maximize his net advantage (whatever that may be)." [Edward S. Lynch, "A Note on Mr. Higgins' 'Indeterminancy in Non-Perfect Competition,'" *American Economic Review,* **XXX**:2 (June 1940), 348.] Also, see the Higgins "Reply," *ibid.*, pp. 348–350. These comments should be borne in mind when reading the next several paragraphs.

It is important to recognize that while each firm will receive a unit price of $P^*$ for its output, output levels may differ among firms and $Q_j^*$ will not necessarily equal $Q_k^*$, nor will $\pi_j$ necessarily equal $\pi_k$. These differences will stem from differences in the firms' $MC$ and $AC$ curves. The latter may differ simply because the entrepreneurs have incorporated into them different normal profits. The more skilled entrepreneur, for instance, may have a higher opportunity cost than the less skilled and consequently may have a higher normal profit requirement and a higher average cost curve. Additionally, the firm with superior technology or knowledge might be producing a given output at lower unit costs than a competitor. In any event, the firm will make an abnormal profit so long as its demand curve lies about the point of minimum average cost. Assuming the average cost curve to be U-shaped, marginal cost will lie above average cost when average cost is increasing. Since at the optimal output level price equals marginal cost, the firm must be making a positive abnormal profit. When, however, the demand curve lies below the point of minimum average cost, the firm suffers a loss. Note that it *may* not actually be suffering a monetary loss. It *could* merely be earning less than the requisite normal profit. In this case, the entrepreneur would be suffering an *opportunity* loss.

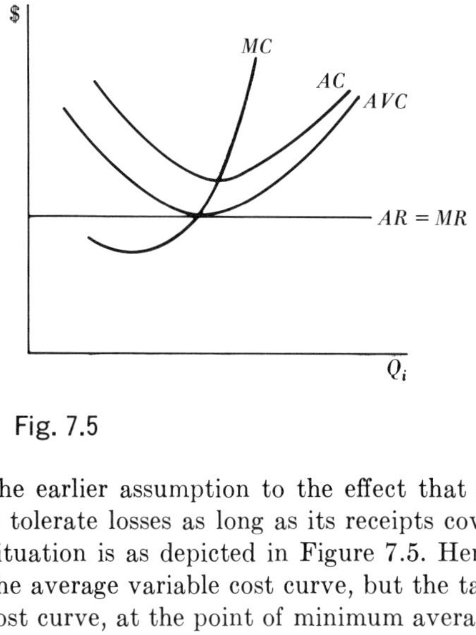


Fig. 7.5

Recall, however, the earlier assumption to the effect that in the short run the firm will continue to tolerate losses as long as its receipts cover its variable costs. Suppose, then, the situation is as depicted in Figure 7.5. Here the firm's demand curve is tangent to the average variable cost curve, but the tangency occurs below the average (total) cost curve, at the point of minimum average variable cost. The firm will be indifferent between producing its optimal output or simply going out of business. The firm suffers a loss through its inability to cover its fixed costs. Since, however, it will be forced to bear these costs anyway, it will continue to produce if it can at least cover its variable costs. This is the *marginal firm*, frequently described as the least efficient producer having the highest average variable cost curve. At prices below minimum average variable cost this marginal firm will be forced to halt all production.

## b. The Long Run

In the long run there are no fixed factors and no fixed costs. Firms are free to enter and leave the industry and to adjust their scales of production. It is also assumed that interfirm differences in technology, efficiency, and knowledge cannot be maintained, for firms will take advantage of their freedom to adjust to the most efficient mode of operation. Hence, not only are all costs variable costs, but each firm will be operating with the most efficient scale of plant and lowest achievable "money" cost curve. This does not mean, however, that each firm will necessarily have the same average cost curve, since entrepreneurs may differ in their normal profit requirements.

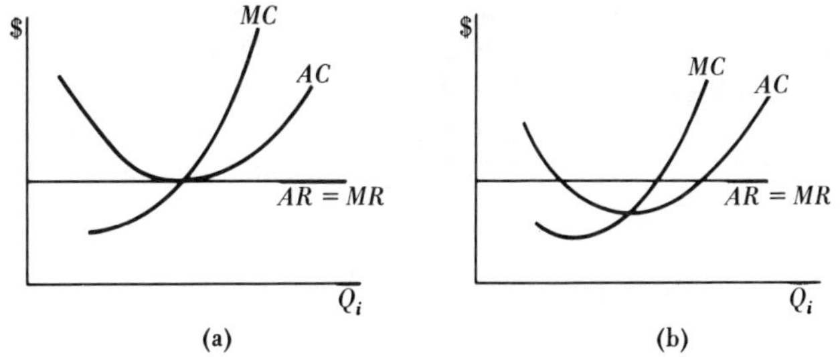


Fig. 7.6

In this situation, the marginal firm will now be the one whose horizontal demand curve is tangent to the $AC$ curve at the point of minimum average total cost, as in Figure 7.6(a). There may, however, be some firms managed by entrepreneurs having lower opportunity costs and consequently lower $AC$ curves. These firms, such as the one depicted in Figure 7.6(b), will be earning above-normal profits even in the long run. In this case, however, their *normal* profits will be lower than those of the marginal firm by the amount of the above-normal profits. Total net earnings above other than the *fixed* entrepreneurial factor cost will be the same for all firms. The division between normal and above-normal profit will be a function of the entrepreneur's opportunity cost. Thus, if all firms were managed by entrepreneurs having the same opportunity cost, each would be a marginal firm and, in the long run, none would earn above-normal profit. In the event that any firms did earn above-normal profit, since technology is the same for all, the profit would have to be effected by cost advantages. Their costs would soon be increased as other entrepreneurs bid up the wages of these favored firms' factors of production. This bidding would continue until all abnormal profit disappeared and all firms became marginal. Where entrepreneurs' opportunity costs differ, the marginal firm will be the one managed by the entrepreneur with the highest opportunity cost. Should factor costs suddenly decrease, the previously marginal firm would earn above-normal profits owing to the fall in the $AC$ curve; some firms standing in the wings would now enter the industry and a new marginal firm make its appearance. All of this, however, would happen only in the long run, when firms are able to come and go as they please and to acquire the knowledge of what constitutes optimal production facilities.

## c. Stability and Equilibrium

A state of equilibrium has been described as one from which there is no tendency to depart. One can go on to distinguish between *equilibria* that are *stable* and those that are *unstable*. The distinguishing characteristic is that in a stable equilibrium there will be a movement to return to that state should there be any slight departure from it. A slight departure from an unstable equilibrium state, however, will result in a still further movement away from it. This further movement will continue until a state is once again reached from which there is no tendency to depart. The state that attracts is stable and the state that repels is unstable.

In the present context, consider the industry demand curve $P^D = D(Q)$ and the industry supply curve $P^S = S(Q)$. Here, *quantity* is the independent variable and price is the dependent variable. The quantities placed on the market will be adjusted until, as at the point $E$ in Figure 7.2(a), the price that consumers are willing to pay, $P^D$, equals the price at which producers are willing to supply, $P^S$. Denote by $Q^E$ the quantity such that $P^D = D(Q^E) = S(Q^E) = P^S$. At quantities greater than $Q^E$, the price that consumers are willing to pay falls short of the price required by producers. The latter will subsequently reduce the amount they place on the market.

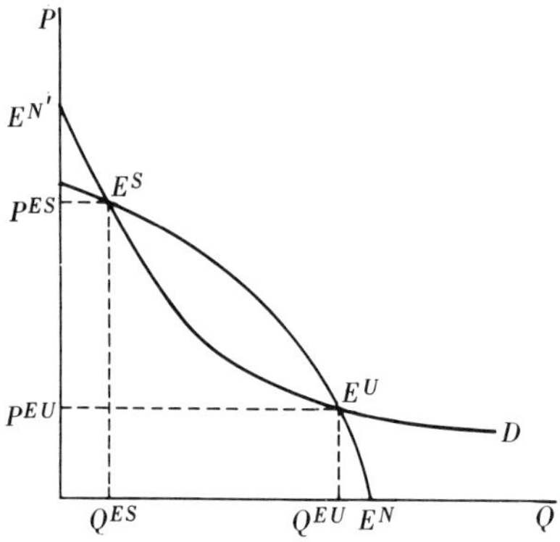


Fig. 7.7

Should a quantity less than $Q^E$ be placed on the market, the price consumers would be willing to pay would exceed that required by producers, who would therefore expand production. Mutual happiness would be attained where $P^S = P^D = P^E$, or where $D(Q) = S(Q)$. To assure the stability of the equilibrium it is necessary that $d[S(Q^E)]/dQ > d[D(Q^E)]/dQ$: that is, the slope of the supply curve must be greater than the slope of the demand curve at $Q^E$. This condition asserts that for values of $Q$ in the neighborhood of $Q^E$, if $Q > Q^E$, then $P^S > P^D$ and quantity will be reduced; whereas if $Q < Q^E$, then $P^D > P^S$ and quantity will be increased. Thus, $E^S$ of Figure 7.7 would be stable, whereas $E^U$ would be unstable. In this case, where $Q^{ES} < Q < Q^{EU}$, $P^S > P^D$ and quantity is reduced until we arrive at $E^S$; when $Q > Q^{EU}$, $P^D > P^S$ and quantity is increased until we arrive at $E^N$ on the quantity axis; when $Q < Q^{ES}$, we again have $P^D > P^S$ and quantity is increased until we return to $E^S$.

Alternatively, suppose price is the independent variable and quantity the dependent variable so that the demand and supply curves are of the form $Q^D = D(P)$ and $Q^S = S(P)$, respectively. Again referring to point $E$ in Figure 7.2(a), at prices below $P^E$ the quantities that consumers are willing to buy exceed those that producers are willing to sell and, consequently, the price will be increased. At prices above $P^E$, price will have to be reduced, since producers cannot sell as much as they wish. Mutual happiness still prevails at $E$, the point to which we are led by each of these reactions. Here, $D(P) = S(P)$. To assure the stability of this equilibrium, then, it is necessary that

$$\frac{d[D(P^E)]}{dP} < \frac{d[S(P^E)]}{dP}$$

—that is, the slope of the supply curve *with respect to the price axis* must be greater than the slope of the demand curve at $P^E$. Thus, the point $E^U$ in Figure 7.7 would now be stable, whereas the point $E^S$ would be unstable. If, for example, when $P^{EU} < P < P^{ES}$ we also have $Q^D < Q^S$, price will be reduced to sell the excess supply, and there will be a movement to $E^U$. If $P > P^{ES}$, $Q^D > Q^S$ and price will be increased until we arrive at $E^{N'}$ on the price axis.

Initially, it is somewhat disconcerting to be confronted with the fact that what are seemingly two perfectly reasonable methods of analysis can lead to quite different results. This difference, however, is not especially troublesome, for the two approaches are not necessarily meant to apply to the same situation. In particular, when *price* is assigned the role of the independent variable, the *Walrasian* approach,[8] the emphasis is on *short-run* situations where the inflexibility of certain factors is reflected in relative fixity of supply. Hence, the industry supply curve will be neither perfectly elastic nor downward sloping, as the fixed factors prevent firms from taking advantage of any potential pecuniary economies available to the industry through expanded purchases of decreasing-cost factors.[9] The difficulty in altering quantity supplied when the industry is out of equilibrium forces price into the role of the independent variable.

In the *long run*, however, with *complete* freedom to alter quantities supplied to take advantage of disparities between demand and supply price—the *Marshallian* approach[10]—*quantity* becomes the independent variable that moves so as to remove these disparities. In this situation, one would not expect the inelastic or backward-bending supply curve that might appear in the short run. One could, however, run into the downward-sloping supply curve occasioned by the cost economies of large-scale *industry* operations that are possible in the long run for a decreasing-cost *industry*. Thus the apparent contradictions of Figure 7.7 are resolved by the fact that if the supply curve is a forward-falling curve, $Q$ will have been assumed to be the independent variable. $E^S$ and $E^N$ are then stable equilibria, while $E^U$ is an unstable equilibrium. If, however, the supply curve is a backward-bending curve, then $E^U$ and $E^{N'}$ are stable equilibria while $E^S$ is unstable. In order to know which mode

[8] Leon Walras, *Elements d'Economie Politique Pure* (Paris: R. Pichon et R. Durand-Auzias, 1926), pp. 54–71 et il faut particulièrement que vous lisiez la 7[me] leçon.

[9] In the purely competitive industry the firm perceives its effects on factor *wages* to be negligible because it is a small producer and hence a small employer. Thus the firm can employ as much of a factor as it desires, in its perception of things, at the going wage. This wage will be determined by the total *industry* demand for the factor. In pure competition, increasing- and decreasing-cost *industries* derive their increasing- and decreasing-cost properties from the fact that the supply curves to the *industry* of various factors of production are either rising or falling. As *industry* output expands with, say, all factors having rising supply curves, when the *industry* demand for the factors increases, the factors' wages will increase. This will in turn cause the individual firms' average cost curves to rise. We shall return to this point in greater detail in the next chapter.

[10] Alfred Marshall, *Principles of Economics* (New York: The Macmillan Company, 1948), pp. 330–350 and particularly pp. 345–346.

of analysis is appropriate, of course, one must know some of the details of the problem. Though one occasionally forgets it, this isn't too bad an idea in general.

Finally, it might be noted that while the supply and demand curves could intersect at several points, resulting in many equilibria, stable and unstable equilibria will always alternate from one equilibrium point to the next, and there will necessarily be one more stable than unstable point. They will alternate since, if (in the Marshallian case, say) the slope of the demand curve exceeds that of the supply curve at one point of intersection, the reverse must be true at the two adjacent points of intersection; or, if there is an unstable point and no adjacent intersection, then points on the axes become stable equilibria. Because of the latter, there will have to be one more stable than unstable point. Examples of *dynamic* stability problems are seen in Exercises 13 and 14.

## 7.5 MONOPOLY

With the now familiar qualification about the difference between short and long run and the fixity of certain factors, the monopolist's solution of the price-quantity problem is essentially the same in the long run as in the short. As noted earlier, he produces so long as price equals or exceeds average variable cost; in the long run, the latter equals average total cost.

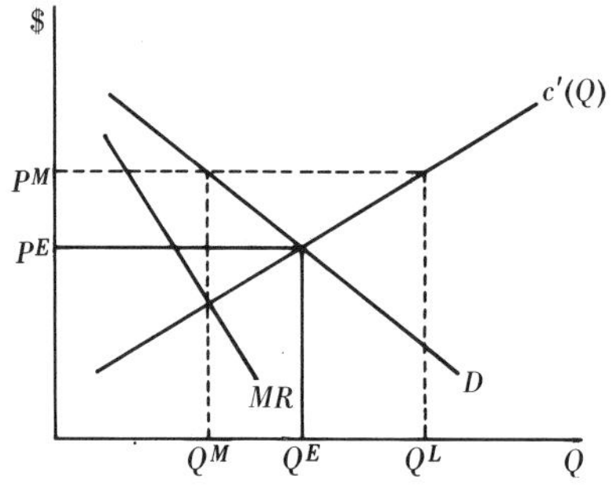


Fig. 7.8

Thus, suppose the monopolist's demand curve is the industry curve of Figure 7.2(a), and his marginal cost curve is the same as the industry supply curve (which, it will be recalled, is obtained by the horizontal summation of the pure competitors' marginal cost curves). The monopolist determines his output by equating $MR$ and $MC$. He therefore derives the curve marginal to the industry demand curve and produces where it and the marginal cost curve intersect. This is illustrated in Figure 7.8. The price he charges is determined by the demand curve at the output where $MR = MC$. With a negatively sloped demand curve, $P^D = D(Q)$, the $MR$ curve is

$$MR = \frac{d[D(Q)Q]}{dQ} = D'(Q)Q + D(Q) < P^D,$$

since $D'(Q) < 0$. Hence, if the competitive industry output is $Q^E$, the monopolist's output $Q^M$ must be such that $Q^M < Q^E$. Also, the monopolist's price $P^M$ must exceed the competitive industry's price of $P^E$. Monopoly therefore carries with it the rather unattractive feature of restricting quantity below, while increasing price above, the levels that would obtain if, as in the purely competitive industry, *price*, rather than marginal revenue and marginal cost were equated. Note again, however, that the monopolist is not actually selling as much as he would like at $P^M$. If he had his druthers he would sell $Q^L$ at $P^M$, for he continues to make a profit on each additional unit, up to $Q^L$ units, that he can sell for $P^M$. But, even monopolists can't have everything. Note also that if a price ceiling of $P^E$, the price at which $MC = D(Q)$, were imposed on the monopolist, he would continue to produce and sell at the maximum price of $P^E$. Indeed, he would produce and sell an output of $Q^E$—the competitive output—the maximum output that one can persuade him to produce. This is because the $MR$ curve now consists of two segments: the horizontal line at $P^E$ for $Q \leq Q^E$, and the original $MR$ curve for $Q > Q^E$; and this line "intersects" the $MC$ curve at $Q^E$ (note again the importance of the second-order condition in this case).

## 7.6 MONOPOLISTIC COMPETITION

The monopolist may be the sole producer of a product, but he still cannot ignore *all* other firms. Indeed, his demand curve, now the industry demand, has embodied into it the presumed reactions of other firms in other industries. As remarked earlier, quantity demanded at each price is determined in light of prices and actions in other industries at each price obtaining for the product in question. As also remarked, however, an "industry" will commonly be a rather imprecisely defined conglomeration of firms producing similar or slightly differentiated products, rather than a distinct set of firms producing a single homogeneous product. The differentiation may be in product quality, packaging, or promotion, and the manner in which it is sold and the services that accompany its sale. The success of a firm's price and output decision, in a world where all other things are treated as if they were certain, will depend upon the firm's ability to correctly assess the intentions and reactions of competitors producing similar products. These competitors may be many or few. The firm will therefore possess some of the uniqueness of product that characterizes the monopolist, and the industry the plurality of firms that characterizes competition. It is this situation that Chamberlin has called monopolistic competition—large-group case where the firms in the industry are many, and small-group case where the firms in the industry are few.[11]

The curve labeled $DD$ in Figure 7.9(a) is the firm's actual demand curve. Embodied into it are the reactions of competitors to the price charged by the firm. Given the results of these reactions, the quantities are those that the firm in question will *actually* be able to sell at any price it establishes. If a price of $P$ were established, because of loyalty to the firm's product and adjustments in price by competitors,

[11] Chamberlin (*The Theory of Monopolistic Competition*) argues that "For one competitor to take into account the alternations of policy which he forces upon the other is simply for him to consider the indirect consequences of his own acts. Let each seller, then, in seeking to maximize his profit, reflect well, and look to the total consequences of his move. He must consider not merely what his competitor is doing now, but also what he will be forced to do in the light of the change which he himself is contemplating . . . (p. 47). Monopolistic competition, then, concerns itself not only with the problem of an *individual* equilibrium (the ordinary theory of monopoly), but also with that of a *group* equilibrium (the adjustment of economic forces within a group of competing monopolists, ordinarily regarded merely as a group of competitors). In this it differs both from the theory of competition and from the theory of monopoly" (p. 69).

as well as the loyalty of the latter's customers, price changes from $P$ would not result in as sweeping quantity variations as might be anticipated in the absence of such loyalties or adjustments. On the one hand, the monopolist of the previous section, Mrs. Robinson's firm of imperfect competition, always behaves as if $DD$ were his demand curve and proceeds to equate $MR$ and $MC$.[12] That is how he arrives at a price of $P$, where he is more than, and properly, content to stay. Professor Chamberlin's firm, on the other hand, can suffer from the sort of myopia that compels it to focus on *dd* of Figure 7.9(a). This curve describes the quantities that the firm would sell if only all of its competitors would hold their prices fixed at whatever

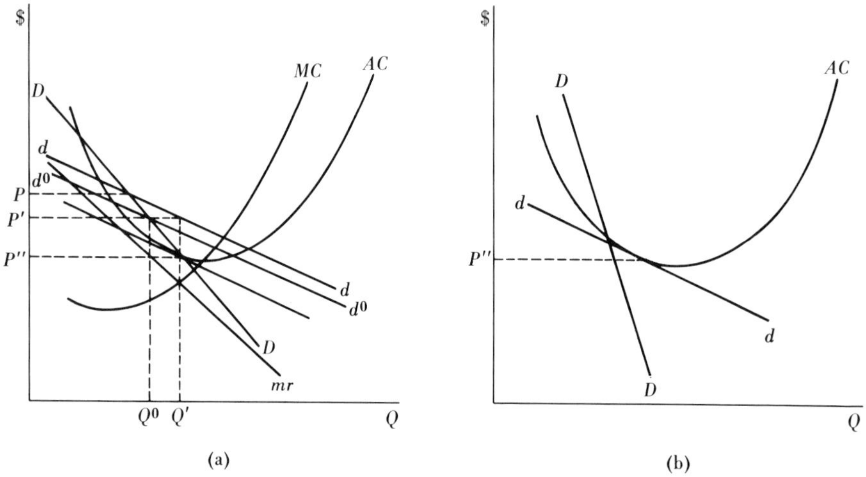


Fig. 7.9

levels happened to be obtaining at the moment. What this means, of course, is that when the price is at $P$, the firm *expects* greater quantity increases (decreases) than would actually result from any decrease (increase) in price. Because of its perception problem, the firm perceives $mr$ to be its marginal revenue curve and reduces price in accordance with the condition that output is established where $mr$, rather than $MR$, equals $MC$. Suppose this price is $P'$. The firm expects to sell $Q'$ but, because of the price-reducing reactions of competitors who have not been asleep through all of this, it actually sells $Q^0$.

[12] "He may be conceived to do this either by estimating the demand price and the cost of various outputs, or by a process of trial and error" [Joan Robinson, *The Economics of Imperfect Competition* (London: Macmillan and Co., Ltd., 1950), pp. 52–53]. For Mrs. Robinson, "The demand curve for the individual firm may be conceived to show the full effect upon the sales of that firm which results from any change in the price which it charges, whether it causes a change in the prices charged by the others or not. It is not to our purpose to consider this question in detail" (p. 21). One might, however, ask what happens to the entrepreneur who is unwilling to risk variations in price and output. For a discussion of Robinson vis-à-vis Chamberlin, see Robert Triffin, *Monopolistic Competition and General Equilibrium Theory* (Cambridge, Mass.: Harvard University Press, 1940), chaps. 1 and 2.

One would think that the firm in question would begin to get at least a hint of what might be going on, but—at least when there are many competitors—it does not. In this, Chamberlin's large-group case, *each and every* firm is in a state of disequilibrium when it arrives at $P$ or $P'$, because *each* entrepreneur *correctly* judges that any price reduction on his part will have an imperceptible effect on *industry* sales. The incremental output that he attains from the price cut will consist primarily of minute quantities attracted from each of his many competitors. Because of his negligible effect on the market, any *one* competitor is justified in ignoring $DD$—since, in fact others do *not* respond to any one firm's price changes. They scarcely notice these. In total, however, with *many* firms behaving in the same manner, the effects on each of the host of competitors are in accordance with the demand curve $DD$. Each firm has, therefore, been disappointed with its additional sales at a level of $Q^0$ when it cut price to $P'$, and each will once again make the correct supposition that its demand curve is a $dd$ curve, this time $d^0d^0$. Now, with each perceiving $d^0d^0$ to be its demand curve, each lowers price, and the previous cycle repeats. Indeed, price will continue to fall until $P''$, where $dd$ is just tangent to the average cost curve, and no further. Thereafter any further price reductions would result only in a loss for the firm, because price would be below average cost. If, moreover, $DD$ also intersects the $dd$ and $AC$ curves at this point of tangency, as in Figure 7.9(a), each firm *and* the industry *as well* will be in equilibrium. This is so, because *every* firm perceives *any* further price changes as resulting in a loss, and the actual demand at $P''$ is just what each firm perceives it to be.

It might not be true, however, that actual and perceived demand are equal at $P''$. In the event that, say, $DD$ intersected $dd$ to the left of the point of tangency, as in Figure 7.9(b), actual demand would be less than perceived demand and each firm would suffer a loss. No one firm will be suffering this alone, however, for there are a multitude of firms characterized by similar demand and cost functions and similar behavior. Not all of these firms will be able to withstand the resultant loss, and in the long run, with exit and entry possible, some will be forced out of business. Those that remain will benefit from this withdrawal by sharing in the custom that previously accrued to the now deceased firms. The effect will be that $DD$ will *shift* to the right, and firms will continue to disappear until, for all survivors, $DD$ and $dd$ intersect at the price at which $dd$ and $AC$ are tangent. At this price, the marginal firms just make normal profit. Should $DD$ and $dd$ intersect to the right of $P''$, the point of tangency, all firms would make above-normal profit, this would attract new firms into the industry, and $DD$ would gradually shift left until it intersected $dd$ at $P''$.

When there are few competitors, Chamberlin's small-group case, each firm is in a much better position to appreciate the potentially disastrous effects of "*dd* myopia"; or, at least, competitors are sufficiently few that each would almost surely be erring in the belief that his own policies, *perceptibly* affecting as they do his brethren, would not provoke them to some counteraction. When they do not fall victim to this error, all firms correctly ignore $dd$ and focus exclusively upon $DD$. Recognizing their mutual interests, all firms act as profit-maximizing monopolists, maintaining a price of $P$ established at an output $Q$ where $MR$ (from $DD$) equals $MC$. Nonetheless, a misguided soul or two can spoil things for everybody else, either by erroneously neglecting $DD$ and competitors' reactions, and focusing exclusively on $dd$, or by focusing on $dd$ and making some judgment as to how competitors *might* be affected and *might* react, as well as making some judgment with respect to their capacities for retaliatory action. In any event, those with greater wisdom stand hopelessly aside watching the results of all of this be played out along the $DD$ curve. Depending upon the situation, some might perceive sufficient incentives to cut price, and might continually err in the belief that others will hold their prices fixed, so as to ultimately drive price down to $P''$.

Because the point at which price settles, or indeed whether price will *ever* settle at one point, is intimately bound to the reactions and beliefs of all members of the group, Chamberlin argued that price is likely to settle somewhere in the range $P$ to $P''$, but no single point in this range compels particular attention as "the" price that will ultimately obtain. Individual financial strength, recognition of mutuality of interests, the flow of information, the antitrust laws, and plain truculence are some of the factors that will undoubtedly be influential. The theory of monopolistic competition does not go much beyond these speculations. It might, however, be noted that if the price were to momentarily settle at, say, $P'$, there is some basis for the belief that the settlement would be permanent. One could argue that as far as the firm is concerned, it is confronted by the *kinked* demand curve consisting of the line segment on $d^0d^0$ at prices above $P'$ and the line segment on $DD$ at prices below $P'$. That is, if the firm were to increase price, it judges that other firms would not follow these increases in order to capture the buyers it has thereby affronted; its subsequent quantity losses would be too great to justify the price increase. Alternatively, if the firm were to reduce price, the judgment is that other firms would feel themselves forced to meet this price reduction in order to retain their customers. As a result, the firm would not gain a substantial amount of business—at least not enough to justify the price cut. Hence, price would stabilize at the kink, thereby effecting a discontinuous marginal revenue curve for each firm.[13]

Finally, note that by advertising and/or by changing the quality of its product, the firm may be able to influence the position of its demand curve. Simultaneously, the firm's cost curves may be affected. It is assumed that all advertising and quality adjustments are such as to maximize the firm's profits, net of advertising costs and costs associated with quality adjustments. Indeed, particularly in view of the potentially disastrous implications of a fierce, toe-to-toe, price-cutting slugfest, there is great and growing sympathy among economists for the argument that firms in

[13] In "The Kinky Oligopoly Demand Curve and Rigid Prices," *Journal of Political Economy*, **LV**:5 (Oct. 1947), George Stigler shows that "The length of the discontinuity in marginal revenue is proportional to the difference between the slopes of the demand curve on the two sides of the kink. The longer this discontinuity, the greater the fluctuations in marginal cost (and in demand, if the kink stays at the same price) that are compatible with price stability and therefore the greater the probability of rigid prices in any interval of time. Some of the factors that affect the length of this discontinuity are: (a) The number of rivals . . . (b). The relative size of rivals . . . (c). The differences among rivals' products . . . (d). The extent of collusion" (p. 435). Stigler goes on to remark that "The theory of the kinky demand curve explains why prices that have been stable should continue to be stable despite certain changes in demand or costs. But the theory does not explain why prices that have once changed should settle down, again acquire stability, and gradually produce a new kink. One possible explanation might be that a period of stability of demand and costs has created a tradition of stable prices, so that, when demand or cost conditions change materially, the kink has emerged to preserve price stability" (p. 436). The desire to avoid price wars, brand loyalty that prevents one from attracting another's customer, implicit agreements among producers,

oligopolistic industries will tend to rely on advertising and quality changes as their major competitive weapons.[14] It is not an argument that will astonish many corporation executives.

## 7.7 SOME OLIGOPOLY MODELS[15]

Certainly the fact that the firm must determine price and quantity even when it has some, rather than infinitely many or no, competitors has not entirely escaped the notice of economists. Resolving the issue has been another matter. The major difficulty here has been the need to incorporate into any proposed model behavioristic assumptions describing the way in which one firm greets, and reacts to, the actions of another. Both monopolistic competition and kinked demand curves provide insights and partial answers to the questions surrounding oligopolistic price-quantity determination. Additionally, both before and after Chamberlin's work, some interesting approaches to the oligopoly problem have been proposed. These run a gamut in which, although the entrepreneurs in question rarely show sparks of brilliance, their understanding and appreciation of competitors' behavior provide a basis for classifying the models as naive versus sophisticated. Though they may seldom if ever be applicable, these models, if not taken too seriously, can provide rewarding insights into the issues surrounding price-quantity determination in an oligopolistic setting.

---

price tradition, or simply the fear of antitrust violations should one producer acquire "too much" of a market share are some of the explanations that have been offered for the price stability. See, for example, K. W. Rothschild, "Price Theory and Oligopoly," *Economic Journal,* **LVII**:227 (Sept. 1947), particularly 312–313, 317; Gardner C. Means, "Looking Around: Is Economic Theory Outmoded?" *Harvard Business Review,* **36**:3 (May–June 1958), 167; Chamberlain, *The Firm,* pp. 203–204; Gary S. Becker, "Irrational Behavior and Economic Theory," *Journal of Political Economy,* **LXX**:1 (Feb. 1962), 1–13, and "A Reply to I. Kirzner," *Journal of Political Economy,* **LXXI**:1 (Feb. 1963), 82–83; and Israel Kirzner, "Rational Action and Economic Theory," *Journal of Political Economy,* **LXX**:4 (August 1962), 380–385.

[14] See, for example, Chamberlin, *Monopolistic Competition,* particularly chap. VII, and Arthur R. Burns, "The Organization of Industry and the Theory of Prices," *Journal of Political Economy,* **XLV**:5 (Oct. 1937), 662–680, and particularly 677, as a pair of the earliest progenitors of the breed. Recently, the potential relationship between market structure and advertising has been exposed to increased empirical attention. Of particular note in this connection is the article by W. S. Comanor and T. A. Wilson, "Advertising, Market Structure and Performance," *Review of Economics and Statistics,* **XLIX**:4 (Nov. 1967), 423–440. Their most penetrating inference is that advertising does indeed have a marked effect on profit rates, and that at least a portion of this influence stems from the barriers to entry and enhanced market power created by advertising. For a useful contrast, see Lester G. Telser, "Advertising and Competition," *Journal of Political Economy,* **LXXII**:6 (Dec. 1964), 537–562, and "Some Aspects of the Economics of Advertising," *Journal of Business,* **XLI**:2 (April 1968), 166–173.

[15] Most of the credit (and a minor share of the blame) for the style and tone of this section must go to an unpublished manuscript by Robert L. Bishop to which many of us have been privileged to have access.

## a. Naïve Behavior

### i. COURNOT[16]

Our tour of naive oligopoly models begins with one of the more interesting models that, after a century, still holds some intrigue for economists: the Cournot model.[17] In this model, there are $n$ firms in the industry producing a homogeneous product. Each firm is a *quantity*-setter. In determining how much to produce during the next production period, the firm assumes that its competitors will not vary production from the levels they happen to be maintaining at the moment. Price is then determined by the *industry* demand curve $P = D(Q)$, where $Q$ is total industry output. Once more denoting the $i$th firm's output by $Q_i$ $(i = 1, \ldots, n)$, price will be given by $P = D(Q) = D(\Sigma\, Q_i)$. If the $i$th firm's total cost function is given by $C_i = c_i(Q_i)$, its profit will be given by $\pi_i = PQ_i - c_i(Q_i)$ and maximized where $\partial\pi_i/\partial Q_i = 0$ (assuming that $\partial^2\pi_i/\partial Q_i^2 < 0$). The partial, rather than the total, derivative is appropriate here, because each firm *assumes* the others' quantities to be fixed. Hence, the $i$th firm calculates

$$\frac{\partial\pi_i}{\partial Q_i} = \left(\frac{\partial P}{\partial Q_i}\right) Q_i + P - \frac{\partial C_i}{\partial Q_i} = \left(\frac{dP}{dQ}\right) Q_i + P - MC_i = 0,$$

where $MC_i$ is the firm's marginal cost and $\partial P/\partial Q_i = dP/dQ$ since $Q = \Sigma\, Q_i$. Thus,

$$Q_i = \frac{[MC_i - P]}{dP/dQ} .$$

If all firms have the same cost curves, $MC_j = MC_k$. In this case, in equilibrium $Q_j = Q_k$ and $Q = nQ_i$. Hence,

$$Q_i = \frac{[MC_i - D(nQ_i)]}{dD(nQ_i)/dQ} .$$

This is an equation with $Q_i$ the only variable and may be solved for $Q_i$ when the specific functional forms are known.

Consider the case of constant average costs, $C_i = aQ_i$, and the linear industry demand curve, $P = B - bQ$. We shall scale the axes in such a way that $B = 1 + a$ and $b = 1$, so that $P = 1 + a - Q$. This is solely an interesting expository convenience. With $MC_i = a$, $P = D(nQ_i) = 1 + a - nQ_i$, and $dD(nQ_i)/dQ = -1$, substitution into the expression derived for the equilibrium $Q_i = Q_i^*$ yields

$$Q_i^* = \frac{[a - (1 + a - nQ_i^*)]}{-1} .$$

[16] A. Cournot, *Researches into the Mathematical Principles of the Theory of Wealth*, tr. N. T. Bacon (New York: The Macmillan Company, 1897).

[17] For some recent applications of the Cournot model, and efforts at drawing inferences about contemporary oligopolistic behavior on the basis of this model, see the following: I. Horowitz, "Research Inclinations of a Cournot Oligopolist," *Review of Economic Studies*, **XXX**:2 (June 1963), 128–130; C. R. Frank, "Entry in a Cournot Market," *Review of Economic Studies*, **XXXII**:3 (July 1965), 245–250; J. Hadar, "Stability of Oligopoly with Product Differentiation," *Review of Economic Studies*, **XXXIII**:1 (Jan. 1966), 57–60; F. M. Scherer, "Research and Development Resource Allocation Under Rivalry," *Quarterly Journal of Economics*, **LXXXI**:3 (August 1967), 359–394.

Solving for $Q_i^*$, we obtain $Q_i^* = 1/(1+n)$. Hence, $Q^* = nQ_i^* = n/(1+n)$, $P^* = 1 + a - [n/(1+n)] = [1 + a(1+n)]/[1+n]$, and

$$\pi_i^* = [P^* - a]Q_i^* = \left[\frac{1 + a - \left[\dfrac{n}{1+n}\right] - a}{1+n}\right] = \frac{1}{(1+n)^2}.$$

In the case of monopoly, $n = 1$ and $P^* = (1+2a)/2$, $Q^* = Q_i^* = \frac{1}{2}$, and $\pi_i = \frac{1}{4}$. This is, of course, the monopoly solution that would be obtained by the earlier $MR = MC$ analysis. In the duopoly case, $n = 2$ and $P^* = (1+3a)/3$, $Q_i^* = \frac{1}{3}$, $Q^* = \frac{2}{3}$, and $\pi_i^* = \frac{1}{9}$. It is of interest that as the number of firms approaches the infinite (that is, as $n \to \infty$) we find

$$\lim_{n\to\infty} Q^* = \lim_{n\to\infty}\left[\frac{n}{1+n}\right] = 1,$$

$$\lim_{n\to\infty} P^* = 1 + a - 1 = a,$$

$$\lim_{n\to\infty} Q_i^* = \lim_{n\to\infty}\left[\frac{1}{1+n}\right] = 0,$$

and

$$\lim_{n\to\infty} \pi_i^* = \lim_{n\to\infty}\left[\frac{1}{(1+n)^2}\right] = 0.$$

As the industry approaches the purely competitive industry, then, each firm's output and profit becomes negligible (that is, approaches zero), price approaches the constant average cost, and industry output is maximized. In general, $Q_i^*$, $P^*$, and $\pi_i^*$ are decreasing functions of $n$, whereas $Q^*$ is an increasing function of $n$. Thus, the model's basic assumptions may stretch one's credulity, but some of the implications, particularly in the limit, would seem to have considerable intuitive appeal.

It is also of particular interest that where firms have different *marginal* cost schedules, the difference in their equilibrium outputs will be given by

$$Q_j^* - Q_k^* = \frac{[MC_j - P^*]}{dP/dQ} - \frac{[MC_k - P^*]}{dP/dQ} = \frac{[MC_j - MC_k]}{dP/dQ}.$$

Recalling that $dP/dQ < 0$, this means that the firm with the *lower marginal cost* will produce the *greater quantity,* with the difference between the firms' outputs being proportional to the difference in marginal costs. The inverse of the slope of the demand curve is the factor of proportionality. This holds, of course, for nonlinear as well as linear functions, but the slopes are nonconstant.

The equation $Q_i = [MC_i - P]/(dP/dQ)$ may also be written as

$$Q_i = \frac{\left[MC_i - D\left(\sum_{j\neq i} Q_j + Q_i\right)\right]}{\dfrac{dD\left(\sum_{j\neq i} Q_j + Q_i\right)}{dQ}}.$$

This form describes $Q_i$ as a function of $\sum_{j\neq i} Q_j$, or as a function of the rest of the industry's output. Such a function is called a reaction curve. The reaction curve describes the *i*th firm's output reaction to any output level maintained in the rest of the industry. This is sometimes called the *conjectural variation* in the firm's output, given its conjectures as to the other firms' behavior.[18]

Each firm follows a course of action whereby it produces in accordance with its reaction curve. Thus if *all* firms are to follow their preferred behavior patterns, each will necessarily produce at the point in $n$-space where these reaction curves intersect. This point will be the *Cournot equilibrium* point—once reached, there will be no inclination to depart from it. The equilibrium will be stable so long as (1) quantity increases in the "rest of the industry" effect quantity *decreases* on the part of the "excluded" firm, and (2) the decreases thus effected in turn encourage further, but successively lesser, increases in "rest of the industry" output, and vice versa. Let $\left(dQ_i/d\left(\sum_{j\neq i} Q_j\right)\right)_i$ denote the change effected in the output of the *i*th firm when the output in the rest of the industry changes, and let $\left(d\left(\sum_{j\neq i} Q_j\right)/dQ_i\right)_R$ denote the change effected in the rest of the industry's output when the output of the *i*th firm changes. The former will measure the slope of the *i*th firm's reaction curve; the latter will be the inverse of the slope of the reaction curve for the rest of the industry, or

$$\left(\frac{dQ_i}{d\left(\sum_{j\neq i} Q_j\right)}\right)_R = \frac{1}{\left(\dfrac{d\left(\sum_{j\neq i} Q_j\right)}{dQ_i}\right)_R}.$$

A stable equilibrium will be achieved where the two reaction curves intersect when

$$0 > \left(\frac{dQ_i}{d\left(\sum_{j\neq i} Q_j\right)}\right)_i > \left(\frac{dQ_i}{d\left(\sum_{j\neq i} Q_j\right)}\right)_R.$$

If the inequalities were reversed, increases in output on any firm's part would encourage increases in the rest of the industry, and vice versa, offering the prospect of a nonending output spiral or a stable monopoly solution.[19]

[18] See William Fellner, *Competition Among the Few* (New York: Augustus M. Kelley, 1960), pp. 71–77. Also see pp. 91–93 for a discussion of conjectural variation with respect to price.

[19] The slopes of the reaction curves will depend upon the industry demand curves and the oligopolists' cost curves. The stability of the Cournot equilibrium will thus depend upon the assumptions made about the shapes of both the latter sets of curves, as well as upon the manner and speed with which the Cournot oligopolists are assumed to adjust their production. See, for example, R. D. Theocharis, "On the Stability of the Cournot Solution of the Oligopoly Problem," *Review of Economic Studies*, **XXVII**:2 (Feb. 1960), 133–134; Franklin M. Fisher, "'The Stability of the Cournot Oligopoly Solution': The Effects of Speeds of Adjustment and Increasing Marginal Costs," *Review of Economic Studies*, **XXVIII**:2 (Feb. 1961), 125–135; Robert L. Bishop, "'The Stability of the Cournot Oligopoly Solution': Further Comment," *Review of Economic Studies*, **XXIX**:4 (Oct. 1962). 332–336; "Dynamic Cournot-type Oligopoly Models—A Correction," *ibid.*, pp. 337–339;

This is illustrated in Figure 7.10 for the duopoly case with linear demand and, for diagrammatic convenience, zero total cost ($a = 0$). Figure 7.10(a) shows the industry demand curve. Point $M$ is the monopoly output, and point $C$ the total Cournot output for a pair of duopolists. Figure 7.10(b) shows the two firms' reaction curves. Firm 1, say, initially produces the monopoly output of $\frac{1}{2}$, thinking that firm 2 will continue not to produce. In the next production period firm 2, noting firm 1's output of $\frac{1}{2}$, determines its output in accordance with the reaction curve

$$Q_2 = \frac{[MC_2 - D(Q_1 + Q_2)]}{dD(Q_1 + Q_2)/dQ} = \frac{[0 - (1 - Q_1 - Q_2)]}{[-1]} = 1 - Q_1 - Q_2$$

or $Q_2 = [1 - Q_1]/2$. The output would be $Q_2 = [1 - \frac{1}{2}]/2 = \frac{1}{4}$. $Q_1$ would remain at $\frac{1}{2}$. Firm 1's reaction curve would similarly be $Q_1 = [1 - Q_2]/2$, so that after witnessing $Q_2 = \frac{1}{4}$, firm 1 would counter with $Q_1 = [1 - \frac{1}{4}]/2 = \frac{3}{8}$ in the following production period. This process would continue over succeeding periods until point

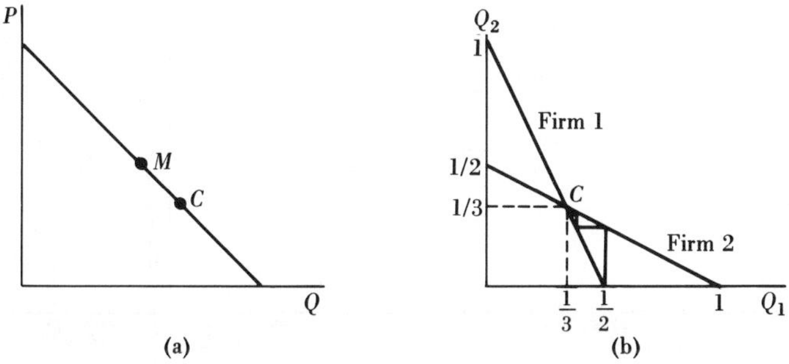


Fig. 7.10

$C$ was reached, where $Q_1^* = Q_2^* = \frac{1}{3}$. Here, $Q^* = Q_1^* + Q_2^* = \frac{2}{3}$, $P^* = \frac{1}{3}$, and $\pi_1^* = \pi_2^* = P^*Q_1^* = P^*Q_2^* = \frac{1}{9}$. Note too that $0 > (dQ_2/dQ_1)_{\text{firm 2}} = -\frac{1}{2} > (dQ_2/dQ_1)_{\text{firm 1}} = -2$. Each firm's reaction curve is negatively sloped and, when either firm is producing below (above) the equilibrium level of $\frac{1}{3}$, the other will react by producing a greater (lesser) quantity than the equilibrium level. Firm 2's quantity increases inspire firm 1 to reduce output, and this reduction inspires firm 2 to a further, but smaller, increase, which in turn effects a further, but smaller, decrease in output on the part of firm 1, and so forth. These reactions drive the firms toward $C$, whereas, were the magnitudes of the slopes of the reaction curves reversed, the firms would be repelled from $C$.

---

and Charles R. Frank, Jr., and Richard E. Quandt, "On the Existence of Cournot Equilibrium," *International Economic Review*, **4**:1 (Jan. 1963), 92–96. The Fisher-Bishop argument, which is more directly related to the present discussion than are the others, is that for a stable equilibrium marginal costs cannot decline as fast as price (Fisher, p. 130), or that "if any one member of the group is producing his monopoly output and all others are producing nothing, at least one of the other producers has an incentive to produce some positive output" (Bishop, p. 332).

### ii. BERTRAND[20]

Bertrand approached the duopoly situation by first endowing his entrepreneurs with the same degree of naiveté as possessed by Cournot duopolists. But, whereas Cournot assumed that each entrepreneur would consider the other's quantities to be fixed, Bertrand assumed that each would consider the other's *prices* to be fixed. In this case, then, the firm is viewed as a *price*-setter. Because the product is homogeneous, all customers are assumed to purchase from the low-price seller. Each firm therefore believes that it can capture the entire industry demand by selling at a price "just below" that charged by the rest of the industry, or the lowest-price seller, in the preceding selling period. In the case where industry demand is $P = 1 + a - Q$ and $C_i = aQ_i$, the result of this naiveté will be an extended series of price cuts from the monopoly price of $P = \frac{1}{2}$ on down, which will continue until unit profit is zero. At this point $P^* = a$ and $Q^* = \Sigma Q_i^* = 1$. As in the Cournot case with $n \to \infty$, the purely competitive solution once again would obtain.

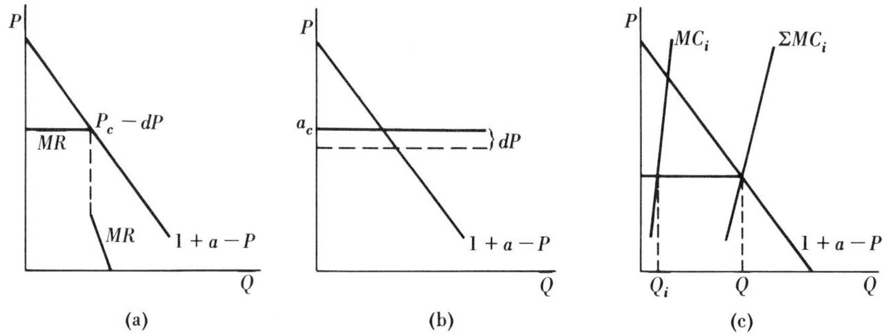


Fig. 7.11

Bertrand's analysis is of greater interest than this rather sterile first situation indicates, when different cost functions are introduced for the various oligopolists. Here, too, however, the Bertrand model takes on a strongly competitive bent. To maximize profit, each firm seeks a price-quantity combination at which $MR = MC$. With $P_c$ the lowest price last charged by any other producer, each firm assumes that in the next period it can sell any desired quantity up to $Q = 1 + a - P$, at a price of $P = P_c - dP$. The latter will be just below the prevailing market price. The firm therefore perceives its demand curve to be discontinuous, as in Fig. 7.11(a). The curve comes in two segments: (1) the horizontal line at $P_c - dP$ up to quantities of $1 + a - P_c + dP$, and (2) the industry demand curve $Q = 1 + a - P$ at greater quantities. The $MR$ curve is therefore also discontinuous, coinciding with the horizontal line at $P_c - dP$ for outputs up to $Q = 1 + a - P_c + dP$ (since each additional unit is sold for the same price of $P_c - dP$), and with the industry $MR$ curve thereafter.

[20] J. Bertrand on Cournot's *Recherches*, reprinted from the *Journal des Savants* (Sept. 1883), in A. Cournot, *Recherches sur les Principes Mathematiques de la Theorie des Richesses* (Paris: Marcel Riviere and Co., 1938), pp. 233–250.

It is assumed that no firm can charge the monopoly price without being undercut by a competitor. Still, throughout the series of naive price cuts, each made with the thought that the cut will neither be met by nor encourage retaliation, each firm will seek the highest price possible. This requires that $dP$ be as small as possible. Where all firms have *constant* but *differing* average equal to marginal cost curves, the low-cost producer will charge a price of $a_c - dP$, where $a_c$ is the average cost of the next lowest-cost producer in the industry. At this price, he will capture the entire market of $Q = 1 + a - a_c + dP$, as illustrated in Figure 7.11(b).

Where the firms have *increasing* marginal costs, the series of price cuts stops only when *each* firm has equated *price* to marginal cost. Each firm initiates its price cuts from the $MR = MC$ position. Beyond the $P = MC$ point, any further reduction in price would mean that the next *unit* would have to be sold for less than it cost to produce. Even for a Bertrand entrepreneur, this would be rather hard to take. Thus, as in the purely competitive industry, equilibrium is reached at a price and output where the curve made up of the horizontal sum of the individual firms' marginal cost curves intersects the industry demand curve. Each firm supplies the quantity indicated by its own marginal cost curve at the price established in the market. This is illustrated in Figure 7.11(c). Note that with constantly decreasing costs, one producer would necessarily drive the others out through a series of price cuts. Price would eventually be driven to the point at which profits are zero—that is to the point where price equals average cost.

### iii. EDGEWORTH[21]

Bertrand enterpreneurs do not appear to be too sharp. In the first place, the invalidity of the assumption of the others' price rigidity should eventually occur to them. Second, even if it does not, their competitors might not be able to satisfy the entire demand at the market price even if any one should step aside. In this event, not only would more than one firm share in industry demand at a given price, but it might even profit a firm to charge a *higher* price than that charged by competitors, who could not supply the entire market anyhow.

The latter thought attràcted Edgeworth. Following Bertrand, he assumed each firm would presume the price rigidity of competitors, but each had limited capacity. Under these circumstances, the firms' exact behavior depends upon their cost functions, the capacity restrictions imposed on them, and the assumptions made about demand when all demand is not satisfied at a given price. Because of the complexity added by the relatively minor reduction in naiveté, only a single possibility is illustrated here.

Suppose there are duopolists operating in an industry whose demand curve is $P = 1 - Q$. Each firm is a cost-free producer (that is, $C_i = aQ_i$ and $a = 0$) but has a capacity restriction of .45 units during each selling period. Thus, if each is a Bertrand price-cutter, when each is producing maximum output, $P = 1 - 2Q_i = 1 - 2(.45) = .10$. There is no incentive to reduce price below .10, for each is already selling all he can produce and earning a profit of $.10(.45) = .045$.

Now, suppose that duopolist 1 keeps cutting price until $P^*$ to assure he sells his maximum output of .45. If the market price is maintained at $P^*$, industry demand will be $Q = 1 - P^*$. But, duopolist 1 can only satisfy .45 units of this demand.

[21] F. Y. Edgeworth, "The Pure Theory of Monopoly," in his *Papers Relating to Political Economy* (London: Macmillan and Co., Ltd. 1925), pp. 116–126.

$Q - .45 = (1 - P^*) - .45 = .55 - P^* = Q_u$ units will go *unsatisfied.* We now make one of *many* possible assumptions about duopolist 2's demand: namely, with total demand of $1 - P^*$ and unsatisfied demand of $Q_u = .55 - P^*$, the ratio of unsatisfied to total demand, $R = Q_u/Q = (.55 - P^*)/(1 - P^*)$, will be the *proportion* of industry demand that duopolist 2 can *always* capture at any price above $P^*$. Moreover, it is assumed buyers do not recontract to sell to other buyers.

Now, neither duopolist can produce the monopoly output of $Q_m = \frac{1}{2}$. In *aggregate* they can, however, and they could sell a total of $Q_m = \frac{1}{2}$ for a price of $P_m = \frac{1}{2}$. Thus, so long as duopolist 1 is producing at, or in excess of, .05 units (that is, $Q_m - .45$), the highest price that duopolist 2 will charge will be the monopoly price. At this price, total demand is $Q_m = \frac{1}{2}$. If duopolist 1 is selling his capacity of .45, duopolist 2's demand when he charges a price of $P_2 = P_m = \frac{1}{2}$ will be $Q_2 =$ (industry demand at $P_2$) (percentage of industry demand going unsatisfied at duopolist 1's price of $P^*$) $= Q_mR = (\frac{1}{2})[(.55 - P^*)/(1 - P^*)]$. His total profit will be $\pi_{mR} = P_2Q_2$, which with $P_2 = P_m$ will be

$$\pi_{mR} = P_m(Q_mR) = \left(\frac{1}{2}\right)\left(\frac{1}{2}\right)\left(\frac{.55 - P^*}{1 - P^*}\right) = \left(\frac{.55 - P^*}{4 - 4P^*}\right).$$

Suppose, now, that in the series of price cuts duopolist 2 refuses to cut price below $P^*$, the price at which he will be able to sell his entire output of .45. At this price, his profit will be $\pi_{P^*} = .45P^*$. Thus, if the lower limit of duopolist 2's price cuts is $P_2 = P^*$, such that $\pi_{P^*} = \pi_{mR}$, he establishes a price yielding him exactly the same profit as the upper bound to price, $P_m = \frac{1}{2}$. This lower bound will be set such that $\pi_{mR} = (.55 - P^*)/(4 - 4P^*) = .45P^* = \pi_{P^*}$; or $36P^{*2} - 56P^* + 11 = 0$. Solving for $P^*$, $P^* \approx .2306$. The profit at this price is .1038. This is higher than the profit of .0450 duopolist 2 would obtain by continued price-cutting to .10. Thus, the Edgeworth duopolist will neither cut price below .2306 nor raise price above $\frac{1}{2}$. Moreover, with $\pi_{mR} = \pi_{P^*} = .1038 = Q_2(\frac{1}{2})$, it immediately follows that $Q_2 = .2076$ when $P_m = \frac{1}{2}$.

As each duopolist cuts price between prices of $\frac{1}{2}$ and .2306, the other keeps assuming that there will be no further cuts, and hence continues to believe he can sell his *entire* output by price-cutting. When duopolist 1 is charging a price of $P_1 < P_2$ and selling his entire output of .45, duopolist 2 can capture at $P_2$ a proportion of industry demand of $(.55 - P_1)/(1 - P_1)$. Duopolist 2's profit if he prices above $P_1$ will therefore be given by $P_2(1 - P_2)[(.55 - P_1)/(1 - P_1)]$. The latter is maximized at $P_2 = \frac{1}{2}$, the monopoly price. Pricing below $P_1$, duopolist 2 earns a profit of $.45P_2$ by selling his total output. To determine his optimum price, he must compare the two profits. When $P_1 = .30$, for example, setting $P_2 = \frac{1}{2}$ yields him a profit of $(\frac{1}{2})(1 - \frac{1}{2})[(.55 - .30)/(1 - .30)] = (\frac{1}{4})(.3573) = .0893$; setting $P_2 = .29$, say, will yield a profit of $.29(.45) = .1305$. Hence, price-cutting is superior to charging a price of $\frac{1}{2}$ and permitting the competitor to produce to capacity. Price-cutting ceases to be attractive at prices below .2306. Indeed, again assuming the other firm will not change price, in lieu of cutting price below .2306 each firm has profit incentive to permit his competitor to sell out his entire output and then to charge the monopoly price for his own output. During the next producing and selling period, the competitor comes back into the market just undercutting the monopoly price. Each firm again acts as a Bertrand duopolist. There will, however, be no incentive to cut price below .2306. Rather, at this point there will be a return to the monopoly price. Note, however, that this lower limit will depend upon the assumptions made about the "unsatisfied" demand. It should be clear, too, that this case can be extended beyond that of duopoly.

## b. Sophisticated Behavior

### i. STACKELBERG[22]

The discussion of naive behavior began with Cournot assumptions, and the discussion of sophisticated behavior begins by returning to Cournot assumptions. It will be convenient to restrict the analysis to the duopoly case, with each duopolist assuming that during the coming production period the other will hold quantity fixed at his current level of output. The additional twist given this situation by Stackelberg is that one or both of the duopolists may be sufficiently sophisticated to recognize that the other will make the Cournot assumption about his behavior. This recognition permits the sophisticated duopolist to determine and incorporate the other's reaction curve and conjectural variation into his own profit-maximizing computations.

Suppose the industry demand curve is $P = 1 + a - bQ$, and that each duopolist has a total cost curve of $C_i = aQ_i + (1 - b)Q_i^2$. With this choice of curves, the monopoly profit of $\pi_m = PQ - C_i = Q + aQ - bQ^2 - aQ - Q^2 + bQ^2 = Q(1 - Q)$ is again maximized at $Q = \frac{1}{2}$, and $b = 1$ yields the previously analyzed simple Cournot case with constant average cost. Further, as $b$ is less than or greater than 1 we have increasing or decreasing costs, but always with monopoly *unit* profit at $(1 - Q)$ and monopoly output at $Q = \frac{1}{2}$.

The profit of duopolist 1 will be

$$\begin{aligned}\pi_1 = PQ_1 - C_1 &= [1 + a - b(Q_1 + Q_2)]Q_1 - aQ_1 - (1 - b)Q_1^2 \\ &= Q_1 - Q_1^2 - bQ_1Q_2,\end{aligned}$$

and that of duopolist 2 will be $\pi_2 = Q_2 - Q_2^2 - bQ_1Q_2$. Assuming the other's output fixed, these profits will be maximized at $\partial\pi_1/\partial Q_1 = \partial\pi_2/\partial Q_2 = 0$ since $\partial^2\pi_i/\partial Q_i^2 = -2$. This yields reaction curves of $Q_1 = (1 - bQ_2)/2$ and $Q_2 = (1 - bQ_1)/2$ for duopolist 1 and 2, respectively. With each behaving in accordance with these reaction curves, these equations may be solved simultaneously to yield $Q_1^* = Q_2^* = 1/(2 + b)$. Substituting $Q^* = Q_1^* + Q_2^* = 2/(2 + b)$ into the demand curve, $P^* = 1 + a - 2b/(2 + b)$. Hence, $\pi_1^* = \pi_2^* = [1/(2 + b)]^2$. Clearly, with $b = 1$ the earlier results are again obtained. Note, however, that unless we restrict $b > 0$ we have $dP/dQ > 0$, which is a bit much; and unless $b < 2$, $(dQ_2/dQ_1)_{\text{firm }2} \leq (dQ_2/dQ_1)_{\text{firm }1}$ and the Cournot equilibrium is unstable.

The function $\pi_1 = Q_1 - Q_1^2 - bQ_1Q_2$ describes duopolist 1's *isoprofit* map. For any attainable profit level $\bar{\pi} = \pi_1 = Q_1 - Q_1^2 - b_1Q_1Q_2$, one can find any number of combinations of the $Q_i$ to yield $\bar{\pi}$. Suppose duopolist 1 is sophisticated in the sense that he knows of duopolist 2's naiveté and determines and allows for the latter's reaction curve. His problem is to maximize his profit subject to the other's reaction curve, or

$$\text{Maximize } \pi_1, \quad \text{subject to} \quad Q_2 = \frac{1 - bQ_1}{2}.$$

[22] H. von Stackelberg, *The Theory of the Market Economy,* tr. A. T. Peacock (London: William Hodge and Co., Ltd., 1952), pp. 194–204.

By substitution of $Q_2$ into the isoprofit function,

$$\pi_1 = Q_1 - Q_1^2 - \frac{bQ_1(1 - bQ_1)}{2} = Q_1\left(1 - \frac{b}{2}\right) - Q_1^2\left(1 - \frac{b^2}{2}\right).$$

For a maximum,

$$\frac{d\pi_1}{dQ_1} = \left(1 - \frac{b}{2}\right) - 2Q_1\left(1 - \frac{b^2}{2}\right) = 0; \quad \text{or} \quad Q_1^* = \frac{2 - b}{2(2 - b^2)}.$$

Therefore,

$$Q_2^* = \frac{1 - bQ_1^*}{2} = \frac{4 - 2b - b^2}{4(2 - b^2)}.$$

We must now further restrict $b$ by requiring $(4 - 2b - b^2) \geq 0$ to assure $Q_2 \geq 0$; or $b \leq \sqrt{5} - 1$.

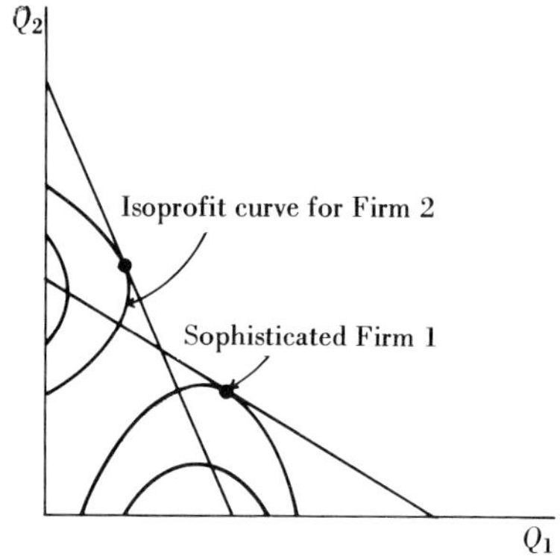


Fig. 7.12

With $b = 1$, it readily follows that $Q_1^* = \frac{1}{2}$, $Q_2^* = \frac{1}{4}$, and $P^* = \frac{1}{4} + a$. Also, $\pi_1^* = \frac{1}{8}$ and $\pi_2^* = \frac{1}{16}$. With both naive, $\pi_i^* = \frac{1}{9}$. The sophisticated duopolist thus gains by maintaining monopoly output. But continued naiveté is costly to his competitor. It may also be seen, by numerical example or by the calculus, that as $b$ increases—that is, as we move from increasing to decreasing costs—the sophisticated (naive) duopolist's gains (losses) in profit and output increase.

With both duopolists sophisticated, each sets $Q_i = (2 - b)/2(2 - b^2)$. With $b = 1$, $Q_i = \frac{1}{2}$ and $P = a$; and, since $C_i/Q_i = a$, $\pi_i = 0$. Thus, each produces the monopoly output and makes zero profit. With increasing costs ($b < 1$) each would earn a profit, but with decreasing costs ($b > 1$) each would suffer a loss. Unit profit is given by $\pi_{iu} = P - C_i/Q_i = 1 - bQ_j - Q_i$, $j \neq i$. Hence, with $b > 1$, $Q_i = Q_j > \frac{1}{2}$ and $\pi_{iu} < 0$; but, with $b < 1$, $Q_i = Q_j < \frac{1}{2}$ and $\pi_i > 0$. The fact of two sophisticated duopolists in a decreasing-cost market would, unless some collusive arrangement were worked out between them, be disastrous for each.

The Stackelberg analysis in the Cournot situation is illustrated in Figure 7.12. The bowed curves are the duopolists' isoprofit curves, as indicated. The further out from the axis an isoprofit curve is, the smaller is the duopolist's profit. The sophisticated duopolist seeks the output such that he will be on his adversary's reaction curve and, simultaneously, on the isoprofit curve that is closest to the relevant axis. At this point his isoprofit curve is just tangent to the other's reaction curve. The present illustration is for the case where $b = 1$.

The Stackelberg case is of considerable interest, for it demonstrates how (1) sophistication in the presence of naiveté can be rewarding, (2) the rewards will be directly related to favorable cost conditions, and (3) in a circumstance when each firm has what are, apparently, favorable cost conditions, sophistication for each of the parties can be particularly disastrous. Moreover, under *all* conditions, when *each* party is sophisticated, each stands to suffer losses in profit that would not be suffered if they were not as sophisticated. It might also be mentioned that sophistication in a Bertrand market would go for nought, since a sophisticated producer could do little about the price-cutting propensities of a naive competitor—except perhaps reinforce his naiveté by doing what the other expects: namely, hold his own price fixed.

It is also possible, however, that if each of the duopolists is sophisticated, his sophistication will extend to the attempt to persuade the other to accept some mutually satisfactory alternative to their "warfare." The attempt might extend from tacit persuasion to overt collusion. This possibility is considered next.

## ii. COLLUSIVE BEHAVIOR[23]

Retaining the Cournot structure, suppose the duopolists collude to achieve output $Q_i$ to maximize *joint* profit of $\pi = \pi_1 + \pi_2 = Q_1 + Q_2 - Q_1^2 - Q_2^2 - 2bQ_1Q_2$.[24] Setting $\partial\pi/\partial Q_1 = \partial\pi/\partial Q_2 = 0$ yields $1 - 2Q_1 - 2bQ_2 = 1 - 2Q_2 - 2bQ_1 = 0$, or $Q_1 = Q_2$. The additional requirements are $\partial^2\pi/\partial Q_i^2 = -2 < 0$ and for a maximum

$$\left[\frac{\partial^2\pi}{\partial Q_1^2}\right]\left[\frac{\partial^2\pi}{\partial Q_2^2}\right] = 4 > \left[\frac{\partial^2\pi}{\partial Q_1\,\partial Q_2}\right]^2 = 4b^2.$$

Thus, a unique joint-profit maximum will obtain at the point where the duopolists share equally in the total output, only if $0 < b < 1$. This means that for maximization of total profit and for both to produce, and to produce equally, costs must be nondecreasing. Indeed, it is quite clear that if the producers have decreasing average cost curves, $b > 1$, the optimal collusive procedure is for one to produce everything and for the profits to be divided between the two. The question remains, however, as to how the profit is to be divided.

On the one hand, it might seem reasonable to assume that irrespective of cost conditions the duopolists would agree to divide the total profits equally. Since, $\partial\pi/\partial Q_i = 1 - 2Q_i - 2bQ_j = 0$ and $Q_i^* = Q_j^*$, with nondecreasing costs $Q_i^* =$

[23] See the following: Chamberlin, *Monopolistic Competition*, pp. 46–51; Fellner, *Competition Among the Few*, chaps. IV–IX; and especially Robert L. Bishop, "Duopoly: Collusion or Warfare?" *American Economic Review*, L:5 (Dec. 1960), 933–961.

[24] The argument is Fellner's (*Competition Among the Few*, p. 130) that "Reaction functions or, if the quasi-agreement relates directly to points, reaction points should be expected to reflect a tendency toward joint-profit maximization. If the aggregate industry profit is not maximized and the less-than-maximum profit is divided in some fashion, it always is possible to give *every single participant* more than he actually gets, by changing the quasi-agreement to a basis on which the aggregate industry profit *is* maximized."

$\dfrac{1}{2[1+b]}$ $(i = 1, 2)$ and $Q^* = Q_1^* + Q_2^* = \dfrac{1}{[1+b]}$. Thus, in an increasing-cost situation with $b < 1$, $Q^* = 1/[1+b] > \frac{1}{2}$ and total output exceeds the monopoly output of $\frac{1}{2}$; with constant costs, $b = 1$, the duopolists combine to produce the monopoly output, and as long as they shared equally in the pooled total profit, it would be a matter of indifference as to who produced what; with decreasing costs, $b > 1$, the previous first-order conditions signal a position to avoid rather than seek, one producer would produce the monopoly output, and the profits would be shared.

On the other hand, with one duopolist on a given isoprofit curve, an arbitrator might seek an output combination such that the other is on his own highest isoprofit curve. Through this combination, the first duopolist becomes no worse off, while the second does as well as he can without forcing a sacrifice from the first. All such output combinations assuring maximum profits for one duopolist, given the other's profit level, lie on the locus of tangency points between the duopolists' isoprofit curves as illustrated in Figure 7.13.

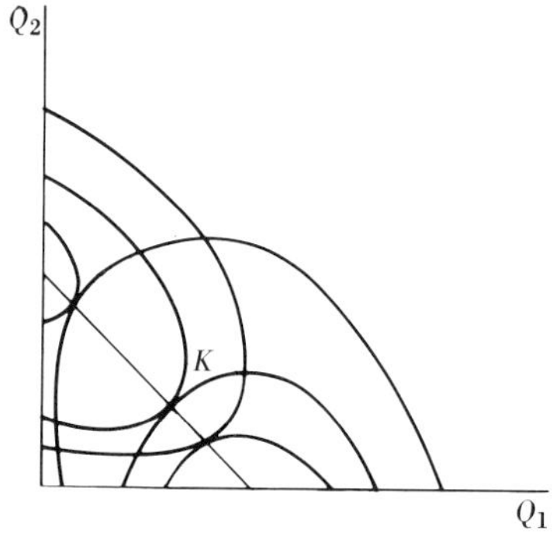


Fig. 7.13

Suppose, for example, we choose to maximize $\pi_1$ subject to the constraint $\pi_2 = \bar{\pi}$. This can be framed as a Lagrangian problem: Maximize $L(\pi_1, \lambda) = \pi_1 - \lambda[\pi_2 - \bar{\pi}]$. The first-order conditions for a maximum require $\partial L/\partial Q_i = \partial\pi_1/\partial Q_i - \lambda(\partial\pi_2/\partial Q_i) = 0$ $(i = 1, 2)$. Therefore

$$\lambda = \frac{\left[\dfrac{\partial\pi_1}{\partial Q_1}\right]}{\left[\dfrac{\partial\pi_2}{\partial Q_1}\right]} = \frac{\left[\dfrac{\partial\pi_1}{\partial Q_2}\right]}{\left[\dfrac{\partial\pi_2}{\partial Q_2}\right]} \quad \text{or} \quad \frac{\left[\dfrac{\partial\pi_1}{\partial Q_1}\right]}{\left[\dfrac{\partial\pi_1}{\partial Q_2}\right]} = \frac{\left[\dfrac{\partial\pi_2}{\partial Q_1}\right]}{\left[\dfrac{\partial\pi_2}{\partial Q_2}\right]}.$$

Now, each one's profit will be a function of *both* output levels, or $\pi_i = \pi_i(Q_1, Q_2)$. Hence,

$$d\pi_i = \left[\frac{\partial\pi_i}{\partial Q_1}\right] dQ_1 + \left[\frac{\partial\pi_i}{\partial Q_2}\right] dQ_2 = 0$$

describes the changes in $Q_1$ and $Q_2$ required to maintain profits fixed for duopolist $i$.

Alternatively, on a given isoprofit curve,

$$-\frac{\left[\dfrac{\partial \pi_i}{\partial Q_1}\right]}{\left[\dfrac{\partial \pi_i}{\partial Q_2}\right]} = \left(\frac{dQ_2}{dQ_1}\right)_{\pi_i=k_i}.$$

The term $(dQ_2/dQ_1)_{\pi_i=k_i}$ is the slope of the isoprofit curve $\pi_i = k_i$. The first-order conditions for an optimum therefore require $(dQ_2/dQ_1)_{\pi_1=k_1} = (dQ_2/dQ_1)_{\pi_2=k_2}$. As long as $\pi_1$ and $\pi_2$ are concave functions of $Q_1$ and $Q_2$, the second-order conditions will also be satisfied at this point—that is, at the point where the slopes of the isoprofit curves are equal, or where an isoprofit curve of duopolist 1 is tangent to duopolist 2's $\pi_2 = \bar{\pi}$ isoprofit curve. In the present case, with $\pi_i = Q_i - Q_i^2 - bQ_iQ_j$ ($i = 1, 2$ and $j \neq i$),

$$\left(\frac{dQ_2}{dQ_1}\right)_{\pi_1=k_1} = \frac{[1 - 2Q_1 - bQ_2]}{bQ_1} \quad \text{and} \quad \left(\frac{dQ_2}{dQ_1}\right)_{\pi_2=k_2} = \frac{bQ_2}{[1 - 2Q_2 - bQ_1]}.$$

The locus of tangencies is found by equating the two slopes, or

$$\frac{[1 - 2Q_1 - bQ_2]}{bQ_1} = \frac{bQ_2}{[1 - 2Q_2 - bQ_1]}.$$

This locus is given by

$$0 = 1 - [2 + b][Q_1 + Q_2] + 2b[Q_1^2 + Q_2^2] + 4Q_1Q_2,$$

which is referred to as the *contract curve.*

With nondecreasing costs, the duopolists share equally in the maximized joint profits at the midpoint on the contract curve, the point $K$ in Figure 7.13, with $b = 1$. With decreasing costs, joint profits are *minimized* at the midpoint. In the absence of objections to being on the contract curve, each firm prefers to operate on the *most favorable* isoprofit curve that the competitor can be persuaded to agree to. The art of tacit persuasion could involve some interesting *strategies.* A strategy is a planned series of actions. In the present instance, for example, a duopolist might agree to operate on the contract curve so long as his profit exceeds that of his competitor by 10 percent. He might thus operate in accordance with the curve so long as his own profit is 10 percent greater than that of his competitor. Should his competitor produce an output that prevents him from taking this 10 percent advantage, with constant costs he could simply produce 10 percent more than the competitor. He could continue to operate in this fashion until total output equaled 1, at which point further output would not be sold. At this point, he could simply produce $1 - Q_j$, $j$ = competitor. With $b = 1$, the contract curve equation can be factored to imply $1 - 2Q_1 - 2Q_2 = 0$. Thus, for duopolist 1 the strategy above would reduce to producing a quantity of $Q_1 = [1 - 2Q_2]/2$ for $Q_2 \leq .238$, producing $Q_1 = 1.1Q_2$ for $.238 < Q_2 \leq .479$, and producing $Q_1 = 1 - Q_2$ for $Q_2 > .479$. The point of this strategy is that duopolist 2 is best off on the contract curve. Hopefully, duopolist 1's self-inflicted losses incurred through his enlightened self-interest will be momentary and will persuade duopolist 2 to accept the smaller share than afforded by an even split. Of course, if duopolist 2 has similar designs, the results are all-out economic warfare, with such factors as willpower and financial strength playing vital roles.[25] The dark line in Figure 7.14 illustrates duopolist 1's output under this strategy.

Clearly, then, even in this relatively simple extension of the Cournot model, aspects of strategy, willpower, and willingness to take risk and withstand loss come into play. But how we handle these and how we determine the actual point at which the firms will operate is not quite as clear. One framework that holds some promise—most of it not yet realized—is offered by game theory. Let us consider some of the opportunities available in the game-theoretic approach.

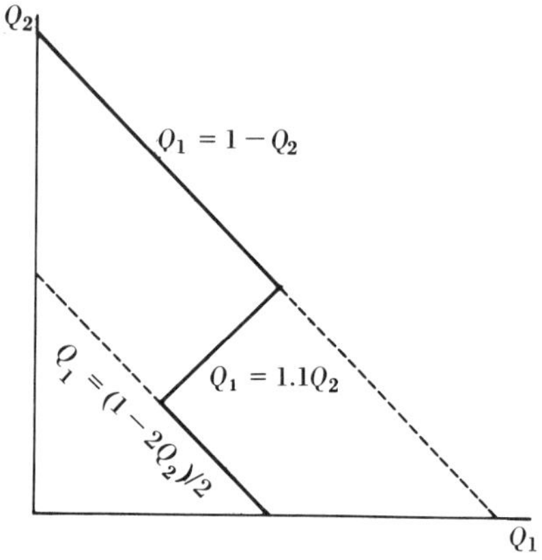


Fig. 7.14

### iii. GAME THEORY[26]

The *theory of games* is concerned with individuals' choices among alternative courses of action, when the results of those decisions will depend upon the selections

[25] The term "warfare" is more than appropriate here. The formulation of price decisions, for example, has been likened to a military campaign with both defensive and offensive strategies [E. G. Nourse, "The Meaning of 'Price Policy,'" *Quarterly Journal of Economics*, **LV**:1 (Feb. 1941), pp. 175–209]. Indeed, Rothschild ("Price Theory and Oligopoly," p. 307) has suggested that "The oligopoly-theorist's classical literature can neither be Newton or Darwin, nor can it be Freud; he will have to turn to Clausewitz's *Principles of War*. There he will not only find numerous striking parallels between military and (oligopolistic) business strategy, but also a method of a *general* approach which—while far less elegant than traditional price theory—promises a more realistic treatment of the oligopoly problem." In this connection, and in light of the remarks on stability in footnote 13, it might be noted that Fellner (*Competition Among the Few*, pp. 177–183) argues that while actual price warfare would tend to result in lower prices in oligopolistic industries than in a monopoly situation, the potential for price warfare, if the warfare is avoided, could lead to the establishment of higher-than-monopoly price levels. Of particular interest is Thomas C. Schelling's *The Strategy of Conflict* (Cambridge, Mass.: Harvard University Press, 1963).

[26] For more extensive discussions and comment see: John von Neumann and Oskar Morgenstern, *Theory of Games and Economic Behavior* (Princeton, N.J.: Princeton University Press, 1944); Leonid Hurwicz, "The Theory of Economic Behavior," *American Economic Review*, **XXXV**:5 (Dec. 1945), 908–925; and R. Duncan Luce and Howard Raiffa, *Games and Decisions* (New York: John Wiley & Sons, Inc., 1957). It is of interest to note

of other individuals. Given the framework of the decision problem, the rules for selection, the options, and the mutually determined payoffs or consequences of all combinations of choices, we have a decision problem or a *game*. The theoretical study of such situations is not terribly well developed beyond the simpler two-person or two-competitor situations. While one can also consider certain quite complex possibilities for $n$-person ($n > 2$) games, this goes beyond our present scope. Our discussion here will be restricted to two-person games, which in the present context will be duopoly situations.

### Two-Person, Constant-Sum Games

First consider two profit-motivated duopolists who, having ascertained that profit is directly related to market share, express their objectives as "the maximization of market shares."[27] Their goals will conflict, because any addition to one's market share must *necessarily* come at the expense of the other. What one duopolist gains the other loses, and the sum of their shares is a constant—in this case, 1. The duopolists may thus be said to be participants in a two-person, *constant*-sum "game." The problem is to devise a strategy aimed at yielding the largest part of the sum. The catch is that *each* duopolist is faced with a similar problem. The success that each has in attaining his objectives will depend upon (1) the set of actions that he contemplates choosing among and (2) the choice that he makes from that set, as well as (3) the actions contemplated and the choice made by his competitor.

Delineating possible actions is in many respects the most difficult task in decision problems. Unnecessary losses are frequently incurred by competitors who fail to consider all the options available to them. It is rare, however, that one can carefully consider or even recognize *all* options, or comprehensively evaluate their potential consequences, making due allowance for each of a competitor's options.[28] Nevertheless, we shall suppose that each competitor has narrowed his alternatives down to a finite few *and* that each is aware of his opponent's options. In the current era of industrial intrigue, this is not too farfetched.

Duopolist 1 is contemplating making either one of two minor product changes or else maintaining the status quo. These actions or *pure strategies* will be denoted by $S_{11}$, $S_{12}$, and $S_{13}$, respectively. Duopolist 2 contemplates initiating one of three

---

that in *The Theory of Business Enterprise* (New York: Charles Scribner's Sons, 1904), written at the turn of the century, Thorstein Veblen discussed proceedings in the business world as a game (pp. 27–35).

[27] The potential of market position as a means of enhancing long-term profits, especially under uncertainty, and the particular ability to extend market share when demand is increasing, has been noted by Rothschild ("Price Theory and Oligopoly," p. 319), and discussed at length by Moses Abramovitz, "Monopolistic Selling in a Changing Economy," *Quarterly Journal of Economics,* **LII** (May 1938), 191–214. Also see Richard B. Heflebower, "Toward a Theory of Industrial Markets and Prices," *American Economic Review,* **XLIV**:2 (May 1954), pp. 121–140.

[28] For discussions of this crucial point see the following: Herman Chernoff, "Rational Selection of Decision Functions," *Econometrica,* **22**:4 (Oct. 1954), 422–443; R. M. Cyert and J. G. March, "Organizational Structure and Pricing Behavior in an Oligopolistic Market," *American Economic Review,* **XLV**:1 (March 1955), 129–139; Herbert A. Simon, *Administrative Behavior* (New York: The Macmillan Company, 1958), particularly p. 81; and James G. March and Herbert A. Simon, *Organizations* (New York: John Wiley & Sons, Inc., 1958).

advertising programs or else maintaining the status quo. His pure strategies will be denoted by $S_{21}$, $S_{22}$, $S_{23}$, and $S_{24}$, respectively. If duopolist 1 chooses strategy $S_{1j}$ and duopolist 2 chooses strategy $S_{2i}$, duopolist 2's share of the market will be $a_{ij}$ and that of duopolist 1 will be $\bar{a}_{ji} = 1 - a_{ij}$. This is a constant-sum game, and the sum of the *payoffs* will be $a_{ij} + \bar{a}_{ji} = a_{ij} + 1 - a_{ij} = 1$. The payoffs are summarized in Table 7.1. This *payoff table* describes the payoff to duopolist 2 from each combination of pure strategies. A similar table could be constructed for duopolist 1 with $\bar{a}_{ji} = 1 - a_{ij}$. In a constant-sum game, the entries in a payoff table will generally be the payoffs to the competitor choosing between "row" strategies.

Because of the conflict inherent in the constant-sum game, it quickly becomes apparent that each duopolist will be attracted to the alternative whose most distasteful consequence is the least unfortunate of any of the misfortunes that might befall him. The attraction is stimulated by the realization that one's opponent will do his best to see that the worst comes to pass. One seeks to avoid this worst by a course of action designed to assure that, *at a minimum*, one will receive as a payoff the best of the worst. In this way, each competitor selects the decision that maximizes his minimum gain (or its equivalent, minimizes the maximum loss). Such a decision is called a maximin (or minimax) decision. To see the desirability of this strategem, note that duopolist 2's minimum share, if he chooses $S_{21}$, will be .50, the payoff when duopolist 1 has chosen $S_{11}$; if he chooses $S_{22}$, then $a_{22} = .35$ is the

TABLE 7.1
Duopolist 2's Market Share

| | | *Duopolist 1's Choices* | | |
|---|---|---|---|---|
| | | $S_{11}$ | $S_{12}$ | $S_{13}$ |
| | $S_{21}$ | .50 | .55 | .65 |
| *Duopolist 2's* | $S_{22}$ | .40 | .35 | .60 |
| *Choices* | $S_{23}$ | .25 | .65 | .55 |
| | $S_{24}$ | .30 | .40 | .50 |

minimum share that he receives, when $S_{12}$ is chosen by duopolist 1. In this manner, the four minima are determined to be $a_{11} = .50$, $a_{22} = .35$, $a_{31} = .25$, and $a_{41} = .30$. By choosing $S_{11}$, duopolist 2 assures himself of no less than half the market, *irrespective* of duopolist 1's decision—this, against a competitor seeking to restrict him to as small a share as possible.

As far as duopolist 1 is concerned, the worst that he can do by choosing $S_{11}$ is $1 - a_{11} = .50$. If he chooses $S_{12}$ or $S_{13}$, he could do as poorly as $1 - a_{32} = .35$ or $1 - a_{13} = .35$. Hence, by choosing $S_{11}$ he maximizes his minimum share. When $S_{11}$ and $S_{21}$ respectively are chosen, each duopolist does, in fact, have his worst fears realized. Note, however, that neither has any inclination to regret his decision, for each has indeed made the choice that is optimal in light of his competitor's action. The seemingly pessimistic outlook on life has turned out to be more than justified.

The entry $a_{11}$ is called a *saddle point*. A saddle point occurs when an entry is the minimum in its row and the maximum in its column. The value $a_{11} = .50$ is called the *value of the game*. This value indicates what duopolist 2's payoff is expected to be. The pure strategies $S_{11}$ and $S_{21}$ yield $a_{11}$ as an *equilibrium* point. Once at the saddle point, one has no inclination to change strategies, even after the competitor's strategy is known. An equilibrium or saddle point occurs whenever

$$\max_i (\min_j a_{ij}) = \min_j (\max_i a_{ij}).$$

Pure-strategy saddle-point solutions are analytically convenient. Unhappily, however, they will not necessarily exist. For example, the payoffs for the same set of pure strategies might appear as in Table 7.2. If once again each duopolist chooses his minimax pure strategy $S_{22}$ and $S_{12}$, the payoff of $a_{22} = .55$ no longer represents an equilibrium point. Now, given the opportunity to choose anew, if he thought that duopolist 2 would stick to $S_{22}$, duopolist 1 would choose $S_{11}$. Suppose that, even before he makes his initial choice, duopolist 1 *assumes* that duopolist 2 will choose $S_{22}$. Acting on this assumption, duopolist 1 might now choose $S_{11}$ rather than $S_{12}$. But duopolist 2 could in turn anticipate duopolist 1's reasoning process, since both have knowledge of the payoff table. He might, therefore, actually choose $S_{23}$. Once again, however, duopolist 1 could carry his own reasoning a step further—and so forth.

It would appear, then, that this situation in which

$$\max_i (\min_j a_{ij}) \neq \min_j (\max_i a_{ij})$$

is not amenable to a clear-cut pure-strategy solution. One may, however, devise a *mixed strategy* for these situations. A mixed strategy is a combination of pure strategies whereby each pure strategy is selected with a given probability. The

TABLE 7.2
Duopolist 2's Market Share

| | | *Duopolist 1's Choices* | | |
|---|---|---|---|---|
| | | $S_{11}$ | $S_{12}$ | $S_{13}$ |
| | $S_{21}$ | .60 | .40 | .65 |
| *Duopolist 2's* | $S_{22}$ | .50 | .55 | .60 |
| *Choices* | $S_{23}$ | .65 | .50 | .35 |
| | $S_{24}$ | .30 | .40 | .50 |

purpose is to achieve an objective *comparable* to maximizing the minimum gain or minimizing the maximum loss. The comparable objective would be to maximize the minimum *expected* gain. The latter is the mathematical expectation or expected value of the possible gains. The probability weights are the probabilities with which the respective pure strategies have been chosen.

To develop these probabilities, suppose that duopolist 2 elects to choose strategy $S_{2i}$ with a *stochastic* mechanism generating his choice of action. *Nobody* can possibly outguess him now or anticipate *with certainty* which pure strategy he will choose. This is because each pure strategy will be selected *at random* with probability $p_i$. The problem is to select the $p_i$ so as to maximize the minimum expected gain. If duopolist 1 should select $S_{11}$, duopolist 2's *expected* gain from the use of his randomizing scheme will be $\sum_i p_i a_{i1}$. Suppose, however, that *some* mixed strategy exists that will assure an expected gain of at least $V$. Then duopolist 2 will want to set the $p_i$ such that $\sum_i p_i a_{i1} \geq V$. That is, his expected gain is at least as great as that of the alternative scheme. Note that we do not specify the value of $V$. But, we can be sure that $V \geq .30$, for nobody could devise a strategy that would earn less than .30 in the present situation. Merely by letting the flip of a fair coin dictate the choice between $S_{21}$ and $S_{22}$, one would necessarily do a lot better than .30. As we shall see, $V$ will be determined concurrently with the $p_i$.

In a similar fashion, we want the choice of the $p_i$ to assure that if duopolist 1 should choose $S_{12}$ or $S_{13}$, it will still be true that $\sum_i p_i a_{i2} \geq V$ and $\sum_i p_i a_{i3} \geq V$. As probabilities, it must also be true that $p_i \geq 0$ and $\sum_i p_i = 1$. Duopolist 2's problem can now be looked upon as the maximization of his expected gain, $V$, subject to the enumerated constraints, or: Maximize $Z = V$, subject to

$$\sum_i p_i a_{ij} - V \geq 0 \quad (j = 1, 2, 3); \qquad \sum_i p_i = 1; \qquad V, p_i \geq 0 \quad (i = 1, \ldots, 4).$$

The specific problem at hand would be fully written out as

$$\text{Maximize} \quad Z = V + 0p_1 + 0p_2 + 0p_3 + 0p_4 \tag{7.1}$$

$$\begin{aligned} \text{subject to} \quad & .60p_1 + .50p_2 + .65p_3 + .30p_4 - V \geq 0, \\ & .40p_1 + .55p_2 + .50p_3 + .40p_4 - V \geq 0, \\ & .65p_1 + .60p_2 + .35p_3 + .50p_4 - V \geq 0, \\ & p_1 + p_2 + p_3 + p_4 = 1, \\ & p_1, p_2, p_3, p_4, V \geq 0. \end{aligned} \tag{7.2}$$

As we shall see in the next section, this problem is readily solved using linear programming techniques. Equation (7.1), the function $Z$, is called the *objective function* or the *criterion function* to be maximized or minimized. $V$ and the $p_i$ are the variables whose levels are to be determined. In the present problem, the weight of $V$ in the objective function is 1, and the weight of each $p_i$ is 0 (the latter actually need not be written in *this* objective function). Equations (7.2) form the constraints. Both the objective function and constraints are linear. As we shall see, the variables *must* be nonnegative to assure that the linear programming technique will work. The $p_i$ are necessarily nonnegative. In general, by adding a constant $k$ to every element in the payoff table, we could assure that $V = V_0 + k$ would *have to* be positive. This addition would not alter the basic structure of the problem. The solution would merely yield a value of $V$ that was greater than $V_0$, the actual value for the original problem, by the amount of the constant; or, $V_0 = V - k$. The $p_i$ would be unaffected.

The solution to this problem, as shown in the Appendix at the end of the chapter, is $p_1 = 0$, $p_2 = .75$, $p_3 = .25$, and $p_4 = .0$. Thus, although the options are available, strategies $S_{21}$ and $S_{24}$ are *never* chosen. In the case of $S_{24}$, at least, the reason is eminently clear: $S_{24}$ is dominated by both $S_{21}$ and $S_{22}$ in the sense that either of the latter would yield at least as high a payoff as $S_{24}$, irrespective of duopolist 1's choice. The *value* of the game is $V = .5375$, duopolist 2's expected gain. By substitution into (7.2), it is readily seen that the constraints are indeed satisfied.

Moreover, duopolist 1 cannot be neglected. He will be following a similar strategy, developed by solving the problem: *Minimize* $Z' = V' + 0 \Sigma q_j$, subject to $\sum_j q_j a_{ij} \leq V'$ $(i = 1, \ldots, 4)$; $\sum_j q_j = 1$; $V', q_j \geq 0$. That is, duopolist 1 seeks to *minimize* his maximum expected loss of $V'$. He does this by selecting among the $j = 1, 2, 3$ strategies at random in accordance with probabilities $q_j$ set to assure that duopolist 2's expected gain will be *less than* $V'$ irrespective of the latter's pure-strategy choice. It is clear (and mathematically demonstrable, too) that for each competitor to achieve his objective—and the linear programming solutions that assure this—it is necessary that $V = V'$. This equality does indeed hold. One competitor's expected gain *is* the other's expected loss. Solving duopolist 1's problem yields $q_1 = .4445$, $q_2 = .3611$, and $q_3 = .1944$, with $V' = .5375$. As advertised, duopolist 2's expected gain is duopolist 1's expected loss. Each chooses his pure strategy *at random* in accordance with the $p_i$ and $q_j$. A spinning wheel or random-number generator might be used to *simulate* the probabilities and determine the actions; then, duopolist 2's expected market share is .5375 and duopolist 1's is .4625.

It is important to note that the actions must be generated *randomly*. The probabilities are not just percentages that must be maintained. Suppose duopolist 1 merely selects $S_{11}$ 44.45 *percent* of the time, $S_{12}$ 36.11 *percent* of the time, and $S_{13}$ 19.44 *percent* of the time over many decision periods with some regular pattern of choice. Duopolist 2 might detect the regularity and take advantage of it. Choosing the pure strategies at random prevents this. It is also important to note that, although duopolist 1's expected market share would still be .4625 if duopolist 2 were to choose $S_{21}$, his expected share would soar to .6250 if he used his optimal mixed strategy and duopolist 2 chose $S_{24}$. It is for precisely this reason that (1) duopolist 2 would never utilize $S_{24}$ even if it were not a dominated strategy, and (2) he must continue to use his own optimal mixed strategy and not presume that his fate is already decided by his competitor's actions.

### Nonconstant-Sum Games

To conclude this brief study of games, again consider the Stackelberg-Cournot situation with an industry demand curve of $P = 1 - Q$ and $C_i = 0$. If both duopolists are nonsophisticated, each produces $\frac{1}{3}$ and earns a profit of $\frac{1}{9}$. If both are sophisticated, each produces $\frac{1}{2}$ and each earns 0. If one is sophisticated and the other not, the sophisticated duopolist produces $\frac{1}{2}$ and earns $\frac{1}{8}$, while the nonsophisticated one produces $\frac{1}{4}$ and earns $\frac{1}{16}$. Alternatively, each can produce half the monopoly output, or $\frac{1}{4}$, and earn $\frac{1}{8}$. The possibilities for the three output levels, or pure strategies, are shown in the payoff table, Table 7.3. The first entry in a pair is duopolist 2's profit, and the second is duopolist 1's profit.

TABLE 7.3

| | | *Duopolist 1's Output* | | |
|---|---|---|---|---|
| | | $\frac{1}{2}$ | $\frac{1}{3}$ | $\frac{1}{4}$ |
| *Duopolist 2's Output* | $\frac{1}{2}$ | (0, 0) | $(\frac{6}{72}, \frac{4}{72})$ | $(\frac{9}{72}, \frac{1}{16})$ |
| | $\frac{1}{3}$ | $(\frac{4}{72}, \frac{6}{72})$ | $(\frac{8}{72}, \frac{8}{72})$ | $(\frac{10}{72}, \frac{5}{48})$ |
| | $\frac{1}{4}$ | $(\frac{1}{16}, \frac{9}{72})$ | $(\frac{5}{48}, \frac{10}{72})$ | $(\frac{9}{72}, \frac{9}{72})$ |

This symmetric game is more complex than the constant-sum game, for one competitor's gain is not necessarily the other's loss. It is immediately clear that the output of $\frac{1}{3}$ is the best strategy for each when the other produces $\frac{1}{3}$ or $\frac{1}{4}$, but $\frac{1}{4}$ is best when the other produces $\frac{1}{2}$. That is, so long as each duopolist ceases to be guided by his reaction curve, but concentrates solely on Table 7.3 and considers only the three specific outputs as possibilities, the naive output of $\frac{1}{3}$ is actually the most profitable output—unless one's competitor produces the monopoly output. Also, $\frac{1}{3}$ is always more profitable than $\frac{1}{2}$, given the other's options. That is, the monopoly output is a dominated strategy. If an arrangement could be worked out whereby each produces $\frac{1}{4}$, then *each* would be better off than with the combined output of $\frac{2}{3}$, equally shared. A formerly monopolistic producer of $\frac{1}{2}$ would benefit by agreeing to restrict output to $\frac{1}{4}$ in lieu of having each produce $\frac{1}{3}$. Were such an agreement worked out, however, the duopolists would be tempted to double-cross one another for the additional $\frac{1}{72}$ one could obtain by producing $\frac{1}{3}$ while the other produced $\frac{1}{4}$. It is also possible that duopolist 2 might continue to produce $\frac{1}{2}$ and make it clear to duopolist 1 that he has no intention of altering this output. In this event, duopolist 1's most profitable counter is to produce $\frac{1}{4}$—precisely what duopolist 2 wants him to do.

It might appear, then, that duopolist 2 should in fact produce $\frac{1}{2}$ and keep doing so in repeated production periods, thereby forcing duopolist 1 to accept his fate and produce $\frac{1}{4}$. But what if duopolist 1 should have similar thoughts and he too were to repeatedly produce $\frac{1}{2}$? Consumers would be delighted, for the price would drop to 0, but each duopolist would earn 0 profit. Moreover, as soon as one duopolist gave in and produced $\frac{1}{4}$, the temptation would exist for the other to switch to $\frac{1}{3}$, though this would leave him open to a $\frac{1}{3}$ "counter-output."

One could devise a mixed strategy for each to maximize his minimum expected gain. In such a strategy an output of $\frac{1}{2}$ would be produced with probability of 0 since $\frac{1}{3}$ *dominates* $\frac{1}{2}$; $\frac{1}{3}$ would be produced with probability of 1 and $\frac{1}{4}$ produced with probability of 0, since $\frac{1}{3}$ is better than $\frac{1}{4}$ as long as $\frac{1}{2}$ is never to be produced by a competitor—and it won't be because it is dominated. The argument against invoking such a strategy here, however, is that one might be better off with a threat, pure stubbornness, or the willingness to momentarily absorb loss, against a weaker-willed or financially weaker competitor who could be forced to acquiesce and produce $\frac{1}{4}$. Further, since $\frac{1}{3}$ dominates $\frac{1}{2}$ and each duopolist might expect the other never to produce $\frac{1}{2}$, each might undertake to produce $\frac{1}{2}$ *precisely because* his competitor would not expect him to do so.

Notice that delay in making one's output known is not necessarily advantageous in this situation. One might tend to feel it best to delay production plans until a competitor has made his intentions clear. Yet, if the competitor moves first, convincing his adversary of his intentions to produce $\frac{1}{2}$, what recourse is left to the short-term profit maximizer but to produce $\frac{1}{4}$? In fact, there might be great urgency to inform a competitor of one's plans and convince him that nothing will change them. It would appear, however, that while there may not be a clear-cut strategem to follow, an arbitrator would have no difficulty in suggesting the $(\frac{1}{4}, \frac{1}{4})$ solution.

The clarity of this arbitrated solution contrasts sharply with the ambiguity encountered in the following symmetric situation. Here the entries in the payoff table, Table 7.4, are profit, and the two duopolists are again profit maximizers. $S_{12}$ and

TABLE 7.4

| | | *Duopolist 1* $S_{11}$ | $S_{12}$ | $S_{13}$ |
|---|---|---|---|---|
| | $S_{21}$ | (1000, 1000) | (500, 2000) | (200, 400) |
| *Duopolist 2* | $S_{22}$ | (2000, 500) | (600, 600) | (3000, 0) |
| | $S_{23}$ | (400, 200) | (0, 3000) | (1000, 1000) |

$S_{22}$ are strategies that dominate the others. *Irrespective* of the other's action, $S_{12}$ and $S_{22}$ are the most profitable policies. Yet, unless one will tolerate reduced profit levels simply to reduce a competitor's profit—and some will—the mutually unsatisfactory solution of (600, 600) will be reached rather than, say, (1000, 1000). Even when the competitors agree to coordinate policies of $S_{21}$-$S_{11}$ or $S_{23}$-$S_{13}$, the temptation to renege and switch to one's second strategy is quite strong—perhaps $2000 worth.

This game is a form of the *prisoner's dilemma*. It is characterized by the payoff promised by a double-cross, and the dominance of a mutually unsatisfactory solution. Figure 7.15 illustrates the payoffs: those of duopolist 1 are shown by the abscissa and those of duopolist 2 by the ordinate. The shaded area represents the average payoffs attainable by alternating between strategy pairs. For example, an average payoff of (1250, 1250) could be attained by the duopolists' agreeing to alternate equally between $S_{21}$-$S_{12}$ and $S_{22}$-$S_{11}$, or by their agreeing to one of the two solutions, with the recipient of 2000 paying the other 750 as a "bribe." The outer line linking the (3000, 0) and (0, 3000) solutions is the *Pareto-optimal* set of solutions.

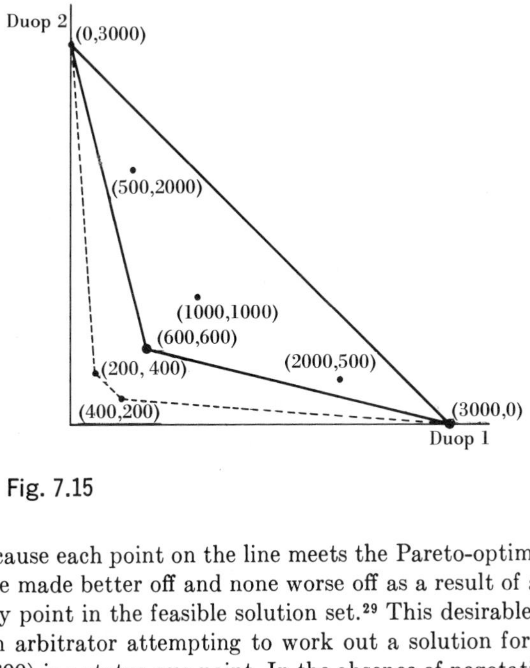


Fig. 7.15

It is so called because each point on the line meets the Pareto-optimality condition: one person can be made better off and none worse off as a result of a move towards this line from any point in the feasible solution set.[29] This desirable property could be utilized by an arbitrator attempting to work out a solution for the duopolists. The point (600, 600) is a status-quo point. In the absence of negotations, it is at this point where the duopolists would find themselves. Any negotiations would proceed from here, since either duopolist could threaten not to participate, stick to his second strategy, and guarantee himself 600.

Most would agree that a (1500, 1500) split would seem reasonable in this situation. This could be achieved by coordinated alteration between (3000, 0) and (0, 3000). One reason for this suggestion is that, starting from the status-quo point and adding

[29] For a good basic discussion of Pareto optimality see James M. Henderson and Richard E. Quandt, *Microeconomic Theory* (New York: McGraw-Hill, Inc., 1958), chap. 7. The heartier souls who tried the original Cournot and Bertrand can push their luck further with Vilfredo Pareto, *Manuel d' Economic Politique* (Paris: Girard, 1909).

equal increments to each duopolist's payoff, we would reach this solution. A more compelling reason has been suggested by Nash.[30] In this instance the *product* of the payoffs is maximized at this particular point.

Now one might feel that the largest *sum* is desirable. But, where the payoffs are not symmetric, and where the situation contains certain inherent advantages for one competitor—say, threat advantages or the ability to assure one's self of a given minimum via a maximin strategy—this sum still has to be divided up in a manner that may somewhat reflect these inherent advantages. A division maximizing the *product* of the payoffs (*perhaps* reduced by the respective security level payoffs to allow for these advantages) rests on the following argument.

Let $(D_{11}, D_{21})$ be the point on the Pareto optimal preferred by duopolist 1, and $(D_{12}, D_{22})$ be the point preferred by duopolist 2. If duopolist 1 moves to duopolist 2's preferred solution, the *relative loss* he incurs from the move will be $(D_{11} - D_{12})/D_{11}$; if duopolist 2 moves, his relative loss will be $(D_{22} - D_{21})/D_{22}$. If the duopolist suffering the smaller relative loss is asked to move, $(D_{11}, D_{21})$ will be selected over $(D_{12}, D_{22})$ so long as $(D_{11} - D_{12})/D_{11} > (D_{22} - D_{21})/D_{22}$, or $D_{22}D_{11} - D_{12}D_{22} > D_{22}D_{11} - D_{11}D_{21}$. Canceling the $D_{22}D_{11}$ term on each side of the inequality, the inequality becomes $D_{11}D_{21} > D_{12}D_{22}$. This states that the point at which the product of the payoffs is the greatest will be the point such that the relative loss incurred by one competitor by a move from this point will exceed the consequent relative gain enjoyed by the other. Thus, let the point at which the product of the payoffs is maximized be on the line segment joining $(d_{11}, d_{21})$ and $(d_{12}, d_{22})$. When $(d_{11}, d_{21})$ is selected $p$ percent of the time and $(d_{12}, d_{22})$ is selected $(1 - p)$ percent of the time, duopolist 1's average payoff is $pd_{11} + (1 - p)d_{12}$; that of duopolist 2 is $pd_{21} + (1 - p)d_{22}$. The product of the payoffs is

$$\pi = p^2[(d_{11} - d_{12})(d_{21} - d_{22})] + p[d_{12}(d_{21} - d_{22}) + d_{22}(d_{11} - d_{12})] + d_{12}d_{22}.$$

This is maximized where $d\pi/dp = 0$ and $d^2\pi/dp^2 < 0$. Setting

$$\frac{d\pi}{dp} = 2p[(d_{11} - d_{12})(d_{21} - d_{22})] + d_{12}(d_{21} - d_{22}) + d_{22}(d_{11} - d_{12}) = 0$$

yields

$$p = \frac{d_{12}(d_{22} - d_{21}) + d_{22}(d_{12} - d_{11})}{2(d_{11} - d_{12})(d_{21} - d_{22})}.$$

This value of $p$ maximizes $\pi$ since $d^2\pi/dp^2 = 2(d_{11} - d_{12})(d_{21} - d_{22}) < 0$, because when $d_{11} > d_{12}$, then $d_{22} > d_{21}$, and conversely. Note, however, that it will not necessarily be true that $0 \leq p \leq 1$, and to incorporate such a constraint on the value of $p$ will require the tools of Chapter 9. Nonetheless, it should be at least intuitively apparent that, assuming say that $d_{11} > d_{12}$ and $d_{22} > d_{21}$, if the $p$ calculated as

[30] See J. F. Nash, "The Bargaining Problem," *Econometrica*, **18**:2 (April 1950), 155–162, and "Two-Person Cooperative Games," *Econometrica*, **21**:1 (Jan. 1953), 128–140. Also see J. C. Harsanyi, "Approaches to the Bargaining Problem Before and After the Theory of Games: A Critical Discussion of Zeuthen's, Hicks', and Nash's Theories," *Econometrica*, **24**:2 (April 1956), 144–157; Luce and Raiffa, *Games and Decisions*, chap. 6; "Game-Theoretic Analysis of Bargaining," *Quarterly Journal of Economics*, **LXXVII**:4 (Nov. 1963), 559–602 and "A Zeuthen-Hicks Theory of Bargaining," *Econometrica*, **32**:3 (July 1964), 410–417, by Robert L. Bishop.

above is $p > 1$, then the optimal feasible Nash solution will be $(d_{11}, d_{21})$; if we compute $p < 0$, then the optimum will be $(d_{12}, d_{22})$. In effect, since neither point can be reached more than 100 percent of the time, we settle for the next best *feasible* option of 100 percent. In the illustration above, the two preferred points are (3000, 0) and (0, 3000). Therefore,

$$p = \frac{0(3000 - 0) + 3000(0 - 3000)}{2(3000 - 0)(0 - 3000)} = \frac{1}{2},$$

and the Nash solution is to alternate between (3000, 0) and (0, 3000).

There are certainly other possible arbitration schemes and other "solutions" and strategies that one could suggest. The possibilities are extended, and in many ways complicated, when instead of monetary payoffs we consider more esoteric measures that attempt to allow for the participants' preferences and their attitudes towards risk. We shall briefly consider this aspect in Section 12.7a.

The possibilities become even less manageable when additional competitors are introduced. Not only are the potential strategies more difficult to evaluate, but the possibilities of bribes and coalitions add additional dimensions that are not readily amenable to determinate solutions. In point of fact, while game theory does hold some promise for analysis of oligopoly situations, the promise has not yet been fully realized.

## 7.8 LINEAR PROGRAMMING[31]

### a. What Linear Programming Is About

The optimal mixed strategies in the two-person constant-sum game were obtained by setting up and solving a pair of *linear programming* (LP) problems. In general, linear programming involves the optimization of a *linear objective function* of $n$ *nonnegative variables* subject to $m$ *linear constraints*. The latter may be equalities or inequalities. Game theory thus introduces us to but one *specific* LP problem, whereas the applicability of linear programming to the problems of the firm and economic theory is much more widespread. It will therefore be useful to develop a *general* procedure for solving LP problems. This procedure will be illustrated in the Appendix at the end of this chapter, wherein we solve the mixed-strategy problem of duopolist 2, as presented in Equations (7.1) and (7.2).

Consider, for example, the following LP problem:

$$\begin{aligned} \text{Maximize} \quad & Z = 2x_1 + 4x_2 \\ \text{subject to} \quad & x_1 + x_2 \leq 10, \\ & 2x_1 + 3x_2 \leq 25, \\ & -x_1 + 2x_2 \leq 12, \\ & x_1, x_2 \geq 0. \end{aligned}$$

[31] The original development of linear programming in the United States is credited to George B. Dantzig. Dantzig's *Linear Programming and Extensions* (Princeton, N.J.: Princeton University Press, 1963) can be perused with profit. Also see Robert Dorfman, Paul A. Samuelson, and Robert M. Solow, *Linear Programming and Economic Analysis* (New York: McGraw-Hill, Inc., 1958), chaps. 1–4, 6–7, and 13–14; and G. Hadley, *Linear Programming* (Reading, Mass.: Addison-Wesley Publishing Company, Inc., 1962).

Since the objective function and all constraints are linear, and since the variables are constrained to be nonnegative, this clearly fits the definition of an LP problem. If the three constraints were strict equalities, they would be graphed as the three solid lines in Figure 7.16. The figure has been restricted to the first quadrant, because of the additional LP constraint that the variables be nonnegative.

The fact that the constraints are inequalities rather than equalities means that in choosing $x_1$ and $x_2$ so as to maximize $Z$, we can make our selection from any point that either lies directly on one of the solid lines in Figure 7.16 or falls within the shaded area. The latter delineates those points satisfying *all* constraints. In the case of the first inequality, for example, any point lying on or to the left of the line $x_1 + x_2 = 10$ will satisfy the constraint; in the case of the third inequality, any point lying on or to the right of the line $-x_1 + 2x_2 = 12$ will satisfy the constraint.

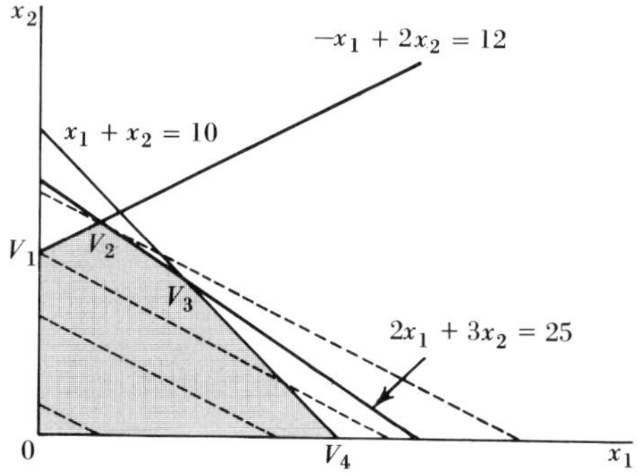


Fig. 7.16

The shaded area, including the lines and the axes, represents the set of feasible solutions—that is, points that satisfy all restrictions. The parallel checked lines represent the objective function $Z = 2x_1 + 4x_2$ drawn for various values of $Z$. The LP problem is to maximize $Z$, or to determine the highest checked line at least one point of which still lies in the shaded area. This point (or points) will be the optimum solution to the problem, for (1) it is feasible, and (2) no other feasible point lies on a checked line drawn for a larger $Z$. In this instance, the optimum solution is easily seen to be at the point of intersection of the lines $2x_1 + 3x_2 = 25$ and $-x_1 + 2x_2 = 12$, or $x_1 = 2$, $x_2 = 7$, and the maximum $Z$ is 32.

Solving LP problems by graphical inspection is not terribly helpful once we are forced to extend the analysis beyond two dimensions. We can, nonetheless, make several important observations with reference to the graph, and this particular problem, that can be extended to the $n$-dimensional LP problem.

It is apparent from Figure 7.16 that, as discussed in Exercises 13 and 14 of Chapter 2, the set of feasible solutions to this LP problem form a convex set. That is, given *any* two points $\mathbf{x}'$ and $\mathbf{x}''$ in the feasible set and given any $\theta$ such that $0 \leq \theta \leq 1$, the point $\mathbf{x} = \theta\mathbf{x}' + (1 - \theta)\mathbf{x}''$ will also be a feasible solution, or the straight line connecting *any* two points in the shaded area will fall wholly within the area. The fact that the feasible solutions form a convex set immediately follows from the previous observations that (1) a linear function $w(\mathbf{y})$ may be considered to be either convex or concave; (2) if $w(\mathbf{y})$ is a convex function, the set of points $Y$ satisfying the constraint $w(\mathbf{y}) \leq 0$, is a convex set; and (3) the intersection of convex sets is also a convex set. Thus, each of the constraints in an LP problem, including the nonnegativity restrictions, defines a convex set, and presuming the constraints are mutually consistent, the sets so defined intersect to form another convex set, the set of feasible solutions.

It is also apparent from the figure that the optimal solution to this simple LP problem will lie on one or more of the solid lines, rather than within the interior of the shaded region itself, and that this will be true *irrespective* of the specific objective function. Indeed, unless the objective function has the same slope as one of the constraining lines, it is apparent that the optimum solution will be at a point where two of the lines intersect—that is, at a *vertex*. These observations may be formalized as follows. We first define the point $\mathbf{y}$ to be an *extreme point* of the convex set $Y$ if and only if there are no other two points $\mathbf{y}'$ and $\mathbf{y}''$ belonging to $Y$ such that $\mathbf{y} = \theta\mathbf{y}' + (1 - \theta)\mathbf{y}''$, $0 < \theta < 1$. The strict inequality restrictions on $\theta$ mean that a point will be an extreme point of a convex set when it is a member of that set, but when there is no convex combination of any other two points in the set that will generate the point in question. In terms of the two-dimensional convex set, a point will be an extreme point if and only if no straight line between any *other* two points in the set passes through the point in question. The convex set of Figure 7.16 contains five extreme points: these are the vertices labeled $O$ (the origin) and $V_i$ $(i = i, \ldots, 4)$.

Now, one can take any point in the present convex set of feasible solutions and assign to it the role of the center of a circle of extremely small radius. That is, for any point $\mathbf{x} = (x_1, x_2)$ we can define the circle $x_1^2 + x_2^2 = \epsilon^2$, where $\epsilon > 0$. No matter how small an $\epsilon$ we take, there will be some points $\mathbf{x}$ that will generate circles enclosing points all of which are also members of the convex set of feasible solutions. Such a point is called an *interior point* of the convex set. If the circle so generated necessarily contains points that are *not* members of the convex set, no matter how small $\epsilon$ becomes, the point is called a *boundary point*. Thus, in pleasantly appealing fashion, the *outermost* line segments connecting the vertices of the convex set of Figure 7.16 are readily seen to be made up of all the boundary points of the convex set of feasible solutions. Moreover, it can be seen that each extreme point is necessarily a boundary point, but not vice versa. If we substitute "sphere" for "circle" and "plane" for "line," these ideas are immediately extended to three dimensions. Beyond three dimensions, we need only refer to hyperspheres and hyperplanes, defined accordingly.

Under these definitions, we shall call a set *closed* if it contains all of its boundary points. The set of feasible solutions in the illustrative problem is thus a *closed convex set*, since it includes *all* points on the surrounding line segments as well as the interior points. In general, when a feasible solution to an LP problem exists, and when the constraints effect finite bounds on the magnitudes of the variables, the set of feasible solutions will be a closed convex set. *Moreover*, and as is intuitively clear from the figure, it can be shown that when the objective function of *any* LP problem has a finite bound, the *optimal* solution to the problem will be an extreme point of the closed convex set of feasible solutions. There may be more than one optimal solution, in which case *any* boundary point that is a convex combination of the optimal extreme points will also be an optimal solution. Thus, if there is more than one optimal solution, there are infinitely many optima, but at least one extreme point will be optimal.

In the general procedure for solving LP problems we shall be taking advantage of these ideas. In particular, we shall develop a procedure whereby we initially select an extreme point of the convex set of feasible solutions and then proceed to evaluate the objective function at that point and through a succession of extreme points. We only need consider extreme points, since we know that one such must be an optimal solution. Moreover, in lieu of considering *all* extreme points, we shall simply inspect those which are immediately "*adjacent*" to the one under immediate consideration. By adjacent, we mean those extreme points connected to the one under consideration by a line segment of boundary points. In terms of Figure 7.16, the points $V_1$ and $V_3$ would be adjacent to $V_2$. If there are adjacent extreme points that lead to a higher objective function, we shall move to one of these; if no adjacent extreme point lies on a higher objective function, we shall be at a maximum. In the present illustration, we might start at the origin, say, and move from there to $V_4$ (in preference, say, to $V_1$), move from $V_4$ to $V_3$ (which is superior to returning to the origin), and move finally from $V_3$ to $V_2$ (which is superior to returning to $V_4$). At $V_2$, we note that neither of the two adjacent extreme points, $V_1$ and $V_3$, yields a higher value for the objective function, and the optimum has been found. We also note that, starting from the origin, had we initially moved to $V_1$ rather than $V_4$, the optimum would have been reached in the very next step. With these general notions in mind, let us now develop the *simplex procedure* for solving linear programming problems.

## b. The Algebraic Foundation of the Simplex Procedure

A problem of the form:

$$\text{Maximize} \quad Z = \sum_{j=1}^{n} c_j x_j,$$

subject to

$$\sum_{j=1}^{n} a_{ij} x_j \leq d_i \quad (i = 1, \ldots, m), \qquad x_j \geq 0 \quad (j = 1, \ldots, n)$$

is a *linear programming* problem. The $c_j$, $a_{ij}$, and $d_i$ are constants. This statement of the problem as one of maximization rather than minimization is solely for expositional convenience.

In this problem there are $m$ linear constraints and $n$ nonnegative variables. The addition of a nonnegative *slack variable* $x_{n+j}$ $(n + j = n + 1, \ldots, n + m)$ to the right-hand side of each of the inequalities converts these to equalities. For example, the inequality

$$a_{i1}x_1 + a_{i2}x_2 + \cdots + a_{in}x_n \leq d_i$$

can be converted to the equality

$$a_{i1}x_1 + a_{i2}x_2 + \cdots + a_{in}x_n + x_{n+i} = d_i.$$

The value of slack variable $x_{n+i} \geq 0$ $(i = 1, \ldots, m)$ will ultimately be determined simultaneously with values for the other variables $x_j$ $(j = 1, \ldots, n)$. With the prime indicating transpose, let $\mathbf{c}'$ be the $1 \times (m + n)$ row vector $\mathbf{c}' = (c_1, \ldots, c_n, 0, \ldots, 0)$, $\mathbf{x}'$ = the $1 \times (m + n)$ row vector $(x_1, \ldots, x_{n+m})$, $\mathbf{d}'$ = the $1 \times m$ row vector $(d_1, \ldots, d_m)$, and $\mathbf{A} = [a_{ij}]$ = the $m \times (m + n)$ matrix of coefficients, $a_{ij}$.

The general LP problem may now be written:

$$\begin{aligned} \text{Maximize} \quad & Z = \mathbf{c}'\mathbf{x} && (7.3a)\\ \text{subject to} \quad & \mathbf{Ax} = \mathbf{d}, && (7.3b)\\ & \mathbf{x} \geq \mathbf{0}, && (7.3c) \end{aligned}$$

where $\mathbf{A} = [\mathbf{a}_1, \ldots, \mathbf{a}_{m+n}]$ and $\mathbf{a}_j$ is an $m \times 1$ column vector whose $m$ elements are the $a_{ij}$ $(i = 1, \ldots, m)$.

Let $\mathbf{B}$ be a matrix $[\mathbf{b}_1, \ldots, \mathbf{b}_m]$ containing exactly $m$ linearly independent columns of $\mathbf{A}$. That is, each $\mathbf{b}_k$ is simply an $\mathbf{a}_j$ that has been momentarily relabeled to distinguish it from the others. Further, we are so distinguishing precisely $m$ of the $\mathbf{a}_j$'s, and we are calling attention to just one of perhaps many sets of $m$ vectors that can be written as

$$\sum_{k=1}^{m} \theta_k \mathbf{b}_k = \mathbf{0}, \text{ only if } \theta_k = 0 \quad (k = 1, \ldots, m).$$

The latter is the manner by which we *define* linear independent vectors. Because there are exactly $m$ rows of $\mathbf{A}$, the $\mathbf{a}_j$ are $m$-component vectors and there can be no more than $m$ linearly independent columns in $\mathbf{A}$. It is assumed the constraints are neither redundant nor incompatible, that there are indeed $m$ independent rows and columns in $\mathbf{A}$, and that *some* matrix $\mathbf{B}$ will exist. Moreover, since the $\mathbf{b}_k$ $(k = 1, \ldots, m)$ are $m$ linearly independent vectors from an $m$-dimensional vector space, any other vector in the space can be written as a linear combination of the $\mathbf{b}_k$—that is, the set $\mathbf{b}_1, \ldots, \mathbf{b}_m$ spans the vector space. By the definition of a basis of a vector space as any set of linearly independent vectors spanning the space, $\mathbf{b}_1, \ldots, \mathbf{b}_k$ is also a *basis* for an $m$-dimensional vector space. Therefore, any vector $\mathbf{a}_j$ contained in $\mathbf{A}$ but not included in $\mathbf{B}$ can be written as a linear combination of $\mathbf{b}_1, \ldots, \mathbf{b}_k$; and, in particular, we can write

$$\mathbf{a}_j = \lambda_{1j}\mathbf{b}_1 + \lambda_{2j}\mathbf{b}_2 + \cdots + \lambda_{mj}\mathbf{b}_m, \text{ or}$$

$$\mathbf{a}_j = \sum_{k=1}^{m} \lambda_{kj}\mathbf{b}_k = \mathbf{B}\boldsymbol{\lambda}_j, \qquad (7.4)$$

where $\boldsymbol{\lambda}_j$ is an $m \times 1$ column vector composed of scalar elements $\lambda_{kj}$ not all of which are zero. Premultiplying both sides of (7.4) by $\mathbf{B}^{-1}$ determines the vector $\boldsymbol{\lambda}_j = \mathbf{B}^{-1}\mathbf{a}_j$. Note that $\mathbf{B}^{-1}$ exists because the columns of $\mathbf{B}$ are linearly independent.

We give special attention to $\mathbf{B}$ because it is through this set of basis vectors that we shall arrive at an extreme point of the convex set of feasible solutions to the LP problem, and it is one of the extreme points that will be the optimal solution. In particular, consider the set of linear equations (7.3b). The set of points satisfying these equations and the nonnegativity constraint (7.3c) is a closed convex set. Further, with respect to (7.3b) or indeed any set of $m$ independent and mutually consistent simultaneous linear equations with $m + n$ variables, one may obtain a *unique* solution for $m$ of the variables (called the *basic* variables) by setting $n$ of the variables equal to zero (these are called the *nonbasic* variables). The solution so obtained is called a *basic* solution. Specifically, by equating to zero those $x_j$ associated with the $n$ vectors $\mathbf{a}_j$ not included in $\mathbf{B}$, *a* basic solution to (7.3b) will be given by $\mathbf{x}_B = \mathbf{B}^{-1}\mathbf{d}$. The elements of $\mathbf{x}_B$ are the $m$ basic variables $x_{B_k} = x_i$ associated with the $m$ vectors $\mathbf{a}_i$ $(i \neq j)$ included in the basis from $\mathbf{B}$. In essence, setting the nonbasic variables equal to zero enables us to write (7.3b) as

$$\sum_{k=1}^{m} x_{B_k}\mathbf{b}_k = \mathbf{d}.$$

This system of $m$ simultaneous equations in $m$ unknowns is readily solved. In the present situation, however, restriction (7.3c) demands that $\mathbf{x} \geq 0$. We shall also require that this restriction be satisfied by *any* basic solution that we consider here. The matrix $\mathbf{B}$ will therefore be *selected* to assure that $x_{B_k} \geq 0$ $(k = 1, \ldots, m)$. The solution thus obtained is called a *basic feasible solution* to the LP problem, because (1) it will be a basic solution and (2) it satisfies *all* constraints. Our concern with such solutions stems from the fact that, as will be shown, if the LP problem has a finite solution, the *optimal* solution will be a basic feasible solution. It can also be shown that every basic feasible solution to $\mathbf{Ax} = \mathbf{d}$ is an extreme point of the closed convex set of feasible solutions, and also that every extreme point of this convex set is a basic feasible solution to $\mathbf{Ax} = \mathbf{d}$. Our method of solving linear programming problems will rest on this principle, and we shall develop a procedure for testing consistently improving basic feasible solutions, until the optimal one has been found —that is, we shall move between adjacent extreme points.

For openers, suppose that $\mathbf{x}_B = \mathbf{B}^{-1}\mathbf{d}$ is indeed a basic feasible solution. Then, associated with any *nonbasic* variable $x_j$ is a vector $\mathbf{a}_j$ satisfying (7.4), $\mathbf{a}_j = \mathbf{B}\boldsymbol{\lambda}_j$. We want to determine whether by replacing some basic variable $x_{B_r}$ with $x_j$, and some basis vector $\mathbf{b}_r$ with $\mathbf{a}_j$, we shall obtain a new basic solution that (1) is feasible and (2) yields a higher value for the objective function than does the present solution. Consider then a particular $\lambda_{kj} \neq 0$, say $\lambda_{rj}$. Dividing both sides of (7.4) by $\lambda_{rj}$ and rearranging terms, we can solve for $\mathbf{b}_r$ in terms of $\mathbf{a}_j$ and the remaining $\mathbf{b}_k$ to obtain

$$\mathbf{b}_r = \frac{1}{\lambda_{rj}}\mathbf{a}_j - \sum_{\substack{k=1 \\ k\neq r}}^{m} \frac{\lambda_{kj}}{\lambda_{rj}}\mathbf{b}_k. \tag{7.5}$$

This operation may be performed for any $\mathbf{a}_j$ not in the basis, so long as $\lambda_{rj} \neq 0$. To get a basic solution containing $x_j$, we need only rewrite the original basic solution,

$$\sum_{k=1}^{m} x_{B_k}\mathbf{b}_k = \mathbf{d},$$

as

$$\sum_{\substack{k=1 \\ k\neq r}}^{m} x_{B_k}\mathbf{b}_k + x_{B_r}\mathbf{b}_r = \mathbf{d},$$

and then substitute (7.5) for $\mathbf{b}_r$. After rearranging terms, we obtain

$$\sum_{\substack{k=1 \\ k\neq r}}^{m} \left(x_{B_k} - x_{B_r}\frac{\lambda_{kj}}{\lambda_{rj}}\right)\mathbf{b}_k + \frac{x_{B_r}}{\lambda_{rj}}\mathbf{a}_j = \mathbf{d}. \tag{7.6}$$

This yields a *new* basic solution to (7.3b), but now the $m$ basis vectors are $\mathbf{b}_k$ ($k = 1, \ldots, m$; $k \neq r$) and $\mathbf{a}_j$.

The nonnegativity requirement on $\mathbf{x}$ demands, however, that (7.6) yield a basic *feasible* solution. That is, we want to move from one extreme point of the convex set of feasible solutions to an adjacent extreme point of that set. To assure that we accomplish this, let us rewrite (7.6) as

$$\sum_{k \neq r} \bar{x}_{B_k}\mathbf{b}_k + \bar{x}_{B_j}\mathbf{a}_j = \mathbf{d}.$$

Then, the requirement that $\bar{x}_{B_k}$ ($k \neq r$) and $\bar{x}_{B_j}$ be nonnegative demands that we respect

$$\bar{x}_{B_k} = x_{B_k} - x_{B_r}\left(\frac{\lambda_{kj}}{\lambda_{rj}}\right) \geq 0 \quad (k \neq r) \quad \text{and} \quad \bar{x}_{B_j} = \frac{x_{B_r}}{\lambda_{rj}} \geq 0. \tag{7.6a}$$

The first expression may be rewritten as

$$\left(\frac{x_{B_k}}{\lambda_{kj}} - \frac{x_{B_r}}{\lambda_{rj}}\right) \geq 0 \qquad (k \neq r).$$

Thus, to determine the column $r$ of $\mathbf{B}$ that will *have to* be replaced if the new basis is to contain $\mathbf{a}_j$ *and* yield a basic *feasible* solution, we *first* require $\lambda_{rj} > 0$. Since the initial solution was feasible, $x_{B_r} \geq 0$ and hence $x_{B_r}/\lambda_{rj} = \theta \geq 0$. The *second* requirement is that

$$\frac{x_{B_r}}{\lambda_{rj}} = \min_k \left\{\frac{x_{B_k}}{\lambda_{kj}}\right\} = \theta.$$

Only if $\theta$ is the *smallest* nonnegative ratio will *all* other ratios $x_{B_k}/\lambda_{kj}$ ($k \neq r$) be nonnegative and satisfy the restriction $x_{B_k} - x_{B_r}(\lambda_{kj}/\lambda_{rj}) \geq 0$. The new basic feasible solution will thus be given by the $\bar{x}_{B_k}$ and $\bar{x}_{B_j} = \theta$. If any element of $\mathbf{x}_B$ should be zero, the basic solution will be called *degenerate*.[32]

It has already been noted, and will soon be shown, that the optimal solution to the LP problem is a basic feasible solution. We now know how to get from one basic feasible solution to another. The LP procedure used here, the *simplex* technique, will be to move from one basic feasible solution to another—that is, from one extreme point of the convex set of feasible solutions to an adjacent extreme point of the set—so long as the level of the objective function is raised by the new solution. When no new basic feasible solution will raise the objective function further, the optimum will have been reached.

To determine whether the new basic feasible solution with $x_j$ is an improvement over the old solution, we must consider the effects on the objective function $Z = \mathbf{c}'\mathbf{x}$. Let $\mathbf{c}'_B$ be composed of the elements of $\mathbf{c}'$ associated with the basic variables $\mathbf{x}_B$.

[32] Degeneracy in a basic feasible solution can lead to "cycling," in the sense that we may be kept going through the same series of solutions. The cycle perpetuates itself and prevents one from reaching an optimal solution. It is commonly held that this difficulty has never occurred in a practical problem. For anyone lucky enough to encounter it, see Hadley, *Linear Programming*, pp. 174–195.

All nonbasic elements of $\mathbf{x}$ will be equal to zero. Thus, for the initial basic feasible solution,

$$Z_1 = \mathbf{c}'_B\mathbf{x}_B = \sum_{k=1}^{m} c_{B_k}x_{B_k}.$$

After introducing $\mathbf{a}_j$ into the basis and eliminating $\mathbf{b}_r$, the objective function becomes

$$Z_2 = \sum_{\substack{k=1\\k\neq r}}^{m} c_{B_k}\left(x_{B_k} - x_{B_r}\frac{\lambda_{kj}}{\lambda_{rj}}\right) + c_j\left(\frac{x_{B_r}}{\lambda_{rj}}\right).$$

But, since $x_{B_r} - x_{B_r}(\lambda_{rj}/\lambda_{rj}) = 0$, the summation term is unaltered when $k = r$, and thus we may omit the $k \neq r$ expression under the summation sign. Thus, the *change* in the objective function in mc .ing from one basic feasible solution to the next is given by

$$Z_2 - Z_1 = \left[c_j\left(\frac{x_{B_r}}{\lambda_{rj}}\right) + \sum_{k=1}^{m} c_{B_k}x_{B_k} - \sum_{k=1}^{m} c_{B_k}x_{B_r}\frac{\lambda_{kj}}{\lambda_{rj}}\right] - \sum_{k=1}^{m} c_{B_k}x_{B_k}$$

$$= c_j\left(\frac{x_{B_r}}{\lambda_{rj}}\right) - \sum_{k=1}^{m} c_{B_k}x_{B_r}\frac{\lambda_{kj}}{\lambda_{rj}}$$

or

$$Z_2 - Z_1 = \frac{x_{B_r}}{\lambda_{rj}}\left[c_j - \sum_{k=1}^{m} c_{B_k}\lambda_{kj}\right] = \theta s_j, \tag{7.7}$$

with $\theta = x_{B_r}/\lambda_{rj}$ as before, and

$$\left[c_j - \sum_{k=1}^{m} c_{B_k}\lambda_{kj}\right] = s_j.$$

In the nondegenerate case with $\theta > 0$, the value of the objective function will be increased and $Z_2 - Z_1 > 0$, so long as $s_j > 0$. The latter is called the *simplex criterion.* $Z_2 - Z_1$ is the increment in the objective function achieved when $x_j$ is set equal to $\theta$ in the new basic solution; $(Z_2 - Z_1)/\theta = s_j$ is the *per unit* increment in the objective function achieved by this selection. The simplex procedure calls for the introduction into solution of that variable having the largest simplex criterion. This variable gives the largest *per unit* increase in $Z$, not necessarily the largest *total* increase. The procedure *is*, however, computationally convenient and orderly. Note, however, that the value of $s_j$ will depend upon the *other* variables in the basis into which $\mathbf{a}_j$ is being introduced. That is, the effects of moving to an extreme point will depend upon the extreme point that one is moving from. If, therefore, we decide to introduce $\mathbf{a}_u$ rather than $\mathbf{a}_v$ into the basis because $s_u$ is greater than all other $s_j$, when we next evaluate the possibility of introducing $\mathbf{a}_v$ into the new basis, we shall have to recompute *all* $s_j$. If an $s_j = 0$, this means that the introduction of $\mathbf{a}_j$ into the basis in place of $\mathbf{b}_r$, and the substitution of $x_j$ for $x_r$ will leave $Z$ unchanged.

The optimal *basic* solution may be written

$$Z^0 = \sum_{k=1}^{m} c_{B_k} x_{B_k}.$$

Since it is optimal,

$$s_j = c_j - \sum_{k=1}^{m} c_{B_k} \lambda_{kj} \leq 0$$

for all $\mathbf{a}_j$ not in the basis. If $s_j \leq 0$, there is no $\mathbf{a}_j$ outside of the basis that can raise the value of $Z$; if $s_j = 0$, there is an alternative optimal basic solution.

Suppose, however, that we consider *any nonbasic feasible* solution yielding

$$Z^* = \sum_{j=1}^{n+m} c_j x_j.$$

In this solution, at least $m + 1$ of the $x_j \neq 0$. This is so, since if exactly $m$ of the $x_j$ were positive, the solution would be basic; and if fewer than $m$ were positive, the solution would be basic but degenerate. As a solution, however, the $x_j$ must satisfy (7.3b) and (7.3c). Thus,

$$\sum_{j=1}^{n+m} x_j \mathbf{a}_j = \mathbf{d} \quad \text{and} \quad x_j \geq 0.$$

But, since each vector $\mathbf{a}_j$ can be written as a linear combination of the basis vectors, taking the $\mathbf{b}_k$ from the optimal basis we may write

$$\mathbf{a}_j = \sum_{k=1}^{m} \lambda_{kj} \mathbf{b}_k.$$

By substituting the latter expression for $\mathbf{a}_j$ into the previous set of equations, (7.3b), we obtain

$$\sum_{j=1}^{n+m} \sum_{k=1}^{m} x_j \lambda_{kj} \mathbf{b}_k = \mathbf{d}.$$

Since the order of summation is reversible, the latter may also be written

$$\sum_{k=1}^{m} \left( \sum_{j=1}^{n+m} x_j \lambda_{kj} \right) \mathbf{b}_k = \mathbf{d}.$$

We know, however, that in the optimal basic solution

$$\sum_{k=1}^{m} x_{B_k} \mathbf{b}_k = \mathbf{d}.$$

Comparing this expression with

$$\sum_{k=1}^{m} \left( \sum_{j=1}^{n+m} x_j \lambda_{kj} \right) \mathbf{b}_k = \mathbf{d},$$

we see that

$$x_{B_k} = \sum_{j=1}^{n+m} x_j \lambda_{kj}.$$

Now, since

$$s_j = c_j - \sum_{k=1}^{m} c_{B_k} \lambda_{kj} \leq 0$$

for all $\mathbf{a}_j$ outside the optimal basis,

$$\sum_{k=1}^{m} c_{B_k} \lambda_{kj} \geq c_j.$$

Thus,

$$Z^* = \sum_{j=1}^{n+m} c_j x_j \leq \sum_{j=1}^{n+m} \left( \sum_{k=1}^{m} c_{Bk} \lambda_{kj} \right) x_j = \sum_{k=1}^{m} \left( \sum_{j=1}^{n+m} \lambda_{kj} x_j \right) c_{B_k}$$

$$= \sum_{k=1}^{m} c_{B_k} x_{B_k} = Z^0,$$

or

$$Z^* \leq Z^0.$$

This shows that the optimal basic feasible solution to the LP problem will be an optimal solution to the problem. There is *no* nonbasic feasible solution that can yield a $Z^*$ greater than $Z^0$.

The latter result is vital, because it implies the following most important theorem: if we have an LP problem with $m + n$ slack plus nonslack variables and $m$ constraints, the optimal solution will contain *at most* $m$ variables at nonzero levels, and fewer than $m$ positive variables if the solution is degenerate. Moreover, there are a finite number of bases, namely $(m + n)!/m!n!$ or $m + n$ things (variables) taken $m$ (equations) at a time. There are thus a finite number of steps to go through before the optimal solution is reached,[33] or a maximum number of extreme points that we might possibly have to inspect.

Note, however, that if at any stage in the process *all* $\lambda_{kj} \leq 0$, the solution is *unbounded*. The solution

$$\sum_{k=1}^{m} x_{B_k} \mathbf{b}_k = \mathbf{d}$$

may be written

$$\sum_{k=1}^{m} x_{B_k} \mathbf{b}_k - \theta \mathbf{a}_j + \theta \mathbf{a}_j = \mathbf{d}.$$

But, since

$$\mathbf{a}_j = \sum_{k=1}^{m} \lambda_{kj} \mathbf{b}_k,$$

[33] See Hadley, *Linear Programming*, pp. 95–104. There may be alternative optima, signaled by zero simplex values in an optimal basic solution.

we may also write

$$-\theta \mathbf{a}_j = -\theta \sum_{k=1}^{m} \lambda_{kj} \mathbf{b}_k.$$

Hence,

$$\sum_{k=1}^{m} x_{B_k} \mathbf{b}_k = \sum_{k=1}^{m} (x_{B_k} - \theta\lambda_{kj}) \mathbf{b}_k + \theta \mathbf{a}_j = \mathbf{d}.$$

With $\lambda_{kj} \leq 0$ $(k = 1, \ldots, m)$, we may *choose* $\theta$ to be any positive number, and all the initial basic variables will remain nonnegative. Since $x_j$ can be made infinitely large, the solution is *unbounded.*

# Appendix to Chapter 7

## 7A.1 AN ILLUSTRATION OF THE SIMPLEX PROCEDURE

Let us illustrate the computations for the simplex procedure by applying it to duopolist 2's problem of (7.1) and (7.2). The first constraint is

$$.60p_1 + .50p_2 + .65p_3 + .30p_4 - V \geq 0.$$

The inequality is first converted to an equality by *subtracting* a nonnegative slack variable $S_1$ from the left-hand side. This gives the equation

$$.60p_1 + .50p_2 + .65p_3 + .30p_4 - V - S_1 = 0.$$

Similarly, nonnegative slack variables $S_2$ and $S_3$ are subtracted in the second and third constraints to produce equalities from these inequalities. The fourth constraint is already an equality. It will, however, be convenient to *momentarily* alter it by *adding* a nonnegative variable $A_4$ to the left side of the fourth constraint, while maintaining the equality. Thereupon, (7.2) becomes

$$\begin{aligned}
.60p_1 + .50p_2 + .65p_3 + .30p_4 - V - S_1 &= 0,\\
.40p_1 + .55p_2 + .50p_3 + .40p_4 - V - S_2 &= 0,\\
.65p_1 + .60p_2 + .35p_3 + .50p_4 - V - S_3 &= 0,\\
p_1 + p_2 + p_3 + p_4 \qquad + A_4 &= 1.
\end{aligned} \tag{7.8}$$

The advantage of adding $A_4$ to the fourth equation is that by setting $p_1 = p_2 = p_3 = p_4 = V = 0$, we immediately obtain a basic feasible solution, $S_1 = S_2 = S_3 = 0$, and $A_4 = 1$. If, however, the *initial* condition that $\sum_{i=1}^{4} p_i = 1$ is to be satisfied, $A_4$ must equal zero in the optimal solution. To assure this, we add $A_4$ to the objective function assigning a large *negative* value of $-M$ as its coefficient. Having $A_4$ *detract* from the value of the objective function assures that it will eventually be forced out of the solution. A variable such as $A_4$, which is designed *solely* to lead to a ready basic feasible solution and will under no circumstances itself appear in the optimal solution, is called an *artificial variable*. The *slack variables*, $S_i$, *may* appear in the optimal solution, and their values in the objective function are zero. Equations (7.8), together with the condition $p_i \geq 0$ $(i = 1, \ldots, 4)$, $S_j \geq 0$ $(j = 1, 2, 3)$, $V \geq 0$, and $A_4 \geq 0$ represent the LP constraints. The objective function may be written:

$$\text{Maximize} \quad Z = 0p_1 + 0p_2 + 0p_3 + 0p_4 + 1V + 0S_1 + 0S_2 + 0S_3 - MA_4.$$

This problem is rewritten in a simplified form in the first *simplex tableau*, labeled I, of Table 7.5. For notational simplicity, the variables are not listed alongside their coefficients. For convenience, the first three equations have been multiplied by $-1$. This makes the coefficients of $S_1$, $S_2$, and $S_3$ 1 rather than $-1$. It does not alter the

TABLE 7.5

| | | | $p_1$ (1) | $p_2$ (2) | $p_3$ (3) | $p_4$ (4) | $V$ (5) | $S_1$ (6) | $S_2$ (7) | $S_3$ (8) | $A_4$ (9) | **d** (10) |
|---|---|---|---|---|---|---|---|---|---|---|---|---|
| | **Maximize** | | 0 | 0 | 0 | 0 | 1 | 0 | 0 | 0 | $-M$ | |
| | $S_1$: | 0 | −.60 | −.50 | −.65 | −.30 | 1 | 1 | 0 | 0 | 0 | 0 |
| | $S_2$: | 0 | −.40 | −.55 | −.50 | −.40 | 1 | 0 | 1 | 0 | 0 | 0 |
| I | $S_3$: | 0 | −.65 | −.60 | −.35 | −.50 | 1 | 0 | 0 | 1 | 0 | 0 |
| | $A_4$: | $-M$ | 1 | 1 | 1 | 1 | 0 | 0 | 0 | 0 | 1 | 1 → |
| | | $s_j$ | $M$ ↑ | $M$ | $M$ | $M$ | $1-M$ | 0 | 0 | 0 | 0 | $Z_1 = -M$ |
| | $S_1$: | 0 | 0 | .10 | −.05 | .30 | 1 | 1 | 0 | 0 | .60 | .60 |
| | $S_2$: | 0 | 0 | −.15 | −.10 | 0 | 1 | 0 | 1 | 0 | .40 | .40 → |
| II | $S_3$: | 0 | 0 | .05 | .30 | .15 | 1 | 0 | 0 | 1 | .65 | .65 |
| | $p_1$: | 0 | 1 | 1 | 1 | 1 | 0 | 0 | 0 | 0 | 1 | 1 |
| | | $s_j$ | 0 | 0 | 0 | 0 | 1 ↑ | 0 | 0 | 0 | $-M$ | $Z_2 = 0$ |
| | $S_1$: | 0 | 0 | .25 | .05 | .30 | 0 | 1 | −1 | 0 | .20 | .20 → |
| | $V$: | 1 | 0 | −.15 | −.10 | 0 | 1 | 0 | 1 | 0 | .40 | .40 |
| III | $S_3$: | 0 | 0 | .20 | .40 | .15 | 0 | 0 | −1 | 1 | .25 | .25 |
| | $p_1$: | 0 | 1 | 1 | 1 | 1 | 0 | 0 | 0 | 0 | 1 | 1 |
| | | $s_j$ | 0 | .15 ↑ | .10 | 0 | 0 | 0 | −1 | 0 | $-M - .40$ | $Z_3 = .40$ |
| | $p_2$: | 0 | 0 | 1 | .20 | 1.20 | 0 | 4 | −4 | 0 | .8 | .8 |
| | $V$: | 1 | 0 | 0 | −.07 | .18 | 1 | .60 | .4 | 0 | .52 | .52 |
| IV | $S_3$: | 0 | 0 | 0 | .36 | .09 | 0 | −.80 | −.2 | 1 | .09 | .09 → |
| | $p_1$: | 0 | 1 | 0 | .80 | −.20 | 0 | −4 | 4 | 0 | .2 | .2 |
| | | $s_j$ | 0 | 0 | .07 ↑ | −.18 | 0 | −.60 | −.4 | 0 | $-M - .52$ | $Z_4 = .52$ |
| | $p_2$: | 0 | 0 | 1 | 0 | 1.25 | 0 | 4.4444 | −3.8889 | −.5555 | .75 | .75 |
| | $V$: | 1 | 0 | 0 | 0 | .1625 | 1 | .4445 | .3611 | .1944 | .5375 | .5375 |
| V | $p_3$: | 0 | 0 | 0 | 1 | −.25 | 0 | −2.2222 | −.5555 | 2.7777 | .25 | .25 |
| | $p_1$: | 0 | 1 | 0 | 0 | 0 | 0 | 2.2222 | 4.4444 | −2.2222 | 0 | 0 |
| | | $s_j$ | 0 | 0 | 0 | −.1625 | 0 | −.4445 | −.3611 | −.1944 | $-M - .5375$ | $Z_5 = .5375$ |

problem and is unnecessary, but it will simplify the exposition. The first row of I reproduces the first constraint equation:

$$-.60p_1 - .50p_2 - .65p_3 - .30p_4 + V + S_1 + 0S_2 + 0S_3 + 0A_4 = 0.$$

$S_2$, $S_3$, and $A_4$ are added with 0 coefficients to maintain the original equality, while assuring that all equations will contain all variables—even if certain variables do not directly enter into the equation. The "$c_i$" are given in the row immediately above tableau I. Hence, $\mathbf{c}' = (0, 0, 0, 0, 1, 0, 0, 0, -M)$. The columns are labeled (1) through (10). Thus the fourth column of each tableau contains coefficients associated with $p_4$. In the first tableau these are the coefficients of the vector $\mathbf{a}_4$. In the previous notation, the tableau reproduces **A** and **d**, where

$$\mathbf{A} = [a_{ij}] = \begin{bmatrix} -.60 & -.50 & -.65 & -.30 & 1 & 1 & 0 & 0 & 0 \\ -.40 & -.55 & -.50 & -.40 & 1 & 0 & 1 & 0 & 0 \\ -.65 & -.60 & -.35 & -.50 & 1 & 0 & 0 & 1 & 0 \\ 1 & 1 & 1 & 1 & 0 & 0 & 0 & 0 & 1 \end{bmatrix}; \qquad \mathbf{d} = \begin{bmatrix} 0 \\ 0 \\ 0 \\ 1 \end{bmatrix}.$$

A basic feasible solution that includes $S_1$, $S_2$, $S_3$, and $A_4$ is readily found. Select $\mathbf{B} = [\mathbf{a}_6, \mathbf{a}_7, \mathbf{a}_8, \mathbf{a}_9] = [\mathbf{b}_1, \mathbf{b}_2, \mathbf{b}_3, \mathbf{b}_4]$, or

$$\mathbf{B} = \begin{bmatrix} 1 & 0 & 0 & 0 \\ 0 & 1 & 0 & 0 \\ 0 & 0 & 1 & 0 \\ 0 & 0 & 0 & 1 \end{bmatrix} = \mathbf{I}.$$

Multiplying the first three equations by $-1$ thus has permitted us to choose for the matrix of basis vectors the unit matrix. Clearly, since the solution indicated in the "constant" column (10) is $S_1 = S_2 = S_3 = 0$ and $A_4 = 1$, $Z = -M$.

The simplex criteria must now be calculated in order to select a new basic feasible solution for which $Z > -M$. Recall that

$$s_j = c_j - \sum_{k=1}^{m} c_{B_k}\lambda_{kj}.$$

In particular, suppose $p_1$ is introduced into solution and therefore $\mathbf{a}_1$ into the basis. To compute $s_1$ in *this* problem requires only $\lambda_{41}$. This is so because the coefficient of $p_1$ in the objective function is $c_1 = 0$; and $c_{B_1} = c_{B_2} = c_{B_3} = 0$ are the coefficients of $S_1$, $S_2$, $S_3$ in the objective function, while $c_{B_4} = -M$ is the coefficient of $A_4$ in the objective function.

Now, to determine the vector $\boldsymbol{\lambda}_j$, recall that $\mathbf{a}_j = \sum_{k=1}^{m} \lambda_{kj}\mathbf{b}_k$. In the present problem, to determine $\boldsymbol{\lambda}_1$,

$$\begin{pmatrix} -.60 \\ -.40 \\ -.65 \\ 1 \end{pmatrix} = \begin{pmatrix} 1 \\ 0 \\ 0 \\ 0 \end{pmatrix}\lambda_{11} + \begin{pmatrix} 0 \\ 1 \\ 0 \\ 0 \end{pmatrix}\lambda_{21} + \begin{pmatrix} 0 \\ 0 \\ 1 \\ 0 \end{pmatrix}\lambda_{31} + \begin{pmatrix} 0 \\ 0 \\ 0 \\ 1 \end{pmatrix}\lambda_{41} \tag{7.9}$$

or $\boldsymbol{\lambda}_1' = (-.60, -.40, -.65, 1)$. Thus, $\lambda_{41} = 1$ and $s_1 = -1(-M) = M$. Writing the expression for $s_1$ explicitly, $s_1 = 0 - 0(-.60) - 0(-.40) - 0(-.65) -$

$(-M)(1) = M$. The simplex criteria for all the variables, calculated in precisely this manner, are given in the row labeled $s_j$ of tableau I.

The simplex procedure, or *algorithm*, moves one to a new basic solution by introducing the variable with the largest positive simplex criterion. With $M$ arbitrarily large there appear to be several equally attractive candidates, as $s_j = M$ for $j = 1, \ldots, 4$. From these $s_j$ let us arbitrarily elect to introduce $\mathbf{a}_1$ into the basis. To determine the variable to omit, we first require that $\lambda_{rj} > 0$. With $j = 1$ there is only one $\lambda_{r1} > 0$, and that is $\lambda_{41} = 1$. Therefore the artificial variable $A_4$ will be eliminated and a new basis associated with variables $p_1$, $S_1$, $S_2$, and $S_3$ will be obtained.

In particular, recall that $\bar{x}_{B_k} = x_{B_k} - x_{B_r}(\lambda_{kj}/\lambda_{rj})$ and $\bar{x}_{B_j} = x_{B_r}/\lambda_{rj}$. Here, since $x_{B_r} = x_{B_4} = 1$, $\bar{x}_{B_j} = 1/1 = 1$. Similarly, $\bar{x}_{B_1} = 0 - 1(-.60/1) = .60$. In general we could write $\bar{x}_{B_k} = (1/\lambda_{rj})(x_{B_k}\lambda_{rj} - x_{B_r}\lambda_{kj})$. Letting $\bar{\mathbf{x}}$ be the $m \times 1$ column vector composed of elements $\bar{x}_{B_k}$, in the present problem we would have

$$\bar{\mathbf{x}} = \frac{1}{1}\left[\begin{pmatrix} 0(1) \\ 0(1) \\ 0(1) \\ 1(1) \end{pmatrix} - \begin{pmatrix} 1(-.60) \\ 1(-.40) \\ 1(-.65) \\ 1(1) \end{pmatrix}\right] = \begin{pmatrix} .60 \\ .40 \\ .65 \\ 0 \end{pmatrix}.$$

Thus, the first three elements of $\bar{\mathbf{x}}$ give the new levels of the variables that remain basic. The 0 in the $r$th (=4th) element indicates that the fourth variable is the $x_{B_r}$ eliminated. Together with $\bar{x}_{B_j} = 1$, the first three elements of $\bar{\mathbf{x}}$ now appear in tableau II as the column vector (10).

At this stage, then, the basic vectors are those of $\mathbf{B}_1 = [\mathbf{a}_1, \mathbf{a}_6, \mathbf{a}_7, \mathbf{a}_8]$. Thus the basic solution is given by the vector $\bar{\mathbf{x}}_{B_1}$ that satisfies $\mathbf{B}_1\mathbf{x}_{B_1} = \mathbf{d}$; or $\bar{\mathbf{x}}_{B_1} = \mathbf{B}_1^{-1}\mathbf{d} = \hat{\mathbf{d}}$. The original equations (7.8) may be written as $\mathbf{Ax} = \mathbf{d}$. Premultiplying both sides by $\mathbf{B}_1^{-1}$, $\mathbf{B}_1^{-1}\mathbf{Ax} = \hat{\mathbf{A}}\mathbf{x} = \mathbf{B}_1^{-1}\mathbf{d} = \hat{\mathbf{d}}$. But, since $\mathbf{B} = \mathbf{I}$,

$$\mathbf{B}_1 = \begin{bmatrix} -.60 & 0 & 0 & 0 \\ -.40 & 1 & 0 & 0 \\ -.65 & 0 & 1 & 0 \\ 1 & 0 & 0 & 1 \end{bmatrix} \quad \text{and} \quad \mathbf{B}_1^{-1} = \begin{bmatrix} 0 & 0 & 0 & 1 \\ 1 & 0 & 0 & .60 \\ 0 & 1 & 0 & .40 \\ 0 & 0 & 1 & .45 \end{bmatrix};$$

or in general

$$\mathbf{B}_1^{-1} = \begin{bmatrix} 0 & 0 & 0 & 1/a_{41} \\ 1 & 0 & 0 & -a_{11}/a_{41} \\ 0 & 1 & 0 & -a_{21}/a_{41} \\ 0 & 0 & 1 & -a_{31}/a_{41} \end{bmatrix} \quad \text{with} \quad \mathbf{B}_1 = \begin{bmatrix} a_{11} & 0 & 0 & 0 \\ a_{21} & 1 & 0 & 0 \\ a_{31} & 0 & 1 & 0 \\ a_{41} & 0 & 0 & 1 \end{bmatrix}.$$

Hence with $\hat{\mathbf{A}} = [\hat{\mathbf{a}}_j]$, $\hat{\mathbf{a}}_j = \mathbf{B}_1^{-1}\mathbf{a}_j$. Specifically,

$$\hat{\mathbf{a}}_j = \begin{bmatrix} 0 & 0 & 0 & 1/a_{41} \\ 1 & 0 & 0 & -a_{11}/a_{41} \\ 0 & 1 & 0 & -a_{21}/a_{41} \\ 0 & 0 & 1 & -a_{31}/a_{41} \end{bmatrix} \begin{pmatrix} a_{1j} \\ a_{2j} \\ a_{3j} \\ a_{4j} \end{pmatrix} = \begin{pmatrix} a_{4j}/a_{41} \\ a_{1j} - a_{4j}(a_{11}/a_{41}) \\ a_{2j} - a_{4j}(a_{21}/a_{41}) \\ a_{3j} - a_{4j}(a_{31}/a_{41}) \end{pmatrix}$$

$$\hat{\mathbf{a}}_j = \begin{pmatrix} 0 \\ a_{1j} \\ a_{2j} \\ a_{3j} \end{pmatrix} - \frac{a_{4j}}{a_{41}} \begin{pmatrix} -1 \\ a_{11} \\ a_{21} \\ a_{31} \end{pmatrix}. \tag{7.10}$$

By applying (7.10) to the elements of tableau I we move directly to tableau II. It is extremely important to recognize, understand, and retain the *fundamental rule* suggested by (7.10): namely, to calculate the element in the position of the vector being introduced, here $\mathbf{a}_{j(=1)}$, divide the element in $\mathbf{a}_j$ in the position corresponding to the basis vector $\mathbf{b}_r$ being eliminated, here $\mathbf{b}_4$, by the $r$th (= 4th) element in $\mathbf{a}_{j(=1)}$. In the present problem we obtain $a_{4j}/a_{41}$, since we are concerned with computing vector $\mathbf{a}_j$, and we are introducing vector $\mathbf{a}_1$ and eliminating basis vector $\mathbf{b}_4$. The remaining components of $\hat{\mathbf{a}}_j$ are computed by subtracting the product of $a_{4j}/a_{11}$ with the corresponding elements in the vector $\mathbf{a}_1$ from the elements in $\mathbf{a}_j$. This is, as a matter of fact, precisely the same way that the constant column $\hat{\mathbf{d}}$ was computed. Stating this procedure in terms of the tableau, in I we want to introduce $\mathbf{a}_1$ and eliminate $\mathbf{b}_4$. Therefore, divide every element in the fourth row by 1, the element $a_{41}$. Rewrite this row as the fourth row of II, since the fourth vector has been replaced. To compute the *rest* of a column, take the *old* column for the vector and subtract from it the product of the element that has already been obtained and the *old* vector of the variable being introduced. For example, we are introducing $\mathbf{a}_1$ and eliminating $\mathbf{b}_4$, so that we "know" the fourth row of II. To compute the first three elements of $\mathbf{a}_2$, we make use of our knowledge of the fourth element, namely $\hat{a}_{42} = 1$. We compute $\hat{\mathbf{a}}_{2.}$, the vector of the first three elements of $\mathbf{a}_2$:

$$\hat{\mathbf{a}}_{2.} = \begin{pmatrix} -.50 \\ -.55 \\ -.60 \end{pmatrix} - 1\begin{pmatrix} -.60 \\ -.40 \\ -.65 \end{pmatrix} = \begin{pmatrix} .10 \\ -.15 \\ .05 \end{pmatrix}.$$

The second column of II is now complete, and the remaining columns are completed in similar fashion.

With the basis vectors given as the unit vectors $\mathbf{e}_i' = (0, \ldots, \overset{i}{1}, \ldots, 0)$, the elements of a column are the associated $\lambda_{kj}$. Thus, the simplex criterion *at any stage* is given by subtracting the sum of the products of the column elements and the contributions to the objective function of the corresponding basic variables from the contribution to the objective function of the variable whose simplex is being computed. The contributions of the basic variables are noted on the left side of each tableau. To determine $s_3$ at this second stage, we would compute $s_3 = 0 - 0(-.05) - 0(-.10) - 0(.30) - 0(1) = 0$.

The highest positive simplex in II is $s_5 = 1$. We shall therefore introduce $V$ into the solution. Thus we must compute

$$\frac{\bar{x}_{B_r}}{\lambda_{r5}} = \min_k \left\{\frac{\bar{x}_{B_k}}{\lambda_{k5}}\right\} = \theta, \ \lambda_{r5} > 0.$$

Since the $\bar{x}_{B_k}$'s are the elements in column (10) and the $\lambda_{k5}$'s are the elements in column (5), we want to omit the variable whose solution is given in the row with the smallest *positive* ratio of column-(10) elements to column-(5) elements. The three positive ratios are .60/1, .40/1, and .65/1, the smallest of which is .40. We therefore set $\theta = .40$. Since the present solution gives a $Z$ value of $Z_2 = 0$, and with the anticipated per unit increment in $Z$ given by $s_5 = 1$, the anticipated new value of $Z$ is $Z_3 = Z_2 + \theta s_5 = 0 + .40(1) = .40$. Tableau III reveals this to be the case.

Tableau III is computed from II by repeated application of the fundamental rule. Since $S_2$ is being eliminated and $V$ introduced, every element in the second row of II is divided by the element in the fifth column, second row, or 1. The resultant row is rewritten as the second row of III. To obtain the new solutions, or column (10), apply the rule to get

$$\hat{\mathbf{d}}_{.} = \begin{pmatrix} .60 \\ .65 \\ 1 \end{pmatrix} - .40 \begin{pmatrix} 1 \\ 1 \\ 0 \end{pmatrix} = \begin{pmatrix} .20 \\ .25 \\ 1 \end{pmatrix} \cdot$$

These elements fill out the first, third, and fourth positions in the column. The remaining columns are filled in the same manner. With all variables but $p_1$, $V$, $S_1$, and $S_3 = 0$, the solution is $p_1 = 1$, $V = .40$, $S_1 = .20$, and $S_3 = .25$. As anticipated $Z_3 = V = .40$. Recalling the original game theory problem, it is interesting to note that this solution, whereby with $p_1 = 1$ the pure strategy of $S_{21}$ is always chosen, has an expected value of $V = .40$. In terms of Table 7.2, if duopolist 2 always chooses $S_{21}$, his opponent will choose $S_{12}$ and hold him to 40 percent of the market. Indeed, if all $s_j$ were negative and we were at an optimum solution, this would be a saddle-point, pure-strategy situation. It is not optimal, however, since $s_2 = .15$. Introducing $p_2$ will raise $Z$ further.

We proceed in this fashion until the fifth tableau, with all nonpositive simplex values, and an optimal $Z$ of .5375. Here, $p_2 = .75$, $V = .5375$, $p_3 = .25$, and $p_1 = 0$. Thus the optimal solution is degenerate—but an optimum nonetheless.

It should be noted that all we have really done is solve the same set of simultaneous equations over and over again for different basic solutions. Any one tableau in Table 7.5 is but a reproduction of linear combinations of the original set of equations, (7.8), to obtain a basic feasible solution. The tableau and the rules for moving from one tableau to another only provide a convenient method of manipulation to assure a solution in a finite number of steps.

Before concluding this discussion of linear programming, let us briefly call attention to the extremely important concept of *duality*. The brevity of the present treatment of this concept is occasioned solely by the fact that a *detailed* discussion of duality will be more fruitful after the foundations of nonlinear programming have been mastered. We shall therefore return to the concept in Section 9.7, restricting the present treatment to a brief introduction.

Consider the linear programming problem: Maximize $Z = \mathbf{c}'\mathbf{x}$, subject to $\mathbf{Ax} \leq \mathbf{d}$, $\mathbf{x} \geq \mathbf{0}$. Intimately bound to this LP problem is a second LP problem called the *dual*. The dual is the problem:

$$\text{Minimize} \quad Z_d = \mathbf{d}'\mathbf{y} \tag{7.11a}$$

$$\text{subject to} \quad \mathbf{A}'\mathbf{y} \geq \mathbf{c}, \tag{7.11b}$$

$$\mathbf{y} \geq \mathbf{0}. \tag{7.11c}$$

The original problem is called the primal problem. If the primal is a maximization problem, the dual is a minimization problem, and vice versa. The vector of coefficients in the objective function is the vector of constants in the constraints of the dual, and vice versa. The transpose of the matrix of coefficients in the constraints of the primal is the matrix of coefficients in the dual. The direction of the inequality signs in the constraints is reversed, but the vector of dual variables $\mathbf{y}$ must be nonnegative. Thus, the dual is an LP problem in which a linear function of $m$ nonnegative variables is to be minimized subject to $n$ linear constraints.

The relationship between primal and dual in programming problems in general, as well as why duals are so very important, will be discussed in some detail in Section 9.7. For the moment, however, we simply note the following ties between the LP primal and its dual: (1) the optimal solutions for the $(j = 1, \ldots, n)$ nonslack variables in the primal are the simplex criteria for the ($j = m + 1, \ldots, m + n$) slack variables in the optimal solution to the dual; (2) the optimal solutions for the ($j = n + 1, \ldots, m + n$) slack variables in the primal, are the simplex criteria for the ($j = 1, \ldots, m$) nonslack variables in the optimal solution to the dual; (3) the negatives of the simplex criteria for the ($j = 1, \ldots, n$) nonslack and ($j = n + 1, \ldots, m + n$) slack variables in the primal are the solutions for the ($j = m + 1, \ldots, m + n$) slack and ($j = 1, \ldots, m$) nonslack variables in the dual; and (4) the maximum $Z$ is equal to the minimum $Z_d$. Thus, all the information obtainable from the dual is contained in the optimal tableau for the primal, and vice versa. Since it would normally be easier to solve an LP problem the fewer the equations in it, the latter condition might dictate the choice of which to solve.

In the context of the two-person constant-sum game, it can be shown that when each competitor is deriving his optimal mixed strategy, the problem that he solves is in fact equivalent to the *dual* of his competitor's mixed-strategy linear programming problem.[34] In particular, with respect to the present problem, the negatives of the simplex values for $S_1$, $S_2$, $S_3$, the slack variables of the primal, give the $q_i$ for duopolist 1: $q_1 = .4445$, $q_2 = .3611$, $q_3 = .1944$. Setting the *arbitrary* $M = 0$, the negative of the simplex of $A_4$, or .5375, gives $V' = V$. The negative of the simplex of $p_4$, or .1625, is the extent to which the expected return from the optimal mixed strategy exceeds $1 - V'$ for duopolist 1 if duopolist 2 should ever select pure strategy 4—which he never does. This result is, of course, equivalent to the earlier observation that if duopolist 2 should select his fourth option, the expected market share of duopolist 1 would be $.4625 + .1625 = .6250$. In general, then, since the optimal solution to an LP problem will *never* contain more variables at nonzero levels than there are constraints, and since $V$ and $V'$ are *always* included in solution, the optimal mixed strategy for one competitor can *never* contain more pure strategies than are available to the other competitor, since the latter plus one is the number of constraints in the mixed-strategy LP problem.

## EXERCISES

1. "The firm under pure competition can sell as much as it wishes at the going price. Should the same firm suddenly find itself in a monopoly position it would be faced with a downward-sloping demand curve and could only increase sales by reducing price. Therefore monopolistic control benefits consumers." Discuss.

2. Industrial concentration ratios compute the percentages of total sales in an industry, say, that accrue to the leading $x$ number of firms in the industry. The concentration ratio is frequently considered important in signaling possible antitrust violations. Between 1944 and 1964 the concentration ratios for the leading 25 firms in the United States brewing industry rose from 39.2 percent to 85.4 percent. Simultaneously, the number of firms declined from 374 to 129.
   (a) What can one say about the trend in the "degree of competition" in the brewing industry?
   (b) What would you expect the effects of these trends to be on the price of beer?
   (c) Is the brewing industry becoming more competitive? oligopolistic? or monopolistic? than it was in 1944?

[34] See D. Gale, H. W. Kuhn, and A. W. Tucker, "Linear Programming and the Theory of Games," and G. B. Dantzig, "A Proof of the Equivalence of the Programming Problem and the Game Problem," in T. C. Koopmans, ed., *Activity Analysis of Production and Allocation* (New York: John Wiley & Sons, Inc., 1951), pp. 317–329, 329–335.

3. To what extent does "the" firm concern itself with whether the industry demand curve upon which it bases its price decisions is short or long run?

4. (a) Consider an industry with a demand curve given by $P = 1000/Q + 4000$, where $P$ is price and $Q$ is quantity. There is one firm in the industry, a profit-maximizing monopoly, with a total cost curve given by $C = 1000 + Q^2$, where $C$ is total cost. What is the profit-maximizing price and output?
   (b) Suppose a second firm with the same cost curve enters the industry. What will the *first* firm's price and output be if:
      (i) Both behave as Bertrand duopolists?
      (ii) Both behave as naive Cournot duopolists?
      (iii) The first firm behaves as a sophisticated Cournot duopolist (in the Stackelberg sense) and the second firm is a naive Cournot duopolist?
   (c) Suppose an *additional* 2008 profit-maximizing firms with, once again, cost curves identical to the first firm's enter the industry. Assume that, for all intents and purposes, pure competition prevails. What will the new price and *industry* output be?
   (d) Suppose all 2010 firms merge to become a single profit-maximizing monopolist. Now, what will be the *industry* price and output?

5. Suppose there are $n$ profit-maximizing firms in a purely competitive industry, each with an average cost curve of $C_i = 1000 + Q_i$. Suppose also that the industry demand curve is $P = 250{,}000 - \frac{1}{2}Q$. Buyers and sellers have free access to one another.
   (a) What is the equilibrium price and quantity?
   (b) By how much will price and quantity *change* if the number of firms quadruples?
   (c) What will happen to price and quantity (give the specific gory details) if the $n$ firms decide to merge?
   (d) Suppose that there are only two firms in the industry. What would be the equilibrium price and quantity if:
      (i) Each behaved as a Bertrand duopolist?
      (ii) Each behaved as a naive Cournot duopolist?
      (iii) One of the latter became "sophisticated" in the Stackelberg sense?
      (iv) Both became "sophisticated"?
      (v) They reached a "Chamberlin" accord?

6. (a) Describe and discuss the use and importance of the so-called "second-order" conditions in the theory of the firm and the theory of consumer behavior.
   (b) Describe and discuss the similarities and differences between the theory of production of the firm and the theory of consumer behavior.
   (c) Describe and discuss the similarities and differences in the derivation of the long-run factor demand curve in the theory of the firm and the long-run product demand curve in the theory of consumer behavior.
   (d) Describe and discuss the similarities and differences between imperfect competition and monopolistic competition.
   (e) Describe and discuss the similarities and differences between the pricing behavior of the pure competitor and that of the monopolist.

7. Is a three-firm industry "less competitive" than a five-firm industry? Discuss.

8. (a) Draw the reaction curves for an unstable Cournot duopoly situation.
   (b) Must Cournot duopolists always have reaction curves that (1) intersect? (2) are negatively sloped? Discuss the possibilities as well as the implications.

9. What would happen if a decreasing MC Cournot duopolist ran up against an increasing MC Bertrand duopolist?

10. Discuss in detail the implications of Stackelberg sophistication in a constant average cost Bertrand-Edgeworth market.

11. Demonstrate the effects and implications of duopolists' having different marginal cost curves for (i) Cournot, (ii) Bertrand, (iii) Edgeworth, and (iv) two sophisticated Stackelberg-Cournot duopolists.

12. Suppose that a pair of duopolists have the same set of cost curves. Derive the second-order conditions for a stable profit-maximization equilibrium under Cournot, Bertrand, Edgeworth, and alternative Stackelbergian assumptions.

13. Assume, with Theocharis ("On the Stability of the Cournot Solution of the Oligopoly Problem") that there are $i = 1, \ldots, n$ Cournot oligopolists producing a homogeneous commodity. Each oligopolist has a constant MC curve. The market demand curve, in period $t$, is given by $P_t = A - a \sum_{i=1}^{n} Q_{it}$,

where $Q_{it}$ is the output in period $t$ of the $i$th firm. Each firm assumes that the price in period $t + 1$ will be given by

$$P_{t+1} = A - aQ_{i(t+1)} - a \sum_{j \neq i} Q_{jt}.$$

Derive an expression for $Q_{it}$. [*Hint:* An equation of the form $\sum_{i=-k}^{m} a_i x_{t+i} = 0$ is a difference equation and has solutions of the form $x_t = br^t$ (how can one show this?), where $b$ and $r$ are constants. If $x_t = b_1 r_1^t$ and $x_t = b_2 r_2^t$ are both solutions, then $x_t = b_1 r_1^t + b_2 r_2^t$ will be a solution (how can one show this?).]

14. Suppose that the competitive industry's demand curve is given by $P_t^d = A - aQ_t$ and its supply curve by $P_t^s = B + bQ_{t-1}$.
   (a) Discuss the meaning of these assumptions.
   (b) What is the equilibrium price and output?
   (c) Is the equilibrium stable?
   (d) Why might this be called a *cobweb* model?

15. Derive and discuss the demand and cost conditions under which a Cournot oligopolist will have a concave isoprofit function.

16. Construct a two-person, zero-sum game having more than one saddle point.

17. Consider the following game:

| | $A_1$ | $A_2$ | $A_3$ | $A_4$ |
|---|---|---|---|---|
| $B_1$ | 60,000 | −4,000 | −1,000 | −5,000 |
| $B_2$ | −10,000 | 10,000 | 10,000 | −10,000 |
| $B_3$ | 1,000 | −10,000 | 20,000 | 40,000 |

The entries are dollar payoffs to duopolist B and losses to duopolist A, given the $B_iA_j$ strategy choices. Derive each duopolist's minimax mixed strategy.

18. The "prisoner's dilemma" is a game of the following form:

| | $A_1$ | $A_2$ |
|---|---|---|
| $B_1$ | (10,000, 10,000) | (0, 100,000) |
| $B_2$ | (100,000, 0 ) | (5,000, 5,000) |

If one thinks of the entries as "hours in jail" and $B_1(A_1)$ and $B_2(A_2)$ as the alternatives "don't confess" and "confess" to a burglary for which two alleged criminals have been apprehended, the nomenclature becomes clear. Thinking of these entries as dollars of profit, discuss the options for (a) overt and tacit collusion, and (b) determining an optimal strategy.

19. Change the entries in the previous payoff table to the following:

| | $A_1$ | $A_2$ |
|---|---|---|
| $B_1$ | (50,000, 10,000) | (0, 0 ) |
| $B_2$ | (0, 0 ) | (10,000, 50,000) |

Now suggest a strategy.

20. Suppose two profit-maximizing entrepreneurs simultaneously spot a $1000 bill in the street. How would you suggest they divide it?

21. Arbitrate the following game (all entries in market shares for "Mr. B"):

| | $A_1$ | $A_2$ | $A_3$ |
|---|---|---|---|
| $B_1$ | .3 | .4 | .7 |
| $B_2$ | .3 | .9 | .2 |
| $B_3$ | .6 | .1 | .1 |
| $B_4$ | .9 | .9 | .5 |

22. Solve the following linear programming problems, and set up and solve their duals:

(a) Maximize $Z = 8x_1 + 5x_2$ subject to

$$\begin{aligned} x_1 + 2x_2 &\geq 10, \\ 3x_1 + x_2 &\leq 40, \\ x_1, x_2 &\geq 0. \end{aligned}$$

(b) Maximize $Z = 3x_1 + 2x_2 - 2x_3$ subject to

$$\begin{aligned} 3x_1 + x_2 - x_3 &\geq 2, \\ 2x_1 + 4x_2 - x_3 &\geq 5, \\ 4x_1 + 2x_2 - 3x_3 &\geq 7, \\ x_1\, x_2, x_3 &\geq 0. \end{aligned}$$

(c) Maximize $Z = x_1 + 3x_2 + 5x_3 + 7x_4$ subject to

$$\begin{aligned} x_1 + x_2 + x_3 + x_4 &\leq 60, \\ 4x_1 + x_2 + x_3 + 4x_4 &\leq 200, \\ 3x_1 + 3x_2 + 2x_3 + x_4 &\leq 85, \\ x_1, x_2, x_3\, x_4 &\geq 0. \end{aligned}$$

23. A profit-maximizing pure competitor is faced with a monthly demand curve of $P = 100$. He produces a single product in three plants. His unit variable costs in these plants are 75, 65, and 80, respectively. His entire output for a month must be stored in a warehouse that holds no more than 1000 units of output in total. The processes used in plants 1 and 2 each make use of a fixed factor, Fixed. Each unit produced in plant 1 takes up 2 units of Fixed, and each unit produced in plant 2 takes up 3 units of Fixed. The firm has a total of 1750 units of Fixed available.

(a) How much should be produced in each plant?

(b) How much would the firm be willing to pay for another unit of Fixed?

(c) Can the firm use a bigger warehouse? Why?

24. Prove that (a) every basic feasible solution to $\mathbf{Ax} = \mathbf{d}$ is an extreme point of the closed convex set of feasible solutions, and (b) every extreme point of this convex set is a basic feasible solution to $\mathbf{Ax} = \mathbf{d}$, thereby proving in the process that (c) at least one extreme point of the convex set will be an optimal solution to the LP problem.

25. Prove that if two alternative solutions are optimal solutions to an LP problem, there are an infinite number of alternative optima.

# 8

# THE NEOCLASSICAL THEORY OF THE FIRM: Effects of Shifts in the Functions

## 8.1 INTRODUCTION

It is not particularly commonplace to discover firms producing a single product via a single process, and managed by profit-maximizing entrepreneurs behaving as if the values of their decision-making parameters were known with certainty. Nevertheless, one studies the behavior of these firms in the hope of gleaning some insights into decision making in the real world. The prospect of realizing these hopes becomes particularly attractive and feasible when one analyzes the firm's *reactions to changes* in the basic functions and parameters through which decisions are reached. It might be quite obvious, for example, that an increase in the demand for a firm's product will do the firm's profit position no harm—indeed it will do it some good; but, the effects on price are, in fact, not quite as obvious—even if one might be *tempted* to jump to the erroneous conclusion that price too will necessarily rise.

This chapter will be concerned with analyzing the *direction* of changes in price and quantity effected by changes in the basic functions underlying price-quantity determination. This analysis is undertaken in the spirit of viewing the neoclassical theory of the firm as a vehicle for determining *general* tendencies, rather than as a precise description of the real world. In this spirit, "Instead of giving a complete explanation of the 'determination' of output, prices, and employment by the firm, marginal analysis really intends to explain the effects which certain *changes* in conditions may have upon the actions of the firm .... Economic theory, static as well as dynamic, is essentially a theory of adjustment to change. The concept of equilibrium is a tool in this theory of change; the marginal calculus is its dominating principle."[1]

[1] Fritz Machlup, "Marginal Analysis and Empirical Research," *American Economic Review*, **XXXVI**:4, part 1 (Sept. 1946), 521. Machlup later comments: "The purpose of the analysis of the firm is not to explain all actions of each and every firm in existence; we are satisfied if we can explain strong tendencies in a representative sector of business. The chief aim of the analysis, moreover, is to show the probable effects of certain changes; if the direction in which output or price is likely to move as a result of a certain change in

## 8.2 SHIFTS IN DEMAND

Let us first consider the effects on price and quantity of *shifts* in product demand. When the quantity demanded increases as a result of a decline in price, this describes a movement *along* a given demand curve. When, however, tastes and preferences change, income changes, or the availability and cost of substitute and complementary goods change, there will be a *shift* in the demand curve. This shift will mean that, at any given price, a greater or lesser quantity will be demanded than prior to the shift. One ordinarily assumes, and the discussion is restricted to, situations in which the shift is unique; that is, quantity demanded *either* increases (or remains unchanged) at every price, *or* quantity demanded decreases (or remains unchanged) at every price. Thus, consider the demand curve $Q = D(P, V)$ of Figure 8.1. Suppose

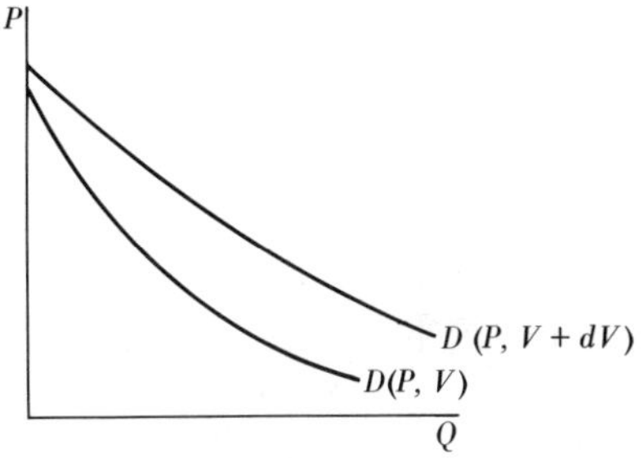


Fig. 8.1

that $V$ changes by an amount $dV$ with $P$ constant. This effects a *shift* in the demand curve to $Q = D(P, V + dV)$. It should be noted that the new demand curve is not necessarily parallel to the old demand curve; the curves might intersect—but not in the relevant range of the positive first quadrant. When $P$ is permitted to change with $V$ constant, a movement *along* a given demand curve in the price-quantity space is effected. The implications of demand shifts for the pure competitor and the monopolist can differ, and the two market situations will therefore be discussed separately.

### a. Pure Competition

Consider a purely competitive industry, and an industry demand curve in which price is the independent variable. The industry demand and supply curves will then be written as $Q^d = D(P, V)$ and $Q^s = S(P)$, respectively. Equilibrium occurs at a point $(P^*, Q^*)$ such that $D(P^*, V) = S(P^*)$. This is the Walrasian case. Suppose

---

'data' is not affected by the existence and strength of nonpecuniary factors in business conduct, their inclusion or exclusion from the marginal analysis of the firm is not a crucial matter'' (p. 527). The Machlup article presents the case for the defense in the classic Lester-Machlup debate. See Richard A. Lester, "Shortcomings of Marginal Analysis for Wage-Employment Problems," *American Economic Review*, **XXXVI**:1 (March 1946), 63–82 and "Marginalism, Minimum Wages, and Labor Markets," *American Economic Review*, **XXXVII**:1 (March 1947), 135–148; Machlup, "Marginal Analysis and Empirical Research," pp. 518–554 and "Rejoinder to an Antimarginalist," *American Economic Review*, **XXXVII**:1 (March 1947), 148–154; and also getting into the act, George J. Stigler, "Professor Lester and the Marginalists," *ibid.*, pp. 154–157.

there is a change in the amount $dV$ in the "other factors" $V$ such that $Q^d + dQ^d = D(P, V + dV)$ with $dQ^d > 0$. Since $Q^* + dQ^* > Q^*$, or the quantity demanded at $P^*$ exceeds the quantity supplied, both the new and the old equilibria will be stable if *price* is increased. Hence, if the supply curve is positively sloped, a new equilibrium will be reached such that both price and quantity are above their previous equilibrium levels of $P^*$ and $Q^*$; if the supply curve is virtually inelastic, price will increase, but quantity will remain unchanged; and, if the supply curve is negatively sloped at $Q^*$—that is, backward bending—the price increase could effect a quantity decrease and, while price will be higher than $P^*$ at the new equilibrium point, the quantity may be less than $Q^*$. The reverse will be true of a decrease or downward shift in demand, as illustrated for the three different supply curves of Figures 8.2(a)–(c).

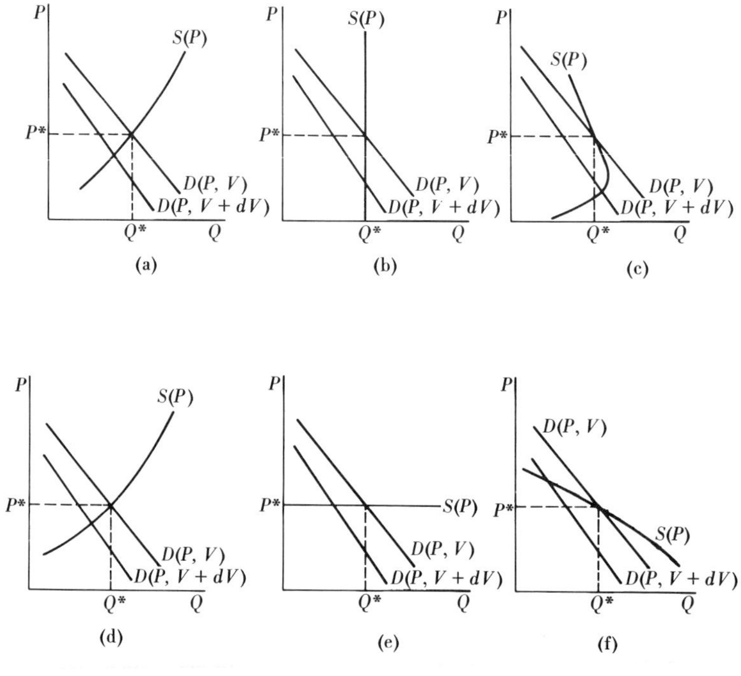


Fig. 8.2

In the Marshallian case price is a function of quantity. Let us write the demand and supply curves as $P^d = D(Q, V)$ and $P^s = S(Q)$, respectively. In this case equilibrium occurs at a point $(P^*, Q^*)$ such that $D(Q^*, V) = S(Q^*)$. Given a change in $V$ that effects an upward shift in demand, the "new" demand curve would be $P^d + dP^d = D(Q, V + dV)$, $dP^d > 0$. At $Q^*$ we would find $P^* + dP^* > P^*$. Again presuming the equilibrium to be a stable one, with demand price exceeding supply price there will be a *quantity* increase. Thus, irrespective of the slope of the supply curve, the new equilibrium quantity will exceed $Q^*$. The new price will exceed, equal, or fall short of $P^*$, however, according as the supply curve is positively sloped, infinitely elastic, or downward sloping. Again, the reverse will be true for a downward shift in demand, as illustrated in Figures 8.2(d)–(f).

Now, the supply curve in the purely competitive industry is the horizontal sum of the individual firms' marginal cost curves. Moreover, *each* firm's marginal cost curve will necessarily be flatter in the long run than in the short. This characteristic will be passed on to the industry supply curve. The less steeply sloping supply curves are thus immediately recognized to be the "longer"-run supply curves. It is then intuitively appealing, although not necessarily correct, to explain the latter phenomenon via the following suggestion: as firms in the industry have the opportunity to adjust greater numbers of their factors of production, *industry* output can be increased without the firms' requiring as much of a price increase in order to profit from the extended production as would be required when more factors are fixed. Indeed, one might even suspect that if the ability to vary factors upon extending output effects sufficient cost savings for the *industry as a whole*, the supply price required might actually be reduced. Similar arguments would hold for reductions in output, or the ability of price alterations to call forth output changes over different short runs.[2] This argument, however, offers only a partial explanation. Despite its initial appeal, it cannot, for example, explain the downward-sloping supply curve, nor fully explain *any* long-run supply curve. In particular, it has already been noted that pure competition *requires* that *each* firm encounter rising average costs, and consequently rising *marginal* costs, at relatively low output levels. *Each* firm will equate price to marginal cost, and price will be no less than minimum average variable cost. Hence, *each* firm must produce at an output at which marginal cost is *increasing*. This is as true in the long run as in the short. How, then, could the long-run supply curve, which is the horizontal sum of *upward*-sloping curves, be *downward* sloping?

The explanation is that the long-run industry supply curve, irrespective of its slope and shape, reflects *both* the complete variability of all factors and the freedom of firms to move into and out of the industry. Prior to an upward shift in demand, the industry depicted in Figure 8.3 is in short-run equilibrium at $P^*$, where the industry demand curve $DD_1$ and short-run supply curve $SS_1$ intersect. With an upward shift in demand to $DD_2$, price and quantity initially increase to $P^{**}$ and $Q^{**}$. At the higher price, each firm's $MRP_i = MR \cdot MPP_i = AR \cdot MPP_i = VMP_i$ curve will also shift upwards, reflecting the firms' increased demands for the $i$th variable factor. That is, with $MR = AR$ increasing, the demands for the factors, or the marginal revenue products, increase. Thus, the total industry demand for the variable factors undergoes an initial increase. Further, firms that previously found it unprofitable to enter the industry may now be attracted to it at the higher price.[3] With the entry of these firms into the industry, the *industry's* demand for the factors of production will undergo an additional upward shift.

Now, the factors will be supplied in accordance with constant, decreasing, or increasing factor cost or factor supply curves. Suppose in the short run associated

[2] Recalling from the previous chapter that the Walrasian approach is essentially short-run and the Marshallian approach essentially long-run in nature, the implication of the previous arguments is that demand increases (decreases) will necessarily effect price increases (decreases) in the short run, and quantity increases (decreases) in the long run. The short-run effects on quantity, and the long-run effects on price, of demand shifts are not quite as unambiguous.

[3] The question of time horizon can also be incorporated into the analysis. In particular, "When the industry . . . is subject to free entry, the increase in the discounted value

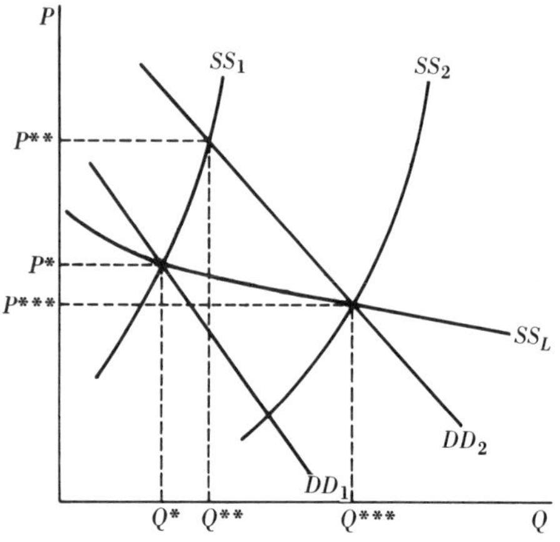


Fig. 8.3

with $SS_1$ there is a single variable factor, and this factor has a downward-sloping supply curve. When industry output is increased to $Q^{**}$, there will be an upward shift in the *industry's* demand for the factor. Consequently, there will be a *reduction* in the factor's unit cost to each firm and a reduction in the *average* cost curve of each firm contributing to $SS_1$. This reduction in the factor's unit cost will be even greater once the new firms attracted to the industry by the higher price enter the factor markets with their demands. The end result is that when the industry once again attains equilibrium, each firm is operating with a *short-run* average variable cost curve *lower* than that which existed at the former equilibria when price was at $P^*$ or $P^{**}$. This is so for, while there are more firms producing the higher industry output, the previously existing firms obtain the cost benefits of the higher industry output. Consequently, they can produce their former outputs at a lower cost than prior to the demand shift. The new equilibrium is established at the intersection of $DD_2$ and the short-run supply curve $SS_2$. $SS_2$ lies to the right of $SS_1$ and reflects the presence of *both* the new and old firms and their total factor demands.

The *long-run* industry supply curve is the curve $SS_L$. The latter describes the locus of points of intersection of the various short-run supply curves, made up of the horizontal sum of different numbers of firms' marginal cost curves, with the industry demand curves. Where there is more than a single factor of production and on balance the industry benefits from pecuniary economies received through the factors of production, the long-run supply curve will be downward sloping, as in Figure 8.3. The long-run effect of an upward shift in demand will then be a reduction in price to accompany the increase in output. In so-called constant-cost industries *all* unit factor costs are constant at all levels of employment. The additional firms entering the industry will be marginal firms initially attracted by the higher price in the most immediate short run. These firms will eventually drive the price down to the point at

of the effective profit attracts new firms into the industry. The influx of new firms continues until the aggregate output of the industry planned for some or all dates increases sufficiently to reduce the discounted value of the effective profit of the firms to zero level." Oscar Lange, "A Note on Innovations," *Review of Economics and Statistics*, XXV:1 (Feb. 1943), 190–191.

which it equals minimum average variable cost—the same price as existed prior to the demand shift. In increasing-cost industries at least one factor has a rising supply curve, on balance factor costs increase with increased output, and the long-run industry supply curve will be upward sloping.

It is important to recognize that the long-run industry supply remains the horizontal sum of the individual firms' long-run marginal cost curves. In the purely competitive industry the firms produce at outputs where marginal cost is increasing. The summation simply involves a different number of firms producing at increasing marginal cost.[4] These firms will, perhaps, have total cost functions that will vary with industry output. The original firms would be *willing*, indeed anxious, to supply the given quantity at prices *above* those reflected in the long-run industry supply curve. Nonetheless, given the presence of additional firms attracted at higher output levels, industry supply reflects the *lowest* price (= marginal cost = minimum average total cost) that producers, in particular marginal firms, are willing to accept.

Finally, note that while the long-run effect of an increase in demand on *industry* output is unambiguous, such is not the case for the individual firm. In the initial short run, say that corresponding to $SS_1$, the current producer's output will also increase;[5] but, his "longer"-run output might increase, decrease, or remain unchanged following the demand shift. This is so since the *firm's* output is determined by the intersection of its marginal revenue equals industry-equilibrium price curve, which is perceived as horizontal, with the firm's marginal cost curve. Although the firm's total and average cost curves might be altered as a result of the change in industry output, the marginal cost curve could remain unchanged or could change in a direction *opposite* to that of the total cost curve. Thus, if *marginal* costs increase but prices do not when industry output increases, the individual firm's output will fall. But there will be more firms in the industry, each producing a smaller output. This is illustrated in Figures 8.4(a) and (b). In the long run, the competitive firm's equilibrium output may increase following an increase in industry demand that

[4] Presumably, however, the number if not the composition of firms producing a given equilibrium output in a particular short run will be fixed. But contrast the following views: "In most industries we are faced, not with a population of transitory firms, each being born, rising to maturity and passing on through old age to death, but with a number of more or less permanent business units or employment nuclei, each with its own individuality, each expanding and contracting from time to time as its luck waxes or wanes, its managers grow slack or make way for new blood, fashion ebbs and flows, but continuing in existence more or less indefinitely; and we must conceive of equilibrium in the industry as a whole as arising, if it arises at all, from a dovetailing of their various phases of efficiency, due to the fact that their fluctuations are in part independent and in part compensatory, the contraction of one leading to the expansion of another." G. F. Shove, "The Representative Firm and Increasing Returns," *Economic Journal*, **XL**:157 (March 1930), 114–115. "It is not difficult to discover industries which appear to be in long-period equilibrium in the sense that their price and output have been reasonably constant for a long time, although these industries are not in equilibrium in the sense that all their component firms are in full long-period equilibrium. What we often observe when we look at an industry is a group of firms, some of which are growing, some declining, some stationary, whose numbers are being augmented by new entry and reduced by the exit of existing firms. A theory which could capture this aspect of reality would clearly be a considerable gain." Peter Newman and J. N. Wolfe, "A Model for the Long-Run Theory of Value," *Review of Economic Studies*, **XXIX**:78 (Oct. 1961), 51.

[5] Except in the special case of a backward-bending supply curve.

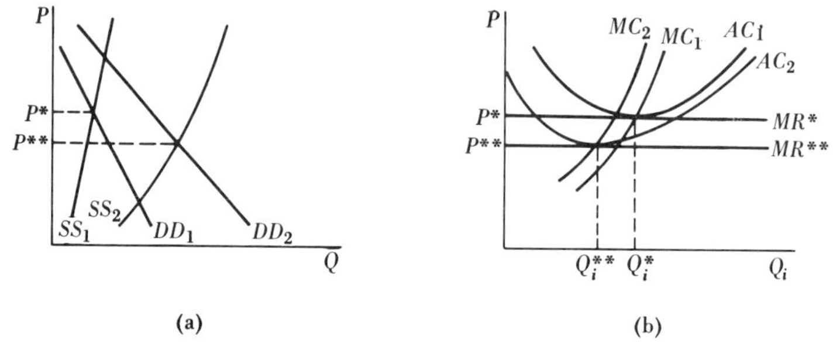


Fig. 8.4

fails to increase price, only if the long-run marginal cost curve is horizontal over the relevant range, *or* if the long-run marginal cost curve shifts downward as a result of changing factor costs following an increase in industry output. Either case can result in a shift "to the right" of the short-run rising marginal cost curve. The particulars of the situation will therefore dictate the effects of upward demand shifts on the individual firm's output level and profits. The effects of demand decreases will be exactly the reverse of the effects of demand increases.

## b. Monopoly[6]

On the one hand, the effects of a shift in demand on a monopolist are particularly interesting for they depend upon the *shape* of the demand curve itself as well as on the determinant of supply, the monopolist's marginal cost curve. On the other hand, since there is and will remain but a single producer of the product, differences between short- and long-run effects of demand shifts will stem solely from differences between short- and long-run marginal cost. We shall, therefore, discuss the short-run effects in some detail, and merely indicate how any conclusions would have to be modified for the long run.

The analysis of the effects of a demand shift on the monopolistic industry is more complex than that for the purely competitive industry, because the monopolist determines his output at the point where marginal revenue, rather than average revenue, equals marginal cost. Once more deleting reference to the "other factors" and writing the firm's (and industry's) demand curve as $P = D(Q)$, marginal revenue is given by $D'(Q)Q + D(Q) = MR$. Dividing both sides of this equation by $D(Q) = P$ yields $D'(Q)Q/P + 1 = MR/P$. But, $D'(Q)Q/P = 1/\eta$, where $\eta < 0$ is the elasticity of demand. Hence, $MR = P(1 + 1/\eta)$. The profit-maximizing price and output will be determined where $MR = MC$ or $P(1 + 1/\eta_P) = MC$. Here $\eta_P$ has replaced $\eta$, the subscript serving as a reminder that the elasticity of demand will, except for demand curves that are rectangular hyperbolas, change with price. It is clear from this formulation that, assuming as we do that $MC$ is everywhere positive, the monopolist *never* produces at a point on his demand curve where demand is inelastic—that is, where $\eta_P > -1$. The latter would yield $1/\eta_P < -1$ and hence $MC < 0$—impossible by assumption. If he produces where $\eta_P = -1$, then

[6]For a more extensive discussion of the issues raised here, see Joan Robinson, *The Economics of Imperfect Competition* (London: Macmillan and Co., Ltd., 1950), chaps. 4 and 5. Unfortunately, however, Joltin' Joe's whereabouts are not discussed.

$MC = 0$. At this point the monopolist's total revenue does not change when price decreases and output increases—but neither do his total costs nor, consequently, his profits.

To analyze the effects of a shift in demand, it is convenient to first consider the case of Figure 8.5 where marginal cost is constant at $MC = k$. Prior to the demand

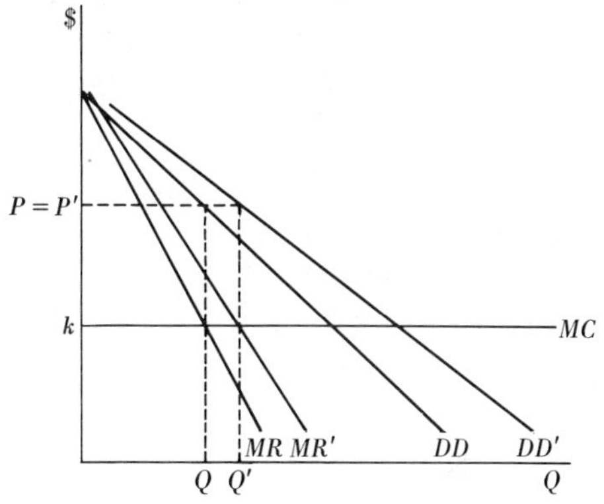


Fig. 8.5

shift, the $MR = MC$ condition implies that $P(1 + 1/\eta_P) = k$ or $P = k\eta_P/(1 + \eta_P)$. Since $dP/d\eta_P = k/(1 + \eta_P)^2 > 0$ for all $P$ and $Q$, the more inelastic is demand, that is, with greater $\eta_P < 0$, the higher will be price. In effect, the less responsive is demand to price changes, the greater will be the price charged by the firm having power to set price.

Suppose that when the demand curve shifts to the right, the new elasticity of demand, $\eta_{P'}$, equals the old elasticity of demand at each old price $P$—that is, $\eta_P = \eta_{P'}$. This is the case for the demand curves of Figure 8.5. Then the new price will be given by $P' = k\eta_{P'}/(1 + \eta_{P'})$; but, with $\eta_P = \eta_{P'}$ we will also have $k\eta_{P'}/(1 + \eta_{P'}) = k\eta_P/(1 + \eta_P)$, or $P' = P$. If demand becomes less elastic at each $P'$ so that $-1 > \eta_{P'} > \eta_P$, it follows that $P' > P$. If demand becomes more elastic, then $P' < P$.

Moreover, whether demand becomes more or less elastic at a given price will depend upon the position of the new demand curve *as well as* its shape. Suppose, for example, that the new demand curve is strictly convex. The greater is the convexity of the curve, the greater will be the positivity of $d^2P'/dQ^2$. But $\eta_{P'} = [1/(dP'/dQ)]P'/Q$. Therefore, for a given $P'$ and $Q$, the greater is the convexity of the new demand curve, the more inelastic will be the demand curve at higher prices, since $dP'/dQ$ becomes more *negative* as quantity *falls*. With a strictly concave demand curve, the greater is the concavity of the curve, the greater will be the negativity of $d^2P'/dQ^2$, and hence the more elastic will be the demand curve at higher prices. Therefore, other things being equal, the greater (lesser) is the tendency to increase price with a demand increase and a convex (concave) demand curve.

Should marginal costs be increasing, the intersection of the new $MR' = P'(1 + 1/\eta_{P'})$ curve with the marginal cost curve will occur at a smaller output than in the constant-cost case. This is so, for in this case the term on the right-hand side of the $MR' = MC$ equality will rise as output rises to meet the declining left-hand term, rather than sit back and wait for the increased output to reduce the left-hand term. Suppose that the preshift output point at which $MR = MC$ is the same point where, in the constant-unit-cost situation, we had $MR = k$. Since the postshift output is smaller than in the constant-cost case, the price must be greater. Further, the price will be greater the greater is the convexity of the marginal cost curve. This is so, for the greater the convexity of $MC$ the greater the positivity of $d^2(MC)/dQ^2$; and with marginal costs increasing at an increasing rate, the *smaller* will be the increased output level at which $MR' = MC$. In contrast, with falling $MC$, $MR' = MC$ at a *higher* output than the $MR' = k$ point. This output will be greater the greater the concavity of the declining $MC$ curve. This is so, for with $MC$ *declining* at an increasing rate of *decline*, it will be necessary to sell a greater output in order to achieve the further reduction in the $MR'$ values necessary to restore the $MR' = MC$ equality. In effect, the falling $MR'$ curve will have a tougher time catching up with the falling $MC$ curve than if the latter were falling with $d^2(MC)/dQ^2 > 0$. In either event, the price will be lower than in the constant-cost case. The effects of a shift in demand from $DD$ to $DD'$ in the case of rising $MC$ are illustrated for a particular set of demand and cost curves in Figure 8.6.

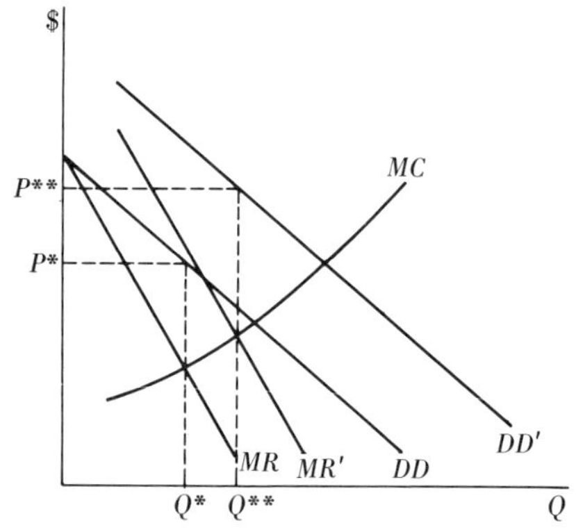


Fig. 8.6

It should be noted that the effects of a demand shift on output are more ambiguous than the effects on price. When price decreases as a result of a demand shift, output *must* have increased. When price increases, however, output may either have increased *or* decreased *or* remained unchanged. It might ordinarily be expected that output will increase when demand increases, even if price should also be increased. Nevertheless, suppose the new demand curve to be much more inelastic than the old at each price. It is quite conceivable that while the new price will exceed the old price, the monopolist will actually reduce his output. Profit *must* increase, however, since with the new demand curve to the right of the old, the monopolist gets a higher price at each and every output level than prior to the shift. Were he to leave his output unaltered, his profits would necessarily rise with the price increase. The effects of a decrease in demand will, of course, be exactly the reverse of those of an increase.

The long-run effects will differ from those of the short run only insofar as the shapes of the long-run and short-run marginal cost curves differ. Long-run $MC$ will be flatter or, with decreasing $MC$, more negatively sloped than short-run $MC$. Hence, following an upward shift in demand, the long-run increase (decrease) in price will be less (more) than the short-run increase (decrease), and the new long-run output will exceed short-run output. Long-run profit will exceed short-run profit, for the monopolist will, in the long run, be able to adjust *all* his factors of production to take advantage of his increased demand. In so doing, he thereby establishes a *new* set of short-run cost curves. If demand decreases, quantity decreases and price increases (decreases) will be accentuated (dampened) in the long run. Profit will be reduced to a lesser extent in the long run than the short, since the entrepreneur will again be able to adjust *all* factors of production in accordance with his reduced demand. The short versus long run is illustrated for a decline in demand, from $DD$ to $DD'$, in Figure 8.7. Here, the monopolist's postdecline preference for $Q_L$ over $Q_S$ and $Q^*$,

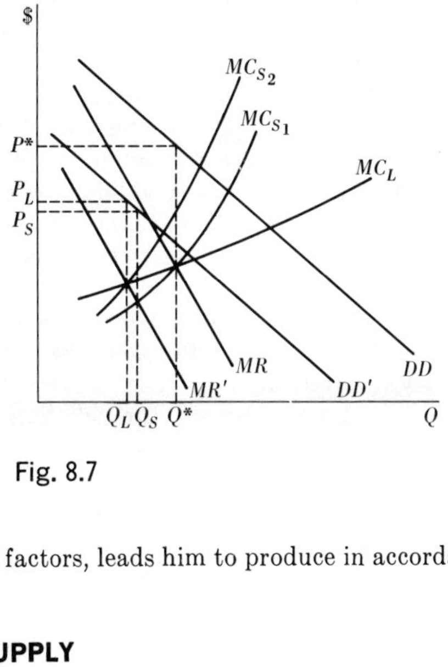


Fig. 8.7

once he can alter *all* factors, leads him to produce in accordance with the new short-run curve, $MC_{S_2}$.

## 8.3 SHIFTS IN SUPPLY

In the purely competitive industry, shifts in supply are occasioned by changes in the underlying cost conditions confronting the firms, or by changes in the number of firms in the industry. The effects of such shifts are analogous to, and analyzed in a similar fashion to, shifts in demand. In Figure 8.3, for example, the short-run industry supply curve shifts from $SS_1$ to $SS_2$ as a result of a change in the number of producers and perhaps a change in factor wages. The exact positioning of the curve will depend upon the manner in which the higher industry output and demand for the factors of production affects the individual firms' cost curves. Just as the increase in industry demand results in a higher short-run price and output, under the same demand conditions with a rising supply curve the increase in short-run industry supply reduces the price and leads to a further increase in output.

Now, a shift in short-run supply, and a concurrent shift in *long-run* supply, could also be brought about by a shift in the firms' cost curves. Suppose, for example, that as a result of a technological breakthrough in an industry supplying a factor of production, this factor's supply curve undergoes a downward shift, and the price of the factor is suddenly reduced. Then the average cost curve of each current producer will also fall. So too will the average cost curves of firms that were unable to produce profitably prior to the cost reduction. Suppose the factor whose cost has fallen is a variable factor selling to the industry at a constant cost for all relevant levels of employment. For both the firms currently producing, as well as the firms sitting on the sidelines, *short-run marginal* costs may decrease, increase, or remain unchanged following the cost decrease. *Long-run average* cost will necessarily decline, however, and there will therefore be more firms willing to supply in accordance with their new short-run marginal cost curves. Therefore, the short-run industry supply curve, the horizontal sum of the individual firms' marginal cost curves, will shift to the right.

Note that we can be confident that the new short-run industry supply curve will lie to the right of the old curve, even when the new short-run $MC$ curves lie to the left of the old. This must be so, for were it otherwise the new short-run price would be above the old short-run price. In this case, even without the lower factor costs a host of firms that were previously marginal would find it profitable to enter the industry. With the lower costs, the new marginal firms will be the ones for which price is equal to the new minimum average variable cost. This new minimum is necessarily going to be no greater than the old minimum, because of the cost advantage, and will be less than the old minimum so long as we continue to assume that (1) firms cannot bid the factor price back up to former levels, in which case the equilibrium point would remain the same, and (2) the industry demand curve is downward sloping.

Again, the new marginal firm will not make above-normal profit, although the previously marginal firms might do so. The latter could be brought about if effects on profit of the cost reduction exceeded, on balance, those of the subsequent price decline. The consumer will necessarily benefit through lower price and greater output. Of course, if the factor itself has an upward-sloping supply curve, the effects of the cost reduction will not be as great as in the constant-cost case, as the price of the factor will be bid up by the new entrants to the industry. The reverse will be true for a decreasing-cost factor. Similarly, the *precise* effects will depend upon the supply conditions for the other factors of production and *their* roles in the production process.

The monopolist's profit position must, of course, be enhanced by any reduction in costs, since he can always produce at his former costs. Like the competitor, his cost reductions can be based on a change in factor supply conditions or on a technological advance. The consumer will only benefit, however, if the monopolist's $MC$ curve shifts to the right. If $MC$ shifts to the right, price will be reduced and quantity increased. Even with a decrease in *total* costs, however, if $MC$ should shift to the left—and this is certainly conceivable—price would be raised and quantity reduced, though the monopolist's profit would still increase. If $MC$ is unaffected by the cost shift, the consumer will also be unaffected.

## 8.4 THE EFFECTS OF A TAX

### a. A Franchise and Profits Tax

A franchise tax or license fee imposed upon the firm is, in the short run, an addition to fixed cost imposed by a government upon the firm. The effect is of a similar nature. In the short run, the franchise tax is unavoidable and, like all other fixed costs, will not affect the firm's operations and production decision. It will reduce short-run profit, or increase short-run loss, by the amount of the tax. So long as *variable* costs are being covered, however, the profit-maximizing firm will continue to operate as it did prior to the tax.

In the long run, however, all costs are variable—including the cost of the franchise tax. In the long run the firm avoids this tax by going out of business, an option that is not available in the short run. Let us first consider the effects on the monopolist. If even after the tax he still makes a long-run profit, the monopolist continues to operate as before. If the tax is $F$, posttax profit is reduced from a pretax $\pi$ to $\pi_F = \pi - F = PQ - C(Q) - F$. Still, $d\pi_F/dQ = d\pi/dQ$, since $F$ is independent of $Q$. Hence posttax profit is maximized at the previous $MR = MC$ position. So long as $\pi_F > 0$, the monopolist may grumble and complain about creeping socialism, but he is not expected to do anything as rash as retire to the farm or enter politics.

Similarly, suppose the monopolist's profits are taxed some proportion $\tau$. In order to avoid presenting the entrepreneur with any tax loopholes, let us assume that the tax comes in the form of an income tax—that is, it is a tax on both fixed normal, and variable above-normal, profits. If normal profits are denoted by a fixed $N$, and with posttax profits of $\pi_\tau = (1 - \tau)\pi$, the monopolist's posttax income of $I_\tau = (1 - \tau)\pi + (1 - \tau)N = (1 - \tau)(\pi + N)$ will be maximized where $dI_\tau/dQ = (1 - \tau)d\pi/dQ = 0$ and $d^2I_\tau/dQ^2 < 0$. This again leads to the pretax $MR = MC$ point. This will be true even with, say, a tax rate that is a function of total income, or $\tau = h(\pi + N)$. Here, $I_\tau = [1 - h(\pi + N)][\pi + N]$. With $N$ fixed, the monopolist seeks a $Q$ such that

$$\frac{dI_\tau}{dQ} = \left(\frac{d\pi}{dQ}\right)[1 - \tau] - \left(\frac{d\tau}{d\pi}\right)\left(\frac{d\pi}{dQ}\right)[\pi + N] = \frac{d\pi}{dQ}\left[(1 - \tau) - \left(\frac{d\tau}{d\pi}\right)(\pi + N)\right] = 0,$$

and $d^2I_\tau/dQ^2 < 0$. If $d\pi/dQ = 0$, we have the former $MR = MC$ position. If the second expression in brackets equals zero, then $d\tau/d\pi$ = the marginal tax rate = $(1 - \tau)/(\pi + N)$. Note, however, that so long as we assume a tax rate such that posttax income is greater the greater is pretax income, we shall always have

$$\frac{dI_\tau}{d\pi} = [1 - \tau] - \left[\frac{d\tau}{d\pi}\right][\pi + N] > 0 \quad \text{or} \quad \frac{1 - \tau}{\pi + N} > \frac{d\tau}{d\pi}\cdot$$

Hence we return to the $MR = MC$ first-order condition, which obtains at the same price and output as prior to the tax. The monopolist thus suffers a decline in profit, but the consumer is unaffected.[7]

[7] In the incidence sense—that is, who "pays" the tax—this argument has led economists to the assumption that a tax on profits cannot be shifted. The latter assumption rests, however, on the basic assumption that the firm operates as a profit maximizer under certainty. [See K. E. Boulding, "The Incidence of a Profits Tax," *American Economic Review*, **XXXIV**:1 (Sept. 1944), 567–572.] Nonetheless, in our world, prices are often increased in response to the imposition of a profits tax. [See Marian Krzyzaniak and Richard A. Musgrave, *The Shifting of the Corporate Income Tax* (Baltimore: Johns Hopkins Press, 1963), p. 100 for the empirical pro, and for the con see R. J. Gordon, "The Incidence of the Corporation Income Tax in U.S. Manufacturing, 1925–62," *American Economic Review*, **LVII**:4 (Sept. 1967), 731–759.] The price increases are ordinarily reconciled with the theory via the argument that the firm had been operating "inefficiently" prior to the tax. In attempting to *maintain* profits, the entrepreneur is once

The effects of an income tax on the pure competitor will be similar to those on the monopolist. In the short run, those competitors enjoying technological advantages will earn the greater income and pay the higher tax. In the long run, however, when these advantages become freely available to all, each pure competitor earns the same *total* of normal plus above-normal profit, each pays the same tax, and the consumer is unaffected. This assumes, however, that all industries are subject to the same tax. If all industries are not subject to the tax, then in the long run there will be some firms who will leave the taxed industries. This exiting of firms will effect a shift to the left in the short-run industry supply curve and, therefore, an eventual rise in price and fall in industry output.

In a similar manner, the long-run effects of a franchise tax on the pure competitor differ from the short-run effects. In the long run, the franchise tax is avoidable and its effects on the consumer may be severe. Specifically, the franchise tax will force some pure competitors out of business because it will keep them from earning their normal profit. With the upward shift in *each* firm's average cost curve in the amount $F/Q$ and the demise of many firms, the long-run industry supply curve will shift upwards. Again, this occurs *not* because the firms' $MC$ curves have necessarily changed, but because there will be fewer firms in the industry, and fewer $MC$ curves to include in the horizontal summation. A new short-run industry supply curve will result with a subsequent lower short-run equilibrium output and higher price. Depending upon the number of firms forced out by the tax, the resultant drop in output, and the ensuing effects on factor costs, a new long-run supply curve to the left of the old supply curve will result. Thus, long-run equilibrium price will increase and output will be reduced. This is so even though in the *immediate* short run there will be no changes in price and quantity. Again, however, if *all* industries are subject to the *same* franchise tax, and if all entrepreneurs insist on remaining entrepreneurs in some industry, consumers will be unaffected by the tax, but entrepreneurs will have to revise their concept of normal profits downward.

### b. Sales Tax

A sales tax is one imposed upon the firm's revenue. The two basic forms are the *ad valorem* tax, which is a tax imposed as a percentage of price, and the *excise* tax, which is a unit tax paid as a fixed amount per unit sold. The effects on price and output of these two forms are quite analogous, and they would be analyzed in similar fashion. We shall therefore discuss in detail just one of them, the excise tax.

Consider a purely competitive industry with a demand curve $P^d = D(Q)$ and supply curve of $P^s = S(Q)$. With the imposition of a tax of $\tau$ per unit, if $Q$ units are sold, sellers will receive a price, net of the tax, of $P^\tau = P^d - \tau = D(Q) - \tau$. Equilibrium will obtain where the price that sellers receive equals the price at which they are willing to supply. This occurs where $P^\tau = P^d - \tau = D(Q) - \tau = P^s$. The resultant quantity is a $Q$ such that $D(Q^\tau) - \tau = S(Q^\tau)$. Assuming the former equilibrium to be stable, the effect on output is akin to that of a downward shift in demand, with consumers now paying a price of $P^\tau + \tau$. Alternatively, we can view the price that sellers receive as $P^d$, and the price at which they are willing to supply

---

again forced back into his role of economic man, and he puts a tighter reign on the firm's operations. For a nice discussion of these issues, see Charles Z. Wilson, "Some Organizational Factors in Tax Shifting," *Western Economic Journal*, **IV**:1 (Fall 1965), pp. 49–71.

as $P^s + \tau$. From this point of view, equilibrium will obtain where $P^s + \tau = P^d$. Thus, equilibrium is attained at the same $Q$ whether we approach the analysis using $P^s + \tau = P^d$ or $P^s = P^d - \tau = P^\tau$. The effect with $P^s + \tau = P^d$ is akin to that of an upward shift in supply. These alternative methods of analysis are illustrated in Figure 8.8(a). Figure 8.8(b) illustrates an ad valorem tax having comparable effects

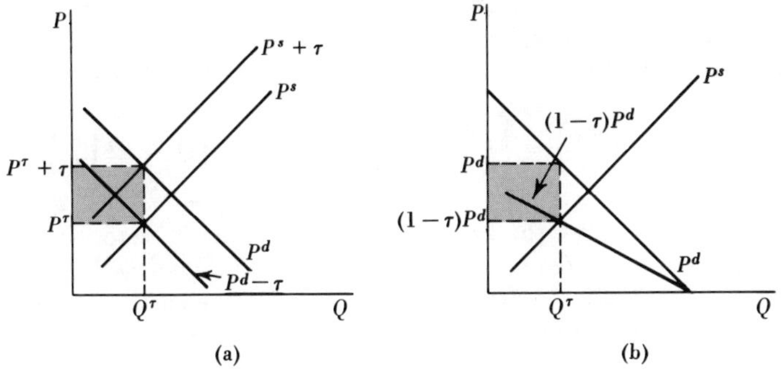


Fig. 8.8

on price and output to those of the excise tax. In this graph, the price producers receive is given by $(1 - \tau)P^d$. We need not discuss here short versus long run, nor the effects on the individual firm, as these will be analogous to the previously discussed effects of shifts in demand and supply in the short run versus the long.

Further, although here we are not especially concerned with the welfare implications of a sales tax, it is interesting to note the following. Suppose the supply curve is upward sloping and that both the industry demand and supply curves are linear. Further, suppose the pretax equilibrium occurs at $Q^*$. If $-dP^d/dQ = dP^s/dQ$, that is, the demand and supply curves are of equal *absolute* slope, the *increase* in the price the consumer is willing to pay when quantity is reduced from an equilibrium level will exactly equal the *decrease* in price the firms are willing to bear. Now, $P^d = P^s$ before the tax, and $P^d - P^s = \tau$ after the tax. Hence, at $Q^\tau$ consumers will pay $P^d + \frac{1}{2}\tau$ and producers will receive $P^s - \frac{1}{2}\tau$. The price consumers pay increases by the same amount as the price that producers receive decreases. In a sense, not a very good one, each pays half the tax. If $-dP^d/dQ > dP^s/dQ$, that is, the demand curve is steeper in absolute slope than the supply curve, the price the consumer pays rises by more than half the tax. This is so, since the price he is willing to pay rises by more than the decline in price suppliers will bear with the same quantity change. Similarly, if $-dP^d/dQ < dP^s/dQ$, the price the producer receives falls by more than half the tax. In either event, the difference between the two prices is $\tau$.

Moreover, with nonlinear demand and supply, the price the consumer pays will be a greater percentage of $\tau$, the greater is the convexity of the demand curve and the lesser is the concavity of the supply curve. This is true since the greater is the convexity of the demand curve the greater is $d^2P^d/dQ^2 > 0$. Hence, the greater is the increase in price that the consumer is willing to pay as quantity falls. Similarly, the lesser is the concavity of the supply curve, the smaller is $-d^2P^s/dQ^2$, and the smaller is the price reduction accepted by firms when quantity falls. Indeed, if the long-run supply curve is downward sloping, the price the consumer pays would actually increase by *more* than $\tau$, and the price received by suppliers would be higher than before the tax—but there would be fewer firms around to enjoy it.

Other things aside, the latter discussion provides a fairly compelling argument against sales taxes levied upon decreasing-cost industries. Note too that the government's tax revenue, indicated by the shaded areas in Figure 8.8(a) and (b), is given by $G = \tau Q^\tau = (P^d - P^s)Q^\tau$. To maximize its tax revenue, the government wishes to set a tax such that the posttax output of $Q^\tau$ assures $dG/d\tau = 0$ (assuming that at this output $d^2G/d\tau^2 < 0$). Now,

$$\frac{dG}{d\tau} = \left(\frac{dG}{dQ}\right)\left(\frac{dQ}{d\tau}\right) = \left[\left(\frac{dP^d}{dQ}\right)Q + P^d - \left(\frac{dP^s}{dQ}\right)Q - P^s\right]\left(\frac{dQ}{d\tau}\right).$$

For $dG/d\tau = 0$, we require the expression in brackets to be zero, since $dQ/d\tau \neq 0$ generally. Therefore, we require $(dP^d/dQ)Q + P^d = (dP^s/dQ)Q + P^s$. The expression on the left is simply the *industry's* marginal revenue curve. The expression on the right is the curve marginal to the curve that would be obtained by considering the industry supply curve to be an "average" curve. Thus, as far as the tax-revenue-maximizing government is concerned, its "average cost" of raising the tax is the price it must pay to suppliers out of total selling price, and the industry supply curve becomes the government's "average cost" curve. Then, the government sets its tax to assure that output will be such as to equate what is for the government $MR$ and "$MC$."

The analysis of a sales tax on a monopoly follows along similar, if slightly more complex lines. Again, the greater complexity stems from the monopolist's equating $MR \neq P$ to $MC$. After a unit tax of $\tau$ is imposed, the monopolist's profit is given by $\pi = [D(Q) - \tau]Q - c(Q)$. This is maximized where $\partial\pi/\partial Q = MR - \tau - MC = 0$ and $\partial^2\pi/\partial Q^2 < 0$. Hence, the newly relevant marginal revenue curve, $MR^\tau = MR - \tau$, is precisely $\tau$ below the old one, and profit is maximized where $MR^\tau = MC$. Analogous to a drop in demand, the effect of the tax is to reduce the optimum $Q$. Therefore, the price the consumer pays increases. The decline in $Q$ is greater in the long run than in the short run because there is a flatter (or a more downward-sloping) $MC$ curve in the long run. The price rise is therefore greater in the long run. Figure 8.9 illustrates a tax on a monopolist.

Moreover, suppose demand is linear of the general form $P^d = A - aQ$ and marginal cost is constant at $MC = k$. To maximize profit the monopolist produces $Q^* = (A - k)/2a$ and charges $P^* = (A + k)/2$. After the tax is imposed, he produces $Q^\tau = (A - k - \tau)/2a$ and charges $(A + k + \tau)/2$. In the case of linear demand and constant average cost, then, the price the consumer pays always increases by half the tax. Further, since in general $MR = D'(Q)Q + D(Q)$, $d(MR)/dQ = D''(Q)Q + 2D'(Q)$. With $D'(Q) < 0$, if demand is linear, $D''(Q) = 0$ and $d(MR)/dQ = 2D'(Q) < 0$; or $dP/dQ = \frac{1}{2}d(MR)/dQ$. If the demand curve is convex, $D''(Q) > 0$. That is, the marginal revenue curve is not as negatively sloped, relative to the demand curve, as in the case of linear demand. With linear demand, the imposition of a tax of $\tau$ causes the original $MR$ to be exactly $\tau$ greater at $Q^\tau$ than at $Q^*$ (since $MR^\tau = MR - \tau = k$). The price increase, however, is exactly half $\tau$, since the demand curve has half the slope of the $MR$ curve. With a convex demand curve, the demand curve has *more than* half the slope of the $MR$ curve because $D''(Q) > 0$. Hence, $MR$ is still increased by $\tau$ at $Q^\tau$, but price is increased by *more than* half $\tau$ as

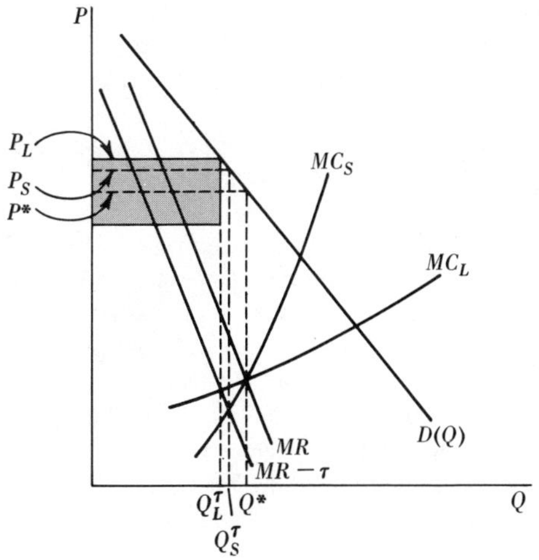


Fig. 8.9

$dP/dQ = \frac{1}{2}d(MR)/dQ - \frac{1}{2}D''(Q)Q < 0$. In the limiting case, where demand is virtually inelastic, price will increase by $\tau$. With concave demand, $D''(Q) < 0$ and the price is less influenced by changing $Q$ than in the linear case; hence, the price increase is less than half $\tau$. Analogous to the analysis for the previously described demand shifts, with linear demand the price will rise by more than half of $\tau$ if $MC$ is falling and by less than half of $\tau$ if $MC$ is rising. This is so since, in the former case the new optimum output, $Q^{\tau'}$, will be such that $Q^{\tau'} < Q^\tau$, and in the latter case $Q^{\tau'} > Q^\tau$. Similarly, the greater the convexity (concavity) of the $MC$ curve, the greater (smaller) the reduction in $Q$ and the greater (smaller) the rise in price paid by the consumer. This is illustrated for a rising $MC$ curve in Figure 8.10.

The rather unlovely implications of a sales tax are emphasized if the government

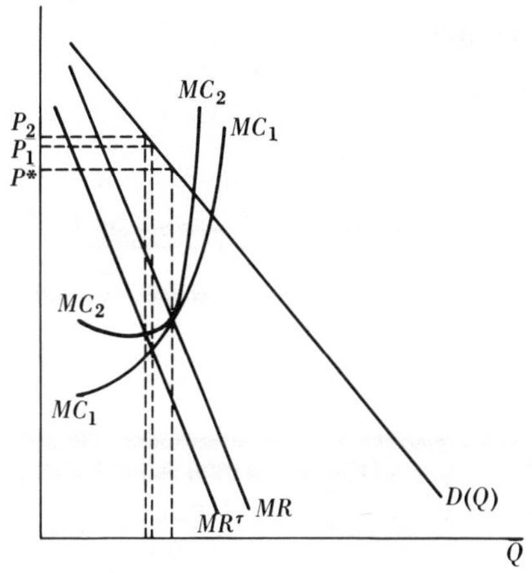


Fig. 8.10

sets the tax so as to maximize tax revenue. The government's revenue again is $G = \tau Q^\tau$—the shaded area in Figure 8.9. Here $G = \tau Q^\tau = (MR - MR^\tau)Q^\tau = (MR - MC)Q^\tau$. To maximize $G$ requires a $\tau$ such that $dG/d\tau = 0$, or

$$\left[\frac{d(MR)}{dQ}\right]Q + MR = \left[\frac{d(MC)}{dQ}\right]Q + MC \quad \text{and} \quad \frac{d^2G}{d\tau^2} < 0.$$

That is, the government looks upon the original $MR$ curve as its "demand" curve and upon the $MC$ curve as its "average cost" curve, and then proceeds to act as a monopolist would act. The tax rate $\tau$ is set such as to generate what is for the government the optimal monopoly output. The restrictive practices of the monopolist are thereby compounded by the imposition of the sales tax.

As a final comment here, it should be mentioned that a subsidy acts as a negative tax. Thus, a subsidy of $\xi$ would have precisely the reverse effects of a tax. In the case where a producer was *paid* an amount of $\xi$ for each unit sold, this would be analogous to the imposition of a unit tax of $-\tau$, and the effects would be analyzed accordingly.

## 8.5 PRICE INSTABILITY IN A COMPETITIVE MARKET

Even the most die-hard of marginalists is unlikely to be overly impressed by the profundity of the inference that, ceteris paribus, firms will derive greater benefits from increases in demand than from demand decreases. Suppose, however, that we consider a pure competitor confronted by either of two short-run situations. In the first situation, industry demand is stable and the price is constant at $\bar{P}$. In the second situation, industry demand is unstable in the sense that it shifts both up *and* down, but in a random manner. Thus, the price that is determined in the market is a random variable $P$, which is judged to be distributed according to the density function $f(P)$. It will be supposed that (1) the mean or expected value of the random variable $P$ is equal to $\bar{P}$—the certainty price in the stable market; and (2) the firm's total cost curve is a convex function of output, $C = c(Q)$—that is, $d^2C/dQ^2 > 0$ or the $MC$ curve is rising. Would the firm prefer the stable first situation or the unstable second situation?

Although the assumption can be modified, at this juncture it will be convenient to assume that the firm is indifferent to risk in the sense that the decision maker or entrepreneur is indifferent between accepting or not accepting a fair bet. In this case, he does not eschew the unstable situation unless the expected value of his profits is less than the certainty equivalent in the stable situation. But the expected value of his profits will depend upon his freedom to adjust output in reaction to price changes!

On the one hand, following Oi,[8] let us assume that production is instantaneously adjustable. Then, denoting by $Q^*$ the optimum ($P = MC$) output for a given price $P$, total profit at $P$ will be $\pi = PQ^* - c(Q^*)$. If there is a small price change of $dP$, profit will change by

$$\frac{d\pi}{dP} = Q^* + \left(\frac{dQ^*}{dP}\right)P - \left(\frac{dc(Q^*)}{dQ^*}\right)\left(\frac{dQ^*}{dP}\right) = Q^* + \left(\frac{dQ^*}{dP}\right)\left[P - \frac{dc}{dQ^*}\right] = Q^*,$$

[8] Walter Y. Oi, "The Desirability of Price Instability Under Perfect Competition," *Econometrica*, **29**:1 (Jan. 1961), 58–64.

since $P = dc/dQ^*$ at $Q^*$. Then, $d^2\pi/dP^2 = dQ^*/dP > 0$, since with a rising $MC$ curve, price increases will call forth greater output. It therefore follows, with $d^2\pi/dP^2 > 0$, that profit is a convex function $\pi(P)$ of price. But, as we saw in Section 6.5, the expectation of a convex function of a random variable is greater than the value of the function evaluated at the expected value of the random variable. That is,

$$E_1[\pi] = \int_P \pi(P)f(P)\,dP > \pi(\bar{P}) = \pi\left(\int_P Pf(P)\,dP\right).$$

Thus, the firm indifferent to risk and capable of instantaneously adjusting production prefers price instability and $E_1[\pi]$ to price stability and $\pi(\bar{P})$. Moreover, as was previously shown, if the probability density is symmetric, the desirability of price instability will increase as the variance in price increases, given a fixed expected price, and given the convexity of the profits function with respect to price.

On the other hand, following Tisdell,[9] let us assume that production is planned in advance and cannot be altered from its preplanned optimal level of $\bar{Q}$. Then, expected profits are given by

$$E_2[\pi] = \int_P P\bar{Q}f(P)\,dP - c(\bar{Q}) = \bar{Q}\int_P Pf(P)\,dP - c(\bar{Q}) = \bar{Q}\,\bar{P} - c(\bar{Q}).$$

$E_2[\pi]$ is maximized at an output where $dE_2(\pi)/d\bar{Q} = \bar{P} - dc/d\bar{Q} = 0$, or $\bar{P} = dc/d\bar{Q}$. Thus, $\bar{Q}$ is the output at which marginal cost equals the expected price. The expected profit of $E_2[\pi]$ is thus exactly equal to the certainty profit secured when a price of $\bar{P}$ always obtains. Hence, since $d^2E_2[\pi]/d\bar{Q}^2 = -d^2c/d\bar{Q}^2 < 0$ and the expected profit is a concave function of $\bar{Q}$, any other preplanned output, or *combination* of preplanned outputs each chosen at random a predetermined percentage of the time, must lead to a lesser expected profit. It follows, then, that when output is not alterable and price is not predictable, price stability is preferred to price instability.

Note, however, that if one had a *perfect* price predictor, then one could predetermine an optimal output and always be correct (in the $P = MC$ sense). Perfect prediction therefore returns us to the instantaneous-adjustment case. It follows, then, that with an *imperfect* prediction mechanism, price stability becomes more desirable for the pure competitor who is indifferent to risk and unable to instantaneously adjust production, the worse is the predictor; and the better is the predictor, the more desirable is price instability. As is all too often the case, the particulars will decide the issue.[10]

[9] Clem Tisdell, "Uncertainty, Instability, Expected Profit," *Econometrica*, **31**:1–2 (Jan.–April 1963), 243–247.

[10] For discussions of some particulars and particular points of interest, see the following: Richard R. Nelson, "Uncertainty, Prediction, and Competitive Equilibrium," *Quarterly Journal of Economics*, **LXXV**:1 (Feb. 1961), 41–62; Walter Y. Oi, "Rejoinder," *Econometrica*, **31**:1–2 (Jan.–April 1963), 248; Albert Zucker, "On the Desirability of Price Instability: An Extension of the Discussion," *Econometrica*, **33**:2 (April 1965), 437–441.

It is of some interest to the discussion to consider the following remarks by Shove ("The Representative Firm and Increasing Returns," p. 110): ". . . the continual fluctuations in luck, ability and other factors affecting cost prevent the advantages of mass-production from enabling a single firm to absorb the whole output. If a firm could enlarge its output to any required size . . . *instantaneously*, then indeed the predominance of internal economies would, on our present hypothesis, be incompatible with competitive equilibrium; but since it cannot, the two conditions can be reconciled."

## 8.6 THE INVENTORY ISSUE

The decision processes of firms of the real world are indeed complicated by the instability of demand, as well as by the inability to store unsold output without cost. In particular, if output is unsold at a given point in time it might spoil and therefore never be sold; or it may be necessary to sell the unsold output at a reduced price—day-old bread, for example. Further, even if the output is certain to be sold within a given amount of time and at its original price, the firm might still incur a cost in keeping the output stored—the cost of maintaining a warehouse, for example, or the cost associated with tying up needed capital in unsold output. Problems such as these introduce us to the general class of *inventory* problems. These are concerned with the determination of optimal policies for producing, ordering, and storing the firm's products. Here, we shall merely posit a couple of the more elementary inventory models in order to introduce some basic concepts that are germane to the more complex issues that can be and have been raised.[11]

### a. Demand Uncertainty

Consider once again an entrepreneur who is indifferent to risk, and who behaves as either a price-taker confronted with a price of $P$, or a price-setter who chooses not to alter his optimal price of $P$ between production periods. For this firm, the uncertainty is with respect to the number of units that can be sold during the period of length $T$ at a price of $P$. The entrepreneur does, however, assess a probability density of $g(Q)$ for the probability that $Q$ units will be sold at the price of $P$. The firm's total cost curve is given by $c(Q)$—which, to simplify the problem, will be assumed linear. Thus, average variable cost is a constant $k$. If the firm does not sell its output during time $T$, all unsold output is sold in what is to all intents and purposes a second market, independent of the first, at a net price $P_n < k$. The net price includes a storage charge and carrying cost for capital tied up in inventory. Thus, if the firm produces $\bar{Q}$, and more than $\bar{Q}$ units are demanded (the probability of which is given by $g(\bar{Q}+) = \int_{\bar{Q}}^{\infty} g(Q)\,dQ$), the firm suffers an *opportunity loss* of $(P - k)$ on each unit it could have sold—but did not produce—and an expected opportunity loss of $(P - k) \int_{\bar{Q}}^{\infty} (Q - \bar{Q})g(Q)\,dQ$. If less than $\bar{Q}$ units are demanded (the probability of which is given by $g(\bar{Q}-) = \int_0^{\bar{Q}} g(Q)\,dQ$), the firm suffers a loss of $k - P_n$ on each of the unsold units, or an expected loss of $(k - P_n) \int_0^{\bar{Q}} (\bar{Q} - Q)g(Q)\,dQ$. The expected *loss* associated with $\bar{Q}$ is therefore given by

$$L = k_1 \int_{\bar{Q}}^{\infty} (Q - \bar{Q})g(Q)\,dQ + k_2 \int_0^{\bar{Q}} (\bar{Q} - Q)g(Q)\,dQ, \tag{8.1}$$

where $k_1 = P - k$ and $k_2 = k - P_n$. The entrepreneur indifferent to risk will want to minimize this loss. This requires $dL/d\bar{Q} = 0$ (assuming that $d^2L/d\bar{Q}^2 > 0$). By

[11] For more extensive discussions see the following: K. J. Arrow, S. Karlin, and H. Scarf, *Studies in the Mathematical Theory of Inventory and Production* (Stanford, Calif.: Stanford University Press, 1958); G. Hadey and T. Whitin, *Analysis of Inventory Systems* (Englewood Cliffs, N.J.: Prentice-Hall, Inc., 1963); and M. Starr and D. Miller, *Inventory Control: Theory and Practice* (Englewood Cliffs, N.J.: Prentice-Hall, Inc., 1963).

the well-known formula for the differentiation of an integral with a parameter,[12]

$$\frac{dL}{d\bar{Q}} = -k_1 \int_{\bar{Q}}^{\infty} g(Q)\,dQ + k_2 \int_0^{\bar{Q}} g(Q)\,dQ = -k_1 g(\bar{Q}+) + k_2 g(\bar{Q}-).$$

But $g(\bar{Q}+) + g(\bar{Q}-) = 1$ or $g(\bar{Q}+) = 1 - g(\bar{Q}-)$. Therefore,

$$\frac{dL}{d\bar{Q}} = -k_1 + k_1 g(\bar{Q}-) + k_2 g(\bar{Q}-) = 0;$$

this occurs where

$$g(\bar{Q}-) = \frac{k_1}{k_1 + k_2}. \tag{8.2}$$

That is, the optimal output level is such that the probability of selling no more than that output is equal to the profit per unit sold divided by the net price reduction per unit ($k_1 + k_2 = P - k + k - P_n = P - P_n$) from having to sell unsold output in the second market. Clearly

$$\frac{\partial g(\bar{Q}-)}{\partial k_1} = \frac{k_2}{(k_1 + k_2)^2} > 0 \quad \text{and} \quad \frac{\partial g(\bar{Q}-)}{\partial k_2} = -\frac{k_1}{(k_1 + k_2)^2} < 0.$$

That is, holding the price reduction fixed and raising the unit profit raises the desired probability and increases $\bar{Q}$—the optimal output. Holding unit profit fixed, but reducing the price at which unsold output can be sold, will reduce the desired probability and reduce $\bar{Q}$.

Suppose, for example, that $Q$ is assumed to be Poisson distributed with a mean of 15. Then, if $P = 1000$, $k = 400$, and $P_n = 100$, we determine $k_1 = 600$ and $k_2 = 300$ so that $k_1/(k_1 + k_2) = \frac{600}{900} = .67$. From tables of the cumulative Poisson distribution, $\bar{Q}$ is readily found to be 17. If $k = 500$, however, $k_1 = 500$ and $k_2 = 400$, so that $k_1/(k_1 + k_2) = \frac{500}{900} = .56$, and $\bar{Q}$ is reduced to 16. In this, the discrete case as implied by the use of the discrete Poisson, we select the *integer* $Q$ that satisfies the condition $g(\bar{Q}-) \leq k_1/(k_1 + k_2) \leq g([\bar{Q} + 1]-)$.

## b. Fixed Demand

Suppose, however, that the firm has determined its optimal output level $Q$ and is certain that during $T$ it will indeed sell $Q$ at the price of $P$. Unfortunately, however, the entire $Q$ is not sold at any one instant during $T$. Rather there is a constant *rate* of demand such that a *total* of $Q$ units will be sold during $T$. The firm sells its output from an outlet. Each time a batch of output is brought to the outlet, the firm incurs a *set-up cost* of $C_1$. This cost is independent of the number of units brought to the outlet. The reason the total $Q$ is not given to the outlet in one fell swoop is because the firm incurs a *carrying cost* of $C_2$ per unit of time, for each unit held at the outlet. Moreover, if a customer asks to purchase a unit but the outlet is out of stock, the customer is mailed the unit prior to the end of $T$, but the mailing charge and cus-

[12] This states that, for the differentiation of an integral of a function $F(x, y)$ whose derivative $\partial F/\partial x$ exists, and where $F$ and $\partial F/\partial x$ are continuous functions of both $x$ and $y$,

$$\frac{d}{dx}\left[\int_{A(x)}^{B(x)} F(x, y)\,dy\right] = \int_{A(x)}^{B(x)} \frac{\partial F}{\partial x}\,dy + F[x, B(x)]\frac{dB}{dx} - F[x, A(x)]\frac{dA}{dx}.$$

tomer irritation are judged to entail a *shortage cost* of $C_3$ per unit of time, for each *unit* that is not immediately supplied. The issue here, then, is to minimize the firm's total *inventory cost*, $C_I$, associated with $m$ shipments to the outlet, containing $Q/m$ units in each shipment.

Suppose the firm holds an initial inventory of $I$ at the beginning of the period of length $T$. The firm will regularly and steadily sell all $I$ units over a period of $t_1$. The rate of sales will be $r = I/t_1$. Thus at any time $t$ during $t_1$, a total of $I - It/t_1$ units will remain in inventory. The total number of units held, per unit of time during the interval from time $t = 0$ to $t = t_1$, will be

$$\int_0^{t_1} \left(I - \frac{It}{t_1}\right) dt = It_1 - \frac{It_1^2}{2t_1} = \frac{It_1}{2}.$$

The inventory set-up cost plus carrying cost for this period will therefore be $C_1 + C_2It_1/2$.

Now, suppose that the firm fails to carry sufficient inventory to satisfy all customers, and in fact fails to provide a *total* of $S$ units after a period of $t_2$, beyond $t_1$ when initial inventory runs out. The shortage will have mounted at a rate of $S/t_2$ per unit of time. The total number of units short, per unit of time, will be

$$\int_0^{t_2} \left(\frac{St}{t_2}\right) dt = \frac{St_2^2}{2t_2} = \frac{St_2}{2}.$$

The total shortage cost will be $C_3St_2/2$. Thus, if the firm ships to its outlet a fixed number of units $Q_s = I + S$ at the beginning of each interval of $t_1 + t_2 = t_s$, and if all previously unsatisfied orders, totaling $S$, are immediately filled, the firm will have to make a total of $Q/Q_s = T/t_s$ shipments during $T$. In doing so, it incurs a total cost associated with inventory of

$$C_I = \frac{T}{t_s}\left[C_1 + \frac{C_2It_1}{2} + \frac{C_3St_2}{2}\right]. \tag{8.3}$$

The firm's problem is to determine values for $I$ and $S$ to minimize inventory costs: that is, the firm must determine an optimum starting inventory and initial order size. To accomplish this, the calculus may be employed as soon as (8.3) is rewritten solely as a function of $I$, $Q_s$, and a set of known parameters.

In particular, $Q_s = I + S$ and $t_s = t_1 + t_2$. Therefore, $Q/(I + S) = T/(t_1 + t_2)$. Since, however, the rate of demand is fixed, $I/t_1$ or the rate of inventory decline must equal $S/t_2$, the rate of shortage buildup. Hence, $t_2 = (S/I)t_1$. Therefore,

$$\frac{Q}{I + S} = \frac{T}{t_1 + \left(\frac{S}{I}\right)t_1} = \frac{IT}{t_1[I + S]}.$$

or $t_1 = IT/Q$, and so $t_2 = ST/Q$, whereupon $t_s = (T/Q)[I + S] = (T/Q)Q_s$. We may therefore rewrite (8.3) as follows:

$$C_I = \left[\frac{Q}{Q_s}\right]\left[C_1 + \frac{C_2I^2T}{2Q} + \frac{C_3S^2T}{2Q}\right]$$

$$= \frac{C_1Q}{Q_s} + \frac{C_2I^2T}{2Q_s} + \frac{C_3(Q_s - I)^2T}{2Q_s}. \tag{8.3a}$$

For a minimum, we seek

$$\frac{\partial C_I}{\partial Q_s} = \frac{-C_1Q - \dfrac{C_2I^2T}{2} + (Q_s^2 - I^2)\left(\dfrac{C_3T}{2}\right)}{Q_s^2} = 0; \tag{8.4a}$$

$$\frac{\partial C_I}{\partial I} = \frac{C_2IT - C_3(Q_s - I)T}{Q_s} = 0. \tag{8.4b}$$

These two nonlinear simultaneous equations yield optimum values of

$$Q_s^* = \text{optimum shipment size} = \sqrt{\frac{2Q}{T}\frac{C_1}{C_2}\left(\frac{C_2 + C_3}{C_3}\right)};$$

$$I^* = \text{optimum inventory size} = \sqrt{\frac{2Q}{T}\frac{C_1}{C_2}\left(\frac{C_3}{C_2 + C_3}\right)};$$

$$t_s^* = \text{optimum time between shipments} = \sqrt{\frac{2T}{Q}\frac{C_1}{C_2}\left(\frac{C_2 + C_3}{C_3}\right)}.$$

It is readily shown that the second-order conditions for a minimum are satisfied by these values. It is interesting to note that if the firm chooses never to run a shortage, in effect the shortage cost $C_3$ is set equal to infinity, $Q_s^* = I^* = \sqrt{2QC_1/TC_2}$, and the optimum initial inventory is the optimum order size. The latter formula, known as the elementary lot-size formula, is quite famous, often quoted, and often abused in the annals of inventory discussions. At best it is suggestive. It should also be noted that we assume instantaneous receipt of orders and instantaneous filling of back-orders. Clearly a real-life problem would require modification of these assumptions (as well as others, depending upon the specifics).

## 8.7 THE QUEUEING PROBLEM

As an additional complication to the firm's problems, suppose management wishes to satisfy all demand at a quoted price of $\bar{P}$; or, more precisely, $\bar{P}$ has been determined to be the optimal price, and sooner or later all demand will have to be satisfied at that price. But, over a time interval $T$, demand at the quoted price is a random variable with mean $\bar{Q}^d$, and the actual output the firm can distribute to its customers with a given set of factors is also a random variable with mean $\bar{Q}^s$. Moreover, $\bar{Q}^d$ and $\bar{Q}^s$ are the means of Poisson processes. The Poisson assumption offers an advantage, since we can then show that the probability of a unit's being demanded during some small time interval $\Delta t \to 0$ will be given by $\bar{Q}^d(\Delta t)$, and the probability that a unit will be distributed during $\Delta t$ will be given by $\bar{Q}^s(\Delta t)$.[13]

These probabilities can be used to determine considerable information of great interest to the firm. For a start, they can be used to determine the probability that, at a given moment of time, $Q_i = i$ units will be demanded, but the customers will be forced to wait before their demands are satisfied. Eventually the demands will be satisfied, and we shall assume they are satisfied in the order in which they have been received. But the delay may well lead to customer irritation, and this irritation

[13] W. Feller, *An Introduction to Probability Theory and its Applications*, vol. I (New York: John Wiley & Sons, Inc., 1950), chap. XVII.

could cause the firm a loss of business in the future. The firm's problem here could be considered to be the determination of the optimum $\bar{Q}^s$, or service rate.

Since the demands will eventually be satisfied, $\bar{Q}^s$ must *exceed* $\bar{Q}^d$, for any alternative would at some point result in an infinite backlog of orders. Indeed, even with $\bar{Q}^s > \bar{Q}^d$ a backlog of demands may not be unusual, because both demand and distribution are *random* variables, and it is assumed an order is filled only after a preceding order has been filled. The ice cream vendor who distributes ice cream cones only upon demand is a case in point. He can serve an average of, say, 180 customers an hour, and he gets an average of only 120 customers an hour. Unhappily, he cannot serve each and every customer in precisely 20 seconds, nor do the customers come to his stand at exactly 30-second intervals. The combination of uncoordinated arrivals and random service time can lead to waiting lines or *queues*. In the present case, we are considering the simplest type of waiting-line problem: there is a single place at which orders are received and processed, and orders are filled as they come in. If we change the way orders are received and processed, the relatively simple model developed below can become much more complex and, possibly, much less tractable.[14]

Suppose, then, that the probability that $n - 1$ orders will be sitting at the firm waiting to be placed, and that one order is in the process of being filled at any time $t$, is given by $f_n(t)$; $n$ will be referred to as the number of units in the system. For $n > 0$, the probability that there will also be $n$ units in the system at time $t + \Delta t$ is given by

$$f_n(t + \Delta t) = f_n(t)[\bar{Q}^d \,\Delta t][\bar{Q}^s \,\Delta t] + f_n(t)[1 - \bar{Q}^d \,\Delta t][1 - \bar{Q}^s \,\Delta t] + f_{n+1}(t)[1 - \bar{Q}^d \,\Delta t][\bar{Q}^s \,\Delta t] + f_{n-1}(t)[\bar{Q}^d \,\Delta t][1 - \bar{Q}^s \,\Delta t] + \phi,$$

where, for example, the first term is the probability that $n$ orders will be in the system at time $t$, one more order will arrive into the system during $\Delta t$, and one order will be filled during $\Delta t$, thereby leaving $n$ orders in the system at time $t + \Delta t$. Similarly, the fourth term is the probability of having $n - 1$ orders in the system at time $t$ (which is why we require here that $n > 0$) and having one more order "enter" the system without an order being filled during $\Delta t$. The $\phi$ encompasses the higher-order probabilities, and these are assumed to be sufficiently small (because $\Delta t$ is small) that they may be taken as zero.

Rearranging terms and dividing by $\Delta t$, we obtain

$$\frac{f_n(t + \Delta t) - f_n(t)}{\Delta t} = f_n(t)[-\bar{Q}^d - \bar{Q}^s + 2\bar{Q}^d\bar{Q}^s \,\Delta t] + f_{n+1}(t)[1 - \bar{Q}^d \,\Delta t][\bar{Q}^s] + f_{n-1}(t)[\bar{Q}^d][1 - \bar{Q}^s \,\Delta t].$$

But, letting $\Delta t \to 0$ and taking limits on both sides of the equation, we find that

$$\lim_{\Delta t \to 0} \left[\frac{f_n(t + \Delta t) - f_n(t)}{\Delta t}\right] = \frac{df_n(t)}{dt} = f_n(t)[-\bar{Q}^d - \bar{Q}^s] + f_{n+1}(t)[\bar{Q}^s] + f_{n-1}(t)[\bar{Q}^d].$$

Moreover, if we assume that the probability $f_n(t)$ is independent of time in the sense that $f_n(t) = f_n(t + \Delta t)$, then $df_n(t)/dt = 0$. We may therefore write

$$f_{n+1}(t) - (1 + \rho)f_n(t) + \rho f_{n-1}(t) = 0, \tag{8.5}$$

[14] See, for example, P. M. Morse, *Queues, Inventories and Maintenance* (New York: John Wiley & Sons, Inc., 1958); and T. L. Saaty, *Elements of Queueing Theory* (New York: McGraw-Hill, Inc., 1961).

where $\rho = \bar{Q}^d/\bar{Q}^s$ is called the *traffic intensity ratio*—the rate of mean demand to mean service.

Equation (8.5) is a second-order homogeneous difference equation (see Exercise 7.13). Solutions to this equation are of the form $f_n(t) = ar^n$, where $a$ and $r$ are constants. To determine $a$ and $r$, substitute into (8.5) to obtain

$$ar^{n+1} - (1 + \rho)ar^n + \rho ar^{n-1} = 0 \quad \text{or} \quad r^2 - (1 + \rho)r + \rho = 0.$$

Thus, $r = 1$ or $r = \rho$, by the familiar quadratic formula. Therefore, $f_n(t) = a_1(1)^n + a_2\rho^n$ (again, see Exercise 7.13).

To determine $a_1$ and $a_2$, note that if $n = 0$, then, comparable to the earlier machinations.

$$f_0(t + \Delta t) = f_0(t)[\bar{Q}^d \Delta t][\bar{Q}^s \Delta t] + f_0(t)[1 - \bar{Q}^d \Delta t][1] + f_1(t)[1 - \bar{Q}^d \Delta t][\bar{Q}^s \Delta t] + \theta,$$

where, for example, if no units are demanded, no orders are filled with probability of 1. Here, notice, we cannot have $f_{-1}(t)$, which accounts for the "shortage" of terms. Repeating the previous gyrations, we determine

$$\frac{df_0(t)}{dt} = 0 = -f_0(t)\bar{Q}^d + f_1(t)\bar{Q}^s$$

or

$$f_1(t) = \rho f_0(t). \tag{8.6}$$

From $f_n(t) = a_1 + a_2\rho^n$, we know that $f_1(t) = a_1 + a_2\rho$. Hence, with $a_1 + a_2\rho = \rho f_0(t)$, $a_1 = 0$ and $a_2 = f_0(t)$. Therefore, $f_n(t) = f_0(t)\rho^n$, and this also holds for $n = 0$, since $\rho^0 = 1$.

Moreover, since the $f_n(t)$ are probabilities, they must sum to unity over all $n$; or

$$\sum_{n=0}^{\infty} f_n(t) = \sum_{n=0}^{\infty} f_0(t)\rho^n = f_0(t) \sum_{n=0}^{\infty} \rho^n = 1.$$

But, with $\rho < 1$, by the well-known series expansion

$$\sum_{n=0}^{\infty} \rho^n = \frac{1}{1 - \rho}.$$

Therefore, $f_0(t)/(1 - \rho) = 1$, or $f_0(t) = 1 - \rho$. Hence $f_n(t) = (1 - \rho)\rho^n$. For example, with $\bar{Q}^d = 120$ and $\bar{Q}^s = 180$, $\rho = \frac{2}{3}$ and the probability of $n = 3$ orders in the system at any given time will be $f_3(t) = (\frac{1}{3})(\frac{8}{27}) = .1$. The probability of *immediate* service for a new *customer*—that is, $f_0(t)$—is $1 - \frac{2}{3} = \frac{1}{3}$.

From this stage, we note that the *expected* number of units being demanded at any time $t$ is given by

$$E[n] = \sum_{n=0}^{\infty} nf_n(t) = \sum_{n=0}^{\infty} n(1 - \rho)\rho^n = (1 - \rho)\rho \sum_{n=0}^{\infty} n\rho^{n-1}.$$

By another well-known series expansion,

$$\sum_{n=0}^{\infty} n\rho^{n-1} = \frac{1}{(1 - \rho)^2}.$$

Hence $E[n] = \rho/(1-\rho)$; or, in the previous numerical example, $E[n] = (\frac{2}{3})/(\frac{1}{3}) = 2$. Since the mean service rate is $\bar{Q}^s$ per time $T$, the mean service time during $T$ will be $1/\bar{Q}^s$. Thus, from the time a unit is demanded until the time the order *begins* to be processed, an expected $E[n]/\bar{Q}^s$ of time will elapse; the unit itself will take an expected $1/\bar{Q}^s$ of time to be processed. Thus, on average, a customer will have to wait for $E[n]/\bar{Q}^s + 1/\bar{Q}^s$ before receiving his order, or the average waiting time for a unit will be

$$W = \frac{\rho}{1-\rho}\frac{1}{\bar{Q}^s} + \frac{1}{\bar{Q}^s} = \frac{1}{\bar{Q}^s - \bar{Q}^d},$$

which in the present example will be $\frac{1}{60}$ of a unit of time.

Suppose, now, that it costs $C_s$ for each unit of average service time that the firm maintains; or, with an average level of $\bar{Q}^s$, the firm's cost for "getting the units out" is $C_s\bar{Q}^s$. Each unit of time that a customer waits before receiving a unit he demands is thought to cost $C_w$. Since there is an average of $\bar{Q}^d$ customers, and each waits an average of $1/(\bar{Q}^s - \bar{Q}^d)$ units of time, the total cost of customer irritation is $C_w\bar{Q}^d/(\bar{Q}^s - \bar{Q}^d)$. The firm's service costs are therefore

$$C = C_s\bar{Q}^s + \frac{C_w\bar{Q}^d}{\bar{Q}^s - \bar{Q}^d}. \tag{8.7}$$

To minimize these service costs, the firm seeks an average service level $\bar{Q}^s$ such that $dC/d\bar{Q}^s = 0$ and $d^2C/d\bar{Q}^{s^2} > 0$. This is readily seen to occur at a level $\bar{Q}^{s*}$, where

$$\bar{Q}^{s*} = \bar{Q}^d + \sqrt{\frac{C_w}{C_s}\bar{Q}^d}\,.$$

Clearly, the optimum service level increases with increases in average demand, increases in the cost of customer irritation, and decreases in the cost of providing service.

Many complications arise, to be sure, in actual service problems. The present model can be extended, but its limitations are severe: people may not wait, there may be more than a single place at which an order may be placed, the order may have to go through a series of channels, and so forth. The simple model does, nevertheless, indicate the potential that the queueing approach holds for solving a very practical and important problem confronting the firm: distribution.

## 8.8 THE DYNAMIC PROGRAMMING APPROACH

As a final related problem, suppose the firm has made a commitment to satisfy demands of $Q_j^d$ over a series of $j = 1, \ldots, n$ production days. The firm's output capability in any given day is, to all intents and purposes, unlimited; and for each day in which a production run is scheduled the firm incurs a set-up cost of $C_1$. Similarly, for each day in which a unit is held in inventory the firm incurs carrying charges at the rate of $C_2$ per unit. The profit-maximizing firm thus is faced with a production-scheduling problem: it needs to determine the number of units $Q_j^s$ to produce on the $j$th day in order to minimize the sum of set-up plus carrying costs.

Problems such as this, indeed a very wide range of problems, can be solved quite efficiently using *dynamic programming*.[15] Dynamic programming is, in effect, a

[15] See Richard Bellman, *Dynamic Programming* (Princeton, N.J.: Princeton University Press, 1957).

*computational* scheme that facilitates the optimization of an objective function, subject to a set of constraints, where the functions and variables are not necessarily continuous.

Suppose, for example, that we wish to maximize an objective function $Z = f(x_1, \ldots, x_n)$ subject to a series of constraints, $g_i(x_1, \ldots, x_n) \leq 0$ $(i = 1, \ldots, m)$. Define the *state parameter* $\mathbf{X}$ to be a vector containing a particular combination of the $x_j$; $\mathbf{X}$ therefore describes the state of the system. Thus, if we were to neglect $x_2, \ldots, x_n$ and then solve the problem solely with respect to $x_1$, some state parameter $\mathbf{X}$ would describe the optimal value of $x_1$. The value of the objective function for this optimal $x_1 = \hat{x}_1$ will be denoted by $H_1(\mathbf{X})$. Similarly, if we neglect $x_{k+1}, \ldots, x_n$ and then solve the problem solely with respect to $x_1, \ldots, x_k$, the value of the objective function will be denoted by $H_k(\mathbf{X})$, where the state parameter $\mathbf{X}$ describes the vector of values $(\hat{x}_1, \ldots, \hat{x}_k) = \hat{\mathbf{x}}_k$. The vector $\hat{\mathbf{x}}_k$ will be called the *k-stage* solution to the problem. What we seek is the vector $\hat{\mathbf{x}}_n = \mathbf{x}_n^*$, or the $n$-stage solution. In the dynamic programming approach, this $n$-stage solution is obtained by taking advantage of the information obtained from the 1- through $(n - 1)$-stage solutions via Bellman's *principle of optimality:* "An optimal policy has the property that whatever the initial state and initial decision are, the remaining decisions must constitute an optimal policy with regard to the state resulting from the first decision."[16]

The principle of optimality suggests, for example, that in the second stage of a two-stage problem, *given* the value(s) for the first stage, we shall want to optimize for the second stage alone; and, if the state parameter $\mathbf{X}$ for the first stage contains the optimal $x_1$ for the two-stage problem, then this optimization at the second stage will yield the optimum for the two-stage problem, or $H_2(\mathbf{X})$. Moreover, if there are $n$ stages and the levels for the first $n - 1$ stages are optimal, then $H_n(\mathbf{X})$ will be obtained by optimizing solely with respect to the *decision variables* at the $n$th stage—that is, with respect to those variables over which we retain control.

With respect to the particular problem posited here, suppose that over a coming five-day period a profit-maximizing firm is committed to satisfying demands of $Q_1^d = 700$, $Q_2^d = 600$, $Q_3^d = 600$; $Q_4^d = 900$, and $Q_5^d = 400$. The output the production force can generate in any one day is virtually unlimited. Set-up costs and carrying costs are $C_1 = 500$ and $C_2 = .75$, respectively. We shall assume that no units are currently held in inventory and that the firm wishes to be certain that none will remain in inventory at the end of the five-day period. We thus know that total output of $\sum_{j=1}^{5} Q_j^s$ will equal $\sum_{j=1}^{5} Q_j^d = 3200$. The objective then is to select the $Q_j^s$ $(j = 1, \ldots, 5)$ so as to minimize

$$Z = 500\delta_j + .75 \sum_{j=2}^{5} I_j,$$

where $\delta_j = 1$ if $Q_j^s > 0$ and $\delta_j = 0$ if $Q_j^s = 0$; and $I_j$ is the number of units held in inventory at the beginning of the $j$th day.

The solution to the one-stage problem demands no sensational algorithms: $\hat{Q}_1^s = 700$, since the firm "seeing" only the single day has no options. There are zero units left in inventory at the end of the day, and this describes the state of the system after the first stage; so, $H_1(0) = 500 =$ the cost of the single set-up.

[16] Bellman, *Dynamic Programming,* p. 83.

For the two-stage problem we again want no inventory on hand at the end of the second stage. The principle of optimality then limits the solution to two possibilities: (1) the first-stage parameter is optimal, so that we need only optimize for the second stage with the first-stage values given; or (2) the first-stage parameter must be readjusted—that is, $Q_1^s$ must be increased, in which case $Q_1^s = 1300$ is readily seen to be the optimal output level. This is true, since the carrying cost per unit of .75 is necessarily less than $500/Q_2^s$, the set-up cost per unit for any feasible second-stage output level. Hence,

$$H_2(0) = \min \begin{cases} 500 + H_1(0) & = 1000, \\ 500 + .75(600) & = 950, \end{cases}$$

or $H_2(0) = 950$. The optimal two-stage solution is thus $(\hat{Q}_1^s = 1300, \hat{Q}_2^s = 0) = \hat{\mathbf{Q}}_2$.

Similarly, the optimal three-stage solution will be determined from

$$H_3(0) = \min \begin{cases} 500 + H_2(0) & = 1450, \\ 500 + .75(600) + H_1(0) & = 1450, \\ 500 + .75(600) + .75(600 + 600) & = 1950, \end{cases}$$

or $H_3(0) = 1450$. The optimal three-stage solution is thus *either* $(\hat{Q}_1^s = 1300, \hat{Q}_2^s = 0, \hat{Q}_3^s = 600)$ or $(\hat{Q}_1^s = 700, \hat{Q}_2^s = 1200, \hat{Q}_3^s = 0)$. In effect there are going to be two set-ups, 600 units are going to be held in inventory for a single day, and it doesn't much matter which day is selected. In this analysis, then, either (1) the two-stage solution is optimal and we need only optimize for the third day, or (2) the one-stage solution is optimal and we need only optimize for the last two days, or (3) neither of the former is optimal and the total output for the three days should be produced at once. That the cost-minimizing solution must be one of these three alternatives becomes apparent when we recognize that, given the fixed set-up cost, if it is worthwhile to undertake *any* production for a given day, the *entire* day's output should be produced.

Proceeding in this fashion, then,

$$H_4(0) = \min \begin{cases} 500 + H_3(0) & = 1950, \\ 500 + .75(900) + H_2(0) & = 2125, \\ 500 + .75(900) + .75(900 + 600) + H_1(0) & = 2800, \\ 500 + .75(900) + .75(900 + 600) + .75(900 + 600 + 600) & = 3875, \end{cases}$$

or $\hat{Q}_4^s = 900$, and either of the three-stage alternative optima will minimize total cost. Finally,

$$H_5(0) = \begin{cases} 500 + H_4(0) & = 2450, \\ 500 + .75(400) + H_3(0) & = 2250, \\ 500 + .75(400) + .75(400 + 900) + H_2(0) & = 2725, \\ 500 + .75(400) + .75(400 + 900) + .75(400 + 900 + 600) & \\ \qquad + H_1(0) & = 3700, \\ 500 + .75(400) + .75(400 + 900) + .75(400 + 900 + 600) & \\ \qquad + .75(400 + 900 + 600 + 600) & = 5075. \end{cases}$$

Hence, the optimal solution is either: (1) $Q_1^{s*} = 1300$; $Q_2^{s*} = 0$; $Q_3^{s*} = 600$; $Q_4^{s*} = 1300$; and $Q_5^{s*} = 0$; or (2) $Q_1^{s*} = 700$; $Q_2^{s*} = 1200$; $Q_3^{s*} = 0$; $Q_4^{s*} = 1300$; and $Q_5^{s*} = 0$. In each case, there are three set-ups costing a total of $3(500) = 1500$, and 600 ($= I_2$ or $I_3$) plus 400 ($= I_5$) or a total of 1000 units held in inventory for a day at a total cost of $.75(1000) = 750$. The cost minimum is thus $Z^* = H_5(0) = 2250$.

As a second illustration, suppose the firm's production function is given by $Q = F_1^{.3}F_2^{.2}F_3^{.5}$, and that the firm is a pure competitor paying the three factors of production wages of 2.0, 1.0, and 3.0, respectively. Total cost is thus given by $C = 2F_1 + F_2 + 3F_3$. Factor employment for the profit maximizer was previously determined via Lagrangian methods. Let us now solve the problem via dynamic programming —not because it is the best means of doing so, but because it is instructive.

To solve the single-stage problem, we wish to maximize $Q = F_1^{.3}$ subject to $C = 2F_1$, or $\hat{F}_1 = C/2$ and $H_1(\mathbf{X}) = (C/2)^{.3}$. For the two-stage problem, $C = 2F_1 + F_2$ or $F_2 = C - 2F_1$. Hence $Q = F_1^{.3}(C - 2F_1)^{.2}$. To maximize $Q$, we require

$$\frac{dQ}{dF_1} = .3F_1^{-.7}(C - 2F_1)^{.2} - .4F_1^{.3}(C - 2F_1)^{-.8} = 0,$$

since $d^2Q/dF_1^2 < 0$; or $\hat{F}_1 = .3C$, $\hat{F}_2 = .4C$, and $H_2(\mathbf{X}) = (.3C)^{.3}(.4C)^{.2} = C^{.5}(.3)^{.3}(.4)^{.2}$.

For the three-stage problem, we note first that $F_3 = (C - 2F_1 - F_2)/3$. But, since the optimal solution to the two-stage problem is $\hat{F}_1 = .3C$ and $\hat{F}_2 = .4C$, we already know that $F_1/F_2 = \frac{3}{4}$. Hence $F_3 = (C - 2F_1 - \frac{4}{3}F_1)/3 = C/3 - \frac{10}{9}F_1$. The problem has thus been reduced to the maximization of $Q = F_1^{.3}(4F_1/3)^{.2}(C/3 - 10F_1/9)^{.5}$. This is easily solved by setting $dQ/dF_1 = 0$ to obtain $F_1^* = 3C/20$, $F_2^* = C/5$, and $F_3^* = C/6$. Then, $H_3(\mathbf{X}) = Q^* = (C/60)(9)^{.3}(12)^{.2}(10)^{.5}$. It is, moreover, readily shown that with this solution, each factor is employed at a level that equates the ratios of marginal physical products to marginal factor costs for all factors.

It should be noted that in each of these two problems we would arrive at an optimal solution either by the "forward" method employed, or by a "backward" approach in which we would first solve the problem at the $n$th stage (for $\hat{Q}_5^s$ or $\hat{F}_3$), then resolve the problem with respect to the last two stages, and so forth. Note also that in each instance optima were obtained by employing appropriate, if differing, optimization procedures. Then the suggestions that were obtained at earlier stages with respect to the properties of optimal solutions were incorporated into the problem in order to facilitate the solution at succeeding stages. In this manner, the dynamic programming approach and the principle of optimality provide a computational framework for the successive revision of a series of solutions to comparatively simple problems, until the optimal solution to the more complex original problem has been obtained.

## 8.9 IDENTIFICATION ONCE AGAIN

We are now better equipped to consider anew a problem that was first broached in Chapter 3—the empirical estimation of demand curves. What is now clear, however, is that the joint observations upon which the estimation will at least in part be based, the prices and quantities, are *interdependently* determined. Specifically, suppose it is hypothesized that short-run industry supply for period $t$ is given by $Q_t^s = \alpha_{00} + \alpha_{10}P_t + \epsilon_{0t}$, and industry demand by $Q_t^d = \alpha_{01} + \alpha_{11}P_t + \epsilon_{1t}$, where the $\alpha_{ij}$ are parameters and $\epsilon_{jt}$ are random disturbances. We always observe purchases = sales at any given $P_t$. In the special case where there are no random disturbances, we will always observe $Q_t^s = \alpha_{00} + \alpha_{10}P_t = Q_t^d = \alpha_{01} + \alpha_{11}P_t$, or

$$P_t = \frac{\alpha_{01} - \alpha_{00}}{\alpha_{10} - \alpha_{11}} \quad \text{and} \quad Q_t^s = Q_t^d = \alpha_{00} + \frac{\alpha_{10}(\alpha_{01} - \alpha_{00})}{\alpha_{10} - \alpha_{11}}.$$

Thus, if $t = 1, \ldots, N$, we will simply have $N$ observations of a single point, and empirical estimation of demand or supply curves will be impossible. If, however, there are random disturbances, then the supply and demand curves will shift as in Figure 8.11(a). As a result, what we observe is the series of intersections of the

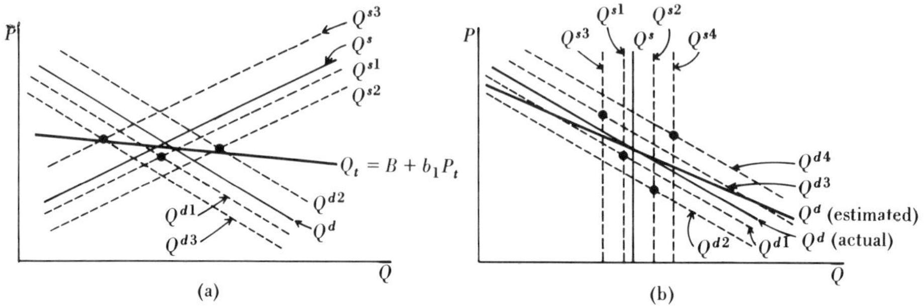


Fig. 8.11

curves labeled $Q^{di}$ with the curves labeled $Q^{si}$. In the absence of random elements, price and quantity would be determined by $Q^d$ and $Q^s$; but, except by chance, the intersection of these curves might actually never be observed. Thus, if market observations are used to obtain a least-squares estimate of the curve described by $Q_t = \beta_0 + \beta_1 P_t + \epsilon_t$, the estimated curve, $Q_t = B_0 + B_1 P_t + e_t$, will simply be a *market relation* that relates *purchases* and *sales* to *market price;* it will not reveal anything about demand and supply—irrespective of the slope of the curve—though it might serve as a mechanism for predicting purchases and sales at *given* prices.

The problem here, as in the estimation of the production function in Chapter 5, is one of identification. For example, if we assume that the true demand relation is in fact given by $Q_t^d = \alpha_{01} + \alpha_{11}P_t + \epsilon_{1t}$, estimates of $\alpha_{01}$ and $\alpha_{11}$, denoted $a_{01}$ and $a_{11}$, may be obtained by placing some a priori restriction on $\alpha_{10}$. One such restriction could be $\alpha_{10} = 0$, or supply is virtually inelastic. Then, as in Figure 8.11(b), the systematic component of the equation $Q_t^d = \alpha_{01} + \alpha_{11}P_t + \epsilon_{1t}$ *can* be estimated by least squares from the series of intersections of the independently shifting supply and demand curves, for there *is* only one equation of this form.

Alternatively, one might be able to distinguish these two relationships from one another, if there were good reason to believe "other factors" were present in either or both equations bearing a systematic relationship with the dependent variable. If, for example, in addition to price the quantity demanded depends upon the population size in period $t$, or $H_t$, then the demand equation could be rewritten $Q_t^d = \alpha_{01} + \alpha_{11}P_t + \alpha_{21}H_t + \epsilon_{1t}$. If in addition to price the quantity supplied depends upon technical efficiency as indicated by unit costs, $C_t$, then the supply curve could be rewritten $Q_t^s = \alpha_{00} + \alpha_{10}P_t + \alpha_{20}C_t + \epsilon_{0t}$. With $Q_t^s = Q_t^d = Q_t$ and $P_t$ as the two endogenous variables, and $H_t$ and $C_t$ as the two exogenous variables, the supply and demand equations are exactly identified. They could thus be estimated via two-stage least squares, indirect least squares, or any other suitable estimation procedure.[17]

[17] See, for example, Arthur S. Goldberger, *Econometric Theory* (New York: John Wiley & Sons, Inc., 1964), pp. 288–364.

Of course, one will not necessarily *have* an exactly identified supply-and-demand model.[18]

As an illustration, consider the data in Table 8.1. These are brewing industry data, the prices and costs having been taken directly from Tables 3.1 and 5.3. Fitting the just-identified supply-and-demand model suggested in the previous paragraph to these data via indirect least squares, the reduced-form equations (standard errors in parentheses) are:

$$Q_t = 78.4139 - \underset{(.0004)}{.0008}C_t + \underset{(.0072)}{.0211}H_t + v_{1t}, \qquad R^2 = .4580; \qquad (8.8a)$$

$$P_t = 17.0431 + \underset{(.0014)}{.0049}C_t + \underset{(.0237)}{.0137}H_t + v_{2t}, \qquad R^2 = .8546. \qquad (8.8b)$$

The structural equations are then readily determined:

$$Q_t^d = 107.6139 - .1713P_t + .0235H_t + e_{1t}, \qquad (8.9a)$$

$$Q_t^s = -183.7144 + 1.5380P_t - .0084C_t + e_{2t}. \qquad (8.9b)$$

It is interesting to note that, just as is alleged in textbooks, the demand curve is downward sloping and the supply curve is upward sloping in the price-quantity space. Also, at any given price, the quantity demanded increases as the population increases, and the quantity supplied decreases as unit costs increase (or, in their current role as a proxy for efficiency, as efficiency decreases). Further, since for our observations $P_t/Q_t$ is consistently in the neighborhood of .4, in the relevant range the elasticity of demand is consistently in the neighborhood of

TABLE 8.1

| Year | $P_t$ | $Q_t$ (Millions of barrels) | $C_t$ | $H_t$ (Millions) |
|---|---|---|---|---|
| 1946 | $34.94 | 79.5 | $32.73 | 141.9 |
| 1947 | 34.51 | 87.2 | 29.58 | 144.7 |
| 1948 | 33.16 | 85.1 | 29.86 | 147.2 |
| 1949 | 33.44 | 84.6 | 30.47 | 149.8 |
| 1950 | 34.04 | 82.8 | 30.68 | 152.3 |
| 1951 | 34.40 | 83.8 | 29.93 | 154.9 |
| 1953 | 35.50 | 86.0 | 33.20 | 160.2 |
| 1954 | 36.31 | 83.3 | 34.59 | 163.0 |
| 1955 | 36.33 | 85.0 | 34.08 | 165.9 |
| 1956 | 36.20 | 85.0 | 34.12 | 168.9 |
| 1957 | 36.86 | 84.4 | 34.72 | 172.0 |
| 1958 | 36.16 | 87.6 | 34.51 | 174.9 |
| 1959 | 37.85 | 87.6 | 35.79 | 177.8 |
| 1960 | 36.05 | 87.9 | 35.31 | 180.7 |

[18] For discussions that are particularly germane here, see Tjalling C. Koopmans, "Identification Problems in Economic Model Construction," in William C. Hood and Tjalling C. Koopmans, eds., *Studies in Econometric Method* (New York: John Wiley & Sons, Inc., 1953), pp. 29–35; Stefan Valavanis, *Econometrics* (New York: McGraw-Hill, Inc., 1959), pp. 89–100; and Franklin M. Fisher, *The Identification Problem in Econometrics* (New York: McGraw-Hill, Inc., 1966).

$\eta = (dQ_t^d/dP_t)(P_t/Q_t^d) \approx (-.1713)(.4) = -.07$. The conclusion that in the relevant range the demand for beer is virtually inelastic corresponds with a similar conclusion reached by entirely different methods elsewhere;[19] similarly the elasticity of supply will be $\eta_s = (dQ_t^s/dP_t)(P_t/Q_t^s) \approx (1.5380)(.4) = .61$. It might also be noted that a simple linear regression of price on quantity results in the equation $Q_t = 68.8929 + .0004P_t + e_t$ ($R^2 = .0803$), which is pleasantly nondescript.

## 8.10 A RECAPITULATION

### a. An Equilibrium Model of the Neoclassical Firm

To illustrate how the closely knit parts of the neoclassical theory of the firm fit together, let us consider the rather simple model described below. The equations are chosen for their easy solution and mutual compatibility. Together they demonstrate how one can draw some very interesting inferences for economic analysis, even when one's knowledge as to the levels of the specific parameters in question is somewhat vague.

Suppose the firm's production function is given by $Q_t = q(F_1, F_2, t) = \alpha F_1^{\alpha_1} F_2^{\alpha_2}$, where $Q_t$ is output at time $t$ during a period of length $T$, $\alpha = \alpha(t) > 0$, and the $\alpha_i = \alpha_i(t) > 0$ $(i = 1, 2)$ are functions of time. $F_1$ and $F_2$ are the levels of the two factors of production. The advantage of making $\alpha$, $\alpha_1$, and $\alpha_2$ functions of time is that we can thereby introduce technological advance directly into the production function via the variable $t$. This is accomplished by making technological advance itself a function of time.

For example, assume $\alpha_1$ and $\alpha_2$ to be constant, and suppose we can write $\alpha = (1 + g)^t$. Let us suppose, too, that $g > 0$. This would imply that given levels of the factors of production yield output levels that are consistently increasing over time, where $g$ is the percentage rate of growth. Alternatively, if $\alpha_1$ say could be written as $\alpha_1 = A_1 + a_1 t$, then the marginal physical product of factor 1 would be given by $\partial Q_t/\partial F_1 = (A_1 + a_1 t)(Q_t/F_1)$. The latter then is also a function of time, and can also reflect technological change.

The two factors supply their services at wage rates of $W_i = (w_i/2)F_i$ $(i = 1, 2)$, where $w_i$ is a constant. We divide by 2 as a later notational convenience. Clearly, $w_i$ can also be made a function of time.

The firm's demand curve is given by $P_t = D(Q_t, t) = \beta Q_t^{-1/\eta}$ $(\eta > 1)$, where $P_t$ is the price at $t$, $\beta = \beta(t)$ is a function of time, and $-\eta < -1$ is the elasticity of demand.

The firm's isocost curves are described by $C = W_1F_1 + W_2F_2 = \frac{1}{2}[w_1F_1^2 + w_2F_2^2]$. The marginal factor cost of factor $i$ is given by $\partial C/\partial F_i = MC_i = w_iF_i$, $i = 1, 2$. From the production function, marginal physical product is given by $\partial Q_t/\partial F_i = MPP_i = \alpha_i Q_t/F_i$. To maximize output for a given cost, we require $\lambda = MPP_1/MC_1 = MPP_2/MC_2$ or

$$\lambda = \frac{\alpha_1}{w_1F_1^2} = \frac{\alpha_2}{w_2F_2^2}, \tag{8.10}$$

since the isoquants will be convex and the isocost curves concave.

[19] Ira Horowitz and Ann R. Horowitz, "Firms in a Declining Market: The Brewing Case," *Journal of Industrial Economics*, **XIV**:2 (March 1965), 129–153.

From (8.10), $F_1 = F_2\,(\alpha_1 w_2/\alpha_2 w_1)^{1/2}$. Substituting into the production function,

$$Q_t = \alpha F_2^{\alpha_1}\left(\frac{\alpha_1 w_2}{\alpha_2 w_1}\right)^{\alpha_1/2} F_2^{\alpha_2} = \alpha H^{\alpha_1/2} F_2^{(\alpha_1+\alpha_2)},$$

where $H = \alpha_1 w_2/\alpha_2 w_1$. Hence,

$$F_2 = Q_t^{1/(\alpha_1+\alpha_2)}[\alpha H^{\alpha_1/2}]^{-1/(\alpha_1+\alpha_2)}.$$

Therefore,

$$F_1 = Q_t^{1/(\alpha_1+\alpha_2)}[\alpha]^{-1/(\alpha_1+\alpha_2)}[H]^{\alpha_2/2(\alpha_1+\alpha_2)}.$$

The firm's total cost curve can thus be written

$$\begin{aligned} C &= \tfrac{1}{2}[w_1 F_1^2 + w_2 F_2^2] \\ &= \tfrac{1}{2}[w_1 Q_t^{2/(\alpha_1+\alpha_2)}\alpha^{-2/(\alpha_1+\alpha_2)}H^{\alpha_2/(\alpha_1+\alpha_2)} + w_2 Q_t^{2/(\alpha_1+\alpha_2)}\alpha^{-2/(\alpha_1+\alpha_2)}H^{-\alpha_1/(\alpha_1+\alpha_2)}] \\ &= \tfrac{1}{2}Q_t^{2/(\alpha_1+\alpha_2)}\alpha^{-2/(\alpha_1+\alpha_2)}[w_1 H^{\alpha_2/(\alpha_1+\alpha_2)} + w_2 H^{-\alpha_1/(\alpha_1+\alpha_2)}], \end{aligned}$$

or, upon combining the constants into the single parameter $C_0$,

$$C = C_0 Q_t^{2/(\alpha_1+\alpha_2)}. \tag{8.11}$$

Marginal cost is thus

$$MC = \frac{\partial C}{\partial Q_t} = \left(\frac{2C_0}{\alpha_1+\alpha_2}\right) Q_t^{(2-\alpha_1-\alpha_2)/(\alpha_1+\alpha_2)}.$$

Marginal revenue is given by $MR = P_t(1 - 1/\eta) = \beta Q_t^{-1/\eta}(1 - 1/\eta)$. To maximize profit, $MR = MC$ or

$$\beta Q_t^{-1/\eta}\left(1 - \frac{1}{\eta}\right) = \left(\frac{2C_0}{\alpha_1+\alpha_2}\right) Q_t^{(2-\alpha_1-\alpha_2)/(\alpha_1+\alpha_2)}$$

or

$$Q_t^* = \left[\beta\left(1 - \frac{1}{\eta}\right)\frac{\alpha_1+\alpha_2}{2C_0}\right]^{\eta(\alpha_1+\alpha_2)/[2\eta+(\alpha_1+\alpha_2)(1-\eta)]}. \tag{8.12}$$

Given $Q_t^*$, we can then determine equilibrium values $F_1^*$, $F_2^*$, and $P_t^*$ from previous equations expressing these as functions of $Q_t$. The marginal revenue product of factor $i$ is determined from

$$MRP_i = (MR)(MPP_i) = \beta Q_t^{-1/\eta}\left(1 - \frac{1}{\eta}\right)\frac{\alpha_i Q_t}{F_i} = \alpha_i\beta\left(1 - \frac{1}{\eta}\right)Q_t^{(1-1/\eta)}F_i^{-1}$$

by substituting for $Q_t$ from the production function. For example,

$$MRP_2 = \alpha_2\beta\left(1 - \frac{1}{\eta}\right)[\alpha H^{\alpha_1/2}F_2^{(\alpha_1+\alpha_2)}]^{(1-1/\eta)}F_2^{-1} = GF_2^{\gamma},$$

where, once again, $G$ and $\gamma$ are but combinations of parameters.

Similarly, total revenue is given by $P_t^* Q_t^*$ and total costs by $C_0 Q_t^{*2/(\alpha_1+\alpha_2)}$. The difference yields total profit. In this manner, the firm's profit-maximizing price, output, and factor-employment position can be determined. Although even in this simple example some of the expressions appear to be quite cumbersome, had we been working with actual numerical values each of the rather complex-looking terms, such as $\eta(\alpha_1+\alpha_2)/[2\eta + (\alpha_1+\alpha_2)(1-\eta)]$, would boil down to a single number.

## b. Sensitivity Analysis

The production function $Q_t = \alpha F_1^{\alpha_1} F_2^{\alpha_2}$ is a homogeneous production function of the Cobb-Douglas class. That is, if the factors are each increased by a factor of $\theta$, $Q_{t\theta} = \alpha(\theta F_1)^{\alpha_1}(\theta F_2)^{\alpha_2} = \alpha\theta^{(\alpha_1+\alpha_2)} F_1^{\alpha_1} F_2^{\alpha_2}$. Hence, if $\alpha_1 + \alpha_2 = 1$, the function is linear homogeneous and we have constant returns to scale; if $\alpha_1 + \alpha_2 > 1$ $(< 1)$ we have increasing (decreasing) returns to scale.

Moreover, we have previously noted that $M = 1/\eta$ has been suggested by Lerner as a measure of the firm's monopoly power. If $-\eta = -1$, $M = 1$; as $-\eta \rightarrow -\infty$, $M \rightarrow 0$. Had we carried out the analysis with $W_i = w_i F_i^{\gamma}$, setting $\gamma_i = 0$ and $\eta = \infty$ we would readily determine the operations of the firm in pure competition in the factor *and* product markets. With $\gamma_i > 0$ $(< 0)$ we would have increasing (decreasing) factor costs. To make the algebra less cumbersome, we have simply set $\gamma_i = 1$ in the illustration above.

It should be clear that by changing the values of *any* of the parameters and studying the subsequent effects on the values of such variables as $Q_t^*, P_t^*, F_1^*, F_2^*$, one can learn both the *direction* in which these variables change as the levels of the parameters change, and the *extent* of the change. For a given set of parameters, one might determine how the firm's output and profit will change over time, or how profit will change with technological advance as embodied in the term $\alpha(t)$, thereby determining whether the firm can justify, on a profit basis, undertaking a research and development program to secure this technological advance; or one can determine the extent to which increased wage demands by a particular factor of production will influence price and output, or factor employment; and one can determine the extent to which the latter depends upon the factor's marginal physical product.

Studying the extent and direction of the influence of particular parameters, or of particular functions, is called *sensitivity analysis*. We are quite literally studying the sensitivity of the model and its implications to the sensitivity of the assumptions and the parameters that comprise it. The two major vehicles of sensitivity analysis are the calculus and the computer. If the functions in the model and the equations for which the model is solved are easily differentiable and the derivatives easily interpreted, then the signs and the magnitudes of the derivatives indicate the manner and magnitude of the changes in the variable in question. In the above example, one might calculate $\partial Q_t^*/\partial\eta$ to determine the effects upon optimum output of a change in the elasticity of demand.

Alternatively, one might simply test various numerical values, and combinations of values of the parameters, and study the subsequent effects on the variables of interest. While this would ordinarily not be a pleasant task to undertake by hand, the high-speed computer makes it a most practical option. Further, this option is available even when the functions are not differentiable, readily or otherwise. Thus, in lieu of calculating $\partial Q_t^*/\partial\eta$, one might simply substitute values such as $\eta = \frac{3}{2}, \frac{7}{2}, \frac{21}{2}$, and $\infty$ into the equation for $Q_t^*$. The numerical changes in $Q_t^*$ could then be studied. By selecting and sketching a wide enough assortment of values, one could interpolate the remaining values in a single graph with $Q_t^*$ on one axis and $\eta$ on another.

One of the benefits of sensitivity analysis is the theoretical insights that are obtained into a problem. In the model above, for instance, once $\partial Q_t^*/\partial\eta$ is determined, and if one accepts a correspondence between $1/\eta$ and monopoly power, some general inferences can be drawn about the relationship between monopoly power and output restrictions; or, for a given $\eta$, one can evaluate the relationship between price and increasing, decreasing, and constant returns to scale. With the time variable $t$ acting as a shift parameter, one can also determine how shifts in demand affect price and output in pure competition as opposed to a monopolistic situation.

These issues, however, may be of more theoretical interest to economists than practical concern to decision makers confronting real problems. For the latter, however, sensitivity analysis can present two great benefits. First, even if the parameters are not precisely known, the firm may be able to establish a range within which it is certain a parameter will fall. In this fashion, a range can be determined within which the optimal output level, say, should fall. Second, if this range of optimal outputs is narrow, it might not be worth the firm's trouble to obtain more precise estimates of the parameters, and the firm can proceed directly with the output decision.

Alternatively, if the range is quite sensitive to the values of particular parameters as revealed by the sensitivity analysis, the firm can concentrate its efforts on obtaining more precise estimates of these particular parameters to the neglect of the others. Thus, sensitivity analysis can help indicate whether a more detailed analysis of a situation is necessary, as well as where efforts toward greater detail and precision should be concentrated.

## EXERCISES

1. Consider an industry in which the demand curve is given by $P^d = 100{,}000Q^{-.5}$. Suppose the purely competitive industry's supply curve is given by $P^s = 10Q^{1.5}$. The $Q$ represents thousands of units of output, and the $P$ is in price per thousand.
   (a) Determine the equilibrium price and output.
   (b) Suppose that $P^s = 10Q^{1.5}$ is a monopolist's $MC$ curve and $P^d = 100{,}000Q^{-1.5}$ is his demand curve. What are the monopoly price and output?
   (c) What happens, in each case, to price and output if the demand elasticity doubles?
   (d) What happens, in each case, to price and output if the supply ($MC$) curve moves up by a factor of 2?

2. "Firms will either increase price following imposition of a corporate profits tax so as to pass the tax on to the consumer, or will operate more efficiently to reduce costs, or some combination of the two." Discuss.

3. "A sales tax is a regressive tax." Discuss.

4. Determine the ad valorem tax that maximizes the government's tax revenue (a) in a purely competitive industry, (b) in a monopoly industry, (c) in a Cournot duopoly industry.

5. "A reduction in demand makes a purely competitive industry less competitive, because it reduces the number of firms in the industry." Discuss.

6. In his article "The Path to Equilibrium" [*Quarterly Journal of Economics*, **LXXXI**:2 (May 1967), 244] Dr. John B. Williams argues that: "*Given* free competition, with every producer a price-taker, price at equilibrium equals *full* cost, not just marginal cost, when the latter is constant or nearly so."
   (a) Is this conclusion compatible with the neoclassical model?
   (b) What are the implicit (and explicit) assumptions that would have to underlie such a conclusion?

7. Consider the model discussed in Section 8.10. Suppose the government levies an excise tax of $\tau$ per unit on the product.
   (a) Develop a relationship between the price increase suffered by the consumer and the elasticity of demand.

(b) Will the price increase be greater if there are increasing, constant, or decreasing returns to scale? Is there a precise tie?

(c) Suppose the government wishes to maximize its tax revenue. What should the tax rate be?

(d) Could the same tax revenue be generated by a profits tax? What would be the advantage of each method over the other?

8. Consider the discriminating monopolist of Exercise 6, Chapter 6.

(a) Suppose the elasticity of demand in the first market increases (that is, becomes more elastic) and that in the second market decreases. By how much must each change in order to leave total output unaltered?

(b) Suppose demand in the first market shifts up and that in the second market shifts down, with the elasticities unaltered. By how much must each shift in order to leave total output unaltered?

(c) Can you guess and answer the third part of this question?

9. Discuss the circumstances under which the pure competitor's long-run $MC$ curve might be constant, and under which (a) his short-run $MC$ curve will be rising and (b) his output will be reduced when industry demand falls.

10. Discuss and contrast the views quoted in footnote 4.

11. Hypothesize and discuss the conditions under which a purely competitive industry might have a backward-bending supply curve.

12. Suppose that instead of receiving all output instantaneously, the firm of Section 8.6b receives output at its outlet at the *rate* of $R$ per unit of time $t$, for each shipment to the outlet, say because the output must undergo additional processing at the outlet before sale. If shortage costs are infinite, determine an optimum shipping and inventory policy. What if they are not infinite?

13. Show that the first-order conditions in Section 8.6 do indeed minimize rather than maximize inventory costs.

14. Suppose the demand and supply curves for the brewing industry are log-linear functions. Estimate them via two-stage least squares.

15. In the queueing model of Section 8.7, suppose customers grow impatient and "leave the system" if $N$ orders are ahead of theirs. How long will the average customer who places an order have to wait before receiving his merchandise?

16. Using a dynamic programming approach, solve Exercise 22(a), Chapter 7, where $x_1$ and $x_2$ must be integers. Did you enjoy doing this? Why or why not? Would someone who wasn't lazy enjoy doing this exercise?

# 9

# SOME EXTENSIONS OF THE NEOCLASSICAL THEORY: Mathematical Programming[1]

## 9.1 INTRODUCTION

Although the neoclassical model provides an interesting and useful framework within which to analyze decision making in the firm, there are several bones that one can pick with it. As cases in point, (1) management could have multiple goals and not be solely profit-oriented; (2) the option to produce more than a single product and utilize more than a single process could be available; and (3) it may be unrealistic to treat the uncertainties that abound in the business world as cavalierly as they are treated in the neoclassical model. There are additional issues that can be raised, but comment on these is deferred until Chapter 11. In this and the following chapter we shall introduce several of the more interesting extensions of the neoclassical theory—extensions that have attempted to make the theory more relevant from the perspective of the real-world decision maker.

In the present chapter we shall continue our preoccupation with the firm's price-quantity determination in a world of certainty. Now, however, we shall be especially concerned with applying techniques of mathematical programming to help resolve problems that relate to the determination of optimum output levels in the firm. *Mathematical programming* refers to the choice or the programming of levels for the activities among which one can choose. The activities might be the products that

[1] For more detailed and extensive discussions of the approaches introduced in this chapter, see G. Hadley, *Nonlinear and Dynamic Programming* (Reading, Mass.: Addison-Wesley Publishing Company, Inc., 1964), chaps. 4, 6, 7, and 8. Some interesting attempts at taking advantage of these approaches within the neoclassical framework are the following: T. C. Koopmans, *Activity Analysis of Production and Allocation* (New York: John Wiley & Sons, Inc., 1951); R. Dorfman, P. A. Samuelson, and R. M. Solow, *Linear Programming and Economic Analysis* (New York: McGraw-Hill, Inc., 1958); K. E. Boulding and W. A. Spivey, *Linear Programming and the Theory of the Firm* (New York: The Macmillan Company, 1960); and Thomas H. Naylor, "A Kuhn-Tucker Model of the Multi-Product, Multi-Factor Firm," *Southern Economic Journal*, **XXXI**:4 (April 1965), 324–330.

the firm produces or the processes that the firm elects to use to produce a given product; the activities might be the advertising media the firm elects to employ in order to promote its products, or the various financial sources, capital markets, and financial arrangements to which the firm has access; the activities might be the inventories of its various products that the firm elects to carry, or, as in Chapter 7, the strategies the firm can employ in its competitive struggles. The applicability of these techniques therefore extends over a wider range of the firm's problems than might be revealed by the fairly narrow contexts in which they are initially introduced here. Because of their widespread applicability, then, the techniques themselves will be of considerable interest; they are indeed most useful tools to include in an analyst's analytical tool kit. Additionally, however, mathematical programming can serve to make the neoclassical theory more operational.[2] While some may not judge this to be the most urgent of the economist's tasks, most would agree that if this goal is achieved, it will be a step, if a small one, in the right direction.

As a preliminary comment, it should be noted that the algebraic manipulation necessary for the solution of problems using these techniques is generally a tedious clerical job most easily and accurately handled by a high-speed clerk or computer. The theoretical foundations for these techniques will therefore be developed in the text, but numerical illustrations of the computations will be reserved for the Appendix at the end of the chapter.

## 9.2 SEPARABLE FUNCTIONS

Consider a profit-maximizing firm owning two plants and a warehouse. The warehouse has a capacity of 5000 square feet. A different product is produced in each plant. The average total cost functions for each product have been determined to be $C_1 = 500 + 5Q_1$ and $C_2 = 300 + 5Q_2$, where $Q_1$ and $Q_2$ are the monthly output levels of the respective plants. The monthly demands for each product have been estimated as $P_1 = 1500 - 45Q_1$ and $P_2 = 700 - 5Q_2$, respectively. The firm's total profit will therefore be given by $\pi = 1000Q_1 - 50Q_1^2 + 400Q_2 - 10Q_2^2$.

To store a unit of $Q_1$ requires 500 square feet of warehouse space, and to store a unit of $Q_2$ requires 300 square feet. Because of the products' bulk, the firm has determined that its best policy is to retain each month's output in the warehouse until the end of the month, and then to distribute the entire output to the firm's retail outlet in a single shipment. The most urgent problem the firm has to resolve is the determination of the output levels $Q_1$ and $Q_2$. These are to be set so as to maximize profit, subject to the constraint that $500Q_1 + 300Q_2 \leq 5000$ = storage capacity. Once the optimum outputs are determined, the prices will be established from the demand equations.

[2] The term "operational" is used in Webster's sense of being "in condition to undertake a destined function"—assist in practical decision making. J. E. Haring and G. C. Smith ["Utility Theory and Profit Maximization," *American Economic Review*, **XLIX**:4 (Sept. 1959), 566–583] have previously used the term in a related, but second sense. They distinguish between three classes of decision involving risk: marginal decisions that "are always associated with small possible losses and often with nonmonetary influences as well"; structual decisions in which "the possible losses are very large relative to total assets"; and operational decisions that involve "neither extremely small nor extremely large losses and for which nonmonetary considerations are insignificant." The latter, it is suggested, "are the very subject matter of economics" (p. 571). We shall use "operational" in a wider sense, to encompass *all* the firm's decision problems—large or small.

In order to contribute to a deeper understanding of the most *general* procedure for attacking this sort of problem (a procedure developed in some detail in the next section), let us first attempt to solve the problem by means of a graph and a few elementary observations. To facilitate these observations, note that the objective function the firm wants to maximize can, after a bit of algebraic manipulation, be rewritten in the form

$$\frac{(Q_1 - 10)^2}{\frac{1}{5}} + \frac{(Q_2 - 20)^2}{1} + \left(\frac{\pi}{10} - 900\right) = 0.$$

In this form, the objective function is seen to describe a set of concentric ellipses with center at the point ($Q_1 = 10$, $Q_2 = 20$). Any specific ellipse is determined once $\pi$ is specified. Moreover, $\pi$ is readily shown to be a strictly concave function of $Q_1$ and $Q_2$. The maximum value that $\pi$ can take on is 9000, in which case the ellipse collapses into the point ($Q_1 = 10$, $Q_2 = 20$). As $\pi$ is reduced from 9000, the ellipse proceeds to expand around this point as its center. The three ellipses shown in Figure 9.1 have

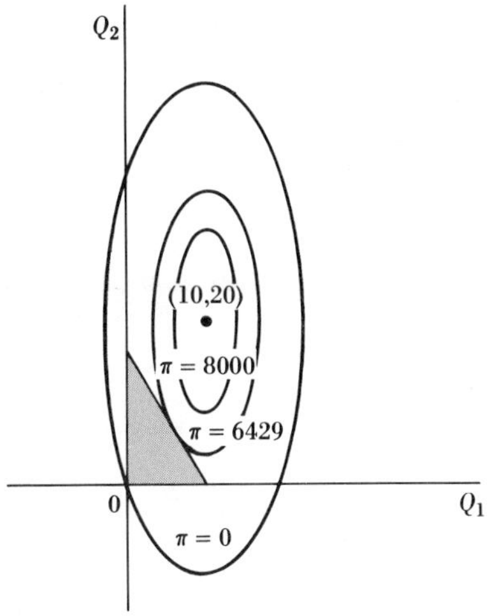


Fig. 9.1

been drawn for $\pi = 0$, $\pi = 6429$, and $\pi = 8000$. The firm seeks that ellipse associated with the maximum attainable $\pi$.

Since $Q_1$ and $Q_2$ must be nonnegative, the single linear constraint and the axes define a closed convex set of feasible solutions shown as the shaded area in the figure. Were it not for the constraints, the optimum production point would be ($Q_1 = 10$, $Q_2 = 20$) with $\pi = 9000$. But all of this "ellipse," namely the center, lies outside of the closed convex set of feasible solutions. If this point and any portion of the ellipse had fallen inside the set, then the problem would be solved: that is, the constraint can be ignored, for the unconstrained optimum is feasible. With the unconstrained optimum *not* a feasible solution, and since the ellipses are growing larger as $\pi$ gets smaller, there is strong visual appeal, as well as later mathematical support, for the notion that the smallest ellipse not lying entirely outside the closed convex set of feasible solutions—that ellipse associated with the largest feasible $\pi$—will be *tangent* to a boundary of the set. That is, we would prefer to be outside the shaded area, but, inasmuch as we cannot accomplish this, we hope to stay as close to the unshaded area as possible.

Note, however, in contrast with the case of linear programming, it would not seem here that the optimum solution need be an *extreme* point of the convex set. The solution process can therefore become much less convenient, for even though we may know that the optimal solution is a boundary point, we must still determine the "boundary" containing the point. In effect, some constraints are going to hold as strict equalities in the optimal feasible solution, and we must determine which these are; the remaining constraints can be ignored. Then, since we are optimizing an objective function subject to a set of strict equalities, we can in effect solve the problem via Lagrangian methods. The facts that there are a finite number of constraints, and that we are dealing with a closed convex set of feasible solutions, are thus of considerable help, for there are only a finite number of boundaries to inspect. Even though the chore may become tedious, then, when the objective function has the appropriate convexity properties, and when the feasible region is convex, we can at least undertake the search for an optimum with an assurance that the local optimum will be a global optimum, and that we can reach it with a finite amount of effort. In the present instance, employing the graphical method, this effort would require sharp enough vision to note that the ellipse drawn for $\pi = 6429$ is just tangent to the boundary of the convex set defined by $500Q_1 + 300Q_2 = 5000$, at the point ($Q_1 = \frac{40}{7}$, $Q_2 = \frac{50}{7}$).

In attacking this particular problem in a less off-the-cuff manner, suppose that we attempted to directly employ the ordinary Lagrange technique, by first adding a nonnegative slack variable $Q_3$ to the left side of the inequality so as to convert it to an equality. The problem would then become:

$$\text{Maximize} \quad \pi = 1000Q_1 - 50Q_1^2 + 400Q_2 - 10Q_2^2 \tag{9.1a}$$

$$\text{subject to} \quad 500Q_1 + 300Q_2 + Q_3 = 5000. \tag{9.1b}$$

The first-order conditions yield $Q_1 = \frac{40}{7}$, $Q_2 = \frac{50}{7}$, and $Q_3 = 0$. Hence, $P_1 = 1244.4$, $P_2 = 664.4$, and $\pi = 6428.6$. Further, the second-order conditions are also satisfied at this point. There are, however, two inhibiting difficulties with this approach to the firm's problem. First, in applying the Lagrange technique we have ignored the unstated fact that all the $Q_j$ ($j = 1, 2, 3$) *must* be nonnegative. As it has turned out, they are nonnegative, but we had no prior assurance that this would be the case. Second, it is not necessarily going to be true that the firm can produce and sell a fraction, namely $\frac{2}{7}$ or $\frac{5}{7}$, of a unit. The statement made by (9.1a) and (9.1b) is, therefore, not a very good description of the problem that the firm must solve. It is generally a good idea to solve the problem you have to solve, not the one you want to solve. Let us therefore first suggest how the firm might *approximate* a solution to a problem such as this one, where additionally $Q_j \geq 0$ ($j = 1, 2, 3$). In later sections we shall consider how to obtain an *exact* solution, as well as how one might approach the additional restriction that the solutions be given in integer form.

Equations such as (9.1a) and (9.1b) are said to be made up of *separable functions*, for each equation or inequation can be written as the finite *sum* of functions of a single variable. A general problem of this form, together with the constraint that the variables be nonnegative, could be written as

$$\text{Maximize} \qquad Z = \sum_{j=1}^{n} f_j(x_j) \tag{9.2a}$$

$$\text{subject to} \quad \sum_{j=1}^{n} g_{ij}(x_j) = d_i, \qquad i = 1, \ldots, m, \tag{9.2b}$$

$$x_j \geq 0, \qquad j = 1, \ldots, n. \tag{9.2c}$$

The $m$ constraints are written as equalities since, where there are originally inequalities, it is assumed that slack and artificial variables have been added to convert these to equalities. There is a total of $n$ variables.

When all the functions of a problem such as (9.2a–c) are (1) separable and (2) have the appropriate convexity properties as indicated in the following section, or when by an appropriate transformation of variables the problem can be converted into an equivalent problem *with* separable functions having the desired properties,[3] it is frequently possible to obtain a fairly accurate solution using approximation methods. In particular, we shall consider the *possibility* of converting *any* nonlinear programming problem of the form of (9.2a–c) into an approximately equivalent linear programming problem,[4] because we already know how to solve these.

Suppose the possible range of values that $x_j$ might take on extends from 0 to $U_j$. As in Figure 9.2, this range may be subdivided into a series of $K$ intervals, not

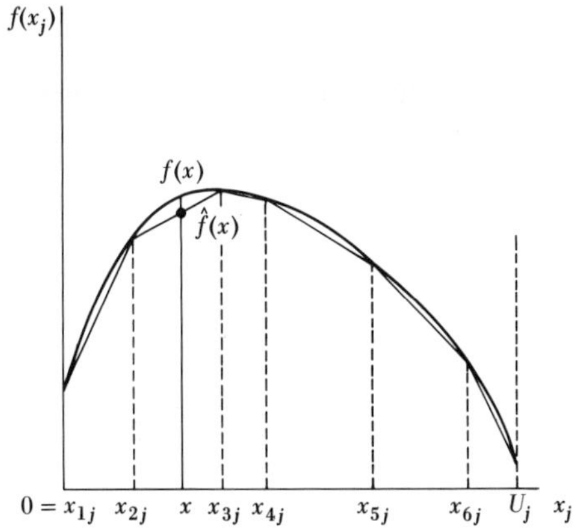


Fig. 9.2

[3] For example, a term such as $x_1x_2 = y$ may be converted to $\log y = \log x_1 + \log x_2$, provided that the $x_i$ are positive. Then $y$ may be substituted for $x_1x_2$ in the original expression, and $\log y = \log x_1 + \log x_2$ added as an additional constraint. A second possibility here would be to set $y_1 = (x_1 + x_2)/2$ and $y_2 = (x_1 - x_2)/2$. Then, $y_1^2 - y_2^2$ would be substituted for $x_1x_2$ in the original expression, and $y_1 = (x_1 + x_2)/2$ and $y_2 = (x_1 - x_2)/2$ added as additional constraints. For additional discussion, see Hadley, *Nonlinear and Dynamic Programming*, pp. 119–123.

[4] See Clair E. Miller, "The Simplex Method for Local Separable Programming," in R. L. Graves and P. Wolfe, eds., *Recent Advances in Mathematical Programming* (New York: McGraw-Hill, Inc., 1963), pp. 89–100.

necessarily equal, such that the lower and upper limits of the $k$th interval ($k = 1, \ldots, K$) are $x_{kj}$ and $x_{(k+1)j}$, respectively. Thus the first interval would be $x_{1j} = 0$ to $x_{2j}$, and the $k$th interval would be $x_{kj}$ to $x_{(k+1)j} = U_j$.

Now, consider any $x_j$ such that $x_{kj} \leq x_j \leq x_{(k+1)j}$—that is, any $x_j$ lying in the $k$th interval. A unique scalar $\beta_{kj}$ exists, $0 \leq \beta_{kj} \leq 1$, such that

$$x_j = \beta_{kj}x_{kj} + (1 - \beta_{kj})x_{(k+1)j}$$

or, letting $\beta_{(k+1)j} = (1 - \beta_{kj})$,

$$x_j = \beta_{kj}x_{kj} + \beta_{(k+1)j}x_{(k+1)j}. \tag{9.3}$$

In effect, $x_j$ is given as a weighted average of the end points of the interval containing it, where the $\beta_{kj}$'s are the weights. We may therefore write any $x_j$ in the form

$$x_j = \sum_{k=1}^{K+1} \beta_{kj}x_{kj},$$

where *at most* two $\beta_{kj}$'s are positive. If $\beta_{tj}$ is positive, either (1) $\beta_{(t-1)j} + \beta_{tj} = 1$, or (2) $\beta_{tj} + \beta_{(t+1)j} = 1$, and (3) all other $\beta_{(t+s)j} = 0$, $s > 1$. It should be reiterated that when we determine $x_j$ we determine the unique $\beta_{kj}$, and at most the two adjacent $\beta_{kj}$ for the $k$th interval containing $x_j$ can be positive; if $x_j = x_{tj}$, then $\beta_{tj} = 1$ and all other $\beta_{kj} = 0$. For example, if $x_{1j} = 6$ and $x_{2j} = 9$, then $x_j = 8 = .33(6) + .67(9)$, or $\beta_{1j} = .33$ and $\beta_{2j} = .67$.

Now, in lieu of determining $f_j(x_j)$ directly by substituting the value of $x_j$ into the function, we might *estimate* it by an approximation procedure utilizing the results of Equation (9.3). Specifically, suppose $x_j$ falls in the $k$th interval. Using the limits of the interval, we could evaluate $f_j(x_{kj})$ and $f_j(x_{(k+1)j})$. Then, since $x_j = \beta_{kj}x_{kj} + \beta_{(k+1)j}x_{(k+1)j}$, $f_j(x_j)$ could be approximated by

$$\hat{f}_j(x_j) = \beta_{kj}f(x_{kj}) + \beta_{(k+1)j}f(x_{(k+1)j}). \tag{9.4}$$

This method of approximation is illustrated in Figure 9.2. The relevant $f(x_j)$ is approximated by $\hat{f}(x_j)$ lying on the line segment having $x_{kj}$ and $x_{(k+1)j}$ as end points. Clearly, the greater the number of intervals and the smaller the length of these intervals, the closer the approximation will be to the actual value of the function.

One can therefore approximate the functions in the objective function by

$$\hat{f}_j(x_j) = \sum_{k=1}^{K+1} \beta_{kj}f_j(x_{kj}) = \sum_{k=1}^{K+1} \beta_{kj}f_{kj},$$

and those in the constraints by

$$\hat{g}_{ij}(x_j) = \sum_{k=1}^{K+1} \beta_{kj}g_{ij}(x_{kj}) = \sum_{k=1}^{K+1} \beta_{kj}g_{kij}$$

subject to the earlier qualification on the $\beta_{kj}$'s. The programming problem of (9.2a–c) can thus be approximated by the problem

$$\text{Maximize} \qquad Z = \sum_{j=1}^{n} \sum_{k=1}^{K+1} \beta_{kj} f_{kj} \tag{9.2$\hat{a}$}$$

$$\text{subject to} \quad \sum_{j=1}^{n} \sum_{k=1}^{K+1} \beta_{kj} g_{kij} = d_i, \qquad i = 1, \ldots, m, \tag{9.2$\hat{b}$}$$

$$\sum_{k=1}^{K+1} \beta_{kj} = 1, \qquad j = 1, \ldots, n, \tag{9.2$\hat{d}$}$$

$$\beta_{kj} \geq 0, \tag{9.2$\hat{e}$}$$

and if $\beta_{tj} > 0$, either $\beta_{(t-1)j} + \beta_{tj} = 1$ or $\beta_{tj} + \beta_{(t+1)j} = 1$, and all other $\beta_{kj} = 0$.

Problem (9.2$\hat{a}$–$\hat{e}$) is a linear programming problem in which the $\beta_{kj}$'s replace the $x_j$'s as the variables. Note that $x_j$ no longer appears in the problem, hence we do not have an Equation (9.2$\hat{c}$) akin to (9.2c). If $f_r(x_r)$ and $g_{ir}(x_r)$ $(i = 1, \ldots, m)$ are already linear functions, there is no need to call upon the approximation procedure, and these functions and the $x_r$ would be carried along as in the original problem. To solve this new LP problem, however, we must utilize a *restricted-basis-entry* variant of the simplex technique. Through restricted basis entry we allow for the fact that at most two of the $\beta_{kj}$'s can appear in a solution, and then these must be adjacent.

To illustrate the technique, consider problem (9.1a–b) with $Q_j \geq 0$ $(j = 1, 2, 3)$. Here we have separable functions: $f_1(Q_1) = 1000Q_1 - 50Q_1^2$, $f_2(Q_2) = 400Q_2 - 10Q_2^2$, $g_{11}(Q_1) = 500Q_1$, $g_{12}(Q_2) = 300Q_2$, and $g_{13}(Q_3) = Q_3$. Assuredly, $0 \leq Q_1 \leq 10$ and $0 \leq Q_2 \leq 16.67$. In the case of $Q_1$ the restriction is in terms of both storage capacity and the fact that $Q_1 = 10$ is the unconstrained marginal revenue equals marginal cost optimum; in the case of $Q_2$, 20 is the unconstrained marginal revenue equals marginal cost optimum, but storage capacity restricts output to a maximum of 16.67. $Q_3$ enters the problem as a linear function only, so we need not fool with it.

*For expository purposes,* let us divide $Q_1$ into the five equal intervals between 0 and 10, and $Q_2$ into the three equal intervals between 0 and 16.67. Each of the functions $f_1$, $f_2$, $g_{11}$, and $g_{12}$ must now be evaluated at the end points of these intervals. This is done in Table 9.1.

TABLE 9.1

| $Q_{k1}$ | $f_1$ | $g_{11}$ | $Q_{k2}$ | $f_2$ | $g_{12}$ |
|---|---|---|---|---|---|
| 0 | 0 | 0 | 0 | 0 | 0 |
| 2 | 1800 | 1000 | 5.56 | 1915 | 1668 |
| 4 | 3200 | 2000 | 11.12 | 3211 | 3336 |
| 6 | 4200 | 3000 | 16.67 | 3889 | 5000 |
| 8 | 4800 | 4000 | | | |
| 10 | 5000 | 5000 | | | |

Thus,

$$\hat{f}_1(Q_1) = \sum_{k=1}^{6} \beta_{k1} f_1(Q_{k1}) = 0\beta_{11} + 1800\beta_{21} + 3200\beta_{31} + 4200\beta_{41} + 4800\beta_{51} + 5000\beta_{61}.$$

Similar expressions are developed for the remaining functions $\hat{f}_2(Q_2)$, $\hat{g}_{11}(Q_1)$, and $\hat{g}_{12}(Q_2)$. The approximation of the original problem thereby becomes

Maximize

$$\hat{Z} = 0\beta_{11} + 1800\beta_{21} + 3200\beta_{31} + 4200\beta_{41} + 4800\beta_{51} + 5000\beta_{61} + 0\beta_{12} + 1915\beta_{22} + 3211\beta_{32} + 3889\beta_{42} + 0Q_3, \qquad (9.1\hat{a})$$

subject to

$$0\beta_{11} + 1000\beta_{21} + 2000\beta_{31} + 3000\beta_{41} + 4000\beta_{51} + 5000\beta_{61} + 0\beta_{12} + 1668\beta_{22} + 3336\beta_{32} + 5000\beta_{42} + Q_3 = 5000, \qquad (9.1\hat{b})$$

$$\beta_{11} + \beta_{21} + \beta_{31} + \beta_{41} + \beta_{51} + \beta_{61} = 1, \qquad (9.1\hat{c})$$
$$\beta_{12} + \beta_{22} + \beta_{32} + \beta_{42} = 1,$$

$$Q_3, \beta_{k1}, \beta_{k2} \geq 0 \qquad \text{for all } k. \qquad (9.1\hat{d})$$

This is a linear programming problem with eleven variables and three constraints, with the additional qualification that at most two, and then only adjacent, $\beta_{kj}$'s may enter the solution. As there are a total of three constraints in (9.1$\hat{b}$) and (9.1$\hat{c}$), the fundamental result of linear programming tells us that *at most* three $\beta_{kj}$'s will be nonzero and hence that at least one $\beta_{k1}$ or $\beta_{k2}$ will necessarily be equal to one. This means that either or both of the approximate optimal $Q_1$ or $Q_2$ will lie exactly on the end point $Q_{k1}$ or $Q_{k2}$. Thus the choice of interval bounds may be particularly important in this example.

The problem is solved in the chapter Appendix to yield the following optimum values to the approximating problem: $\beta_{41} = 1$, so that $\hat{Q}_1 = 6$; $\beta_{22} = .8010$, $\beta_{32} = .1990$, and $\hat{Q}_2 = 6.67$; $Q_3 = 0$ and $\hat{Z} = 6373$. The $\hat{Q}_i$ are quite close to the values obtained earlier of $Q_1 = \frac{40}{7}$ and $Q_2 = \frac{50}{7}$. One reason why the approximation is so good is that the single initial constraint is already in linear form. $\hat{Z}$ differs from the earlier $\pi$ of 6429, however, for two reasons: (1) because the values for $Q_1$ and $Q_2$ are slightly different, (2) because of the nonlinearity in the objective function, which is being approximated by a series of linear segments. Having solved the problem for values of $\hat{Q}_1$ and $\hat{Q}_2$, however, we would determine the *actual* prices and costs from the actual demand and cost curves, and the *actual* $\pi$ by substitution into (9.1a) rather than (9.1$\hat{a}$). $\hat{Z}$ underestimates $\pi$ because of the *concavity* of the objective function. Note, however, that given the concavity or convexity of the constraints, the amount absorbed by the "left side" will be under- or overestimated by the approximating function. Thus, while the solution obtained will be feasible for the approximating problem, it will not necessarily be feasible for the actual problem.

Moreover, unless the functions involved have the appropriate convexity properties noted below, the approximating technique may simply lead one to a local rather than global optimum. That is, if "in the neighborhood" of a point (that is, a finitely small interval about the point) there is no value of the function higher than that of the point, there is a local optimum; if nowhere is there a value of the function exceeding that at the point, it is a global optimum. Thus, if in the optimal approximating solution $\beta_{kj}$ and $\beta_{(k+1)j}$ are positive, then $x_{kj} \leq \hat{x}_{kj} \leq x_{(k+1)j}$. Any $x$ "in the neighborhood" of $\hat{x}_{kj}$ also lies in this interval and $\beta_{tj} = 0$, $t \neq k$, $k + 1$. When only $\beta_{kj} = 1$, $\hat{x}_j = x_{kj}$, and only $\beta_{(k-1)j}$ or $\beta_{(k+1)j}$ can become positive "in the neighborhood" of $x_j$. The simplex technique assures that, in the former case permitting $\beta_{(k-1)j}$ or $\beta_{(k+2)j}$ to enter the basis, or in the latter case permitting $\beta_{(k-1)j}$ or $\beta_{(k+1)j}$ to enter the basis, would lower the value of the objective function, for their simplex values are negative. We have therefore attained the highest local maximum in the interval about $\hat{x}_j$. Because of the restricted-basis-entry condition whereby *non-adjacent* $\beta_{tj}$'s might have positive simplex values but not be permitted into the basis, we cannot be certain that we have a global maximum.[5]

## 9.3 THE KUHN-TUCKER CONDITIONS

As a further generalization of the firm's output decision, suppose the firm produces $i = 1, \ldots, n$ products, each of which may be produced via $k = 1, \ldots, q$ different processes.[6,7] In the case of a single process, $q = 1$. These processes may differ in terms of, say, the facilities used or the technology employed. Let $Q_{ik}$ denote the amount of the $i$th product produced via the $k$th process. Then the total output of product $i$ is the sum over all $q$ processes, or

$$Q_i = \sum_{k=1}^{q} Q_{ik}.$$

Suppose that during a time period of $T$ the demand for $Q_i$ is given by $P_i = D(Q_i)$. The total cost curve for $Q_{ik}$—that is, the cost of producing $i$ via the $k$th process—is given by $C_{ik} = c_{ik}(Q_{ik})$. Total profit will be

$$\pi = \sum_i P_i Q_i - \sum_i \sum_k C_{ik} = \sum_i D(Q_i)Q_i - \sum_i \sum_k c_{ik}(Q_{ik}).$$

Suppose too that during this time period different numbers of the firm's products *each* require the use of $j = 1, \ldots, m$ fixed factors of production. Let $a_{ikj}$ be the

[5] If, however, the functions have the proper convexity requirements, then restricted basis entry is not required. See Hadley, *Nonlinear and Dynamic Programming*, pp. 123–126.

[6] Although this would seem to further stretch the firm's information requirements, Julius C. Margolis ["The Analysis of the Firm: Rationalism, Conventionalism, and Behaviorism," *Journal of Business*, **XXXI**:3 (July 1958), 187–199] has argued as follows: "The development of a set of products with varying designs and prices is both more profitable and less risky than... simple price variation... because of the exploitation of the different sections of the demand curve which are sequentially discovered, and... since it involves less information directly accessible to the firm" (p. 197).

[7] This type of decision has been beyond the capacity of the traditional marginal analysis. In "The Equilibrium of the Firm in Multi-Process Industries" [*Quarterly Journal of Economics*, **LIX**:1 (Feb. 1945), 280–286] Wilford J. Eiteman suggests that "it is absurd to claim that entrepreneurs strive, consciously or unconsciously, to expand their scale of operations until marginal costs equal marginal returns. As a matter of fact, the concept of marginal output is foreign to the thinking of the average plant manager, possibly because the simplest practical application of marginal analysis to multi-process industry is too complex to constitute a working guide in practice" (p. 284). Note, however, that we shall herein be using a "type" of marginal analysis that, while indeed complex, is not sufficiently so to make it impractical as a working guide in practice.

amount of the $j$th fixed factor required by a unit of product $i$ produced via process $k$. Also, denote the available amount of the $j$th fixed factor by $\bar{F}_j$. Then, we require that

$$\sum_{i=1}^{n} \sum_{k=1}^{q} a_{ikj}Q_{ik} \leq \bar{F}_j, \qquad j = 1, \ldots, m$$

—that is, total output of all products cannot take up more of the $j$th fixed factor than is available.

Finally, suppose the firm has negotiated an agreement—for example, a labor contract—whereby the proportion of product $r$ produced by process $s$ must be *at least* 25 percent; but suppose also that the proportion declines as total output of product $r$ increases. The specific requirement is that $Q_{rs}/Q_r \geq .25 + Q_r^{-a}$ (where $a$ is a positive constant), or $Q_{rs} \geq .25Q_r + Q_r^{1-a}$. Further, at least $\bar{Q}_{rs} > 0$ units of $Q_{rs}$ *must be* produced or $Q_{rs} \geq \bar{Q}_{rs}$.

The firm's production problem may now be summarized as

$$\text{Maximize} \qquad \pi = \sum_{i=1}^{n} D(Q_i)Q_i - \sum_{i=1}^{n} \sum_{k=1}^{q} c_{ik}(Q_{ik}) \tag{9.5a}$$

$$\text{subject to} \qquad \sum_{i=1}^{n} \sum_{k=1}^{q} a_{ikj}Q_{ik} \leq \bar{F}_j, \qquad j = 1, \ldots, m, \tag{9.5b}$$

$$Q_{rs} - .25Q_r - Q_r^{1-a} \geq 0, \tag{9.5c}$$

$$Q_{rs} \geq \bar{Q}_{rs}, \tag{9.5d}$$

$$\sum_{k=1}^{q} Q_{ik} - Q_i = 0, \qquad i = 1, \ldots, n, \tag{9.5e}$$

$$Q_i, Q_{ik} \geq 0, \qquad i = 1, \ldots, n; k = 1, \ldots, q. \tag{9.5f}$$

This is a problem in *nonlinear programming*. Here, an objective function that need not be linear is maximized subject to a series of constraints that (1) also may contain nonlinear terms; (2) may be expressed as equalities or inequalities; and (3) may place certain restrictions, such as nonnegativity, on the variables. Since one can always convert inequalities to equalities by the introduction of slack variables, it is the restrictions on the levels of the variables that prevent the use of Lagrangian techniques. A problem such as (9.5a–f) can, however, frequently be solved via an approach based on a set of conditions that *must be* fulfilled if the objective function is to be maximized or minimized. These conditions are due to Kuhn and Tucker.[8] The Kuhn-Tucker conditions will be sufficient as well as necessary when the functions in question have certain curvature properties to be noted below.

To develop the Kuhn-Tucker conditions, let us consider the problem:

$$\text{Maximize} \qquad Z = f(x_1, \ldots, x_n) \tag{9.6a}$$

$$\text{subject to} \quad g_i(x_1, \ldots, x_n, x_{si}) = d_i, \qquad i = 1, \ldots, m, \tag{9.6b}$$

$$x_{si}, x_j \geq 0. \tag{9.6c}$$

[8] H. W. Kuhn and A. W. Tucker, "Nonlinear Programming," in J. Neyman, ed., *Proceedings of the Second Berkeley Symposium on Mathematical Statistics and Probability* (Berkeley, Calif.: University of California Press, 1951), pp. 481–492.

Here, $x_{si}$ is a slack variable added linearly to the $i$th constraint such that $x_{si}$ appears as an addition (subtraction) to the left side if the original constraint is a less (greater) than inequality. If $x_{si}$ does not appear in the $i$th constraint of (9.6b), the original constraint is initially an equality.

Now, were it not for the restriction (9.6c), the problem could be formulated and solved as a Lagrangian problem involving (9.6a) and (9.6b). The Lagrangian objective function would be

$$L(x_1, \ldots, x_n; x_{s1}, \ldots, x_{sm}; \lambda_1, \ldots, \lambda_m) = f(x_1, \ldots, x_{sm}) - \sum_{i=1}^{m} \lambda_i[g_i(x_1, \ldots, x_n, x_{si}) - d_i],$$

and the problem would be

$$\text{Maximize} \quad L(\mathbf{x}, \boldsymbol{\lambda}) = f(\mathbf{x}) + (-\boldsymbol{\lambda}')[\mathbf{g} - \mathbf{d}], \tag{9.7}$$

where $\mathbf{x}'$ is the $1 \times (n + m)$ row vector $(x_1, \ldots, x_{sm})$; $\boldsymbol{\lambda}'$ is a $1 \times m$ row vector $\boldsymbol{\lambda}' = (\lambda_1, \ldots, \lambda_m)$; $\mathbf{d}' = (d_1, \ldots, d_m)$ or $\mathbf{d}$ is an $m \times 1$ column vector; and $\mathbf{g}$ is an $m \times 1$ column vector, where $\mathbf{g}' = (g_1, \ldots, g_m)$. The "prime" will be used to indicate transpose.

To solve (9.7) we seek (1) an $\mathbf{x} = \mathbf{x}^*$ such that $L(\mathbf{x}^*, \bar{\boldsymbol{\lambda}}) \geq L(\mathbf{x}, \bar{\boldsymbol{\lambda}})$ for all $\mathbf{x} \neq \mathbf{x}^*$ and $\boldsymbol{\lambda} = \bar{\boldsymbol{\lambda}}$, the specific set of $\lambda_i$'s selected; simultaneously, we seek (2) a $\boldsymbol{\lambda} = \boldsymbol{\lambda}^*$ such that $L(\bar{\mathbf{x}}, \boldsymbol{\lambda}^*) \leq L(\bar{\mathbf{x}}, \boldsymbol{\lambda})$ for all $\boldsymbol{\lambda} \neq \boldsymbol{\lambda}^*$ and $\mathbf{x} = \bar{\mathbf{x}}$, the specific set of $x_j$'s selected. In the first instance, the problem is to determine $\mathbf{x}$ such that once $\boldsymbol{\lambda}$ has been chosen, the Lagrangian function will be maximized. In the second instance, the problem is to determine $-\boldsymbol{\lambda}$ such that once $\mathbf{x}$ has been chosen, the Lagrangian function is *maximized;* or alternatively $+\boldsymbol{\lambda}$ must be determined such that once $\mathbf{x}$ has been chosen, the Lagrangian function is *minimized* (because of the minus sign in parentheses). These two conditions combine into the single condition $L(\mathbf{x}, \boldsymbol{\lambda}^*) \leq L(\mathbf{x}^*, \boldsymbol{\lambda}^*) \leq L(\mathbf{x}^*, \boldsymbol{\lambda})$. When this condition holds for all $\mathbf{x}$ and $\boldsymbol{\lambda}$ in the neighborhood of $(\mathbf{x}^*, \boldsymbol{\lambda}^*)$, the point $(\mathbf{x}^*, \boldsymbol{\lambda}^*)$ is said to be a *saddle point.* At the saddle point, the Lagrangian is *maximized* with respect to $\mathbf{x}$, given the *optimal* $\boldsymbol{\lambda}$, and *minimized* with respect to $\boldsymbol{\lambda}$, given the optimal $\mathbf{x}$. This terminology calls forth the image of the saddle whose center is a minimum from one standpoint, and a maximum from another. This is consistent with the use of the term saddle point in the game-theoretic sense. Moreover, a mixed-strategy pair that *minimizes* one player's expected loss while *maximizing* the other player's expected gain is also a saddle point.

In seeking the solution to (9.7), then, we are seeking a saddle point of the Lagrangian. Consider a particular $x_j$, say $x_t$. Set all other $x_j$ at their optimal levels of $x_j^*$ $(j \neq t)$; and, let $\boldsymbol{\lambda} = \boldsymbol{\lambda}^*$. It is assumed that $L(\mathbf{x}, \boldsymbol{\lambda})$ is continuous and differentiable. Let us first graph $L(\mathbf{x}, \boldsymbol{\lambda})$ as a function of $x_t$. In particular, suppose the function is a *concave* function of $x_t$ as in Figure 9.3(a)(i). As long as $x_t$ is not required to be nonpositive, *this* function will take on its global maximum where $\partial L/\partial x_t = 0$ and $x_t > 0$. If $x_t$ *is* required to be nonpositive, *this* function will be maximized with respect to $x_t$ at the upper bound of $x_t$. Here, $x_t = 0$ and $\partial L/\partial x_t > 0$. If the concave function is like that of Figure 9.3(a)(ii), as long as $x_t$ is not required to be nonnegative, *this* function will take on its global maximum where $\partial L/\partial x_t = 0$ and $x_t < 0$. If $x_t$ *is* required to be nonnegative, then *this* function will be maximized with respect to $x_t$ where $x_t = 0$ and $\partial L/\partial x_t < 0$.

Alternatively, suppose $L(\mathbf{x}, \boldsymbol{\lambda})$ is a *convex* function of $\lambda_i = \lambda_{t'}$. Let all other $\lambda_i = \lambda_i^*$ $(i \neq t')$ and $x_j = x_j^*$, such as in Figure 9.3(b). This function will take on its unrestricted minimum where $\partial L/\partial \lambda_{t'} = 0$. To minimize $L(\mathbf{x}, \boldsymbol{\lambda})$ with respect to $\lambda_{t'}$ we shall want to set $\lambda_{t'}$ such that $\partial L/\partial \lambda_{t'} = 0$ unless $\lambda_{t'}$ is restricted in sign. If $\lambda_{t'}$ must be nonnegative, either $\partial L/\partial \lambda_{t'} = 0$ or, as in Figure 9.3(b)(i), $\lambda_{t'} = 0$ and $\partial L/\partial \lambda_{t'} > 0$; if $\lambda_{t'}$ must be nonpositive, either $\partial L/\partial \lambda_{t'} = 0$ or, as in Figure 9.3(b)(ii), $\lambda_{t'} = 0$ and $\partial L/\partial \lambda_{t'} < 0$.

Moreover, as Figure 9.3 suggests, a convex function necessarily takes on its global maximum, and a concave function necessarily takes on its global minimum, at one of its bounds. Thus, the maximization (minimization) of a convex (concave) function of a single variable requires no terribly seductive algorithms. Further, if the function is convex over certain ranges and concave over others, as in Figure 9.3(c), determining the global max or min will require one to test alternative local optima. One can, however, take advantage of the observations that have just been made with respect to the functions in Figures 9.3(a) and 9.3(b), as well as those made previously

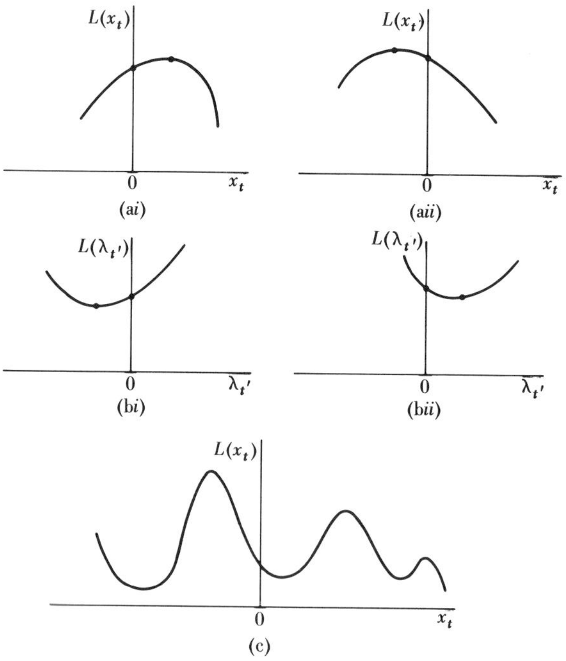


Fig. 9.3

with respect to Figure 9.1, and arrive at some conclusions about where a concave function of several variables takes on its maximum, and where a convex function takes on its minimum, in the presence or absence of certain constraints.

In particular, suppose that $L(\mathbf{x}, \boldsymbol{\lambda})$ of (9.7) is a concave function that we seek to maximize. We seek a saddle point $(\mathbf{x}^*, \boldsymbol{\lambda}^*)$. If a saddle point is to obtain at $(\mathbf{x}^*, \boldsymbol{\lambda}^*)$, and if $x_t$ say is restricted by $x_t \geq 0$, then $\partial L(\mathbf{x}^*, \boldsymbol{\lambda}^*)/\partial x_t^* \leq 0$, with $x_t^* = 0$ when $\partial L(\mathbf{x}^*, \boldsymbol{\lambda}^*)/\partial x_t < 0$. This holds, for if $\partial L(\mathbf{x}^*, \boldsymbol{\lambda}^*)/\partial x_t > 0$ a further increase in

$x_t$ beyond $x_t^*$ would raise $L(\mathbf{x}^*, \boldsymbol{\lambda}^*)$. Generalizing this, a saddle point requires as necessary conditions:

$$\begin{aligned}
&\text{(1a)} \quad \frac{\partial L(\mathbf{x}^*, \boldsymbol{\lambda}^*)}{\partial x_j} \{\leq, =, \geq\}\ 0 \text{ for } x_j\{\geq 0, \text{unrestricted}, \leq 0\},\\
&\text{(1b)} \quad \frac{\partial L(\mathbf{x}^*, \boldsymbol{\lambda}^*)}{\partial \lambda_i} \{\leq, =, \geq\}\ 0 \text{ for } \lambda_i\{\leq 0, \text{unrestricted}, \geq 0\},\\
&\text{(2a)} \quad x_j^* \left(\frac{\partial L(\mathbf{x}^*, \boldsymbol{\lambda}^*)}{\partial x_j}\right) = 0, \qquad j = 1, \ldots, n, s1, \ldots, sm,\\
&\text{(2b)} \quad \lambda_i^* \left(\frac{\partial L(\mathbf{x}^*, \boldsymbol{\lambda}^*)}{\partial \lambda_i}\right) = 0, \qquad i = 1, \ldots, m.
\end{aligned} \tag{9.8}$$

It can also be shown[9] that if $L(\mathbf{x}, \boldsymbol{\lambda}^*)$ is a concave function of $\mathbf{x}$, and if $L(\mathbf{x}^*, \boldsymbol{\lambda})$ is a convex function of $\boldsymbol{\lambda}$, the necessary conditions (9.8) are sufficient.

Now the problem we started with, or (9.6a–c), is: Max $Z = f(\mathbf{x})$, subject to $g_i(\mathbf{x}) = d_i$; $x_j, x_{si} \geq 0$ for all $j$ and $i$. It is assumed the functions are continuous and differentiable. The Lagrangian function is

$$L(\mathbf{x},\boldsymbol{\lambda}) = f(\mathbf{x}) - \sum_{i=1}^{m} \lambda_i[g_i(\mathbf{x}) - d_i]$$

so that at all points, including the saddle point,

$$\frac{\partial L}{\partial x_t} = \frac{\partial f(\mathbf{x})}{\partial x_t} - \sum_{i=1}^{m} \lambda_i \left(\frac{\partial g_i(\mathbf{x})}{\partial x_t}\right).$$

Specifically at the saddle point, if $x_t^* > 0$, then $\partial L(\mathbf{x}^*, \boldsymbol{\lambda}^*)/\partial x_t = 0$. If $x_t^* = 0$, then *either* $\partial L(\mathbf{x}^*, \boldsymbol{\lambda}^*)/\partial x_t = 0$ or $\partial L(\mathbf{x}^*, \boldsymbol{\lambda}^*)/\partial x_t < 0$ by condition (1a) of (9.8). Thus, it is necessarily true that for a solution to (9.6a–c) to occur at $(\mathbf{x}^*, \boldsymbol{\lambda}^*)$,

$$\frac{\partial f(\mathbf{x}^*)}{\partial x_t} - \sum_{i=1}^{m} \lambda_i^* \left(\frac{\partial g_i(\mathbf{x}^*)}{\partial x_t}\right) \leq 0,$$

or

$$\frac{\partial f(\mathbf{x}^*)}{\partial x_t} \leq \sum_{i=1}^{m} \lambda_i^* \left(\frac{\partial g_i(\mathbf{x}^*)}{\partial x_t}\right). \tag{9.9}$$

That is, the constraints must be such that as $x_t$ increases beyond $x_t^*$, the effects of the increase on the constraints outweigh the effects on the objective function. If this were not so, we could simply go on to increase $x_t$ without bound. Moreover, $\partial L(\mathbf{x}^*, \boldsymbol{\lambda}^*)/\partial d_i = \lambda_i^*$ and it is clear that where $x_{si} = 0$ and the constraint is of the $\geq$ form, an increase in $d_i$ can only *reduce* $f(\mathbf{x})$ as the constraint is being made tighter; alternatively, a reduction in $d_i$ can leave $f(\mathbf{x})$ unchanged and force $x_{si} > 0$, or increase $f(\mathbf{x})$ (and *perhaps* force $x_{si} > 0$). Thus, with the constraint of the $\geq$ form, $\partial L(\mathbf{x}^*, \boldsymbol{\lambda}^*)/\partial d_i = \lambda_i^* \leq 0$. Similarly, where the constraint is of the $\leq$ form and $x_{si} = 0$, a decrease

[9] See Hadley, *Nonlinear and Dynamic Programming*, pp. 85–87, 191–193.

in $d_i$ can only reduce $f(\mathbf{x})$ as the constraint is being made tighter; alternatively, an increase in $d_i$ *might* increase $f(\mathbf{x})$. Hence, with the constraint of the $\leq$ form, $L(\mathbf{x}^*, \boldsymbol{\lambda}^*)/\partial d_i = \lambda_i^* \geq 0$. Where the constraints are originally equalities, the $\lambda_i^*$ may take on either sign. This analysis also indicates that where a constraint is not binding, so that $x_{si} > 0$, $\lambda_i^* = 0$ since $\partial L(\mathbf{x}^*, \boldsymbol{\lambda}^*)/\partial d_i = \lambda_i^* = 0$. Specifically, all that is affected at the margin is $x_{si}$, and the latter does not enter into $f(\mathbf{x})$—that is, $x_{si}$ is altered, but it does not contribute to the objective function.

Recalling that $L(\mathbf{x}, \boldsymbol{\lambda}) = f(x_1, \ldots, x_n) - \sum_{i=1}^{m} \lambda_i[g_i(x_1, \ldots, x_n, x_{si}) - d_i]$ will have an *absolute* maximum at $\mathbf{x}^*$ for a given set of $\lambda_i = \lambda_i^*$ if the function is a concave function of $\mathbf{x}$, it is now apparent that $L(\mathbf{x}, \boldsymbol{\lambda})$ will indeed satisfy this condition if: (1) $f(\mathbf{x})$ is concave for $\mathbf{x} \geq 0$; and (2) $g_i(\mathbf{x})$ is concave when $\lambda_i^* < 0$ or $g_i(\mathbf{x}) \geq d_i$ and binding. The latter assures that $\sum_{i=1}^{m} \lambda_i[g_i(x_1, \ldots, x_{si}) - d_i]$ will be a convex function of $\mathbf{x}$ and hence *the negative of this will be a concave function* of $\mathbf{x}$ and the sum of concave functions is concave. Further, $L(\mathbf{x}, \boldsymbol{\lambda})$ is a linear, and hence convex (or concave), function of $\boldsymbol{\lambda}$. Thus both $f(\mathbf{x}, \boldsymbol{\lambda}^*) \leq f(\mathbf{x}^*, \boldsymbol{\lambda}^*)$ and $f(\mathbf{x}^*, \boldsymbol{\lambda}^*) \leq f(\mathbf{x}^*, \boldsymbol{\lambda})$; or, $(\mathbf{x}^*, \boldsymbol{\lambda}^*)$ is a global saddle point. If the appropriate convexity or concavity in the constraints is absent, we may simply have a local maximum for $f(\mathbf{x}^*)$, say, or indeed, $\mathbf{x}^*$ may be a minimum point or a saddle point.

The vitally important Kuhn-Tucker optimality conditions for solving problems of the form (9.6a–c) are therefore as follows: with $f(\mathbf{x})$ a concave function of $\mathbf{x}$, conditions (9.8), the necessary conditions for a saddle point must hold at $(\mathbf{x}^*, \boldsymbol{\lambda}^*)$ for a relative maximum to exist at this point. It is also true, moreover, that when $g_i(\mathbf{x})$ is convex (concave) if $\lambda_i^* > (<) \ 0$, (9.8) becomes necessary *and* sufficient for $(\mathbf{x}^*, \boldsymbol{\lambda}^*)$ to be a global saddle point.

To illustrate these powerful concepts, let us apply them to a problem of the form of (9.5a–f). We suppose that the firm produces two products in the amounts $Q_1$ and $Q_2$; the demand curves are $P_1 = 500 - 2Q_1$ and $P_2 = 1000 - 3Q_2$. There are two processes available for producing $Q_1$. The output of the first process is denoted by $Q_{11}$ and that of the second by $Q_{12}$. The total costs of producing $Q_{11}$, $Q_{12}$, and $Q_2$ are given by $C_{11} = 100 + 50Q_{11}$, $C_{12} = 500 + 25Q_{12}^2$, and $C_2 = 400 + 100Q_2$. Total profit is therefore given by

$$\pi = 500Q_1 - 2Q_1^2 + 900Q_2 - 3Q_2^2 - 50Q_{11} - 25Q_{12}^2 - 1000. \qquad (9.10a)$$

$Q_{11}$, $Q_{12}$, and $Q_2$ each require the use of a single fixed factor, thereby imposing upon the firm the constraint that

$$2Q_{11} + 5Q_{12} + 2Q_2 \leq 230. \qquad (9.10b)$$

Moreover, by prior union agreement, at least half the output of product 1 must be produced by the first process and at least one unit must be produced; or,

$$\frac{Q_{11}}{Q_1} \geq .5 \quad \text{and} \quad Q_1 \geq 1,$$

so that

$$Q_{11} - .5Q_1 \geq 0, \qquad (9.10c)$$

$$Q_1 \geq 1, \qquad (9.10d)$$

and $Q_{11} + Q_{12} = Q_1$, or

$$Q_{11} + Q_{12} - Q_1 = 0, \tag{9.10e}$$

$$Q_1, Q_{11}, Q_{12}, Q_2 \geq 0. \tag{9.10f}$$

The functions in (9.10a–e) do in fact have the appropriate convexity properties such that the application of the Kuhn-Tucker conditions will be sufficient as well as necessary for a global optimum. The problem's solution is shown in the chapter Appendix to be $Q_1^* = 24$, $Q_2^* = 91$, $Q_{11}^* = 24$, $Q_{12}^* = 0$; and from the demand curves, $P_1 = 452$, $P_2 = 727$, and $\pi^* = 66{,}905$.

To complement the algebraic solution and further clarify the fundamentals of the present approach, suppose we are considering the optimum production point with $Q_{12}^* = 0$, and let us seek a solution to the problem via the graphical approach. With $Q_{12} = 0$, $Q_{11} = Q_1$ and the objective function can be written

$$\frac{(Q_1 - 112.5)^2}{\frac{1}{2}} + \frac{(Q_2 - 150)^2}{\frac{1}{3}} + (\pi - 91{,}812.5) = 0. \tag{9.10a'}$$

This equation describes a set of concentric ellipses with the center at ($Q_1 = 112.5$, $Q_2 = 150$). At this point, $\pi$ takes on its maximum value of 91,812.5. As $\pi$ diminishes, the ellipses expand. As in the problem of the previous section, once again the constraints prevent the firm from attaining an $MR = MC$ position for either product. In the case of $Q_2$, the $MR = MC$ output would be 150. With $Q_{12} = 0$, the $MR = MC$ output for $Q_{11}$ would be 112.50 (with $Q_{11} = 0$, the $MR = MC$ output for $Q_{12}$ would be 9.36). In particular, with $Q_{12} = 0$, the shaded area of Figure 9.4 represents the

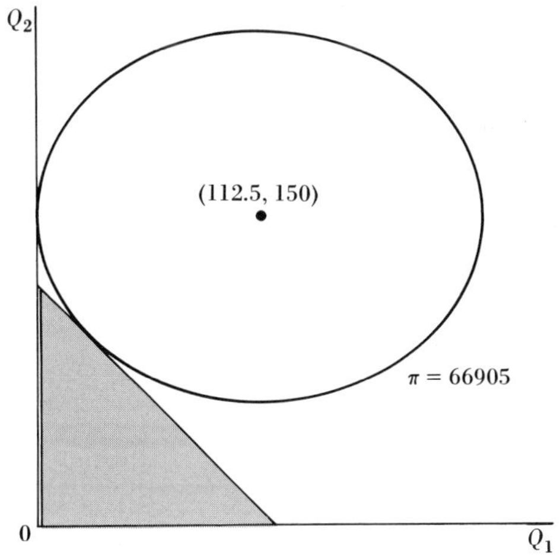


Fig. 9.4

closed convex set of feasible solutions. The smallest ellipse of the form of (9.10a′) having at least one point in the shaded area is the ellipse drawn for $\pi = 66{,}905$. This ellipse is tangent to the line $2Q_1 + 2Q_2 = 230$ at the optimum production point ($Q_1 = 24$, $Q_2 = 91$). For this problem, then, the Kuhn-Tucker conditions demand that we perform this same operation, but in four dimensions, and this is what the algebra in the Appendix is doing: it is testing various boundaries.

It should also be noted that while a solution to the nonlinear programming problem may be found, as a rule the task is by no means easy. For example, if in the present problem $\lambda_2 \neq 0$, then since $\lambda_2^*(\partial L(\mathbf{Q}^*, \boldsymbol{\lambda}^*)/\partial\lambda_2) = 0$, we have as an equality

$$\frac{\partial L(\mathbf{Q}^*, \boldsymbol{\lambda}^*)}{\partial \lambda_2} = Q_{11} - .5Q_1 = 0;$$

if $Q_1 \neq 0$, then since $Q_1^*(\partial L(\mathbf{Q}^*, \boldsymbol{\lambda}^*)/\partial Q_1) = 0$, we have as an equality

$$\frac{\partial L(\mathbf{Q}^*, \boldsymbol{\lambda}^*)}{\partial Q_1} = 500 - 4Q_1 + .5\lambda_2 - \lambda_3 + \lambda_4 = 0.$$

In general, since any $\lambda_i$ $(i = 1, \ldots, m)$ may be zero or not zero, the number of ways in which combinations of the constraints may hold as equalities equals the number of ways in which $m$ things may be divided into 2 groups, or $2^m$; the number of ways in which combinations of the $\partial L(\mathbf{x}, \boldsymbol{\lambda})/\partial x_j$ $(j = 1, \ldots, n + m)$ may equal zero will be equal to the number of ways in which $n + m$ things may be divided into 2 groups, or $2^{n+m}$. Thus, there may be as many as $2^m 2^{n+m} = 2^{2m+n}$ combinations of simultaneous equations to solve, and solutions to test. As in the present instance, with constraints holding as equalities and certain variables necessarily positive, these combinations are reduced, but the task of solution can still be formidable.

It should be noted too that, by contrast with linear programming, with the introduction of nonlinearities the number of constraints no longer restricts the number of variables at nonzero levels in the optimal solution. Moreover, note that if the feasible set of solutions looked like that of Figure 9.5 rather than Figure 9.4, more than one ellipse would be tangent to a boundary. In this case, the feasible set is not convex, and a local optimum will not necessarily be a global optimum. When, however, we

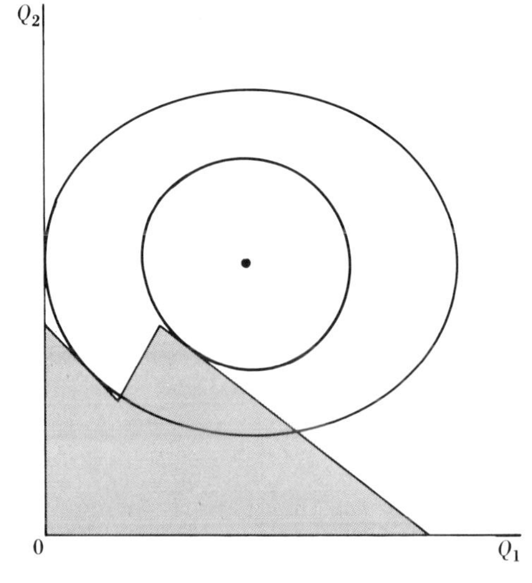


Fig. 9.5

require $g_i(\mathbf{x})$ to be convex for $g_i(\mathbf{x}) - d_1 \leq 0$, recall that we are demanding that this constraint define a convex set of feasible solutions; and, since the intersection of convex sets is also convex, the sufficiency conditions are equivalent to requiring that the set of feasible solutions be convex.

## 9.4 QUADRATIC PROGRAMMING

Let us now consider the special case in which the constraints of a programming problem are linear and the objective function is of a quadratic form. That is, the objective function is a second-degree polynomial so that all variables are raised to positive integer powers and the sum of the powers in any single term does not exceed two. This problem is a *quadratic programming* problem. Through the application of the Kuhn-Tucker conditions to such a problem, there evolves a series of necessary and sufficient conditions that are amenable to solution by several methods, one of which is another variant on the simplex technique of linear programming.[10] In effect, the Kuhn-Tucker conditions transform the original quadratic programming problem into an equivalent linear programming problem. It might be remarked that the quadratic formulation, while a special case of nonlinearity, is by no means a remote possibility. Indeed, the previous two problems described were quadratic programming problems.

As a case in point, suppose a firm produces a product in accordance with the production function $Q = 2HF_1F_2 - aF_1^2 - bF_2^2 + cF_1 + dF_2$ and subject to the cost constraint $w_1F_1 + w_2F_2 \leq C$, where $H$, $a$, $b$, $c$, $d$, $w_1$, $w_2$, and $C$ are constants, and $F_1$ and $F_2$ are the factor service inputs. Thus we assume only that costs *cannot exceed* an amount $C$. Suppose too an agreement has been made to employ the factors in a fashion such that $F_1/F_2 \geq d_1$, $F_2 \geq d_2$, and $F_2 \leq d_3$, all $d_i$ positive constants, $d_2 \leq d_3$. For example, the manufacturer might require the firm to use no more than 16 and no fewer than 10 type-A machines, and at least twice as many type-B machines. This would define a quadratic programming problem: namely, to maximize the quadratic function $Q$ subject to the four constraints (since $F_1$ and $F_2$ are necessarily positive). Since the constraints are linear, there will be a global maximum if $Q$ is concave. This requires that

$$\begin{vmatrix} \partial^2Q/\partial F_1^2 = -2a & \partial^2Q/\partial F_1\,\partial F_2 = 2H \\ \partial^2Q/\partial F_2\,\partial F_1 = 2H & \partial^2Q/\partial F_2^2 = -2b \end{vmatrix} > 0$$

or $H^2 < ab$, and $a$ and $b > 0$ (so that $\partial^2Q/\partial F_1^2$ and $\partial^2Q/\partial F_2^2 < 0$). Graphically, once again the problem is to reach a point on the smallest ellipse defined by the quadratic objective function, any point of which lies within the convex feasible region established by the constraints.

For the general formulation of the problem, suppose that $\mathbf{x}' = (x_1, \ldots, x_n)$, $\mathbf{d}' = (d_1, \ldots, d_m)$, $\mathbf{c}' = (c_1, \ldots, c_n)$, $\mathbf{D}$ is a negative semidefinite $n \times n$ symmetric matrix,[11] and $\mathbf{A} = [a_{ij}]$ $(i = 1, \ldots, m; j = 1, \ldots, n)$. The quadratic objective function may be written $Z = \mathbf{c}'\mathbf{x} + \mathbf{x}'\mathbf{D}\mathbf{x}$, and the quadratic programming problem

[10] See P. Wolfe, "The Simplex Method for Quadratic Programming," *Econometrica*, **27**:3 (July 1959), 382–398. For alternative approaches and further discussion see Hadley, *Nonlinear and Dynamic Programming*, chap. 7, and C. Van de Panne and Andrew Whinston, "A Parametric Simplicial Formulation of Houthakker's Capacity Method," *Econometrica*, **34**:2 (April 1966), 354–380.

[11] A matrix $\mathbf{D}$ is negative semidefinite if and only if $\mathbf{x}'\mathbf{D}\mathbf{x} \leq 0$ for all $\mathbf{x}$.

may be written

$$\text{Maximize} \quad Z = \mathbf{c}'\mathbf{x} + \mathbf{x}'\mathbf{D}\mathbf{x} \tag{9.11a}$$

$$\text{subject to} \quad \mathbf{A}\mathbf{x} = \mathbf{d}, \tag{9.11b}$$

$$\mathbf{x} \geq \mathbf{0}, \tag{9.11c}$$

where the slack variables have already been included in the constraints (9.11b) and for convenience we assume there is a total of $n$ variables. The assumption that $\mathbf{D}$ is symmetric is not at all very restrictive, since we might make it so where necessary via an appropriate transformation of coefficients; the assumption that it is negative semidefinite is necessary to assure the concavity of the objective function.[12]

First form the function $L(\mathbf{x},\boldsymbol{\lambda}) = \mathbf{c}'\mathbf{x} + \mathbf{x}'\mathbf{D}\mathbf{x} - \boldsymbol{\lambda}'[\mathbf{A}\mathbf{x} - \mathbf{d}]$, where $\boldsymbol{\lambda}' = (\lambda_1, \ldots, \lambda_m)$. Since $\mathbf{x} \geq \mathbf{0}$, application of (1a) of (9.8), the Kuhn-Tucker conditions, requires that $\partial L(\mathbf{x}^*, \boldsymbol{\lambda}^*)/\partial x_j \leq 0$ or

$$\frac{\partial L(\mathbf{x}^*, \boldsymbol{\lambda}^*)}{\partial \mathbf{x}} = \mathbf{c} + 2\mathbf{D}'\mathbf{x}^* - \mathbf{A}'\boldsymbol{\lambda}^* \leq \mathbf{0}.$$

Note that $\partial L/\partial \mathbf{x}$ is an $n \times 1$ column *vector* and $\mathbf{0}$ is the zero *vector*. We may now add an $n \times 1$ slack *vector* $\mathbf{x}_s^* \geq \mathbf{0}$ to the left side of the preceding inequality to obtain $\mathbf{c} + 2\mathbf{D}'\mathbf{x}^* - \mathbf{A}'\boldsymbol{\lambda}^* + \mathbf{x}_s^* = \mathbf{0}$, or after moving $\mathbf{c}$ to the right-hand side,

$$2\mathbf{D}'\mathbf{x}^* - \mathbf{A}'\boldsymbol{\lambda}^* + \mathbf{x}_s^* = -\mathbf{c}. \tag{9.12a}$$

Further, application of (2a) of (9.8) requires that $(\mathbf{x}^*)'[\partial L(\mathbf{x}^*, \boldsymbol{\lambda}^*)/\partial \mathbf{x}^*] = 0$. But,

$$(\mathbf{x}^*)'\left[\frac{\partial L(\mathbf{x}^*, \boldsymbol{\lambda}^*)}{\partial \mathbf{x}^*}\right] = (\mathbf{x}^*)'[\mathbf{c} + 2\mathbf{D}'\mathbf{x}^* - \mathbf{A}'\boldsymbol{\lambda}^*] = -(\mathbf{x}^*)'\mathbf{x}_s^*$$

by substitution from (9.12a). Hence (2a) of (9.8) requires $-(\mathbf{x}^*)'\mathbf{x}_s^* = 0$, or

$$(\mathbf{x}^*)'\mathbf{x}_s^* = 0. \tag{9.12b}$$

Moreover, since the constraints of (9.11b) hold as equalities, the components of $\boldsymbol{\lambda}$ are unrestricted in sign. Thus, (1b) and (2b) of (9.8) require that the column vector $\partial L(\mathbf{x}^*, \boldsymbol{\lambda}^*)/\partial \boldsymbol{\lambda}^* = \mathbf{0}$, or

$$\mathbf{A}\mathbf{x}^* - \mathbf{d} = \mathbf{0}. \tag{9.12c}$$

Since the constraints are linear and the objective function is concave, (9.12a–c), the Kuhn-Tucker constraints, are both necessary and sufficient for an optimal solution to (9.11a–c). We thus seek vectors $\mathbf{x} \geq \mathbf{0}$, $\mathbf{x}_s \geq \mathbf{0}$, and $\boldsymbol{\lambda}$ satisfying (9.12a–c); or, in matrix notation, we must solve the equations

$$\begin{bmatrix} 2\mathbf{D}' & -\mathbf{A}' & \mathbf{I} \\ \mathbf{A} & \bar{\mathbf{0}} & \bar{\mathbf{0}} \end{bmatrix} \begin{bmatrix} \mathbf{x} \\ \boldsymbol{\lambda} \\ \mathbf{x}_s \end{bmatrix} = \begin{bmatrix} -\mathbf{c} \\ \mathbf{d} \end{bmatrix}, \tag{9.13}$$

[12] More appropriately, to avoid possible computational difficulties $\mathbf{D}$ will be assumed to be negative definite, so that $\mathbf{x}'\mathbf{D}\mathbf{x} < 0$ for all $\mathbf{x}$.

If $\mathbf{D} = [d_{ij}]$ were not symmetric, the coefficient of $x_i x_j$ $(i \neq j)$, which is $d_{ij} + d_{ji}$, would be derived with $d_{ij} \neq d_{ji}$. One can then define $\tilde{d}_{ij} = \tilde{d}_{ji} = (d_{ij} + d_{ji})/2$, form the matrix $\tilde{\mathbf{D}} = [\tilde{d}_{ij}]$, and restate the objective function in terms of $\tilde{\mathbf{D}}$.

where $\mathbf{I}$ is an $n \times n$ identity matrix, and $\bar{\mathbf{0}}$ is a zero *matrix*, subject to $\mathbf{x} \geq \mathbf{0}, \mathbf{x}_s \geq \mathbf{0}$, and $\mathbf{x}'\mathbf{x}_s = 0$.

Now, (9.13) contains $n + m + n$ unknowns and $n + m$ equations. Since

$$\mathbf{x}'\mathbf{x}_s = \sum_j x_j x_{sj} = 0,$$

but $x_j \geq 0$ and $x_{sj} \geq 0$, it must then follow that $x_j x_{sj} = 0$ $(j = 1, \ldots, n)$. Therefore no more than $n$ of the $\mathbf{x}$ and $\mathbf{x}_s$ variables may be positive. As there are $m$ components in $\boldsymbol{\lambda}$, there will be at most $n + m$ variables in the solution. Hence, we seek a *basic* solution to (9.13) such that $\mathbf{x} \geq 0$, $\mathbf{x}_s \geq 0$, and $\mathbf{x}'\mathbf{x}_s = 0$.

The simplex method will be used to obtain this basic solution. To initiate the process, artificial variables are introduced into (9.12a). This equation then becomes

$$2\mathbf{D}'\mathbf{x} - \mathbf{A}'\boldsymbol{\lambda} + \mathbf{x}_s + \mathbf{E}\mathbf{x}_A = -\mathbf{c}, \tag{9.12a$'$}$$

with $\mathbf{E} = [e_{ij}]$ an $n \times n$ matrix, where $e_{ij} = 0$ for $i \neq j$; and $e_{jj} = +1$ if $c_j$ is negative and $e_{jj} = -1$ if $c_j$ is positive; $\mathbf{x}_A$ is an $n \times 1$ column vector. We can now set the $j$th component of $\mathbf{x}_A$ equal to $c_j$ if $c_j$ is positive, or to $-c_j$ if $c_j$ is negative and thereby obtain an initial basic feasible solution to (9.12a′) solely in terms of the components of $\mathbf{x}_A$. We require these to be nonnegative in order to apply linear programming to solve (9.13). That is, we can now form $Z = -\mathbf{i}'\mathbf{x}_A$, where $\mathbf{i}'$ is the sum vector, as the objective function in a linear programming problem with the objective to maximize $Z$. As an LP problem, however, we require $\mathbf{x}_A \geq \mathbf{0}$. Clearly, the components of $\mathbf{x}_A$ will be forced out of the solution to assure $Z = 0$, and we shall return to the original equations (9.13).

An additional problem in applying the simplex technique is that $\lambda_i$ is unrestricted in sign. To deal with this problem, we set $\lambda_j = \lambda_{+j} - \lambda_{-j}$ and require $\lambda_{+j} \geq 0$ and $\lambda_{-j} \geq 0$. Hence, either $\lambda_{+j}$ or $\lambda_{-j}$ will enter the solution, but not both, as the coefficient vectors associated with each will be exactly the same, but opposite in sign. Hence their simplex criteria will differ only in sign. Writing $\boldsymbol{\lambda} = \boldsymbol{\lambda}_+ - \boldsymbol{\lambda}_-$, we therefore have transformed (9.13) into the LP problem:

Maximize $Z = -\mathbf{i}'\mathbf{x}_A$ subject to

$$\begin{bmatrix} 2\mathbf{D}' & -\mathbf{A}' & \mathbf{A}' & \mathbf{I} & \mathbf{E} \\ \mathbf{A} & \bar{\mathbf{0}} & \bar{\mathbf{0}} & \bar{\mathbf{0}} & \bar{\mathbf{0}} \end{bmatrix} \begin{bmatrix} \mathbf{x} \\ \boldsymbol{\lambda}_+ \\ \boldsymbol{\lambda}_- \\ \mathbf{x}_s \\ \mathbf{x}_A \end{bmatrix} = \begin{bmatrix} -\mathbf{c} \\ \mathbf{d} \end{bmatrix}, \tag{9.13$'$}$$

$$\mathbf{x}, \boldsymbol{\lambda}_+, \boldsymbol{\lambda}_-, \mathbf{x}_s, \mathbf{x}_A \geq \mathbf{0}; \qquad \mathbf{x}'\mathbf{x}_s = 0.$$

As illustrated in the Appendix to this chapter, the problem may be solved via the simplex technique with restricted basis entry. That is, just as the separable-functions approach permitted the admission of at most two, and then only adjacent, $\beta_{kj}$ in solution, here entry to the solution is restricted by the condition $x_j x_{sj} = 0$.

As a specific problem, suppose the firm's production function is given by $Q = 30F_1F_2 - 20F_1^2 - 15F_2^2 + 20F_1 + 10F_2$. If factors 1 and 2 are available for hire at unit prices of $w_1 = 3$ and $w_2 = 2$, and if the firm's expenditures on the factors must be less than 10, the firm's cost constraint becomes

$$3F_1 + 2F_2 \leq 10.$$

Further, suppose that the additional restriction is imposed that $F_1/F_2 \geq 1$, $F_2 > 0$. Then the firm's production problem becomes the quadratic programming problem:

$$\text{Maximize} \quad Q = 30F_1F_2 - 20F_1^2 - 15F_2^2 + 20F_1 + 10F_2 \tag{9.14a}$$

$$\text{subject to} \quad 3F_1 + 2F_2 + F_3 = 10, \tag{9.14b}$$

$$F_1 - F_2 - F_4 = 0, \tag{9.14c}$$

$F_1, F_2 > 0$, $F_3, F_4 \geq 0$. The strict inequality on $F_1$ and $F_2$ means that the convex set of feasible solutions does not contain all of its boundary points. Though this could be troublesome, in the present instance it is not. The optimal solution, as obtained in the Appendix, is $F_1^* = 2$, $F_2^* = 2$, $F_3^* = 0$, $F_4^* = 0$, and $Q^* = 40$; $\lambda_{+1} = 2$ and $\lambda_{-2} = 6$, so that the $\lambda_i$'s have the "correct" sign. It should be noted that the unconstrained maximum is $F_1 = 3$, $F_2 = 3.33$, and $Q = 46.7$.

## 9.5 INTEGER PROGRAMMING

As indicated earlier in this chapter, it will frequently be imperative to obtain the solution to a programming problem strictly in terms of integers. When the variables normally assume large values such as $x_1^* = 2{,}371{,}462.15$ and $x_2^* = 381{,}641.72$, and when their coefficients in the objective function are small, it is unlikely that one can justify any additional effort beyond a simple rounding of the optimal solutions, so long as care is taken to maintain their feasibility under the constraints. When, however, the problem involves comparatively small magnitudes for variables making comparatively large contributions to the objective function, it can be most important that the *optimal integer* solution be obtained. This is the task of *integer programming.* In this section we shall illustrate the possibilities of integer programming using the Gomory technique.[13] This is a procedure for obtaining optimal integer solutions for a linear programming problem in which *all* variables must be integers.

Consider the integer programming problem:

$$\text{Maximize } Z_I = \sum_{j=1}^{n} c_j x_j,$$

$$\text{subject to} \sum_{j=1}^{n} a_{ij}x_j \leq d_i, \quad i = 1, \ldots, m,$$

$$x_j = 0, 1, 2, \ldots, \text{integer}, \quad j = 1, \ldots, n.$$

If we add a slack variable $x_{n+i}$ to the $i$th constraint such as to make it an equality, we shall also want this variable to be a nonnegative integer. This is because the technique to be developed requires that *all* variables be integers. In order to assure that $x_{n+i} = 0, 1, 2, \ldots$, integer, the coefficients $a_{ij}$ and $d_i$ must be integers. It is *always* possible to state these as integers, simply by multiplying both sides of a constraint by a large enough constant to eliminate all fractions, while maintaining the inequality. For example, we may write the constraint $1.21x_1 + 1.35x_2 \leq 71.61$ as $121x_1 + 135x_2 \leq 7161$ by multiplying both sides by 100. We may therefore assume that when we start the procedure, $a_{ij}$ and $d_i$ will be integers.

[13] See Ralph E. Gomory, "An Algorithm for Integer Solutions to Linear Programs," in Graves and Wolfe, eds., *Recent Advances in Mathematical Programming*, pp. 269–302.

If we ignore the integer condition, we are confronted by an ordinary *linear* programming problem whose optimal solution may be found using the simplex technique. Since the optimal solution to the LP problem may itself be an integer solution, our procedure is to first obtain the optimal LP solution and hope. If this solution is an integer solution, the task is completed. If this solution is a noninteger solution, we attempt to move from *it* to an integer solution. The procedure involves the imposition of further restrictions on the solution; hence, the optimal integer solution can yield a value of the objective function that is *at best equal* to the value of the objective function for the optimal LP solution.

In particular, suppose the optimal LP solution to the integer programming problem above includes $x_1, \ldots, x_m$ at nonzero levels. These are indexed as such only for notational convenience. Suppose also that $x_k = K > 0$ is not an integer. The final tableau in the application of the simplex technique will therefore include an equation that would appear as follows:

$$0x_1 + 0x_2 + \cdots + x_k + \cdots + 0x_m + b_{m+1}x_{m+1} + \cdots + b_{m+n}x_{m+n} = K, \qquad (9.15)$$

where $x_{m+1}, \ldots, x_{m+n}$ equal zero, as they are not in the solution. Since $K$ is not an integer, it may be written as $K = I + F$, where $I$ is a nonnegative integer or zero, and $F$ is a positive fraction such that $0 < F < 1$. Similarly, any of the $b_{m+j}$ may be written as $b_{m+j} = I_{m+j} + f_{m+j}$, where $I_{m+j}$ is an integer, *not necessarily positive*, or zero; and, $f_{m+j}$ is a nonnegative fraction such that $0 \leq f_{m+j} < 1$.[14] Thus, if $K = 17.5$, $I = 17$ and $F = .5$; if $b_{m+j} = -2.3$, $I_{m+j} = -3$ and $f_{m+j} = .7$. Hence, (9.15) may be rewritten as

$$x_k + \sum_{j=1}^{n} (I_{m+j} + f_{m+j})x_{m+j} = I + F. \qquad (9.16)$$

But in the optimal *integer* solution $x_k$ will equal some integer $I_k$, or be zero; and $x_{m+j}$ will equal an integer $I_j$, or be zero. Hence $(I_{m+j} + f_{m+j})x_{m+j}$ will equal $I_{m+j}I_j + f_{m+j}x_{m+j} = I'_{m+j} + f_{m+j}x_{m+j}$ in the optimal integer solution, where $I'_{m+j} = 0, 1, 2, \ldots,$ integer. We may therefore subtract $I_k$ and the $I'_{m+j}$ from both sides of (9.16) to obtain

$$\sum_{j=1}^{n} f_{m+j}x_{m+j} = I + F - I_k - \sum_{j=1}^{n} I'_{m+j} = I^* + F, \qquad (9.16a)$$

where $I^*$, as the difference or sum of of integers, is itself an integer or zero.

Certainly any optimal integer solution must satisfy (9.16a). Further, because $f_{m+j} \geq 0$ and $x_{m+j} \geq 0$ $(j = 1, \ldots, n)$, the left side of (9.16a) is necessarily nonnegative. Hence the right side is nonnegative. This implies that $I^* = 0, 1, 2, \ldots,$ *positive* integer. This follows inasmuch as $0 < F < 1$, and if $I^*$ were negative, the

[14] $f_{m+j}$ and $b_{m+j}$ are then said to be *congruent*, for the difference between them is $b_{m+j} - f_{m+j} = I_{m+j}$ or an integer. Two numbers $a$ and $b$ are said to be congruent modulo $M$ if the difference between them, $a - b$, is divisible by $M$—that is, $(a - b)/M =$ integer. In determining the $f_{m+j}$, we seek the smallest positive fraction congruent (modulo 1) to $b_{m+j}$. One could also develop the procedure that follows by taking advantage of the properties of congruent numbers.

right side of (9.16a) would be negative. Therefore (9.16a) implies

$$\sum_{j=1}^{n} f_{m+j}x_{m+j} \geq F. \tag{9.16b}$$

The latter is an additional constraint, *the cutting plane*, that the programming problem must satisfy if an integer solution is to be obtained. It literally cuts away solutions that were previously considered feasible, making them nonfeasible. In particular, the original constraints define a closed convex set of solutions, but the only points in this set that are feasible solutions are the integer solutions. If the optimal extreme point to the LP problem is an integer solution, the integer programming problem is solved. If this extreme point is not an integer solution, we then utilize additional information about the properties of the optimal integer solution to reduce the original convex set of solutions. That is, we impose an additional boundary on this convex set. We then determine the optimal LP extreme point for the reduced convex set: if this extreme point is an integer solution, the original problem is solved; if not, we shall further reduce the convex set of solutions, and proceed anew. For example, the dots in Figure 9.6 represent feasible integer solutions

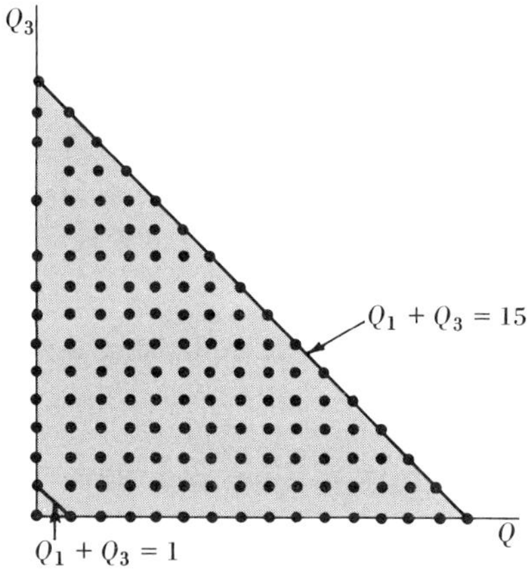


Fig. 9.6

in the $Q_1$-$Q_3$ space for a problem discussed in the Appendix. The line labeled $Q_1 + Q_3 = 1$ is a cutting plane developed for this problem, and the shaded area contains the reduced set of feasible integer solutions.

Adding and subtracting artificial and slack variables $x_{S1}$ and $x_{A1} = 0, 1, 2, \ldots,$ integer to make (9.16b) an equality, we may rewrite (9.16b) as

$$0x_1 + 0x_2 + \cdots + 0x_m + f_{m+1}x_{m+1} + \cdots + f_{m+n}x_{m+n} - x_{S1} + x_{A1} = F. \tag{9.17}$$

In the Gomory technique, we now add (9.17) to the final LP tableau, after adding $0x_{S1} + 0x_{A1}$ to the other equations in the tableau. The original LP problem is thereby replaced by a new LP problem with one additional constraint—(9.17). An immediate basic solution to the problem is available containing $x_1, \ldots, x_m$ and $x_{A1}$ in the basis.

In this solution, $x_1, \ldots, x_m$ are at their optimal LP levels, and $x_{A1} = F$. Proceeding from this solution, the new set of $m + 1$ constraints is manipulated via the simplex technique to yield new basic solutions until a second optimum is obtained—this time for the LP problem with $m + 1$ constraints. If in this new optimum solution all variables are integers, the problem is completed; if not, a second cutting plane must be developed and constraint $m + 2$ added to the problem. Additional constraints are added until the simplex technique yields, for the LP problem containing these and the original constraints, an optimum solution that is in integer form. Thus additional variables may enter into the optimal solution to push the number of nonzero variables beyond the number of *original* constraints.

It should be noted that only a single cutting plane will be added for each noninteger optimum solution. This is true even though at any stage more than one variable may be in noninteger form. In the latter instance there is no single "best" equation from which to develop the cutting plane, although one choice can *turn out* to have been more efficient than another. An arbitrary rule is to develop the cutting plane from that equation whose "$K$" has the largest fractional part "$F$". It should also be noted that this procedure can all too often demand the addition of several cutting planes, and will not necessarily yield an optimum integer solution in one's lifetime. Sometimes we reach a solution quickly and sometimes we do not. At some point it might be well to inspect the solution and to compare the value of the objective function for a rounded solution at that stage with the optimal LP solution. It could then become clear that the rounded solution is in fact the optimal integer solution. For example, if the coefficients in the objective function are integers, then the highest value that an integer solution can yield will also be an integer. If the optimal LP solution is $Z^* = 217{,}616.9$, since $Z_I \leq Z^*$ the optimal integer solution can be no greater than $Z_I^* = 217{,}616$. If this is indeed the value of $Z_I$ obtained with the rounded variables, then simply rounding off yields an optimum solution. Moreover, if the rounded solution is, say, 217,610, one might question whether the *possible* addition of 6 to the objective function is worth the additional effort entailed by further application of the Gomory technique.

Consider, for example, the firm producing a single product via two processes. Management believes that to all intents and purposes the firm operates in a purely competitive market, and that in the relevant range its demand curve is perfectly elastic at a price of \$10,000. Production costs are a constant \$9000 and \$8000 per unit in processes 1 and 2, respectively. The processes require the joint use of a single fixed factor of which a total of 15 units are available. Each unit produced via process 1, $Q_1$, takes up a single unit of the fixed factor; each unit produced by process 2, $Q_2$, takes up two units of the fixed factor; total output is $Q = Q_1 + Q_2$. The profit-maximizing firm's production problem is thus

$$\begin{aligned} \text{Maximize} \quad & \pi = 10{,}000Q - 9000Q_1 - 8000Q_2 \\ \text{subject to} \quad & Q_1 + 2Q_2 \leq 15, \\ & Q - Q_1 - Q_2 = 0, \\ & Q, Q_1, Q_2 = 0, 1, 2, \ldots, \text{integer}. \end{aligned}$$

If this were treated as a linear programming problem with two constraints, at most two of the variables would be positive; and it is quite apparent that there will be exactly two because of the second constraint. These are $Q_2^* = Q^* = \frac{15}{2}$, and

$\pi^* = 15{,}000$. As shown in the Appendix to this chapter, the integer solution admits the third variable into solution. Nevertheless, and although the optimal integer solution of $Q^* = 8$, $Q_1^* = 1$, and $Q_2^* = 7$ differs from the optimal LP solution, the profit at this optimum remains $\pi^* = 15{,}000$. This will not, however, generally be the case.

## 9.6 THE TRANSPORTATION PROBLEM

A second special class of linear programming problems are the so-called *transportation problems*. The latter invoke a special LP technique, one commonly applied in connection with problems that involve determining the optimal allocation of shipments from a set of $m$ starting points to a set of $n$ final locales. The nomenclature can be misleading, however, for the technique may have somewhat broader application whenever a problem can be conveniently couched within the basic framework of a transportation problem.

Suppose that a firm produces a single product at three different plants. Average production cost is constant and equal at all plants. The product is subsequently shipped to five different retail outlets. The $c_{ij}$ entries in the first three rows and five columns of Table 9.2 represent the unit shipping costs from plant $i = 1, \ldots, 3$ to outlet $j = 1, \ldots, 5$. The marginal entries denoted $K_i$ and $O_j$ represent the plant capacities and the outlets' requirements, respectively. The zero entries for $c_{i6}$ ($i = 1, \ldots, 3$) in the sixth column occur since "outlet" 6 is a "slack outlet." This is included because the plants' capacities exceed the outlets' requirements. Thus, there is zero transportation cost associated with a nonshipment. The inclusion of the slack outlet enables us to generalize that the total plant capacity always equals the total outlet requirement. Along with the optimal shipping pattern, we shall therefore determine the plant or plants having excess capacity.[15]

TABLE 9.2

Unit Cost Table

| | $O_1$ | $O_2$ | $O_3$ | $O_4$ | $O_5$ | $O_6$ | $K_i$ |
|---|---|---|---|---|---|---|---|
| $K_1$ | 8 | 2 | 6 | 5 | 3 | 0 | 15 |
| $K_2$ | 5 | 7 | 6 | 3 | 6 | 0 | 25 |
| $K_3$ | 3 | 6 | 2 | 5 | 4 | 0 | 15 |
| $O_j$ | 10 | 15 | 10 | 5 | 10 | 5 | 55 |

The objective in the transportation problem of Table 9.2 would be to minimize total shipping cost. If we let $x_{ij}$ denote the number of units shipped from plant $i$

[15] If the outlets' requirements exceed the total plant capacity, this presents the additional difficulty that in order to resolve the shipment question, we also require some notion as to the cost of failing to satisfy each outlet's requirements.

to outlet $j$, the problem is:

$$\text{Minimize} \qquad C = \sum_{i=1}^{3} \sum_{j=1}^{6} c_{ij} x_{ij} \tag{9.18a}$$

$$\text{subject to} \quad \sum_{i=1}^{3} x_{ij} = O_j \qquad (j = 1, \ldots, 6), \tag{9.18b}$$

$$\sum_{j=1}^{6} x_{ij} = K_i \qquad (i = 1, \ldots, 3), \tag{9.18c}$$

$$\sum_{j=1}^{6} O_j = \sum_{i=1}^{3} K_i, \tag{9.18d}$$

$$x_{ij} \geq 0. \tag{9.18e}$$

As shown in the Appendix, an optimal solution is $x_{12}^* = 15$; $x_{21}^* = 5$, $x_{24}^* = 5$, $x_{25}^* = 10$, $x_{26}^* = 5$, $x_{31}^* = 5$, $x_{33}^* = 10$; and, the cost minimum is $C^* = 2(15) + 5(5) + 3(5) + 6(10) + 0(5) + 3(5) + 2(10) = 165$. As is also indicated, there is an alternative solution yielding the same cost minimum.

The problem framed by equations (9.18a–e) is readily seen to be a linear programming problem in which the coefficient matrix is of a rather special sort. In the general case, the problem would be:

$$\text{Minimize} \qquad C = \sum_{i=1}^{m} \sum_{j=1}^{n} c_{ij} x_{ij}$$

$$\text{subject to} \quad \sum_{i=1}^{m} x_{ij} = O_j \qquad (j = 1, \ldots, n),$$

$$\sum_{j=1}^{n} x_{ij} = K_i \qquad (i = 1, \ldots, m),$$

$$\sum_{j=1}^{n} O_j = \sum_{i=1}^{m} K_i,$$

$$x_{ij} \geq 0.$$

There are a total of $m \times n$ variables, $x_{ij}$; and, in addition to nonnegativity, there are a total of $m + n$ constraints on the $x_{ij}$. *Any one* of these constraints may be considered to be redundant, however, since

$$\sum_{j=1}^{n} O_j = \sum_{i=1}^{m} K_i.$$

For example, the latter equality implies that

$$O_k = \sum_{i=1}^{m} K_i - \sum_{\substack{j=1 \\ j \neq k}}^{n} O_j = \sum_{i=1}^{m} \Big( \sum_{j=1}^{n} x_{ij} \Big) - \sum_{\substack{j=1 \\ j \neq k}}^{n} \Big( \sum_{i=1}^{m} x_{ij} \Big) = \sum_{i=1}^{m} x_{ik}.$$

That is, the $m$ constraints involving the $K_i$, and the $n - 1$ constraints involving the $O_j$, but excluding $O_k$, imply the $k$th constraint established by $O_k$; or $\sum_{i=1}^{m} x_{ik} = O_k$. Hence, we actually have only $m + n - 1$ *independent* constraints. A basic solution to the problem will therefore include at most $m + n - 1$ variables at nonzero levels. In the problem above, there are $3 + 6 - 1 = 8$ independent constraints, but only 7 variables at nonzero levels in the optimal basic solution; the latter is degenerate.

It will help us understand subsequent algebraic manipulations if we set the stage by making some initial probes toward solving the problem of Table 9.2. The first step is to get a basic feasible solution. One such possibility, first suggested by A. Victor Hunt and E. Wainright Peck, is given in Table 9.2′. A more efficient method for obtaining an initial basic feasible solution is suggested in the Appendix.

TABLE 9.2′

Initial Basic Feasible Solution

| | $O_1$ | $O_2$ | $O_3$ | $O_4$ | $O_5$ | $O_6$ | |
|---|---|---|---|---|---|---|---|
| $K_1$ | | 10 | | | 5 | | 15 |
| $K_2$ | 10 | 5 | | 5 | | 5 | 25 |
| $K_3$ | | | 10 | | 5 | | 15 |
| $O_j$ | 10 | 15 | 10 | 5 | 10 | 5 | 55 |

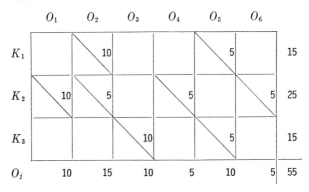

There are eight allocations, so that this basic feasible solution is nondegenerate (but only because of Mr. Peck's influence). The cost of this scheme is $C_1 = 2(10) + 3(5) + 5(10) + 7(5) + 3(5) + 0(5) + 2(10) + 4(5) = 175$. We shall want to consider the effect on the cost of an allocation to any one of the $x_{ij}$ that currently equals zero. In particular, suppose we were to allocate some units to $x_{25}$. We could accomplish this, *starting from the present pattern*, by reducing $x_{15}$, increasing $x_{12}$, and reducing $x_{22}$, all by the amount allocated to $x_{25}$. In this way, all row and column totals are left unchanged. Each unit so rerouted costs 6 to ship to $x_{25}$ and 2 to ship to $x_{12}$; but the saving from *not* having to ship the unit to $x_{15}$ is 3, and the saving from not having to ship to $x_{22}$ is 7. The *net* saving in rerouting a single unit will therefore be $(3 + 7) - 2 - 6 = 2$. The total of $3 + 7 - 2 = 8$ will be referred to as an indirect cost savings of making a shipment to $x_{25}$; 6 will be called the direct cost. Their difference is the net cost savings. Since each unit so reallocated results in a savings of 2, we shall want to reallocate in this way as many units as possible. The maximum number possible is 5, since neither $x_{15}$ nor $x_{22}$ can be reduced by more than 5. If no other reallocation offers a greater per unit net cost savings—and none does—we shall reallocate in this manner. If any other single reallocation would promise a higher net cost saving, per unit, we would select that reallocation. In the transportation technique, we proceed in this fashion, going from one basic feasible solution to the next, until there is no reallocation that promises a positive net cost saving.

More generally, suppose that an initial nondegenerate basic feasible solution to the general transportation problem is found such that $m + n - 1$ of the $x_{ij} > 0$. Consider a nonbasic variable $x_{rt} = 0$; this is equivalent to the previous $x_{25}$. Suppose we introduce $x_{rt}$ into the current basic solution at a level of $\theta$. Since

$$\sum_{i=1}^{m} x_{it} = O_t,$$

some currently basic variable $x_{ut}$ (equivalent to $x_{15}$) will have to be reduced by $\theta$ when $x_{rt}$ is set at $\theta$. But

$$\sum_{j=1}^{n} x_{uj} = K_u.$$

Hence, when $x_{ut}$ is reduced by $\theta$, some other basic variable $x_{uv}$ (equivalent to $x_{12}$) will have to be increased by $\theta$. But increasing $x_{uv}$ by $\theta$ will require that another basic variable $x_{wv}$ (equivalent to $x_{22}$) be reduced by $\theta$, since

$$\sum_{i=1}^{m} x_{iv} = O_v.$$

This process continues until we determine that the basic variable $x_{rz}$ must be reduced by $\theta$. Then, since

$$\sum_{j=1}^{n} x_{rj} = K_j,$$

we shall have to increase an $x_{rj}$ by $\theta$; and, the selected $x_{rj}$ is, of course, the originally increased variable $x_{rt}$. Now, the complete system of equations is once again in balance. If $x_{B_{ij}}$ is a basic variable with a contribution coefficient of $c_{B_{ij}}$, when $x_{rt}$ is introduced in the amount of $\theta$, the objective function is initially increased by $\theta c_{rt}$. The objective function is then further changed by

$$\sum_{ij} (\pm)\theta c_{B_{ij}} = \theta \sum_{ij} (\pm) c_{B_{ij}},$$

where the sign of $c_{B_{ij}}$ is $(+)$ if $x_{B_{ij}}$ is decreased, and $(-)$ if $x_{B_{ij}}$ is increased when $x_{rt}$ is introduced. Since each $x_{B_{ij}}$ that is affected changes by $\theta$, the net change in the objective function is given by

$$\Delta_{rt} = \theta \left[ c_{rt} - \sum_{ij} (\pm) c_{B_{ij}} \right].$$

The term in the brackets is simply the simplex criterion. This gives the per unit change in the objective function effected by introducing $\theta$ units of $x_{rt}$ into the solution. To determine the variable to introduce, we choose that nonbasic variable with the largest *negative* simplex, since the problem is one of cost minimization. Given that $x_{rt}$ is to be introduced, we wish to make $\theta$ as big as possible in order to make $\Delta_{rt}$ as large a reduction as possible. In setting $x_{rt} = \theta$, we need to consider that all $x_{ij}$ must be nonnegative. The only constraints on $\theta$ are, however, those imposed by the $x_{B_{ij}}$ being reduced by $\theta$. Hence we shall set $\theta = \min x_{B_{ij}^-}$ where the $B_{ij}^-$ signals the fact that the basic variable will be *reduced* by $\theta$.

The $c_{rt}$ term in $\Delta_{rt}$ is called the *direct cost* per unit of "shipping" from $r$ to $t$; the $\sum_{ij} (\pm) c_{B_{ij}}$ is called the *indirect cost savings* of rescheduling one unit throughout the current basic solution's "shipping" pattern. To solve the transportation problem, a table of indirect costs is calculated for each basic solution considered and the entries are compared with the corresponding entries in the direct cost table. The variable with the largest excess of indirect cost to direct cost is introduced to the solution. The procedure continues until there are no indirect cost savings exceeding the direct costs. At this point an optimum solution is reached. Where some of the $c_{rt} = \sum_{ij} (\pm) c_{B_{ij}}$ but none are less, there are alternative optima.

The advantage of this computational procedure is the following. Let $\bar{c}_{rt}$ be the indirect cost associated with $x_{rt}$. Then it can be shown that $\bar{c}_{rt} - \bar{c}_{r(t+k)} = c_{t+k} =$ a constant, and $\bar{c}_{rt} - \bar{c}_{(r+q)t} = c_{r+q} =$ a constant. That is, the difference between the elements in any two columns (the first expression) or any two rows (the second expression) of an indirect cost table is constant. To see this, note that when $x_{rt}$ was introduced at a level of $\theta$ we first reduced $x_{ut}$. Had we introduced $x_{(r+q)t}$, again we could first reduce $x_{ut}$, as this same variable is a basic variable in the $t$th column. The series of increases and decreases in the $x_{B_{ij}}$ would be comparable in either case, and the indirect costs would thus involve the same $c_{B_{ij}}$ terms. Whereas, however, the adjustments associated with the introduction of $x_{rt}$ stopped when the basic variable $x_{rz}$ was reduced, those associated with the introduction of $x_{(r+q)t}$ stop when the basic variable $x_{(r+q)z}$ is reduced. The difference in the two indirect costs, per unit, thus boils down to the difference between $c_{rz}$ and $c_{(r+q)z}$, the only two cost terms that differ. This difference is independent of $t$. That is $\bar{c}_{rt} - \bar{c}_{(r+q)t} = c_{rz} - c_{(r+q)z} = c_{r+q}$ $(t = 1, \ldots, n)$. Moreover, since the simplex criterion for a basic variable is zero, the indirect and direct costs of the basic variables are equal. Thus, to compute an indirect cost table, we need merely enter into the table the known direct costs of those variables in the solution, and compute the remaining entries by maintaining a constant difference between any two rows and any two columns. This is illustrated in the end-of-chapter Appendix for the problem of Table 9.2.[16]

## 9.7 DUALITY

We have seen that solving the nonlinear programming problem

$$\begin{aligned} &\text{Maximize} & Z &= f(\mathbf{x}) & & \\ &\text{subject to} & g_i(\mathbf{x}) &= d_i & &(i = 1, \ldots, m), \\ &\text{or} & \mathbf{g}(\mathbf{x}) &= \mathbf{d}, & &\mathbf{x} \geq \mathbf{0} \end{aligned} \tag{9.19}$$

[16] Note that if the entries in the direct cost table, Table 9.2, were actually profits, and if the problem were one of profit maximization, the sole difference in the procedure would be that we would wish to *increase* the value of the objective function at each stage. Thus, we would choose to introduce into the solution that variable with the largest excess of direct "profits" over indirect "profits."

is equivalent to finding the saddle point of the Lagrangian function

$$L(\mathbf{x}, \boldsymbol{\lambda}) = f(\mathbf{x}) - \sum_{i=1}^{m} \lambda_i[\mathbf{g}_i(\mathbf{x}) - d_i],$$

or

$$L(\mathbf{x}, \boldsymbol{\lambda}) = f(\mathbf{x}) - \boldsymbol{\lambda}'[\mathbf{g}(\mathbf{x}) - \mathbf{d}], \mathbf{x} \geq \mathbf{0}.$$

For notational convenience, the slack variables $x_{si}$ have once again been included as part of an $n \times 1$ vector $\mathbf{x}$. Suppose that $L(\mathbf{x}, \boldsymbol{\lambda})$ has a saddle point at $(\mathbf{x}^*, \boldsymbol{\lambda}^*)$. If $L(\mathbf{x}, \boldsymbol{\lambda})$ is to be *maximized* with respect to $\mathbf{x}$ for *any* $m \times 1$ vector $\boldsymbol{\lambda}$ that we might choose, and for the moment ignoring the $\mathbf{x} \geq \mathbf{0}$ qualification, we would *require* $\partial L/\partial \mathbf{x} = \partial f(\mathbf{x})/\partial \mathbf{x} - [\partial \mathbf{g}(\mathbf{x})/\partial \mathbf{x}]\boldsymbol{\lambda} = \mathbf{0}$. But, to determine the saddle point of $L(\mathbf{x}, \boldsymbol{\lambda})$, we wish to *minimize* $L(\mathbf{x}, \boldsymbol{\lambda})$ with respect to $\boldsymbol{\lambda}$, while *simultaneously* satisfying the requirement that $\partial L/\partial \mathbf{x} = \mathbf{0}$. Then we will have maximized $L(\mathbf{x}, \boldsymbol{\lambda})$ with respect to $\mathbf{x}$ and minimized it with respect to $\boldsymbol{\lambda}$. We have thereby *defined* a second problem, called the *dual* to the *primal* problem of (9.19):

$$\begin{aligned} &\text{Minimize} \quad Z_d = L(\mathbf{x}, \boldsymbol{\lambda}) = f(\mathbf{x}) - \boldsymbol{\lambda}'[\mathbf{g}(\mathbf{x}) - \mathbf{d}] \\ &\text{subject to} \quad \frac{\partial f(\mathbf{x})}{\partial \mathbf{x}} - \left[\frac{\partial \mathbf{g}}{\partial \mathbf{x}}\right]\boldsymbol{\lambda} = \mathbf{0}. \end{aligned} \tag{9.19$'$}$$

In the dual problem, we attempt to $\min_{\boldsymbol{\lambda}} [\max_{\mathbf{x}} L(\mathbf{x}, \boldsymbol{\lambda})] = Z_d^*$; in the primal problem we attempt to $\max_{\mathbf{x}} [\min_{\boldsymbol{\lambda}} L(\mathbf{x}, \boldsymbol{\lambda})] = Z^*$. So long as the function $L(\mathbf{x}, \boldsymbol{\lambda})$ has a global saddle point at $(\mathbf{x}^*, \boldsymbol{\lambda}^*)$, and the $\mathbf{x} \geq \mathbf{0}$ condition is respected in the dual as well as the primal, $Z^* = Z_d^*$, and the solutions to the primal and the dual will be one and the same. The $\lambda_i$ are called the *dual variables.*

In particular, consider the linear programming problem

$$\begin{aligned} &\text{Maximize} \quad Z = \mathbf{c}'\mathbf{x} \\ &\text{subject to} \quad \mathbf{A}\mathbf{x} = \mathbf{d}, \qquad \mathbf{x} \geq \mathbf{0}. \end{aligned} \tag{9.20}$$

Here, it will be useful to define $\mathbf{x}' = (x_1, \ldots, x_n, x_{n+1}, \ldots, x_{n+m})$ to be a $1 \times (n + m)$ vector, including slacks. We seek the saddle point of the Lagrangian function $L(\mathbf{x}, \boldsymbol{\lambda}) = \mathbf{c}'\mathbf{x} - \boldsymbol{\lambda}'[\mathbf{A}\mathbf{x} - \mathbf{d}]$. In this case $f(\mathbf{x}) = \mathbf{c}'\mathbf{x}$ and $\mathbf{g}(\mathbf{x}) = \mathbf{A}\mathbf{x}$; hence $\partial f(\mathbf{x})/\partial \mathbf{x} = \mathbf{c}$ and $\partial \mathbf{g}(\mathbf{x})/\partial \mathbf{x} = \mathbf{A}'$. Therefore, the first equation in the dual (9.19′) becomes

$$\text{Minimize} \quad Z_d = L(\mathbf{x}, \boldsymbol{\lambda}) = \mathbf{c}'\mathbf{x} - \boldsymbol{\lambda}'[\mathbf{A}\mathbf{x} - \mathbf{d}]; \tag{9.20$'$a}$$

and the second equation becomes

$$\text{subject to} \quad \mathbf{c} - \mathbf{A}'\boldsymbol{\lambda} = \mathbf{0}. \tag{9.20$'$b}$$

But from (9.20′a) we have $Z_d = \mathbf{c}'\mathbf{x} - \boldsymbol{\lambda}'[\mathbf{A}\mathbf{x} - \mathbf{d}] = (\mathbf{c}' - \boldsymbol{\lambda}'\mathbf{A})\mathbf{x} + \boldsymbol{\lambda}'\mathbf{d}$. Transposing (9.20′b) and substituting for the expression in parentheses, $Z_d = \boldsymbol{\lambda}'\mathbf{d}$. Therefore we may rewrite the dual to the LP problem (9.20) as

$$\begin{aligned} &\text{Minimize} \quad Z_d = \boldsymbol{\lambda}'\mathbf{d} \\ &\text{subject to} \quad \mathbf{A}'\boldsymbol{\lambda} = \mathbf{c}. \end{aligned} \tag{9.20$'$}$$

If, in addition, we require $\boldsymbol{\lambda} \geq \mathbf{0}$, (9.20′) will be a second LP problem. As we shall soon indicate, this requirement is indeed satisfied, and (9.20′) with $\boldsymbol{\lambda} \geq \mathbf{0}$ is also an

LP problem. It should be noted that as a dual, min $Z_d$ = max $Z$, and in *this* case the dual of the dual is the primal. Moreover, recall that $\lambda_i = \partial Z/\partial d_i$ equals the change in the objective function effected when the $i$th constraint is relaxed. $\lambda_i$ can thus be interpreted as an opportunity cost or *shadow price* assigned to an increment in $d_i$, or to the *marginal* unit of the $i$th "resource," since in general $d_i$ plays the role of a limiting resource, or a restraining factor that must be respected. This shadow price $\lambda_i$ reflects the extent to which the *maximum* $Z$ (= minimum $Z_d$) will be reduced should there be a decline of $\partial d_i$ in the available amount of the $i$th resource; the shadow price thus reflects the value of this increment of resource in terms of the sacrifice in the level of the objective function of the *primal* problem that need *not* be made, simply because the increment in the $i$th resource *is* available. This last increment of $\partial d_i$ thus is worth exactly $\lambda_i$ units of $Z$.

To see the relationship between the primal and dual LP problems and variables more clearly, suppose a unit of the *nonbasic* slack variable $x_{n+v}$ is introduced into the optimal solution to the primal problem. This slack variable is associated with the $v$th constraint. Hence, the *available* portion of $d_v$ to distribute to the basic variables in the optimal solution would change. This is equivalent to *reducing* $d_v$ by one unit. But $\partial Z/\partial d_v = \lambda_v$; therefore the value of the objective function would fall by $\lambda_v$. This change, however, is precisely what the simplex criterion, $s_{n+v}$, of the nonbasic variable $x_{n+v}$ computes: namely, the change in $Z$ from introducing a unit of $x_{n+v}$. Thus $s_{n+v} = -\lambda_v$; that is, introducing slack where the constraint is $\leq$ and binding reduces $d_v$, and $\partial Z/\partial d_v = \lambda_v = -s_{n+v}$. If the $v$th constraint is not binding, $s_{n+v} = 0$ and $d_v$ may be reduced (at least by *some* small amount) without affecting $Z$, so that $\lambda_v = 0$.

Similarly, if a nonslack, nonbasic variable $x_u$ is introduced into the optimal solution, each unit of $x_u$ will reduce the objective function by the amount of this variable's simplex criterion or $s_u$. The reason the objective function would be reduced is that the contribution of a unit of $x_u$ to the objective function, or $c_u$, is *less than* the value of the resources that would be absorbed by the unit of $x_u$. Since $a_{ij}$ is the amount of the $i$th resource absorbed by a unit of $x_j$,[17] for a primal problem with $n$ nonslack variables and $m$ inequality constraints, $\sum_{i=1}^{m} a_{ij}\lambda_i$ = the *total value* of the resources, evaluated at the margin, absorbed by a *unit* of variable $x_j$. This is so, since $\lambda_i$ is the *shadow* price or unit value assigned to the marginal unit of the $i$th resource, $a_{ij}\lambda_i$ is thus the value of the $i$th resource absorbed by a unit of $x_j$, and the total value is obtained by summing over all $i$ resources. Hence if a unit of a nonslack variable $x_u$ is brought into the optimal solution of the primal problem, the change in $Z$ will be $s_u$; or, the excess of the value of resources absorbed $\left(\sum_{i=1}^{m} a_{iu}\lambda_i\right)$ over the contribution made by the variable ($c_u$) is given by

$$\sum_{i=1}^{m} a_{iu}\lambda_i - c_u = -s_u.$$

[17] For example, if the $i$th constraint is $6x_1 + 3x_2 + 4x_3 \leq 8$, then $a_{i2} = 3$ units of the total of $d_i = 8$ available units are absorbed for each unit of $x_2$ that is introduced into the solution.

But the $u$th constraint in the dual would be

$$\sum_{i=1}^{m} a_{iu}\lambda_i - \lambda_{m+u} = c_u.$$

Hence,

$$\lambda_{m+u} = \sum_{i=1}^{m} a_{iu}\lambda_i - c_u = -s_u.$$

Thus, $\lambda_{m+u}$ is equal to the change in the objective function, or $-s_u$, that would result if a unit of the nonslack variable $x_u$ were brought into solution. Moreover, since the simplexes in the optimal primal solution are all nonpositive, the dual variables *must* be nonnegative. We can, therefore, add $\boldsymbol{\lambda} \geq \mathbf{0}$ to (9.20′).

It might also be noted that in the present formulation all constraints are of the $\leq$ variety. From Section 9.3 we know, however, that if the $v$th constraint is of the $\geq$ variety, $\partial Z/\partial d_v = \lambda_v \leq 0$. We get around this problem by first multiplying the constraint by $(-1)$, which converts $\geq$ to $\leq$. Then the "$\lambda_v$" that we calculate will be nonnegative, but we must bear in mind that the $\lambda_v$ of the *original* constraint will be equal in absolute magnitude, but opposite in sign, to the "$\lambda_v$" that has been calculated.

Although we have dwelt on the LP aspect of duality, it is clear that, for *any* programming problem, since $\partial Z/\partial d_i = \lambda_i$, where the $d_i$ are binding resource limitations that restrict the allocations of the $x_j$, the $\lambda_i$'s are shadow prices reflecting the value of the marginal unit of a resource. This, of course, is precisely why in the theory of consumer behavior the Lagrangian multiplier $\lambda$ was found to equal the marginal utility of income—in effect the "value" of the "resource" income—evaluated at the margin. Similarly, for the short-run production problem,

$$\begin{aligned} &\text{Maximize} \quad Q = q(F_1, \ldots, F_m) \\ &\text{subject to} \quad C = \sum_{i=1}^{m} W_i F_i, \qquad F_i = \bar{F}_i \ (i = k+1, \ldots, m) \quad F_i \geq 0, \end{aligned}$$

the dual variables $(\lambda_i)$ associated with the $F_i = \bar{F}_i$ $(i = k+1, \ldots, m)$ constraints would yield the $i$th factor's marginal physical product—given the levels determined for the other factors. In the case of the dual to the quadratic programming problem of (9.11a–c), $\mathbf{g}(\mathbf{x}) = \mathbf{Ax}$ and $f(\mathbf{x}) = \mathbf{c}'\mathbf{x} + \mathbf{x}'\mathbf{Dx}$; hence, $\partial \mathbf{g}(\mathbf{x})/\partial \mathbf{x} = \mathbf{A}'$ and $\partial f(\mathbf{x})/\partial \mathbf{x} = \mathbf{c} + 2\mathbf{D}'\mathbf{x}$. Therefore, the first equation in the dual (9.19′) becomes

$$\text{Minimize} \quad Z_d = L(\mathbf{x},\boldsymbol{\lambda}) = \mathbf{c}'\mathbf{x} + \mathbf{x}'\mathbf{Dx} - \boldsymbol{\lambda}'[\mathbf{Ax} - \mathbf{d}], \tag{9.11′a}$$

and the second equation becomes

$$\text{subject to} \quad \mathbf{c} + 2\mathbf{D}'\mathbf{x} - \mathbf{A}'\boldsymbol{\lambda} = \mathbf{0}. \tag{9.11′b}$$

Transposing and postmultiplying (9.11′b) by $\mathbf{x}$ and rearranging terms yields $\mathbf{c}'\mathbf{x} - \boldsymbol{\lambda}'\mathbf{Ax} = -2\mathbf{x}'\mathbf{Dx}$. Substituting this expression into (9.11′a), we write the quadratic programming dual

$$\begin{aligned} \text{Minimize} \quad & Z_d = -\mathbf{x}'\mathbf{Dx} + \boldsymbol{\lambda}'\mathbf{d} \\ \text{subject to} \quad & -2\mathbf{Dx} + \mathbf{A}'\boldsymbol{\lambda} = \mathbf{c}, \\ & \mathbf{x} \geq \mathbf{0}. \end{aligned} \tag{9.11′}$$

The latter is a second quadratic programming problem with $\mathbf{x}$ and $\boldsymbol{\lambda}$ as the vectors of variables. The optimal solution to (9.11′) is $(\mathbf{x}^*, \boldsymbol{\lambda}^*)$, the optimal solution to (9.11). The interpretation of the dual variables as opportunity costs or shadow prices is not altered. For example, as derived in Table 9.4 of the Appendix, the value of $\lambda_1 = \lambda_{+1}$ is 2, and that of $-\lambda_2 = \lambda_{-2}$ is 6, for the illustrative quadratic programming problem defined by Equations (9.14a–c). $\lambda_{+1} = 2$ implies that reducing the firm's expenditures on its factors of production would result in a reduction of approximately 2 units of output per unit of a small increment $dC$ in cost; put in a more familiar form, $(\frac{1}{2})$ is the extra cost per unit associated with the last increment in output, or marginal cost. $\lambda_2 = -6$ suggests that the firm suffers a loss in output by requiring $F_1/F_2 \geq 1$—it would not do so without the requirement. It would therefore appear that while the primary initial focus in a programming problem might be on determining optima for the variables $x_j$, the dual variables $\lambda_i$ may ultimately turn out to be of even greater interest, for they shed considerable light on the *valuation* problem. That is, they assign prices to the marginal units of the resources used. Even when the optimal solution for the $x_j$ in a programming problem is known, then, there might still be considerable interest in "resolving" the problem or its dual in order to obtain the $\lambda_i$'s and thus assign values to the firm's resources.[18]

## 9.8 A DIGRESSION ON MATHEMATICAL PROGRAMMING AND LEAST-SQUARES CURVE-FITTING

In Chapter 4 we noted that one might wish to incorporate prior judgments into the estimation of least-squares parameters. Specifically, we indicated how one might constrain a single parameter $a_i$ to assure that $a_i = \alpha_i^*$. Given our new mathematical tools, however, it is now possible to generalize the previous analysis.

In particular, suppose one is interested in estimating the production function $Q_t = \alpha F_{1t}^{\alpha_1} F_{2t}^{\alpha_2} \epsilon_t$. Further, suppose one is absolutely certain that there are nonincreasing returns to scale and seeks to have this certainty reflected in the least-squares estimates of $\alpha_1$ and $\alpha_2$. Specifically, one seeks estimates $a_1$ and $a_2$ such that $a_1 + a_2 \leq 1$ and $a_1, a_2 \geq 0$, which will minimize

$$\sum_t \hat{e}_t^2 = \sum_t (\hat{Q}_t - \hat{a} - a_1\hat{F}_{1t} - a_2\hat{F}_{2t})^2,$$

where the circumflex indicates logarithm. Absent the need to recognize the possible presence of simultaneous relationships, and the need to estimate a system of simultaneous equations, this estimation problem would entail minimizing a quadratic function subject to a single linear constraint—that is, we would have a quadratic programming problem.

In general, we wish to estimate a set of parameters, $\alpha_i$, of the function

$$Q_t = \sum_{i=0}^{m} \alpha_i V_{it} + \epsilon_t \tag{9.21}$$

subject to a set of constraints on the estimates $a_i$ of the $\alpha_i$. Translated into the familiar vector-matrix notation, (9.21) or its equivalent (3.1) becomes $\mathbf{Q} = \mathbf{V}\boldsymbol{\alpha} + \boldsymbol{\epsilon}$

[18] For a more detailed discussion, see M. L. Balinski and W. J. Baumol, "The Dual in Nonlinear Programming and its Economic Interpretation," *Review of Economic Studies*, **XXXV**:103 (July 1968), 237–256.

(9.21a) or its equivalent (3.1a). The problem of Equation (3.2), or

$$\text{Minimize} \quad \mathbf{e'e} = \mathbf{Q'Q} - 2\mathbf{a'V'Q} + \mathbf{a'V'Va}, \tag{3.2}$$

now becomes

$$\text{Minimize} \quad \mathbf{e'e} = \mathbf{Q'Q} - 2\mathbf{\tilde{a}'V'Q} + \mathbf{\tilde{a}'V'V\tilde{a}} + \bar{k} \tag{9.22}$$

$$\text{subject to} \quad G_j(\tilde{a}_1, \ldots, \tilde{a}_m, a_{sj}) = d_j, \qquad j = 1, \ldots, r, \tag{9.22a}$$

$$\tilde{a}_i, a_{sj} \geq 0, \qquad i = 1, \ldots, m; j = 1, \ldots, r, \tag{9.22b}$$

where $a_{sj}$ is a slack variable added linearly to the $j$th constraint, $\tilde{a}_i = a_i + k_i$ where $k_i$ is a "large enough" positive *constant* added to $a_i$ to assure that $\tilde{a}_i \geq 0$ and $\mathbf{\tilde{a}}' = (\tilde{a}_1, \ldots, \tilde{a}_m)$, and $\mathbf{k}' = (k_1, \ldots, k_m)$; $G_j$ is some function of the $\tilde{a}_i$ and $a_{sj}$; and, $\bar{k} = -2\mathbf{k'V'Q} + \mathbf{k'V'Vk}$ = a constant. For example, if we require $a_1 + a_2 \geq 1$ and it is suspected (or known) that unconstrained estimates of $a_1 = -6$ and $a_2 = -3$ would be obtained, we might set $\tilde{a}_1 = a_1 + 10$ and $\tilde{a}_2 = a_2 + 10$, and require $\tilde{a}_1 + \tilde{a}_2 \geq 21$.

In the specific case where (9.22a) is linear, we can let $\mathbf{\bar{\tilde{a}}}' = (\tilde{a}_1, \ldots, \tilde{a}_m, a_{s1}, \ldots, a_{sr})$ and rewrite the estimation problem as

$$\text{Minimize} \quad \mathbf{e'e} = \mathbf{Q'Q} - 2\mathbf{\tilde{a}'V'Q} + \mathbf{\tilde{a}'V'V\tilde{a}} + \bar{k} \tag{9.22}$$

$$\text{subject to} \quad \mathbf{A\bar{\tilde{a}}} = \mathbf{d}, \tag{9.22a$'$}$$

$$\mathbf{\bar{\tilde{a}}} \geq \mathbf{0}, \tag{9.22b$'$}$$

where $\mathbf{A}$ is an $r \times (m + r)$ known matrix of coefficients.

The latter problem is a quadratic programming problem comparable to (9.11a–c). Here, $\mathbf{V'Q} = \mathbf{c}$ and $\mathbf{V'V} = \mathbf{D}$; $\mathbf{A}$ and $\mathbf{d}$ are as in the previous formulation. Thus, except for the additional computational burdens involved (and these are not terribly burdensome in the age of the high-speed computer), constrained least-squares estimation, where the constraints are linear, is a most feasible option; and it will be illustrated in Section 14.6 where the need for it arises. Where the constraints are nonlinear, however, the problem may remain *conceptually* tractable, but will not necessarily be pleasant to handle—even with the computer. Nonetheless, from a *practical* standpoint, the sorts of constraints that arise in economic problems, such as that in the production function problem, will ordinarily be linear. Hence, the estimation problem will ordinarily be of the quadratic programming variety.

# Appendix to Chapter 9

## 9A.1 SEPARABLE FUNCTIONS

The separable function problem of Section 9.2 is solved in Table 9.3. The first tableau gives a solution in terms of $Q_3$, $\beta_{11}$, and $\beta_{12}$. The highest simplex value is for $\beta_{61}$. Since only adjacent $\beta_{k1}$'s can appear in a solution, when $\beta_{61}$ is introduced, $\beta_{11}$ is eliminated. In the second tableau $\beta_{42}$ has the highest simplex value, 3811. Nonetheless, we introduce $\beta_{22}$, since only adjacent $\beta_{k2}$'s can appear in a solution, and $\beta_{22}$ has a positive simplex criterion. Similarly, in the third tableau, $\beta_{31}$ has the highest simplex value, but we must introduce $\beta_{51}$ whose simplex criterion is also positive, since $\beta_{61}$ is already in the solution. The process continues until all simplex criteria are nonpositive. The optimal solution is $\beta_{41} = 1$, $\beta_{22} = .8010$, and $\beta_{32} = .1990$.

## 9A.2 KUHN-TUCKER CONDITIONS

The Lagrangian function associated with Equations (9.10a–f) could be written

$$\begin{aligned} L(Q, \lambda) = {} & 500Q_1 - 2Q_1^2 + 900Q_2 - 3Q_2^2 - 50Q_{11} - 25Q_{12}^2 - 1000 \\ & - \lambda_1[2Q_{11} + 5Q_{12} + 2Q_2 + Q_{S1} - 230] - \lambda_2[Q_{11} - .5Q_1 - Q_{S2}] \\ & - \lambda_3[Q_1 - Q_{S3} - 1] - \lambda_4[Q_{11} + Q_{12} - Q_1], \end{aligned}$$

where the $Q_{Si}$ are nonnegative slack variables. Hence,

$$\begin{aligned} \partial L/\partial Q_1 &= 500 - 4Q_1 + .5\lambda_2 - \lambda_3 + \lambda_4 \leq 0, \\ \partial L/\partial Q_2 &= 900 - 6Q_2 - 2\lambda_1 \leq 0, \\ \partial L/\partial Q_{11} &= -50 - 2\lambda_1 - \lambda_2 - \lambda_4 \leq 0, \\ \partial L/\partial Q_{12} &= -50Q_{12} - 5\lambda_1 - \lambda_4 \leq 0, \\ \partial L/\partial Q_{S1} &= -\lambda_1 \leq 0, \\ \partial L/\partial Q_{S2} &= \lambda_2 \leq 0, \\ \partial L/\partial Q_{S3} &= \lambda_3 \leq 0. \end{aligned}$$

The $\partial L/\partial \lambda_i$ yield the original constraint conditions, and $\lambda_4$ is unrestricted in sign.

All possible cases are not enumerated here. Rather, we merely detail two of the more likely candidates for optimal solutions. It should be emphasized, however, that *all* possibilities must be checked out. In particular, the two cases explicitly considered here are: (1) $\lambda_2 = \lambda_3 = 0$, $Q_{12} = 0$, all other variables nonzero; (2) $\lambda_2 = \lambda_3 = 0$, all other variables nonzero.

*Case 1.* This situation requires the following to hold as equalities:

$$\begin{aligned} 500 - 4Q_1 + \lambda_4 &= 0 \qquad (\partial L/\partial Q_1 = 0), \\ 900 - 6Q_2 - 2\lambda_1 &= 0 \qquad (\partial L/\partial Q_2 = 0), \\ -50 - 2\lambda_1 - \lambda_4 &= 0 \qquad (\partial L/\partial Q_{11} = 0), \\ 2Q_{11} + 2Q_2 - 230 &= 0 \qquad (\partial L/\partial \lambda_1 = 0), \\ Q_{11} - Q_1 &= 0 \qquad (\partial L/\partial \lambda_4 = 0). \end{aligned}$$

Solving these simultaneous equations yields a solution: $Q_1^* = Q_{11}^* = 24$; $Q_2^* = 91$; $\lambda_1^* = 177$; $\lambda_4^* = -404$.

TABLE 9.3

| Maximize | | $\beta_{11}$ 0 | $\beta_{21}$ 1800 | $\beta_{31}$ 3200 | $\beta_{41}$ 4200 | $\beta_{51}$ 4800 | $\beta_{61}$ 5000 | $\beta_{12}$ 0 | $\beta_{22}$ 1915 | $\beta_{32}$ 3211 | $\beta_{42}$ 3889 | $Q_3$ 0 | **d** |
|---|---|---|---|---|---|---|---|---|---|---|---|---|---|
| $Q_3$: | 0 | 0 | 1000 | 2000 | 3000 | 4000 | 5000 | 0 | 1668 | 3336 | 5000 | 1 | 5000 |
| $\beta_{11}$: | 0 | 1 | 1 | 1 | 1 | 1 | 1 | 0 | 0 | 0 | 0 | 0 | 1 → |
| $\beta_{12}$: | 0 | 0 | 0 | 0 | 0 | 0 | 0 | 1 | 1 | 1 | 1 | 0 | 1 |
| $s_j$ | | 0 | 1800 | 3200 | 4200 | 4800 | 5000 | 0 | 1915 | 3211 | 3889 | 0 | $Z_1 = 0$ |
| | | | | | | | ↑ | | | | | | |
| $Q_3$: | 0 | −5000 | −4000 | −3000 | −2000 | −1000 | 0 | 0 | 1668 | 3336 | 5000 | 1 | 0 → |
| $\beta_{61}$: | 5000 | 1 | 1 | 1 | 1 | 1 | 1 | 0 | 0 | 0 | 0 | 0 | 1 |
| $\beta_{12}$: | 0 | 0 | 0 | 0 | 0 | 0 | 0 | 1 | 1 | 1 | 1 | 0 | 1 |
| $s_j$ | | −5000 | −3200 | −1800 | −800 | −200 | 0 | 0 | 1915 | 3211 | 3889 | 0 | $Z_2 = 5000$ |
| | | | | | | | | | ↑ | | | | |
| $\beta_{22}$: | 1915 | −2.9976 | −2.3981 | −1.7986 | −1.1990 | −.5995 | 0 | 0 | 1 | 2 | 2.9976 | .0001 | 0 |
| $\beta_{61}$: | 5000 | 1 | 1 | 1 | 1 | 1 | 1 | 0 | 0 | 0 | 0 | 0 | 1 → |
| $\beta_{12}$: | 0 | 2.9976 | 2.3981 | 1.7986 | 1.1990 | .5995 | 0 | 1 | 0 | −1 | −1.9976 | −.0001 | 1 |
| $s_j$ | | 740.4 | 1392.4 | 1644.3 | 1496.1 | 948.0 | 0 | 0 | 0 | −619 | −1851.4 | −.1915 | $Z_3 = 5000$ |
| | | | | | | ↑ | | | | | | | |
| $\beta_{22}$: | 1915 | −2.3981 | −1.7986 | −1.1991 | −.5995 | 0 | .5995 | 0 | 1 | 2 | 2.9976 | .0001 | .5995 |
| $\beta_{51}$: | 4800 | 1 | 1 | 1 | 1 | 1 | 1 | 0 | 0 | 0 | 0 | 0 | 1 |
| $\beta_{12}$: | 0 | 2.3981 | 1.7986 | 1.1991 | .5995 | 0 | −.5995 | 1 | 0 | −1 | −1.9976 | −.0001 | .4005 → |
| $s_j$ | | −207.6 | 444.4 | 696.3 | 548.1 | 0 | −948.0 | 0 | 0 | −619 | −1851.4 | −.1915 | $Z_4 = 5948$ |
| | | | | | ↑ | | | | | | | | |
| $\beta_{22}$: | 1915 | 0 | 0 | 0 | 0 | 0 | 0 | 1 | 1 | 1 | 1 | 0 | 1 |
| $\beta_{51}$: | 4800 | −3 | −2 | −1 | 0 | 1 | 2 | −1.6681 | 0 | 1.6681 | 3.3321 | .0002 | .3319 → |
| $\beta_{41}$: | 4200 | 4 | 3 | 2 | 1 | 0 | −1 | 1.6681 | 0 | −1.6681 | −3.3321 | −.0002 | .6681 |
| $s_j$ | | −2400 | −1200 | −400 | 0 | 0 | −400 | −914.3 | 0 | 295.2 | −25.1 | −.0819 | $Z_5 = 6314$ |
| | | | | | | | | | | ↑ | | | |
| $\beta_{22}$: | 1915 | 1.7985 | 1.1900 | .5995 | 0 | −.5995 | −1.1900 | 2 | 1 | 0 | −.9975 | −.0001 | .8010 |
| $\beta_{32}$: | 3211 | −1.7985 | −1.1900 | −.5995 | 0 | .5995 | 1.1900 | −1 | 0 | 1 | 1.9975 | .0001 | .1990 |
| $\beta_{41}$: | 4200 | 1 | 1 | 1 | 1 | 1 | 1 | 0 | 0 | 0 | 0 | 0 | 1 |
| $s_j$ | | −1869.1 | −848.7 | −223.0 | 0 | −177.0 | −751.3 | −619 | 0 | 0 | −614.8 | −.1114 | $Z_6 = 6373$ |

*Case 2.* This situation requires the following to hold as equalities:

$$\begin{aligned} 500 - 4Q_1 + \lambda_4 &= 0 & (\partial L/\partial Q_1 = 0),\\ 900 - 6Q_2 - 2\lambda_1 &= 0 & (\partial L/\partial Q_2 = 0),\\ -50 - 2\lambda_1 - \lambda_4 &= 0 & (\partial L/\partial Q_{11} = 0),\\ -50Q_{12} - 5\lambda_1 - \lambda_4 &= 0 & (\partial L/\partial Q_{12} = 0),\\ 2Q_{11} + 5Q_{12} + 2Q_2 - 230 &= 0 & (\partial L/\partial \lambda_1 = 0),\\ Q_{11} + Q_{12} - Q_1 &= 0 & (\partial L/\partial \lambda_4 = 0). \end{aligned}$$

Solving these simultaneous equations yields an inadmissible solution—that is, $Q_{12}$ becomes negative. In this manner, case 1 is shown to yield the optimal solution with $\pi^* = 66{,}905$.

## 9A.3 QUADRATIC PROGRAMMING

The quadratic programming problem of Section 9.4 is solved in Table 9.4. In this problem, $\mathbf{c}' = (20, 10, 0, 0)$, $\mathbf{d}' = (10, 0)$, and

$$\mathbf{D} = \begin{bmatrix} -20 & 15 & 0 & 0\\ 15 & -15 & 0 & 0\\ 0 & 0 & 0 & 0\\ 0 & 0 & 0 & 0 \end{bmatrix}, \qquad \mathbf{A} = \begin{bmatrix} 3 & 2 & 1 & 0\\ 1 & -1 & 0 & -1 \end{bmatrix}.$$

Table 9.4 is a simplex tableau in which our problem is to drive the artificial variables out of the solution. Moreover, we require $F_jF_{sj} = 0$ in all solutions; and $\lambda_1 \geq 0$ and $\lambda_2 \leq 0$ because of the direction of the inequality constraints. Hence, if $\lambda_i$ enters the solution it will be through $\lambda_{+1}$ and $\lambda_{-2}$.

The first tableau gives a solution in terms of $F_{A1}, F_{A2}, F_{A3}, F_{A4}, F_3$, and $F_4$. Because we require $F_1$ and $F_2$ *greater* than zero, these are immediately introduced in the second and third tableaus. Note that once $F_4$ is driven out of solution in the second tableau, we can *simultaneously* substitute $F_{S4}$ for $F_{A4}$, since their coefficients coincide. This rids us of one artificial variable. $\lambda_{+1}$ and $\lambda_{-2}$ are introduced in the fourth and fifth tableaus, for under the constraints of this particular application of simplex we have little other choice. We go where we are led. In the fifth and final tableau, with $F_3$ out of the solution, we can replace $F_{A3}$ with $F_{S3}$. The final tableau reveals an optimum solution of $F_1^* = 2$, $F_2^* = 2$, $F_3^* = 0$, $F_4^* = 0$, $\lambda_{+1}^* = 2$, and $\lambda_{-2}^* = 6$; $Q^* = 40$. Note that $-\lambda_2^* = \lambda_{-2} = 6$, since $F_4^* = 0$ and the second constraint $(\geq)$ is binding. The first constraint $(\leq)$ is also binding, and $F_3^* = 0$; and $\lambda_1^* = \lambda_{+1}^* = 2$. Thus, total output would increase if total cost were increased, or if it were not necessary to have at least as much $F_1$ as $F_2$.

## 9A.4 INTEGER PROGRAMMING

Table 9.5 contains the solution for the integer programming problem of Section 9.5. The optimal LP solution is given in the second tableau as $Q_2 = Q = \frac{15}{2}$. The cutting plane is derived from the second row in the optimal LP tableau $0Q + (\frac{1}{2})Q_1 + 0Q_2 + (\frac{1}{2})Q_3 \geq \frac{1}{2}$. Figure 9.6 demonstrates the way in which the cutting plane narrows down the feasible solution set in the $Q_1 - Q_3$ space.

After adding slack and artificial variables, we introduce the cutting plane in the third tableau. Since $Q_1$ has the highest positive simplex criterion, we introduce it in the fourth and optimal tableau. The optimal solution is $Q_1^* = 1$, $Q_2^* = 7$, $Q^* = 8$.

| | Z | $F_1$ | $F_2$ | $F_3$ | $F_4$ | $\lambda_{+1}$ | $\lambda_{+2}$ | $\lambda_{-1}$ | $\lambda_{-2}$ | $F_{S1}$ | $F_{S2}$ | $F_{S3}$ | $F_{S4}$ | $F_{A1}$ | $F_{A2}$ | $F_{A3}$ | $F_{A4}$ | |
|---|---|---|---|---|---|---|---|---|---|---|---|---|---|---|---|---|---|---|
| | | 0 | 0 | 0 | 0 | 0 | 0 | 0 | 0 | 0 | 0 | 0 | 0 | −1 | −1 | −1 | −1 | |
| $F_{A1}$: | −1 | −40 | 30 | 0 | 0 | −3 | −1 | 3 | 1 | 1 | 0 | 0 | 0 | −1 | 0 | 0 | 0 | −20 |
| $F_{A2}$: | −1 | 30 | −30 | 0 | 0 | −2 | 1 | 2 | −1 | 0 | 1 | 0 | 0 | 0 | −1 | 0 | 0 | −10 |
| $F_{A3}$: | −1 | 0 | 0 | 0 | 0 | −1 | 0 | 1 | 0 | 0 | 0 | 1 | 0 | 0 | 0 | 1 | 0 | 0 |
| $F_{A4}$: | −1 | 0 | 0 | 0 | 0 | 0 | 1 | 0 | −1 | 0 | 0 | 0 | 1 | 0 | 0 | 0 | 1 | 0 |
| $F_3$: | 0 | 3 | 2 | 1 | 0 | 0 | 0 | 0 | 0 | 0 | 0 | 0 | 0 | 0 | 0 | 0 | 0 | 10 |
| $F_4$: | 0 | 1 | −1 | 0 | −1 | 0 | 0 | 0 | 0 | 0 | 0 | 0 | 0 | 0 | 0 | 0 | 0 | 0 → |
| | $s_j$ | −10 ↑ | 0 | 0 | 0 | −6 | 1 | 6 | −1 | 1 | 1 | 1 | 1 | 0 | 0 | 0 | 0 | $Z = -30$ |
| $F_{A1}$: | −1 | 0 | −10 | 0 | −40 | −3 | −1 | 3 | 1 | 1 | 0 | 0 | 0 | −1 | 0 | 0 | 0 | −20 → |
| $F_{A2}$: | −1 | 0 | 0 | 0 | 30 | −2 | 1 | 2 | −1 | 0 | 1 | 0 | 0 | 0 | −1 | 0 | 0 | −10 |
| $F_{A3}$: | −1 | 0 | 0 | 0 | 0 | −1 | 0 | 1 | 0 | 0 | 0 | 1 | 0 | 0 | 0 | 1 | 0 | 0 |
| $F_{S4}$: | 0 | 0 | 0 | 0 | 0 | 0 | 1 | 0 | −1 | 0 | 0 | 0 | 1 | 0 | 0 | 0 | 1 | 0 |
| $F_3$: | 0 | 0 | 5 | 1 | 3 | 0 | 0 | 0 | 0 | 0 | 0 | 0 | 0 | 0 | 0 | 0 | 0 | 10 |
| $F_1$: | 0 | 1 | −1 | 0 | −1 | 0 | 0 | 0 | 0 | 0 | 0 | 0 | 0 | 0 | 0 | 0 | 0 | 0 |
| | $s_j$ | 0 | −10 ↑ | 0 | −10 | −6 | 0 | 6 | 0 | 1 | 1 | 1 | 0 | 0 | 0 | 0 | 0 | $Z = -30$ |
| $F_2$: | 0 | 0 | 1 | 0 | 4 | .3 | .1 | −.3 | −.1 | −.1 | 0 | 0 | 0 | .1 | 0 | 0 | 0 | 2 |
| $F_{A2}$: | −1 | 0 | 0 | 0 | 30 | −2 | 1 | 2 | −1 | 0 | 1 | 0 | 0 | 0 | −1 | 0 | 0 | −10 → |
| $F_{A3}$: | −1 | 0 | 0 | 0 | 0 | −1 | 0 | 1 | 0 | 0 | 0 | 1 | 0 | 0 | 0 | 1 | 0 | 0 |
| $F_{S4}$: | 0 | 0 | 0 | 0 | 0 | 0 | 1 | 0 | −1 | 0 | 0 | 0 | 1 | 0 | 0 | 0 | 1 | 0 |
| $F_3$: | 0 | 0 | 0 | 1 | −17 | −1.5 | −.5 | 1.5 | .5 | .5 | 0 | 0 | 0 | −.5 | 0 | 0 | 0 | 0 |
| $F_1$: | 0 | 1 | 0 | 0 | 3 | .3 | .1 | −.3 | −.1 | −.1 | 0 | 0 | 0 | .1 | 0 | 0 | 0 | 2 |
| | $s_j$ | 0 | 0 | 0 | 30 | −3 ↑ | 1 | 3 | −1 | 0 | 1 | 1 | 0 | −1 | 0 | 0 | −1 | $Z = -10$ |
| $F_2$: | 0 | 0 | 1 | 0 | 8.5 | 0 | .25 | 0 | −.25 | −.1 | .15 | 0 | 0 | .1 | −.15 | 0 | 0 | .5 |
| $\lambda_{+1}$: | 0 | 0 | 0 | 0 | −15 | 1 | −.5 | −1 | .5 | 0 | −.5 | 0 | 0 | 0 | .5 | 0 | 0 | 5 |
| $F_{A3}$: | −1 | 0 | 0 | 0 | −15 | 0 | −.5 | 0 | .5 | 0 | −.5 | 1 | 0 | 0 | .5 | 1 | 0 | 5 |
| $F_{S4}$: | 0 | 0 | 0 | 0 | 0 | 0 | 1 | 0 | −1 | 0 | 0 | 0 | 1 | 0 | 0 | 0 | 1 | 0 |
| $F_3$: | 0 | 0 | 0 | 1 | −39.5 | 0 | −1.25 | 0 | 1.25 | .5 | −.75 | 0 | 0 | −.5 | .75 | 0 | 0 | 7.5 → |
| $F_1$: | 0 | 1 | 0 | 0 | 7.5 | 0 | .25 | 0 | −.25 | −.1 | .15 | 0 | 0 | .1 | −.15 | 0 | 0 | .5 |
| | $s_j$ | 0 | 0 | 0 | −15 | 0 | −.5 | 0 | .5 ↑ | 0 | −.5 | 1 | 0 | −1 | −.5 | 0 | −1 | $Z = -5$ |
| $F_2$: | 0 | 0 | 1 | .2 | .6 | 0 | 0 | 0 | 0 | 0 | 0 | 0 | 0 | 0 | 0 | 0 | 0 | 2 |
| $\lambda_{+1}$: | 0 | 0 | 0 | −.4 | .8 | 1 | 0 | −1 | 0 | −.2 | −.2 | 0 | 0 | .2 | .2 | 0 | 0 | 2 |
| $F_{S3}$: | 0 | 0 | 0 | −.4 | .8 | 0 | 0 | 0 | 0 | −.2 | −.2 | 1 | 0 | .2 | .2 | 1 | 0 | 2 |
| $F_{S4}$: | 0 | 0 | 0 | .8 | −31.6 | 0 | 0 | 0 | 0 | .4 | −.6 | 0 | 1 | −.4 | .6 | 0 | 1 | 6 |
| $\lambda_{-2}$: | 0 | 0 | 0 | .8 | −31.6 | 0 | −1 | 0 | 1 | .4 | −.6 | 0 | 0 | −.4 | .6 | 0 | 0 | 6 |
| $F_1$: | 0 | 1 | 0 | .2 | −.4 | 0 | 0 | 0 | 0 | 0 | 0 | 0 | 0 | 0 | 0 | 0 | 0 | 2 |
| | $s_j$ | 0 | 0 | 0 | 0 | 0 | 0 | 0 | 0 | 0 | 0 | 0 | 0 | −1 | −1 | −1 | −1 | $Z = 0$ |

TABLE 9.5

| **Maximize** | | $Q$ | $Q_1$ | $Q_2$ | $Q_3$ | | | **d** |
|---|---|---|---|---|---|---|---|---|
| | | 10,000 | −9,000 | −8,000 | 0 | | | |
| $Q_3$: | 0 | 0 | 1 | 2 | 1 | | | 15 → |
| $Q$: | 10,000 | 1 | −1 | −1 | 0 | | | 0 |
| | $s_j$ | 0 | 1,000 | 2,000 | 0 | | | $Z_1 = 0$ |
| | | | | ↑ | | | | |
| $Q_2$: | −8,000 | 0 | $\frac{1}{2}$ | 1 | $\frac{1}{2}$ | | | $\frac{15}{2}$ |
| $Q$: | 10,000 | 1 | $-\frac{1}{2}$ | 0 | $\frac{1}{2}$ | | | $\frac{15}{2}$ |
| | $s_j$ | 0 | 0 | 0 | −1,000 | | | $Z_2 = 15{,}000$ |
| | | $Q$ | $Q_1$ | $Q_2$ | $Q_3$ | $Q_{S1}$ | $Q_{A1}$ | **d** |
| $Q_2$: | −8,000 | 0 | $\frac{1}{2}$ | 1 | $\frac{1}{2}$ | 0 | 0 | $\frac{15}{2}$ |
| $Q$: | 10,000 | 1 | $-\frac{1}{2}$ | 0 | $\frac{1}{2}$ | 0 | 0 | $\frac{15}{2}$ |
| $Q_A$: | $-M$ | 0 | $\frac{1}{2}$ | 0 | $\frac{1}{2}$ | −1 | 1 | $\frac{1}{2}$ → |
| | $s_j$ | 0 | $0 + M/2$ | 0 | $-1{,}000 + M/2$ | $-M$ | 0 | $Z_3 = 15{,}000 - M/2$ |
| | | | ↑ | | | | | |
| $Q_2$: | −8,000 | 0 | 0 | 1 | 0 | 1 | −1 | 7 |
| $Q$: | 10,000 | 1 | 0 | 0 | 1 | −1 | 1 | 8 |
| $Q_1$: | −9,000 | 0 | 1 | 0 | 1 | −2 | 2 | 1 |
| | $s_j$ | 0 | 0 | 0 | −1,000 | 0 | $-M$ | $Z_4 = 15{,}000$ |

## 9A.5 THE TRANSPORTATION PROBLEM

Given the direct cost table of Section 9.6, let us obtain a basic feasible solution by assigning the largest possible amounts to locations having the smallest unit shipping costs, while respecting the outlet requirements and plant capacities. We thus assign, in order, $x_{12} = 15$, $x_{33} = 10$, $x_{31} = 5$, $x_{24} = 5$, $x_{21} = 5$, and the remaining $x_{25} = 10$ and $x_{26} = 5$. These are entered in the corner triangles of Table 9.6. The entries in the body of the table are the direct = indirect costs of those outlets to which shipments are being made from each plant, as well as those indirect costs that are calculable.

TABLE 9.6

| | $O_1$ | $O_2$ | $O_3$ | $O_4$ | $O_5$ | $O_6$ | $K_i$ |
|---|---|---|---|---|---|---|---|
| $K_1$ | | 2 (15) | | | | | 15 |
| $K_2$ | 5 (5) | | 4 | 3 (5) | 6 (10) | 0 (5) | 25 |
| $K_3$ | 3 (5) | | 2 (10) | 1 | 4 | −2 | 15 |
| $O_j$ | 10 | 15 | 10 | 5 | 10 | 5 | 55 |

TABLE 9.7

| | $O_1$ | $O_2$ | $O_3$ | $O_4$ | $O_5$ | $O_6$ | $K_i$ |
|---|---|---|---|---|---|---|---|
| $K_1$ | 0 | 2 (15) | −1 | −2 | 1 | −5 | 15 |
| $K_2$ | 5 (5) | 7 ($\epsilon$) | 4 | 3 (5) | 6 (10) | 0 (5) | $25 + \epsilon$ |
| $K_3$ | 3 (5) | 5 | 2 (10) | 1 | 4 | −2 | 15 |
| $O_j$ | 10 | $15 + \epsilon$ | 10 | 5 | 10 | 5 | $55 + \epsilon$ |

TABLE 9.8

| | $O_1$ | $O_2$ | $O_3$ | $O_4$ | $O_5$ | $O_6$ | $K_i$ |
|---|---|---|---|---|---|---|---|
| $K_1$ | 0 | 2 (15) | −1 | −2 | 1 | −5 | 15 |
| $K_2$ | 5 (10) | 7 (0) | 4 | 3 (5) | 6 (5) | 0 (5) | 25 |
| $K_3$ | 3 | 5 | 2 (10) | 1 | 4 (5) | −2 | 15 |
| $O_j$ | 10 | 15 | 10 | 5 | 10 | 5 | 55 |

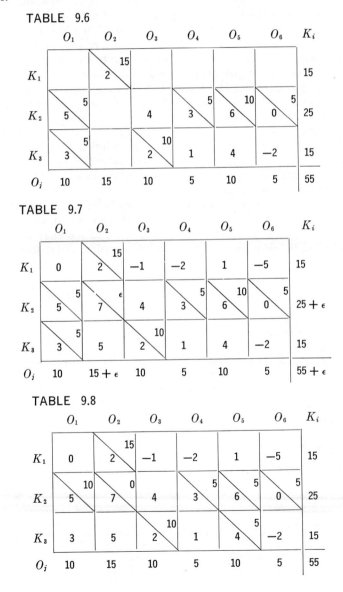

Note that we cannot determine *all* indirect costs from the rule that the difference between any two rows and any two columns in an indirect cost table is constant. This is so since we have only a single entry for the first row and second column. The problem arises as the current solution is degenerate. That is, a nondegenerate basic feasible solution would contain $m + n - 1 = 8$ positive variables, and the present solution contains but 7. We can, however, set up what is to all intents and purposes a second problem with margin entries as in Table 9.7 and with $\epsilon$ an arbitrarily small quantity. Now, setting $x_{22} = \epsilon$, we can complete the indirect cost table for this "new" problem and nondegenerate basic feasible solution. These are the entries in the body of Table 9.7. Here all indirect costs save $\bar{c}_{35} = c_{35}$ lie below the direct costs. Hence the allocation scheme is already optimal, but there is an equivalent optimal alternative. Having attained the optimal for the "new" problem, we merely set the arbitrary $\epsilon = 0$ and obtain the optimal solution to the original problem.

To find an alternative optimum, note that we wish to allocate units to $x_{35}$, where $\bar{c}_{35} = c_{35}$. To do this via the current optimum, we can reduce $x_{25}$ by 5, increase $x_{35}$ by 5, reduce $x_{31}$ by 5, and increase $x_{21}$ by 5. Note that the 5 units by which $x_{35}$ is increased is the maximum amount by which $x_{31}$ may be reduced. Clearly, we could also reduce $x_{31}$ by 1 unit, and so on. Table 9.8 shows the new indirect costs, again with $x_{22} = 0$ as part of the basic solution, and none exceeding the associated direct costs. Hence, the corner entries present an alternative optimum solution. The reader will find it instructive to set up the indirect cost table, and resolve the problem, with $x_{13} = \epsilon$. Then, the algorithm will suggest that units be added to $x_{15}$. This can be accomplished, using the current pattern, by reducing $x_{13} = \epsilon$, increasing $x_{33}$ and $x_{21}$, and reducing $x_{25}$ and $x_{31}$. The change made will necessarily be in the amount $\epsilon$, which is the minimum allocation to a variable to be reduced. Thus, in general, when we wish to introduce an $x_{ij}$ into the solution, we first reduce an $x_{ik}$ already in the solution, increase an $x_{sk}$ in the solution, reduce an $x_{st}$ in the solution, and so forth until an $x_{rj}$ in the solution is reduced.

## EXERCISES

1. Consider the following problem:

$$\begin{array}{ll} \text{Maximize} & Z = 10x^2 - 15y^2 - 20x + 50y \\ \text{subject to} & x^2 \geq 1, \\ & -x^3 + y^2 \leq 1.25, \\ & y \geq 0, \quad x \text{ unconstrained.} \end{array}$$

   (a) Solve this problem using the separable functions approach.
   (b) Solve this problem as a nonlinear programming problem using the Kuhn-Tucker conditions.
   (c) Solve this problem graphically.
   (d) Set up and solve the dual to this problem.

2. Consider the following problem:

$$\begin{array}{ll} \text{Maximize} & Z = 20xy - 10x^2 - 15y^2 - 20x + 50y \\ \text{subject to} & 2x + y \geq 8, \\ & -3x + 4y \leq 5, \\ & x, y \geq 0. \end{array}$$

(a) Solve this problem as a general nonlinear programming problem.
(b) Solve this problem as a quadratic programming problem.
(c) Solve this problem graphically.
(d) Set up and solve the dual to this problem.

3. (a) Solve the LP problems of Exercise 22, Chapter 7, where the solutions must be integer solutions.
(b) Solve these LP problems, using the Kuhn-Tucker conditions, as nonlinear programming problems.
(c) Set up and solve the duals to these problems.

4. Consider the following LP problem:

$$\begin{aligned} \text{Maximize} \quad & Z = \mathbf{c}'\mathbf{x} \\ \text{subject to} \quad & \mathbf{Ax} = \mathbf{d}, \\ & \mathbf{x} \geq \mathbf{0}. \end{aligned}$$

(a) Could this be solved as a Lagrangian problem? Why not do it that way?
(b) Could this be solved as a quadratic programming problem? What does this suggest?

5. Consider the direct cost table for the following transportation problem:

| | $K_1$ | $K_2$ | $K_3$ | $K_4$ | $K_5$ | |
|---|---|---|---|---|---|---|
| $O_1$ | 5 | 3 | 7 | 8 | 10 | 35 |
| $O_2$ | 2 | 3 | 2 | 6 | 1 | 20 |
| $O_3$ | 7 | 3 | 6 | 5 | 5 | 45 |
| $O_4$ | 8 | 5 | 4 | 9 | 9 | 25 |
| | 50 | 10 | 20 | 25 | 20 | |

What allocations will minimize the transportation costs?

6. Consider a firm that produces two products. The firm determines that its monthly output of product 1 will be $Q_1 = 1000$ and of product 2 will be $Q_2 = 3000$. Both products are to be sold from a retail outlet. Product 1 requires 5 cubic feet of space and product 2 requires 2 cubic feet of space per unit. All told, the outlet has 3000 cubic feet of space.

The set-up cost associated with deliveries of the two products to the outlet are \$100 and \$50 for deliveries of products 1 and 2, respectively. The average costs of producing products 1 and 2 are \$50 and \$100, respectively. The company calculates its rate of interest on funds tied up in inventory at 6 percent per year. Product 1 sells for $\$P_1$ and produce 2 for $\$P_2$. Shortage costs are infinite.

(a) Determine an optimum inventory policy for the firm.
(b) Generalize this problem and its solution for $n$ products.

7. Consider the production function $Q = 1000F_1^{.2}F_2^{.3}F_3^{.4}$; also, consider the following factor supply curves: $W_1 = 10F_1$, $W_2 = 5F_2$, and $W_3 = 10F_3$. The firm wishes to restrict its expenditures on each of the three factors to a maximum of \$1000, \$500, and \$2000, respectively.

(a) Determine the maximum output the firm can get for its money, by solving this as a nonlinear programming problem.
(b) Convert this to a linear programming problem and solve.
(c) Set up, solve, and interpret the dual to this problem.

8. Show that if $L(\mathbf{x}, \boldsymbol{\lambda}^*)$ is a concave function of $\mathbf{x}$ for all $\mathbf{x}$, and if $L(\mathbf{x}^*, \boldsymbol{\lambda})$ is a convex function of $\boldsymbol{\lambda}$ for all $\boldsymbol{\lambda}$, then $L(\mathbf{x}, \boldsymbol{\lambda})$ has a global saddle point at $(\mathbf{x}^*, \boldsymbol{\lambda}^*)$.

9. Suppose that, for the short-run demand curve of DURK in the Appendix to Chapter 3, the DURK analysts are convinced that the sum of the income and price elasticities of demand is not negative. Estimate the long-run demand elasticities.

10. Suppose a discriminating monopolist has a total cost curve given by $C = 1000 + 10Q^2$. His demand curve in one market is given by $P_1 = 10{,}000 - 2Q_1$, and in the second market by $P_2 = 10{,}000 - 3Q_2$. The monopolist does not wish to charge more than a 10 percent differential per unit in the two markets, because if the differential is any greater, buyers will find it profitable to travel to the lower-price market for their purchases. How much should the monopolist produce, and at what price should he sell in each market?

11. Suppose the firm discussed in Section 9.2 has a management that is primarily interested in maximizing total sales revenue. Management recognizes, however, a need to maintain profits at a respectable level. The current level of respectability is \$6000. How much of what should be produced?

12. A monopolist produces two products jointly. The total cost function for their joint production is given by $C = (5Q_1 + Q_2)^2 + 1000$. The demand curves for $Q_1$ and $Q_2$ are given by $P_1 = 20{,}000 - 5Q_1 - 3P_2$ and $P_2 = 1500 - 2Q_2 - 2P_1$.
   (a) How much should he produce of what in order to maximize profit?
   (b) Suppose the monopolist wishes to maximize sales revenue, but insists on earning at least \$1500 in profit. Now how much of what should he produce?
   (c) Set up, solve, and interpret the dual to the latter problem.

13. Derive the solutions for, and interpret the values of, the dual variables in the general integer programming problem.

14. Given a just-identified system of two simultaneous equations with two exogenous variables, suppose the sum of the parameters in each of the two structural equations is to be constrained. Develop a procedure for estimating all the parameters of the model using constrained least squares.

15. A consumer with a total expenditure potential of \$10,000 may purchase three goods: $q_1$ selling at \$2, $q_2$ selling at \$3, and $q_3$ selling at \$4. His needs and market limitations demand that he purchase no more than 1000 units of $q_1$ and no less than 750 units of $q_3$. His utility function is given by $U = q_1^{1/2}q_2^{1/4}q_3^{1/8}$.
   (a) How much $q_i$ $(i = 1, 2, 3)$ should he purchase?
   (b) Derive his demand curve for $q_2$.
   (c) Set up, solve, and interpret the dual to the problem you solved in the first part of this exercise.

16. Suppose the firm of Section 9.4 faces a demand curve given by $P = 10{,}000 - Q/2$. Derive the firm's short-run demand curve for $F_2$.

17. Suppose the entries in Table 9.2 are unit profits. Determine a shipping pattern to maximize total profit.

18. Formulate the dual to the general quadratic programming problem of Equations (9.11a–c), where **D** is positive semidefinite and the problem is a minimization problem.

19. (a) Formulate the dual to the problem of Equations (9.22) and (9.22a, b) and interpret the meaning of the values of the dual variables.
   (b) Formulate the dual to the general integer programming problem and interpret the meaning of the values of the dual variables.

20. Solve Equations (9.14a–c), first with the 10 in the first constraint replaced by 9, and second with $F_1/F_2 \geq 1$ replaced by $F_1/F_2 \geq 1.1$. Compare the change effected in $Q^*$ with the changes suggested by the values of the dual variables in the original problem. How will $Q^*$ change if both constraints are changed simultaneously?

# 10

# SOME EXTENSIONS OF THE NEOCLASSICAL THEORY: Alternatives to Profit Maximization

## 10.1 INTRODUCTION

In most of the preceding discussion it has been assumed that the goal of entrepreneurial decisions would be profit maximization or, where equivalent, cost minimization. The economist's traditional concern with, and interest in, the implications of profit-maximizing behavior is certainly not misplaced. If one is to operate a business, and if the business is to survive, it seems a rather good idea that the business make some money.[1] Failing any compelling alternative, making as much money as possible

[1] In *The Theory of Business Enterprise* (New York: Charles Scribner's Sons, 1904), written at the turn of the century, Thorstein Veblen commented: "The motive of business is pecuniary gain, the method is essentially purchase and sale. The aim and usual outcome is an accumulation of wealth. Men whose aim is not increase of possessions do not go into business, particularly not on an independent footing" (p. 20). In "Uncertainty, Evolution and Economic Theory" [*Journal of Political Economy*, **LVIII**:3 (June 1950), 211–221], Armen A. Alchian suggests that "realized profits, not *maximum* profits, are the mark of success and viability" (p. 213). One might consider these remarks, and the profit-maximization assumption, when reading the following excerpts from an article that appeared in the Louisville *Courier-Journal* (April 2, 1968) shortly after men's necklaces became fashionable (in some circles): "Jewelers are moving cautiously when they're working in expensive metals, but they are ready to sell men's necklaces if the fad continues. Not Tiffany's, however. Walter Hoving, the store's chairman, is putting up a militant resistance to the whole idea. 'We don't think they are attractive and we don't care how much business we lose on them,' Hoving said recently. 'We don't carry diamond rings for men, either, and we pass up about $3 million worth of business a year on them.' Hoving added that he couldn't prevent a man from shopping in the women's department 'But if we know a man is buying a necklace for himself, we will refuse to sell it.'. . . If Tiffany's shuns the necklace, Cartier, five blocks down Fifth Avenue, has no such inhibitions. . . . When men like Richard Burton go around sporting necklaces and starting fads, jewelers argue that it would be foolish to resist."

It might be noted that some feel profit maximization is unrealistic because it is too *difficult* and it is *immoral* [Robert N. Anthony, "The Trouble with Profit Maximization,"

seems like another good idea—especially since, given knowledge of the relevant functions and the calculus, profit maximization may require little effort beyond what the entrepreneur-manager would have to expend anyhow. Moreover, in the purely competitive industry, one may have only two options: either maximize profits or suffer a loss. The latter is a consequence that only the most philanthropic of entrepreneurs can afford to accept—and probably not for an extended period.

In contrast, the monopolist or oligopolist *may* be able to exercise some discretion over whether to maximize profit. Indeed, as we have seen, the interdependencies introduced in oligopolistic industries may encourage the replacement of strict profit maximization with some alternative criterion, such as maximizing the minimum *expected* market share.

The discretion to choose among alternative goals, or to give weight to alternative and perhaps conflicting criteria, can be particularly important in a firm in which management and ownership are separated. On the one hand, the *owners* of the firm, the stockholders, could be concerned solely with the firm's long-term profit position. The *stream* of profits generated by the firm over time would presumably affect dividends and the value of the firm's shares—and these are the things that concern the stockholders.[2] On the other hand, *management* could be concerned with maintaining the firm's market position, adding to the firm's sales revenue, or increasing the total assets controlled by the firm. This could be the case when managerial salaries and/or job security are thought to be related to variables such as the firm's market share, sales, or assets, rather than to profits.[3]

---

*Harvard Business Review*, **XXXVIII**:6 (Nov.–Dec. 1960), 134]; some feel it is socially the most efficient device [Peter F. Drucker, *Concept of the Corporation* (New York: The John Day Company, Inc., 1946), p. 240]; and some feel it is inconsistent to hold that profit maximization brings out the worst in people and also that it is socially undesirable to discriminate on the basis of race, color, and creed [Almen A. Alchian and Reuben A. Kessel, "Competition, Monopoly, and the Pursuit of Pecuniary Gain," in *Aspects of Labor Economics* (Princeton, N.J.: Princeton University Press, 1962), pp. 174–175].

[2] For interesting discussions of this point, see the following: R. A. Gordon, *Business Leadership in the Large Corporation* (Berkeley, Calif.: University of California Press, 1945); P. W. S. Andrews, *Manufacturing Business* (London: Macmillan and Co., Ltd., 1949); Joseph W. McGuire, *Theories of Business Behavior* (Englewood Cliffs, N.J.: Prentice-Hall, Inc., 1964), particularly p. 53; and R. Joseph Monsen, Jr., and Anthony Downs, "A Theory of Large Managerial Firms," *Journal of Political Economy*, **LXXIII**:3 (June 1965), 221–236.

[3] One can discuss this and related issues at some length, and many have done so. In the beginning, there was the classic study by A. A. Berle, Jr., and Gardiner C. Means, *The Modern Corporation and Private Profits* (New York: The Macmillan Company, 1933). Herrymon Maurer [*Great Enterprise* (New York: The Macmillan Company, 1955)] has put forth the view that "It is the common habit of contemporary managers to reach decisions on the basis of what will be good for the company, not on the basis of what will produce the highest immediate dividends or the greatest rise in stock values. . . . [Regular recompense] could be cited as an incentive to make executives stay at their job. But . . . rarely does premium or penalty attach to executive performance" (pp. 78–79). Gordon (*Business Leadership in the Large Corporation*, p. 278) has argued that nonpecuniary motives alone, such as power, prestige, desire for security, an urge for creative work, and group loyalty, "are sufficient to account for substantial differences in the compensation of executives of approximately comparable ability." Alternatively, it has been held that "The assumption of profit maximization obscures the fact that the entrepreneur often

The notion that management might view profit as just one of many variables to consider in decision making is by no means of recent vintage. It has long been recognized that such diverse factors as return on investment and entrepreneurial leisure preferences, as well as such similar factors as market share and sales revenue, frequently play key roles in real-world decision making.[4] By and large, however, this variety of goals has remained on the perimeter of neoclassical economic theory, rather than being included in the core. One reason is that such goals frequently imply a brand of economic irrationality that economists tend to be reluctant to support with elegant models. Another, perhaps more practical, reason is that inclusion of these goals in a precise analytical framework is difficult to accomplish and carry out to the bitter and meaningful end without certain advanced mathematical techniques. The techniques of mathematical programming, in particular, can be especially useful in this connection. Now that these are part of our analytical hardware, we shall turn to some of the suggested alternatives to profit-maximization myopia.

## 10.2 PROFIT VERSUS LEISURE

The business world is quite demanding of the entrepreneur who must produce or perish. Whether he has to produce so as to *maximize* profit is, however, another matter. Hicks, for example, has suggested that the owner-manager may be

---

maximizes *his* equity and not the present value of the firm's net worth. And where control is at stake, the two objectives may prompt different behavior." [M. W. Reder, "A Reconsideration of the Marginal Productivity Theory," *Journal of Political Economy*, **LV**:5 (Oct. 1947), 455.] Others have, however, been quite taken with the notion that management will be concerned with events in the securities market, and with maintaining the firm's market value and ability to generate capital. See, for example, Franco Modigliani and Merton H. Miller, "The Cost of Capital, Corporation Finance and the Theory of Investment," *American Economic Review*, **XLVIII**:3 (June 1958), 261–297; John Lintner, "The Financing of Corporations," in Edward S. Mason, ed., *The Corporation in Modern Society* (Cambridge, Mass.: Harvard University Press, 1960), pp. 166–201; and Carl Kaysen, "Another View of Corporate Capitalism," *Quarterly Journal of Economics*, **LXXIX**:1 (Feb. 1965), 41–51.

In some early empirical work, Arch Patton ["Current Practices in Executive Compensation," *Harvard Business Review*, **XXIX**:1 (Jan. 1951), 56–64] concluded that profit was the prime mover behind executive compensation and that, *within industries*, "the profit level of the individual company is by far the most important determinant of executive compensation" (p. 58). Alternatively, empirical studies by David R. Roberts ["A General Theory of Executive Compensation Based on Statistically Tested Propositions," *Quarterly Journal of Economics*, **LXX**:2 (May 1956), 270–294] and J. W. McGuire, J. S. Y. Chiu, and A. O. Elbing ["Executive Incomes, Sales and Profits," *American Economic Review*, **LII**:4 (Sept. 1962), 753–761] conclude that it is corporate sales, and not corporate profits, to which executive salaries are actually tied. As an interesting theoretical argument in support of the latter work, Herbert A. Simon ["The Compensation of Executives," *Sociometry*, **20**:1 (March 1957), 32–35] develops a model grounded in the hypothesis that "an executive's salary 'should' be *b* times the salary of his immediate subordinates, no matter what his level" (p. 33). Also see George J. Staubus, "Payments for the Use of Capital and the Matching Process," *Accounting Review*, **XXVII**:1 (Jan. 1952), 104–113.

[4] For an empirical view of business pricing policies and their motivation, see Robert F. Lanzillotti, "Pricing Objectives in Large Companies," *American Economic Review*, **XLVIII**:5 (Dec. 1958), 921–940.

motivated by a variety of objectives including the "quiet life."[5] Unfortunately, and the poets notwithstanding, the best things in life are rarely free. Thus, when the firm's profit position is directly related to entrepreneurial effort, the owner-manager will have to reconcile his desires for leisure and for all the things that money can buy. It is to this reconcilation that Scitovsky addressed himself.[6]

Let us summarize the entrepreneur's preferences for profits versus leisure in a utility function comparable to that encountered in the theory of consumer behavior.[7] Let $U = u(\pi, \rho)$ describe this function, where $\pi$ denotes profits and $\rho$ denotes leisure (or relaxation or recreation). The entrepreneur is assumed to have a positive preference for both profits and leisure. Further, suppose that the firm's technology links profits to entrepreneurial effort, $F_e = -\rho$, by the function $\pi = g(F_e)$. That is, entrepreneurial effort, or negative leisure, is a factor of production. *Given* the levels at which the other factors are to be employed, and *given* the firm's production function, profits can be written as a function of $F_e$, entrepreneurial effort, alone. Then with $\pi = g(F_e)$, $\pi - g(F_e) = f(\pi, F_e) = 0$. The latter will be referred to as the *transformation* function between profits and leisure. The terminology reflects the fact that $f(\pi, F_e)$ summarizes the *alternatives* from which the entrepreneur *must* choose. Presumably, the greater the effort the greater the profit, with the possibilities running the gamut from maximum profit and minimum leisure, to maximum leisure leading to zero profit. As in Figure 10.1, it is assumed the function is concave, with profits increasing at a decreasing rate as effort increases (or as leisure, which is negative effort, decreases).

Just as the consumer is assumed to maximize his utility subject to a budget con-

[5] Specifically, "It seems not at all unlikely that people in monopolistic positions will very often be people with sharply rising subjective costs; if this is so, they are likely to exploit their advantage much more by not bothering to get very near the position of maximum profits, than by straining themselves to get very close to it. The best of all monopoly profits is a quiet life." [J. R. Hicks, "The Theory of Monopoly," *Econometrica*, **3** (Jan. 1935), 8.]

[6] T. Scitovsky, "A Note on Profit Maximization and Its Implications," *Review of Economic Studies*, **XI**:1 (Winter 1943), 57–60.

[7] In so doing, it is implicitly assumed that the entrepreneur has incorporated into the function his notions of how the profits would be spent. For related discussions of entrepreneurial preferences and their role in decision making see the following: Benjamin Higgins, "Elements of Indeterminacy in the Theory of Non-Perfect Competition," *American Economic Review*, **XXIX**:3 (Sept. 1939), 468–479; Talcott Parsons, "The Motivation of Economic Activities," *Canadian Journal of Economics and Political Science*, **VI**:2 (May 1940), 187–202; E. G. Nourse, "The Meaning of 'Price Policy'," *Quarterly Journal of Economics*, **LV**:1 (Feb. 1941), 175–209; Gerhard Tintner, "The Theory of Production Under Nonstatic Conditions," *Journal of Political Economy*, **L**:5 (Oct. 1942), 645–667; Chester I. Barnard, *The Functions of the Executive* (Cambridge, Mass.: Harvard University Press, 1950), p. 145; J. P. Nettl, "A Note on Entrepreneurial Behaviour," *Review of Economic Studies*, **XXIV**:64 (Feb. 1957), 87–94; J. E. Haring and G. C. Smith, "Utility Theory and Profit Maximization," *American Economic Review*, **XLIX**:4 (Sept. 1959), 566–583; Harold L. Johnson, "A Behavioral Approach to the Business Enterprise," *Southern Economic Journal*, **XXVII**:1 (July 1960), 1–10; Jose Encarnación, Jr., "Constraints and the Firm's Utility Function," *Review of Economic Studies*, **XXXI**:86 (April 1964), 113–120; and C. E. Ferguson, "The Theory of Multidimensional Utility Analysis in Relation to Multiple-Goal Business Behavior: A Synthesis," *Southern Economic Journal*, **XXXII**:2 (Oct. 1965), 169–175.

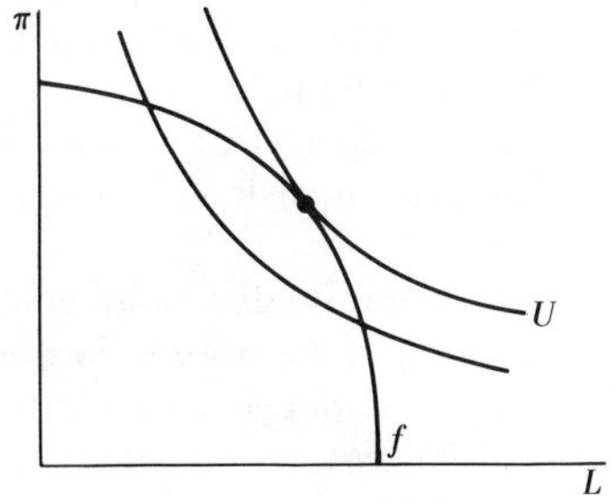


Fig. 10.1

straint, the entrepreneur is assumed to maximize his utility subject to the transformation constraint. The entrepreneur's problem is thus to choose $\pi$ and $F_e$ so as to maximize $U = u(\pi, \rho)$, subject to $f(\pi, F_e) = 0$. Setting up the Lagrangian, we have, $L(\pi, F_e; \lambda) = u(\pi, \rho) - \lambda f(\pi, F_e)$. Assuming the differentiability of the functions and that we have a convex indifference curve between profits and leisure to go with our concave transformation function, the second-order conditions hold and the maximization requires that

$$\frac{\partial L(\pi, F_e; \lambda)}{\partial \pi} = \frac{\partial u}{\partial \pi} - \lambda \frac{\partial f}{\partial \pi} = 0, \tag{10.1a}$$

$$\frac{\partial L(\pi, F_e; \lambda)}{\partial F_e} = \frac{\partial u}{\partial \rho}\frac{\partial \rho}{\partial F_e} - \lambda \frac{\partial f}{\partial F_e} = -\frac{\partial u}{\partial \rho} - \lambda \frac{\partial f}{\partial F_e} = 0, \tag{10.1b}$$

$$f(\pi, F_e) = 0. \tag{10.1c}$$

Equations (10.1a–c) imply that

$$\lambda = \frac{\partial u}{\partial \pi}\Big/\frac{\partial f}{\partial \pi} = -\frac{\partial u}{\partial \rho}\Big/\frac{\partial f}{\partial F_e}$$

or

$$-\frac{\partial u}{\partial \rho}\Big/\frac{\partial u}{\partial \pi} = \frac{\partial f}{\partial F_e}\Big/\frac{\partial f}{\partial \pi}. \tag{10.2}$$

But $df = (\partial f/\partial \pi)\, d\pi + (\partial f/\partial F_e)\, dF_e = 0$, or

$$\frac{\partial f}{\partial F_e}\Big/\frac{\partial f}{\partial \pi} = -\left(\frac{d\pi}{dF_e}\right)_{f=0}.$$

The latter expression will be called the rate of transformation of entrepreneurial effort for profit. Similarly, let $dU = (\partial u/\partial \pi)\, d\pi + (\partial u/\partial \rho)\, d\rho = 0$, or

$$\frac{\partial u}{\partial \rho}\Big/\frac{\partial u}{\partial \pi} = -\left(\frac{d\pi}{d\rho}\right)_{U=\text{constant}}.$$

The latter expression will be called the rate of substitution in preference of leisure for profit. Hence, by substitution into (10.2), the first-order conditions for utility maximization are seen to imply that

$$\left(\frac{d\pi}{d\rho}\right)_{U=\text{constant}} = -\left(\frac{d\pi}{dF_e}\right)_{f=0}, \tag{10.3}$$

or entrepreneurial effort should be expended to the point at which the additional profit that the additional effort *will generate* exactly equals the additional profit that the entrepreneur *will demand*, before he is willing to make the sacrifice in leisure time necessitated by the additional effort. This is the tangency point between the transformation function and the entrepreneur's highest indifference curve in Figure 10.1.

One might, however, question the profundity of an analysis that suggests that an entrepreneur will work only so long as he deems the rewards worth the effort of attaining them[8]—especially since it is not at all clear whether the entrepreneur's potential laxity in deigning not to seek the maximum profit position will lead to a greater or lesser output or price than in the classical $MR = MC$ case. That is, there may be some point beyond which additional entrepreneurial effort will not increase profit, and there may be a continuum of profit levels that are attainable with the same maximum effort. But it may require the same effort on the behalf of the *entrepreneur* in his decision-making role to produce beyond the $MR = MC$ point as to produce below it, even though increased production would require greater effort from the *other* factors than would lesser production.

## 10.3 SALES MAXIMIZATION

One of the more recent thought-provoking additions to the lore of the theory of the firm is Baumol's sales-maximization model.[9] Having been impressed with what classical economists would view as a possibly inappropriate, and certainly disproportionate, management emphasis on sales *revenue*, Baumol has suggested that modern corporate management may in fact seek to maximize *sales* and not profits, subject only to a minimum *acceptable* profits constraint.

There are some very sound reasons why management might seek to maximize sales, rather than profits, particularly where management and ownership are sepa-

[8] And it has been so questioned in K. E. Boulding, "Implications for General Economics of More Realistic Theories of the Firm," *American Economic Review*, **XLII**:2 (May 1952), 35–44.

[9] W. J. Baumol has developed the model in twin packages. In the chronologically first package ["On the Theory of Oligopoly," *Economica*, **XXV**:99 (Aug. 1958), 187–198], he sets forth the view that "*once his profit exceeds some vaguely defined minimum level,* [the businessman] is prepared to sacrifice further increments in profits if he can thereby obtain large revenues" (p. 187). In the second package ["On the Theory of Expansion of the Firm," *American Economic Review*, **LII**:5 (Dec. 1962), 1078–1087], "maximization of rate of growth of sales revenue seems a somewhat better approximation to the goals of many management groups in large firms than is maximization of the current level of sales" (p. 1085). Some early empirical support for the role of business volume was inferred from his "preliminary investigations" in George Katona's study *Psychological Analysis of Economic Behavior* (New York: McGraw-Hill Inc., 1951), pp. 202–203. In a more recent study [Marshall Hall, "Sales Revenue Maximization: An Empirical Examination," *Journal of Industrial Economics*, **XV**:2 (April 1967), 143–156] empirical support could not be found for *either* sales *or* profit maximization. It has also been suggested that, given oligopolistic interdependence, it is precisely in these sorts of situations that sales maximization is not a tenable hypothesis [William G. Shepherd, "On Sales-Maximizing and Oligopoly Behaviour," *Economica*, **XXIX**:116 (Nov. 1962), 420–424]. Alternatively, it has been suggested that managers might seek to maximize *growth*, subject to a *security* constraint [Robin Marris, "A Model of the 'Managerial' Enterprise," *Quarterly Journal of Economics*, **LXXVII**:2 (May 1963), 185–209].

rate. First, there is the previously alluded to evidence (footnote 3) to suggest that managerial salaries may be directly related to sales. Second, sales is a very popular surrogate for measuring firm size, and size implies several things to which owners and managers alike might wish the firm to aspire. The ability to attract capital, the sense if not fact of security that a substantial market position may engender, and the ability to survive, may all be associated with size of firm. Still, neither management nor the firm can survive in the absence of some minimum level of profitability to satisfy the *owners'* demands—hence, the minimum-profits constraint to go along with the sales-maximization objective.

Consider again a firm producing a single product via a single process. Given the familiar definitions of $P$ and $Q$, and letting $A$ be the level of the firm's advertising expenditures, we shall write the firm's demand curve as $P = D(Q, A)$. The relationship between advertising and demand is perhaps best described by the hypothesis that the greater the level of advertising, the greater the number of units that will be demanded at a given price. For algebraic convenience, however, it is assumed that consumers will be willing to pay a higher price for a given quantity, the greater the level of advertising expenditure. This is not to say that there may not be diminishing returns to advertising programs, nor that a good TV aspirin commercial may not drive one to a good nonadvertised alcoholic beverage.

Let $F$ denote fixed costs, $C = c(Q)$ denote total variable cost, $\tau < 1$ denote the profits-tax rate, and $\bar{\pi}$ denote the minimum-profit requirement, net of taxes. The sales-maximizing firm's problem may be stated as:

$$\text{Maximize} \qquad R = PQ = D(Q, A)Q \tag{10.4a}$$

$$\text{subject to} \quad (1 - \tau)[D(Q, A)Q - c(Q) - A - F] \geq \bar{\pi}, \tag{10.4b}$$

$$Q, A \geq 0, \tag{10.4c}$$

where $[D(Q, A)Q - c(Q) - A - F]$ is pretax profit.

The Lagrangian function for (10.4a–c) is

$$L(Q, A; \lambda) = D(Q, A)Q - \lambda[(1 - \tau)[D(Q, A)Q - c(Q) - A - F] - \bar{\pi}].$$

Assuming the appropriate curvature properties, the Kuhn-Tucker conditions to maximize $R$ require that

$$\frac{\partial L}{\partial Q} = MR - \lambda(1 - \tau)(MR - MC) \leq 0, \tag{10.5a}$$

$$\frac{\partial L}{\partial A} = \left(\frac{\partial D}{\partial A}\right) Q - \lambda(1 - \tau)\left(\frac{\partial D}{\partial A}\right) Q + \lambda(1 - \tau) \leq 0, \tag{10.5b}$$

$$\frac{\partial L}{\partial \lambda} = (1 - \tau)[D(Q, A)Q - c(Q) - A - F] - \bar{\pi} \geq 0. \tag{10.5c}$$

Some quite interesting inferences can be drawn from (10.5a–c). First, if $Q > 0$, that is if the firm chooses to produce, (10.5a) holds as an equality. Then, $\partial L/\partial Q = 0$, or $MR/(MR - MC) = \lambda(1 - \tau)$. But the $\geq$ in (10.4b) implies $\lambda \leq 0$. Since $\tau < 1$, it follows that $MC \geq MR$. That is, the firm produces at or beyond the point at which $MR = MC$, selling the greater output at a price that with $\partial D/\partial Q < 0$ is less than the profit-maximizing price. The profit constraint means, however, that the firm will not necessarily produce the revenue-maximizing output—that is, the output at which $MR = 0$.

Similarly, $\partial L/\partial A \leq 0$ implies that $\partial D/\partial A \leq -\lambda(1-\tau)/Q[1-\lambda(1-\tau)]$. To help interpret the latter result, note that the profit-maximizing firm would set advertising expenditures and output so as to maximize $(1-\tau)\pi$. This occurs where $\partial\pi/\partial A = \partial\pi/\partial Q = 0$, given that the second-order conditions hold. The first-order conditions for the profit maximizer are

$$\left[\frac{\partial D(Q, A)}{\partial Q}\right] Q + D(Q, A) = MC \quad \text{and} \quad \left[\frac{\partial D(Q, A)}{\partial A}\right] Q = 1.$$

Solving these two equations simultaneously, the first equality is the $MR = MC$ condition, where marginal revenue is evaluated with advertising expenditure at its optimal level $A^*$. The left side of the second equality is the change in total revenue at the $MR = MC$ output (that is, change in price multiplied by total output) effected by a small increment in advertising expenditure. The equality thus implies that advertising expenditure will increase in the profit-maximizing firm so long as the incremental expenditure adds as much or more to total revenue as it adds to total cost.[10]

In the sales-revenue-maximizing firm, there are two cases to consider: (1) $(1-\tau)\pi = \bar{\pi}$ and $\lambda < 0$; and (2) $(1-\tau)\pi > \bar{\pi}$ and $\lambda = 0$. In the *second* case, the revenue-maximizing position occurs at a smaller output than that at which profit equals the minimum requirement. Hence, as seen from (10.5a) and (10.5b) with $Q$ and $A > 0$ and $\lambda = 0$, $MR = 0$ and $[\partial D(Q, A)/\partial A]Q = 0$. That is, advertising is pushed to the point where it is no longer effective in increasing the price consumers are willing to pay, and the firm operates at the point of unit elasticity ($MR = 0$) on this highest possible demand curve.[11] In the *first* case, when profits just equal the minimum requirement, with $Q$ and $A > 0$ and $\lambda < 0$, $0 < MR < MC$ and

$$\left[\frac{\partial D(Q, A)}{\partial A}\right] Q = \frac{1-\tau}{(1-\tau) - \dfrac{1}{\lambda}} < 1.$$

In this case, advertising is not undertaken to the point where it is no longer effective; nevertheless, the level of advertising will extent *beyond* the point at which it is *economically* justified—that is, beyond the point at which it adds more to total revenue than it costs to undertake. Because of the profit constraint, however, this tendency to advertise will be lessened as the tax rate increases and as fixed costs increase. Thus, unlike the profit maximizer, the sales maximizer's production *and* advertising policies *may* be influenced by *both* the profits tax rate and the level of fixed costs. These will exercise influence when the profit constraint is binding. Then, increases in $\tau$ or $F$ will mean the constraint will be violated and will necessitate cutbacks in advertising and production more in accord with an $MR = MC$ decision. These cutbacks are required in order to achieve greater pretax profits and restore the constraint equality.

[10] For the early neoclassical treatment, see Edward H. Chamberlin, *The Theory of Monopolistic Competition* (Cambridge, Mass.: Harvard University Press, 1960), chaps. VI–VII. Also see Roy W. Jastram, "Advertising Outlays Under Oligopoly," *Review of Economics and Statistics*, **XXXI**:2 (May 1949), 106–109.

[11] Assuming that this point exists, which for this second case would rule out the class of constant-elasticity demand curves, except for unit elasticity, where sales *revenue* is unalterable.

The sales-maximization model does yield some interesting analytical implications to contrast with the classical model. Moreover, it recognizes and admits some additional characteristics of the modern corporation—the oligopolistic firm with the nonowner manager—seeking greater volume and the security that is purported to go with it. The question arises, however, as to why the manager who has been able to determine the relevant functions and parameters with the certainty that enables him to reach the Lagrangian saddle point should be security motivated. Presumably, if his world is indeed one of certainty, the decision maker can choose to operate at *any* point on his demand and cost curves. That he does not choose the profit-maximizing point would suggest to some that his world is not worry-free: and it is not worry-free precisely because of the uncertainty that surrounds the relevant functions and parameters. This same criticism can be raised against the similar "managerial emoluments" model suggested by Williamson. Nonetheless, and with good reason, the latter has had sufficient impact on the theory of the firm to warrant its detailed consideration.

## 10.4 DISCRETIONARY PROFITS AND MANAGERIAL EMOLUMENTS

Although it is unique in the substantive issues that it raises, some of the roots of the Williamson model[12] may be found in each of the two models previously considered. First, the Williamson model recognizes the possibility that management will be able to exert some discretion over the level of profit the firm earns for, and the proportion of this profit that is distributed to, the firm's stockholders. The model leans heavily on the notion that the earnings distributed to the firm's ownership during a specified planning period must not fall below some minimum level of $\bar{\pi}$. Management may, however, exercise discretion as to how any earnings over and above $\bar{\pi}$ are to be distributed. In particular, all profit can be reported as such and the (corporate) profits tax paid on it. Alternatively, with stockholder contentment assured so long as *their* earnings do not fall below $\bar{\pi}$, the total amount the firm earns in excess of $\bar{\pi}$ can be spent as management sees fit.

On the one hand, a portion of these expenditures may be for staff or supporting personnel making some positive contribution to the firm's activities. These expenditures are denoted by $S$. $S$ may encompass expenditures for the sales force, service personnel, or others affecting the operating efficiency of the organization. In this

[12] O. E. Williamson, "Managerial Discretion and Business Behavior," *American Economic Review*, **LIII**:5 (Dec. 1963), 1032–1057; also, *The Economics of Discretionary Behavior: Managerial Objectives in a Theory of the Firm* (Englewood Cliffs, N.J.: Prentice-Hall, Inc., 1964). For related discussions, primarily some most interesting antecedents, see the following: Veblen, *The Theory of Business Enterprise*, pp. 156–157; Reder, "A Reconsideration of the Marginal Productivity Theory," p. 453; Richard A. Lester, "Equilibrium of the Firm," *American Economic Review*, **XXXIX**:2 (March 1949), 478–484; Maurer, *Great Enterprise*, pp. 108–109; R. M. Cyert and James G. March, "Organizational Factors in the Theory of Oligopoly," *Quarterly Journal of Economics*, **LXX**:1 (Feb. 1956), 44–64; Gardner C. Means, "Looking Around: Is Economic Theory Outmoded?" *Harvard Business Review*, **XXXVI**:3 (May–June 1958), 167; Anthony, "Profit Maximization"; Almarin Phillips, "Operations Research and the Theory of the Firm," *Southern Economic Journal*, **XXVIII**:4 (April 1962), 357–364; Adolf A. Berle, "The Impact of the Corporation on Classical Economic Theory," *Quarterly Journal of Economics*, **LXXIX**:1 (Feb. 1965), 25–40; and Monsen and Downs, "A Theory of Large Managerial Firms."

manner, $S$ is assumed to influence the price that one is willing to pay for the organization's product(s). Hence, $S$ plays a role in the Williamson model, comparable to the role played by $A$ in the Baumol model. On the other hand, a portion of management's distribution of earnings in excess of $\bar{\pi}$ may be allocated to emoluments that are not making a positive contribution to the firm. These are denoted by $M$. The emoluments could be in the form of additions to salary, office fixtures, or a paper-towel dispenser to replace the inoperative hot-air hand dryer in the men's washroom. Thus, management is assumed to exhibit a preference for supporting staff and personal consumption financed out of corporate profits, and the availability of above-minimum satisfactory profits makes feasible such fringe expenditures.

As a second feature, the Williamson model also allows for *management's* preferences and the earnings constraint by introducing a *management* utility function. This function, $U = u(S, M, \pi_d)$, expresses management's utility as a function of staff, emoluments, and *discretionary profit*. The latter, representing profits earned above the minimum required which management may spend as it sees fit, is given by $\pi_d = (1 - \tau)[D(Q, S)Q - c(Q) - S - M - F] - \bar{\pi}$. This expression is comparable to (10.4b) in the Baumol model. That is, it will be assumed that the firm produces a single product, subject to a total variable cost curve $c(Q)$. The demand for the product is described by $P = D(Q, S)$ and will be a function of the expenditures for staff. $\tau < 1$ is the tax rate on profits, $F$ is fixed cost, and $(1 - \tau)[D(Q, S) - c(Q) - S - M - F]$ is posttax profit.

It is assumed that management strives to maximize its own utility rather than the firm's profits. This will have to be accomplished, however, subject to the satisfaction of the minimum-profits constraint. Management's problem is therefore to select levels of output ($Q$), staff ($S$), and emoluments ($M$) so as to maximize $U$, subject to $\pi_d \geq 0$. The Lagrangian function is $L(Q, S, M; \lambda) = U - \lambda\pi_d$. The solution to the problem therefore requires the determination of $Q$, $S$, $M$, and $\lambda$ such that $(\partial L/\partial Q)Q = (\partial L/\partial S)S = (\partial L/\partial M)M = (\partial L/\partial \lambda)\lambda = 0$. Assume first that $Q$, $S$, $M$, and $\pi_d$ are positive, and that the functions have the appropriate curvature properties so that the Kuhn-Tucker conditions are necessary and sufficient to assure a global maximum. Under these conditions, we require that $\partial L/\partial Q = \partial L/\partial S = \partial L/\partial M = \lambda = 0$, or

$$\frac{\partial L}{\partial Q} = \frac{\partial u}{\partial \pi_d}\frac{\partial \pi_d}{\partial Q} - \lambda\frac{\partial \pi_d}{\partial Q} = \frac{\partial u}{\partial \pi_d}(1 - \tau)(MR - MC) = 0, \tag{10.6a}$$

$$\frac{\partial L}{\partial S} = \frac{\partial u}{\partial S} + \frac{\partial u}{\partial \pi_d}\frac{\partial \pi_d}{\partial S} - \lambda\frac{\partial \pi_d}{\partial S} = \frac{\partial u}{\partial S} + \frac{\partial u}{\partial \pi_d}(1 - \tau)\left[\frac{\partial R}{\partial S} - 1\right] = 0, \tag{10.6b}$$

$$\frac{\partial L}{\partial M} = \frac{\partial u}{\partial M} + \frac{\partial u}{\partial \pi_d}\frac{\partial \pi_d}{\partial M} - \lambda\frac{\partial \pi_d}{\partial M} = \frac{\partial u}{\partial M} + \frac{\partial u}{\partial \pi_d}(1 - \tau)(-1) = 0. \tag{10.6c}$$

Whenever management asserts a preference for discretionary profit, (10.6a) reduces to $MR = MC$, since $(1 - \tau)$ and $\partial u/\partial \pi_d > 0$. This is an extremely important implication of the model, for it suggests that even if some of the firm's earnings *are* diverted to staff and emoluments, and even if management is first concerned with its own preferences and only secondarily with those of the stockholders, the production operation itself is carried on in a manner that would be a comfort and joy to economic man himself.

Condition (10.6b) reduces to

$$\frac{\partial R}{\partial S} = \frac{-\dfrac{\partial u}{\partial S} + \dfrac{\partial u}{\partial \pi_d}(1-\tau)}{(1-\tau)\left(\dfrac{\partial u}{\partial \pi_d}\right)} = 1 - \frac{\dfrac{\partial u}{\partial S}}{\dfrac{\partial u}{\partial \pi_d}(1-\tau)}.$$

Since management asserts a preference for staff and discretionary profit, $\partial u/\partial S$ and $\partial u/\partial \pi_d > 0$. Hence, $[\partial u/\partial S]/[\partial u/\partial \pi_d](1-\tau) > 0$ and $\partial R/\partial S < 1$. That is, unlike the situation in the profit-maximizing firm, where staff is hired only to the point where it adds as much to revenue as it does to cost (that is, $\partial R/\partial S = 1$), here staff is hired *beyond* this point. This is comparable to the conclusions with respect to advertising in the Baumol model.

Similarly, from (10.6c)

$$\frac{\partial u}{\partial M} = \frac{\partial u}{\partial \pi_d}(1-\tau).$$

Note that with $dU = (\partial u/\partial M)\,dM + (\partial u/\partial \pi_d)\,d\pi_d = 0$, the previous equation implies that $-(d\pi_d/dM)_{U=\text{constant}} = (\partial u/\partial M)/(\partial u/\partial \pi_d) = (1-\tau)$ is the rate of substitution of emoluments for discretionary profits. We thus see that at the optimum, the rate of substitution of emoluments for discretionary profit is a function of the tax rate. With $\tau > 0$, emoluments are extended *beyond* the point at which the marginal utility of emoluments equals the marginal utility of discretionary profits. Without a tax on profits, management would extend its emoluments only so long as the additional satisfaction gleaned therefrom more than compensated for the sacrifice entailed in the reduction of discretionary profits. As the tax rate increases, $\pi_d$ will be decreased (and $\partial u/\partial \pi_d$ will thereby *increase*) and $M$ will be increased (and $\partial u/\partial M$ will thereby *decrease*). This will restore $(\partial u/\partial M)/(\partial u/\partial \pi_d) = (1-\tau)$, but at a lower ratio. In effect, management takes its rewards as emoluments in preference to sharing them with the government through taxes on profits.

It should also be noted, that unlike profit-maximizing behavior, not only will management utility-maximizing behavior be influenced by the tax rate on profits, but fixed costs will also be influential. The latter exert an influence through their effect on discretionary profits. Thus, an increase in fixed costs, $F$, will reduce $\pi_d$, ceteris paribus, and this reduction will in turn lead to a reduction in staff and emoluments. Again, however, output will remain at the $MR = MC$ point.

Finally, it should be noted that with $\pi_d = 0$ we may have $\lambda < 0$. In this case, (10.6a) still implies $MR = MC$; but from (10.6b) and (10.6c) we see that wherever a $\partial u/\partial \pi_d$ term appears in an earlier expression, this must now be replaced with a $[(\partial u/\partial \pi_d) - \lambda]$ term. With $\pi_d = 0$, $\partial u/\partial \pi_d$ will be higher. Hence with $\lambda < 0$, this means that the new expressions for $\partial R/\partial S$ and $\partial u/\partial M$ will be increased, or that there will be a cutback in staff and emoluments. The latter will, however, be as large as they can be under these very trying minimum-earnings circumstances. The value of $\lambda < 0$ is, in effect, an opportunity cost (in terms of "marginal utility") that reflects the "worth"to management of having the owners be content with a lower minimum-earnings requirement.

Unlike the previous two models, the Williamson model does retain the key profit-maximizing *production* condition of the neoclassical model. This is true even though profit maximization is not an explicit goal. This feature is not without some appeal, particularly to neoclassical diehards. The recognition that management will also serve its own ends, to the partial neglect of stockholder interests, by behaving at least somewhat like the neoclassical entrepreneur, is also quite attractive.[13] Again, however, one's ability to accomplish all of this in our uncertain world is open to considerable doubt, as is management's apparent neglect of the omnipresent issues raised by risk.

## 10.5 DIVERSIFICATION

In the real world, of course, management cannot and does not take quite so callous an attitude towards risk. Indeed, the previously noted objectives of size, growth, and security may influence the very nature of the business, *or businesses*, in which the firm is engaged; specifically, they may affect the firm's choice of which product(s) to produce and which process(es) to employ, as well as the input mix and level of output of a particular commodity. The desire for security, in combination with the profits lure, is the basis for the firm's decision to *diversify* in a *variety* of directions.[14] The conglomerate corporation of the modern world is a complex producer of many different products via many different processes. Any one of these products might not seem to the casual observer to contribute sufficiently to profit to make its production worthwhile—as it might not be in a world of certainty. In a world of uncertainty, however, a variety of products may yield a variety of "hedges" against the normal risk of business. As one observes the ever-increasing number of conglomerate firms, management's desire to temper business risk via diversification becomes apparent.[15]

[13] H. T. Koplin ["The Profit Maximization Assumption," *Oxford Economic Papers*, **15**:2 (July 1963), 130–139] has argued that "the failure of the firm to maximize profits will usually indicate the existence of economic inefficiency" (pp. 136–137). Hence, because it effects "maximum internal economy in the running of the business," one can even endow social value to the profit motive (Andrews, *Manufacturing Business*, p. 21). Whether management need strive for "maximum internal economy" would clearly seem to depend, however, upon the definition of "profits" and *whose* profits management is concerned about. This does not argue against the "principle that is implied in all rational behavior: the criterion of efficiency. In its broadest sense, to be efficient merely means to take the shortest path, the cheapest means, toward the attainment of the desired goals." Herbert A. Simon, *Administrative Behavior* (New York: The Macmillan Company, 1958), p. 14.] Also, see Edward S. Mason, "The Apologetics of Managerialism," *Journal of Business*, **XXXI**:1 (Jan. 1958), 1–11.

[14] Writing in *1738* Daniel Bernoulli deduced "the rule that it is advisable to divide goods which are exposed to some danger into several portions rather than risk them altogether" ["Exposition of a New Theory on the Measurement of Risk" (1738), trans. Louise Sommer, *Econometrica*, **XXII**:1 (Jan. 1954), 30]. For discussions of the various motives, see the following: W. Rupert Maclaurin, "The Sequence from Invention to Innovation and Its Relation to Economic Growth," *Quarterly Journal of Economics*, **LXVII**:1 (Feb. 1953), 97–111; A. D. H. Kaplan, *Big Enterprise in a Competitive System* (Washington, D.C.: The Brookings Institution, 1954); D. Schwartzman, "Multiple Company Mergers and the Theory of the Firm," *Oxford Economic Papers*, **7**:2 (June 1955), 197–214; Edith T. Penrose, *The Theory of the Growth of the Firm* (New York: John Wiley & Sons, Inc., 1959), particularly pp. 129–130; H. B. Malmgren, "Information, Expectations and the Theory of the Firm," *Quarterly Journal of Economics*, **LXXV** (Aug. 1961), 399–421; and H. R. Jensen, E. W. Kehrberg, and D. W. Thomas, "Integration as an Adjustment to Risk and Uncertainty," *Southern Economic Journal*, **XXVII**:4 (April 1962), 378–384.

[15] For a most interesting discussion, see L. A. Dow and W. E. Cullison, "Oligopoly,

One very interesting, widely applicable *and* applied approach for achieving diversification has been suggested by Markowitz. The following is a variant on the basic Markowitz model for investment in a *portfolio* of *securities*.[16] In the present context, the firm has the capability to produce each of $n$ different products. The products the firm elects to produce, together with their respective output levels, describe the firm's *product portfolio*. Although different from one another, the products constituting the product portfolio will not necessarily be unrelated. Thus, in establishing this portfolio, management will want to allow for the possibility that the demand for one product might tend to increase when the demand for another decreases. The producer of gun casings and washing machines is a case in point. Demand for the former may rise and that for the latter may fall when the economy's choice tends to favor "guns versus butter"; in a peacetime economy, the reverse will tend to be true. Alternatively, the demands might tend to move in the same direction. When new housing starts are on the rise, for example, the demands for hot-water heaters and central air conditioning units are also likely to rise. And, remember we are uncertain as to precisely what these demands are or will be, and how they are related. Similar remarks could be made with respect to costs.

The specific problem we shall deal with here is to determine that proportion of currently available production facilities to be set aside during the coming year for each of the $n$ products. Denote by $x_i$ the *proportion* of production facilities to be devoted to producing product $Q_i$. Clearly $\sum_{i=1}^{n} x_i \leq 1$, since no more than 100 percent of the available facilities can be utilized.

Management feels justified in assuming that the yearly profit contributed by $Q_i$, per unit of production facility diverted towards its production, is a constant, but management is uncertain as to what this contribution is. For example, in the firm with 100 machines it might not be too distortive to assume that each machine, or percent of facility, used to produce DURK will result in $\$\pi$ of profit per year, but there is some doubt as to the specific value of $\pi$. Fortunately, however, the firm has a well-trained management with a strong Bayesian bent. The management is willing to make a series of $m_i$ probability statements about this contribution. These statements will be to the effect that, for each unit of production facility devoted to product $Q_i$, the probability is $p_{ij}$ that profit will be $\pi_{ij}$. Thus,

$$r_i = \sum_{j=1}^{m_i} p_{ij}\pi_{ij}$$

is the *expected profit*, per year, from a unit of production facility used to produce $Q_i$; $\sigma_i^2$ is the *variance in profit*, where

$$\sigma_i^2 = \sum_{j=1}^{m_i} p_{ij}(\pi_{ij} - r_i)^2.$$

A $\int d\pi$ would replace the $\Sigma$ in the continuous case.

---

Intergroup Conflict and the Growth of the Firm," *American Journal of Economics and Sociology*, **24**:3 (July 1965), 273–288.

[16] H. M. Markowitz, *Portfolio Selection* (New York: John Wiley & Sons, Inc., 1959). A well-known variant on the Markowitz model is offered by William F. Sharpe, "A Simplified Model of Portfolio Selection," *Management Science*, **9**:1 (Jan. 1963), 277–293.

The firm's expected return per unit from a "portfolio" of products will therefore be

$$\bar{r} = \sum_{i=1}^{n} x_i r_i.$$

By the rule for determining the variance of a function of several variables (Appendix to Chapter 3) the variance in the "portfolio" of products will be given by

$$\sigma^2 = \sum_{i=1}^{n} \sum_{k=1}^{n} x_i x_k \sigma_{r_i r_k}.$$

This follows since the function in question is simply $\bar{r}$, which is a weighted sum of the $r_i$, the $x_i$ being the weights.[17]

The variance is frequently interpreted as a measure of risk, for it indicates the extent of the potential deviation of the actual return from expected return. With certainty there is zero variance; but where there is uncertainty, there is a good deal of intuitive appeal in the suggestion that the wider is the dispersion of the possible returns around the expected return—that is, the greater is the variance—the greater is the extent to which one will be unprepared for the outcome, and the greater is the risk. Thus the security-oriented, or at least security-conscious, management might choose as the primary basis for its decisions the minimization of risk, or the minimization of its surrogate $\sigma^2$. In the business world, however, this primary goal cannot be sought to the neglect of considerations of return or profit earned. In the world of uncertainty, it *may not* be possible to utilize production facilities so as to *assure* a prespecified *minimum-profits* level, but these facilities can be employed to assure that *expected* profit exceeds some preestablished minimum: that is,

$$\sum_{i=1}^{n} x_i r_i \geq \bar{\pi}.$$

Suppose, too, that because certain assets are fixed or because of contractual obligations, at least $100\bar{x}_k$ percent of the firm's production facilities *cannot be* devoted to the production of anything but $Q_k$; this requires that $x_k \geq \bar{x}_k$. The firm's problem then becomes:

$$\text{Minimize} \quad \sigma^2 = \sum_{i=1}^{n} \sum_{k=1}^{n} x_i x_k \, \sigma_{r_i r_k} \tag{10.7a}$$

$$\text{subject to} \quad \sum_{i=1}^{n} x_i \leq 1, \tag{10.7b}$$

$$\sum_{i=1}^{n} x_i r_i \geq \bar{\pi}, \tag{10.7c}$$

$$x_k \geq \bar{x}_k, \qquad k = 1, \ldots, n, \tag{10.7d}$$

$$x_i \geq 0, \qquad i = 1, \ldots, n. \tag{10.7e}$$

[17] Recall that the correlation between $r_i$ and $r_k$ will be given by $\sigma_{r_i r_k}/\sigma_{r_i}\sigma_{r_k}$. Thus, the $\sigma_{r_i r_k}$ term actually reflects the *correlation* between the profits from the two projects. Assigning an internally consistent value to this correlation will not be easy. From the

Equations (10.7a–e) describe a quadratic programming problem. One could, of course, establish a wider variety of constraints. So long as the objective function is convex and the constraints are mutually consistent and consistent with the goal of minimizing $\sigma^2$, the problem can be solved to yield the optimal $x_i$—that is, the proportion of facilities to be devoted to $Q_i$. These proportions will not necessarily be fixed for all time. As new information is received, the $p_{ij}$ may be revised; and as new opportunities become available, the set of $Q_i$ from which the firm will select may be altered. Either condition can effect a change in the optimal solution.

It should be recognized that one can formulate an equivalent second problem that has as its objective function the maximization of expected return, subject to a maximum-acceptable-risk constraint. The firm's complete set of options between risk and expected return as we let $\bar{\pi}$ vary in (10.7c) would appear as the curve *PO* in Figure 10.2. This locus of points is called the efficiency set of solutions, since each point describes the availability of a "portfolio" that, for a given risk, yields the maximum return or, for a given return, the minimum risk. In essence management must choose the point on the efficiency locus that it prefers. This choice will reflect management's options, constraints, and risk-taking propensities.

In effecting this choice, management is required to portray its preferences for risk versus return in a set of indifference curves. Just as the efficiency locus *PO* describes what management *can achieve* between risk and return, the indifference curves, such as *RR* in Figure 10.2, describe what management is *willing to accept*

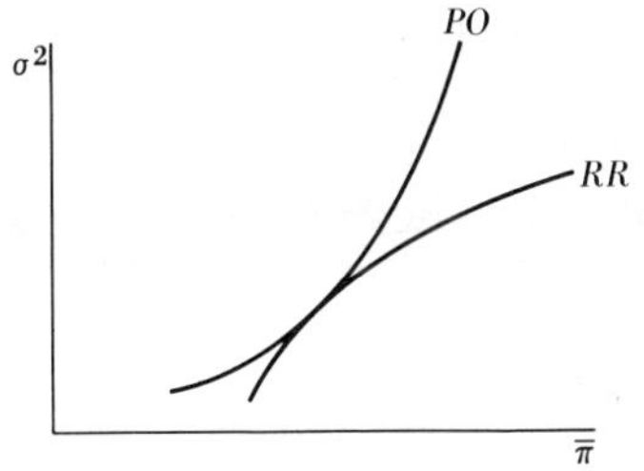


Fig. 10.2

as tradeoffs between equally preferred combinations of risk and return. The combination is chosen that places management on the indifference curve lying furthest to the right, or the combination that is at the point of tangency of the efficiency locus *PO* and the indifference curve *RR*. Once again, however, the choice is made under comparatively static conditions to the neglect of the potential opportunities that might await the firm in the future; the "grand design" is ignored and an immediate problem is placed in a vacuum and solved. But, as one probes into these complex areas of decision making, it is indeed necessary to learn to walk before you can run; and the Markowitz model provides an extremely adaptable vehicle for realistic advancement.

---

practical standpoint, simple *historical* estimates based on past data alone have traditionally been employed. Where such past data are not available, one must meet the problem head-on and rely on subjective judgments.

## 10.6 UNCERTAINTY AND MATHEMATICAL PROGRAMMING

The specter of uncertainty has hovered over much of the preceding discussion. The Markowitz model provides one of the more meaningful and suggestive means by which some of the issues arising out of uncertainty may be handled. Although one may question a decision maker's ability to arrive at a mutually consistent set of probability judgments in complex situations—or, even more hazardous, his ability to assign a consistent set of *covariances*—and although one may question the use of *variance* as a proxy for *risk* and *expected return* as a proxy for *profitability*, the Markowitz model is at least conceptually tractable and heads us in the right direction. It is implicit in this approach, and justifiably so, that in the presence of uncertainty, such goals as profit maximization or cost minimization will be operationally meaningless. They will become meaningless so long as the decision-making parameters are not known with certainty. One cannot be certain of maximizing profits if one has no *certain* knowledge as to the price that will obtain in the market, the quantity demanded at each price, or the costs that will be incurred in getting the product to the consumer.[18]

It has been seen that even when (or perhaps *particularly* when) sophisticated econometric methods are employed in parameter estimation, the values that are assigned will, except for extraordinary circumstances, be just that—estimates. At best they will be estimates about which one can make probability statements, and this is true even when we grant the frequently heroic assumption that the model has been "correctly" specified. Moreover, in the case of a cost equation such as $w_1F_1 + w_2F_2 = C$, even when one is prepared to accept specific values for $w_1$ and $w_2$, the value of $C$ or the total costs to which output must be constrained may also be subject to some variation. Management might, for example, be "90 per cent certain" that funds of up to $C_1$ will be available to support a current production operation, but it is "highly unlikely," say "less than one chance out of a hundred," that costs in excess of $C_2$ can be incurred without seriously impairing the firm's financial credibility. Under these circumstances, the optimal decision requires a bit more effort than simply taking a few derivatives and solving sets of simultaneous equations.

The possibility of variability in the relevant parameters can be particularly disconcerting and raise particular havoc with mathematical programming approaches to decision making. For example, consider all the potential trouble spots in the simple linear programming problem in the now familiar notation: Maximize $Z = \mathbf{c}'\mathbf{x}$, subject to $\mathbf{Ax} \leq \mathbf{d}$, $\mathbf{x} \geq \mathbf{0}$. Suppose the $x_j$'s represent product output levels, the $c_j$'s are contributions to profit, the $d_i$'s are resource-capacity restrictions, and the $a_{ij}$'s represent the amount of resource $i$ required by a unit of product $j$. The problem is to maximize total profit. But, even granting a fixed vector $\mathbf{c}$, uncertainty can arise on the demand and cost side to prevent *certain* knowledge of exactly what this vector $\mathbf{c}$ is; even granting a fixed vector $\mathbf{d}$, the decision maker need not be certain as to the exact resource limitation to which he will be subject; and similar uncertainty can prevail with respect to the amount of a resource that a particular product will ultimately require.

Several approaches have been offered for dealing with these sorts of problems,

[18] For a discussion, see Charles J. Hitch and Roland N. McKean, "What Can Managerial Economics Contribute to Economic Theory?" *American Economic Review*, **LI**:2 (May 1961), 147–154.

and here we shall consider a couple of the less strenuous excursions. As a start, suppose one assigns a probability of $p_{kj}$ to the likelihood that $c_{kj}$ will obtain as product $j$'s contribution. Suppose, too, it is felt to be absolutely *imperative* that the constraints be satisfied. One possibility for dealing with parameter uncertainty is to replace the vector $\mathbf{c}'$ with the vector $E[\mathbf{c}'] = (\bar{c}_1, \ldots, \bar{c}_m)$, where $\bar{c}_j = \sum_{k=1}^{t_j} p_{kj}c_{kj}$ is the *expected* contribution of each unit of $j$ to the objective function. Letting $\Sigma\, a_{ij}^*x_j \leq d_i^*$ represent the *most restrictive* member of the $i$th set of uncertain constraints, the original LP problem might be replaced by another LP problem: Maximize $\hat{Z} = E[\mathbf{c}']\mathbf{x}$, subject to $\mathbf{A}^*\mathbf{x} \leq \mathbf{d}^*$, $\mathbf{x} \geq \mathbf{0}$. Here, $\mathbf{A}^*$ is the matrix $\mathbf{A}$ and $\mathbf{d}^*$ the vector $\mathbf{d}$, in which in *every* instance the $i$th row contains the parameters for the most restrictive constraint of the $i$th class. Where there is no single "most restrictive" constraint, the most restrictive *collection* of these constraints would *all* be added to the problem, so that $\mathbf{A}^*$ and $\mathbf{d}^*$ would be of larger dimension than $\mathbf{A}$ and $\mathbf{d}$. In this approach, we seek a solution within the convex set of feasible solutions defined by any and all constraints that might *possibly* obtain. Thus, if a constraint might be $3x_1 + 4x_2 \leq 60$ *or* it might turn out to be $4x_1 + 3x_2 \leq 60$, we demand that the solution satisfy both constraints; if a constraint might be $3x_1 + 4x_2 \leq 60$ *or* it might be $3x_1 + 4x_2 \leq 90$, we demand only that it satisfy the first constraint, for the second now becomes superfluous.

We cannot simply take some sort of "average" of constraints emanating from the same source, for then we would have no guarantee that one or more of these will not be violated. This is not the case when we use some sort of averaging process to define the objective function. Then, we know that we will still choose an extreme point of the convex set of feasible solutions, but we do not know whether the extreme point selected will turn out to be optimal in light of those values that actually obtain for the objective function's parameters. Moreover, if the objective functions $Z' = 2x_1 + 5x_2$ and $Z'' = 3x_1 + 3x_2$ are considered to be equally likely, the optimal solution with respect to the averaged function $Z_a = 2.5x_1 + 4x_2$ will not necessarily be either one of the optima with respect to $Z'$ or $Z''$; further, unless these optima are adjacent extreme points, if one should select as the decision the average of the individual optima, this average solution must be an interior point of the convex set, and therefore nonoptimal for *any* objective function. One might still choose this point as a form of compromise; but if there is any compromising to be done, it would seem usually to be preferable to do it along a boundary of the convex set. This method for handling uncertainty therefore assumes *both* that (1) it is reasonable to replace a criterion function with its mathematical expectation, and (2) it is not reasonable to *ever* consider violating a constraint. We shall look into the former assumption at greater length in Chapter 12. For the moment, however, we merely call attention to the *possibility* of maximizing expected value—or, in a more popularized and intuitive vein, the "average payoff"—as a criterion for decision making under uncertainty.

The second assumption, that a constraint may *never* be violated, raises some additional issues. It might, for example, be most reasonable to attempt simply to restrict the probability that a constraint will be violated to some preestablished maximum. For example, one might wish to be "90 percent certain" that costs will not exceed some prespecified level. One possibility for accomplishing this arises where the $d_i$ are assumed to be stochastic and independent of other parameters. It will also be convenient to assume that they are normally distributed with means of $E[d_i] = \bar{d}_i$. The present approach is that suggested by Charnes and Cooper.[19]

The Charnes and Cooper approach to the *chance-constrained* programming problem is as follows. Suppose the decision maker wishes to assure that the probability the $i$th constraint is violated is no greater than $\alpha_i$. Commonly $\alpha_i$ will be comparatively small. It will be smaller, (1) the lesser is the decision maker's risk-taking propensity, and (2) the greater is the cost associated with violating the constraint. For example, the $i$th constraint, $\Sigma\, a_{ij}x_j \leq d_i$, might involve available storage space. If the constraint is violated, it might be necessary to destroy some output, $x_j$, or store output elsewhere at a high cost. In this case one would want to set the probability of violating the $i$th constraint, denoted by $P(\Sigma\, a_{ij}x_j > d_i)$, at a lower level than might otherwise be the case. In particular, we will want

$$P(\Sigma\, a_{ij}x_j > d_i) \leq \alpha_i,$$

or, since $P(\Sigma\, a_{ij}x_j > d_i) + P(\Sigma\, a_{ij}x_j \leq d_i) = 1$, we will want to require

$$P(\Sigma\, a_{ij}x_j \leq d_i) \geq 1 - \alpha_i.$$

Now, denote the mean and standard deviation of the random variable $d_i$ by $\bar{d}_i$ and $\sigma_i$, respectively. By subtracting $\bar{d}_i$ from either side of the inequality and dividing by $\sigma_i$, we may rewrite $P(\Sigma\, a_{ij}x_j \leq d_i)$ as

$$P\left(\frac{\Sigma\, a_{ij}x_j - \bar{d}_i}{\sigma_i} \leq \frac{d_i - \bar{d}_i}{\sigma_i}\right).$$

But it is well known that with $d_i$ normally distributed $(d_i - \bar{d}_i)/\sigma_i = N_i$ is a normally distributed random variate with mean zero and standard deviation of one. Therefore, in seeking a set of $x_j$ such that $P[(\Sigma\, a_{ij}x_j - \bar{d}_i)/\sigma_i \leq N_i] \geq 1 - \alpha_i$, we equivalently require $P[\Sigma\, a_{ij}x_j \leq \sigma_i N_i + \bar{d}_i] \geq 1 - \alpha_i$, or simply

$$\Sigma\, a_{ij}x_j \leq \sigma_i N_i + \bar{d}_i, \tag{10.8}$$

where the value of $N_i$ and the right hand side of the inequality are determined by the value assigned to $\alpha_i$.

Assume, for example, that $\alpha_i = .05$. That is, we want the probability to be no greater than .05 that the $i$th constraint is violated. From a table of the cumulative normal distribution we determine that the probability is .05 that the *actual* value of a randomly generated $d_i$ will be more than $|N_i| = 1.645$ standard deviations below the mean of $\bar{d}_i$. Hence, if we set $N_i = -1.645$ and require that $\Sigma\, a_{ij}x_j \leq \bar{d}_i - 1.645\sigma_i$ we will assure that *the probability* that the $i$th constraint will be violated, or that $\Sigma\, a_{ij}x_j > d_i$, does not exceed .05. To limit the probability of violating the $i$th constraint to .01, we set $N_i = -2.33$. Then, we require $\Sigma\, a_{ij}x_j \leq \bar{d}_i - 2.33\sigma_i$. In effect, when we wish to reduce the probability of violating a constraint, we reduce the "quantity" of the available "resource." Moreover, by a series of alterations in $\alpha_i$, one can perform a sensitivity analysis to analyze the effects on the objective function of alternative "levels of risk."

In chance-constrained programming, then, (10.8) replaces the original constraint and the ordinary LP procedure is applied to the new problem with the probability-

[19] See A. Charnes and W. W. Cooper, "Chance-Constrained Programming," *Management Science,* **6**:1 (Oct. 1959), 73–79; also, "Deterministic Equivalents for Optimizing and Satisficing Under Chance Constraints," *Operations Research,* **11**:1 (Jan.–Feb. 1963), 18–39.

adjusted constraints. The advantage of the normality assumption is that the right side, $\sigma_i N_i + \bar{d}_i$, is easily determined from readily accessible tables of the normal distribution. Where the normality assumption is unreasonable, the specific distribution assessed must be examined.

In this case, then, a programming problem, say the maximization of an expected value, is undertaken subject to a series of restrictions the exact nature of which is determined by risk-taking propensities and the costs of violating particular constraints. Again, we note the *need* to replace a strict profit-maximization problem with an alternative problem that reflects personal judgments, goals, and attitudes.

## 10.7 TIME PREFERENCE

Among management's attitudes that can most radically affect its decisions is time preference. Specifically, those costs and benefits associated with a decision that are felt immediately will not bear the same instantaneous impact, nor be as influential in decision making, were they anticipated to occur say a decade later. Moreover, firms and individuals can logically disagree as to the precise extent to which the payoff from an activity should be adjusted to reflect the time delay before the payoff is received. The present discussion will emphasize the impact of this adjustment for time delay where the firm is primarily profit-oriented. Strictly speaking, then, one can quarrel with couching this discussion among nonprofit-maximizing approaches to decision making. But, as will be seen, the discussion does have additional aspects to justify the choice, and the *principles* illuminated are of sufficiently general applicability to warrant the intrusion.

Suppose a firm or individual always has the option of investing in a particular project, be it a government bond, a savings account, or a new machine, that will yield a guaranteed return of $r$ percent a year on each dollar so invested. The immediate investment of $A$ dollars, the yearly earnings from which are reinvested over the investment period of $t$ years, will result in an *assured* total of no more nor less than $R_t = A(1 + r)^t$ dollars at the period's end. If $r$ is the percentage return *guaranteed* by the *most profitable alternative* option that could *always* be chosen, ceteris paribus one would be reluctant, if downright unwilling, to invest $A$ dollars in a project that promised *less than* $R_t$ dollars at the end of $t$ years. Indeed, if one *is* offered a promise of $R_t$ dollars to be received $t$ years hence, and assuming that one always prefers more money to less, the most one would be willing to pay for this promise is $A = R_t/(1 + r)^t$ dollars. This is so because of the *assumption* that $R_t$ dollars can *always* be accumulated after $t$ years by the current investment of $A$ dollars in the certain alternative. $R_t/(1 + r)^t$ is called the *present discounted value* of $R_t$ dollars—a payoff positive or negative—to be received at the end of $t$ years. The guaranteed alternative is called the *marginal* project. The marginal project is thus one that may not as yet have been undertaken, presumably because its return after $t$ years does not exceed that of the chosen alternatives, but it promises with certainty a return of $r$ per dollar that is at least as great as the return on all other certain options that have not been selected. The only reason for not investing some, or additional, funds in the marginal project is that these funds are not available. When they become available, they will be invested in the marginal project unless an alternative investment comes along that promises rewards having a higher present discounted value than that of the marginal project. The *rate of discount*, $r = r^*$, used in the computation is called the *marginal cost of capital*. Again, it is the return on the most profitable certain *alternative* available; or, equivalently, $r^*$ is the *minimum rate of return* that the investor *demands* before being willing to invest in a project.[20]

Suppose, then, that a firm can invest in a project involving capital outlays of $K_t$ in period $t$. It will be assumed that all costs and receipts are incurred or enjoyed at time $t$, the end of period $t$. The capital is subject to depreciation write-offs of $D_t$ dollars in period $t$. The capital outlays are used to construct a plant of known size producing a product the demand curve for which is judged to be $P_t = D(Q_t, t)$. This describes the demand curve assumed *with certainty* to face the firm in period $t$ as a function of time. The total cost curve is estimated as $C_t = c(Q_t)$. This does not include a depreciation charge. Profit, net of depreciation, in period $t$ will be given by $\pi_t = P_tQ_t - C_t - D_t = D(Q_t, t)Q_t - C_t - D_t$. With a fixed profits tax of $\tau$, net profit will be given by $(1 - \tau)\pi_t = (1 - \tau)[D(Q_t, t)Q_t - C_t] - (1 - \tau)D_t$. *Net cash flow*—the amount of funds actually retained by the firm—will, however, include the depreciation write-off $D_t$. The latter is a "cost," but one for which funds are actually not expended. Cash flow in period $t$, $R_t$, will therefore be given by

$$R_t = -K_t + (1 - \tau)\pi_t + D_t = -K_t + (1 - \tau)[D(Q_t, t)Q_t - C_t] + \tau D_t.$$

Suppose the plant is expected to last for $m$ years, at the end of which it will be scrapped for a net value or cost of $S_m$ dollars. The present discounted value of the project will be given by the sum of the cash flows over all $m + 1$ time periods, or

$$V_1 = \sum_{t=0}^{m} \frac{R_t}{(1 + r)^t} + \frac{S_m}{(1 + r)^m}.$$

In detail,

$$V_1 = \sum_{t=0}^{m} \frac{-K_t + (1 - \tau)[D(Q_t, t)Q_t - C_t] + \tau D_t}{(1 + r)^t} + \frac{S_m}{(1 + r)^m}. \qquad (10.9)$$

Clearly, if $\tau = 0$—that is, without a corporate profits tax—depreciation charges are conspicuously irrelevant to determining present value and the worth of a project. Also, the earlier the time at which depreciation is charged, the higher is $V_1$. That is, as long as there is a profits tax, we want faster depreciation write-offs, for this gives additional cash flow at an earlier date.[21] To determine output levels to maximize

[20] The issue of "what $r$?" to use is discussed at length in various articles in Ezra Solomon, ed., *The Management of Corporate Capital* (New York: The Free Press of Glencoe, 1959). In particular, see the following: J. H. Lorie and L. J. Savage, "Three Problems in Rationing Capital," pp. 56–66; Ezra Solomon, "The Arithmetic of Capital-Budgeting Decisions," pp. 74–79; E. Renshaw, "A Note on the Arithmetic of Capital Budgeting Decisions," pp. 80–88; Ezra Solomon, "Measuring a Company's Cost of Capital," pp. 128–140; H. V. Roberts, "Current Problems in the Economics of Capital Budgeting," pp. 198–202; and J. Hirshleifer, "On the Theory of Optimal Investment Decision," pp. 205–228.

[21] Ira Horowitz, "Depreciation and User Cost in Decision Making," *Quarterly Review of Economics and Business*, **2**:2 (May 1962), 55–62. The previous formulation makes the mathematically convenient assumptions that, should the project entail a loss in any period, the firm will earn sufficient profits elsewhere to permit the tax deduction, and the firm will always be in a position to enjoy the tax advantages of depreciation write-offs. Given the complexity of the tax laws, a specific project in a particular firm would have to be evaluated under a set of assumptions appropriate to *that* firm's situation, but the present generalities do not misrepresent the fundamental issues.

$V_1$, the firm sets $\partial V_1/\partial Q_t = 0$. This is readily seen from (10.9) to be equivalent to equating marginal revenue to marginal cost in each period.[22]

With $Q$ determined so as to equate each period's $MR$ and $MC$, $V_1$ will be a function of $r$ alone. This function, $V_1 = v_1(r)$, will *ordinarily*, but not necessarily, be a monotonically decreasing function. The curve traced out by this function will correspond to that in Figure 10.3. The curve crosses the abscissa where $V_1 = 0$ at a discount

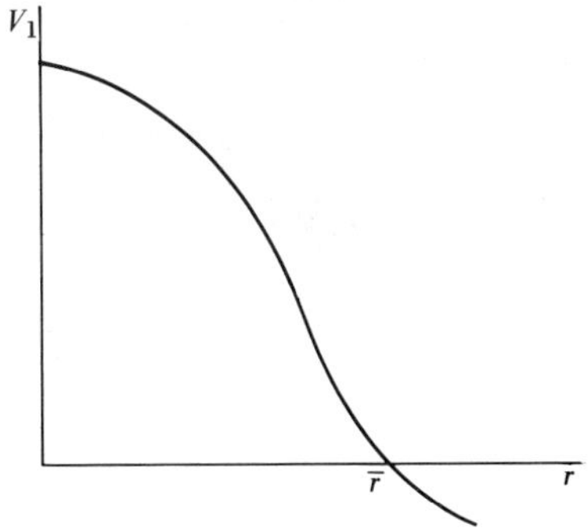


Fig. 10.3

rate $\bar{r}$. This discount rate, at which the present discounted value of an income stream equals zero, has been variously called the *internal rate of return*,[23] the marginal efficiency of capital,[24] and the profitability index.[25] To determine $\bar{r}$, note that by writing $y = 1/(1 + r)$ and combining terms in the numerator, (10.9) may be written

$$V_1 = \sum_{t=0}^{m} a_t y^t.$$

[22] The role of time in influencing price-quantity determination, and the need to consider the establishment of a price *policy* or set of price *strategies*, have been discussed from a variety of viewpoints. For a sampling of the economist's outlook see the following: Alfred C. Neal, "Marginal Cost and Dynamic Equilibrium of the Firm," *Journal of Political Economy*, **L**:1 (Feb. 1942), 45–64; Oscar Lange, "A Note on Innovations," *Review of Economics and Statistics*, **XXV**:1 (Feb. 1943), 19–25; Peter L. Bernstein, "Profit Theory—Where Do We Go From Here?," *Quarterly Journal of Economics*, **LXVII**:3 (Aug. 1953), 407–422; Kaplan, *Big Enterprise in a Competitive System*, particularly pp. 166–167; Gordon, *Business Leadership in the Large Corporation*, particularly p. 328; James S. Early, "Marginal Policies of 'Excellently Managed' Companies," *American Economic Review*, **XLVI**:1 (March 1956), 44–70; Penrose, *The Theory of the Growth of the Firm*, particularly pp. 29–30; Ira Horowitz, "Formulation of the Price-Cost Relationship in a Class of Plant Investment Decisions," *Journal of Industrial Engineering*, **XIV**:6 (Nov.–Dec. 1963), 300–306.

[23] Kenneth Boulding, "The Theory of a Single Investment," *Quarterly Journal of Economics*, **XLIX**:2 (May 1935), 475–494.

[24] J. M. Keynes, *The General Theory of Employment, Interest and Money* (London: Macmillan and Co., Ltd., 1951), pp. 135–146.

[25] Ray I. Reul, "Profitability Index for Investments," *Harvard Business Review*, **35**:4 (July–Aug. 1957), 121.

Setting $V_1 = 0$, the latter becomes

$$0 = \sum_{t=0}^{m} a_t y^t,$$

a polynomial of degree $m$. From "the" solution for $y = \bar{y}$ we obtain $\bar{r} = (1 - \bar{y})/\bar{y}$. Unhappily there will not necessarily be a unique $\bar{y}$ nor, therefore, a unique $\bar{r}$. The equation may have *many* real roots. Specifically, it follows from Descartes' rule that there may be as many real roots to (10.9) with $V_1 = 0$ as there are changes of sign between successive $a_t$.[26] Thus, where there are sporadic cash losses or negative flows scattered among an income stream, it might not be possible to calculate a unique internal rate of return.

Suppose now that management's problem is to choose between engaging in the latter project or the alternative option of selecting a project with a present discounted value of $V_2$. It is assumed that this project too is evaluated at the optimal output levels. The firm can select either one or neither of the two projects, but not both. From management's standpoint the projects are mutually exclusive. $V_2$ will also be a function of the discount rate. This function $V_2 = v_2(r)$ is superimposed on that for $V_1$ in Figure 10.4. Note that $V_1 = V_2$ at a discount rate of $\hat{r}$. That dis-

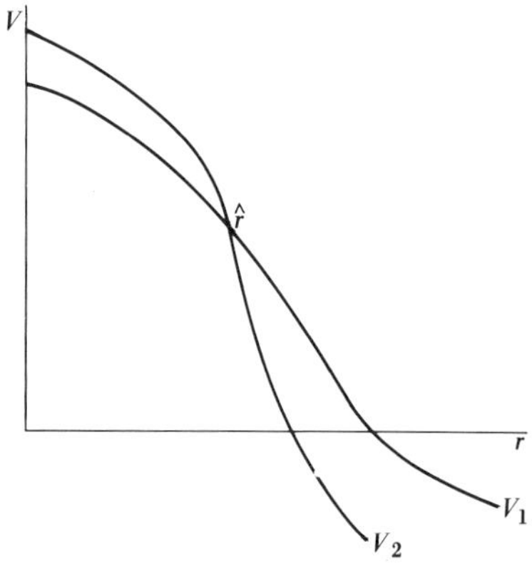


Fig. 10.4

count rate, $\hat{r}$, at which the present discounted value of alternative projects is equal, is called the *rate of return over cost*.[27] As with $\bar{r}$, $\hat{r}$ is determined by equating $V_1$ and $V_2$, combining corresponding terms in the numerators, and then determining the roots of the resultant polynomial equation. Thus, there is no particular reason why $\hat{r}$ should be unique. As in Figure 10.5, there may be many such rates as to equate $V_1$ and $V_2$.

[26] Descartes' rule states that the number of positive real roots of a polynomial equation with real coefficients is equal to the number of variations in sign that obtain in the equation, or else is less than that number by a positive even integer. For an excellent discussion of this and related matters, see Hirshleifer, "On the Theory of Optimal Investment Decision," pp. 222–227.

[27] Irving Fisher, *The Theory of Interest* (New York: The Macmillan Company, 1930), p. 155.

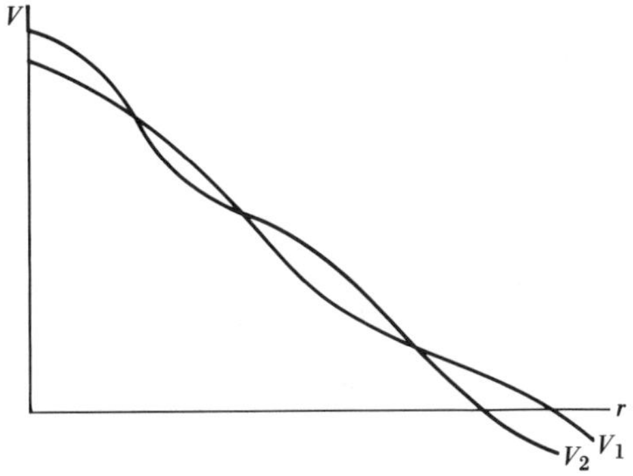


Fig. 10.5

Now, it will profit a firm to invest in *either* one of the two projects so long as the project's present discounted value is positive, discounted at the marginal cost of capital $r^*$. This is so, for the costs of the investment are already incorporated into the income streams via the $K_t$; and, since the marginal project has a present value of 0 when discounted at $r^*$ (that's how $r^*$ was determined), a positive present value reveals that a project has a higher worth, at the current decision time, than that of the guaranteed alternative. Similarly, in choosing between two alternatives each of which has a positive present value when discounted at $r^*$, that project should be chosen which has the higher present value. It is important to note that, as in Figure 10.4 and the numerical illustration of Table 10.1, the optimal project is not necessarily the one yielding the higher internal rate of return, $\bar{r}$. This is true, since choosing the project with the higher $\bar{r}$, or maximizing the rate of return, erroneously assumes that a project's receipts can be reinvested at the rate of $\bar{r}$, the internal rate of return. This is the rate that is being implicitly used as the discount factor when maximizing the rate of return. This procedure fails to recognize that, by assumption, the cash flows generated by the projects can only be reinvested *with certainty* at the marginal cost of capital, $r^*$. Thus, their present value must be determined by discounting at a rate of $r^*$.[28]

The first four columns of Table 10.1 give the year, capital outlay, depreciation charge, and pretax profit (before depreciation) for two alternative projects. The fifth column gives the cash flow. The last two columns give the discounted cash flow. In the sixth column, the flows are discounted at the internal rate of return, as revealed in the row labeled $\Sigma$ which sums all the values in a column. The sum of the values in the sixth column is, in each case, approximately zero. At a marginal cost of capital of .065, each project has a present value of approximately 150; or $.065 = \hat{r}$ is the rate of return over cost. It is readily seen that at values of $r^* > .065$, $V_1 > V_2$.

[28] The "pro-$\bar{r}$" forces were initially led by Boulding ("The Theory of a Single Investment," p. 482), and immediately headed off by P. A. Samuelson, "Some Aspects of the Pure Theory of Capital," *Quarterly Journal of Economics,* **LI**:3 (May 1937), 469–496. For other early defenses of this now well-accepted preference, see the following: F. A. Lutz, "The Criterion of Maximum Profit in the Theory of Investment," *Quarterly Journal of Economics,* **LX** (Nov. 1945), 56–77; F. A. and Vera Lutz, *The Theory of Investment of the Firm* (Princeton, N.J.: Princeton University Press, 1951), p. 21; and Harry Markowitz, "Portfolio Selection," *Journal of Finance,* **VII**:1 (March 1952), 77–91.

TABLE 10.1

| | | | PROJECT 1 ($\tau = .50$, $\bar{r} = .103$, $\hat{r} = .065$) | | | |
|---|---|---|---|---|---|---|
| **Year** | $K$ | $D$ | $D(Q)Q - c(Q)$ | $R$ | $R/(1.103)$ | $R/(1.065)$ |
| 0 | 1000 | 0 | 0 | −1000 | −1000 | −1000 |
| 1 | 1000 | 334 | 350 | −658 | −597 | −618 |
| 2 | —— | 667 | 700 | 683 | 561 | 602 |
| 3 | —— | 666 | 900 | 783 | 583 | 648 |
| 4 | —— | 333 | 500 | 667 | 451 | 518 |
| Σ | 2000 | 2000 | 2450 | 475 | −2 | 150 |

| | | | PROJECT 2 ($\tau = .50$, $\bar{r} = .095$, $\hat{r} = .065$) | | | |
|---|---|---|---|---|---|---|
| **Year** | $K$ | $D$ | $D(Q)Q - c(Q)$ | $R$ | $R/(1.095)$ | $R/(1.065)$ |
| 0 | 2000 | 0 | 0 | −2000 | −2000 | −2000 |
| 1 | —— | 500 | 500 | 500 | 457 | 470 |
| 2 | —— | 500 | 500 | 500 | 417 | 441 |
| 3 | —— | 500 | 900 | 700 | 533 | 579 |
| 4 | —— | 500 | 1200 | 850 | 591 | 661 |
| Σ | 2000 | 2000 | 3100 | 550 | −2 | 151 |

Indeed, the internal rate of return is $\bar{r} = .103$ for project 1 and $\bar{r} = .095$ for project 2. At values of $0 \leq r^* < .065$, however, $V_2 > V_1$. In fact, with $r^* = 0$ (the fifth column), $V_2 = 550$ and $V_1 = 475$. All of this is simply by way of demonstrating that before one is able to determine which is the superior of two mutually exclusive alternatives, one must know something about the time value of money, or how important it is to get your hands on the cash flow sooner as opposed to later.

It is, of course, possible that $r^*$ itself will change as a function of time. In this case the expression $1/(1 + r^*)^t$ would be replaced by $1\Big/\Big[\prod_{j=0}^{t} (1 + r_j^*)\Big]$, where $r_j^*$ is the marginal cost of capital in period $j$. Further, if in lieu of a discrete rate of $r$ per year, the marginal investment is assumed to "grow" at a compound rate of $r^*$ per year, compounded $n$ times a year, $1/(1 + r^*)^t$ would be replaced by $1/(1 + r^*/n)^{nt}$. With continuous growth or infinite compounding (that is, as $n \to \infty$) $1/(1 + r^*/n)^{nt} \to e^{-r^*t}$. In this case, (10.9) would be written

$$V_1 = \int_0^m [-K_t + (1 - \tau)[D(Q_t, t)Q_t - C_t] + \tau D_t]e^{-rt}\,dt + S_m e^{-rm}. \quad (10.9')$$

It would, of course, also be possible, perhaps quite reasonable, to write the functions $K_t$, $D(Q_t, t)$, $C_t$, and $D_t$ as continuous functions of $t$ through a minor notational change.

Since the impact of decisions is commonly felt over a period of time, equations such as (10.9) and (10.9′) will commonly enter into one's decision-making calculus. These equations point up the need and importance to recognize (1) opportunity costs in terms of the marginal cost of capital, (2) the timing of cash flows, and (3) the period over which the decision will haunt you—the $m$. There are, however, some serious questions to raise about one's ability to determine the various terms in the equations, as well as the generality of the assumptions underlying the previous discussion. One does not necessarily know, nor can one necessarily determine, with certainty, the cash flows. Further, these flows will not necessarily be independent of one another. Where a *set* of projects is to be chosen, we do not actually know the marginal cost of capital until *after* the invesments have been made.[29] It is only then that we know the return from the *marginal* project.

From a practical standpoint, one can always select some cutoff rate to use as the discount factor. It is unlikely that the choice between $r^* = .07$ or $r^* = .08$ will result in too many differing decisions. Where the cash flows of a project are uncertain, one might choose to determine their *expected* present values. Then, a procedure such as the Markowitz model could be used to determine the choice among projects. Where the uncertain *returns* from a project in *successive* years are *interrelated*, one can still determine *expected* present values and appropriately discounted variances, say, to use in the Markowitz model. The variances will now depend upon the assumptions made about the extent of the interrelationship between the yearly cash flows.[30] Similarly, the *interrelationships among projects* may be handled with varying degrees of sophistication.[31] Finally, where the actions in one period will influence those in another period, this must also be allowed for. One technique for handling such problems is the dynamic programming approach of Section 8.8.

In essence, then, we must be aware of the need to recognize time preferences in decision making, and this awareness can raise some extremely important and difficult complications. Some of these complications can be, and have been, dealt with; many others remain a challenge. In dealing with this challenge, it should be remembered that decisions *must* get themselves made. The decision maker should, therefore, go as far as is practical in the direction of a theoretically correct analysis; but, when a theoretical impasse is reached, he should not be reluctant to invoke whatever heuristic tools and understanding his experience and immediate needs call forth.

## 10.8 DECISION MAKING Sans MAXIMIZATION (OF ANYTHING)

Implicit in the preceding models is the assumption that the decision-making unit will have some goal(s) and a criterion function that it will make some effort to maximize. Despite the obvious theoretical and mathematical attraction of having the decision maker maximize *something*, from a practical standpoint the need, ability, or indeed desire on the part of decision makers to exert the effort required to maximize *anything* can be and has been cast in serious doubt. These doubts have been raised in a variety of quarters and from a variety of directions. The present discussion is restricted to two of the more basic contentions.

The first of these, and a friend of long standing, stems from observation rather than speculation about the businessman's decision-making process. It suggests that

[29] See Hirshleifer, "On the Theory of Optimal Investment Decision," p. 213.

[30] Frederick S. Hillier, "Comparative Evaluation of Performance Using Multiple Criteria," *Management Science*, **9**:3 (April 1963), 443–457; also see Ira Horowitz, "The Plant Investment Decision Revisited," *Journal of Industrial Engineering*, **XVII**:8 (August 1966), 416–422.

[31] For an excellent overview of the related literature, see H. Martin Weingartner, "Capital Budgeting of Interrelated Projects: Survey and Synthesis," *Management Science*, **12**:7 (March 1966), 485–516.

the absence of complete data, the imperfect knowledge and foresight, and the interdependencies among firms that characterize the business world encourage the decision maker to rely on a variety of rules of thumb in reaching decisions.[32] This may be particularly prevalent where pricing decisions are concerned and competitive reactions, demand, and cost parameters are at best rather crude guesses. In this case, price might reflect the entrepreneur's considered judgment as to the price level that will discourage *potential* competitors from entering the industry or will maintain the firm's market position;[33] or, price could simply evolve as a matter of industry custom, which, in oligopolistic situations, reflects the *industry's* best interests rather than those of any one firm.[34]

To effect these prices, the most serious candidate for a pricing guide to replace $MR = MC$ has been the "full cost" principle.[35] The latter suggests that, in the absence of full knowledge about the elasticity of demand, the entrepreneur will price his product simply by adding some fixed percentage or markup to production costs. The exact percentage will depend upon industry custom or particular circumstances. The pleasant feature of this procedure is that its application does not take too much thought, analysis, or information; and, so long as one sells his total output for more than the cost of putting it on the market, the probability that a profit will be made is fairly impressive. Nonetheless, the profit earned will not necessarily be as great as that which might be earned with no more effort, but a slightly different

[32] See the following: R. F. Harrod, "Price and Cost in Entrepreneur's Policy," *Oxford Economic Papers*, no. 2 (May 1939), pp. 1–11; D. C. Hague, "Economic Theory and Business Behavior," *Review of Economic Studies*, **XVI**(3):41 (1949–1950), 144–157; Henry M. Oliver, Jr., "Average Cost and Long-Run Elasticity of Demand," *Journal of Political Economy*, **LV**:3 (June 1947), 212–221; Richard Alt, "The Internal Organization of the Firm and Price Formation: An Illustrative Case," *Quarterly Journal of Economics*, **LXIII**:1 (Feb. 1949), 92–110; W. J. Baumol and R. E. Quandt, "Rules of Thumb and Optimally Imperfect Decisions," *American Economic Review*, **LIV**:2, part I (March 1964), 23–46; and Shorey Peterson, "Corporate Control and Capitalism," *Quarterly Journal of Economics*, **LXXIX**:1 (Feb. 1965), 1–24, and 11–12 in particular.

[33] Moses Abramovitz, "Monopolistic Selling in a Changing Economy," *Quarterly Journal of Economics*, **LII**:1 (Feb. 1938), 191–214; Lester, "Equilibrium of the Firm," pp. 480–481; Richard B. Heflebower, "Toward a Theory of Industrial Markets and Prices," *American Economic Review*, **XLIV**:2 (May 1954), 121–140; and Oswald Knauth, *Business Practices, Trade Position, and Competition* (New York: Columbia University Press, 1956).

[34] Richard A. Lester, "Absence of Elasticity Considerations in Demand to the Firm," *Southern Economic Journal*, **XIV**:3 (Jan. 1948), 287; Oswald Knauth, *Managerial Enterprise* (New York: W. W. Norton & Company, Inc., 1948), pp. 124, 134; and William Fellner, *Competition Among the Few* (New York: Augustus M. Kelley, 1960), chaps. VII–VIII.

[35] The classical exposition of the cause is by R. L. Hall and C. J. Hitch, "Price Theory and Business Behavior," *Oxford Economic Papers*, no. 2 (May 1939), pp. 12–45. Also see George Katona, "Psychological Analysis of Business Decisions and Expectations," *American Economic Review*, **XXXVI**:1 (March 1946), 44–62; William Fellner, "Average-Cost Pricing and the Theory of Uncertainty," *Journal of Political Economy*, **LVI**:3 (June 1948), 249–252; Edward H. Chamberlin, "'Full Cost' and Monopolistic Competition," *Economic Journal*, **LXII**:246 (June 1948), 318–325; Andrews, *Manufacturing Business*, p. 157; and Neil W. Chamberlain, *The Firm: Microeconomic Planning and Action* (New York: McGraw-Hill, Inc., 1962), p. 195. For a more recent rekindling of the full-cost urge, see John B. Williams, "The Path to Equilibrium," *Quarterly Journal of Economics*, **LXXXI**:2 (May 1967), 241–255.

markup, and the precise markup must still be determined. It has, in fact, been argued that although entrepreneurs may not actually seek to equate $MR$ and $MC$, or may not have marginal analysis in mind when establishing their markups, through a series of trials and errors they will come to establish that markup which, whether or not they are conscious of it, effects the $MR = MC$ price and output.[36]

The second contention is that decision makers may not have either the information, the information-processing capabilities, or the inclination to achieve maximization. In most decision problems there are simply too many options to seriously and realistically consider in detail. Indeed, one might not be capable of enumerating or even determining all the options. In this situation, one might seek, or settle for, a *satisfactory* solution to the problem.[37] In the case of pricing, for example, the firm might undertake a series of price increases or decreases until a level of profits is attained that is deemed satisfactory by the decision-making powers. There is, of course, the question of establishing the level at which profits, if profits are the central issue, become satisfactory. One interesting suggestion is that this level will be determined by the decision maker's aspirations. This suggestion is of particular interest, for it can then be argued that once the aspiration level is attained, aspirations rise. Thus, once earned, satisfactory profits are no longer satisfactory and one's satisficing level rises. This leads to a search for options that will provide higher profits. After a series of increases in the aspiration level and subsequently profitability, the maximum profit, $MR = MC$, position is eventually reached.[38] Any further increases in the level of aspirations will result in frustration rather than profit.

[36] In effect, this is the Machlup argument as set forth in his "Marginal Analysis and Empirical Research," *American Economic Review*, **XXXVI**:4, part I (Sept. 1946), 518–554, and more recently in his "Theories of the Firm: Marginalist, Behavioral, Managerial," *American Economic Review*, **LVII**:1 (March 1967), 1–33. Also, see Oliver, "Average Cost and Long-Run Elasticity of Demand," pp. 213–214.

[37] See R. A. Gordon, "Short-Period Price Determination in Theory and Practice," *American Economic Review*, **XXXVIII**:3 (June 1948), 265–288, and 271 in particular; Richard M. Cyert, Herbert A. Simon, and Donald B. Trow, "Observation of a Business Decision," *Journal of Business*, **XXIX**:4 (Oct. 1956), 327–348; Herbert A. Simon, *Models of Man* (New York: John Wiley & Sons, Inc., 1957), particularly pp. 202, 272–273; Peter F. Drucker, "Business Objectives and Survival Needs: Notes on a Discipline of Business Enterprise," *Journal of Business*, **XXXI**:2 (April 1958), 81–90; and Monsen and Downs, "A Theory of Large Managerial Firms," p. 226. And, for an interesting comparison of profit maximization and satisficing behavior through linear programming, see J. Odhnoff, "On the Techniques of Optimizing and Satisficing," *Swedish Journal of Economics*, **LXVII**:1 (March 1965), 24–39.

[38] See Julius Margolis, "The Analysis of the Firm: Rationalism, Conventionalism, and Behaviorism," *Journal of Business*, **XXXI**:3 (July 1958), 187–199; Diran Bodenhorn, "A Note on the Theory of Firm," *Journal of Business*, **XXXII**:2 (April 1959), 164–174; Julius Margolis, "Traditional and Revisionist Theories of the Firm: A Comment," *ibid.*, pp. 178–182; and, more recently, in precisely the same vein, R. H. Day, "Profits, Learning and the Convergence of Satisficing to Marginalism," *Quarterly Journal of Economics*, **LXXXI**:2 (May 1967), 302–311. For some interesting psychological sidelights, see Katona, *Psychological Analysis of Economic Behavior*, p. 202; James Morgan, "A Review of Recent Research on Consumer Behavior," in Lincoln H. Clark, ed., *Consumer Behavior* (New York: Harper & Row, 1958), p. 103; and Mason Haire, "Psychological Problems Relevant to Business and Industry," *Psychological Bulletin*, **56**:3 (May 1959), 169–194. For some related antecedent views, see Boulding, "Implications for General Economics of More Realistic Theories of the Firm."

## 10.9 A BRIEF COMMENT ON NONPROFIT-MAXIMIZING GOALS AND THE THEORY OF THE FIRM

It is quite common for persons unfamiliar with the economics literature to criticize the theory of the firm, and the view that economists take of the firm, on the grounds that its narrow focus on profit maximization makes the theory impotent as a vehicle for the analysis of decision making in the modern corporation, or even in the feudal proprietorship. While the criticism is not without some foundation, as the preceding *sample* of alternatives reveals, economists have not been unaware of the need to give the theory of the firm wider scope than that afforded through myopic analysis of the behavior of the neoclassical firm owned and managed by an entrepreneur who is economic man in disguise. Moreover, this awareness has stimulated serious efforts to embody alternative goals into the theory, and to place the decision maker's problems into a more realistic and less restrictive framework.

Unfortunately, many of the earliest efforts were aborted by the absence of, or the economist's ignorance of, the analytical tools necessary to build and handle the sorts of elegant models that a more sophisticated approach to the problems of the modern firm demands. In a discipline aspiring to scientific rigor, institutional wisdom can lay a foundation for theoretical elegance; but, standing by itself, institutional wisdom is at best an imperfect substitute for theoretical elegance. Nevertheless, as in the theory of consumer behavior, the substitution effect is symmetrical, and theoretical constructions should not neglect observed behavior. Recognition of multiple goals is important for economic theory.

But profit maximization is not the only assumption that the neoclassical theory makes. If the theory is not without its faults, the defects must stem from the assumptions. Thus if the theory is to be advanced, we must consider which of the assumptions to retain and which to dispose of. A critique of the basic assumptions in the neoclassical theory therefore introduces the next major portion of the book, which considers the most recent developments in the theory of the firm. As part of this critique, the contribution made by the nonprofit-maximizing approaches will be evaluated in a bit more detail.

## EXERCISES

1. Consider a firm with a production function given by $Q = 1000F_1^{.3}F_2^{.3}F_3^{.3}F_4^{.1}$, where the $F_i$ $(i = 1, 2, 3)$ are services from factors of production, and $F_4$ is in hours of entrepreneurial effort. The $F_i$ $(i = 1, 2, 3)$ are supplied at fixed wages of \$2, \$3, and \$4, respectively. The firm's demand curve is given by $P = 10{,}000Q^{-1/2}$. The entrepreneur's utility function in terms of profits $(\pi)$ versus leisure $(L = 24 - F_4)$ is $U = \pi^{.6}L^{.2}$. Determine the price charged for the product in order to maximize the entrepreneur's utility.

2. A firm's total cost curve is given by $C = 1000 - 20Q + .25Q^2$; the demand curve is given by $P = 980 - .75Q$.
   (a) Determine the price and output that maximize sales revenue.
   (b) Determine the price and output that maximize sales revenue, subject to the constraint that profits exceed 100,000.
   (c) Determine the effects on price and output in the latter case if a profits tax of 10 percent is imposed on the firm.
   (d) How will price and output differ from the previous two cases for the profit maximizer?
   (e) How will they differ for an entrepreneur who "satisfices" at the 100,000 mark?

3. Suppose that the firm's total cost curve (exclusive of advertising costs) is given by $C = 100 + Q^2$ and the demand curve by $P = 1000Q^{-1/2}A^{1/2}$, where $A$ is advertising expenditure.

(a) Determine price, quantity, and the level of advertising in the profit-maximizing firm.

(b) Suppose the firm maximizes sales revenue, subject to the constraint that profits exceed 500. What are the new price, output, and advertising levels?

4. Suppose that the firm of the previous problem is run by a management having a utility function of $U = \pi_d^{.2} M^{.5} A^{.1}$, where $\pi_d$ is discretionary profit and $M$ is managerial emoluments. The firm's owners require a profit of 100, after taxes. The tax rate is 10 percent. Determine the utility-maximizing levels of price, output, advertising, and emoluments. How do these change when the tax is removed?

5. In the past 10 years, a firm has sold brands X, Y, and Z. The profits on the brands, per 100 dollars of advertising expenditure, were as follows:

| Year | Brand X | Brand Y | Brand Z |
|---|---|---|---|
| 1959 | 500 | 200 | 550 |
| 1960 | 500 | 150 | 200 |
| 1961 | 1000 | 400 | 1050 |
| 1962 | 1000 | 400 | 950 |
| 1963 | 700 | 350 | 1000 |
| 1964 | 600 | 350 | 1100 |
| 1965 | 800 | 400 | 1250 |
| 1966 | 1000 | 500 | 1450 |
| 1967 | 1000 | 500 | 1550 |
| 1968 | 500 | 100 | 0 |

Management's judgments of 1969 profits are based exclusively on past performance. Each year is assumed to be independent of other years.

Management requires an expected profit of $300 for each $100 spent on advertising. How should the advertising budget be spent so as to minimize risk (as measured by historical variance)?

6. Assume that one assesses correlations of $r_{12} = .65$ and $r_{13} = .42$, to describe the relationship between random variables 1 and 2, and 1 and 3, respectively. Derive and discuss the constraints imposed upon $r_{23}$. Generalize these constraints.

7. A firm must choose between two research programs. The expenditures and receipts associated with each are as follows:

| | | PROJECT 1 | | |
|---|---|---|---|---|
| Year | Research | Development | Capital | Receipts |
| 0 | 100 | | | |
| 1 | 150 | | | |
| 2 | 300 | 50 | | |
| 3 | 150 | 100 | | |
| 4 | | 150 | 1000 | |
| 5 | | | 2000 | 800 |
| 6 | | | | 1200 |
| 7 | | | | 1200 |
| 8 | | | | 1000 |
| 9 | | | | 600 |
| 10 | | | | 280 |

| Year | Research | PROJECT 2 Development | Capital | Receipts |
|---|---|---|---|---|
| 0 | 150 | | | |
| 1 | 200 | | | |
| 2 | 300 | 100 | | |
| 3 | | 150 | | |
| 4 | | 100 | 1500 | |
| 5 | | | 1500 | 200 |
| 6 | | | | 200 |
| 7 | | | | 300 |
| 8 | | | | 1000 |
| 9 | | | | 3000 |
| 10 | | | | 495 |

The firm assumes a 20 percent annual depreciation rate on its capital assets and a 50 percent tax rate. Discuss the circumstances under which one project will be preferred to the other.

8. Consider the firm of Exercise 12, Chapter 9. Suppose that the monopolist wishes to maximize sales revenue, subject to the minimum-profits constraint. Also, suppose that the firm is uncertain as to the exact level of its fixed costs, since it is committed to employ the fixed factors, but it receives an "end of the month" bill to cover their costs. The \$1000 figure is the mean of the distribution of fixed costs. The variance is \$400. Management wishes to be "82 percent certain" that profits exceed \$1500. How much of what should be produced?

9. Consider zero-cost Cournot duopolists with an industry demand curve of $P = 1 - Q$. Both are now sales maximizers, but they demand minimum profits of $\frac{1}{10}$ and $\frac{1}{15}$, respectively.

(a) Is there a stable equilibrium price and industry output?

(b) How does the situation change if the $\frac{1}{10}$ demander is sophisticated in the Stackelberg sense?

10. Discuss conditions under which utility maximization and profit maximization will lead the firm to the same price and production policy.

11. Will a sales-maximizing pure competitor (short run), subject to a minimum abnormal-profits constraint, prefer price stability or price instability (in the Oi sense)?

12. Construct and interpret the duals to the Scitovsky, Baumol, and Williamson models.

13. The Poseyville Manufacturing Company manufactures DURK at four factories and ships it for sale at six outlets. The monthly quantity produced, outlet requirements, and unit shipping costs (dollars) are as indicated in the following table:

| | | *Outlet* | | | | | | |
|---|---|---|---|---|---|---|---|---|
| | | $O_1$ | $O_2$ | $O_3$ | $O_4$ | $O_5$ | $O_6$ | |
| *Factory* | $F_1$ | 12 | 10 | 6 | 12 | 16 | 4 | 100 |
| | $F_2$ | 14 | 4 | 8 | 8 | 18 | 2 | 200 |
| | $F_3$ | 8 | 16 | 10 | 6 | 12 | 8 | 150 |
| | $F_4$ | 8 | 4 | 12 | 10 | 12 | 14 | 150 |
| | | 50 | 150 | 150 | 100 | 50 | 50 | |

The Poseyville people usually sell DURK for $18 at outlets $O_1$, $O_2$, and $O_3$. Half the time, however, DURK is sold for $19 at outlet $O_5$, and half the time for $21. They justify the higher prices by pointing to the higher shipping costs. The price of DURK at outlet $O_6$ is independent of the price at outlet $O_5$. About one-fourth of the time DURK is sold at $O_6$ for $15, and the remainder of the time for $11, because of a "weak" market. The price of DURK at outlet $O_4$ is *always* set at the average price at which a unit is sold in outlets $O_5$ and $O_6$. What shipping pattern should Poseyville employ next month?

14. A book store specializing in used textbooks has room left on its shelves for 70 additional books. The manager feels that except for economics, sociology, and psychology books he has no need for additional books. In general, economics texts weigh 4 ounces, sociology texts 2 ounces, and psychology texts 3 ounces. The strain on his remaining shelves being what it is, they can only bear 170 ounces worth of textbooks without collapsing under the weight of knowledge. Further, the manager can purchase only $20 worth of books since his current balance isn't in too good shape. Used economics texts wholesale for 20 cents, whereas psychology and sociology texts cost 30 cents.

Most of the time the book dealer nets 5 cents, 15 cents, and 10 cents on economics, sociology, and psychology texts, respectively. That is, he anticipates, with probability of .8, that this is what he will net. Sometimes, when people are particularly troubled with money matters, he nets 15, 5, and 25 cents, respectively; at other times it is 20, 5, and 5 cents, respectively. The latter, he feels, are equally likely outcomes.

(a) How many of each type of book should the profit-maximizing dealer purchase?
(b) Suppose the dealer wishes to maximize sales revenue, subject to the constraint that, with probability of no less than .67, he wants profits to be at least $4. What should he purchase?
(c) Interpret the duals to problems (a) and (b).

15. An airplane freight service has planes located at five sites as indicated in the accompanying table. It is required to send the planes to four localities, pick up a cargo, and return the planes to their original destinations. The table indicates mileage from site to locality, together with the requirement of the locality and number of planes at each site.

| | | *Site* | | | | | |
|---|---|---|---|---|---|---|---|
| | | **A** | **B** | **C** | **D** | **E** | **Requirements** |
| *Locality* | **W** | 100 | 60 | 20 | 25 | 40 | 4 |
| | **X** | 50 | 70 | 60 | 50 | 62 | 6 |
| | **Y** | 75 | 40 | 15 | 75 | 35 | 5 |
| | **Z** | 40 | 50 | 40 | 70 | 40 | 5 |
| | **Planes** | 2 | 4 | 6 | 4 | 4 | 20 |

It costs $3/mile to fly an empty plane, and $7/mile to fly a loaded plane. The probability that all localities will fill up the planes is .5; the probability that locality **Z** will not fill up any planes and will return them empty is .25; the probability that locality **W** will not fill up any planes and will return them empty is .2.

How many planes would you advise sending from each site to each locality?

# 11

# RECENT DEVELOPMENTS AND THE THEORY OF THE FIRM: A Critique of the Basic Assumptions in the Neoclassical Theory

## 11.1 INTRODUCTION

The severest criticism to which the theory of the firm has been, and continues to be, subjected is that it creates a credibility gap between business as it is and as it is depicted by neoclassical theory. The temptation to describe the applicability of the neoclassical model to real-world decision problems as strictly "marginal" is almost overwhelming. There is, however, nothing inherently objectionable about this discrepancy. Indeed, even the model's staunchest proponents would not necessarily maintain that through neoclassical theory one can resolve actual business problems, for such is not ordinarily envisioned as the theory's major objective. A more defensible position is that the neoclassical model is a simple logical exercise in which the assumptions directly imply the conclusions and the conclusions directly imply the assumptions. For example, the profit-maximization assumption immediately suggests that the firm will continue to expand production so long as the increments in revenue attributable to the sale of the additional output exceed the cost increments incurred in producing the additional output. Alternatively, the firm that is hiring its factors of production so as to equate for each marginal revenue product to marginal factor cost is necessarily a profit-maximizing firm. Even if considered as primarily an exercise in logic, however, the neoclassical theory would still be of particular interest and great importance, for it presents useful generalizable information about the effects of *changes* in the system, and it helps to *establish standards* for the allocation of resources upon which to judge real-world market performance.

Moreover, one can also argue that the basic tenets of the theory, and marginalism as a method of analysis, do in fact have much to offer the decision maker. It *is* important to recognize that it is the impact of *incremental* output on the criterion function that must be evaluated, and it is the *incremental* revenues and *incremental* costs that will be germane when profits are the overriding consideration. While many of the assumptions are so unpalatable that the theory's *direct applicability* to actual decision problems is somewhat suspect, the neoclassical model can serve as a point of departure upon which more realistic and/or sophisticated models may be based.

In either event, if one is concerned with actual price and production decisions in the firm, neoclassical economic theory and what it has to say on the subject should not be ignored. Despite long and vigorous debate with respect to the theory and its merits,[1] and despite the many conscientious efforts to provide a suitable substitute candidate for serious consideration, the proponents of the theory refuse to be discouraged and their number refuses to stop growing. Furthermore, until such time as a theory is developed that is *clearly* a better predictor, or that *clearly* provides a better explanation of economic behavior and phenomena than does the neoclassical model, the ranks of the supporters will continue to swell. This is to the good, since the theory *has*, in fact, served us well; and it makes little sense to discard it in the absence of a discernibly superior alternative. Rather, one concerned with solving business problems should reach a judgment as to (1) which aspects of the theory are appealing and should be retained, and (2) which are so offensive to the sensibilities, and so incompatible with the need to arrive at and evaluate actual decisions in practical problems, as to warrant immediate rejection. Since the model's implications follow directly on the heels of its assumptions, the process of selection and rejection requires a careful assessment and critique of these assumptions. That is the purpose of this chapter.

## 11.2 THE RELEVANT FUNCTIONS

The neoclassical firm determines price, output, and factor employment on the basis of a specific set of demand and cost functions. These functions may be either known or determinable, or may simply represent datum accepted by the decision maker as the pertinent information for decision-making purposes. The essential assumption, however, is that the decision maker behaves *as if* the parameters of the relevant functions were known to obtain with certainty. Whether or not he *does* know them with certainty, or, perhaps more important, whether or not he ever *can* know them with certainty, are issues that expositors of the neoclassical theory tend to treat as minor irritants of which they must simply demonstrate some awareness.

[1] The major thrusts of the debate have centered on whether managers equate *MR* and *MC* either consciously or subconsciously, whether managers have even heard of *MR* and *MC* and whether the overt recognition of these concepts is a prerequisite to achieve their equation, and whether one should even be troubled about the whole affair. For a healthy sampling of the most pertinent considerations, see the following: Richard A. Lester, "Shortcomings of Marginal Analysis for Wage Employment Problems," *American Economic Review*, **XXXVI**:1 (March 1946), 63–82, and "Marginalism, Minimum Wages, and Labor Markets," *American Economic Review*, **XXXVII**:1 (March 1947), 135–148; Fritz Machlup, "Marginal Analysis and Empirical Research," *American Economic Review*, **XXXVI**:4, part 1 (Sept. 1946), 518–554, and "Rejoinder to an Antimarginalist," *American Economic Review*, **XXXVII**:1 (March 1947), 148–154; George J. Stigler, " Professor Lester and the Marginalists," *ibid.*, pp. 154–157; Henry M. Oliver, Jr., "Marginal Theory and Business Behavior," *American Economic Review*, **XXXVII**:3 (June 1947), 375–383; D. C. Hague, "Economic Theory and Business Behavior," *Review of Economic Studies*, **XVI**(3):41 (1949–1950), 144–157; and James S. Early, "Marginal Policies of 'Excellently Managed' Companies," *American Economic Review*, **XLVI**:1 (March 1956), 44–70. I have previously discussed this at length in a paper upon which this chapter is in large measure based, and which has been freely borrowed from here: "The Advance of the Theory of the Firm: One Step Forward, One Step Back," *Quarterly Review of Economics and Business*, **7**:2 (Summer 1967), 53–64.

It suffices that decision makers employ marginal analysis with respect to what they *believe* the appropriate decision-making parameters to be. They then proceed to equate a *subjectively* assessed marginal revenue to a *subjectively* assessed marginal cost in determining price and output.[2]

It is, of course, possible that a specific result anticipated by an entrepreneur, such as the price that his output will bring, will not be realized. But the consequences of any lack of omniscience, and their potential effects on the initial decision, have tended to be treated almost tangentially to the central issues, or as the basis for additional definitions, or else entirely ignored.[3] Moreover, by the judicious choice of definitions in subjectively assessing the relevant functions, the issues raised by uncertainty and human fallibility can be slowly but surely washed away. Thus, the entrepreneur managing the neoclassical firm suffers a rather unpleasant surprise upon discovering he is unable to dispose of his entire output at the established price. Surprise may turn to veritable gloom when it develops that the unsold output must

[2] In "Marginal Analysis and Empirical Research" Machlup almost casually comments as follows: "The proposition that the firm will attempt to equate marginal cost and marginal revenue is logically implied in the assumption that the firm will attempt to maximize its profit (or minimize its losses). It should hardly be necessary to mention that all the relevant magnitudes involved—cost, revenue, profit—are subjective—that is, perceived or fancied by the men whose actions are to be explained (the businessmen)—rather than 'objective'—that is, calculated by disinterested men who are observing these actions from the outside and are explaining them" (p. 521). Yet, as Oliver ("Marginal Theory and Business Behavior") among others has commented, "If marginal revenue is defined to include every possible consideration concerning rises and falls in gross income, and if marginal cost is defined to include every possible consideration concerning avoidable costs, the statement that a businessman trying to maximize profits will attempt to equate marginal revenue and marginal cost is merely a 'highbrow' and awkward way of saying that he will consider everything that may increase his income and everything that may increase his outgo and then try to strike the best balance" (p. 376). Similarly, and in lieu of leaving well enough alone, Richard A. Lester ["Absence of Elasticity Considerations in Demand to the Firm," *Southern Economic Journal*, **XIV**:3 (Jan. 1948), 285–289] has noted that "One may seek to include all such 'institutional' and 'psychological' factors within demand and marginal revenue schedules. To do so indiscriminately, however, would deprive such terms as 'demand elasticity' and 'marginal revenue' of much of their analytical value and would render them practically meaningless" (p. 287).

[3] In *The Theory of Monopolistic Competition* (Cambridge Mass.: Harvard University Press, 1960) Chamberlin devotes a small portion of his chapter, "Duopoly and Oligopoly," to the effects of uncertainty (pp. 51–54). His conclusion is that uncertainty leads to an indeterminate outcome (with respect to price and output). Recall that Mrs. Robinson characterizes the firm's demand curve as embodying the reactions of other firms to the given firm's price changes. These are reactions of which the other firms themselves are unlikely to be certain a priori. Yet Mrs. Robinson asserts: "It is not to our purpose to consider this question in detail." [Joan Robinson, *The Economics of Imperfect Competition* (London: Macmillan and Co., Ltd., 1950), p. 21.] For Machlup, the marginal concepts "are to be understood as referring to subjective estimates and conjectures. . . [and] the estimates need not be reduced to definite numerical values" ("Marginal Analysis and Empirical Research," p. 533). It would appear that although uncertainty is omnipresent and certainly the real-world decision maker *must* be concerned with how to deal with it, neoclassical theory may essentially ignore it, because its presence renders the model intractable, the issues that it raises are not directly within the scope of the theory, or the whole problem is merely terminological.

be scrapped, and somebody paid to haul it away. Nonetheless, so long as an additional cost term is embodied into the cost function to allow for contingencies such as this, or so long as the assessment of the demand curve includes a discount factor on price to reflect the possibility that, at any given price, the firm may not sell quite as many units as the entrepreneur's best judgment suggests it will sell, the $MR = MC$ calculus remains the profit-maximizing procedure.

There have been a wide variety of suggestions as to how the relevant functions would be determined. Guesswork is a distinct possibility, not to be lightly dismissed. By learning through doing, and by a series of readjustments in one's guesses on the basis of further experience, it may be possible to get a better understanding of the appropriate parameters and modes of behavior. This involves what is essentially a hunt-and-peck analysis that bypasses direct determination. In this procedure, as, say, price quotes are varied, the effects on profits and sales are analyzed. As long as price increases result in higher profits, price is increased further. Should a price increase result in a decline in profits, price is reduced. In this trial-and-error manner the neoclassical firm is able to determine the elasticity of demand and, concurrently, the profit-maximizing, $MR = MC$, position.[4] This approach implicitly assumes sufficient stability on both the demand *and* cost side to assure that the learning process will be helpful, and presumes that there are no institutional barriers, or long-term considerations, to prevent continual readjustments in price and output. If, however, we cannot always count on these assumptions being valid—that is, if management does not necessarily have sufficient data to permit reliable inferences to be drawn about costs, and if demand is in fact subject to random influences—then chance and good fortune must play a much more vital role in determining entrepreneurial success than is generally specified by the theory.[5]

[4] Robinson, *The Economics of Imperfect Competition*, p. 52. Oliver ("Marginal Theory and Business Behavior") has argued that while "few businessmen would make price or other changes if they did not expect *greater profits* (or smaller losses) to ensue, the more restricted conclusion that the new prices are selected because they are expected to *equate marginal revenue and marginal cost* does not necessarily follow" (p. 382). In the limit, however, the drive for *greater* profits will, even in the entrepreneur's ignorance, necessarily drive him to the $MR = MC$, profit-maximizing position. This is seen in the previously mentioned Margolis-Day type of analysis where the entrepreneur is a satisficer, but one with a rising aspiration level. In this analysis, $MR = MC$ "is not a decision rule but is a condition of 'equilibrium' which encourages the firm to select another variable for possible adjustment to achieve higher profits" [Julius Margolis, "The Analysis of the Firm: Rationalism, Conventionalism, and Behaviorism," *Journal of Business*, **XXXI**:3 (July 1958), 196]. It is thus meaningful to question whether *any* theory in which *greater* profits present an irresistible lure can tell us anything more about market behavior than does the neoclassical theory. For related comment see Diran Bodenhorn, "A Note on the Theory of the Firm," *Journal of Business*, **XXXII**:2 (April 1959), 164–174.

[5] For an exceptionally stimulating inquiry into the effects of uncertainty on the economic analysis of the firm, see Armen A. Alchian, "Uncertainty, Evolution and Economic Theory," *Journal of Political Economy*, **LVIII**:3 (June 1950), 211–221. In this paper, Alchian sets out his "viability" hypothesis under which at any point in time certain firms or certain courses of behavior might be more viable than others, given the society's requisites for survival; but management may neither know nor seek the optimum set of conditions. The aggregate set of actions that are observed are akin to a stochastic process, some of the outcomes of which are, however, likely to give the appearance of having been selected by a decision maker blessed with perfect foresight. In reacting to the viability

Depicting a decision maker as groping around for information about the pertinent decision-making parameters is a somewhat misleading portrayal of this aspect of real-world decision processes—but only somewhat. Decision makers do evaluate information and they do learn from experience. Thus, the suggestions that the relevant functions represent *best estimates*, or the *expected values* of probability-weighted magnitudes, or *present discounted values* encompassing factors to reflect the future effects of current decisions, in effect suggest that the information gleaned through trial and error will be evaluated, processed, and used in a very orderly and specific fashion.[6] Nonetheless, even when a "guess" becomes a "best estimate," one can still reach a decision that, in retrospect, will be acknowledged to have been unfortunate. Even with the new information provided by the experience, one might *again* make exactly the same decision inasmuch as an unfortunate outcome need not imply

---

hypothesis, Mrs. Penrose has made the point that man *can* reduce uncertainty (in the sense of the risks that he accepts or the knowledge he fails to acquire) and *can* affect his environment, and that if survival is his goal and only the fit survive, then some analytical goal such as profit maximization may well be a requisite of his behavior. See E. T. Penrose, "Biological Analogies in the Theory of the Firm," *American Economic Review*, **XLII**:5 (Dec. 1952), 804–819. Richard B. Heflebower ["Toward a Theory of Industrial Markets and Prices," *American Economic Review*, **XLIV**:2 (May 1954), 121–140] sees the firm as "consciously adapting to its environment or as 'adopted' when its successful moves are accidentally good" (p. 124); and Neil W. Chamberlain [*The Firm: Micro-Economic Planning and Action* (New York: McGraw-Hill Inc., 1962)] attributes success "not to a firm's actually making ex ante the decisions which are described in market theory, but to a firm's finding itself ex post in a position *as if* it had made such decisions" (p. 4). But if there is something to all of this, then surely the entrepreneur's attitude toward risk will influence the courses of action that he chooses! and surely this should be explicitly recognized.

[6] For example F. E. Balderston ["Scale of Output and Internal Organization of the Firm," *Quarterly Journal of Economics*, **LXIX**:1 (Feb. 1955), 45–70] suggests that "the best course for the firm is to estimate most probable (i.e., mean or modal) values for the net revenue function, and then to account for the presence of uncertainty by correcting (upward or downward, depending on the risk-preferences of the entrepreneur) the estimated values of the turnover rate..." (p. 51). Harrod suggests that a true valuation of marginal revenue would require "the addition of a sum representing the present value of superior goodwill of the customer through future time, due to his not having gone elsewhere on this occasion" [R. F. Harrod, "Price and Cost in Entrepreneur's Policy," *Oxford Economic Papers*, no. 2 (May 1939), p. 4]. In several studies the firm has been presented with a set of functions and probabilities, and the standard marginal analysis has been performed on the mathematical expectation of the functions. For example: Edwin S. Mills, "Uncertainty and Price Theory," *Quarterly Journal of Economics*, **LXXIII**:1 (Feb. 1959), 116–130; Richard R. Nelson, "Uncertainty, Prediction, and Competitive Equilibrium," *Quarterly Journal of Economics*, **LXXV**:1 (Feb. 1961), 41–62; and Arthur S. Nevins, "Some Effects of Uncertainty: Simulation of a Model of Price," *Quarterly Journal of Economics*, **LXXX**:1 (Feb. 1966), 73–88. Also see Oscar Lange, "A Note on Innovations," *Review of Economics and Statistics*, **XXV**:1 (Feb. 1943), 19–25; William Fellner, "Average-Cost Pricing and the Theory of Uncertainty," *Journal of Political Economy*, **LVI**:3 (June 1948), 250; R. M. Cyert, W. R. Dill, and J. G. March, "The Role of Expectations in Business Decision Making," *Administrative Science Quarterly*, **3**:3 (Dec. 1958), 309; and E. A. G. Robinson, "The Pricing of Manufactured Products and the Case Against Imperfect Competition: A Rejoinder," *Economic Journal*, **LXI**:242 (June 1951), 430.

an incorrect decision. Moreover, if we endow the entrepreneur with additional sophistication enabling him to employ engineering data and econometric methods to estimate the parameters of the required functions, these estimates, too, may be nothing more than mathematical expectations. Actually, such estimates are also guesses based on historical sample information; but this partial information has been processed in such an orderly and sophisticated fashion, and the parameters offered to us with such precision, that there is a tendency to forget that we have simply turned our "guessing proxy" over to an equation, and very likely to a computer.

There would, therefore, seem to be little justification for rejecting the neoclassical model on the grounds that it assumes knowledge of a set of functions and parameters of which one cannot possibly be certain. In point of fact, one *can* always make an assessment, however vague, of these functions, and this is exactly what the real-world decision maker does. The theory has concerned itself with how the decision maker should behave, if he wants to maximize profit, *after* he has secured the information upon which a decision is to be based. From the standpoint of microeconomic *theory*, the question of *how* the information would be obtained, and the form in which it would be presented, has been considered to be interesting but not basic. It has been implicitly assumed, and correctly so, that the entrepreneur must (and he will) somewhow arrive at a set of figures to describe the relevant functions. The theory further assumes, however, that once this has been accomplished, the data will be placed into a format that permits them to be treated as *certain* observations. It is therefore not necessary for the neoclassical entrepreneur to worry about uncertainty, or to concern himself with the possible consequences of error, for he is consistently assumed to behave *as if* he can never err.

It is the latter assumption, rather than the assumption that the relevant functions can be determined, that separates the real world and the neoclassical world. Unlike the neoclassical entrepreneur, the corporate manager must not only recognize the existence of uncertainty, he must allow for it and be prepared to deal with it. Economic theorists have tended to place undue emphasis on the role that uncertainty plays in influencing the *success* of a business decision as opposed to its role in the initial decision *selection*. In this former role, the firm's "normal" profit becomes the level of profit anticipated from the $MR = MC$ decision, and the "abnormal" profit becomes that difference between normal profit and actual profit effected by chance elements.[7] Only recently have there been attempts to *explicitly* recognize the *several* ways and means by which uncertainty will exert an *ex ante* influence on the actual decisions taken by the neoclassical firm.[8] When this aspect of uncertainty is empha-

[7] See J. Fred Weston, "A Generalized Uncertainty Theory of Profit," *American Economic Review*, **XL**:1 (March 1950), 40–60; William Fellner, *Probability and Profit* (Homewood, Ill.: Richard D. Irwin, Inc., 1965), pp. 109–138. For a discussion in this vein of profits as a return for the risk-bearing aspect of the entrepreneurial function, see M. L. Greenhut, "The Decision Process and Entrepreneurial Returns," *Manchester School of Economic and Social Studies*, **XXXIV**:3 (Sept. 1966), 247–268.

[8] See, for example, Phoebus J. Dhrymes, "On the Theory of the Monopolistic Multiproduct Firm Under Uncertainty," *International Economic Review*, **5**:3 (Sept. 1964), 239–257; Saul H. Hymans, "The Price-Taker: Uncertainty, Utility, and the Supply Function," *International Economic Review*, **7**:3 (Sept. 1966), 346–356; and Rudolph G. Penner, "Uncertainty and the Short-Run Shifting of the Corporation Tax," *Oxford Economic Papers*, **19**:1 (March 1967), 99–110.

sized and *directly* incorporated into the neoclassical theory, the gap between theory and practice is considerably shortened, and the nature of the relevant functions is considerably sharpened. For the moment, we offer this statement without proof, but Chapter 13 is devoted to substantiating it.

## 11.3 THE PROFIT-MAXIMIZATION ASSUMPTION

The most popular grounds for criticism of the neoclassical theory is almost surely the profit-maximization assumption that forces the entrepreneur into the role of economic man. The attacks on the economic man portrayal run a gamut: at one end are the views that businessmen do not know how to maximize profits,[9] that they do not have the information-processing network necessary to permit profit maximization even if they knew how to achieve it with such a network,[10] and that, even if they knew how to achieve profit maximization and had the required information-processing capabilities, they would not necessarily want to achieve it;[11] at the other end is the view that in the uncertain world in which we live, the profit-maximization goal is operationally meaningless and equivocal.[12]

Attempts to modify, refine, or replace the profit-maximization assumption have taken three main paths. In the first of these the profit-maximization motive is no

[9] See Hague, "Economic Theory and Business Behavior," and Henry M. Oliver, Jr., "Discussion," *American Economic Review*, **XLIV**:2 (May 1954), 157–160. Hague comments: "Even if businessmen took the trouble to estimate the marginal cost of each product (and it would only be an estimate), they could never know enough about the marginal revenue from each product to be able to say how much of each they ought to produce or at what price. So, while it seems certain that most businessmen have never heard of marginal cost or marginal revenue, it seems clear that they would be very little better off if they had" (p. 147).

[10] See, for example, Martin Shubik, "Information, Risk, Ignorance and Indeterminacy," *Quarterly Journal of Economics*, **LXVIII**:4 (Nov. 1954), 629–640; Herbert A. Simon, "A Behavioral Model of Rational Choice," *Quarterly Journal of Economics*, **LXIX**:1 (Feb. 1955), 99–118; and Sherrill Cleland, "A Short Essay on a Managerial Theory of the Firm," in Kenneth E. Boulding and W. Allen Spivey, eds., *Linear Programming and the Theory of the Firm* (New York: The Macmillan Company, 1960), pp. 202–216, particularly p. 211.

[11] The profit-maximization assumption, as well as the proffered substitutes, is the subject of any number of recent studies. For some good surveys of what people are complaining about and what is being done to rectify the complaints, see the following: Herbert A. Simon, "New Developments in the Theory of the Firm," *American Economic Review*, **LII**:2 (May 1962), 1–15; H. T. Koplin, "The Profit Maximization Assumption," *Oxford Economic Papers*, **15**:22 (July 1963), 130–139; E. Grunberg, "The Profit-Maximizing Assumption: Comment," *Oxford Economic Papers*, **16**:2 (July 1964), 286–290; William L. Baldwin, "The Motives of Managers, Environmental Restraints, and the Theory of Managerial Enterprise," *Quarterly Journal of Economics*, **LXXVIII**:2 (May 1964), 238–256; Armen A. Alchian, "The Basis of Some Recent Advances in the Theory of Management of the Firm," *Journal of Industrial Economics*, **XIV**:1 (May 1965), 30–41; and Gerald L. Nordquist, "The Breakup of the Maximization Principle," *Quarterly Review of Economics and Business*, **5**:3 (Fall 1965), 33–46.

[12] Armen A. Alchian, "Uncertainty, Evolution and Economic Theory"; Stephen Enke, "On Maximizing Profits: A Distinction Between Chamberlin and Robinson," *American Economic Review*, **XLI**:4 (Sept. 1951), 566–578; Charles J. Hitch and Roland N. McKean, "What Can Managerial Economics Contribute to Economic Theory?," *American Economic Review*, **LI**:2 (May 1961), 147–154.

longer the beacon guiding the firm's behavior. Instead, it is replaced with more complex alternatives that also imply the optimizing, or the maximizing, of *some* objective function.[13] In the previous chapter, we considered maximization of sales, maximization of present value, maximization of managerial emoluments or utility, or just the quiet life, perhaps with consideration given to a minimum-profits constraint, as alternative behavioral postulates under which the firm might be assumed to operate.

The implications of such refinements for the neoclassical firm's behavior were seen to provide some interesting insights into certain facets of real-world decision making. The fact of the matter is, however, that their major achievement has been to provide precise, and probably valid, rationales to indicate why the neoclassical firm—given the same knowledge, given the same cost, production, and demand considerations, and given the same economic environment—would produce at other than the $MR = MC$ point, and charge a price other than that charged by the profit-maximizing firm. These theories commonly do not question the entrepreneur's ability to attain *any* feasible preestablished goal; they merely question the *oversimplification* of the statement of the goal.

A second path taken by some innovators of economic theory has led to the establishment of uncertainty-related motives for the firm. Among these are survival, security, worry avoidance, maintaining balance among the firm's assets, acquiring and maintaining a secure market position, and growth.[14] In general, however, it is

[13] In contrast to the satisficing school, there remain staunch defenders of the maximizing school. Their arguments are that, on the one hand, goals are typically expressed in optimal terms, and that once one has formulated a set of goals and criteria it is *required* and *essential* that, within the constraints imposed upon the system, an optimum be sought. See, for example, C. Michael White, "Multiple Goals in the Theory of the Firm," in Boulding and Spivey, eds., *Linear Programming and the Theory of the Firm*, pp. 186–187. On the other hand, it has been suggested that managers are maximizers whose goals differ and who do not necessarily seek *profit* maximization. Nonetheless, it is then argued that the *results* of their behavior will not differ markedly from those of profit maximizers. See Robert C. Turner, "The 'Apologetics of Managerialism': Comment," *Journal of Business*, **XXXI**:3 (July 1958), 246. Shubik has also suggested that corporations will have many objectives, some of which may be in conflict, but others of which will lead to the same policy decision. See Martin Shubik, "Objective Functions and Models of Corporate Optimization," *Quarterly Journal of Economics*, **LXXV**:3 (August 1961), 345–375. For a pox on both the maximizing and satisficing houses, stemming from the notion that individual firms must reconcile their actions with respect to the *groups* of which they are members, see Almarin Phillips, "A Theory of Interfirm Organization," *Quarterly Journal of Economics*, **LXXIV**:4 (Nov. 1960), 602–613.

[14] See the following for a representative sampling. Survival: Oswald Knauth, *Managerial Enterprise* (New York: W. W. Norton & Company, Inc., 1948); Edward S. Mason, "Various Views on the Monopoly Problem: Introduction," *Review of Economics and Statistics*, **XXXI**:2 (May 1949), 104–106; Carl Kaysen, "A Dynamic Aspect of the Monopoly Problem," *ibid.*, pp. 119–113; Alchian, "Uncertainty, Evolution and Economic Theory"; Peter F. Drucker, "Business Objectives and Survival Needs: Notes on a Discipline of Business Enterprise," *Journal of Business*, **XXXI**:2 (April 1958), 81–90. Security: K. W. Rothschild, "Price Theory and Oligopoly," *Economic Journal*, **LVII**:227 (Sept. 1947), 299–320; T. W. Easterbrook, "The Climate of Enterprise," *American Economic Review*, **XXXIX**:3 (May 1949), 322–335. Worry avoidance: Hague, "Economic Theory and Business Behavior." Maintaining balance among the firm's assets: Leonid Hurwicz, "Theory of the Firm and of Investment," *Econometrica*, **14**:2 (April 1946),

not obvious how the firm is to attain these objectives. Nonetheless, the *attempt* to maximize profits, or the attempt to achieve *situations* where profits might be maximized, have been suggested as perhaps offering means to these ends.[15] Thus it has been speculated that firms that survive and grow are the firms whose management has, perhaps coincidentally in the light of subsequent circumstances, made decisions *as if* the maximization of profits were in truth the primary goal.[16]

Viewing the entrepreneur as a risk-avoider attempting to reduce uncertainty helps to explain why he behaves in certain ways. Nevertheless, by itself this generally fails to provide a *predictive* model to indicate the precise pricing and production decisions reached by the firm. As we have seen, the drive for security could enhance the attractiveness of product diversification. A pair of additional security-seeking alternatives, however, would be for the firm to either charge a "low enough" price to forestall possible entry into a market, or simply fail to increase price when government pressure urges against a price increase; and, on the occasions when either of these policies is followed, it might not appear to be "economically" justified.[17] With the exception of the sort of model dealt with in the previous chapter (and these have generally been developed *outside* the framework of economic theory), the uncertainty models are usually restricted to providing an *ex post* explanation of the firm's behavior, rather than an *ex ante* predictive mechanism for determining *when* the firm will behave in a particular manner in response to a particular stimulus. Their major

---

109–136; W. W. Cooper, "Theory of the Firm: Some Suggestions for Revision," *American Economic Review*, **XXXIX**:6 (Dec. 1949), 1204–1222; Kenneth E. Boulding, *A Reconstruction of Economics* (New York: John Wiley & Sons, Inc., 1950). Acquiring and maintaining market position: Moses Abramovitz, "Monopolistic Selling in a Changing Economy," *Quarterly Journal of Economics*, **LII**:1 (Feb. 1938), 191–214; Heflebower, "Toward a Theory of Industrial Markets and Prices"; Oswald Knauth, *Business Practices, Trade Position, and Competition* (New York: Columbia University Press, 1956); Yale Brozen, "Time, Demand, and Market Position," *Journal of Business*, **XXXI**:2 (April 1958), 95–106. Growth: Chester I. Barnard, *The Functions of the Executive* (Cambridge, Mass.: Harvard University Press, 1950), p. 159; George Katona, *Psychological Analysis of Economic Behavior* (New York: McGraw-Hill, Inc., 1951), p. 203; Edith T. Penrose, *The Theory of the Growth of the Firm* (New York: John Wiley & Sons, Inc., 1959); Robin Marris, "A Model of the Managerial Enterprise," *Quarterly Journal of Economics*, **LXXVII**:2 (May 1963), 185–209; K. George, "The Growth of Firms: An Empirical Study," *Australian Economic Papers*, **3**:1–2 (June–Dec. 1964), 80–81.

[15] Rothschild, "Price Theory and Oligopoly," p. 309; Penrose, "Biological Analogies in the Theory of the Firm," pp. 809–816; Weston, "A Generalized Uncertainty Theory of Profit," p. 54.

[16] In "Pricing Objectives in Large Companies" [*American Economic Review*, **XLVIII**:5 (Dec. 1958)] Robert F. Lanzillotti cites as the most typical pricing objectives of the firms he surveys: "(1) pricing to achieve a target return on investment; (2) stabilization of price and margin; (3) pricing to realize a target market share; (4) pricing to meet or prevent competition" (p. 923). It can, however, be argued that these objectives simply provide rules of thumb that are in fact perfectly consistent with the goal of maximizing profits. See Alfred E. Kahn, "Pricing Objectives in Large Companies: Comment," *American Economic Review*, **XLIX**:4 (Sept. 1959), 670–678; also see Lanzillotti's "Reply," *ibid.*, pp. 679–687 and recall the comments of footnote 5.

[17] For a discussion, with emphasis on the "goodwill" aspects of business pricing policy, see H. R. Edwards, "Price Formation in Manufacturing Industry and Excess Capacity," *Oxford Economic Papers*, **7**:1 (Feb. 1955), 94–118.

impact is to emphasize the firm's tendency to make those decisions which will reduce uncertainty and enhance its security and prospects for survival.

The third, and perhaps the most significant, path that the critics of the neoclassical theory have taken has called into question an individual's willingness as well as his ability to process information. As we have noted, the issue has been raised as to whether it is either practical or possible for the firm to obtain all the information necessary to reach "profit-maximizing" decisions—in particular, whether the cost of such information in terms of dollars, time, or effort is necessarily going to be economically justifiable. One can also question whether individuals have the information-processing capability to permit them and the firm to use all available information in an optimal manner and in a way that will lead the firm to the optimal decision, or whether, in fact, individuals actually desire to reach optimum decisions, irrespective of the criterion of optimality. It has therefore been suggested that individuals operate under bounded rationality through satisficing behavior. These individuals have aspiration levels that, though subject to change over time, provide them with lower bounds within which to evaluate alternatives. Unlike the classical entrepreneur who experiments with various price-quantity solutions until equilibrium is reached where $MR = MC$, the quasi-rational entrepreneur would not necessarily experiment further, once his profit levels reach the minimum acceptable point.[18]

Like the previous paths, the bounded-rationality route does not bring the neoclassical theory onto much firmer ground. Indeed, it shakes the foundations for a theory of decision making to a considerable extent, and with what may well be considerable justification. When it goes beyond "simply" questioning man's ability to reach an optimal decision, however, the bounded-rationality train of thought tends to submerge to the level of its predecessors. That is, it merely suggests why an alternative to the $MR = MC$ solution might be reached, while it concurrently argues that individuals know how to achieve definite ends, that they are able to achieve definite ends, and that, up to a point, there are certain ends that will be sought by the most rational process of which the individual is aware.

Unfortunately, none of these refinements resolves the most essential issues that create the discrepancies between reality and the theory of the firm, or at least none does so in a explicit manner and within a specific framework that offers a significant advance over neoclassical theory. If neoclassical theory is to be replaced, its substitutes must bring us closer to reality, yet retain the inherent simplicity and elegance of the original model. The position taken here is that the divergence from reality in the neoclassical theory stems mainly from its failure to explicitly recognize and deal with the uncertain environment within which the firm is constrained to operate. This uncertainty renders the profit-maximization goal, *as well as* such alternatives as sales or rate-of-return maximization, operationally impotent. What it does encourage, however, is the incorporation of the individual's attitude toward risk as a crucial variable influencing the decisions made by the firm. In Chapter 13 we respond to this encouragement.

[18] See Simon, "A Behavioral Model of Rational Choice," and Margolis, "The Analysis of the Firm." Also see R. A. Gordon, "Short-Period Price Determination in Theory and Practice," *American Economic Review*, **XXXVIII**:3 (June 1948), 265–288; and R. M. Cyert and James G. March, "Organizational Factors in the Theory of Oligopoly," *Quarterly Journal of Economics*, **LXX**:1 (Feb. 1956), 44–64.

## 11.4 THE TREATMENT OF TIME

Time is introduced into the theory of the firm from three distinct directions and in three distinct roles. Unhappily, the most emphasized aspect of time, the distinction between short and long run, is of little or no consequence to the real-world decision maker concerned with the need to reach, and live with, a current decision. Indeed, the relationship between time and the short versus the long run is itself tenuous. The short and the long runs of economic theory are distinguished from one another by the variability, or lack thereof, of the factors of production, number of firms, or consumer purchases.

It is of considerable interest to the economic theorist to note the ultimate and immediate consequences of a shift in demand, and to distinguish between these consequences. He does this by focusing on the long-run effects of change on price and quantity and number of firms in the industry, comparing these to the short-run effects. The real-world decision maker must also be concerned with how these variables will change *over time* in response to a demand shift. Ordinarily, however, he cannot be satisfied with a vague generality such as that, following an increase in demand, there will be an increase in the number of his competitors and a decrease in price below the short-run price, once firms have had an opportunity to adjust all factors of production. If the modern manager is to design an appropriate price and production *policy* to carry his firm through a sequence of days, months, or years, he must consider *precisely* when and how these variables will change. The timing of decisions and their consequences is often vital, and cannot be relegated to a generality centered around the variability of firms and factors.

If, however, this emphasis on the short and the long run is misplaced from the standpoint of the corporate manager, it certainly does not do anybody any harm. Some of the theoretician's attention may thereby be diverted from more practical issues (and this in itself may occasionally be a positive contribution), but this emphasis need not have any other harmful side effects. The real-world decision maker may not concern himself with whether his is a short-, intermediate-, or long-*run* decision. But, if he should ever figure it out, the firm's profits and sales, and his emoluments, are unlikely to be altered. He will, however, concern himself with whether his is a short-, intermediate-, or long-*term* decision in the sense of recognizing the length of time with which he must live with the decision and its consequences, and balancing these with his own time preferences.

Time also becomes a relevant consideration in interpreting the functions guiding the neoclassical entrepreneur's decisions. One simply does not employ 30 laborers, 5 units of capital, and 2 acres of land and, by adding a drop or two of entrepreneurial talent, *instantaneously* produce and sell 1243 units of output. Surely things are not quite that easy for the real-world decision maker. In fact, they are not quite that easy for the economic strawman with whom we have been concerned, although there has not been complete agreement on the matter among theoreticians.[19] As with the length of run, this aspect of time has been handled with a vagueness, or lack of concern, that the corporate manager cannot share. The latter must know the *exact* period of time over which the factors are being employed and the output is being generated, and the *exact* period of time being referred to when we talk about

[19] For an illuminating discussion see Armen A. Alchian, "Costs and Outputs," in *The Allocation of Economic Resources* (Stanford, Calif.: Stanford University Press, 1959), pp. 23–40.

*the* demand for his product. Again, however, this issue is more important for a specific decision than for a general method of analysis, and the neglect of the issue, like the distortive concern with factor variability, should not lead one to dismiss the entire package. In the real world, the variables that economic theory is concerned about, such as the quantity demanded at a given price, or the output of a production function, are rates per unit of time. If the theory or the theoretician frequently fails to specify them as such, this is an oversight that we can surely live with. Moreover, if the theory goes on to lump these variables into convenient packages for analytical purposes, one can sympathize with this too, for this is precisely what decision making in the real world requires. That is, in either theory or fact, it is not practical to deal with every unit of output as it comes along. Rather, we necessarily confine ourselves to the week's output, or the day's output, or the morning's output. The time period of concern is that which is pertinent for decision-making purposes, or that which is *made* pertinent by the constraints imposed by the data upon which a decision will be based. If after an initial statement to this effect, microeconomic theory turns its attention to other things, it certainly does not suffer therefrom.

The third important aspect of time stems from the need to discount future events. If, however, the need to consider time as a variable can be satisfied by incorporating a discount factor into one's computations, then, as has been previously indicated, the tenets of microeconomic theory require very little adjustment. Profit-maximizing entrepreneurs will still want to equate *some* $MR$ to *some* $MC$ in every time period during which a decision must be reached, or will incorporate a time discount factor *directly* into their $MR$ and $MC$ computations. Business operations may appear to be less profitable (or costly) as a result of the time factor, and one's choice among alternatives may be influenced by the time factor, but aside from a change of degree in the input data used by the entrepreneur the neoclassical theory is unaltered. Further, as noted, such changes as do occur in the basic functions and data can always be made a matter of definition and the whole issue delicately defined away.

There are, however, two additional properties of the future and its relationship to the present that the real-world decision maker can neither ignore, define, nor discount away. First, if there is any uncertainty in his world, then this will commonly be magnified as he studies the future. The manager who can only guess about current demand will almost certainly become much more vague about the future. Second, *successful* managers do not participate in a series of isolated decisions. Rather, they establish *policies*, or *planned sequences* of decisions that recognize the potential dependence of one decision upon future decisions, and the effects that the results of past decisions will have on a present decision. Both of these issues are very important and influential in real-world decision making. They too can be defined away and buried in the definitions of demand, cost, and the production function. If, however, the theory of the firm is to rise above the role of logical exercise and provide a basis for decision making in the complex and hopefully long-lived world in which we live, then these aspects of time cannot be treated negligently, but must receive explicit recognition.

## 11.5 ENTRY, EXIT, AND COMPETITIVE ASSUMPTIONS

When the firm of economic theory has many competitors and competes in a purely competitive industry, it behaves as a price-taker, and the entrepreneur-manager has basically very little to do. He either operates so as to maximize profits or he suffers a loss; and to maximize profits he must simply determine the output at which marginal cost equals price. Since he can determine the relevant functions, his problems are by no means manifold. Similarly, the monopolist must work out a few of the computational details, but once he is willing to accept a set of functions upon which to base his decisions, there is very little to trouble him about the firm's operations. Of course, the real world does not see too many genuine monopolists or purely competitive industries, and economists have not been unaware of this fact.[20] Unfortunately, once we turn from these polar cases and direct attention to the intermediate oligopoly cases, we discover a multitude of suggestions, frequently conflicting, with respect to how firms will or should behave.

Essentially the same can be said for the serious issues created by the opportunities for entry to, and exit from, an industry. In the purely competitive industry one either can (in the long run) or cannot (in the short run) have cost-free entry or exit from an industry, and the effects on other firms and the industry in question are determinable; and in the monopolistic industry, the firm in question will either produce or not in the short run or the long, and will either leave the industry or not in the long run; but there are no potential entrants. The intermediate case, where firms may or may not enter or exit and there is some definite cost in doing so, receives little attention in microeconomic theory.

It is, however, with these intermediate cases that the real-world decision maker is concerned. The failure to deal adequately and fully with them has been interpreted by some to mean that microeconomic theory devotes most of its attention to the detailed solution of problems for firms that do not exist.[21] The defense of the theory, once again, turns on the definitions of the relevant functions. If the demand curve is *defined* so as to incorporate the effects of *potential* entrants on the quantity the firm will sell at a given price, as well as to incorporate the effects of the policies followed by the *unspecified number* of competitors, the profit-maximizing firm will continue to seek an $MR = MC$ output. Viewed in this light, the difficulty is not one of determining a new theory to handle a variety of assumptions with respect to actual and potential competition. Rather, the problem is strictly that of the entrepreneur's attempt to determine the parameters of his demand curve or the elasticity of demand for his product. The entrepreneur must, however, recognize that competitive factors will influence this determination, and he must assess and incorporate these factors into his analysis.

It is, on the one hand, tempting to cry out in protest against the methodological device of combating potential criticism with potent definitions, and to counterattack with the assertion that this defense is all right if theoretical elegance is more important than practical problem-solving. On the other hand, it may well be that the all-encompassing definition of the demand curve is not merely the most useful one from the theoretical standpoint but from the practical standpoint as well. The

[20] Economic theory develops, perhaps with an unfortunate time lag, as an outgrowth of institutional needs. Just as firms are commonly neither pure competitors nor monopolists, neither are the most important of them "representative." And the way in which firms are viewed by economists changes as societies change. See, for example, E. A. G. Robinson, "The Pricing of Manufactured Products," *Economic Journal*, **LX**:240 (Dec. 1950), 771–780; and Adolf A. Berle, "The Impact of the Corporation on Classical Economic Theory," *Quarterly Journal of Economics*, **LXXIX**:1 (Feb. 1965), 25–40.

[21] For example, P. W. S. Andrews, *On Competition in Economic Theory*, (London: Macmillan and Co., Ltd., 1964).

corporate manager making a judgment with respect to the firm's possible sales at a particular price, *like the neoclassical entrepreneur*, must make this judgment on the basis of a set of assumptions regarding the actions and reactions of current and potential competitors. The strength and number of this competition will affect the ease with which a judgment is reached and may affect the uncertainty surrounding the judgment and the confidence one has in it, but it need not affect the process of reaching this judgment nor the format for presenting the final assessments. Thus, the modern manager and neoclassical entrepreneur may each assert that, in his best judgment, if the firm charges a price of $P$ dollars it will be able to sell an estimated $Q$ units per week. In arriving at this estimate, *each* will have considered competitive conditions, even though neither may take the trouble to tell us precisely how this was done.

What we are suggesting, then, is that if microeconomic theory is to be made more meaningful and operational, the exact nature of, and means of determining, the firm's demand curve cannot be glossed over. Rather, the need to distinguish between different industrial structures for analytical purposes in price and quantity determination will disappear once we provide a clear-cut operational statement of (1) precisely what the demand curve means, (2) what assumptions underlie the demand curve, and (3) precisely how the behavior of current and potential competitors will be reflected in the demand curve. In this manner we are also able to successfully handle the difficult questions of what constitutes an industry and a product. The discussion of the firm's demand curve in Section 4.4f is offered in this spirit, and we shall return to this interpretation in subsequent chapters.

## 11.6 PRODUCTS AND PROCESSES

For the most part the neoclassical firm produces a single product in a single place via a single process. That assumption does not suffer from excess generality. Its restrictiveness will be reflected in the limited number of firms to which it can be applied. As we have seen, it is certainly *possible* to modify the neoclassical model, and to formulate the firm's problem, so as to incorporate the case of multiple products and multiple processes and multiple locations. We soon discover, however, that we are also immersed in multiple problems, including the practical difficulties of obtaining a solution and obtaining the parameters to be used as inputs to the model. As one complication, it might not be feasible to treat multiple products individually where the problem of allocating joint costs arises, or where one product is a by-product of another. As a contrasting complication, it might not be practical to treat them otherwise when the mathematical operations required for the solution of the more complex problem are exceedingly exacting and difficult to carry out.

From the standpoint of theoretical problem formulation and analysis, it is by no means obvious that a more generalized model of the firm will be any more informative with respect to general tendencies than the single-product single-process version of the neoclassical model. Nor is it obvious that, from the standpoint of *actual* problem solution, a more generalized model will be any more useful. In the operational sense, it will almost surely be necessary, in every instance, to solve a specific and unique problem, making specific assumptions and using specific parameters. To help solve such problems, however, we can use certain general and widely applicable mathematical and statistical tools.

What we require from economic theory, then, is a set of convincing arguments as to factors that are important for decision making in the firm, and why these factors are important, as well as an indication of what their influence *might* be. Concurrently, the theory can provide the insights and framework upon which to build the model required to describe the particular problem at hand. That is, the theory should help to indicate to the decision maker those factors that he *ought* be concerned with, and how he *might* go about formulating the problem to suit a set of objectives. If one is to improve upon the neoclassical model, the improvement must take us further in the latter direction. The addition of several products and processes to the firm's area of concern does not, in our view, accomplish this purpose. Once management is provided with the necessary mathematical and statistical tool kit, the problem becomes more cumbersome with the latter additional complications—but it can be dealt with.

To advance the theory of the firm we do not need more complex *mathematical* problems: we need a more practical statement of the essential *economic* problem. The position taken here is that this economic problem is how to deal with uncertainty. In succeeding chapters we shall, therefore, demonstrate that even within the seemingly narrow context of the neoclassical model the influence of uncertainty can be profound, and we shall indicate the manner in which uncertainty can be quantified and explicitly incorporated into a decision-making calculus. Once this is accomplished, the resolution of the more complex problems of the firm under uncertainty becomes a realistic possibility, although it remains a practical problem. Then, however, the problem is indeed one of mathematics and statistics, rather than one of economics.

## 11.7 THE FIRM AS A WELL-OILED MACHINE

Although the previous statements are not specifically designed to irritate organization theorists, sociologists, psychologists, and persons of similar persuasion, they will undoubtedly have that effect. Many economists may be similarly inclined. For many persons the critical assumptions implicit in the neoclassical theory are that the firm has somehow resolved all of the organizational issues: there is a vice-president of finance who, with his staff, has determined optimal financial arrangements such as whether to float a bond or water a stock, the personnel and production managers have determined the optimal number of washrooms to have on the third floor and where to locate them, and the consulting psychologist has indicated that the men's room should not be designated a powder room even if there are economies in purchasing signs, and the corporate polity have been able to agree on a common goal for the firm, preferably the maximization of profits. Economists are troubled by the fact that the neoclassical entrepreneur does very little to influence the firm's destinies. It is only sporadically and tangentially that economic theory concerns itself with the possibilities of advertising to shift the demand curve, or of research-and-development activity to develop a new product or improve upon an old process. Moreover, in the light of the separation of ownership and management that pervades modern firms, there is widespread interdisciplinary concern and distrust of *any* theory that rests on the behavior of an entrepreneur-manager who seemingly resolves all of the former problems and, in so doing, needs to be concerned only with his own goals and emotions.

These qualms about microeconomic theory are, of course, extremely important, and they raise issues that are well taken. It is unquestionably true that decision making in the modern firm is an exceedingly complex process. Whereas economists are inclined to talk about the firm *as if* it were being managed by a single entrepreneur with well-defined tastes and preferences, attitudes, and opinions, they are forced to live with firms whose managements are arranged in bureaucratic hierarchies frequently distinct and isolated from the firms' owners. Economic theory *assumes* that somehow the interpersonal questions have been resolved: somehow, differing judgments have been combined and reconciled. These are indeed heroic assumptions that stretch the credulity of many economists, to say nothing of sociologists and organization theorists.

Although the skepticism is warranted, there are some blanks in economic theory that are beyond the purview of economists per se and that should and do remain for others to fill in. It is the sociologist's and organization theorist's task to shed light on the processes through which conflicting preferences, and preferences of varying intensities, eventually blend in the decision-making process. It is the statistician's (and perhaps the philosopher's) task to determine how differing probability judgments are reached and reconciled. These may be difficult problems, but the economist is as justified in accepting their resolution as "givens" as he is in accepting the fact that, for example, engineers will provide the firm with the necessary technical information and know-how upon which to base certain production decisions. The details of mechanical engineering—for example, *how* the technical issues are resolved —are no more the economist's concern than the details of *how* the interpersonal issues are resolved. In his role as an economic theorist, the economist is being properly presumptive when he accepts the assumption that somehow these issues get themselves resolved, by fiat or vote, by fair means or foul. Subsequently, starting from the point of resolution, it is the economist's task to indicate those *economic* policy decisions that would be most compatible with existing capabilities, opportunities, preferences, and judgments.[22]

## 11.8 INFORMATION-PROCESSING CONSTRAINTS

It has also been assumed that the firm will be guided by a *rational* individual who behaves as an economic man. That is, his single goal is the maximization of profits and he will attempt to reach this goal via a reasoned and orderly process of decision making, eschewing modes of behavior that lead him away from the central objective. We shall reserve discussion of the rationality assumption for the next chapter. It is mentioned here because the assumption of rationality implies the need to obtain, consider, and evaluate information. To all intents and purposes, the neoclassical model assumes that entrepreneurs either know everything they need to know in order to reach a rational decision or else can obtain, apparently cost-free, the information needed to fill in whatever gaps might exist in their knowledge; and, in their calculations, they can seemingly allow for anything that might come up, and do so instantaneously subject only to the fixity of certain factors of production. Moreover, the decision maker can process infinite amounts of complex data, and he

[22] For an interesting debate on these issues, see Talcott Parsons, "The Motivation of Economic Activities," *Canadian Journal of Economics and Political Science*, VI:2 (May 1940), 187–202; Frank H. Knight, "Professor Parsons on Economic Motivation," *Canadian Journal of Economics and Political Science*, VI:3 (August 1940), 460–465; and Talcott Parsons, "Reply to Professor Knight," *ibid.*, pp. 466–472. It should be mentioned that this debate was not a case of length over strength.

can isolate and consider all possible ways in which he might behave. Thus, the decision maker eventually considers enough price and production policies, and evaluates a sufficient stock of data, to permit him to achieve an $MR = MC$ output position.

Such a decision maker is certainly a very fortunate and capable chap. Indeed, if only in this one respect, he is quite unlike the vast majority of persons who have to reach decisions, and the latter includes quite an impressive array of individuals. In the real world important constraints *are* imposed in the decision process, because obtaining and evaluating information entails costs in terms of time, money, and effort.[23] The crucial problems for the decision maker are: (1) how much information to seek, and (2) how much to pay for it in time and money; (3) how to reach an *optimal* solution on the basis of *partial* information and a limited number of options; (4) how to narrow down the options that one can seriously evaluate to a feasible and finite few; and (5) how much effort to put into "rational" decision processes.

These important problems for the real-world decision maker are all but ignored by the neoclassical theory of the firm. Still, their resolution, or indeed merely the *need* to resolve them, can have an impressive impact on the theory and its implications. Individuals differ, and they differ as decision makers. In a world immersed in uncertainty one *can* be irrational and survive. In our world, one's attitudes and judgments are *vital* to the decisions that are reached. In our world, not all decision makers have the same information and not all evaluate it in the same manner. In our world, there are no universally *best* decisions, only individually *preferred* decisions, and one will not necessarily suffer from a failure to employ the most sophisticated decision-making tools. Indeed, one might actually prefer not to employ them and could very well benefit from the failure to do so.

In attempting to make microeconomic theory more realistic, then, one should indicate how information can be used and evaluated in order to permit a rational decision maker, who *wishes* to do so, to reach preferred decisions. In so doing, however, one should recognize that not all decision makers will necessarily behave rationally, reaching decisions through an orderly decision process—and not all will want to do so.

## 11.9 AN OVERALL EVALUATION

Although the neoclassical model paints a very abstract picture of the firm, this chapter has suggested that the picture can be most revealing and can provide most rewarding insights. But the picture can certainly use a few careful and major touches.

The neoclassical theory of the firm may fail to live up to all that has been demanded of it by those outside the economics profession and all that has been claimed for it from those within the profession. The response to these failures has been an attempt to refine, reformulate, or redirect the theory to bring it closer to reality and, presumably, to close the gap between what the theory achieves and what the profession requires. In an effort at accomplishing this reorientation of the theory, the organizational structure of the firm, the motives of its management, the extent to which certainty can be presumed, and the rationality or desire for rationality of the decision maker have been called to the fore as influential variables.

[23] See Shubik, "Information, Risk, Ignorance and Indeterminancy," and H. B. Malmgren, "Information, Expectations, and the Theory of the Firm," *Quarterly Journal of Economics*, **LXXV**:3 (August 1961), 399–421.

We have argued that the obligation of the economic theorist is to recognize the importance of these issues, and in particular we have argued that the crucial variable with which he must begin to be concerned is uncertainty. This done, the other factors will fall or be encouraged into place. It has been argued that uncertainty will influence the decisions that the firm reaches, and that the nature of this influence should be directly incorporated into the neoclassical theory in lieu of sliding it in through the back door. Further, in a world of uncertainty populated by decision makers who may, perhaps, prefer not to react in a completely rational fashion, we may be demanding too much of a theory in requiring that it predict perfectly and in an orderly way, and we shall always be claiming too much if we blatantly suggest that the theory describes the way in which all decision makers behave. An economic theory can be developed that will describe how a rational decision-making unit will behave when placed in a given situation. Such a theory can indicate the role that chance and uncertainty, as well as irrationality, have played in the degree of success attained by a firm. It can suggest how firms will *tend to* react in given situations. It cannot, and it should not, be required to predict with certainty in a world in which uncertainty abounds. It is with this qualification in mind that we proceed.

# 12

# RECENT DEVELOPMENTS AND THE THEORY OF THE FIRM: Decision Making under Risk

## 12.1 INTRODUCTION

Although one of the more terrifying joys of life is rendered by the sweet trauma of decision making, in the overwhelming majority of situations into which they have thus far been thrust, neither the consumer nor the entrepreneur will necessarily find decision making to be an overly traumatic experience. Each, of course, will have his problems. The consumer must order his preferences and live within a budget constraint; the entrepreneur must establish his objectives and determine the maximum price at which he will be able to sell, and the minimum cost at which he will be able to produce, alternative levels of output. Nevertheless, given sufficient patience and insight, or given sufficient understanding of geometry and/or the calculus, each will make his selection absent of fear that the outcome will be other than that which had been anticipated.

In the real world, however, few persons, even if blessed with patience, insight, and mathematical talents, can behave as if their futures were determinate. Indeed, many of us who all too frequently make decisions that in light of succeeding events *turn out* to have been nonoptimal, might strive to *improve* our predictive accuracy or to reduce the number of variables over which we exercise at best only imperfect control; but we might well find the life of a *perfect* predictor rather tiresome. Since there is little we can do about them, it is fortunate that the periodic disappointments and pleasant surprises of our world of uncertainty do add spice to what otherwise might be a dull way to pass the time.[1] Even if we commonly do so in a very vague and

[1] As noted in Chapter 4, one may be able to refine and revise probability assignments and, say, in the case of repetitive events, bring them more in line with long-term frequencies, or in relation to some criterion function, evaluate them ex post as having been better or worse than other assignments. But one cannot ordinarily eliminate the randomness in a system. Rather, one can attempt to isolate the random components of a system from its systematic components, and then attempt to understand better the nature of the random process involved. As H. Working remarks, "The most perfect expectations possible in economic affairs must be subject to substantial error because the outcome

haphazard manner, then, daily problems of choice require that we give consideration to the various consequences that a decision can have, and make some assessment of the likelihood that a given result will obtain. For example, in his role of consumer one might prefer good duck to good steak. Before ordering one or the other in a restaurant, however, he should consider the possibility that the duck will be greasy or the steak will be tough, as well as make some allowance for the fact that *nothing* is worse than greasy duck.

Similarly, in his role of entrepreneur, the decision maker will not be restricted to choosing among a set of profit-maximizing, sales-maximizing, or utility-maximizing prices and outputs. Instead, his problem is to choose among alternative policies *each* of which tempts him with the *possibility* of *various* levels of profits and sales. In a world of uncertainty, a single policy can seldom be guaranteed to be optimal against all possible contingencies. In the absence of such a policy, the decision maker's problem is not simply to assert a preference for a $5000 profit to profits of $4000, $2000, or $1000. That's easy. Instead, he will ordinarily have to choose between, say, a policy that offers the *prospects* of $5000 and $1000 with equal probabilities of .5, and a second policy that he judges will yield $4000 with probability of .7 and $2000 with probability of .3. Under these circumstances, the choice is not quite so obvious, although each of us may have definite *preferences* with respect to one alternative or the other. Put to a vote, one choice might prove more popular than the other, but there will not necessarily be unanimous agreement, and there is no point in asserting that one choice is "right" and the other is "wrong."

There is certainly nothing particularly novel in these characterizations. As Frank Knight commented a half century ago: "It is correct to treat all instances of economic uncertainty as cases of choice between a smaller reward more confidently and a larger one less confidently anticipated."[2] Indeed, this very *lack* of novelty leads one to wonder why so very little had been done, until recently, to *explicitly* recognize this dilemma in the theory of the firm. The failure to do so can be traced in large measure to the historic unavailability of a tractable method for dealing with the issues raised by uncertainty. The basic difficulty in developing a model to deal with uncertainty is that one must not only assign and allow for the *probabilities* involved, but one must also incorporate the decision maker's *attitude towards risk.* In deciding whether to undertake a research venture, for example, management must have some understanding of both (1) what the "chances are" of achieving any of the various possible

---

depends on unpredictable future events. Market expectations, therefore, have a certain *necessary inaccuracy*...that irreducible minimum of inaccuracy...". ["The Investigation of Economic Expectations," *American Economic Review*, **XXXIX**:3 (May 1949), 159.]

[2] Frank H. Knight, *Risk, Uncertainty and Profit* (Boston: Houghton Mifflin Company, 1921), p. 237. Knight went on to remark that "those with confidence in their judgment and disposition to 'back it up' in action specialize in risk-taking" (p. 270). Recall, however, that Knight distinguished between risk and uncertainty, although those with Bayesian tendencies need not do so.

Even those who do not outwardly profess to be Bayesians, or to be championing the subjectivist cause, may count in their number some economists who are quite aware of the central issues. Consider, for example, Stephen Enke's nail-on-the-head comment: "Unless people have beliefs concerning the likelihood of certain future events occurring, a specific motivation cannot provide them with a criterion for selecting one alternative over another." ["On Maximizing Profits: A Distinction Between Chamberlin and Robinson," *American Economic Review*, **XLI**:4, (Sept. 1951), 569].

degrees of success or failure, *and* (2) whether these sorts of payoffs and odds are sufficiently attractive to be "worth" the gamble.

Like all fairy tales, however, ours has a happy ending. A *practical* method for handling these issues was suggested by John von Neumann and Oskar Morgenstern in their modern classic, *Theory of Games and Economic Behavior*.[3] It is somewhat surprising that microeconomic theorists have been so reticent towards exploiting the advantages of the von Neumann-Morgenstern analysis, or at least that the economist's perspective has been so narrow. But this reticence is rapidly disappearing and the perspective broadening, if by stealthy leaps and restrained bounds. In this chapter we shall present the von Neumann-Morgenstern approach to decision problems and indicate its ties to the Bayesian approach to probability. In the next chapter we shall consider the potential of the analysis for the theory of the firm.

## 12.2 THE VON NEUMANN-MORGENSTERN APPROACH

Chapter 2 introduced the notion of utility. It emphasized that the consumer's problems of choice, as formulated therein, could be handled using an *ordinal* concept of utility. Cardinality, and the measurability of utility or individual preferences under certainty, was not necessary to the tasks at hand. In order to avoid the use of measurable utility, we stressed *rates of substitution* as opposed to marginal utilities. In that analysis, the statement that one basket of goods has more or less utility than another for a particular individual would merely imply that the person *prefers* one basket to the other. The issue becomes much more complex, however, when the individual must choose between, say, one basket of goods (or nothing) offered with probability of $p_1$ and a more desirable second basket of goods (or nothing) offered with probability of $p_2 < p_1$. It would seem apparent that ingredients of the earlier notion of utility are important here too; but it is also apparent that they provide only partial assistance in the selection progress.

As might be expected, there have been a wide assortment of approaches to the problem of quantifying individual preferences and incorporating them into a decision-making framework.[4] Perhaps the earliest serious attempt to solve the problem in a situation under risk is due to Bernoulli. He suggested that "the utility resulting from any small increase in wealth will be inversely proportionate to the quantity of goods previously possessed.... Any gain must be added to the fortune previously possessed, then this sum must be raised to the power given by the number of possible ways in which the gain may be obtained; these terms should then be multiplied together. Then of this product a root must be extracted the degree of which is given by the number of all possible cases, and finally the value of the initial possessions must be subtracted therefrom; what then remains indicates the value of the risky proposition in question."[5] These ideas opened the gates to a succession of views with respect to what exactly is meant by the term "utility," whether in any of its varied

[3] Third edition published by Princeton University Press in 1953. The first edition appeared in 1944.

[4] For particularly interesting summaries, see Kenneth J. Arrow, "Alternative Approaches to the Theory of Choice in Risk-Taking Situations," *Econometrica*, **19**:4 (Oct. 1951), 404–437; and Ward Edwards, "The Theory of Decision Making," *Psychological Bulletin*, **51**:4 (July 1954), 380–417.

[5] Daniel Bernoulli, "Exposition of a New Theory on the Measurement of Risk" (1738), trans. Louise Sommer, *Econometrica*, **22**:1 (Jan. 1954), 25, 28.

connotations "utility" is measurable, and whether resolution of the latter issues will in turn lead to the resolution of problems of choice. Since any present discussion is likely to add to the confusion rather than alleviate it, we shall restrict usage of the term *utility* to its previous interpretation (an ordinal expression of preference under certainty), and we shall simply comment that it is unfortunate that von Neumann and Morgenstern did not do likewise. Their use of the term utility in a second, if related, context does not, however, in any way detract from the singular importance of their contribution.

The von Neumann-Morgenstern model for decision making under risk rests on the acceptance of a set of behavior postulates. These are implied in a series of axioms upon which the model is based.[6] Considered individually, these axioms seem to be remarkably innocent, or at least quite reasonable, and one is unlikely to be overly reluctant about accepting any particular axiom. As a set, however, they have powerful implications.

## a. The Axioms

### i. THE FIRST AXIOM

The first axiom states: A *transitive preference* or indifference *relation* exists between *any* two entities. Thus, either $X_1$ is at least as desirable as $X_2$ ($X_1 \gtrsim X_2$), or $X_2$ is at least as desirable as $X_1$ ($X_2 \gtrsim X_1$). Moreover, if one exhibits a preference for $X_1$ over $X_2$ and for $X_2$ over $X_3$, then in a paired comparison one should prefer $X_1$ to $X_3$. Formally, $X_1 \gtrsim X_2$ and $X_2 \gtrsim X_3$ implies that $X_1 \gtrsim X_3$. $X_1$ might be a lonely old age, $X_2$ might be a son and a daughter, and $X_3$ might be a happy family complete with lots of grandchildren; or the $X_i$ might represent various combinations of profits and sales. Further, the $X_i$ could represent risky undertakings or projects composed of sets of potential payoffs $x_j$, each of which is promised with a specific probability $p_{ij}$. Each of the payoffs $x_j$ is also subject to a transitive prefence or indifference relation. To describe this risky alternative, we shall write

$$X_i = ([p_{i1}]x_1; [p_{i2}]x_2; \ldots ; [p_{ij}]x_j; \ldots ; [p_{in}]x_n), \qquad i = 1, \ldots, m.$$

It will be convenient to arbitrarily number the payoffs such that $x_1 \gtrsim x_2 \gtrsim \cdots \gtrsim x_{j-1} \gtrsim x_j \gtrsim x_{j+1} \gtrsim \cdots \gtrsim x_n$. Thus, $x_1$ will always denote the most preferred payoff, and $x_n$ the least preferred.

For example, suppose one is considering three alternative investments: $X_1$, $X_2$,

[6] The axioms described here are a minor variant on those offered by R. Duncan Luce and Howard Raiffa in *Games and Decisions* (New York: John Wiley & Sons, Inc., 1957), pp. 23–31. See also von Neumann and Morgenstern, *Theory of Games and Economic Behavior*, pp. 15–31 and 617–628; Jacob Marschak, "Rational Behavior, Uncertain Prospects, and Measurable Utility," *Econometrica*, **18**:2 (April 1950), 111–141; L. J. Savage, *The Foundations of Statistics* (New York: John Wiley & Sons, Inc., 1954), pp. 69–91; L. J. Savage, "Bayesian Statistics," in R. E. Machol and Paul Gray, eds., *Recent Developments in Information and Decision Processes* (New York: The Macmillan Company, 1962), pp. 161–182; J. Wolfowitz, "Bayesian Inference and Axioms of Consistent Decision," *Econometrica*, **30**:3 (July 1962), 470–479; and John W. Pratt, Howard Raiffa, and Robert Schlaifer, "The Foundations of Decisions Under Uncertainty: An Elementary Exposition," *Journal of the American Statistical Association*, **59**:306 (June 1964), 353–375.

and $X_3$. Suppose too that present discounted value, determined to be the only datum of concern to management, is uncertain for each project. Nonetheless, given management's probability judgments, the projects may be fully described as follows:

$$X_1 = ([.3]500; [.2]300; [.2]100; [.3]0);$$
$$X_2 = ([.2]500; [.3]400; [.3]200; [.2]100);$$
$$X_3 = ([.1]500; [.2]400; [.2]300; [.2]200; [.2]100; [.1]0).$$

Here, $x_1 = 500 \gtrsim x_2 = 400 \gtrsim \cdots \gtrsim x_6 = 0$; and, for example, $p_{12} = 0$, $p_{22} = .3$, and $p_{33} = .2$. Note that not all projects offer the possibility of the same set of payoffs. One could, however, always rewrite $X_1$ as

$$X_1 = ([.3]500; [0]400; [.2]300; [0]200; [.2]100; [.3]0),$$

and similarly for $X_2$. In effect, all projects can be considered to contain each of the $n$ payoffs, even though in the $i$th project the $j$th payoff is offered with probability $p_{ij} = 0$.

It should be understood that while the ordering of the payoffs was, in this example, quite straightforward, if the payoffs had been more complex the specific ordering might have been more difficult, but could have been accomplished. If, for instance, management is concerned with discounted *sales* as well as profits, the payoffs could then be written as couples, such as (sales, profits). A trio of such couples might be (1500, 500), (1800, 400), and (2000, 300). When present discounted profit is management's *sole* concern, $(1500, 500) \succ (1800, 400) \succ (2000, 300)$. To order these payoffs we need simply consider the second entity, or $500 \succ 400 \succ 300$. If management were interested in sales position along with profits, it might rank the payoffs as follows: $(1800, 400) \gtrsim (1500, 500) \gtrsim (2000, 300)$.

The first axiom thus implies that some things will be preferred to others (a suggestion that is not too hard to take) and that individuals are *consistent* in their preferences (which is a bit more difficult to swallow). As indicated in Chapter 2, those of us subject to human fallibility may well be inconsistent when our leanings are not terribly strong, and our preferences may be subject to quite radical shifts over very short time intervals. Conceptually, however, most would (1) probably admit to being discriminators in the sense of having preferences, and (2) very likely consider it desirable for these prererences to be mutually consistent. It may be particularly difficult to reach a preferred decision, or to order preferences, among alternative *projects*—that is, to choose among the $X_i$ as opposed to the $x_j$—when the payoffs are complex and when the additional consideration of uncertainty clouds the air. The purpose of the set of axioms and the present analysis, however, is to facilitate the ordering of risky alternatives in a manner consistent with one's actual preferences. Thus, this analysis will not indicate an alternative that *all* persons *should necessarily select*, but it will indicate the alternative that a *given* person *does in fact prefer*. This preference will be *deduced* on the basis of the person's attitude towards risk and his prior ordering of *payoffs*.

A mechanism that accomplishes the foregoing is important for two reasons. First, one will regularly be led to make the decision that is actually preferred, and although the elements of chance might cause one to bemoan one's fortunes, the original decision need not be regretted. Indeed, unless one's preferences have been altered, under the same circumstances the same decision would be preferred, and hopefully a happier outcome will obtain. Second, the analysis will enable a second party to determine that choice preferred by a specific individual. Thus, an individual could delegate decision-making authority to another in confidence that this other person will reach the decision that the delegating individual prefers. In the modern world, with its layers of bureaucracy and its complex systems that demand the delegation of decision-making authority, this second feature is of considerable importance.

### ii. THE SECOND AXIOM

The second axiom states: When the projects $X_i$ ($i = 1, \ldots, m$) are themselves offered with probabilities of $q_i$, say as part of a superproject

$$Y_k = ([q_1]X_1; [q_2]X_2; \ldots; [q_i]X_i; \ldots; [q_m]X_m),$$

a project $X^* = ([p_1]x_1; \ldots; [p_j]x_j; \ldots; [p_n]x_n)$ containing only the original payoffs $x_j$ ($j = 1, \ldots, n$) can be determined such that one is indifferent between $Y_k$ and $X^*$ ($Y_k \sim X^*$). Further, the $p_j$ are determined by combining the original $p_{ij}$ and $q_i$ via the ordinary probability calculus. Specifically,

$$p_j = \sum_{i=1}^{m} q_i p_{ij}.$$

Suppose, for example, that the previous $X_1$, $X_2$, and $X_3$ had been offered with probabilities $q_i$ ($i = 1, 2, 3$) of .2, .3, and .5, respectively. Then, $Y_k = ([.2]X_1; [.3]X_2; [.5]X_3)$. Suppose, now, that there are four urns labeled $X_1$, $X_2$, $X_3$, and $Y_k$. The urn labeled $Y_k$ contains ten balls. Two of the balls are labeled $X_1$, three are labeled $X_2$, and five are labeled $X_3$. The superproject $Y_k$ may thus be likened to dipping into the $Y_k$ urn and drawing a single ball with the outcome dictating the $X_i$ to be obtained. The label on the ball will send the dipper to one of the other three urns. Each of the other urns also contains ten balls, but these are marked 500, 400, 300, 200, 100, or 0. The distribution of the balls is given by the $p_{ij}$ in each $X_i$. Thus, for the urn marked $X_1$, there are three balls marked 500, two marked 300, two marked 100, and three marked 0. There are none with the 400 or 200 labels, for these payoffs are not possible with $X_1$. Similarly for the urns marked $X_2$ and $X_3$. The payoff after drawing from $Y_k$ and the subsequent $X_i$ will be determined by the label on the last ball drawn. The probability of a 500 payoff is therefore given by the probability of drawing from urn $X_1$ times the probability of drawing a 500 ball from $X_1$, plus the probability of drawing from $X_2$ times the probability of drawing a 500 ball from $X_2$, plus the probability of drawing from $X_3$ times the probability of drawing a 500 ball from $X_3$; or, since the successive draws are assumed to be independent, $p_1 = .2(.3) + .3(.2) + .5(.1) = .17$. In precisely the same fashion, $p_2 = .2(.0) + .3(.3) + .5(.2) = .19$; and $p_3 = .14$, $p_4 = .19$, $p_5 = .20$, and $p_6 = .11$. Of course, $\sum_{j=1}^{n} p_j = 1$, since *some* payoff must be earned.

The axiom suggests that one will be indifferent between a project $X^* = ([.17]500; [.19]400; [.14]300; [.19]200; [.20]100; [.11]0)$ and $Y_k$. That is, setting aside the joys of dipping into urns, one should be indifferent between reaching into a single urn marked $X^*$ containing one hundred balls of which seventeen are labeled 500, nineteen are labeled 400, and so forth, or engaging in the successive series of draws from different urns. By the combining process, the $Y_k$ option has been simplified, without altering the payoffs or the relative likelihoods of receiving them.

### iii. THE THIRD AXIOM

The third axiom states: An individual can express preference and indifference between a guaranteed payoff $x_j$ and a risky alternative $\tilde{x}_j$ that involves only the most preferred payoff $x_1$ and the least preferred payoff $x_n$. Moreover, probabilities $r_j$ and $1 - r_j$ can be found such that (1) $\tilde{x}_j = ([r_j]x_1; [1 - r_j]x_n)$ is indifferent to $x_j$ ($\tilde{x}_j \sim x_j$); and, (2) where $\tilde{x}'_j = ([r'_j]x_1; [1 - r'_j]x_n)$ for $r'_j \neq r_j$, $\tilde{x}'_j \succ \tilde{x}_j$ if and only if $r'_j > r_j$; and $\tilde{x}_j \succ \tilde{x}'_j$ if and only if $r_j > r'_j$. Note that $\succ$ means "preferred" and $>$ means "greater than."

Clearly, if the probability of receiving $x_1$ is greater than $r_j$, the risky alternative will be preferred to the guaranteed $x_j$; and if $x_j = x_1$, then $r_j = 1$; if $x_j = x_n$, then $r_j = 0$. That is, one will be indifferent between having the best of the possible worlds with certainty and participating in a game of chance in which the best of the possible worlds is a payoff, only if one is absolutely certain of gaining the payoff. Similarly, it should not matter if one is simply handed the worst of all possible worlds, or if one draws from an urn in which the only possible outcome is the receipt of the worst of the possible worlds. But if one is indifferent between accepting a payoff with certainty or drawing once from an urn containing 100 green and 100 purple balls, and if a green ball awards the most preferred payoff and a purple ball awards the least preferred payoff, then drawing from an urn with 101 green balls and 99 purple balls should be preferable to *either* of the previous alternatives. This follows, since the chance of getting the most preferred alternative has improved, and concurrently the chance of getting the least preferred alternative has been reduced.

All of this assumes that the gambling act *itself* is not inherently desired or objectionable. That is, irrespective of one's risk-taking propensities, when the sole possibilities are that one will either win or lose, that option will be preferred that offers the highest probability of winning. This also assumes that the *indifference probabilities* $r_j$ are determinable. They would in fact be determined via some process analogous to the following procedure. The payoff $x_j$ is on one side of a scale and the urn with the green (most preferred payoff) and purple (least preferred payoff) balls is on the other side. As soon as the proportion of green balls in the urn is such that the individual is willing to permit *any* second party, be it friend or foe, to select either $x_j$ or the urn for him, the point of indifference is reached. If the individual is unwilling to permit a second party to make the selection, and prefers to choose himself, he indicates a preference for the selected alternative.[7]

Now, an individual will be referred to as being *linear in risk* if he is indifferent between participating in a game of chance, or receiving the expected value of the game with certainty. This is what was previously referred to as "indifferent" to risk. Hence, for the discounted values comprising the illustrative set of payoffs, $x_1 = 500$, $x_n = 0$, and for an individual who is linear in risk, $500 \sim ([1]500; [0]0)$; $400 \sim ([.8]500; [.2]0)$; $300 \sim ([.6]500; [.4]0)$; $200 \sim ([.4]500; [.6]0)$; $100 \sim ([.2]500; [.8]0)$; and $0 \sim ([0]500; [1]0)$; or, in general, $\tilde{x}_j = r_j x_1 + (1 - r_j)x_n$. An individual will be called a *risk-evader* if he demands that the expected value of the risky alternative exceeds that of a guaranteed payoff before being willing to accept it; a *risk-taker* will be willing to accept the risky alternative in lieu of the guaranteed payoff, even though the expected value of the former is *less than* the value of the latter. Hence, for a

[7] It is assumed that the act of selection is not itself an attraction, and that a foe, say, does not have "inside information" that would lead him to select an alternative that is other than it appears to be (such as an urn in which the purple balls tend to the top).

*particular* risk-evader it may be that 400 ~ ([.95]500; [.05]0); and, for a *particular* risk-taker, 400 ~ ([.3]500; [.7]0). In the former case, the individual demands more favorable odds than are offered by a fair bet before being willing to gamble; in the latter case, the individual is even willing to gamble if the odds are unfavorable, in the fair-bet sense.

It should be apparent that not all risk-evaders will require the same probability of winning, nor will all risk-takers. Further, not all of us will *always* and *consistently* behave as risk-evaders or risk-takers. The time and the stakes can make a difference. This axiom requires only that, in a given situation, an individual will be indifferent to accepting a risky alternative or a guaranteed alternative payoff, for *some* pair of probabilities $r_j$ and $1 - r_j$ of receiving a most preferred and least preferred award.

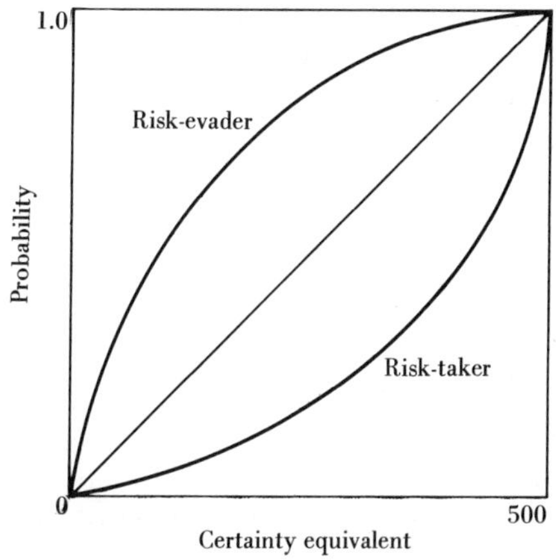


Fig. 12.1

Figure 12.1 presents a fairly stereotyped portrait used to describe the risk preferences of the risk-evader, the risk-taker, and the person linear in risk. The payoffs appear on the abscissa and the probabilities of winning in the risky alternative, the $r_j$'s, appear on the ordinate. The straight line depicting the demands of one who is linear in risk simply traces out the expected value of a gamble involving the most and least preferred payoffs at the particular $r_j$. Since the risk-evader (-taker) requires less than (more than) the expected value of the gamble before being willing to exchange it for a guaranteed payoff, his demands are depicted on a curve that lies above (below) the straight line. The assumption that one will always prefer a higher probability of winning the most preferred payoff to a lower probability of winning means that the curves will always be assumed to be monotonically increasing.

Although we commonly do not think of it as doing so, at some points an individual's curve might lie above the straight line of expected value, and at other points lie below it. Generally, however, we tend to classify individuals as being *either* risk-evaders or risk-takers; we attempt to draw these curves by extracting information from the person involved about his preferences at several points on the curve. Since to fill in all points on a continuous curve by this process might take a considerable amount of time, the remaining points are filled in by extrapolation. Because they offer nice mathematical properties that need not be distortive and in fact may be quite realistic, the curve for the risk-evader is frequently assumed to be strictly concave, and that for the risk-taker assumed strictly convex.[8] The latter curvature properties are apparent in the curves of Figure 12.1. It should be emphasized that while the convexity (concavity) property will be generally assumed for the risk-taker (-evader) in succeeding discussions, this will be done out of mathematical convenience as opposed to behavioral necessity.

### iv. THE FOURTH AXIOM

The fourth axiom states: If the risky alternative $\tilde{x}_j$ replaces the payoff $x_j$ in a project $X_i$, the new project containing $\tilde{x}_j$ is equally preferred to the old project containing $x_j$. The justification is that since $\tilde{x}_j$ is equally preferred to $x_j$ it should not matter which one of the two is promised. Formally, if $\tilde{x}_j \sim x_j$, letting $X_i' = ([p_{i1}]x_1; \ldots; [p_{ij}]\tilde{x}_j; \ldots; [p_{in}]x_n)$, $X_i' \sim X_i$.

Although this axiom seems quite harmless in the sense that if one is truly indifferent between $\tilde{x}_j$ and $x_j$ one should not care which is promised as a potential payoff, it is also quite powerful and essential. This is so, for by repeated use of the axiom *all* of the $x_j$'s in $X_i$ may be replaced by their risky equivalents $\tilde{x}_j$. In this manner, the project $X_i = ([p_{i1}]x_1; \ldots; [p_{ij}]x_j; \ldots; [p_{in}]x_n)$ can be replaced in the analysis by *its* equivalent $\tilde{X}_i = ([p_{i1}]\tilde{x}_1; \ldots; [p_{ij}]\tilde{x}_j; \ldots; [p_{in}]\tilde{x}_n)$. That is, $X_i \sim \tilde{X}_i$. Moreover, by the second axiom, $\tilde{X}_i$ is actually nothing but a superproject involving smaller *projects* $\tilde{x}_j = ([r_j]x_1; [1 - r_j]x_n)$; hence, we can employ the probability calculus to determine a project $\tilde{X}_i^* \sim \tilde{X}_i$, where $X_i^* = ([p_i]x_1; [1 - p_i]x_n)$, since $x_1$ and $x_n$ are the only original payoffs left in the analysis; and because $X_i^* \sim \tilde{X}_i$ and $\tilde{X}_i \sim X_i$, from the transitivity property $X_i^* \sim X_i$. Thus, the original $X_i$ may now be replaced by the $X_i^*$. The latter involve alternatives promising the most and least preferred payoffs, *exclusively*.[9] The most preferred $X_i^*$ will be the one that offers the highest probability of the most preferred alternative. That is, $X_i^* \succ X_k^*$ whenever $p_i > p_k$. In effect, we shall use a $>$ property that we can compute to signal a $\succ$ property that we must impute.

[8] Additional curvature properties, beyond concavity and convexity, may also be of interest. In particular, as discussed in Section 12.6, if persons who are risk-evaders, say, tend to become more or less risk-averse as their total wealth changes, this too will affect their behavior.

[9] Not only does this provide an *analytically* attractive procedure, but it also introduces a *behavioral* feature that some other models ascribe to decision makers: namely, the tendency to view or describe risky alternatives in terms of "best" and "worst" features, and to choose between them on this basis—for example, the notion that investors contrast the "most likely" gain with the "most likely" loss in choosing between alternative investments [James W. Angell, "Uncertainty, Likelihoods and Investment Decisions," *Quarterly Journal of Economics*, **LXXIV**:1 (Feb. 1960), 1–28], or that an individual will tend "to concentrate his fears at some specific point, selecting *one particular* degree of misfortune to represent what he 'stands to lose,'" and a similar "focus-value" for what he "stands to gain" [G. L. Shackle, "The Expectational Dynamics of the Individual," *Economica*, **X**:38 (May 1943), 99–129, and 101–106 in particular], or that "entrepreneurs try to maximize 'best guesses' of profits...but...the presumption is strong that the possibility of less favorable outcomes is taken into account with a higher weight than the possibility of more favorable outcomes" [William Fellner, *Competition Among the Few* (New York: Augustus M. Kelley, 1960), pp. 38–39].

In particular, consider the risk-evader depicted in Figure 12.1. Let us confront him with the choice among $X_1$, $X_2$, and $X_3$. Suppose he asserts the following equivalences: $500 \sim ([1]500; [0]0)$; $400 \sim ([.95]500; [.05]0)$; $300 \sim ([.85]500; [.15]0)$; $200 \sim ([.70]500; [.30]0)$; $100 \sim ([.50]500; [.50]0)$; $0 \sim ([0]500; [1]0)$. For *this one person*, then: $X_1 \sim \tilde{X}_1 = ([.3]([1]500; [0]0); [0]([.95]500; [.05]0); [.2]([.85]500; [.15]0); [0]([.70]500; [.30]0); [.2]([.50]500; [.50]0); [.3]([0]500; [1]0)$. Thus, $\tilde{X}_1$ offers a .3 probability of gaining 500 as a certainty, a 0 probability of gaining 500 with probability of .95, a .2 probability of gaining 500 with probability of .85, and so forth; or, by the second axiom, $\tilde{X}_1 \sim X_1^* = ([.57]500; [.43]0)$. In similar fashion, $\tilde{X}_2 \sim X_2^* = ([.795]500; [.205]0)$; and $\tilde{X}_3 \sim X_3^* = ([.70]500; [.30]0)$. Hence, since $p_2 > p_3 > p_1$, $X_2^* \succ X_3^* \succ X_1^*$; and since $X_2^* \sim X_2$, $X_1^* \sim X_1$ and $X_3^* \sim X_3$, $X_2 \succ X_3 \succ X_1$. *Given* the expressed risk preferences and attitudes about the specific payoffs, we can infer that $X_2$ is the preferred project for this particular individual. $X_2$ will also be preferred by one who is linear in risk, since it has the highest expected value, and we can easily show (as we do below) that one who is linear in risk orders alternatives in accordance with expected value. But $X_2$ will not necessarily be preferred by all persons. Indeed, the risk-taker of Figure 12.1 will prefer $X_1$. His risk-taking propensities are quite strong, and he is strongly encouraged to choose $X_1$ because it offers the highest probability of 500. It also offers the highest probability of 0—but that is why he is called a risk-taker.

As this example makes clear, then, different persons with different sets of preferences and different attitudes towards risk can and logically should prefer different choices in *certain*, though not necessarily *all*, situations under risk, and this will hold even when their probability judgments coincide. It should also be clear that, even when different persons hold similar sets of preferences and attitudes towards risk, they can prefer different choices when their probability judgments differ. In the context of the firm under risk, we must therefore move our discussion away from "the" single *best* decision and toward the decision that is most *preferred* by a given decision maker at a given time.

## b. Maximizing Expected Utiles

The previous analysis is intended to permit the determination of a preference ordering among alternatives under risk for a particular decision maker. It must be emphasized that the analysis will not tell a decision maker which decision he *should* prefer. Rather, it will indicate to him which decision he actually *does* prefer. Specifically, $X_i \succ X_k$ not *because* $p_i > p_k$; instead, because $X_i \succ X_k$, the analysis *forces* $p_i > p_k$. The fact that $p_i$ is greater than $p_k$ merely *signals the fact* that $X_i$ is preferred to $X_k$. To repeat, this signaling is important, for it permits one to behave *purposefully* and *consistently* in complex situations under risk in accordance with one's own preferences, or in accordance with the preferences of another.[10]

An equivalent means of accomplishing this same objective, or of getting the same set of signals, involves the use of a function $V = v(x_i)$ designed to reflect *ordinal*

[10] "The concept of *purposiveness* involves a notion of a hierarchy consisting in an implementation of the goals set forth in the step immediately above. Behavior is purposive insofar as it is guided by general goals or objectives; it is rational insofar as it selects alternatives which are conducive to the achievement of the previously selected goals." [Herbert A. Simon, *Administrative Behavior* (New York: The Macmillan Company, 1958), p. 5.]

risk preferences, or one's attitude towards a given entity in a given situation under risk. This risk-preference function is a very special type of *linear relation*. By linear relation, we mean the following. A *number* $V = v(x_j)$ is the measure assigned to the entity $x_j$ in accordance with the function $V$. If $x_k \succ x_j$, this will be reflected in the ordinal function by assigning $v(x_k) > v(x_j)$. Suppose, now, that $x_k \succ x \succ x_j$. Also, suppose that $x \sim \tilde{x} = ([r]x_k; [1 - r]x_j)$. That is, the individual concerned is indifferent between having $x$ with certainty, or participating in a game of chance in which the probability of gaining $x_k$ is $r$, and the probability of gaining $x_j$ is $1 - r$. In this system, since $x \sim \tilde{x}$, we will want to assign $v(x) = v(\tilde{x})$, where $v(x_k) > v(x) > v(x_j)$. By assumption, however, the individual is indifferent between the payoff $x$ and a risky alternative in which the probability of receiving $v(x_k)$ is $r$ and the probability of receiving $v(x_j)$ is $1 - r$. The *expected* payoff in terms of the risk-preference function $V$ is therefore $rv(x_k) + (1 - r)v(x_j)$.

The risk-preference function is thus a linear *relation* in the following special sense: we *require* that the value assigned to a given entity be equal to the mathematical expectation of the function for the risky alternative to which the entity is indifferent. Formally, $v(x)$ *must* be assigned to assure that $v(x) = rv(x_k) + (1 - r)v(x_j)$. The latter is the sense in which linearity *necessarily* obtains in the *relation*. It should be noted that the function $V$ will itself *not necessarily* be a linear *function*. As we shall see, it will only be a linear *function* (that is, $V = v_1 + v_2x_j$) for one who is linear in risk. It will, however, be a linear *relation* in the expectation sense.

In the latter sense, consider a linear *transformation* $\hat{V}$ such that $\hat{v}(x_j) = \alpha + \beta v(x_j)$. We require that $\hat{v}(x) = r\hat{v}(x_k) + (1 - r)\hat{v}(x_j)$. Hence,

$$\begin{aligned}\hat{v}(x) &= r\alpha + r\beta v(x_k) + (1 - r)\alpha + (1 - r)\beta v(x_j)\\ &= \alpha + \beta(rv(x_k) + (1 - r)v(x_j))\\ &= \alpha + \beta v(x).\end{aligned}$$

That is, the linear *transformation* preserves the ordering and linear *relation* property of $V$. Thus, for present purposes either $V$ or $\hat{V}$ would be a suitable risk-preference function, given the requirements that have been imposed upon such a function. It would therefore seem that although the preference function is *cardinal* in that it assigns specific numbers in ranking each entity in accordance with preferences, its true flavor is that of an *ordinal* ranking mechanism. One cannot, therefore, use the function to compare the strength of different persons' preferences (that is, interpersonal comparisons via the risk-preference function are meaningless); nor is it reasonable to conclude that one would prefer a move from $x_j$ to $x_k$ to a move from $x_s$ to $x_t$ simply because $v(x_k) - v(x_j) > v(x_t) - v(x_s)$. There is, nonetheless, a good deal of ambiguity in the cardinality-versus-ordinality issue.

Suppose, then, that we assign values of $V_1 = v(500)$ and $V_0 = v(0)$ for the risk-preference function of the risk-evader of Fig. 12.1, where $V_0 < V_1$. To determine $v(400)$, we need only recall that the risk-evader has *already* expressed the view that $400 \sim ([.95]500; [.05]0)$; or, $v(400) = v([.95]500; [.05]0)$. By the linear *relation* property,

$$v(400) = .95v(500) + .05v(0) = .95V_1 + .05V_0.$$

Similarly, $v(300) = .85V_1 + .15V_0$, $v(200) = .70V_1 + .30V_0$, and $v(100) = .50V_1 + .50V_0$. Hence,

$$v(X_1) = v([.3]V_1; [.2](.85V_1 + .15V_0); [.2](.50V_1 + .50V_0); [.3]V_0).$$

Again applying the linear relation property,

$$v(X_1) = .3V_1 + .2(.85V_1 + .15V_0) + .2(.50V_1 + .50V_0) + .3V_0 = .57V_1 + .43V_0.$$

In similar fashion, $v(X_2) = .795V_1 + .205V_0$ and $v(X_3) = .70V_1 + .30V_0$. But, since $V_1 > V_0$, $v(X_2) > v(X_3) > v(X_1)$. This too *signals* the fact that $X_2$ is preferred to $X_3$ is preferred to $X_1$, by this *particular* risk-evader. Since, however, the risk-preference ordering holds for any linear transformation, letting $V_1 = 1$ and $V_0 = 0$ immediately yields $v(X_1) = .57$, $v(X_2) = .795$, and $v(X_3) = .70$. The latter are exactly the probabilities $p_i$ previously computed to reveal risky alternatives, involving only the most and least preferred payoffs, that would be equivalent to the projects $X_i$. Therefore, the project yielding the greatest *expected* $v(X_i)$ will equivalently be the one associated with the highest $p_i$, and therefore it also *signals* the preferred alternative. Indeed, since $V_1$ and $V_0$ are arbitrary, one may *always* assign $V_1 = 1$ and $V_0 = 0$. If they are so assigned, expected $v(X_i)$ and $p_i$ are *always* equal.

The units of risk preference are commonly called *utiles*, and their mathematical expectation, or expected $v(X_i)$, is the *expected utiles*.[11] In selecting the alternative that maximizes expected utiles, one will therefore be selecting the preferred alternative. This is the alternative equivalent to a game that offers the highest probability of getting the most preferred payoff, and the lowest probability of getting the least preferred payoff, among all such game equivalents.

Further, for an individual with linear risk preferences,

$$\bar{x}_j = rx_1 + (1 - r)x_n = x_j.$$

That is, the expected value of the risky alternative is equal to the required guaranteed payoff. Hence,

$$v(\bar{x}_j) = v(rx_1 + (1 - r)x_n) = rV_1 + (1 - r)V_0 = v(x_j).$$

Let $V_1 = x_1$ and $V_0 = x_n$. Then,

$$v(\bar{x}_j) = rx_1 + (1 - r)x_n = \bar{x}_j.$$

That is, expected utiles and expected value become one and the same. Thus, for an individual with a linear risk-preference *function*, ordering alternatives via expected *value* will be equivalent to ordering alternatives via expected *utiles*. For greater expository latitude, in the following sections we shall assume that all values have been assigned in accordance with some risk-preference function in mind. In particular, we shall focus on that of the risk-evader of Figure 12.1, with $V_1 = 1$ and $V_0 = 0$.

## 12.3 THE GENERAL DECISION PROBLEM UNDER RISK

Once the previous set of axioms and the von Neumann-Morgenstern approach are accepted, then—theoretically, at least—determination of the preferred decision

[11] When, for pedagogical or editorial convenience, it seems like a good idea to refer to it at all, we shall refer to expected *utiles* as opposed to the more widely used term expected *utility*. Similarly, we shall always refer to the decision maker's *risk-preference* function as opposed to the widely employed term *utility* function. The latter will be reserved exclusively for its earlier meaning in the theory of consumer behavior, as a function describing an *ordinal* ranking of preferences under *certainty*. We call attention to the point in the hope of heading off possible, indeed likely, misinterpretation on the part of those delving further into the literature where the terms may be used interchangeably.

becomes a comparatively manageable chore. There may be some tiresome computational burdens, but your friendly computer is always blinking in the background, ready and willing to lend a helping core. As a practical matter, however, actually obtaining a decision maker's risk-preference function could become a very trying and unsatisfactory experience, particularly when the payoffs to be considered are complex $n$-tuples of data. For example, when a payoff is evaluated with respect to sales, rate of return, present discounted value, and market share, the decision maker will not necessarily express his preferences in a consistent fashion, no matter how vigorously we insist that he should be able to do so (or how often we tell him about the first axiom). Moreover, whenever more than one person is involved in the decision process, it may not be clear just who's risk preferences we should be concerned with, or how to reconcile conflicting sets of risk preferences (that is, risk preferences that do not coincide and that would lead to different decisions).

It is also clear that the preferred decision will depend upon the initial inputs and that we cannot always know or consider all alternatives or recognize all of the possible outcomes and their consequences. Further, the probability assignments may be vital in the choice between one option and another, and there will not necessarily be unanimous agreement with respect to what these assignments should be.

It is an unhappy fact that we shall have to live with these difficulties when we employ the von Neumann-Morgenstern approach. It is also an unhappy fact that we shall have to live with them even if we should not employ the von Neumann-Morgenstern approach. One ordinarily must choose between making a specific decision, delaying a decision (perhaps in the hopes of obtaining more information, or relying on the powers of prayer to make the problem go away), or avoiding a decision (perhaps by transferring the problem to someone else's shoulders). In any event an alternative is being chosen, and the influential variables will be precisely those that are incorporated into the von Neumann-Morgenstern calculus. Perhaps the greatest distinction between the less sophisticated decision-making procedures and the present approach is that in the former the relevant information may either be overlooked or dealt with in an ad hoc manner, whereas in the latter all of the available information is *explicitly* incorporated in a *consistent* and *purposeful* manner. In any one instance, the present approach will not necessarily suggest a course of action different from that suggested by a less sophisticated procedure. But it assures that one singles out, on the basis of the best *available* information, the decision that is *optimal*, in the sense of being truly preferred by the decision maker. There is not much more that can be asked of a decision-making model.

Let us suppose, then, that a decision maker is initially faced with a set of $m + 1$ known alternatives: he may either select an $X_i = ([p_{i1}]x_1; \ldots; [p_{ij}]x_j; \ldots; [p_{in}]x_n)$, $i = 1, \ldots, m$, or he may acquire additional information that will lead him to revise his judgments with respect to the $p_{ij}$. The problem is described graphically by the *game* or *decision tree* of Figure 12.2. In this tree, the alternatives are limited to $X_1$, $X_2$, or $X_3$, plus the information alternative denoted by $S$. The decision maker's first problem is to decide whether to take the *branch* of the tree labeled $D$ for decision, or to take the branch labeled $S$ for obtaining *sample* information.

The decision maker has a risk preference function $V$ such that

$$v(X_i) = \sum_{j=1}^{n} p_{ij}v(x_j)$$

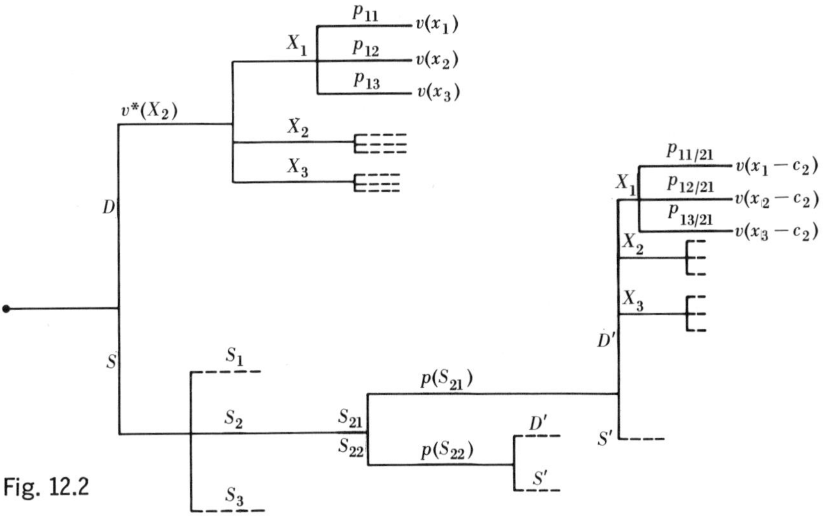


Fig. 12.2

is an ordinal measure of his preference towards alternative $X_i$.[12] We denote by $v^*(X_\omega)$ that $v(X_i)$ such that $v(X_\omega) \geq v(X_i)$, $i = 1, \ldots, m$. That is, $v(X_\omega)$, the expected utiles associated with alternative $X_i = X_\omega$, is at least as great as the expected utiles associated with any other alternative. Hence, there is no alternative that is preferred to $X_\omega$. If the equality sign should hold for an $i \neq \omega$ such that $v(X_\omega) = v(X_y)$, then alternatives $X_\omega$ and $X_y$ are each *optimal choices*, in the sense of being equally preferred. This is illustrated along the upper branch of the game tree, which itself expands into a series of branches. The $D$ branch leads into three branches, each reflecting a possible choice, $X_i$ $(i = 1, 2, 3)$. Each of the three branches itself expands into a series of branches, the end points of which are labeled with the utile equivalents of possible $x_j$. The associated $p_{ij}$, or the probability of receiving $v(x_j)$ when alternative $X_i$ is selected, is indicated along the top limb of the branch. To avoid our being overwhelmed in a morass of twigs, only the uppermost branch of $X_1$ is fully labeled, and the possible payoffs are also limited to three. To provide a frame of reference, let us assume that $v^*(X_\omega) = v(X_2) > v(X_1) > v(X_3)$. Hence, if a decision is made immediately, the preferred choice is project $X_2$.

Suppose, however, that the decision maker chooses the branch $S$ and obtains additional, *sample,* information. He will, perhaps, have the choice between $K$ different sampling *procedures*, $S_k$ $(k = 1, \ldots, K)$. In the game tree of Figure 12.2 he will have to select the branch labeled $S_1$, $S_2$, or $S_3$. Again, for simplicity only the branch labeled $S_2$ is filled in with any detail, and we shall continue to use this particular branch as a frame of reference. Suppose that the choice of $S_k$ could result in any one of $K'$ different observations or samples. Each such sample will be labeled $S_{kk'}$ $(k' = 1, \ldots, K')$. In the game tree, there are two possible sample results, and hence two branches evolving from the $S_2$ branch. As indicated in the earlier development of Bayes' rule, the sample information will lead to a set of revised probabilities $p_{ij|kk'}$. The latter gives the probability that the payoff $x_j$ will be received when alternative $X_i$ is chosen, and sample $S_{kk'}$ has been observed. Concurrently, $p(S_{kk'})$,

[12] Where the probability distributions and the payoffs are given as continuous functions, an integral would replace the sum.

the probability that the sample $S_{kk'}$ will be observed, would be computed. The latter terms appear along the tops of the possible branches, $S_{21}$ and $S_{22}$, of the game tree.

Information is not ordinarily cost-free. Denote the cost of procedure $S_k$ by $c_k$. Each payoff in alternative $X_i$ will therefore be reduced by $c_k$ as a result of employing $S_k$. Hence, for each sample, the decision maker must now order his preferences with respect to

$$X_{i|kk'} = ([p_{i1|kk'}]x_1 - c_k; \ldots; [p_{ij|kk'}]x_j - c_k; \ldots; [p_{in|kk'}]x_n - c_k), \qquad i = 1, \ldots, m.$$

That is, the choice of the sampling procedure reduces the payoffs, and the sample information alters the probabilities of the payoffs, thereby resulting in what is essentially a *new* set of alternatives to choose from. Given an $S_{kk'}$, the preferred choice will now be that $X_\omega$ such that $v^*(X_{\omega|kk'}) = v(X_{\omega|kk'}) \geq v(X_{i|kk'})$, $i = 1, \ldots, m$, with the earlier qualification holding when the equality sign holds for $i \neq \omega$. Note that

$$v(X_{i|kk'}) = \sum_{j=1}^{n} p_{ij|kk'}v(x_j - c_k).$$

In general, this is *not* equal to

$$\sum_{j=1}^{n} p_{ij|kk'}v(x_j) - v(c_k).$$

That is, the expected utiles of the payoffs less their sampling costs is generally not equal to the expected utiles of the payoffs less the utiles associated with the costs. The cost of sampling must be subtracted from the payoffs *before* we substitute the payoffs into the risk-preference function. The second procedure *is* applicable, however, when the decision maker has a *linear* risk-preference function, for, as before, it is easily demonstrated that then and then only $v(x_j - c_k) = v(x_j) - v(c_k)$ for all $x_j$ and all $c_k$.

Now, $S_{kk'}$ will result in $v^*(X_{\omega|kk'})$ with probability $p(S_{kk'})$. Note that the $X_\omega$ need not be the same for all $k'$, but will be determined after observing $S_{kk'}$. Sampling procedure $S_k$ will thus have an associated ordinal preference measure of

$$v(S_k) = \sum_{k'=1}^{K'} p(S_{kk'})v^*(X_{\omega|kk'})$$

—provided that a decision is made immediately after the procedure $S_k$ has been employed. One might, however, have the option of obtaining still more sample information. In this situation, the decision maker's problem is comparable to his initial problem: whether to take a branch labeled $D'$ and make a selection, or whether to elect a branch labeled $S'$ and sample further. This, too, is indicated in the game tree.[13]

[13] As part of a particular sampling procedure $S_N$, one might have the options of either purchasing a total of $N$ observations at a cost of $c_N$, or of purchasing individual observations, or groups of observations, at a cost of $c_{N'}$ per observation, with the additional option of halting purchases at any stage. Inasmuch as the revised probabilities obtained via Bayes' rule will be the same whether revised on the basis of all $N$ observations considered as a group, or on the basis of $N$ observations considered one at a time, the latter *sequential sampling* procedure will be at least as attractive as the former procedure so long as $Nc_{N'} \leq c_N$—that is, so long as it costs no more per observation to purchase all $N$

In this manner, the various sampling procedures may be ordered in terms of the $v(S_k)$. The optimal sampling procedure will be that $S_k = S_\omega$ such that $v^*(S_\omega) = v(S_\omega) \geq v(S_k)$, $k = 1, \ldots, K$. The earlier qualification again holds when the equality holds for $k \neq \omega$. An immediate decision will thus be preferred to *any* sampling procedure considered, whenever $v^*(X_\omega) > v^*(S_\omega)$. When the inequality is reversed, sampling will be preferred to immediate selection; and, should $v^*(X_\omega) = v^*(S_\omega)$, the decision maker is found to be indifferent as to whether to sample or select.

In terms of the game tree, whenever it is up to the decision maker to make a decision—that is, to choose a branch along which to proceed—he will always prefer that branch labeled with a $V^*$. He then judges that he will be *sent* along another branch in accordance with a stochastic process based upon the assigned probabilities. Either the "game" will end—that is, his decision has a payoff—or he must make another decision. He may therefore look upon his problem as one of selecting the optimal *strategy*. For example, select sample procedure $S_\omega$ and if $S_{\omega v}$ occurs then sample further; and then if $S_{\omega v v'}$ occurs, make a final choice of $X_\omega$; if, however, any other sample occurs, then sample once again before making a final choice, and so forth.

When all *optimal strategies* are enumerated so as to give due consideration to the *optimal reactions* to the probabilistic outcomes, the nonoptimal strategies, those that will never be employed, are ignored, and the decision problem is said to have been reduced to *normal* form. Where we simply record the game tree in its entirety and then sit back and wait to *observe* the probabilistic outcome before making the next decision, the decision problem is said to be in *extensive* form. If in the latter case the decision maker is to make the optimal choice following any outcome, and if in the former case the decision maker is to be able to narrow down all possible strategies to those which will be optimal under all possible contingencies, then both ways of handling the problem will require the same collection of data and will result in the same sequence of decisions. In the former case, that of the normal form, we simply ignore certain options, in effect we cut off the dead branches, once it has been determined that these options will never be preferred. The distinction, then, is more one of portraying the problem than of resolving it.

## 12.4 A NUMERICAL ILLUSTRATION OF DECISION MAKING UNDER RISK

To illustrate the decision procedure, consider a firm producing KNIFS. This firm, Associated KNIF, behaves as a price-setter. A "new" price is established each year when a new model is introduced in the market. Industry custom prompts the firm to either hold the price line ($X_1$), increase price by 10 percent ($X_2$), or reduce price by 10 percent ($X_3$). Once a price is quoted, Associated KNIF follows the practice of sticking to that price for a six-month period, whereupon price policy is again reviewed.

---

observations. One can presume, however, that sequential sampling *will* cost more, per observation, for it will be at least as expensive to undertake and at least as desirable as the block sample. Still, sequential sampling may be preferred because of the likelihood that fewer than $N$ observations will be purchased. Indeed, this analysis enables one to determine the sampling plan to purchase as well as the maximum number of observations to purchase in any *sequential* sampling plan. For a discussion, see Robert Schlaifer, *Probability and Statistics for Business Decisions* (New York: McGraw-Hill, Inc., 1959), pp. 590–602.

The management of Associated is concerned solely with profit. Management believes that this profit will depend upon Associated's price, as well as upon the price quoted by its chief competitor, Consolidated KNIF. Specifically, given Associated's price, profit is believed to depend upon whether Consolidated raises price (also by 10 percent), holds the price line, or lowers price (by 10 percent). Associated's management judges the probability of each of these three possibilities to be $p(R) = .50$, $p(H) = .25$, and $p(L) = .25$, respectively. Given these *prior* assessments and the related profitability estimates, the three "projects" or price policies that Associated must select from are as follows:

$$X_1 = ([.50]400; [.25]300; [.25]125);$$
$$X_2 = ([.50]500; [.25]225; [.25]50);$$
$$X_3 = ([.50]300; [.25]375; [.25]150).$$

For convenience, then, we have denoted $p_{11} = p_{21} = p_{31} = p(R)$, and similarly for the remaining $p_{ij}$. These alternatives are most conveniently summarized in a payoff table, Table 12.1.

TABLE 12.1
Profits

| | | CONSOLIDATED KNIF | | |
|---|---|---|---|---|
| | | **Raises Price** $p(R) = .50$ | **Holds Price** $p(H) = .25$ | **Lowers Price** $p(L) = .25$ |
| **ASSOCIATED KNIF ELECTS** | $X_1$ | 400 | 300 | 125 |
| | $X_2$ | 500 | 225 | 50 |
| | $X_3$ | 300 | 375 | 150 |

Let us assume the risk-preference function guiding Associated's management to be that of the risk-evader of Figure 12.1. If we set $V_1 = 1$ and $V_0 = 0$, Table 12.2 then gives the risk-preference equivalent of Table 12.1. The expected utiles figure

TABLE 12.2
Utiles

| | | CONSOLIDATED KNIF | | |
|---|---|---|---|---|
| | | **Raises Price** $p(R) = .50$ | **Holds Price** $p(H) = .25$ | **Lowers Price** $p(L) = .25$ |
| **ASSOCIATED KNIF ELECTS** | $X_1$ | .95 | .85 | .57 |
| | $X_2$ | 1 | .75 | .30 |
| | $X_3$ | .85 | .94 | .62 |

for $X_1$ is therefore $v(x_1) = .50(.95) + .25(.85) + .25(.57) = .8300$. Similarly, $v(X_2) = .7625$ and $v(X_3) = .8150$. Thus, $v^*(X_\omega) = v^*(X_1) = v(X_1)$, and $X_1$ is the preferred alternative. In this instance, then, the risk-evading management in question, selecting a price policy without further information, would decide upon $X_1$—no price change. Note that on the basis of expected *profit*—that is, for one with linear risk preferences—$X_2$, the price increase, is preferred, and $X_2 \succ X_1 \succ X_3$.

Suppose, now, that in lieu of establishing the new price at the present time, Associated KNIF can delay placing the new-model KNIFS on the market. Each week's delay is estimated to cost the company 25 units of profit. The sole purpose in delaying is to obtain information with respect to Consolidated's future action by observing the pricing pattern on used Consolidated KNIFS—specifically, whether or not Consolidated runs a used-KNIF sale. On the basis of past experience, it is judged that if Consolidated does intend to increase price, the probability that it will run a used-KNIF sale is $p(S_{11} \mid R) = .1$, and the probability that Consolidated will not run a used-KNIF sale is $p(S_{12} \mid R) = .9$. Similarly, where $H$ denotes Consolidated's holding the price line, and $L$ denotes Consolidated's lowering the price line, it is judged that $p(S_{11} \mid H) = .2$, $p(S_{12} \mid H) = .8$, $p(S_{11} \mid L) = .7$, and $p(S_{12} \mid L) = .3$. Therefore using Bayes' rule, the *prior* probabilities can be revised on the basis of samples $S_{11}$ and $S_{12}$. The *posterior* probabilities thus obtained are as follows:

$$p(H \mid S_{11}) = \frac{p(H)p(S_{11} \mid H)}{p(H)p(S_{11} \mid H) + p(R)p(S_{11} \mid R) + p(L)p(S_{11} \mid L)}$$

$$= \frac{.25(.2)}{.25(.2) + .50(.1) + .25(.7)}$$

$$= \frac{.050}{.275} = .1818.$$

The notation $p(H \mid S_{11})$ is a convenient alternative to the previous $p_{12|11} = p_{22|11} = p_{32|11}$ (equals $p(H \mid S_{11})$ in the present instance). Similarly, $p(R \mid S_{11}) = .1818$, $p(L \mid S_{11}) = .6364$, $p(H \mid S_{12}) = .2759$, $p(R \mid S_{12}) = .6207$, and $p(L \mid S_{12}) = .1034$. The denominator in the expression for $p(H \mid S_{11})$, or $p(H)p(S_{11} \mid H) + p(R)p(S_{11} \mid R) + p(L)p(S_{11} \mid L) = .275$, equals $p(S_{11})$, the probability of sample 1, a used-KNIF sale; similarly, $p(S_{12}) = .725$.

After allowing for the reduction of 25 in profits resulting from the week's delay, the risk-preference equivalents of the three alternatives are as given in Table 12.3 (estimated from Figure 12.1).

TABLE 12.3
Utiles

| | | CONSOLIDATED KNIF | | |
|---|---|---|---|---|
| | | **Raises Price** | **Holds Price** | **Lowers Price** |
| **ASSOCIATED KNIF ELECTS** | $X_1$ | .94 | .83 | .50 |
| | $X_2$ | .99 | .70 | .20 |
| | $X_3$ | .83 | .92 | .57 |

Thus, if $S_{11}$ is observed, we determine

$$v(X_1 \mid S_{11}) = .639986, \quad v(X_2 \mid S_{11}) = .434522, \quad v(X_3 \mid S_{11}) = .680898.$$

If $S_{12}$ is observed, we determine

$$v(X_1 \mid S_{12}) = .864155, \quad v(X_2 \mid S_{12}) = .828303, \quad v(X_3 \mid S_{12}) = .827947,$$

where, to be consistent within the present notation, we denote $v(X_2 \mid S_{12}) = .6207(.99) + .2759(.70) + .1034(.20) = .828303 = v(X_{2|12})$ in the previous notation. Hence, $v^*(X_3 \mid S_{11}) = .680898$ and $v^*(X_1 \mid S_{12}) = .864155$. To compute the expected utiles of the sampling procedure,

$$v(S) = p(S_{11})v^*(X_3 \mid S_{11}) + p(S_{12})v^*(X_1 \mid S_{12}) = .275(.680898) + .725(.864155) = .8138.$$

Since $v(S) < v^*(X_1) = .8300$, an immediate decision is preferred to the one-week delay.

It is important to recognize, however, that the option of delaying is rejected not because the information gleaned would be worthless, but rather because this information is simply not worth the cost of 25. Indeed, even if one were offered infinitely large quantities of information, or a superlative and infallible predictor guaranteeing *perfect information* or a perfect prediction of Consolidated's actions, the *value of this perfect information* would be limited. In particular, with perfect information, Associated would earn either 500, 375, or 150 in profits, depending upon whether a price increase, no change, or price decrease were predicted for Consolidated. Since the prior probabilities of obtaining such predictions are .50, .25, and .25, respectively, the expected *utiles* associated with perfect information is determined to be $v(PI) = .50(1) + .25(.94) + .25(.62) = .8900$. The *monetary* equivalent of this is estimated from Figure 12.1 to be about 325. The monetary equivalent of the optimal decision ($X_1$ with $v^*(X_1) = .8300$) is estimated to be about 275. Perfect information would thus be worth no more than 50 to Associated KNIF.

## 12.5 LINEAR RISK PREFERENCES—A SPECIAL CASE

It is frequently assumed that over small ranges, or for supposedly impersonal corporate managements, the risk-preference function will be linear. The justification for the assumption is commonly some combination of (1) genuine belief in the proposition that corporations as such are involved in a sufficiently large number of decisions to enable, if not compel, them to take advantage of their ability to ride out the short-term ups and downs and consider only the long-term averages, and a commitment to the view that the corporate polity is sufficiently devoid of emotion, or comprised of sufficiently diverse individuals, to make the assumption of nonlinearity unwarranted, and (2) the recognition that the algebraic convenience of the linearity assumption may more than compensate for any minor distortions that would result if the appropriate risk-preference function were "almost" if "not quite" linear. At any rate, the assumption is made often enough that we should at least consider its advantages in the analysis of decision problems under risk.

We continue to focus on the previous KNIF problem. When the decision maker is linear in risk, maximizing expected value is equivalent to maximizing expected utiles. In the present instance, the expected values of the three alternatives are $E(X_1) = .50(400) + .25(300) + .25(125) = 306.25$, $E(X_2) = 318.75$, and $E(X_3) = 281.25$. $X_2$ is thus the preferred alternative. With perfect information, the expected value is $E(PI) = .50(500) + .25(375) + .25(150) = 381.25$. The *value of perfect information* is therefore given by $E(PI) - E^*(X_2) = 381.25 - 318.75 = 62.50$. The latter is the difference between one's *expected* gain with and without perfect information, and it represents the *maximum* that one would be willing to pay for an infinite amount of information.

Given the *sample information* contained in $S_{11}$ and $S_{12}$, the expected values are now as follows:

$$E(X_1|S_{11}) = .1818(400) + .1818(300) + .6364(125) = 206.8100,$$
$$E(X_2|S_{11}) = 163.6250 \text{ and } E(X_3|S_{11}) = 218.1750,$$
$$E(X_1|S_{12}) = .6207(400) + .2759(300) + .1034(125) = 343.9750,$$
$$E(X_2|S_{12}) = 377.5975 \text{ and } E(X_3|S_{12}) = 305.1825.$$

We thus have $E^*(X_3|S_{11})$ and $E^*(X_2|S_{12})$ as the maxima for each sample result, and $X_3$ is preferred if $S_{11}$ is observed, while $X_2$ is preferred if $S_{12}$ is observed. The expected value with sample information is determined by weighting these expected values by the probabilities of receiving them, or

$$E(S) = .275(218.1750) + .725(377.5975) = 333.7563125.$$

Since $E^*(X_2) = 318.75$ would be obtained without the sample information, the difference of 15.0063125 is the *value of sample information.* That is, one with linear risk preferences would spend *no more than* about 15 for this sample information.

To obtain additional insight, let us take a second view of this situation and consider what the decision maker's partial ignorance is costing Associated. The loss to Associated for failing to make the optimal decision, *in light of* Consolidated's action, will depend upon what the latter's action turns out to be. If Consolidated holds the price line, for example, Associated will not have lost anything from the prior choice of $X_3$. When Consolidated does not alter price, Associated is best off for having lowered its own price. But the prior choice of $X_1$ will result in an *opportunity loss* of 75. This is so termed because the gain of 300 is 75 less than the 375 *maximum* that would have been earned with the optimal decision $X_3$. Similarly, the opportunity loss of choosing $X_2$, given no price change on Consolidated's part, is 150. This is the difference between the potential 375 and the actual 225. The entire *opportunity-loss* table is given here as Table 12.4.

TABLE 12.4
Opportunity Loss

| | | CONSOLIDATED KNIF | | |
|---|---|---|---|---|
| | | **Raises Price** $p(R) = .50$ | **Holds Price** $p(H) = .25$ | **Lowers Price** $p(L) = .25$ |
| **ASSOCIATED KNIF ELECTS** | $X_1$ | 100 | 75 | 25 |
| | $X_2$ | 0 | 150 | 100 |
| | $X_3$ | 200 | 0 | 0 |

Now, the choice of $X_1$ will result in an *expected opportunity loss* of $EL(X_1) = .50(100) + .25(75) + .25(25) = 75.00$. Similarly, $EL(X_2) = 62.50$ and $EL(X_3) = 100.00$. With perfect information there will be no opportunity loss, since a non-optimal decision will never be made. The absence of perfect information will thus result in an expected opportunity loss of 62.50 if the previously determined optimum of $X_2$ is chosen, and still higher opportunity losses will result if the other alternatives are chosen. With perfect information, this 62.50 opportunity loss is avoided. We thus determine that perfect information is worth, as before, as much as 62.50. Further, $X_2$ is again revealed to be the optimal decision, for it *minimizes expected opportunity loss.* That the latter is equivalent to maximizing expected value when risk preferences are linear is readily seen as follows. Let $x_{ij}(x_{ij}^*)$ be the (highest) possible return obtainable when the $j$th outcome obtains, and let $p_j$ be the probability of the $j$th outcome. Then,

$$E(X_i) = \sum_j p_j x_{ij} \qquad \text{and} \qquad E(PI) = \sum_j p_j x_{ij}^*.$$

The initial approach was to choose the maximum $E(X_i)$. Since $E(PI)$ is a constant, however, maximum $E(X_i)$ and maximum $[E(X_i) - E(PI)]$ lead to equivalent decisions. The very same choice will therefore *minimize* $[E(PI) - E(X_i)]$. But

$$E(PI) - E(X_i) = \sum_j p_j x_{ij}^* - \sum_j p_j x_{ij} = \sum_j p_j(x_{ij}^* - x_{ij}) = EL(X_i).$$

Since, in general, minimizing a function is equivalent to maximizing the negative of the function,

$$\min EL(X_i) = -\max\,[E(X_i) - E(PI)].$$

Hence, minimizing expected opportunity loss is equivalent to maximizing expected value, and the minimum expected opportunity loss is the value of perfect information. And, as a final touch on this particular aspect of the problem, since $E(PI) = 381.25$ and $E(S) = 333.7563125$, $E(PI) - E(S) = 47.4936875 = EL(S)$ is the expected opportunity loss of the sample information as opposed to possession of perfect information. The expected opportunity loss of the optimal decision, absent any information, is $EL(X_2) = 62.50$. Thus $EL(X_2) - EL(S) = 15.0063125$ is the reduction in expected opportunity loss that is offered by the sample information, and this once again determines the (maximum) value of the sample information.

This sort of analysis could also be performed where the risk-preference function is nonlinear. To do so, we must determine the opportunity losses in terms of utiles. For example, the opportunity losses associated with Table 12.2 would be given by Table 12.5. Then, upon taking the mathematical expectations, $Lv(X_1) = .50(.05) + .25(.09) + .25(.05) = .0600$, $Lv(X_2) = .1275$, and $Lv(X_3) = .0750$. This is minimized for $X_1$. Comparable to the linear case, $Lv^*(X_1) = .0600 = v(PI) - v^*(X_1) = .8900 - .8300 = .0600$, or the expected utile loss is the extent to which a decision results in a utile reduction below the level attained with perfect information. Inasmuch as the .0600 figure will suggest different monetary equivalents depending upon the level of $v(PI)$, when risk preferences are nonlinear, approaching the problem via opportunity loss is not as interesting as in the linearity case.

TABLE 12.5
Utile Loss

| | | CONSOLIDATED KNIF | | |
|---|---|---|---|---|
| | | Raises Price $p(R) = .50$ | Holds Price $p(H) = .25$ | Lowers Price $p(L) = .25$ |
| ASSOCIATED KNIF ELECTS | $X_1$ | .05 | .09 | .05 |
| | $X_2$ | 0 | .19 | .32 |
| | $X_3$ | .15 | 0 | 0 |

Note, however, that in certain instances, as in inventory problems of the sort mentioned in Section 8.6a with variable demand, management might have greater confidence in its ability to assess the loss associated with a nonoptimal decision than in its ability to assess the possible gains from all decisions. In essence the revenues could be invariant (but unknown) with respect to different decisions, while the costs are known but variable. Minimizing expected opportunity loss would then lead to the optimal decision.

As an illustration, suppose that with each unit it produces but does not sell, a firm incurs a cost of $C_1$. Each unit demanded that the firm fails to supply entails a cost of $C_2$. Let $p(Q < I)$ denote the probability that demand will be less than $I$ units, and let $p(Q \geq I)$ denote the probability that demand will be at least $I$ units. The expected loss from stocking the last unit is $p(Q < I)C_1$—the expected cost of producing and not selling that unit; the expected loss of not having that last unit on hand to sell is $p(Q \geq I)C_2$. With linear risk preferences, the unit will be stocked so long as $p(Q \geq I)C_2 \geq p(Q < I)C_1$. But $p(Q \geq I) + p(Q < I) = 1$. Hence, the unit will be stocked so long as

$$[1 - p(Q < I)]C_2 \geq p(Q < I)C_1 \quad \text{or} \quad p(Q < I) \leq \frac{C_2}{C_1 + C_2}.$$

This is the same stocking rule as was developed in Section 8.6a; but to develop it here it was not necessary to explicitly detail all prices, production costs, shortage costs, holding costs, and the like.

It might also be noted that one could describe risk preferences entirely in terms of opportunity losses. Based upon some arbitrary $x^*$, for example, one could assign a loss function $L(x^* - x_i)$ to order one's "preferences" with respect to payoffs that are below some "target" level. The preferred decision thereupon becomes the decision that minimizes the associated mathematical expectation of the loss function. Indeed, this is how we selected our least-squares estimators, as discussed in Section 3.5.

## 12.6 A DIGRESSION ON RISK AVERSION

In a paper of considerable interest and importance, Pratt[14] has considered the possibility of measuring the extent to which an individual seeks to avoid risk (or alternatively, his propensity to gamble). Pratt's measure of *risk aversion* is a *function* that is directly related to the difference between the expected *value* of a risky alternative and the cash equivalent to which the individual whose preferences are being considered would be indifferent. The latter difference is called the *risk premium*. To facilitate discussion and draw out the full impact of the measure, we shall concentrate on *monetary* values. The risk-preference function $V = v(Y)$ will therefore assign utile equivalents $V$ to monetary values $Y$.

The payoff of a project $X$ is a random variable $x$ distributed by $f(x)$. The expected value of the project is denoted by $E(X) = E[x] = \int xf(x)\,dx$. In terms of risk preferences, $v(X) = v(\tilde{\$})$, or $X \sim \tilde{\$}$. Let us focus on the risk-evader, while recognizing that the risk-taker's behavior would be analyzed in similar fashion (but for certain changes of sign). In accordance with the previous definition, $E(X) - \tilde{\$} = \rho > 0$ will measure the risk premium. In effect, the risk premium is a "load" that

[14] John W. Pratt, "Risk Aversion in the Small and in the Large," *Econometrica*, **32**:1–2 (Jan.–April 1964), 122–136.

one is willing to pay in order to avoid a gamble. $\rho$ is thus a function of the risky alternative $X$ and the certain monetary equivalent $\tilde{\$}$. In the present development, we shall be requiring the decision maker to determine the risk premium he would demand before he would be willing to exchange his assets for the risky alternative $X$.

Suppose the decision maker has assets of exactly \$. Note that \$ measures his assets, and $\tilde{\$}$ the cash equivalent of $X$. Given a continuous and uniquely defined risk-preference function $V$, we are able to assign a utile equivalent of $v(\$ + E(X) - \rho)$ to $\$ + E(X) - \rho$. Further, $E(X) - \rho = \tilde{\$}$ and $\tilde{\$} \sim X$. Therefore, by the transitivity property, $E(X) - \rho \sim X$. The individual is indifferent between holding (1) his assets of \$ plus the cash equivalent of the risky project, and (2) his assets of \$ and the risky project. Hence, he assigns an equal $V$ to $\$ + E(X) - \rho$ and the expectation of $v(Y)$, where $Y = \$ + x$. This is so, since he is willing to substitute $X$ for $E(X) - \rho$ in the $\$ + E(X) - \rho$ expression; and in so doing, he receives $\$ + x$ in accordance with the density $f(x)$. Thus $E[v(Y)] = E[v(\$ + x)] = \int v(\$ + x)f(x)\,dx = v(\$ + E(X) - \rho)$, or

$$E[v(\$ + x)] = v(\$ + E(X) - \rho). \tag{12.1}$$

Let us consider a project $X$ for which $E(X) = 0$ and the variance in the payoffs $\sigma_x^2 = E[x^2] = \int x^2 f(x)\,dx \to 0$. That is, the project offers a fair gamble, and the dispersion in the returns is comparatively small. In this case, $v(\$ + E(X) - \rho)$ reduces to $v(\$ - \rho)$. Computing the Taylor's series expansion around \$ for the latter expression, we have

$$v(\$ - \rho) = v(\$) - \rho \frac{dv(\$)}{d\$} + \theta, \tag{12.2a}$$

where $\theta$ comprises the higher-order terms. Similarly,

$$E[v(\$ + x)] = E\left[v(\$) + x\frac{dv(\$)}{d\$} + \frac{1}{2}x^2\frac{d^2v(\$)}{d\$^2} + \phi\right], \tag{12.2b}$$

where $\phi$ comprises the higher-order terms. Note that the higher-order terms $\to 0$ since $\sigma_x^2 \to 0$. Since $E[v(\$)] = v(\$)$, $E[x] = E(X) = 0$, and $E[x^2] = \sigma_x^2$, (12.2b) reduces to

$$E[v(\$ + x)] = v(\$) + \frac{1}{2}\sigma_x^2\frac{d^2v(\$)}{d\$^2} + E(\phi). \tag{12.2b$'$}$$

If we denote $dv/d\$$ by $v'$ and $d^2v/d\$^2$ by $v''$, and substitute (12.2a) and (12.2b′) into (12.1), the latter becomes $v(\$) - \rho v'(\$) + \theta = v(\$) + \frac{1}{2}\sigma_x^2 v''(\$) + E(\phi)$, or

$$\rho = -\left(\frac{1}{2}\right)\sigma_x^2\left[\frac{v''(\$)}{v'(\$)}\right] - \frac{E(\phi) - \theta}{v'(\$)}. \tag{12.3}$$

The risk premium $\rho$ is thus an increasing function of $-[v''(\$)/v'(\$)]$. That is, the bigger is $-v''(\$)/v'(\$)$, the greater is the premium that the risk-evader will pay in order to avoid the risky alternative. Hence, we *define*

$$r(\$) = -\frac{v''(\$)}{v'(\$)} \tag{12.4}$$

to be the measure of *risk aversion* (in the "small," since we measure risk aversion locally, for a particular asset level of \$); $-r(\$)$ would measure the propensity to gamble.

Clearly, since $v'(\$) > 0$ by the assumption that greater \$ is preferred to lesser \$, the risk-evader with a concave risk-preference function will have $v''(\$) < 0$ and hence $r(\$) > 0$. That is, he will demonstrate an aversion to risk. The interesting aspect of Pratt's risk-aversion measure is that it specifically measures risk aversion as a function of an individual's assets. With this measure, one may therefore speak about increasing, constant, or decreasing risk aversion. This is important, for if it is ordinarily true, as we might expect it would be, that the greater an individual's assets the smaller the risk premium he would be willing to pay to avoid a given risk (that is, decreasing risk aversion), this would suggest certain classes of risk-preference functions to employ in an analysis of decision making under risk.[15]

## 12.7 A SECOND LOOK AT SOME PREVIOUSLY CONSIDERED PROBLEMS

In the earlier chapters we sporadically introduced problems into which uncertainty entered. Then, however, it was assumed that the decision makers involved were concerned solely with expected *values* with respect to specific criterion functions exclusive of risk-preference functions. That is, it was assumed that the decision makers had linear risk preferences and were indifferent to making fair bets. In this section we reintroduce three of these problems and consider the potential effects of nonlinearity in risk.

### a. The Market-Share Game

Chapter 7 introduced the duopoly problem wherein each of two competitors is interested solely in his share of the market. In particular, we formulated the two-person constant-sum game summarized in Table 7.2, and reproduced here as Table 12.6(a). With each duopolist adopting a mixed strategy in order to maximize his minimum expected market share duopolist 1 would select his strategies with probabilities of $q_1 = .4445$, $q_2 = .3611$, and $q_3 = .1944$; duopolist 2 would never select his fourth strategy, since it is dominated by the first strategy. As it turns out, however, he never selects the first strategy either. Rather, he alternates between $S_{22}$ and $S_{23}$, choosing the former with probability of $p_2 = .75$ and the latter with probability of $p_3 = .25$. The value of the game, or duopolist 2's expected market share, is .5375.

TABLE 12.6(a)
Duopolist 2's Market Share

| | | *Duopolist 1's Choices* | | |
|---|---|---|---|---|
| | | $S_{11}$ | $S_{12}$ | $S_{13}$ |
| | $S_{21}$ | .60 | .40 | .65 |
| *Duopolist 2's* | $S_{22}$ | .50 | .55 | .60 |
| *Choices* | $S_{23}$ | .65 | .50 | .35 |
| | $S_{24}$ | .30 | .40 | .50 |

Suppose, however, that the duopolists have nonlinear risk preferences with respect to market share. Specifically, and for illustrative purposes only, we shall assume that duopolist 1 has a risk-preference function described by $V_1 = (1 + a)^{3/4}$, and duopolist 2 has a risk-preference function described by $V_2 = (1 + b)^{1/4}$, where

[15] For a discussion, see Pratt, "Risk Aversion in the Small and in the Large," pp. 131–135.

$a$ and $b$ are their respective market shares. Thus, $d^2V_1/da^2 = -\frac{3}{16}(1 + a)^{-5/4}$ and $d^2V_2/db^2 = -\frac{3}{16}(1 + b)^{-7/4}$; and both duopolists have concave risk-preference functions and are risk-evaders. Further, considering Pratt's measure of risk aversion for duopolists 1 and 2, respectively, we have $r_1(a) = \frac{1}{4}(1 + a)^{-1}$ and $r_2(b) = \frac{3}{4}(1 + b)^{-1}$. Hence, $r_1(a) < r_2(b)$ for all $a = b$, and duopolist 2 is more risk-averse than duopolist 1 at any given level of market share, although both demonstrate decreasing risk aversion. In Pratt's sense, duopolist 2 would be willing to pay a higher premium in market share to avoid *a given risk* than would duopolist 1.

When we convert the duopolists' respective market shares into their risk equivalents, Table 12.6(a) is converted into Table 12.6(b). Table 12.6(b) describes a two-person *non*constant-sum game. Allowance for nonlinear risk preferences has therefore converted a constant-sum game into a nonconstant-sum game. When individuals are risk-evaders or risk-takers, then, it is apparent that constant-sum games would evolve only by the most extraordinary of coincidences.

TABLE 12.6(b)

| | | *Duopolist 1's Choices* $S_{11}$ | $S_{12}$ | $S_{13}$ |
|---|---|---|---|---|
| | $S_{21}$ | (1.125, 1.287) | (1.088, 1.423) | (1.133, 1.252) |
| *Duopolist 2's* | $S_{22}$ | (1.107, 1.355) | (1.116, 1.321) | (1.125, 1.287) |
| *Choices* | $S_{23}$ | (1.133, 1.252) | (1.107, 1.355) | (1.078, 1.456) |
| | $S_{24}$ | (1.068, 1.489) | (1.088, 1.423) | (1.107, 1.355) |

Although a clear mode of behavior is not obvious, the duopolists still have the possibility of developing mixed strategies to maximize their minimum expected *utiles*. Duopolist 1's optimum strategy calls for probabilities of $q_1' = .4417$, $q_2' = .3619$, and $q_3' = .1964$, for $S_{11}$, $S_{12}$, and $S_{13}$, respectively; duopolist 2 will select among his first three options (the fourth is still dominated by the first) with probabilities of $p_1' = .0090$, $p_2' = .7457$, and $p_3' = .2453$, respectively. Thus, $a_{22} = .55$, the market share accruing to duopolist 2 when he selects $S_{22}$ and duopolist 1 selects $S_{12}$, will obtain with probability of $q_2'p_2' = (.3619)(.7457) = .269869$; similarly for the other entries in the table. Proceeding in this manner, we then find the expected market share for duopolist 2 to be .53750175. In *this* case, then, neither duopolist will find his optimal mixed strategy altered much by converting market shares into utiles, nor will the expected market share of .5375 be altered to any significant extent. But the latter *has been* altered, and $S_{21}$ *is* selected, if only upon exceedingly rare occasions. Attitude towards risk can make a difference in games of conflict, and ordinarily it will.

## b. Uncertainty in the Production Function

As in Section 6.5, let us suppose that the production function is written $Q = q(u, F_1, \ldots, F_m)$, where $u$ is a random variable described by the density function $f(u)$. The $F_i$ are factor service levels, and the total cost curve is

$$C = \sum_{i=1}^{m} W_i F_i.$$

Suppose also that the firm perceives itself to be a purely competitive seller in the product market, and believes it can sell as much as it wishes at a price of $P$. If the entrepreneur is linear in risk and maximizes expected profit, he will maximize

$$E[\pi] = \int_u PQ(u)f(u)\, du - C, \tag{12.5}$$

with respect to the $F_i$, or he will seek a set of $F_i$ such that

$$\frac{\partial E[\pi]}{\partial F_i} = P \int_u \left[\frac{\partial Q(u)}{\partial F_i}\right] f(u)\, du - \frac{\partial C}{\partial F_i} = 0, \qquad i = 1, \ldots, m. \tag{12.6}$$

In order to make the succeeding analysis more tractable without detracting from its major purpose, we assume in (12.6) that the random variable $u$ is independent of the $F_i$. It will also be assumed that the second-order conditions are satisfied. Thus, we require that

$$MR\cdot(E[MPP_i]) = MC_i, \qquad i = 1, \ldots, m, \tag{12.6$'$}$$

or that the firm hires each factor of production to the point where marginal revenue $(= P)$ times the *expected* marginal physical product of each factor $(= \int_u [\partial Q(u)/\partial F_i] f(u)\, du)$ is equated to the factor's marginal cost $(= \partial C/\partial F_i)$.

Now, however, let us suppose the entrepreneur is nonlinear in risk and inquire into the implications of this supposition for factor employment. Specifically assume his risk-preference function in terms of profits to be $V = v(\pi)$. Then he will wish to maximize the expectation of $V$, or maximize

$$E[V] = \int_u v(PQ(u) - C)f(u)\, du. \tag{12.7}$$

The $F_i$ must therefore be chosen so as to set $\partial E[V]/\partial F_i = 0$ $(i = 1, \ldots, m)$, assuming as we shall that the second-order conditions are satisfied. Thus, we compute

$$\begin{aligned} \frac{\partial E[V]}{\partial F_i} &= \int_u \left(\frac{dv}{d\pi(u)}\right)\left(\frac{\partial \pi(u)}{\partial F_i}\right) f(u)\, du \\ &= \int_u \left[\frac{dv}{d\pi(u)}\right]\left[P\frac{\partial Q(u)}{\partial F_i} - \frac{\partial C}{\partial F_i}\right] f(u)\, du = 0. \end{aligned} \tag{12.8}$$

Note that $\pi$ is now a function of $u$, since $\pi$ is a function of $Q(u)$.

Rearranging terms in (12.8), we can rewrite the latter as

$$P \int_u \left[\frac{dv}{d\pi(u)}\right]\left[\frac{\partial Q(u)}{\partial F_i}\right] f(u)\, du = \int_u \left[\frac{dv}{d\pi(u)}\right]\left[\frac{\partial C}{\partial F_i}\right] f(u)\, du.$$

But, since $\partial C/\partial F_i$ is independent of the random variable $u$, this term can be factored out of the integral on the right. With $P = MR$, the entire expression can be rewritten in a form comparable to (12.6′):

$$\frac{MR\left[\int_u \left[\frac{dv}{d\pi(u)}\right] MPP_i(u)f(u)\, du\right]}{\int_u \left[\frac{dv}{d\pi(u)}\right] f(u)\, du} = MC_i, \qquad i = 1, \ldots, m. \tag{12.8$'$}$$

With linear risk preferences, $dv/d\pi(u)$ is a constant, and since $\int_u f(u)\,du = 1$, (12.8′) reduces to (12.6′).

Note, now, that the bracketed expression in the numerator is simply the mathematical expectation of the product of two random variables, $[dv/d\pi(u)] = MV(u)$ and $MPP_i(u)$. In general, if $x$ and $y$ are random variables, then $E[xy] - E[x]E[y] = \sigma_{xy}$. That is, the expectation of their product less the product of their individual expectations is equal to their covariance. Hence, $E[MV \cdot MPP_i] - E[MV]E[MPP_i] = \sigma_{VP_i}$, where $MV(u)$ and $MPP_i(u)$ are both distributed in accordance with $f(u)$. Note further that the denominator on the left side of (12.8′) is $E[MV]$. Therefore, the left side of (12.8′) may be rewritten as

$$\begin{aligned}\frac{MR \cdot (E[MV \cdot MPP_i])}{E[MV]} &= \frac{MR \cdot (\sigma_{VP_i} + E[MV]E[MPP_i])}{E[MV]} \\ &= MR \cdot \left(\frac{\sigma_{VP_i}}{E[MV]} + E[MPP_i]\right) \\ &= MR \cdot (E[MPP_i]) + \sigma_{VP_i}\left(\frac{MR}{E[MV]}\right).\end{aligned}$$

Substituting this expression into (12.8′), we determine the following equilibrium condition:

$$MR \cdot (E[MPP_i]) + \sigma_{VP_i}\left(\frac{MR}{E[MV]}\right) = MC_i, \qquad i = 1, \ldots, m. \qquad (12.8'')$$

Comparing (12.8″) with (12.6′) it is clear that the only discrepancy is in the $\sigma_{VP_i}(MR/E[MV])$ term that appears in (12.8″) but not in (12.6′). It is "missing" from (12.6′) since with linear risk preferences, $dv/d\pi(u) = MV =$ *marginal utiles with respect to profit* is constant. In the latter circumstance, $MV$ and $MPP_i$ will be uncorrelated and $\sigma_{VP_i} = 0$. It will necessarily be true, however, that $MR > 0$ and $E[MV] > 0$, by the implicit assumptions of a positive price and a positive preference for higher profits, so that $MR/E[MV] > 0$. Assume first that $MC_i$ is constant ($i = 1, \ldots, m$) and equals $MR \cdot (E[MPP_i])$ at a level of employment of $F_i^*$. We shall also assume that at this level each factor is employed where its marginal physical product, given $u$, is decreasing. Then, the left side of (12.8″) will be greater or less than the left side of (12.6′) at $F_i^*$, depending upon whether $\sigma_{VP_i}$ is positive or negative. If $\sigma_{VP_i} > 0$, say, then to assure that the equality is achieved, the left side must be reduced. The assumption that the second-order conditions hold implies in turn that the reduction can only be accomplished by increasing $F_i$ above $F_i^*$; $F_i$ would have to be below $F_i^*$ if $\sigma_{VP_i} < 0$.

Now, we can make the general presumption that $u$ affects $Q$ in a regular manner such that higher $u$ induces greater $Q$, and hence effects greater $\pi$ for a given level of employment. Moreover, if the entrepreneur is a risk-evader with a strictly concave risk-preference function, $MV$ will be a monotonically decreasing function of $\pi$ and hence of $u$; if the entrepreneur is a risk-taker with a strictly convex risk-preference function, $MV$ will be a monotonically increasing function of $\pi$ and hence of $u$. More rigorously,

$$\frac{\partial\left(\dfrac{dv}{d\pi}\right)}{\partial u} = \left(\frac{d^2v}{d\pi^2}\right)\left(\frac{\partial \pi}{\partial u}\right).$$

With $\partial\pi/\partial u > 0$ by assumption, the sign of $d^2v/d\pi^2$ will dictate the sign of the entire expression; and the sign will be positive (negative) when the risk-preference function is strictly convex (concave).

Unfortunately, the relationship between the magnitude of $u$ and $MPP_i$ is not quite as clear. Notice, however, that when $MPP_i$ is, say, a decreasing function of $u$, then for the risk-evader for whom $MV$ is also a decreasing function of $u$, $MPP_i$ and $MV$ are *positively* correlated, and $\sigma_{VP_i} > 0$. The risk-evader therefore *prefers* to hire $F_i^{**} > F_i^*$. Analogously, for the risk-taker, $\sigma_{VP_i}$ is necessarily negative in this case, and he prefers to employ $F_i^{***} < F_i^*$. Each one's preferences will be exactly reversed when $MPP_i$ is an increasing function of $u$. Hence, their preferences can *only* coincide when $MPP_i$ is independent of $u$. In this case, $\sigma_{VP_i} = 0$ and linear and nonlinear preference functions lead to the same employment levels. In effect, risk preferences will only affect employment under this type of uncertainty when the random elements in the production process affect the factors' marginal physical products in a very systematic way.

Moreover, if $MC_i$ is an increasing function of $F_i$, it will require fewer additional units to achieve the equality in the case when $\sigma_{VP_i} > 0$, for then the right side increases with increasing $F_i$ to meet the falling left side; similarly, when $\sigma_{VP_i} < 0$, a lesser reduction is required in $F_i$. Thus, any discrepancies in preferred employment positions will tend to be less for factors with increasing marginal cost curves than for those with constant costs. By an analogous argument, the differences will be even more pronounced when the factors have decreasing marginal cost curves. All of this assumes, however, that second-order conditions obtain for all sets of risk-preference functions at the point at which the first-order conditions obtain. As we shall see in the next chapter, this assumption may be more heroic than it initially appears. Nonetheless, the major point of the analysis is quite clear: uncertainty and attitudes towards risk can lead even neoclassical entrepreneurs to prefer different levels of factor employment, although their decisions are based on precisely the same information.

### c. Price Instability in a Competitive Market

Let us consider anew the situation that arose in Section 8.5. There, a pure competitor was producing with a rising and strictly convex total cost curve, $C = c(Q)$, for a market in which price is a random variable distributed in accordance with the density function $f(P)$. The expected price is given by $\bar{P} = \int_P Pf(P)\,dP$, and equals the certainty price in the stable market.

Oi's firm can instantaneously adjust production in response to price changes. Its output decisions are therefore always made under certainty (of *price*). If the $P = MC$ output is $Q^*$, profit is given by $\pi = PQ^* - c(Q^*)$. It was seen, moreover, that the competitor who seeks to maximize expected profit (that is, one with linear risk preferences), will prefer price instability to price stability at $\bar{P}$, inasmuch as expected profits of $E[\pi] = \int_P [PQ^* - c(Q^*)]f(P)\,dP$ exceed the certainty profits of $\bar{\pi}^* = \bar{P}\bar{Q}^* - c\bar{Q}^*$. Suppose, however, that the entrepreneur has a risk-preference function with respect to profits of $V = v(\pi)$. Then the expectation of this function will be $E_1[V] = \int_P v(\pi)f(P)\,dP$.

Let us consider the curvature of $V(\pi)$ in order to make use of the previously deduced fact that the expected value of a strictly convex (concave) function of a random variable will be greater (less) than the value of the function evaluated at the expected value of the random variable. It was previously shown that in the Oi case $d\pi/dP > 0$ and $d^2\pi/dP^2 > 0$. Further,

$$\frac{dv}{dP} = \left(\frac{dv}{d\pi}\right)\left(\frac{d\pi}{dP}\right) \quad \text{and} \quad \frac{d^2v}{dP^2} = \left(\frac{d^2v}{d\pi^2}\right)\left(\frac{d\pi}{dP}\right)^2 + \left(\frac{d^2\pi}{dP^2}\right)\left(\frac{dv}{d\pi}\right).$$

For a risk-taker with a strictly convex risk-preference function, $d^2v/d\pi^2 > 0$. Hence, since $(d\pi/dP)^2 > 0$, $d^2\pi/dP^2 > 0$, and $dv/d\pi > 0$, it follows directly that $d^2v/dP^2 > 0$. Therefore, the risk-taker's risk-preference function is a convex function of price, its expectation is higher than is the function evaluated at the certainty price, and price instability is preferred to price stability. For the risk-evader, however, with a strictly concave risk-preference function, $d^2v/d\pi^2 < 0$ and hence $d^2v/dP^2 \gtreqless 0$. That is, even though over the long term he stands to gain more therefrom, on the average, if he is sufficiently abhorrent of risk, the risk-evader *may* prefer to do without the price instability, and would gladly substitute price stability at the certainty price. The apprehensions that Oi's results raise in some of us who tend to think of instability as being "bad" may well stem from latent risk-evasive tendencies, successfully suppressed in a misspent risk-taking youth.

In Tisdell's case, production is planned in advance at some optimal $\bar{Q}$. Profits are given by $\pi = P\bar{Q} - c(\bar{Q})$ and $E_2[V] = \int_P v(P\bar{Q} - c(\bar{Q}))f(P)\,dP$. To determine the optimum $\bar{Q}$, we require

$$\begin{aligned}\frac{dE_2[V]}{d\bar{Q}} &= \int_P \left(\frac{dv}{d\pi}\right)\left(\frac{d\pi}{d\bar{Q}}\right) f(P)\,dP \\ &= \int_P \left(\frac{dv}{d\pi}\right)\left(P - \frac{dc}{d\bar{Q}}\right) f(P)\,dP \\ &= \int_P P\left(\frac{dv}{d\pi}\right) f(P)\,dP - \frac{dc}{d\bar{Q}}\int_P \left(\frac{dv}{d\pi}\right) f(P)\,dP = 0;\end{aligned}$$

and $d^2E_2[V]/dP^2 < 0$. Solving $dE_2[V]/d\bar{Q} = 0$,

$$\frac{dc}{d\bar{Q}} = \frac{\int P\left(\frac{dv}{d\pi}\right) f(P)\,dP}{\int \left(\frac{dv}{d\pi}\right) f(P)\,dP}. \tag{12.9}$$

In the case of linear risk preferences, $dv/d\pi$ is a constant and may be factored out of the numerator and denominator. Since $f(P)$ is a probability density function, in the denominator $\int f(P)\,dP = 1$ and the previous $dc/d\bar{Q} = \bar{P}$ condition is restored. That is, output is maintained at the point where marginal cost equals the expected price. Further, denoting $dv/d\pi = MV$, as in the preceding subsection, we may write the numerator on the right side of (12.9) as $E[(MV)(P)] = E[MV]E[P] + \sigma_{VP}$, where $\sigma_{VP}$ is the covariance between $dv/d\pi$ and $P$. The denominator is simply $E[MV]$.

Hence, the right side of (12.9) is

$$\frac{E[MV]E[P] + \sigma_{VP}}{E[MV]} = \bar{P} + \frac{\sigma_{VP}}{E[MV]} \cdot$$

Note further that $dP/dP = 1 > 0$ and $d(dv/d\pi)/dP = d^2v/d\pi\, dP = (d^2v/d\pi^2)(d\pi/dP)$. Given $Q$ held fixed at $\bar{Q}$, $d\pi/dP = \bar{Q}$. Hence $d^2v/d\pi\, dP = (d^2v/d\pi^2)\bar{Q}$. The latter expression will be positive when $d^2v/d\pi^2 > 0$ and negative when $d^2v/d\pi^2 < 0$. That is, $dv/d\pi$ will be an increasing (decreasing) function of $P$ if $V = v(\pi)$ is a strictly convex (concave) function, and the entrepreneur is a risk-taker (-evader). But with $dv/d\pi$ an increasing function of $P$, $P$ and $dv/d\pi$ are positively correlated and $\sigma_{VP} > 0$. In this case, then, $\sigma_{VP}/E(MV) > 0$ and $\bar{P} + \sigma_{VP}/E(MV) > \bar{P}$. Therefore, to achieve the equality of (12.9), $dc/d\bar{Q}$ must be increased above the $\bar{P} = dc/d\bar{Q}$ level; or, since marginal cost is an increasing function of $Q$, output for the risk-taker will lie *above* the output for one with linear risk preferences. With precisely the same arguments, output for the risk-evader will lie below the output level for one with linear risk preferences. With linearity, note that $\sigma_{VP} = 0$. The second-order conditions for a maximum are readily seen to hold, except *perhaps* for risk-takers, at the point where the first-order conditions are satisfied.[16]

Again, it is apparent that once risk preferences are introduced into a model, the optimal decision can be affected. Moreover, it is not simply a matter of risk-takers behaving differently from risk-evaders. Rather, the *shape* of the risk-preference function, given similar overall attitudes towards risk, can also result in the choice of different decisions by different individuals.

## 12.8 RATIONALITY, INDIVIDUALITY, AND THE REPRESENTATIVE FIRM

It has long been commonplace for microeconomic theorists to devote considerable energy to studying the "representative firm. . . one which has had a fairly long life, and fair success, which is managed with normal ability, and which has normal access

[16] For the second-order conditions, we require $d^2E_2[V]/d\bar{Q}^2$. This is found to be

$$\frac{d^2E_2[V]}{d\bar{Q}^2} = \int \frac{d^2v}{d\pi^2}\frac{d\pi}{d\bar{Q}} Pf(P)\, dP - \frac{d^2c}{d\bar{Q}^2}\int \frac{dv}{d\pi} f(P)\, dP - \frac{dc}{d\bar{Q}}\int \frac{d^2v}{d\pi^2}\frac{d\pi}{d\bar{Q}} f(P)\, dP.$$

Rearranging terms,

$$\frac{d^2E_2[V]}{d\bar{Q}^2} = \int \frac{d^2v}{d\pi^2}\left[P - \frac{dc}{d\bar{Q}}\right]^2 f(P)\, dP - \frac{d^2c}{d\bar{Q}^2}\int \frac{dv}{d\pi} f(P)\, dP.$$

The second expression is always positive, since $d^2c/d\bar{Q}^2$ and $\int [dv/d\pi]f(P)\, dP$ are necessarily positive. When $d^2v/d\pi^2$ is negative the first integral is necessarily negative, and $d^2E_2[v]/d\bar{Q}^2 < 0$, and the second-order conditions for a maximum are indeed satisfied. Hence, the second-order conditions *necessarily* hold for the risk-evader and *might* hold for the risk-taker.

This approach to the problem has been employed by Rudolph G. Penner, "Uncertainty and the Short-Run Shifting of the Corporation Tax," *Oxford Economic Papers*, **19**:1 (March 1967), 99–110. The same conclusion regarding the output levels for the three types of individuals confronted with this price-instability situation was derived by an alternative method for a specific risk-preference function by J. J. McCall in his article, "Competitive Production for Constant Risk Utility Functions," *Review of Economic Studies*, **XXXIV**:100 (Oct. 1967), 417–420.

to the economies, external and internal, which belong to that aggregate volume of production .... Thus a representative firm is in a sense an average firm... at which we need to look in order to see how far the economies, *internal and external*, of production on a large scale have extended generally in the industry and country .... We cannot see this by looking at one or two firms taken at random."[17] On the one hand, this emphasis can be justified by the desire to predict and explain *aggregate* behavior, or the behavior of the *bulk* of firms. To do so, it would indeed seem advisable to concentrate on modal forms of behavior rather than on the radical extremes. On the other hand, the emphasis on "representative" carries with it the connotation that something is to be said about the way in which most firms do in fact behave and that it is meaningful to allude to the "representative" firm for, while there may be a deviationist or two in their midst, firms and entrepreneurs tend to be conforming organisms. There is a paradoxical tendency for us to romanticize the great entrepreneurs of history as free-wheeling risk-taking individualists, and the great entrepreneurs of neoclassical firms as rational profit-maximizing conformists. Thus in treading the previous theoretical paths, the specter of rationality and conformity has been our constant companion.

In this spirit, the thrust of our efforts has been towards the construction of models and decision rules to assist a set of carefully selected decision makers in their attempts to attain certain preestablished goals. Although profit maximization in the neoclassical world attracted most of our attention, the goals considered have been, in fact, many and varied. For example, we developed rules for the consumer seeking to maximize utility subject to a budget constraint, rules for the neoclassical firm seeking to employ its factors of production so as to maximize profits, rules for the corporate management seeking to maximize its own utility in a world of certainty while simultaneously keeping the stockholders content, and rules for recognizing the most preferred of a set of risky alternatives. The setting in which the decision maker was placed differed from model to model, the assumptions made about the decision maker's objectives differed from model to model, but the models were tied together by a common thread wherein *efficient* decision making was sought. *Irrespective* of his problems or motivations, it has been assumed throughout that the decision maker will make an effort to utilize the *best* of his ability and knowledge to resolve these problems, in light of his recognized alternatives and their perceived consequences. He may be a maximizing perfectionist, or a somewhat more human and lackadaisical satisficer, but he takes advantage of the high-speed computer, the available data, and the decision-making algorithms of which he is aware, to make his decisions in a conscientious and *reasoned* manner. In the sense that he will *want* his decisions to be based on *reason*, the decision maker is presumed to *want* to behave *rationally*.

The notion that decision makers prefer to make their decisions in a rational manner is quite attractive, and most of us are only too ready to accept it. For one thing, *irrational* behavior is just not something about which one ordinarily brags. For another, the rationality assumption enables the model builder to take advantage of some very powerful mathematical tools in the application of classical optimization principles to well-defined criterion functions. And for yet another, if decision makers do not *choose* to behave rationally, there is not an awful lot that the student of

[17] Alfred Marshall, *Principles of Economics* (New York: The Macmillan Company, 1948), pp. 317–318.

decision making can say about how the practitioner either *will* or *should* behave. Nonetheless, and despite the philosophical and practical attractions of the rationality assumption, individuals will not *necessarily* feel compelled to behave rationally, nor should one assume that even when all the pertinent data can be quantified, decision problems will *necessarily* be dealt with in a precise, orderly, and reasoned fashion. There is more than a little truth in the observation: "We all expect other people to have rational motives, though we know very well that our own acts are half of them due to impulse."[18]

This is not to deny that many, if not most, individuals attempt to run their lives in a depressingly rational way. Nor do we deny the possibility that individuals may behave with complete rationality when they *intentionally elect* to ignore certain principles of rational decision making in favor of, say, ad hoc devices that are less troublesome to employ. It is not at all clear that an entrepreneur is behaving irrationally when, although he is aware of the defects and the alternatives, he still chooses to employ a rule-of-thumb markup in pricing his product because it is "easier to handle and is customary"; nor is it necessarily irrational to fail to act in accordance with one's best judgment when, for example, one introduces an implicit "fudge factor" to allow for an inherent streak of optimism or pessimism of which others tend to be unaware. In a sense, in these instances one might be said to have recourse to a "higher order" of rationality.[19] Furthermore, individuals who upon occasion fail to select the alternative that in light of their preferences would be their most rational choice might very well prefer to behave in a consistently rational

[18] Geoffrey Household, *The Courtesy of Death* (New York: Bantam Books, Inc., 1968), p. 21.

Writing shortly after the turn of the century, Thorstein Veblen commented: "Both the classical school in general and its specialized variant, the marginal-utility school, in particular, take as their common point of departure the traditional psychology of the early nineteenth-century hedonists, which is accepted as a matter of course or of common notoriety and is held quite uncritically.... [But] men's activities differ...in respect of the alertness of the response and nicety of adjustment of irksome pain-cost to apprehended future sensuous gain; but, on the whole, no other ground or line or guidance of conduct than this rationalistic calculus falls properly within the cognizance of the economic hedonists. Such a theory can take account of conduct only insofar as it is rational conduct, guided by deliberate and exhaustively intelligent choice-wise adaptation to the demands of the main chance." ["The Limitations of Marginal Utility," *Journal of Political Economy,* **17**:9 (Nov. 1909), 622–623.]

[19] For an interesting discussion of this point with specific respect to consumer behavior, see James Morgan, "A Review of Recent Research on Consumer Behavior," in Lincoln H. Clark, ed., *Consumer Behavior* (New York: Harper & Row, 1958), pp. 93–219, and p. 104 in particular.

R. M. Cyert, W. R. Dill, and J. G. March, "The Role of Expectations in Business Decision Making," *Administrative Science Quarterly,* **3**:3 (Dec. 1958), 339, point out a tendency for decision makers to *unconsciously* or *semiconsciously* adjust perceptions to hopes. If this be the case, then it might indeed be considered "rational" to *consciously* reassess decisions by presuming that this *subconscious* adjustment has previously occurred. This is different from the possibility of recognizing that another person has provided distorted information—as when, say, the probabilistic judgments of a lower-level manager contain inherent biases that will make him "look good" [see, for example, Donald H. Woods, "Improving Estimates that Involve Uncertainty," *Harvard Business Review,* **44**:4 (July–August 1966), 91–98]—and adjusting this information to correct the biases. In this instance, it would not be rational to do otherwise.

manner, even though human frailties sometimes lead them astray.[20] Nevertheless, none of this precludes the possibility that many of us who are fully aware of certain techniques for rational decision making, and who have the information, capability, and opportunity to behave rationally, will elect not to take advantage of the rationality option.

Decision making, particularly with respect to the business world, has traditionally been considered to be an art, although it is rapidly evolving into a science. Aided and abetted by recent developments in computer technology, and encouraged by the increasing complexity of the modern business world, scientific management and scientific decision making have surged toward the commonplace.[21] In this age, the very thought of bending, folding, or mutilating strikes terror into men's hearts. There is some comfort in the notion that "Computers for heuristic problem solving will replace executives only when the costs per unit of problem-solving capacity are competitive with the costs of executives."[22] But if computers *are* to be given more of our decision-making proxies, this would imply that future decisions will *necessarily* be made in a more rational and precise fashion, as only rational decision rules are likely to be fed to the computer. We suggest that such will indeed be the case, at least for the more mundane problems of choice that management faces. This belief has encouraged the quantitative model-building approach stressed herein. The *need to delegate* decision-making authority in the modern corporation is a concomitant of the replacement of the individual entrepreneur by a managerial hierarchy, as well as the separation of the ownership and management functions. When a single individual can no longer make all of the decisions in which he holds some interest, and when he is compelled to relinquish some responsibility for decision making to others, it is our belief that he will be inclined to look favorably upon decision procedures that tend to generate the selections he would have made himself. We suggest that this is one of the attractions of rules of thumb—to guide the decisions of subordinates in recurrent situations in which the alternatives and their consequences are held within fairly limited bounds.[23]

[20] In "Risk, Ambiguity, and the Savage Axioms," *Quarterly Journal of Economics*, **LXXV**:4 (Nov. 1961), 643–669, Daniel Ellsberg discusses the tendency of decision makers to violate axioms of rational decision making *of which they are aware*, and with particular relish calls attention to occasions upon which such staunch proponents of rational decision processes as L. J. Savage and Howard Raiffa failed to act in accordance with such axioms. From his standpoint, however, Raiffa comments that the axioms do not describe or predict behavior, but merely indicate how people should behave "in complicated situations, *provided* [they] can make choices in a coherent manner in relatively simple, uncomplicated situations" [Howard Raiffa, "Comment," *Quarterly Journal of Economics*, **LXXV**:4 (Nov. 1961), 690]. He goes on to express his gratitude for having his sins of irrationality called to his attention, and asserts that others would adhere to the axioms, as he makes an effort to do, once they saw what it cost them not to do so, and once they really understood the procedures.

[21] For a discussion of the historical evolvement of this movement, see Harold F. Snoddy and Lionel Naum, "Evolution of a 'Science of Managing' in America," *Management Science*, **1**:1 (Oct. 1954), 1–31.

[22] Herbert A. Simon and Allen Newell, "Heuristic Problem Solving: The Next Advance in Operations Research," *Operations Research*, **6**:1 (Jan.–Feb. 1958), 8.

[23] For some extremely thought-provoking discussions of rationality in decision making, and the role of the organization in the development of decision procedures, see James G. March and Herbert A. Simon, *Organizations* (New York: John Wiley & Sons, Inc.,

It is one thing, however, to teach and preach rational decision making, and quite another to impose it on one's self! It is one thing to pay the piper for your own errors of judgment, and quite another to bear the consequences for someone else's errors. It is our view that rational decision making suffers from two very serious defects. First, it is just not very much fun.[24] It is like playing bridge in a foursome where every player knows what he is doing and pays strict attention to the game, or like watching the Green Bay Packers play football. This is not to say that as soon as one proceeds to gather information, consider alternatives, and weigh possible consequences before arriving at a decision, he commits himself to a series of moves from one dull rut to another. The point, rather, is that it is far more pleasant and interesting to make decisions by processing the appropriate information with at least some degree of lassitude and fallibility, instead of transferring the processing function *entirely* into the hands of an insensitive equation and an infallible computer. Since each of us is likely to visit this world but once, he might as well make the most of his all-too-brief stay.

Second, there are some decisions that are simply *too important* to trust to a decision-making algorithm.[25] Many persons are willing to permit a computer service

---

1958). Also see Herbert Simon, *Models of Man* (New York: John Wiley & Sons, Inc., 1957).

In "Oligopoly Theory and Retail Food Pricing" [*Journal of Business*, **XXXVII**:4 (Oct. 1964), 346–363] William J. Baumol, Richard E. Quandt, and Harold T. Shapiro suggest empirical support for the hypothesis that "many firms ignore their competitors when making routine decisions. They are, of course, not unaware of their competitors' existence. But, because of the cost and complexity of the decision process, and the imperfection of the data with which management must work, they are forced to reply on crude rules of thumb which take no explicit account of the likely response by their competitors. It must be emphasized that this hypothesis does not require all of a company's decisions will be based on explicit calculations of good competitive strategy. This view merely applies to day-to-day company decisions, each of which is of limited importance only, even though their cumulative significance for the firm may be very great" (p. 347).

Theodore Levitt ["The Lonely Crowd and the Economic Man," *Quarterly Journal of Economics*, **LXX**:1 (Feb. 1956), 95–116] has remarked that "while the newly emerging other-directed society seems offhand to impose the torpor of conformity and acquiescence upon itself. . . it does not follow either that the concept of the economic man. . . is therefore obsoleted or that. . . the capitalist spirit, with all the vigor and creativeness that this implies, will degenerate into nothing more than the sterile manipulation of impotent symbols. What it may more realistically mean is the generation of a more energetic, a more scientific, a more conscientious, and a more elaborately creative engine for human welfare than even the most romantic and imaginative proselyters of capitalism have been able to conjure in their two hundred years of outspoken advocacy" (p. 116).

[24] The following remarks are directly on the target: "But is it desirable to reduce the field of irrationality? The mind, weary of reasoning, takes refuge in the irrational, finds rest in it. It is useless to turn to reason to resolve the incessant little problems of our daily life; far better to allow the free play of automatic mechanisms and to address ourselves to reason only in important cases. . . . The irrational is not only necessary, it is pleasant, it is the salt of life; irrationality must be credited for carrying us through dreams and away to fairyland, for throwing into the monotony of daily life a note of fantasy. Intense and prolonged rational behavior tends to destroy man's vitality." [Louis Baudin, "Irrationality in Economics," *Quarterly Journal of Economics*, **LXVIII**:4 (Nov. 1954), 501–502.]

[25] Ernest H. Weinwurm, "Limitations of the Scientific Method in Management Science," *Management Science*, **3**:3 (April 1957), 225–233.

to select their *potential* merger candidates of the opposite sex, and to initiate the preliminary negotiations on the basis of the computer's suggestions, but few would allow the computer to make the ultimate choice of whom they should marry (which is not to say that the computer might not do a better job than some have done). Similarly, many who are willing to have their firm's inventory policy guided solely by a computer algorithm, or who will accept the computer's suggestions with respect to *prospective* merger candidates, are likely to be reluctant to have the computer decide when, where, and with whom their firms should merge.

The failure to subscribe to the most appropriate decision procedures and to take advantage of the best available information may have serious consequences. Sacrifices may be exacted for the psychic pleasures accompanying the irrationality of the occasional and traditional "flyer." We suspect, however, that many, if not most, individuals find these sporadic sacrifices tolerable and well worth making. Moreover, in the world of uncertainty in which one makes comparatively few truly monumental decisions, the vagaries of chance could actually work to the benefit of the less rational of two decision makers. Although *on balance* rationality reaps its rewards, an *individual* decision maker's failure to utilize the most appropriate decision-making tools for any *individual* decision does not *have* to have deleterious consequences, nor will his meticulous employment of these tools guarantee uniform success.

Our point is not to argue for irrationality in decision making: we have come too far for that. Instead, we wish to point out that in the real world decision makers with varying objectives will behave with varying degrees of rationality. Still further, these decision makers are *individuals* in every sense of the word. They are not selfless automatons, each one like the other. It is pointless to worry about whether man is basically a risk-evader or a risk-taker, or whether managements tend to be sales, growth, or profits oriented. Different persons have different preferences, and these preferences may rival or complement each other; additionally, interpersonal differences may rival or complement each other.

Therefore, models that we build upon a foundation of the rational entrepreneur guiding the representative firm can only hint at the sacrifices that may accompany irrationality, or the implications of stressing certain objectives rather than others. These models may also indicate the *directions* that decisions will *tend* to take in the real world. They cannot, and should not, be expected to be *perfect* predictors. They are there to be used; they can be helpful; they can point out the relevant considerations and indicate the lines along which a rational decision should proceed. But the models demand a degree of perfection that we are unlikely to achieve in our imperfect world, and we would do well to view them with greater tolerance than that with which they have been endowed by their intolerant proponents.

## EXERCISES

1. Suppose that Associated KNIF's decision-making authority passes into the hands of the risk-taker of Figure 12.1.
   (a) Draw the game tree to correspond to the problem of Section 12.4.
   (b) Estimate the value of sample information to this decision maker.

2. Consider a quantity-setting firm with a total cost curve given by $C = 10Q + 8Q^2$. Management is uncertain as to whether the demand curve is given by $P = 100 - Q$ or $P = 104.5 - Q$. Each of these possibilities is thought to be equally likely. Suppose,

further, that management's risk-preference function in terms of profits $\pi$ is given by $V = \pi^\alpha$.

(a) Determine the optimum output for (i) $\alpha = .5$; (ii) $\alpha = 1$; (iii) $\alpha = 1.5$; (iv) $\alpha = 2.5$; (v) $\alpha = 3.5$.
(b) On the basis of these results, what unwarranted generalizations might one make with respect to the relative output policies of risk-evaders versus risk-takers, and both versus individuals who are linear in risk?
(c) Does risk aversion in Pratt's sense appear to be important?

3. Suppose that the previous management's risk-preference function in terms of profits $\pi$ and sales $R$ is given by $V = 10\pi^\alpha + R^\beta$.

(a) Determine the optimum policy for (i) $\alpha = 1$ and $\beta = 0$; (ii) $\alpha = 0$ and $\beta = 1$; (iii) $\alpha = .5$ and $\beta = .3$; (iv) $\alpha = 2.5$ and $\beta = .3$; (v) $\alpha = .5$ and $\beta = 2.3$.
(b) Do these results suggest anything?

4. A hot dog vendor at the zoo must decide upon the number of hot dogs to prepare for the day. Any "dogs" that he prepares but does not sell are surreptitiously fed to the yaks at the day's end. Hot dogs wholesale for 6¢ and retail for 15¢. The demand for "dogs" may, for all intents and purposes, be assumed to be normally distributed with a mean of $\mu$ and a standard deviation of $\sigma = \mu/10$. The mean, however, is assumed to be a function of the weather. On clear days $\mu \approx 1000$; on overcast days $\mu \approx 600$; on drizzling days $\mu \approx 200$; on pouring-rain days $\mu = 0$.

The hot dog vendor looks out his window and judges the probability of a clear day to be .5, the probability of an overcast day to be .2, and the probability of a drizzle to be .2. His five next-door neighbors all have weather-sensitive but independent corns. Their corns never ache prior to clear days, and they always ache if it is going to pour rain. The probability of a corn's aching, given that an overcast or drizzling day is to occur, is .5 and .8, respectively. Each of the vendor's neighbors is willing to tell the vendor about the state of his corns for $5.

(a) If the vendor is linear in risk and doesn't consult his neighbors, how many hot dogs should he prepare?
(b) If the vendor does consult his neighbors, but determines *in advance* how many neighbors he will consult, how many should he consult?
(c) If all five neighbors collude, how much is the most they could expect the vendor to pay to hear about their troubles?
(d) Determine the answers to these corny questions if the vendor's risk-preference function for profits is given by $V = (1000 + \pi)^{.5}$. What if it is $V = (1000 + \pi)^{2.5}$?

5. (a) Show that for a risk-evading individual with a quadratic risk-preference function, the greater the variance of the potential payoffs in a project, the lesser will be the expected utiles of the project. In the process, develop the underlying basis for the Markowitz portfolio model, and resolve Exercise 5 of Chapter 10 for a specific quadratic risk-preference function.
(b) Discuss the implications of employing the Markowitz model to develop a portfolio for an individual who is a risk-evader with a risk-preference function that is not quadratic, and for individuals who are either linear in risk or risk-takers.

6. Consider the firm of Exercise 12, Chapter 9. Suppose the monopolist judges the probability to be .50 that the total cost function is as stated. He thinks that his fixed costs might actually turn out to be either $500 or $1500, and that these are equally likely possibilities. The unknown factor is the state's pending action on the current franchise tax of $500, and whether it will be doubled, maintained, or repealed (the only alternatives under discussion).

One can learn something about the possible actions of the legislature from after-dinner table-talk with certain well-placed politicos. The probability that a dinner guest from the legislature will hint at a cut, given that there will be a cut, is assessed as $P(HC \mid C) = .8$. The probability that he will hint at a cut, given there will be no change, is assessed as $P(HC \mid N) = .4$; the probability that he will hint at a cut, given an increase, is assessed as $P(HC \mid R) = .2$. Similarly, for the hint that there will not be a change in the tax, the probabilities are assessed as $P(HN \mid C) = .1$, $P(HN \mid N) = .5$, and $P(HN \mid R) = .3$.

Suppose one were to invite a group of independent thinkers to dinner, and that it costs $20 to feed a legislator.

(a) If the entrepreneur is concerned solely with profits and is linear in risk, should he invite anybody to dinner—and, if so, how many persons?

(b) Devise hypothetical risk-preference functions, and indicate whether the previous answer is altered if the entrepreneur is a risk-taker or a risk-evader.

7. Determine the value of perfect information for each of the three entrepreneurs in the previous problem, and resolve the problem using opportunity loss.

8. Combine the statement of the previous problem with the question of Exercise 3(a).

9. How would the answers to Exercises 13, 14, and 15 of Chapter 10 be affected by the assumption of nonlinear risk preferences?

10. Consider the two-person, nonconstant-sum game of Table 7.3. Suppose that one person has a risk-preference function of $V_1 = \pi_1^{.5}$ and the other has a function given by $V_2 = (.0000001)\pi_2^{.3}$.

(a) Suggest strategies for each duopolist.

(b) What would be the Nash solution?

11. Consider a firm that is faced with the following payoff table (in profits):

| | $E_1$ | $E_2$ | $E_3$ | $E_4$ | $E_5$ |
|---|---|---|---|---|---|
| $X_1$ | 100 | 70 | 50 | 100 | 200 |
| $X_2$ | 200 | 50 | 80 | 70 | 60 |
| $X_3$ | 40 | 80 | 100 | 70 | 150 |
| $X_4$ | 75 | 100 | 200 | 200 | 50 |

The firm's analysts are being very vague in their impressions with respect to $P(E_j)$, the probabilities of the $E_j$ ($j = 1, \ldots, 5$). They do believe, however, that the following relationships hold: $P(E_1) \geq 2P(E_2)$; $P(E_1) + P(E_2) \geq P(E_3) + P(E_4) + P(E_5)$; $P(E_3) \geq P(E_4) + P(E_5)$; and $P(E_2) \leq P(E_4)$. What $X_i$ would you suggest for a specific risk-evader, a specific risk-taker, and for one who is linear in risk?

12. Formulate the general case of the previous problem.

13. (a) Discuss conditions under which the following functions suggested by Pratt ("Risk Aversion in the Small and in the Large," p. 133) will be strictly decreasing risk-averse risk-preference functions ($x > 0$):

(1) $V = (x + d)^q$. (2) $V = \log (x + d)$.
(3) $V = -(x + d)^{-q}$. (4) $V = [1 + (\alpha x + \beta)^{-2}]^{-1/2}$.
(5) $V = -c_1 e^{-cx} - c_2 e^{-dx}$. (6) $V = \log (x + d + [(x + d)^2 + b])$.
(7) $V = \arctan (\alpha x + \beta)$. (8) $V = \log (1 - (\alpha x + \beta)^{-1})$.
(9) $V = -[1 - (\alpha x + \beta)^{-2}]^{-1/2}$. (10) $V = \log (d_1 + \log (x + d_2))$.

(b) Discuss the properties of the following functions, also suggested by Pratt:

(1) $V = x^{1-c}$.
(2) $V = \log x$.
(3) $V = -x^{-(c-1)}$.

14. By analyzing the risk-preference function $V = -e^{-x}$, discuss the advantages of $r(x)$ as opposed to $-d^2v(x)/dx^2$ as a measure of risk aversion.

# 13

# RECENT DEVELOPMENTS AND THE THEORY OF THE FIRM: Price-Quantity Determination under Uncertainty

## 13.1 INTRODUCTION

After a good deal of time and effort, we mave managed to reach a conclusion that might not appear very striking: namely, different people can be cast into the same situation and react differently, and the course of action chosen by any one person will depend upon the circumstances surrounding the situation into which he has been thrust.[1] This suggests that if, on the one hand, the economist wishes to don his analyst's hat and build models to assist in managerial decision making, he will have to tailor his general *models* to the specific *needs* of a particular management. The model builder thereby constructs impersonal models for management's personal use, and these require the injection of subjective ingredients that are unlikely to be invariant from one managerial unit to another.

On the other hand, if the economist wishes to don his theorist's hat and build models to help him speculate about the directions that managerial decisions might be *anticipated* to take, he can do this too, provided he tailors the general *conclusions* to the specific *characteristics* of particular classes of management. The model builder thereby infers from impersonal models the behavioral *tendencies* of managements endowed with certain personal characteristics, and the potential variation in these characteristics suggests that his models will not be amenable to dogmatic generalities that will be invariant from one situation to another.

[1] This is not to oppose Simon's position that: "Two persons, given the same possible alternatives, the same values, the same knowledge, can rationally reach only the same decision." [Herbert A. Simon, *Administrative Behavior* (New York: The Macmillan Company, 1958), p. 241.] In the present context, however, even if one accepts the assumption that rationality reigns supreme, the likelihood that decision makers will share similar values (including attitudes towards risk) and similar knowledge would seem fairly remote. Assuming, as we do, a set of continuous functions and, in effect, an *infinite* set of decisions to choose from, the scope for departures from sameness among entrepreneurs of neoclassical firms would seem to be comparably greater. The sameness that we often feel we see in decision making would stem from the need to select from a fairly small, finite set of alternatives.

In this chapter we shall emphasize the rather significant differences that can arise in the inferences drawn about entrepreneurial behavior when both uncertainty *and* attitude towards risk are injected into the neoclassical model. These ingredients can enter the model in a variety of ways; in each case their implications can differ. We shall therefore support the previous arguments with several of the more interesting models suggested for the analysis of price-quantity determination under uncertainty.

## 13.2 LINEAR RISK PREFERENCES

Despite the recognition that in reality uncertainty will pervade the functions employed in the traditional marginal analysis, and despite the awareness that probabilistic elements would thereby be implicitly involved in price-quantity determination in the real world as well as in the neoclassical firm, economists have tended to neglect the implications of probability and uncertainty for the firm's decision variables.[2] This neglect ended in 1959 with Edwin Mills' article "Uncertainty and Price Theory."[3] Mills showed that even when we assume the entrepreneur to have linear risk preferences, the *explicit* incorporation of randomness in the demand curve will have unanticipated and perhaps ungeneralizable consequences.

Directly on the heels of the Mills article, A. A. Walters considered the *explicit* incorporation of randomness into the services derived from the factors of production.[4] Walters showed, for the special case of fixed technological coefficients, as we previously showed for the more general class of production functions, that even assuming *linear* risk preferences uncertainty will have unanticipated and perhaps ungeneralizable consequences for the factors' marginal physical product curves and, as previously indicated, for factor demand and output as well.

The procession of ensuing efforts has concentrated on introducing random elements into microeconomic theory via the demand curve. The certainty that is assumed on the product and cost side is certainly debatable; but, since our twofold purpose here is to point out that the effects of uncertainty can be many and varied, and to indicate how uncertainty can and should be incorporated into an otherwise deterministic model, the attention that we shall now give to these recent developments is not misplaced, nor are the implications misleading. As ground rules, in this section

[2] For brief remarks showing varying degrees of awareness or the lack thereof with respect to the importance of uncertainty see the following: Fritz Machlup, "Marginal Analysis and Empirical Research," *American Economic Review*, **XXXVI**:4, part 1 (Sept. 1946), 521; A. G. Hart, "Risk, Uncertainty, and the Unprofitability of Compounding Probabilities," in the American Economic Association's *Readings in the Theory of Income Distribution* (Philadelphia: The Blakiston Co., 1949), p. 549; J. Fred Weston, "A Generalized Uncertainty Theory of Profit," *American Economic Review*, **XL**:1 (March 1950), 49; R. M. Cyert, W. R. Dill, and J. G. March, "The Role of Expectations in Business Decision Making," *Administrative Science*, **3**:3 (Dec. 1958), 309; Edith T. Penrose, *The Theory of the Growth of the Firm* (New York: John Wiley & Sons, Inc., 1959), p. 13; Julius Margolis, "Traditional and Revisionist Theories of the Firm: A Comment," *Journal of Business*, **XXXII**:2 (April 1959), 182; and more extensively, Karl H. Borch, *The Economics of Uncertainty* (Princeton, N.J.: Princeton University Press, 1968).

[3] *Quarterly Journal of Economics*, **LXXIII**:1 (Feb. 1959), 116–130.

[4] "Marginal Productivity and Probability Distributions of Factor Services," *Economic Journal*, **LXX**:278 (June 1960), 325–330.

we shall consider two models that assume linear risk preferences; in later sections we shall consider models in which this assumption is dropped.

## a. Random Demand and the Price- and Quantity-Setter

Mills posits a situation in which the firm's known total cost function is given by $C = c(Q^*)$, where $Q^*$ is the predetermined and unalterable production for a time period of length $T$. Demand at a price of $P$ is given by $Q = D(P, u)$, where $u$ is a random variable, distributed by $g(u)$ with zero mean. Thus

$$\bar{u} = E[u] = \int_{-\infty}^{\infty} ug(u)\, du = 0.$$

Further, $u$ is distributed independently of $P$, so that we can write $Q = D(P, u) = D(P) + u$.[5] Thus, for any price $P^*$, expected demand is given by $\bar{Q} = E[Q \mid P^*] = E[D(P^*) + u] = E[D(P^*)] + E[u] = D(P^*)$.

Consider the case of a single-period time horizon. By assumption, output not sold during $T$ is scrapped without bringing in any revenue. The firm's total revenue from producing $Q^*$ and setting a price of $P$ will be a two-segment function: (1) $R_1 = PQ$ for $Q \leq Q^*$; (2) $R_2 = PQ^*$ for $Q \geq Q^*$. The first segment is the total revenue received when no more units are demanded at a price of $P$ than have been produced; the second segment is the total revenue received from selling total output when at least as many units are demanded at $P$ as have been produced.

Profit is given by either $\pi_1 = PQ - c(Q^*)$ or $\pi_2 = PQ^* - c(Q^*)$, depending upon demand. *Expected* profit is therefore given by

$$E[\pi] = \int_0^{Q^*} PQf(Q)\, dQ + \int_{Q^*}^{\infty} PQ^*f(Q)\, dQ - c(Q^*), \tag{13.1}$$

where for convenience we have written $g(u) \equiv g(Q - D(P)) \equiv f(Q)$. If the entrepreneur has linear risk preferences in terms of profits, and assuming his sole interest is profit, then (13.1) becomes his criterion function and the maximization of expected profit becomes his goal.

Expected profit will be maximized at values of $P$ and $Q^*$ such that $\partial E[\pi]/\partial P = 0$ and $\partial E[\pi]/\partial Q^* = 0$; and, $\partial^2 E[\pi]/\partial Q^{*2} < 0$ and $[\partial^2 E[\pi]/\partial Q^{*2}][\partial^2 E[\pi]/\partial P^2] > [\partial^2 E[\pi]/\partial P\, \partial Q^*]^2$. First, differentiating with respect to price, we determine

$$\frac{\partial E[\pi]}{\partial P} = \int_0^{Q^*} Qf(Q)\, dQ + P \int_0^{Q^*} \frac{dQ}{dP} f(Q)\, dQ + Q^* \int_{Q^*}^{\infty} f(Q)\, dQ, \tag{13.2}$$

since (1) $df(Q)/dP = 0$ by the additivity assumption with respect to the random variable $u$, and (2) $Q^*$ is held fixed. Writing $\bar{Q} = \int_0^{\infty} Qf(Q)\, dQ = \int_0^{Q^*} Qf(Q)\, dQ + \int_{Q^*}^{\infty} Qf(Q)\, dQ$, we have $\int_0^{Q^*} Qf(Q)\, dQ = \bar{Q} - \int_{Q^*}^{\infty} Qf(Q)\, dQ$. Hence, the first of the first-order conditions can be written

$$\frac{\partial E[\pi]}{\partial P} = \bar{Q} - \int_{Q^*}^{\infty} Qf(Q)\, dQ + P \int_0^{Q^*} \frac{dQ}{dP} f(Q)\, dQ + Q^* \int_{Q^*}^{\infty} f(Q)\, dQ = 0,$$

[5] Throughout this and succeeding discussions we shall assume continuity and differentiability, including the higher-order differentiation, of the functions posited. Here, although we treat $u$ as if $-\infty \leq u \leq \infty$, within "the relevant range" of $Q$ and $P$, the requirement that consumers remain buyers and not sellers demands $Q \geq 0$, so that $g(u)$ is truncated to assure $D(P) + u \geq 0$.

or

$$P^* = \frac{\bar{Q} - \int_{Q^*}^{\infty} (Q - Q^*)f(Q)\, dQ}{-\int_0^{Q^*} \frac{dQ}{dP} f(Q)\, dQ}. \tag{13.3}$$

Note that $\int_{Q^*}^{\infty} (Q - Q^*)f(Q)\, dQ$ is simply the mean *excess* demand. Under the common assumption that $dQ/dP < 0$, the denominator will be positive. Hence, we determine an optimal price $P^* > 0$ so long as the mean demand at $P^*$ exceeds the mean excess, or *unsatisfied*, demand at $P^*$ with respect to $Q^*$.

To give economic meaning to (13.3), note that the expression in the denominator of (13.3) may be written as $-\int_0^{Q^*} (dQ/dP)f(Q)\, dQ = \int_{Q^*}^{\infty} (dQ/dP)f(Q)\, dQ - \int_0^{\infty} (dQ/dP)f(Q)\, dQ$. Upon our making this substitution into (13.3), combining terms and rearranging, (13.3) becomes

$$P^* \int_0^{\infty} \left(\frac{dQ}{dP}\right) f(Q)\, dQ + \bar{Q} = P^* \int_{Q^*}^{\infty} \left(\frac{dQ}{dP}\right) f(Q)\, dQ + \int_{Q^*}^{\infty} (Q - Q^*)f(Q)\, dQ. \tag{13.3'}$$

In the certainty case with certain demand of $\bar{Q} = D(P^*)$ at $P^*$, total revenue is given by $\bar{R} = P^*\bar{Q}$, and $d\bar{R}/dP^* = \bar{Q} + (d\bar{Q}/dP^*)P^*$. Now, in the *present uncertainty* case, $Q = D(P) + u$ because $dQ/dP$ is independent of $u$. Thus, $dQ/dP$ may be factored out of both integrals in (13.3') in which it appears. With $\int_0^{\infty} f(Q)\, dQ = 1$, the left side of (13.3') is therefore exactly $d\bar{R}/dP^*$, or the change in expected revenue when price changes. Further, $\bar{L} = P^* \int_{Q^*}^{\infty} (Q - Q^*)f(Q)\, dQ$ is the expected (opportunity) *loss* from a failure to have more than $Q^*$ units available to sell at $P^*$. Hence $d\bar{L}/dP^* = \int_{Q^*}^{\infty} (Q - Q^*)f(Q)\, dQ + P^* \int_{Q^*}^{\infty} (dQ/dP)f(Q)\, dQ$, evaluated at $P^*$, is the change in expected loss when price changes. (13.3'), together with the second-order conditions noted below, therefore suggests that price is lowered to the point where the increase in expected revenue exactly equals the increase in expected (opportunity) loss. A lower price will fail to increase expected revenue to the extent that it increases the expected loss; a higher price will reduce expected revenue to a greater extent than it reduces the expected loss.

To determine the optimum output level, we first differentiate $E[\pi]$ with respect to $Q^*$,

$$\frac{\partial E[\pi]}{\partial Q^*} = P \int_{Q^*}^{\infty} f(Q)\, dQ - \frac{dc}{dQ^*}.\text{[6]} \tag{13.4}$$

[6] It is important to recognize here and in succeeding analysis that we are differentiating integrals in which the variable of differentiation appears as a limit. Thus, when differentiating the first term in (13.1) with respect to $Q^*$ we obtain $+PQ^*f(Q^*)$, since $Q^*$ is the upper limit; the derivative of the second term is $P \int_{Q^*}^{\infty} f(Q)\, dQ - PQ^*f(Q^*)$, since $Q^*$ is the lower limit. The $PQ^*f(Q^*)$ expressions cancel each other.

As the second of the first-order conditions, then, $\partial E[\pi]/\partial Q^* = 0$, or

$$P \int_{Q^*}^{\infty} f(Q)\, dQ = \frac{dc}{dQ^*} = MC(Q^*). \tag{13.5}$$

Since $\int_{Q^*}^{\infty} f(Q)\, dQ$ is the probability of selling the marginal unit produced in the batch of $Q^*$ units, $P \int_{Q^*}^{\infty} f(Q)\, dQ$ is conveniently defined as *expected* marginal revenue. Given a price of $P$, the firm produces $Q^*$ units so as to equate expected marginal revenue to marginal cost.

For both first-order conditions to hold simultaneously, we note that with (13.5) satisfied at $P^*$ we have $P^* = \dfrac{dc}{dQ^*} \Big/ \int_{Q^*}^{\infty} f(Q)\, dQ$. Recalling the crucial assumption that $dQ/dP$ is independent of $u$, we may rewrite (13.3′) as $d\bar{R}/dP^* = P^* (d\bar{Q}/dP^*) \int_{Q^*}^{\infty} f(Q)\, dQ + \int_{Q^*}^{\infty} (Q - Q^*)f(Q)\, dQ$. Substituting the expression for $P^*$ obtained from (13.5) into the latter, we determine

$$\frac{d\bar{R}}{dP^*} = \left(\frac{dc}{dQ^*}\right)\left(\frac{d\bar{Q}}{dP^*}\right) + \int_{Q^*}^{\infty} (Q - Q^*)f(Q)\, dQ. \tag{13.6}$$

Since in the certainty case $\bar{R} = P^*\bar{Q}$, the *riskless* marginal revenue is given by $MR = d\bar{R}/d\bar{Q} = (d\bar{R}/dP^*)(dP^*/d\bar{Q}) = (d\bar{R}/dP^*)/(d\bar{Q}/dP^*)$. Upon dividing both sides of (13.6) by $d\bar{Q}/dP^*$, we obtain

$$MR = MC + \frac{\int_{Q^*}^{\infty} (Q - Q^*)f(Q)\, dQ}{d\bar{Q}/dP^*}, \tag{13.6′}$$

where the second term on the right side is necessarily nonpositive. Assuming the second-order conditions hold,[7] (13.6′) therefore states that under this form of uncertainty, price and output will be determined such that riskless marginal revenue is something *less than* (or at most equal to) marginal cost.

[7] The second-order conditions require the following assumptions:

(1) $$\frac{\partial^2 E[\pi]}{\partial Q^{*2}} = -\frac{d^2c}{dQ^{*2}} - Pf(Q^*) < 0,$$

which holds when the total cost curve is convex, or in effect when the expected marginal revenue declines more rapidly than marginal cost;

(2) $$\frac{\partial^2 E[\pi]}{\partial P^2} = \left[2\left(\frac{dQ}{dP}\right) + P\left(\frac{d^2Q}{dP^2}\right)\right] \int_0^{Q^*} f(Q)\, dQ < 0,$$

or the riskless marginal revenue curve must be downward sloping;

(3) $$\left[\frac{\partial^2 E[\pi]}{\partial P^2}\right]\left[\frac{\partial^2 E[\pi]}{\partial Q^{*2}}\right] = -\left[\frac{d^2c}{dQ^{*2}} + Pf(Q^*)\right]\left[2\left(\frac{dQ}{dP}\right) + P\left(\frac{d^2Q}{dP^2}\right)\right] \int_0^{Q^*} f(Q)\, dQ > \left[\int_{Q^*}^{\infty} f(Q)\, dQ\right]^2 = \left[\frac{\partial^2 E[\pi]}{\partial Q^*\, \partial P}\right]^2,$$

the latter placing a restriction on the probability density.

To see the implications of this, define $P^0$ as the price that equates riskless marginal revenue evaluated at $P^0$ to marginal cost evaluated at an output of $Q^*$, or $MR(P^0) = MC(Q^*)$. It immediately follows from (13.6′), and the second-order conditions, that with $MR(P^*) \leq MC(Q^*)$, $P^* \leq P^0$. The equalities hold only when there is no expected excess demand at $P^*$. When marginal cost is constant, the certainty output would be some $Q = \bar{Q}$ to be sold at a price of $\hat{P}$, and such that $MC(\bar{Q}) = MC(Q^*)$. Hence $MR(P^0) = MC(Q^*) = MC(\bar{Q}) = MR(\hat{P})$, and $P^0 = \hat{P}$. Therefore $P^* \leq P^0 = \hat{P}$, or the optimal price under uncertainty is *less than or equal to* the optimal certainty price. In effect, a lower price is charged to lessen the probability of not being able to sell all that is produced.

Although it is clear that with constant marginal cost risk effects a lower price from the price-quantity-setter than would obtain under certainty, the effects on output are not generalizable. That is, with optimal certainty output of $\bar{Q}$, we can have $\bar{Q} \gtreqless Q^*$. With rising (falling) marginal cost, if $\bar{Q} \geq (\leq)\ Q^*$, then $MC(\bar{Q}) \geq MC(Q^*)$. Hence, $MR(\hat{P}) \geq MR(P^0)$ and $\hat{P} \geq P^0 \geq P^*$. Moreover, even with rising (falling) marginal cost and $\bar{Q} \leq (\geq)\ Q^*$ so that $MC(\bar{Q}) \leq MC(Q^*)$, we might still find $\hat{P} \geq P^*$. This can occur if average demand under uncertainty is great enough to cause large expected excess demand if $Q^*$ were to be sold at a price of $\hat{P}$. Then, a reduction in price below $\hat{P}$ could lower *riskless marginal* revenue substantially while not appreciably influencing expected excess demand. That is, the left side of (13.6′) is greater than the right side at $\hat{P}$, and a price below $\hat{P}$ reduces $MR$ without creating much more expected *or* unsatisfied demand.

It is apparent from these results that even in the case of linear risk preferences the effects of *explicitly* incorporating elements of uncertainty into a microeconomic model of the firm can be profound. It should also be noted that this analysis can be extended to cover more than a single period. If this is done, one might also allow for the possibility of selling unsold output in succeeding periods. Mills demonstrates the intuitively appealing fact that this will tend to raise the optimal level of output when, after allowing for carrying charges and the like, excess output brings in *some* revenue (as opposed to zero revenue in the one-period case). When marginal cost is constant, we will have $P^* \leq \hat{P}$ in any case, but: "When marginal cost is falling, the effect of long-run considerations is to strengthen the tendency for price to be less than its riskless level. When marginal cost is rising, there is a greater likelihood that price will exceed its riskless level than there is in the one-period case."[8]

## b. Random Demand and the Price-Taker

A second demonstration of the potential impact of uncertainty on a neoclassical firm is due to Jacques H. Drèze and Jean J. Gabszewicz.[9] They analyze an industry in which there are $n$ like firms each of which has a known *cubic* total cost curve, $C_i = \gamma + Q_i - (\alpha/2)Q_i^2 + (\beta/3)Q_i^3$, where $Q_i$ is the $i$th firm's output. It is assumed that fixed costs $\gamma \geq 0$, and that $\alpha, \beta > 0$ to assure a U-shaped average cost curve. Industry demand is perfectly inelastic, but is a random variable with *symmetric* probability density of $f(Q)$ such that $E[Q] = \int Qf(Q)\,dQ = \bar{Q}$, $E[(Q - \bar{Q})^2] = \sigma_Q^2 > 0$. Because of the symmetry, $E[(Q - \bar{Q})^3] = 0$.

[8] Edwin S. Mills, *Price, Output, and Inventory Policy* (New York: John Wiley & Sons, Inc., 1962), p. 117. For further discussion, see Chapters 6 and 7.

[9] "Demand Fluctuations, Capacity Utilization and Prices," *Operations Research Verfahren*, **3** (1967), 119–141.

In the purely competitive industry under certainty, this situation would lead to the equation of the horizontal sum of the individual marginal cost curves (that is, the industry supply curve) with the fixed demand curve. Each firm would be a price-taker and produce at the point of minimum average cost (since they all have the same cost functions, with free entry the number of firms under certainty $\hat{n}$ is such that they are *all* marginal firms). Among the *several* issues raised by Drèze and Gabszewicz is whether they will also produce at minimum average cost under uncertainty. The answer, as we shall see, is in the negative.

Under uncertainty, it is assumed that with free entry and linear risk preferences, firms will continue to enter the industry so long as expected profits are nonnegative. The industry will thus evolve into an $n^*$-firm industry in which each firm produces so as to equate the price determined in the market to marginal cost. This output will be $Q_i = Q/n^*$, as the firms are alike in every respect, and they share equally in industry output. The probability of $Q_i$ is given by $h(Q_i) = f(Q)$. Equilibrium is achieved when *expected* profit $E[\pi] = 0$, or when $E[PQ_i - C_i] = E[MC_i \cdot Q_i - C_i] = E[MC_i \cdot Q_i] - E[C_i] = 0$, since $P = MC_i$. Note that $MC_i = dC_i/dQ_i$. The issue we shall be concerned with here is whether under these circumstances *expected* output will be at the point of minimum average cost.

To determine this, we shall obtain the Taylor's expansions for $E[MC_i \cdot Q_i]$ and $E[C_i]$. The expressions are simplified by the following: (1) $d^kC_i/dQ_i^k = 0$ for $k > 3$ because $C_i$ is a cubic function of $Q_i$; (2) $E[(Q_i - \bar{Q})^3] = 0$ by the assumption that $f(Q)$, and hence $h(Q_i)$, is symmetric. Expanding around $E[Q_i] = \bar{Q}_i$, and taking the expectations on both sides, we therefore obtain the following:

$$E[MC_i \cdot Q_i] = MC_i \cdot \bar{Q}_i + E\left[(Q_i - \bar{Q}_i)\frac{d(MC_i \cdot Q_i)}{dQ_i}\right] + \left(\frac{1}{2}\right)E\left[(Q_i - \bar{Q}_i)^2\frac{d^2(MC_i \cdot Q_i)}{dQ_i^2}\right]; \qquad (13.7)$$

$$E[C_i] = C_i + E\left[(Q_i - \bar{Q}_i)\frac{dC_i}{dQ_i}\right] + \left(\frac{1}{2}\right)E\left[(Q_i - \bar{Q}_i)^2\frac{d^2C_i}{dQ_i^2}\right], \qquad (13.8)$$

where terms such as $MC_i$, $C_i$, $d^k(MC_i \cdot Q_i)/dQ_i^k$ and $d^kC_i/dQ_i^k$ are evaluated at $\bar{Q}_i$. Because of the two simplifications noted, the higher-order terms disappear. Thus, (13.7) and (13.8) may be written as follows:

$$E[MC_i \cdot Q_i] = MC_i \cdot \bar{Q}_i + \left(\frac{\sigma_{Q_i}^2}{2}\right)\left(\frac{2d^2C_i}{dQ_i^2} + \frac{\bar{Q}_i d^3C_i}{dQ_i^3}\right); \qquad (13.7')$$

$$E[C_i] = C_i + \left(\frac{\sigma_{Q_i}^2}{2}\right)\left(\frac{d^2C_i}{dQ_i^2}\right). \qquad (13.8')$$

When expected profit is zero, (13.7′) and (13.8′) will be equal. Equating the two aud rearranging terms yields

$$MC_i = \left(\frac{C_i}{\bar{Q}_i}\right) - \left(\frac{\sigma_{Q_i}^2}{2}\right)\left[\frac{d^3C_i}{dQ_i^3} + \frac{\frac{d^2C_i}{dQ_i^2}}{\bar{Q}_i}\right]. \qquad (13.9)$$

$C_i/\bar{Q}_i$ is the *average* cost of producing $\bar{Q}_i$, since as noted $C_i$ is evaluated at $\bar{Q}_i$. Similarly, $MC_i$ is the *marginal* cost of producing $\bar{Q}_i$. The expression in brackets is readily determined to be positive for $\bar{Q}_i > \alpha/4\beta$, and $\sigma^2_{Q_i}$ is necessarily positive when demand is random (it is zero otherwise). It therefore follows that with marginal and average costs evaluated at the $i$th firm's *expected* output, $MC_i < AC_i$; or, since the average cost curve is convex, *expected* output is *less than* that output which would minimize average cost. Under certainty, $\sigma^2_{Q_i} = 0$ and $MC_i = AC_i$. Drèze and Gabszewicz therefore conclude that "under demand fluctuations, free entry and competition may lead to excess capacity *on the average*. Hence, any inference, drawn from average underutilization of capacity, to the effect that imperfect or monopolistic competition prevails, is unwarranted if the data comes from firms confronted with demand fluctuations."[10]

Once more, then, we see that even if we make the simplest assumption about risk preferences, and even if we assume the universality of the assumption, the explicit recognition of a very simple form of uncertainty can markedly alter the inferences drawn from the neoclassical model.

## 13.3 NONLINEAR RISK PREFERENCES

We have already seen that the introduction of nonlinear risk preferences will affect the inferences drawn from the Oi and Tisdell cases. We shall next consider several alternative models offering additional support for the argument that attitude towards risk is too crucial a factor to ignore in the presence of uncertainty.

### a. Random Demand and the Price-Taker

Hymans[11] has analyzed a situation analogous to that considered by Mills. In Hymans' case, however, it is assumed that the firm is one of *many* profit-oriented firms and cannot set price. Instead, the firm is a price-taker in a "competitive environment" in which industry demand is random. Each firm produces its output of $Q^*$ (the subscript $i$ is deleted for convenience) under the assumption that, at the market price of $P$ at which all sellers sell, the demand for its product will be given by $Q = D(P, u)$, where $u$ is a random variable distributed by $g(u)$. Thus, given the market price of $P$, $Q$ itself becomes a random variable. In accordance with our earlier notation, we denote the probability density of $Q$ by $f(Q)$.

It is assumed that the firm scraps all unsold output. Thus, as in Mills' case, the profit function is defined in two segments: $\pi_1 = PQ - c(Q^*)$ for $Q \leq Q^*$; $\pi_2 = PQ^* - c(Q^*)$ for $Q \geq Q^*$, where the total cost curve $C = c(Q)$ is assumed to be a convex function of $Q$.

Expected profit is once again given by (13.1). With a risk-preference function in terms of profits of $V = v(\pi)$, the equation comparable to (13.1) is

$$E[V] = \int_0^{Q^*} v[PQ - c(Q^*)]f(Q)\, dQ + \int_{Q^*}^{\infty} v[PQ^* - c(Q^*)]f(Q)\, dQ. \tag{13.10}$$

Since the firm only exercises control over $Q^*$, the entrepreneur prefers an output of $Q^*$ such that $dE[V]/dQ^* = 0$ and $d^2E[V]/dQ^{*2} < 0$. We therefore determine

$$\frac{dE[V]}{dQ^*} = \int_0^{Q^*} \frac{dv}{d\pi}\frac{d\pi_1}{dQ^*} f(Q)\, dQ + \int_{Q^*}^{\infty} \frac{dv}{d\pi}\frac{d\pi_2}{dQ^*} f(Q)\, dQ.$$

[10] *Ibid.*, p. 140.

[11] Saul H. Hymans, "The Price-Taker: Uncertainty, Utility, and the Supply Function," *International Economic Review*, **7**:3 (Sept. 1966), 346–366.

Letting $dv/d\pi = v'$, the latter becomes

$$\frac{dE[V]}{dQ^*} = \int_0^{Q^*} v'\left(-\frac{dc}{dQ^*}\right) f(Q)\, dQ + \int_{Q^*}^{\infty} v'\left(P - \frac{dc}{dQ^*}\right) f(Q)\, dQ. \qquad (13.11)$$

Writing

$$\int_0^{\infty} v' f(Q)\, dQ = \int_0^{Q^*} v' f(Q)\, dQ + \int_{Q^*}^{\infty} v' f(Q)\, dQ,$$

noting that $P$ and $dc/dQ^*$ are constants and may be taken outside the integrals, and rearranging terms, we may write (13.11) as

$$\frac{dE[V]}{dQ^*} = \left(P - \frac{dc}{dQ^*}\right) \int_0^{\infty} v' f(Q)\, dQ - P \int_0^{Q^*} v' f(Q)\, dQ. \qquad (13.11')$$

The second-order condition $d^2E[V]/dQ^{*2} < 0$ can be shown to hold where $dE[V]/dQ^* = 0$.[12] Hence, $E[V]$ is maximized at an output $Q^*$ such that[13]

$$\frac{P - \dfrac{dc}{dQ^*}}{P} = \frac{\int_0^{Q^*} v' f(Q)\, dQ}{\int_0^{\infty} v' f(Q)\, dQ}. \qquad (13.12)$$

In the case of linear risk preferences, $v'$ is a constant and can be factored out of both numerator and denominator on the right side of (13.12) and then canceled; and $\int_0^{\infty} f(Q)\, dQ = 1$. When we rearrange terms and note that $1 - \int_0^{Q^*} f(Q)\, dQ = \int_{Q^*}^{\infty} f(Q)\, dQ$, (13.12) results in the equilibrium condition $P \int_{Q^*}^{\infty} f(Q)\, dQ = dc/dQ^*$. The latter is precisely (13.5). Now, however, the firm does not control price, only output.

[12] This remark must be qualified for the risk-taker. Specifically,

$$\frac{d^2E[V]}{dQ^{*2}} = -\left(\frac{d^2c}{dQ^{*2}}\right) \int_0^{\infty} v' f(Q)\, dQ + \left(-\frac{dc}{dQ^*}\right)^2 \int_0^{Q^*} v'' f(Q)\, dQ + \left(P - \frac{dc}{dQ^*}\right)^2 \int_{Q^*}^{\infty} v'' f(Q)\, dQ.$$

For one linear in risk, $v' > 0$ and $v'' = 0$; $d^2c/dQ^{*2} > 0$ by assumption, and therefore $d^2E[V]/dQ^{*2} < 0$. If $V$ is a strictly concave function, $v' > 0$ and $v'' < 0$. Again, then, with all three terms in the equation negative, $d^2E[V]/dQ^{*2} < 0$. If, however, we have a risk-taker and $V$ is a strictly convex function, $v'' > 0$. In this case, we *might* have $d^2E[V]/dQ^2 > 0$, and the first-order condition would define a minimum rather than a maximum. Succeeding statements about the risk-taker must therefore be evaluated with this qualification in mind.

[13] It is interesting to note that the term on the left, $(P - dc/dQ^*)/P$, is Lerner's index of monopoly power. With price fixed and $d^2c/dQ^{*2} > 0$, (13.12) suggests that the firm's monopoly power is a decreasing function of its output level—at any price. As we shall see, the greater the willingness to accept risk, the greater will be the output level, at a given price; but in any event the output level will be less than the certainty level. This leads to the further suggestion that as the competitor's propensity to take risk increases, his monopoly power decreases. In effect, he comes closer to behaving as would a pure competitor under certainty having no monopoly power.

In the case of nonlinear risk preferences, rearranging terms, we may rewrite (13.12) as

$$P\left[\frac{\int_{Q*}^{\infty} v'f(Q)\,dQ}{\int_{0}^{\infty} v'f(Q)\,dQ}\right] = \frac{dc}{dQ*}. \tag{13.12$'$}$$

We are interested in determining whether the optimal $Q*$ will be greater or lesser as we consider the risk-evader versus the risk-taker versus the entrepreneur who is linear in risk. To analyze this, let us compare (13.12′) for a risk-evader with a (strictly) concave risk-preference function, with (13.12′) for an entrepreneur who is linear in risk. For the latter, let $v' = k =$ a constant. In particular, we shall be interested in whether

$$\left[\frac{\int_{Q*}^{\infty} v'f(Q)\,dQ}{\int_{0}^{\infty} v'f(Q)\,dQ}\right] \lesseqgtr \int_{Q*}^{\infty} f(Q)\,dQ, \tag{13.13}$$

where $Q*$ is the risk-evader's preferred output level. If $<$ ($>$) holds, then the entrepreneur who is linear in risk will want to increase (reduce) his output above (below) $Q*$ in order to achieve the equality in (13.12′). Let us rewrite (13.13) as follows:

$$\int_{Q*}^{\infty} v'f(Q)\,dQ \;?\; \int_{0}^{\infty} v'f(Q)\,dQ \int_{Q*}^{\infty} f(Q)\,dQ. \tag{13.13$'$}$$

Noting that $dv/d\pi$ is *constant* at $dv(Q*)/d\pi(Q*) = \hat{v}'$ for $Q \geq Q*$ (since profits do not increase above the $\pi_2$ level even when demand exceeds $Q*$), we may write (13.13′) as

$$\hat{v}' \int_{Q*}^{\infty} f(Q)\,dQ \;?\; \int_{0}^{\infty} v'f(Q)\,dQ \int_{Q*}^{\infty} f(Q)\,dQ$$

or

$$\hat{v}' \;?\; \int_{0}^{\infty} v'f(Q)\,dQ. \tag{13.13$''$}$$

But $\int_{0}^{\infty} v'f(Q)\,dQ = \int_{0}^{Q*} v'f(Q)\,dQ + \hat{v}' \int_{Q*}^{\infty} f(Q)\,dQ$. Hence, (13.13″) may be written as

$$\hat{v}'\left[\int_{0}^{Q*} f(Q)\,dQ\right] \;?\; \int_{0}^{Q*} v'f(Q)\,dQ. \tag{13.13$'''$}$$

Now, $dv'/dQ = v''(d\pi/dQ) = v''P$. Therefore with $V$ a concave function and $v'' < 0$, $v'$ is a decreasing function of $Q$. Hence $\hat{v}'$ is necessarily no greater than any $v'$ term on the right side of (13.13‴). They are equal at $Q*$. It immediately follows that $? = <$, and the risk-evader prefers a smaller output to that preferred by the entrepreneur who is linear in risk. By an analogous argument, and with the qualification of footnote 12, the risk-taker prefers a larger output to that preferred by the "linear" entrepreneur. It should also be remarked, however, that if the solution to (13.12′) is unique, and if the second-order condition is violated for the risk-taker, he will want to move as far away as possible from this $Q*$. Thus he will produce either 0 or $\infty$, the latter being the more likely of the two, as the former imposes a lower bound. It is more plausible to expect, however, that at some "high" level of output the first-order condition, or perhaps the addition of a capacity restriction, will yield a global optimum where the second-order condition is satisfied.

It is interesting to note that, irrespective of the shape of the risk-preference function, the bracketed term in (13.12′) is necessarily less than unity. It immediately follows that $P > dc/dQ^*$. Since it has been assumed that the marginal cost curve is rising, this implies that under the present form of uncertainty the price-taking firm *always* produces less than it would produce under certainty. As the entrepreneur's willingness to accept risk increases, however, $\int_{Q^*}^{\infty} v'f(Q)\,dQ$ tends to account for an increasing portion of $\int_{0}^{\infty} v'f(Q)\,dQ$, for all $Q^*$. Hence, the expression in brackets approaches unity, and output approaches the $P = MC$ output. In effect, the greater is the entrepreneur's risk-taking propensity, the closer he comes to a willingness to gamble on the certainty optimum. Moreover, the intuitively appealing result is implied that if the market sets the price at $P^0$ where under certainty $P^0$ would merely equal average cost, then under uncertainty, when it is no longer *guaranteed* that the firm will cover its variable costs, the nonrisk-taking firm will prefer not to produce at all. The reason is the convexity of the total cost function, which implies that at any $Q$ *except* that which minimizes average cost, where minimum $AC = P^0, P > MC(Q)$ means $P^0 < AC(Q)$. Hence, the producing firm would not anticipate being able to cover its variable costs.

### b. Random Demand and the Quantity-Setter

There are several ways in which uncertainty can enter into the *monopolist's* demand curve. Dhrymes[14] has analyzed a situation in which price is a random variable such that $P = D(Q, u)$ is the firm's demand curve, where $u$ is distributed by $g(u)$. In particular, $E[u] = 0$, and $E[u^2] = \sigma_u^2 > 0$. In this case, then, the firm's problem is to determine a level of output, and all output is to be sold for a single maximum price that will clear the market, but the firm is uncertain as to what the market-clearing price will turn out to be.

Profit is given by $\pi = PQ - c(Q)$, and, once again, the entrepreneur is assumed to be concerned solely with profit. This is reflected in his risk-preference function, which is assumed to be a quadratic function of profit of the form

$$V = v(\pi) = \pi(Q, u) + \tfrac{1}{2}\alpha[\pi(Q, u) - \pi(Q, 0)]^2,$$

where $\alpha$ is a parameter that can serve as *a* measure of the propensity to take risk. If $\alpha = 0$, we have a case of linear risk preferences; if $\alpha < 0$, $V$ is strictly concave and we have a risk-evader; if $\alpha > 0$, $V$ is strictly convex and we have a risk-taker.[15]

Taking the expectation of $V$ yields

$$E[V] = \int \pi(Q, u)g(u)\,du + \tfrac{1}{2}\alpha \int [\pi(Q, u) - \pi(Q, 0)]^2 g(u)\,du. \qquad (13.14)$$

If, as in some of the earlier analyses, we once again make the crucial and ever so simplifying assumption that $u$ enters into the demand curve additively so that

[14] Phoebus J. Dhrymes, "On the Theory of the Monopolistic Multiproduct Firm Under Uncertainty," *International Economic Review*, **5**:3 (Sept. 1964), 239–257.

[15] The quadratic form of $V$ can be justified through a Taylor's series expansion of a more general risk-preference function. Upon taking expectations we derive (13.14′) below in which $E[V]$ is a function of $\alpha\sigma_u^2$. It is just such a formulation that encourages a Markowitz model in which the variance serves as a surrogate for risk, and in which $\alpha$ serves as a measure of propensity to take or avoid risk. We refrain from referring to $\alpha$ as a coefficient of risk aversion, as it *is* sometimes referred to, in order to avoid possible confusion with Pratt's measure.

$P = D(Q) + u$, then the first expression in (13.14) becomes $\int \pi(Q, u)g(u)\, du = \pi(Q)$, since $\int ug(u)\, du = E[u] = 0$ by assumption. Further,

$$\begin{aligned}\int [\pi(Q, u) - \pi(Q, 0)]^2 g(u)\, du &= \int [(D(Q, u)Q - c(Q)) - (D(Q, 0)Q - c(Q))]^2 g(u)\, du \\ &= \int [D(Q, u)Q - D(Q, 0)Q]^2 g(u)\, du \\ &= Q^2 \int [D(Q, u) - D(Q, 0)]^2 g(u)\, du \\ &= Q^2\sigma_u^2,\end{aligned}$$

since $\int u^2 g(u)\, du = \sigma_u^2$ by assumption. Thus, (13.14) may be written as

$$E[V] = \pi(Q) + \tfrac{1}{2}\alpha Q^2\sigma_u^2. \tag{13.14'}$$

To determine $Q$ to maximize $E[V]$ we compute

$$\frac{dE[V]}{dQ} = \frac{d\pi}{dQ} + \alpha Q\sigma_u^2; \qquad \frac{d^2E[V]}{dQ^2} = \frac{d^2\pi}{dQ^2} + \alpha\sigma_u^2.$$

Setting $dE[V]/dQ = 0$, and recognizing that $d\pi/dQ = MR - MC$, where $MR$ is evaluated at $u = 0$ (that is, on the "riskless" demand curve, at the mean of the random variable $u$), the first-order condition for a maximum becomes

$$MR = MC - \alpha Q\sigma_u^2. \tag{13.15}$$

Let us assume that in the riskless case the second-order condition for a maximum ($d^2\pi/dQ^2 < 0$) is satisfied at the $MR = MC$ output level, and that the firm is not suffering a loss. If $\alpha = 0$, we return to the equilibrium conditions for the certainty case. That is, under this *specialized* form of uncertainty, the entrepreneur who is linear in risk behaves *as if* the mean demand curve were his certain demand curve. Since $\sigma_u^2 > 0$, it also follows that the second-order condition will necessarily be satisfied for the risk-evader, with $\alpha < 0$. For him, however, $MR > MC$ for $Q > 0$; consequently the risk-evader will prefer a smaller output than that preferred by the entrepreneur who is linear in risk. If $\alpha > 0$, the second-order condition *might* still be satisfied. Should this be the case, this would mean that the risk-taker prefers an output level such that $MR < MC$; or, he prefers a *higher* output level than the certainty level, and a greater output than that preferred by the risk-evader.

As a further generalization, we can determine how changes in $\alpha$ will affect $Q$ by taking the total differential of (13.15) with respect to $\alpha$. Differentiating the left side of (13.15) with respect to $\alpha$ yields $(d(MR)/dQ)(dQ/d\alpha)$; differentiating the right side, we obtain $(d(MC)/dQ)(dQ/d\alpha) - Q\sigma_u^2 - \alpha\sigma_u^2(dQ/d\alpha)$. Setting these two expressions equal to one another and rearranging terms, we obtain

$$\left[\frac{d(MR)}{dQ} - \frac{d(MC)}{dQ} + \alpha\sigma_u^2\right]\frac{dQ}{d\alpha} + Q\sigma_u^2 = 0. \tag{13.16}$$

The expression in brackets is $d^2E[V]/dQ^2$ and will be negative (when we assume that this, the second-order condition, is in fact satisfied). With $Q\sigma_u^2$ necessarily positive, we can therefore deduce that $dQ/d\alpha > 0$, for the equality to hold. We can infer from this result that increasing $\alpha$, or *decreasing* the entrepreneur's propensity to avoid risk and *increasing* his propensity to take risk, will increase his preferred level of output. This is consistent with our previous conclusion, tempered by the qualification with respect to the risk-taker. Moreover, the ordering of preferred output levels in accordance with propensity to take risk is consistent with the ordering suggested in Hymans' model—including the need to qualify the results for risk-takers. The unique conclusion does emerge, however, that uncertainty could lead to output levels *in excess of* the riskless level, when the firm is a risk-taking quantity-setter, faced with a downward-sloping demand curve.[16]

## c. Random Demand and the Profits Tax

### i. THE DHRYMES CASE

Suppose a fixed profits tax of $\tau$ with perfect loss offset is imposed on Dhrymes' entrepreneur. By perfect loss offset we mean that losses are written off against other income. Then, $V = v(\pi_\tau) = v((1 - \tau)\pi)$, since it is only the posttax profits that are assumed to affect preferences. If we repeat the previous analysis, (13.14′) becomes

$$E[V] = (1 - \tau)\pi(Q) + \tfrac{1}{2}\alpha(1 - \tau)^2 Q^2 \sigma_u^2, \tag{13.14''}$$

and the first-order condition for a maximum, (13.15), becomes

$$MR = MC - \alpha(1 - \tau)Q\sigma_u^2. \tag{13.15'}$$

As in the certainty case, if $\alpha = 0$ and the entrepreneur is linear in risk, the profits tax does not affect his preferred output level. If $\alpha \neq 0$, then the effect of a profits tax is to bring $MR$ closer to $MC$ *irrespective* of the entrepreneur's attitude towards risk. That is, the risk-evader will increase his output, while the risk-taker will reduce his output. When the effects of a profits tax were discussed in Chapter 8, it was noted that the observed (if disputed) changes in policy of firms upon whom a profits tax is imposed are often explained by attributing to these firms pretax inefficiency that cannot be tolerated posttax. Thus, it is argued that these firms are forced to operate more in accord with neoclassical dictates. Equation (13.15′) would suggest that if these firms are coming closer to the riskless $MR = MC$ policy, it is because their implicit (or do we dare to believe explicit?) recognition of the omnipresence of uncertainty *demands* that they do so. That is, they are behaving exactly as Dhrymes' model would suggest they *should* behave.

### ii. THE HYMANS CASE

The reactions of Hymans' firm to a perfect-loss-offset profits tax are not quite as clear-cut as those of Dhrymes' firm. The output optimum is still achieved where (13.12′) is satisfied. Now, however, $V = v(\pi_\tau)$, and the $v'$ term is $dv/d\pi_\tau = v'(\pi_\tau)$. The optimum output level at the market price of $P$ will increase with the imposition of a profits tax if the bracketed term in (13.12′) increases when $\tau$ increases, that is, if $\partial[\quad]/\partial\tau > 0$, for then $MC$ and thus output will have to be increased to restore the equality; the reverse is true if $\partial[\quad]/\partial\tau < 0$.

[16] The term "multiproduct" in the title of Dhrymes' article is by no means misleading. Dhrymes does deal with the multiproduct firm. It does not serve our purpose to do so here, however, since the analysis is much more complex and does not yield unique and generalizable conclusions. The analysis does support the general proposition that uncertainty can have far-reaching and unforeseen implications for the firm's behavior, and these implications may differ from those inferred from the certainty model. The interested reader who goes directly to Dhrymes' paper should be cautioned that in his discussion Dhrymes has misinterpreted his results and the effects on output levels of variations in $\alpha$.

Upon taking this derivative, we obtain

$$\frac{\partial[\ \ ]}{\partial\tau} = \frac{\begin{array}{l}\int_{Q^*}^{\infty} v''[c(Q^*) - PQ^*]f(Q)\,dQ \int_0^{\infty} v'f(Q)\,dQ \\ \qquad - \int_0^{\infty} v''[c(Q^*) - PQ]f(Q)\,dQ \int_{Q^*}^{\infty} v'f(Q)\,dQ\end{array}}{\left[\int_0^{\infty} v'f(Q)\,dQ\right]^2},$$

since with $\pi_\tau = (1 - \tau)\pi$, $\partial v'/\partial\tau = v''[\partial\pi_\tau/\partial\tau] = v''[-\pi]$. Noting that for $Q \geq Q^*$ both $v''$ and $v'$ are constant at $v''^*$ and $v'^*$, with both evaluated at $(PQ^* - c(Q^*))(1 - \tau)$, we may write the numerator in $\partial[\ \ ]/\partial\tau$ as

$$v''^*[c(Q^*) - PQ^*] \int_{Q^*}^{\infty} f(Q)\,dQ \int_0^{\infty} v'f(Q)\,dQ$$
$$- v'^* \int_0^{\infty} v''[c(Q^*) - PQ]f(Q)\,dQ \int_{Q^*}^{\infty} f(Q)\,dQ$$
$$= v'^* \int_{Q^*}^{\infty} f(Q)\,dQ \left[\int_0^{\infty}\left[\left(\frac{v'}{v'^*}\right) v''^*[c(Q^*) - PQ^*] - v''[c(Q^*) - PQ]\right] f(Q)\,dQ\right].$$

Further, with $Q \geq Q^*$, $v' = v'^*$, $v'' = v''^*$, and $c(Q^*) - PQ^* = c(Q^*) - PQ$. Hence, the integration can be truncated at $Q^*$, for the terms under the integral will cancel when $Q \geq Q^*$. We thus determine that

$$\frac{\partial[\ \ ]}{\partial\tau} = \frac{v'^* \int_{Q^*}^{\infty} f(Q)\,dQ}{\left[\int_0^{\infty} v'f(Q)\,(d)Q\right]^2}\left[\int_0^{Q^*}\left[\left(\frac{v'}{v'^*}\right) v''^*[c(Q^*) - PQ^*] - v''[c(Q^*) - PQ]\right] f(Q)dQ\right]. \quad (13.16)$$

The term outside the major brackets is necessarily positive. If the entrepreneur is linear in risk, then $v'' = 0$ and the bracketed term and $\partial[\ \ ]/\partial\tau = 0$. Thus, the output of the entrepreneur who is linear in risk will not be altered in the face of a profits tax or changes therein. If the entrepreneur is a risk-evader with a concave and *quadratic* risk-preference function, then $v''$ is a negative constant and can be factored out of the integral. Moreover, $v' > v'^*$ for $Q < Q^*$; and in this same range, $0 > [c(Q^*) - PQ^*] < [c(Q^*) - PQ]$. Thus $0 > (v'/v'^*)[c(Q^*) - PQ^*] \leq [c(Q^*) - PQ]$ for $Q \leq Q^*$. It immediately follows that the bracketed term, as the product of negative terms, is positive, and therefore that $\partial[\ \ ]/\partial\tau > 0$. That is, the "quadratic"' risk-evader will increase his output upon being confronted with the profits tax. He will also increase his output so long as $v''$ is not a decreasing function of $\pi_\tau$ and hence of $Q$. It is only if $v''$ is such a decreasing function—that is, if $v'$ is a *concave* function of $\pi_\tau$ and the marginal "utiles" decrease at an increasing rate—that $v''^*$ can be less than $v''$, and hence the second term in the brackets in (13.16) might outweigh the first. Note, however, that even if $v'$ is a concave function, $\partial[\ \ ]/\partial\tau$ will not *necessarily* be negative.

The case for the risk-taker is not at all clear. Even with a convex and *quadratic* risk-preference function, and with $v''$ a positive *constant*, since $v' < v'^*$ for $Q < Q^*$, we cannot be certain of the sign of the integral. The sign of $\partial[\ \ ]/\partial\tau$ and the exact reaction will depend upon the shape of the risk-preference function.

It might be noted that $-v''^*/v'^* = r(\pi_\tau)$, where $r(\pi_\tau)$ is Pratt's measure of risk aversion. The negative of this term appears in the first expression under the integral in (13.16). Ceteris paribus, the greater the absolute value of $v''^*/v'^*$, the larger will be the value of $\partial[\quad]/\partial\tau > 0$ for the risk-evader, and the greater will be the risk-evader's aversion to risk. Thus, the greater the risk-evading entrepreneur's aversion to risk, the greater will be the extent to which he increases production on the heels of a profits tax.

### iii. THE TISDELL CASE

The effects of a profits tax in a competitive market of the Tisdell type, where the firm produces in advance and can sell its *total* output at the market price, are similar to the effects in Hymans' case. This is as it should be, for both are competitive markets in the sense that the producers are price-takers; but in Tisdell's market the firm sells all its output, whereas in Hymans' market it will not necessarily do so. Thus, Hymans firm necessarily produces less than a comparable Tisdell firm, but the effects of a profits tax are similar, and similarly ambiguous.

This case has been studied by Penner.[17] Specifically, output is assumed to be a function of a single variable factor $F$, so that $Q = q(F)$. Price is a random variable. Posttax profits are given by $\pi_\tau = (1 - \tau)(PQ - wF)$, where $w$ is the fixed factor wage. With $V = v(\pi_\tau)$, $E[V] = E[v((1 - \tau)(PQ - wF))]$. The analysis of Section 12.7c is replicated here, but with the maximization of $E[V]$ undertaken with respect to the variable factor $F$. Output is determined simultaneously with $F$. As before, we determine $dE[V]/dF = (1 - \tau)E\,[v'\,(P\,\partial Q/\partial F - w)]$, where $v' = dv/d\pi_\tau$. As the first-order maximizing condition, setting $dE[V]/dF = 0$, we require that

$$E[v'(P\,\partial Q/\partial F - w)] = E[v']E[P\,\partial Q/\partial F - w] + \sigma_{v'm} = 0,$$

where $\sigma_{v'm}$ is the covariance between $v'$ and $P(\partial Q/\partial F) - w$. For an entrepreneur who is linear in risk, $v' = E[v']$ is a constant, and therefore $\sigma_{v'm} = 0$. Hence, given that the second-order condition is satisfied, $E[V]$ is maximized where $E[P\,\partial Q/\partial F - w] = (\partial Q/\partial F)E[P] - w = 0$; that is, where the variable factor is employed to the point at which *expected* price times the factor's marginal physical product is equal to the factor's marginal cost (equaling here the factor wage).

Given an optimum level of $F = F^*$, profits and $P(\partial Q/\partial F) - w$ will be greater the greater is $P$. Hence, as in Section 12.7c, for the risk-evader with a strictly concave risk-preference function, $v'$ and $P(\partial Q/\partial F) - w$ will be negatively correlated, while for the risk-taker with a strictly convex $V$, they will be positively correlated. Rearranging terms in $dE[V]/dF = 0$, we obtain the equivalent condition:

$$\frac{\partial Q}{\partial F} = \frac{-\sigma_{v'm}}{E[v']E[P]} + \frac{w}{E[P]}\,. \tag{13.17}$$

Thus, for the risk-evader with $\sigma_{v'm} < 0$, $\partial Q/\partial F$ is greater than for an entrepreneur who is linear in risk with $\sigma_{v'm} = 0$, and greater still than for the risk-taker with $\sigma_{v'm} > 0$.[18] Thus, if the firms indeed prefer to produce at all, our earlier results again

[17] Rudolph G. Penner, "Uncertainty and the Short-Run Shifting of the Corporation Tax," *Oxford Economic Papers*, **19**:1 (March 1967), 99–110.

[18] The second-order condition for a maximum requires $d^2E[V]/dF^2 < 0$, and

$$\frac{d^2E[V]}{dF^2} = (1 - \tau)\left(E\left[v''\left(P\frac{\partial Q}{\partial F} - w\right)^2 (1 - \tau) + P\frac{\partial^2 Q}{\partial F^2}v'\right]\right).$$

$\partial^2 Q/\partial F^2 < 0$, by assumption. With the exception of the risk-taker for whom $v'' > 0$, we can therefore be certain that the arguments within the expectation will be negative, and

obtain. Factor employment (and output) will be less for the risk-evader than for the risk-taker, with the "linear" entrepreneur in the middle, producing as he would if the expected price obtained with certainty.

To analyze the effects on employment of a perfect-loss-offset profits tax, we want to compute $dF/d\tau$. First, let us differentiate $dE[V]/dF$ totally with respect to $\tau$. This differentiation yields

$$\frac{d^2E[V]}{dF\,d\tau} = \left(\frac{\partial^2 E[V]}{\partial F^2}\right)\left(\frac{dF}{d\tau}\right) + \left(\frac{\partial^2 E[V]}{\partial F\,\partial \tau}\right) = 0 \text{ at } F^*,$$

since $dE[V]/dF = 0$ at $F^*$. If the second-order condition obtains, $\partial^2 E[V]/\partial F^2 < 0$ at $F^*$. Hence, $dF/d\tau$ and $\partial^2 E[V]/\partial F\,\partial\tau$ must be of like sign. Computing $\partial^2 E[V]/\partial F\,\partial\tau$, we determine

$$\frac{\partial^2 E[V]}{\partial F\,\partial \tau} = -E\left[v'\left(P\frac{\partial Q}{\partial F} - w\right)\right] + (1-\tau)E\left[v''\left(P\frac{\partial Q}{\partial F} - w\right)(wF - PQ)\right]$$

The first expectation is zero by the first-order condition. The sign of $\partial^2 E[V]/\partial F\,\partial\tau$ will thus depend solely upon the sign of the second expectation. The latter can be written as

$$E[v'']E\left[\left(P\frac{\partial Q}{\partial F} - w\right)(wF - PQ)\right] + \sigma_{v''k},$$

where $\sigma_{v''k}$ is the covariance between $v''$ and $(P(\partial Q/\partial F) - w)(wF - PQ)$. If we have a risk-evader with a concave and *quadratic* risk-preference function, $v''$ is a negative constant and $\sigma_{v''k} = 0$. We may write

$$E\left[\left(P\frac{\partial Q}{\partial F} - w\right)(wF - PQ)\right] = E\left[P\frac{\partial Q}{\partial F} - w\right]E[wF - PQ] + \sigma_{m\pi},$$

where $\sigma_{m\pi}$ is the covariance between $(P(\partial Q/\partial F) - w)$ and $(wF - PQ)$. $\sigma_{m\pi}$ is negative, since the first term is an increasing function of $P$ and the second is a decreasing function of $P$. Also, by the first-order condition, $E[P(\partial Q/\partial F) - w] > 0$. $E[wF - PQ] < 0$ or else the nonrisk-taking firm would prefer not to produce, since $E[PQ - wF]$ is expected profit. Hence, $E[(P(\partial Q/\partial F) - w)(wF - PQ)] < 0$, and both $\partial^2 E[V]/\partial F\,\partial\tau$ and $dF/d\tau > 0$. Thus, as in Hymans' case, the risk-evader increases factor employment and hence output. If $v'' = 0$ and the entrepreneur is linear in risk, $dF/d\tau = 0$ and output is unaffected by the profits tax.

For a risk-taker, the situation is once again quite open-ended. Suppose, for example, that $v$ is a convex and *quadratic* risk-preference function. The first-order condition still requires that $E[v'(P\,\partial Q/\partial F - w)] = 0$. But, with $v$ quadratic, $v'$ will be a linear function of $\pi_\tau$ and $v''$ will be a positive constant. Once again, then, $\sigma_{v''k} = 0$, so that the sign of $\partial^2 E[V]/\partial F\,\partial\tau$ will be the same as that of $E[v'']E[(P\,\partial Q/\partial F - w)(wF - PQ)]$; or, since $E[v''] = v'' > 0$, $\partial^2 E[V]/\partial F\,\partial\tau$ will be of the same sign as $E[(P\,\partial Q/\partial F - w)(wF - PQ)] = E[(P\,\partial Q/\partial F - w)]E[wF - PQ] + \sigma_{m\pi}$. By the first-order condition $E[(P\,\partial Q/\partial F - w)] < 0$, since $\sigma_{v'm} > 0$. But, since the risk-taker *may* produce even if expected profits are negative, we cannot be certain of the sign of $E[wF - PQ]$. It is therefore not possible to generalize about the effects of the

that the second-order condition will hold. The general behavioral proposition with respect to their output levels was, however, already established in Section 12.7c, and the second-order condition was seen to hold for the risk-evader in footnote 16 of Chapter 12.

profits tax on the risk-taker, even when the risk-preference function is quadratic. In any event, irrespective of risk preferences, if $v''$ is not constant, the implications of a profits tax depend on the *exact* shapes of $v'$ and of $(P(\partial Q/\partial F) - w)(wF - PQ)$ as functions of $P$.[19]

### d. Summary

The results of the preceding analyses do not lead to many ready-made generalities. Indeed, one of the most consistent features is the disparity in the individual conclusions. Notwithstanding the fact that we know better, let us attempt to bring some order into the previous conglomeration of manipulations and results.

The Tisdell and Dhrymes models suggest that with linear risk preferences and price a random variable, either under pure competition or monopoly the expected profit-maximizing firm will produce an output equivalent to the certainty output at the expected price. This output will, however, be greater than the output of Drèze and Gabszewicz firms under pure competition. The latter firms also express linear risk preferences, but free entry regulates output levels to assure zero expected profit, and this leads firms to underproduce. The output of Mills' monopolistic firm with linear risk preferences is not unambiguous, for this firm must set price as well as output. Mills' firm will, however, usually—though not always—set a lower price than the certainty price for a given output.

With nonlinear risk preferences, the Dhrymes and Tisdell firms are seen to behave in a manner such that risk-evasive tendencies lead to a preference for lower output levels, and risk-taking tendencies to a preference for higher output levels, than obtain under certainty at the expected price. In Hymans' competitive world, the ordering of output preferences follows the same pattern, with risk aversion leading to the lowest output; but, in Hymans' world, uncertainty *necessarily* leads to output levels *below* the certainty output at the expected price. There is, however, one overriding element of consistency in these models: namely, a profits tax tends to draw entrepreneurs with differing risk and output preferences towards the output level preferred by an entrepreneur who is linear in risk. Beyond this, however, the particulars and the assumptions would seem to be preeminent in dictating the conclusions.

## 13.4 A MODEL OF THE PRICE-QUOTER

We shall now discuss at some length the behavior of the price-quoting firm producing to satisfy demand at the quoted price. Although the production capability of firms of the real world will not necessarily be as flexible as is suggested by this model, price-quoting behavior would seem to be the prevailing modus operandi of the business world (even if the quoted price is only the market price). While some customers may be turned away or asked to defer their purchases, firms do generally stand ready to supply the market demands at the quoted price.[20]

[19] Penner also shows that taxes without loss offsets would result in a lower output than with perfect loss offset, and that progressive profits taxes would likely cause lower output levels.

[20] For a discussion, see P. W. S. Andrews, *Manufacturing Business* (London: Macmillan and Co., Ltd., 1949), particularly pp. 153, 174. Portions of this section are based on the author's article, "The Price-Quoter under Risk," *Western Economic Journal*, **7**:2 (June 1969), 129–136.

At a price of $P$, the demand for the product $Q$ over a period of length $T$ is assumed to be a random variable distributed by the density $f(P; Q \mid P_1, \ldots, P_k; Y)$. The latter expression suggests, as discussed in Section 4.4f, that this probability will depend upon the prices $P_i$ charged for comparable products by other firms ($i = 1, \ldots, k$), and upon "other factors" $Y$. As noted in the earlier discussion, the probability can be simplified to $f(P; Q)$, given a set of probability assessments with respect to $Y$ and the $P_i$. The price elasticity of demand was also defined in terms of *expected* demand as

$$\eta = \frac{d \int Qf(P; Q)\, dQ}{dP} \frac{P}{\int Qf(P; Q)\, dQ}. \tag{13.18}$$

Corresponding to the certainty assumption of a downward-sloping demand curve and negative price elasticity, we assume that $\eta < 0$. This requires $d[\int Qf(P; Q)\, dQ]/dP < 0$, since price and expected demand are positive. We shall first consider the price preferences of the entrepreneur who is linear in risk, and then contrast these preferences with those of the entrepreneur who is nonlinear in risk.

## a. Linear Risk Preferences

The profit-centered entrepreneur who is linear in risk will quote a price to maximize expected profits. Given demand of $Q$ at a price of $P$, profit will be $\pi = PQ - c(Q)$. It will be assumed that the firm satisfies all demand at the price of $P$, unless a loss is incurred in the process. This assumption gives rise to the qualification that the firm with a rising marginal cost curve will halt production at the output $Q_m$ at which $\partial\pi/\partial Q = P - dc/dQ = 0$, or price equals marginal cost, and $\partial^2\pi/\partial Q^2 < 0$. Thus, the firm will halt production as soon as additional units cost more to produce than they return in terms of revenue; with constant or falling marginal cost, the firm will satisfy all comers at the price of $P$.

Expected profit is therefore given by

$$E[\pi] = \int_0^{Q_m} (PQ - c(Q))f(P; Q)\, dQ + (PQ_m - c(Q_m)) \int_{Q_m}^{\infty} f(P; Q)\, dQ.$$

To maximize $E[\pi]$, the firm seeks a price such that $dE[\pi]/dP = 0$ and $d^2E[\pi]/dP^2 < 0$. For the first-order condition,

$$\begin{aligned}
\frac{dE[\pi]}{dP} &= \int_0^{Q_m} Qf(P; Q)\, dQ + \int_0^{Q_m} (PQ - c(Q)) \frac{df(P; Q)}{dP}\, dQ \\
&\quad + \frac{dQ_m}{dP} (PQ_m - c(Q_m))f(P; Q_m) + Q_m \int_{Q_m}^{\infty} f(P; Q)\, dQ \\
&\quad + P \frac{dQ_m}{dP} \int_{Q_m}^{\infty} f(P; Q)\, dQ - \frac{dc(Q_m)}{dQ_m} \frac{dQ_m}{dP} \int_{Q_m}^{\infty} f(P; \dot{Q})\, dQ \\
&\quad + (PQ_m - c(Q_m)) \left[ \int_{Q_m}^{\infty} \frac{df(P; Q)}{dP}\, dQ - \frac{dQ_m}{dP} f(P; Q_m) \right] \\
&= \int_0^{Q_m} Qf(P; Q)\, dQ + Q_m \int_{Q_m}^{\infty} f(P; Q)\, dQ \\
&\quad + \int_0^{Q_m} (PQ - c(Q)) \frac{df(P; Q)}{dQ}\, dQ + (PQ_m - c(Q_m)) \int_{Q_m}^{\infty} \frac{df(P; Q)}{dP}\, dQ,
\end{aligned}$$

because the terms that enter when we differentiate with respect to the limits of the integral cancel, and $Q_m$ is defined such that at the optimal price, $P = dc(Q_m)/dQ_m$. This enables us to cancel the quartet of terms "disappearing" from one step to the next. The first-order condition thus leads to an optimum price quote of

$$P^* = \frac{\int_0^{Q_m} c(Q)f'\,dQ + c(Q_m)F' - E[Q]}{\int_0^{Q_m} Qf'\,dQ + Q_mF'}, \tag{13.19}$$

where $f = f(P^*; Q)$; $df(P^*; Q)/dP = f'$;

$$F = \int_{Q_m}^{\infty} f(P; Q)\,dQ; \qquad F' = \int_{Q_m}^{\infty} f'\,dQ;$$

and $E[Q] = \int_0^{Q_m} Qf\,dQ + Q_mF$ = expected sales at the price of $P^*$. It will be assumed that the second-order conditions are satisfied at $P^*$.[21] It is also assumed that the $f(P; Q)$ are assigned to assure that as $P$ increases, the *expected* quantity demanded will decrease. For goods consistent with a downward-sloping demand curve, this decrease in expected quantity is achieved in the following manner. Increasing price from $P$ to $P + dP$ in essence changes the densities from $f(P; Q)$ to $f(P + dP; Q)$. This change is effected by reducing the probabilities of selling the larger quantities, while concomitantly increasing the probabilities of selling the smaller quantities, because buyers will prefer to purchase less at higher prices. Moreover, since $f(P; Q)$ is a probability density and $\int f(P; Q)\,dQ = 1$ for all $P$,

$$\frac{d^k[\int f(P; Q)\,dQ]}{dP^k} = \int \left(\frac{d^kf}{dP^k}\right) dQ = \frac{d[1]}{dP} = 0 \qquad \text{for all } k \geq 1.$$

Hence, say in the $\int c(Q)f'\,dQ$ term, the higher $c(Q)$'s obtaining at the higher $Q$'s are "weighted" by the negative or smaller $f'$ values; the lower $c(Q)$'s obtaining at the lower $Q$'s are "weighted" by the positive $f'$ values; and $\int_0^{Q_m} f'\,dQ + F' = 0$. Therefore, $\int_0^{Q_m} c(Q)f'\,dQ + c(Q_m)F'$ and $\int_0^{Q_m} Qf'\,dQ + Q_mF'$ will each necessarily be negative. Further, $E[Q]$, the expected quantity *sold*, is positive, thereby guaranteeing $P^* > 0$. It should be noted that $E[Q]$ is expected *sales* and can be no greater than expected demand. That is, $\int_0^{Q_m} Qf\,dQ + Q_m \int_{Q_m}^{\infty} f\,dQ \leq \int_0^{\infty} Qf\,dQ$.

To clarify the economic implications of (13.19) and its various components, we first define the *effective* elasticity of demand $\hat{\eta}$ as that elasticity computed from Equation (13.18) when the upper limit on sales is fixed at $Q_m$. Then,

$$\frac{d\left[\int_0^{Q_m} Qf\,dQ + Q_mF\right]}{dP} = \int_0^{Q_m} Qf'\,dQ + Q_mF' + \left(\frac{dQ_m}{dP}\right)F.$$

We may, therefore, replace the denominator of (13.19) with the equivalent expression $(\hat{\eta}/P^*)E[Q] - (dQ_m/dP)F$, obtained from (13.18). After making the substitution

[21] Irrespective of risk preferences, the firm will compare $E[V]$ at the optimum price with $E[V]$ when the firm fails to operate. The firm that is linear in risk therefore requires the optimum expected revenue to exceed the known variable costs. Throughout the succeeding analyses we shall assume that this condition is met.

and rearranging terms, we can write (13.19) as

$$P^*\left[1 + \frac{1}{\hat{\eta}}\right] = \frac{\displaystyle\int_0^{Q_m} c(Q)f'\,dQ + c(Q_m)F' + P^*\left(\frac{dQ_m}{dP}\right)F}{\displaystyle\int_0^{Q_m} Qf'\,dQ + Q_mF' + \left(\frac{dQ_m}{dP}\right)F}. \qquad (13.19')$$

Now, *expected* total revenue at a price of $P$ is given by $\bar{R} = PE[Q]$. Computing the change in expected revenue from a small increment in expected *sales*, or in the *effective expected* quantity demanded—that is, $d\bar{R}/dE[Q]$—we obtain

$$\frac{d\bar{R}}{dE[Q]} = P + \frac{dP}{dE[Q]}E[Q] = P + \frac{P}{\hat{\eta}} = P\left[1 + \frac{1}{\hat{\eta}}\right].$$

The latter expression is equivalent to one previously developed for the certainty case where $MR = P(1 + 1/\hat{\eta})$. Here, however, the "marginal revenue" is attributable to a change in an *expected* quantity. $\eta$ will replace $\hat{\eta}$ when marginal cost is a nonincreasing function, for then the firm places no restrictions on sales at the going price. Similarly, with total expected cost at a price of $P$ given by

$$\bar{C} = \int_0^{Q_m} c(Q)f\,dQ + c(Q_m)F,$$

the change in expected cost that would result from an increment in *expected* quantity produced, or $d\bar{C}/dE[Q]$, is given by

$$\frac{d\bar{C}}{dE[Q]} = \frac{d\left[\displaystyle\int_0^{Q_m} c(Q)f\,dQ + c(Q_m)F\right]}{dP}\,\frac{dP}{dE[Q]}$$

$$= \frac{\displaystyle\int_0^{Q_m} c(Q)f'\,dQ + c(Q_m)F' + \left(\frac{dc(Q_m)}{dQ_m}\right)\left(\frac{dQ_m}{dP}\right)F}{\displaystyle\int_0^{Q_m} Qf'\,dQ + Q_mF' + \left(\frac{dQ_m}{dP}\right)F}.$$

At a price of $P^*, P^* = dc(Q_m)/dQ_m$. Hence, $d\bar{C}/dE[Q]$ equals $P^*(1 + 1/\hat{\eta})$, from Equation (13.19′). Thus, $d\bar{R}/dE[Q] = d\bar{C}/dE[Q]$: or, analogous to the certainty case, the firm quotes a price assuring an expected output that will equate a species of "marginal revenue" to a species of "marginal cost." That is, from (13.19) we immediately determine that the entrepreneur who is linear in risk sets $P^*$ to assure his preferred expected output of

$$E_L^*[Q] = \int_0^{Q_m} c(Q)f'\,dQ + c(Q_m)F' - P^*\left[\int_0^{Q_m} Qf'\,dQ + Q_mF'\right]. \qquad (13.19'')$$

### b. Nonlinear Risk Preferences

In general, the profit-centered entrepreneur sets price to maximize

$$E[V] = E[v(\pi)] = \int_0^{Q_m} v(\pi)f\,dQ + v(\pi_m)\int_{Q_m}^{\infty} f\,dQ,$$

where $\pi_m = PQ_m - c(Q_m)$. The first-order condition for a maximum is

$$\frac{dE[V]}{dP} = \int_0^{Q_m} v'\left(\frac{d\pi}{dP}\right) f\,dQ + \int_0^{Q_m} v(\pi) f'\,dQ + \frac{dQ_m}{dP} v(\pi_m) f(P; Q_m)$$
$$+ \frac{dv}{d\pi_m}\frac{d\pi_m}{dP}\int_{Q_m}^{\infty} f\,dQ + v(\pi_m)\left[\int_{Q_m}^{\infty} f'\,dQ - \frac{dQ_m}{dP} f(P; Q_m)\right]$$
$$= \int_0^{Q_m} v'\left(\frac{d\pi}{dP}\right) f\,dQ + \frac{dv}{d\pi_m}\left(\frac{d\pi_m}{dP}\right) F + \int_0^{Q_m} vf'\,dQ + v(\pi_m)F' = 0. \tag{13.20}$$

Because $d\pi/dP = Q$, (13.20) may be written

$$\int_0^{Q_m} v'Q\hat{f}\,dQ = -\int_0^{Q_m} v\hat{f}'\,dQ, \tag{13.20'}$$

where

$$\int_0^{Q_m} v'Q\hat{f}\,dQ = \int_0^{Q_m} v'Qf\,dQ + \left(\frac{dv(\pi_m)}{d\pi}\right) Q_m \int_{Q_m}^{\infty} f\,dQ.$$

Thus $\hat{f}$ is a density function equivalent to $f$, except that the entire area $\int_{Q_m}^{\infty} f\,dQ$ is massed at $Q_m$; or $\hat{f}(P; Q_m) = \int_{Q_m}^{\infty} f\,dQ$; $\hat{f}'$ is similarly defined. Then, in the now familiar fashion, and with the expectations taken with respect to $\hat{f}$, write the integral on the left of (13.20′) as $E[v'Q] = E[v']E[Q] + \sigma_{v'Q}$, where $\sigma_{v'Q}$ is the covariance between $v'$ and the truncated $Q$. The first-order condition is thus satisfied when

$$E[Q] = \frac{-\int v\hat{f}'\,dQ - \sigma_{v'Q}}{E[v']}. \tag{13.21}$$

For the entrepreneur linear in risk, we can write $V_L = v_L(\pi) = \pi$, $v'_L = 1$, and therefore $\sigma_{v'Q} = 0$. Equation (13.21) immediately reduces to (13.19″), or

$$E_L^*[Q] = -\int_0^{Q_m} \pi f'\,dQ - \pi_m F'.$$

To determine whether attitudes towards risk affect price preferences, note that for the entrepreneur who is nonlinear in risk, we can *always* write $V_N = v_N(\pi) = \pi + w(\pi)$. As depicted in Figure 13.1, for both the least or most desired profits of $\pi_{\min}$ and $\pi_{\max}$, $v_L(\pi_{\min}) = v_N(\pi_{\min})$ and $v_L(\pi_{\max}) = v_N(\pi_{\max})$; and $w(\pi_{\min}) = w(\pi_{\max}) = 0$. For the risk-evader, $w(\pi) \geq 0$; for the risk-taker, $w(\pi) \leq 0$. In either case, $v'_N(\pi) = 1 + w' \geq 0$, or $w' \geq -1$. For convenience, we shall assume a strictly concave (convex) risk-preference function for the risk-evader (-taker), so that $v'' = w'' <$ ($>$) 0.

Now, suppose an entrepreneur with nonlinear risk preferences is evaluating the price of $P^*$ preferred by the "linear" firm. At this price, $dE[V_N]/dP^* = E[v'_N]E[Q] + \sigma_{v'Q} + \int v_N\hat{f}'\,dQ$. Further, $E[v'_N] = E[1 + w'] = 1 + E[w']$ and $\int v_N\hat{f}'\,dQ = \int \pi\hat{f}'\,dQ + \int w\hat{f}'\,dQ$. But at $P^*$, $E[Q] = -\int \pi\hat{f}'\,dQ = E_L^*(Q)$. After substituting the latter expressions for their counterparts,

$$\frac{dE[V_N]}{dP^*} = E_L^*[Q]E[w'] + \int w\hat{f}'\,dQ + \sigma_{v'Q}. \tag{13.22}$$

Equation (13.22) also holds for the "linear" firm, as it should, with $w = w' = \sigma_{v'Q} = 0$ and $dE[V_L]/dP^* = 0$. For the "nonlinear" firm, if $dE[V_N]/dP^* > 0$, the firm will have to increase price above $P^*$ in order to drive $dE[V_N]/dP$ down to zero;

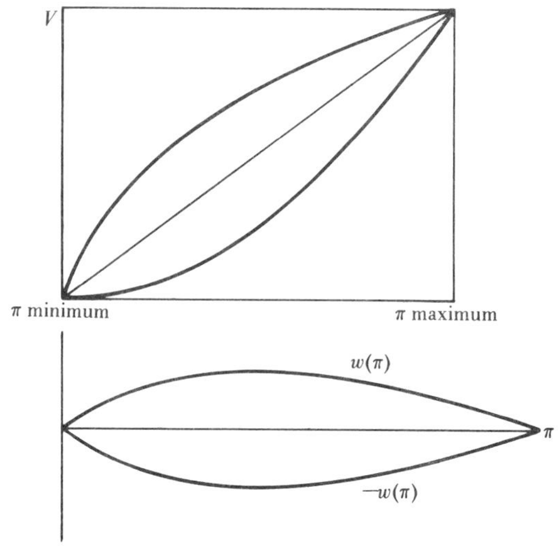


Fig. 13.1

if $dE[V_N]/dP^* < 0$, a price below $P^*$ will be preferred. For the moment we assume the second-order condition holds for both nonlinear and linear risk preferences when (13.20) holds.

For the risk-evader, $\sigma_{v'Q} < 0$ because $v'_N(\pi)$ is a decreasing function of $\pi$, and $\pi$ is an increasing function of $Q$. $Q$ and $v'$ are thus negatively correlated, for increases in $Q$ produce decreases in $v'$. By an analogous argument, $\sigma_{v'Q} > 0$ for the risk-taker. Complicating matters is the unpleasant observation that for neither the risk-evader nor the risk-taker are the signs of $E[w']$ and $\int w\hat{f}'\,dQ$ unique. Nevertheless, with $V_{NE} = \pi + w(\pi)$ and $w(\pi) \geq 0$ for the risk-evader, and with $V_{NT} = \pi + (-w(\pi))$ for the risk-taker, $E[w']$ and $\int w\hat{f}'\,dQ$ will be of opposing sign for opposing risk preferences. With all three terms of opposing sign, other things (that is, the magnitudes) being equal, if $dE[V_N]/dP^* \neq 0$ and the risk-evader prefers a higher price than $P^*$, the risk-taker will prefer a lower price, and vice versa—provided the second-order condition is satisfied for both.[22]

Considering the matter a bit further, let us focus on the risk-evader. For him, $w'(\pi)$ goes from positive to negative as $\pi$ increases. Thus, if at $P^*$ the only possible profit levels are such that $w'(\pi) < 0$, then $w(\pi)$ will be a decreasing function of $\pi$, and whereas $E[w'] < 0$, $\int w\hat{f}'\,dQ > 0$. If all $w'(\pi) > 0$, then $E[w'] > 0$, but $\int w\hat{f}'\,dQ < 0$. The sign of $E_L^*[Q]E[w'] + \int w\hat{f}'\,dQ$ is thus hazy indeed. When the potential profit levels are all high "enough" or low "enough," however, the $w(\pi)$ expression will approach zero, whereas the $w'(\pi)$ expressions will become relatively large. Further, for the risk-evader $\sigma_{v'Q}$ is *always* negative. With considerable trepidation, we therefore hazard the following hedged suggestion: if potential profits at the price the "linear" firm prefers are all at levels such that $w'(\pi) < 0$, $dE[V_N]/dP^*$ will *tend* to be negative (positive) for the risk-evader (-taker); hence, the risk-evader (-taker)

[22] Unless $V$ is linear in the relevant profit range. If $V$ is linear with the risk-taker accepting $E[\pi] < 0$ and the risk-evader demanding $E[\pi] > 0$, then, since $v'$ is constant, risk preferences do not affect price preferences.

will tend to prefer lower (higher) prices to those set by the entrepreneur linear in risk.

It should be understood that there is nothing mandatory in this tendency, and the latter will likely decline as profit levels decline. Indeed, while it is the curvature of the risk-preference function that will ultimately dictate the direction in which the "nonlinear" entrepreneur's price differs from $P^*$, it would seem that as decreases are effected in the relevant profit levels, the risk-evader (-taker) will become more likely to raise (lower) his price relative to $P^*$. One must continually hedge, however, replacing conclusions with conjectures, because of the potentially varied behavior of $V$, $\hat{f}$, and $\hat{f}'$. The second-order condition requires

$$\frac{d^2E[V]}{dP^2} = \int v''Q^2\hat{f}\,dQ + 2\int v'Q\hat{f}'\,dQ + \int v\hat{f}''\,dQ < 0$$

at the optimal $P$, with $\hat{f}''$ defined accordingly. The effects of nonlinearity on $2\int v'Q\hat{f}'\,dQ + \int v\hat{f}''\,dQ$ are not clear. By assumption the condition is satisfied for linear risk preferences with $v'' = 0$. It will also be true, however, that for $V$ strictly concave (convex), $\int v''Q^2\hat{f}\,dQ$ will be negative (positive) since $v''$ will be negative (positive). While we are *not* in a position to assert that when the second-order condition holds for one who is linear in risk, it will *unquestionably* hold for those who are nonlinear in risk, we have every reason to expect that it *will* hold for the risk-evader, and *might* hold for the risk-taker.

Suppose, nonetheless, that $d^2E[V]/dP^2 > 0$, where the first-order condition holds. Then $E[V]$ is *minimized* at this point. Assuming (13.21) to have a unique solution, this would suggest that the entrepreneur will want to move as far away as possible from this point. That is, $E[V]$ would be a convex function of price and *either* the highest or the lowest quotable price will be preferred, depending upon which yields the greater $E[V]$. Moreover, the maximum $E[V]$ occurs at a bound, and there *always* is a lower bound of zero at which a price can be quoted; but the upper bound is effectively unrestricted, so long as there is *some* possibility of a sale at this higher price. Thus the risk-taking entrepreneur is particularly likely to prefer a higher price than that preferred by his "linear" and risk-evading colleagues when the second-order condition for a maximum is not satisfied; but, should he prefer a lower price, he goes all the way and charges the lowest feasible price. The risk-taker doesn't do things half-way, although he might if the solution to (13.21) is not unique.

It should also be mentioned that, as (13.21) makes evident, if the firm is forced to sell to every buyer at the quoted price, the firm linear in risk will charge a price no less than $P^*$. This is so, because then the highest $Q$ and negative $\hat{f}'$ values *may* be associated with lower $v(\pi)$ values than previously, if the possibility exists of some demand greater than the $P^* = MC$ output. Hence, $-\int v\hat{f}'\,dQ$ is reduced, requiring a reduction in $E[Q]$; the latter will be effected by a price boost. This tendency is accentuated for the risk-evader, because not only does $-\int v\hat{f}'\,dQ$ decline, but $E[v']$ is increased, because $v'$ is a decreasing function of $\pi$, and $\sigma_{v'Q}$ becomes less negative. When this risk-evader may be forced to sell more than he would like to sell, he too raises price. The situation is cloudy for the risk-taker, however, because *both* $E[v']$ and $-\int v\hat{f}'\,dQ$ decline, and $\sigma_{v'Q} > 0$ is reduced. It would seem intuitively plausible that at the very least he will not reduce price, but it is not clearly demonstrable that he will raise price (particularly if he has already elected to price at the upper bound, though he might if he elected the lower bound).

Once more, then, we observe the profound effects that attitudes towards risk and uncertainty can have on entrepreneurial behavior, and once more we observe the individuality of this behavior. We shall also consider how this behavior is affected by changes in some of the relevant parameters, but first we present a numerical illustration to help place these results in better perspective.

### c. A Numerical Illustration

Consider a neoclassical firm whose demand curve is $P = 50 - .40Q$, and whose total cost curve is $C = 50 + .10Q^2$. The profit-maximizing price and output are readily determined to be $P^* = 30$ and $Q^* = 50$. Suppose this same firm is to operate under demand uncertainty such that the probabilities of selling quantities between 45 and 55 units at prices of 29.99, 30.00, and 30.01, as well as the associated profit levels, are those in the upper halves of Tables 13.1(a) and (b). The probabilities

TABLE 13.1(a)

| | $\pi = 50Q - .50Q^2 - 50$ | | |
|---|---|---|---|
| $Q$ | $P = 29.99$ | $P = 30.00$ | $P = 30.01$ |
| 45 | | | 1097.95 |
| 46 | 1117.94 | 1118.40 | 1118.86 |
| 47 | 1138.63 | 1139.10 | 1139.57 |
| 48 | 1159.12 | 1159.60 | 1160.08 |
| 49 | 1179.41 | 1179.90 | 1180.39 |
| 50 | 1199.50 | 1200.00 | 1200.50 |
| 51 | 1219.39 | 1219.90 | 1220.41 |
| 52 | 1239.08 | 1239.60 | 1240.12 |
| 53 | 1258.57 | 1259.10 | 1259.63 |
| 54 | 1277.86 | 1278.40 | 1278.94 |
| 55 | 1296.95 | | |
| $E[\pi]$ | 1199.7553 | 1199.7580 | 1199.7553 |

| | $\pi = 40Q - .40Q^2 - 50$ | | |
|---|---|---|---|
| $Q$ | $P = 24.99$ | $P = 25.00$ | $P = 25.01$ |
| 45 | | | 872.95 |
| 46 | 887.94 | 888.40 | 888.86 |
| 47 | 903.63 | 904.10 | 904.57 |
| 48 | 919.12 | 919.60 | 920.08 |
| 49 | 934.41 | 934.90 | 935.39 |
| 50 | 949.50 | 950.00 | 950.50 |
| 51 | 964.39 | 964.90 | 965.41 |
| 52 | 979.08 | 979.60 | 980.12 |
| 53 | 993.57 | 994.10 | 994.63 |
| 54 | 1007.86 | 1008.40 | 1008.94 |
| 55 | 1021.95 | | |
| $E[\pi]$ | 949.7518 | 949.7580 | 949.7570 |

TABLE 13.1(b)
$f(P;Q)$

| $Q$ | $P = 29.99$ | $P = 30.00$ | $P = 30.01$ |
|---|---|---|---|
| 45 | 0 | 0 | .001 |
| 46 | .019 | .02 | .021 |
| 47 | .039 | .04 | .041 |
| 48 | .079 | .08 | .081 |
| 49 | .209 | .21 | .211 |
| 50 | .299 | .30 | .299 |
| 51 | .211 | .21 | .209 |
| 52 | .081 | .08 | .079 |
| 53 | .041 | .04 | .039 |
| 54 | .021 | .02 | .019 |
| 55 | .001 | 0 | 0 |
| $Q$ | $P = 24.99$ | $P = 25.00$ | $P = 25.01$ |
| 45 | 0 | 0 | .00132 |
| 46 | .01868 | .02 | .02133 |
| 47 | .03867 | .04 | .04133 |
| 48 | .07867 | .08 | .08133 |
| 49 | .20867 | .21 | .21133 |
| 50 | .29867 | .30 | .29867 |
| 51 | .21133 | .21 | .20867 |
| 52 | .08133 | .08 | .07867 |
| 53 | .04133 | .04 | .03867 |
| 54 | .02133 | .02 | .01868 |
| 55 | .00132 | 0 | 0 |

have been assigned to assure *expected* demand at each price equivalent to that for the certainty demand curve. Expected profit, given in the row labeled $E[\pi]$, is maximized at the certainty optimum of 30.00.

The upper halves of Tables 13.2 and 13.3 give one *illustrative* set of risk-preference equivalents associated with the profit figures of Table 13.1(a), for a risk-evader ($V = -1{,}440{,}000 + 2600\pi - \pi^2$) and a risk-taker ($V = 640{,}000 - 1600\pi + \pi^2$), respectively. The rows labeled $E[V]$ give the expected "utiles" for each of the three prices, determined with respect to the probability distributions of Table 13.1(b).

Although for *these* three prices $E[V]$ like $E[\pi]$ is maximized for *this* risk-evader at 30, he prefers the price of 29.99 to the price of 30.01. $E[V]$ will not be symmetric about its maximum with respect to $P$, however, because $V$ is a quadratic function of $\pi$ and $\pi$ is a quadratic function of $Q$, and $Q$ can be written as a linear function of $P$. Hence $V$ will be a *quartic* function of $P$, and will be asymmetric with respect to $P$. At these levels of $P$, however, any asymmetry will be minute; and, in point of fact, if the entrepreneur considers fractional prices beyond two decimals, as indeed is often the case in industrial pricing, a price between 29.99 and 30.00 will be preferred.

For the risk-taker, however, the price of 30 is not at all desirable. Indeed, *either* alternative is preferred to 30, with the higher price being preferred to the lower. This

TABLE 13.2
Risk-Evader: $V = -1{,}440{,}000 + 2600\pi - \pi^2$

| $Q$ | $P$ = **29.99** | $P$ = **30.00** | $P$ = **30.01** |
|---|---|---|---|
| 45 | | | 209175.80 |
| 46 | 216854.16 | 217021.44 | 217188.33 |
| 47 | 223959.72 | 224111.19 | 224262.22 |
| 48 | 230152.83 | 230287.84 | 230422.39 |
| 49 | 235458.05 | 235575.99 | 235693.45 |
| 50 | 239899.75 | 240000.00 | 240099.75 |
| 51 | 243502.03 | 243583.99 | 243665.43 |
| 52 | 246288.75 | 246351.84 | 246414.39 |
| 53 | 248283.56 | 248327.19 | 248370.26 |
| 54 | 249509.82 | 249533.44 | 249556.48 |
| 55 | 249990.70 | | |
| $E[V]$ | 238975.13 | 238983.40 | 238971.06 |
| $Q$ | $P$ = **24.99** | $P$ = **25.00** | $P$ = **25.01** |
| 45 | | | 67628.30 |
| 46 | 80206.56 | 80585.44 | 80963.90 |
| 47 | 92890.82 | 93263.19 | 93635.12 |
| 48 | 104930.43 | 105295.84 | 105660.79 |
| 49 | 116343.95 | 116701.99 | 117059.55 |
| 50 | 127149.75 | 127500.00 | 127849.75 |
| 51 | 137365.93 | 137707.99 | 138049.53 |
| 52 | 147010.35 | 147343.84 | 147676.79 |
| 53 | 156100.66 | 156425.19 | 156749.16 |
| 54 | 164654.22 | 164969.44 | 165284.08 |
| 55 | 172688.20 | | |
| $E[V]$ | 126776.09 | 126785.90 | 126776.17 |

also holds in the lower half of the table, derived for the "lower" certainty demand curve of $P = 40 - .30Q$. Profit is maximized for the latter at $P^* = 25$ and $E[Q] = 50$. It should be noted that in assigning the probabilities here, rounding slightly exaggerates the expected quantities below and above $Q = 50$ away from the certainty demand curve. The lesser expected quantities are too small, and the greater are too large. This accounts for the lack of symmetry in the $E[\pi]$ figures in the lower half of Table 13.1(a), but again the asymmetry is negligible.

On the one hand, as indicated in the $E[V]$ row in the lower half of Table 13.2, the lower demand and profits not only dampen the desirability for the risk-evader of a price a shade below 25, but in view of the slight asymmetry, the risk-evader might prefer a price *above* 25. On the other hand, the risk-taker again simply wants to avoid the expected profit maximizer's optimum of 25. Their behavior perhaps suggests the following. In real-world pricing situations, one is necessarily going to choose from a set of *discrete* alternatives. Whether one is linear in risk or a risk-

TABLE 13.3
Risk-Taker: $V = 640{,}000 - 1600\pi + \pi^2$

| $Q$ | $P = 29.99$ | $P = 30.00$ | $P = 30.01$ |
|---|---|---|---|
| 45 | | | 88774.20 |
| 46 | 101085.84 | 101378.56 | 101671.70 |
| 47 | 114670.28 | 114988.81 | 115307.78 |
| 48 | 128967.17 | 129312.16 | 129657.61 |
| 49 | 143951.95 | 144324.01 | 144696.55 |
| 50 | 159600.25 | 160000.00 | 160400.25 |
| 51 | 175887.97 | 176316.01 | 176744.57 |
| 52 | 192791.25 | 193248.16 | 193705.61 |
| 53 | 210286.44 | 210772.81 | 211259.74 |
| 54 | 228350.18 | 228866.56 | 229383.52 |
| 55 | 246959.30 | | |
| $E[V]$ | 160780.12 | 160774.60 | 160784.19 |
| $Q$ | $P = 24.99$ | $P = 25.00$ | $P = 25.01$ |
| 45 | | | 5321.70 |
| 46 | 7733.44 | 7814.56 | 7896.10 |
| 47 | 10739.18 | 10836.81 | 10934.88 |
| 48 | 14189.57 | 14304.16 | 14419.21 |
| 49 | 18066.05 | 18198.01 | 18330.45 |
| 50 | 22350.25 | 22500.00 | 22650.25 |
| 51 | 27024.07 | 27192.01 | 27360.47 |
| 52 | 32069.65 | 32256.16 | 32443.21 |
| 53 | 37469.34 | 37674.81 | 37880.84 |
| 54 | 43205.78 | 43430.56 | 43655.92 |
| 55 | 49261.80 | | |
| $E[V]$ | 22975.66 | 22972.10 | 22980.79 |

evader, unless aversion to risk is extremely pronounced, the price that is an optimum for one entrepreneur will also be the optimum for the others—as far as the *considered* alternatives are concerned. This price is, however, precisely the price that the risk-taker eschews. In effect, and depending upon the range of alternatives he evaluates, it is the risk-taker who will behave *either* as a "price-cutter" *or* as a "price-raiser." The risk-taker looks at a situation with an entirely different perspective from everybody else. He does not conform; he does not view a lower price or a higher price as being "too risky." He is willing to lead—and in any direction.

Closer inspection of the figures in Tables 13.2 and 13.3 helps to shed some light on what motivates the actions of entrepreneurs nonlinear in risk. On the one hand, from Table 13.3 we note that prices *either* above *or* below 30 afford the risk-taker the *possibility* of higher profits, and consequently the *possibility* of *relatively* sizable boosts in the $v(\pi)$ because of the convexity of $V$. Prices away from $P^*$ have increased the dispersion in profits without decreasing their expectation sufficiently to cause the risk-taker to lean towards $P^* = 30$. On the other hand, for the risk-evader the changes in possible $v(\pi)$ effected by a price *lower* than $P^*$ are scarcely apparent when the $\pi$ levels are high, and the lower price might increase the likelihood of the higher $v(\pi)$ sufficiently to warrant this lower price. A price above $P^*$ brings with it the *possibility* of a lower $v(\pi)$ well out of line with all the others. At the lower profit levels, however, there are *relatively* sizable changes in the $v(\pi)$ as price changes. Depending upon how the probabilities of receiving these $v(\pi)$ are affected, the risk-evader may be willing to chance the possibility of the low $v(\pi)$, for now it is not all that out of line with the others.

## d. A Special Case

As an interesting special case, suppose that uncertainty is introduced into the demand curve through the random variable $u$ and the density $g(u)$, such that $Q = D(P) + u$. We shall assume that for all relevant $P$, $Q \geq 0$ and that $E[u] = 0$, $E[u^2] > 0$. The entrepreneur will seek to maximize

$$E[V] = \int_0^{Q_m} v(PQ - c(Q))f(Q)\,dQ + \int_{Q_m}^{\infty} v(PQ_m - c(Q_m))f(Q)\,dQ$$

with respect to $P$, where $f(Q) \equiv g(Q - D(P))$. Assuming that $d^2E[V]/dP^2 < 0$ at the optimal $P^*$, the maximum obtains at a $P^*$ where

$$\int_0^{Q_m} v'\left[Q + \left(\frac{dQ}{dP^*}\right)P^* - \left(\frac{dc}{dQ}\right)\left(\frac{dQ}{dP^*}\right)\right]f(Q)\,dQ + \int_{Q_m}^{\infty} v'\left[Q_m + \left(\frac{dQ_m}{dP^*}\right)P^* - \left(\frac{dc}{dQ_m}\right)\left(\frac{dQ_m}{dP^*}\right)\right]f(Q)\,dQ = 0,$$

since $dQ/dP = d[D(P) + u]/dP$, which is independent of $u$. At $P^*$, however, $P^* = dc/dQ_m$. The previous equation thus reduces to the condition $E[v'Q] + (dQ/dP^*)(E[v'P^*] - E[v'(dc/dQ)]) = 0$, where the expectations are, as before, taken with the entire area $\int_{Q_m}^{\infty} f(Q)\,dQ$ massed at $Q_m$, after adding $v'(dQ/dP^*)(P^* - dc/dQ_m)$ $\int_{Q_m}^{\infty} f(Q)\,dQ = 0$, and canceling the $dQ_m/dP^*$ terms. The latter expression may then be rewritten as

$$E[v']E[Q] + \sigma_{v'Q} + \left(\frac{dQ}{dP^*}\right)P^*E[v'] = \left(\frac{dQ}{dP^*}\right)\left(E[v']E\left[\frac{dc}{dQ}\right] + \sigma_{v'M}\right),$$

where $\sigma_{v'Q}$ and $\sigma_{v'M}$ are the truncated covariances between $v'$ and output, and $v'$ and marginal cost, respectively. Rearranging terms,

$$E[Q] + \left(\frac{dQ}{dP^*}\right)P^* = \left(\frac{dQ}{dP^*}\right)\left(E\left[\frac{dc}{dQ}\right] + \frac{\sigma_{v'M}}{E[v']}\right) - \frac{\sigma_{v'Q}}{E[v']}.$$

Now, expected total revenue at $P^*$ will be given by $E[R] = PE[Q]$. Defining expected marginal revenue as $dE[R]/dE[Q] = E[Q]/(dQ/dP) + P$ (because $dE[Q]/dP = dQ/dP$ by the additivity assumption), and after substituting into the previous equation, and rearranging terms, we then determine the expected utility-maximizing condition:

$$MR = E\left[\frac{dc}{dQ}\right] + \frac{\sigma_{v'M} - \sigma_{v'Q}/(dQ/dP^*)}{E[v']}.$$

In the case of linear risk preferences, the $\sigma_{v'M}$ and $\sigma_{v'Q}$ terms disappear. We then return to a "marginal revenue equals marginal cost" equality, but in terms of expected sales. With increasing marginal cost, $\sigma_{v'Q} < 0$ and $\sigma_{v'M} < 0$ for the risk-evader. But, $dQ/dP^* < 0$ with a downward-sloping demand curve, and hence $\sigma_{v'M}$ *and* $-\sigma_{v'Q}/(dQ/dP^*)$ are negative. Thus, the risk-evader prefers a price such that expected marginal revenue is *less than* expected marginal cost. This implies that he prefers a lower price to that preferred by one who is linear in risk. Analogously, the risk-taker prefers to price such that expected marginal revenue is *above* expected marginal cost. This implies that he prefers a higher price to that preferred by one who is linear in risk. With constant $MC$ the same result holds, for then only $\sigma_{v'M} = 0$; but, with decreasing $MC$, $\sigma_{v'M} > 0$ for the risk-evader (and $< 0$ for the risk-taker), and their relative price preferences cannot be uniquely specified. Overall, the results of this special case do, nonetheless, lend support to the previous suggestions.

## 13.5 THE REACTION OF THE PRICE-QUOTER TO CHANGE

As we have seen, the comparative prices quoted by like firms can be as divergent and unamenable to definitive statements as the attitudes towards risk held by different entrepreneurs. Although one is forced to be equally hesitant in predicting reactions to change when risk preferences are nonlinear, these reactions are, nonetheless, well worth consideration.

### a. The Effects of a Profits Tax

If a perfect-loss-offset profits tax of $\tau$ is imposed on the price-quoter, the first-order condition to maximize $E[V = v(\pi_\tau) = v((1 - \tau)\pi)]$ becomes

$$\frac{dE[V]}{dP} = (1 - \tau) \int v'Q\hat{f}\, dQ + \int v\hat{f}'\, dQ = 0. \tag{13.20''}$$

As shown previously, the effects of the tax on price will be directly proportional to $\partial^2 E[V]/\partial P \partial \tau$. The latter is readily found to be

$$\frac{\partial^2 E}{\partial P \partial \tau} = \int \left[ \frac{v}{(1 - \tau)} - v'\pi \right] \hat{f}'\, dQ - [1 - \tau] \int v''\pi Q\hat{f}\, dQ, \tag{13.23}$$

by partially differentiating (13.20'') with respect to $\tau$, and setting $-\int v'Q\hat{f}\, dQ = \int v\hat{f}'\, dQ/(1 - \tau)$ from the first-order condition.

When $V$ is linear, $v'' = 0$. Setting $v(\pi_\tau) = \pi_\tau = \pi(1 - \tau)$, $v' = 1$ and the bracketed term also becomes zero. Thus $\partial^2 E/\partial P\, \partial \tau = 0$, and the entrepreneur with linear risk preferences does not alter his price when the profits tax is imposed.

If $V$ is nonlinear, the sign of the first integral is quite obscure; but, if $V$ is strictly concave (convex), the second integral is necessarily negative (positive). For the risk-evader with a concave risk-preference function, then, $-[1 - \tau] \int v''\pi Q\hat{f}\, dQ > 0$. The *opposite* will hold for the risk-taker. Failing compelling arguments to the contrary, it would seem as if the risk-evader would "lean" towards price increases when a profits tax is imposed, whereas the risk-taker will "tend to" reduce price. These speculations aside, the crucial point is that in contrast with the traditional theory, we note that *some* change in price is a virtual certainty. Moreover, since the effect of the tax is to reduce the relevant profit levels, the posited effects on price are precisely those previously inferred for risk-evaders and risk-takers. In fact, if in the absence of a profits tax the risk-evader is charging a lower price than that charged by the risk-taker, this situation could be reversed when a profits tax is imposed. The most apparent tendency, however, would be to move each closer to the price preferred by the entrepreneur linear in risk. This reaction is similar to that of the quantity-setter responding to a profits tax.

## b. Shifts in Demand

There are various ways of describing demand shifts. By analogy with the certainty case, such shifts would involve changes in expected quantity demanded at each price; the latter could be effected by changing the shape of the probability distribution, shifting the entire distribution, or a combination of the two. For nondistortive simplicity, we consider only the case where the entire distribution shifts, and we focus on the price effects of increases in *expected* demand. In lieu of having $f(P; Q)$ change, however, we can equivalently have $Q$ change in the amount $dQ > 0$ at all levels of $Q$. With $f(P; Q + dQ)$ equal to $f(P; Q)$, expected quantity will change by $dQ > 0$.

To consider the effects on price of an increase in demand, first differentiate $dE[V]/dP = 0$ totally with respect to $Q$. This differentiation yields

$$\frac{\partial^2 E[V]}{\partial P^2}\frac{dP}{dQ} + \frac{\partial^2 E[V]}{\partial P \partial Q} = 0 \quad \text{or} \quad \frac{dP}{dQ} = \frac{-\partial^2 E[V]}{\partial P \partial Q} \Big/ \frac{\partial^2 E[V]}{\partial P^2}\,.$$

If satisfying the first-order condition does indeed maximize $E[V]$, then $\partial^2 E[V]/\partial P^2 < 0$, and $dP/dQ$ and $\partial^2 E[V]/\partial P \partial Q$ will have the same sign. Computing the latter,

$$\frac{\partial^2 E[V]}{\partial P \partial Q} = \int\left(v'' \frac{\partial \pi}{\partial Q} Q\hat{f} + v'\hat{f}\right) dQ + \int v' \frac{\partial \pi}{\partial Q} \hat{f}'\, dQ. \tag{13.24}$$

But $\partial \pi/\partial Q = P - dc/dQ$. Hence,

$$\frac{\partial^2 E[V]}{\partial P \partial Q} = \int v'' \left[P - \frac{dc}{dQ}\right] Q\hat{f}\, dQ + \int v'\hat{f}\, dQ + \int v' \left[P - \frac{dc}{dQ}\right] \hat{f}'\, dQ. \tag{13.24$'$}$$

Consider the entrepreneur linear in risk with $v(\pi) = \pi$. For him, $v'' = 0$ and $v' = 1$. Hence, $\int v'\hat{f}\, dQ = 1$, and $\int v'[P - dc/dQ]\hat{f}'dQ = P \int \hat{f}'\, dQ - \int (dc/dQ)\hat{f}'\, dQ = -\int (dc/dQ)\hat{f}'\, dQ$, since $\int \hat{f}'\, dQ = 0$. Thus,

$$\frac{\partial^2 E[V_L]}{\partial P \partial Q} = 1 - \int\left(\frac{dc}{dQ}\right)\hat{f}'\, dQ. \tag{13.24$''$}$$

If marginal costs are constant, the integral is zero; if marginal costs are increasing (with $Q$), the integral is negative. In either event, $\partial^2 E[V_L]/\partial P \partial Q > 0$. *Only* if marginal costs are decreasing can $\partial^2 E[V_L]/\partial P \partial Q$ become negative. Since $dP/dQ$ is proportional to $\partial^2 E[V]/\partial P\, \partial Q$, we can assert that one who is linear in risk will increase price for this upward demand shift, so long as marginal cost is not a decreasing function of output—and even then he *might* increase price.

For entrepreneurs who are nonlinear in risk, once again the situation is quite complicated. By assumption $P - dc/dQ \geq 0$. Consider a risk-evader with constant $dc/dQ$. $\int v'(P - dc/dQ)\hat{f}'\, dQ$ is positive, since $v'$ is a decreasing function of $Q$, and the smaller $v'$ values are "weighted" by the negative $\hat{f}'$ values. $\int v'\hat{f}\, dQ$ is necessarily positive. But, if $V$ is strictly concave, both $v''$ and $\int v''[P - dc/dQ]Q\hat{f}\, dQ$

will be negative, and the sign of $\partial^2 E[V]/\partial P \partial Q$ is not clear. If $dc/dQ$ is increasing, then $\int v'[P - dc/dQ]\hat{f}'\,dQ$ will show a greater positive tendency and $\int v''[P - dc/dQ]Q\hat{f}\,dQ$ a lesser negative tendency, and the likelihood of a price increase will be greater. If $dc/dQ$ is decreasing, the likelihood of a price decrease is enhanced. In effect, the upward shift in demand has raised the firm's profit *potential*, and this encourages the risk-evader either to reduce price, or to increase it less than one who is linear in risk would increase it.

In contrast, for the risk-taker with $V$ strictly convex, $v'' > 0$ and $\int v''[P - dc/dQ]Q\hat{f}\,dQ > 0$. With constant marginal cost, $\int v'[P - dc/dQ]\hat{f}'\,dQ < 0$, since $v'$ is an increasing function; and $\int v'\hat{f}\,dQ > 0$, always. Hence, we might expect, but cannot be certain of, a price increase. If $MC$ is increasing, $\int v'[P - dc/dQ]\hat{f}'\,dQ$ will become less negative (or positive); and if $MC$ is decreasing, it will become more negative. The exact effects on $\int v''[P - dc/dQ]Q\hat{f}\,dQ$ will depend upon the shape of $v'$ (which will determine how $v''$ changes with $Q$). It seems likely that the risk-taker will be persuaded to increase price (because $v'' > 0$), a result that is in line with our expectations when the potential profits are increased, but the particulars will decide the issue.

It might be noted that for this type of upward shift in demand,

$$\frac{\partial \hat{\eta}}{\partial Q} = -P\left[\int Q\hat{f}'\,dQ + \left(\frac{dQ_m}{dP}\right)F\right] \Big/ (E[Q])^2 = -\frac{\hat{\eta}}{E[Q]} > 0.$$

That is, effective demand becomes more inelastic at each and every price. The prospect of a price increase with constant $MC$, for one who is linear in risk and viewing an upward shift in demand to a less elastic demand curve, is directly in line with the certainty expectation. Further, suppose demand shifts such that the effective elasticity $\hat{\eta}$ is constant at $P^*$. With constant $MC$, or linear $c(Q) = B + bQ$, (13.19′) becomes

$$P^* = \frac{\int [B + bQ]\hat{f}'\,dQ}{[\int Q\hat{f}'\,dQ]}\left[\frac{\hat{\eta}}{1 + \hat{\eta}}\right] = \frac{b\hat{\eta}}{1 + \hat{\eta}}.$$

Hence, as in the certainty case, the optimal price is unaltered for one who is linear in risk when, with constant $MC$ and a shift in demand, the demand elasticity is unchanged at the optimal price.

## c. Changes in Cost

### i. FIXED COSTS

In the neoclassical theory changes in fixed costs do not affect the firm's decisions. This will not necessarily be true, however, under uncertainty.

As in previous analyses, the effects on price of changes in fixed costs $K$, or $dP/dK$, will be directly proportional to $\partial^2 E[V]/\partial P \partial K$. With profit given by $\pi = PQ - c(Q)$, and writing $c(Q) = K + c_q(Q)$, where $c_q(Q)$ denotes variable costs, $\partial \pi/\partial K = -1$. Therefore,

$$\frac{\partial^2 E[V]}{\partial P \partial K} = -\int v''Q\hat{f}\,dQ - \int v'\hat{f}'\,dQ. \tag{13.25}$$

When the entrepreneur is linear in risk, $v'' = 0$, and $v'$ is a constant, so that $\partial^2 E[V]/\partial P \partial K = 0$; price is indeed unaffected by a change in fixed cost. Again, things are not as clear for the entrepreneur with nonlinear risk preferences. Then, *neither* integral disappears, and in general $\partial^2 E[V]/\partial P\, \partial K \neq 0$. Price will be altered, but the direction is indeterminate.

In the case of the risk-evader, for example, with $V$ strictly concave we will have $v'' < 0$ and $-\int v''Qf\, dQ > 0$. Since $v'$ is a decreasing function of $Q$, however, $\int v'\hat{f}'\, dQ$ will also be positive and $\partial^2 E[V]/\partial P \partial K$ will be the difference of positive quantities. Repeating earlier arguments, one might think it highly likely that the first term will tend to outweigh the second. Then the risk-evader will prefer a higher price when increases in fixed costs are incurred, and this conforms with the suggestion that reductions in the relevant profit levels will *tend* to raise the price preferred by the risk-evader. Precisely the reverse will be true for the risk-taker. Again, however, the suggestion is built on a very shaky foundation; but again the fact that *something* can happen—price may be altered—is apparent.

### ii. VARIABLE COSTS

If variable costs change, the situation holds additional complications. First, suppose variable costs are changed without altering marginal costs. The effects on price would then be seen through the sign of $\partial^2 E[V]/\partial P \partial c_q = \partial^2 E[V]/\partial P \partial K$. That is, the effects would be precisely the same as those in the case of fixed costs. With linear risk preferences, as in the certainty case, the optimal decision will be unaffected when the *marginal* cost curve is fixed.

If marginal costs change, suppose first that this does not influence the number of units that the firm *might* choose to sell. That is, the firm has planned on selling units so long as marginal cost does not exceed the quoted price. We first suppose marginal cost changes, but at the previous optimum $P^*$ the number of units the firm *might* sell does not change, say because the probability is zero of having the number of units demanded that would equate $P^*$ and $MC$. This assumption is important, for it permits us to retain the same upper limit on the integrals. For the entrepreneur who is linear in risk, given a reduction in total costs of $h(Q) > 0$, the first-order condition becomes

$$\frac{dE[\pi]}{dP} = \int Q\hat{f}\, dQ + P \int Q\hat{f}'\, dQ - \int [c(Q) - h(Q)]\hat{f}'\, dQ.$$

At $P^*$, this reduces to $\int h(Q)\hat{f}'\, dQ$. If $h(Q)$ is constant and marginal costs are unaffected, this term disappears and we still have $dE[\pi]/dP^* = 0$; if $h(Q)$ is an increasing function of $Q$ so that $MC$ *falls*, $\int h(Q)\hat{f}'\, dQ$ is negative, so is $dE[\pi]/dP^*$, and hence price will be reduced; if $h(Q)$ is a decreasing function of $Q$, marginal cost and price will be increased—as in the certainty case.

With nonlinear risk preferences, we must consider the effects on $dE[V]/dP^* = \int v'Q\hat{f}\, dQ + \int v\hat{f}'\, dQ$. For the risk-evader, if marginal costs are unchanged, as in the case of changes in fixed costs, when total variable costs decline the first integral will be reduced (since $v'$ is a decreasing function of $\pi$, and the latter has gone up), and the second integral will be increased (since $v$ is increasing, but at a decreasing rate, with $\pi$). If $h(Q)$ is an increasing function of $Q$, the greatest increases in profit are felt at the higher output and profit levels where the $v'$ terms are small, and the effects on the positive first term (which declines) are almost as great as with constant $MC$. Similarly, it is the $v(\pi)$ associated with the negative $\hat{f}'$ that get the bigger boosts. Thus, the second term either will not increase, or might decrease. Again we can only speculate in terms of tendencies, but the risk-evader's tendency to price below $P^*$

will apparently be increased with a decline in total and marginal cost. Similarly, any tendency to increase price when total costs decline will be accentuated by an increase in marginal costs. The opposite will be true for the risk-taker.

Finally, note that if the entrepreneur *might* be able to sell more (or less) at $P^*$ than he previously anticipated he would elect to sell, shifts in marginal cost will change the upper limit on the integrals with which we have been working. This adds an additional complication, since it means that *both* the effective expected demand and the cost curves change. Where the marginal cost curve falls, the effective and actual expected demand are brought more in line with one another, and there is less probability of unsatisfied demand; where the marginal cost is raised, the opposite would be true. The effects on quoted price are not at all apparent.

### d. Advertising Expenditures and Risk Preferences

The effect of advertising is to shift the firm's demand curve to the right; or, in the current context, to effect an increase in expected demand at every price. It will be convenient to analyze advertising policy by considering advertising to raise the quantities at which a given probability distribution of demand obtains.

Denoting advertising expenditures by $A$, $\pi = PQ - c(Q) - A$, and $E[\pi] = \int PQ\hat{f}\,dQ - \int c(Q)\hat{f}\,dQ - \int A\hat{f}\,dQ$. The entrepreneur who is linear in risk requires, as first-order conditions for a maximum, $\partial E[\pi]/\partial P = 0$ and $\partial E[\pi]/\partial A = 0$. The first equality is unaltered from the previous formulation with $A = 0$. The second is given by

$$\frac{\partial E[\pi]}{\partial A} = \int P^*\left(\frac{\partial Q}{\partial A}\right)\hat{f}\,dQ - \int\left(\frac{dc}{dQ}\right)\left(\frac{\partial Q}{\partial A}\right)\hat{f}\,dQ - 1 = 0,$$

by the assumption that advertising expenditures will increase the quantity at which a *given* $f(P;Q)$ will obtain. The second-order conditions then require that this increase in quantity take place at a decreasing rate. Hence, analogous to the certainty case, advertising monies are expended to the point at which $E[(P^* - dc/dQ)(\partial Q/\partial A)] = 1$, or until the *expected* increase in total revenue due to advertising, less the expected additional costs of production stemming from the higher expected output levels, equals the cost of undertaking that advertising. When marginal costs are decreasing, we have an *addition* to the total expected revenue increase.

With nonlinear risk preferences, in addition to $\partial E[V]/\partial P$, we must now consider $\partial E[V]/\partial A = \int v'[(P^* - dc/dQ)(\partial Q/\partial A) - 1]\hat{f}\,dQ$. Setting $\partial E[V]/\partial A = 0$, and again writing

$$E\left[v'\left(P^* - \frac{dc}{dQ}\right)\left(\frac{\partial Q}{\partial A}\right)\right] = E[v']E\left[\left(P^* - \frac{dc}{dQ}\right)\left(\frac{\partial Q}{\partial A}\right)\right] + \sigma_{v'N},$$

we determine

$$E\left[\left(P^* - \frac{dc}{dQ}\right)\left(\frac{\partial Q}{\partial A}\right)\right] = 1 - \frac{\sigma_{v'N}}{E[v']}\cdot \tag{13.26}$$

where $\sigma_{v'N}$ is the covariance between $v'$ and $[(P^* - dc/dQ)(\partial Q/\partial A)]$. In the case of linear risk preferences, $v'$ is constant, $\sigma_{v'N} = 0$, and we return to the earlier equality.

Let us assume for simplicity that $\partial Q/\partial A$ is independent of $Q$, in the sense that a particular increase in advertising expenditures calls forth the same increment in each of the $Q$'s at the *given* $f(P; Q)$'s; but increases in $A$ lead to successively smaller increases in $E[Q]$. In this case, *both* $P^*$ and $\partial Q/\partial A$ are independent of $Q$ per se, and therefore $E[(P^* - dc/dQ)(\partial Q/\partial A)]$ is a function of $dc/dQ$ alone. When marginal costs are increasing over the relevant range of $Q$'s, then $-dc/dQ$ becomes more negative *and* $\pi$ becomes bigger as $Q$ increases. Hence, for the risk-evader, $v'(\pi)$ also declines with increases in $Q$, and thus $\sigma_{v'N} > 0$; for the risk-taker, then, $\sigma_{v'N} < 0$. Therefore, the risk-evader will want to advertise to the point where $E[(P^* - dc/dQ)(\partial Q/\partial A)] < 1$, and for any price level $P^* > E[dc/dQ]$ he will advertise more than the entrepreneur who is linear in risk; analogously, the risk-taker will advertise less. If marginal cost is a decreasing function of output, the risk-taker will advertise more, and the risk-evader will advertise less, than one who is linear in risk. With constant $MC$, all three will have the same advertising preferences for a given $P^*$.

Note, however, that $E[(P^* - dc/dQ)(\partial Q/\partial A)]$ will be smaller the smaller is $P^*$ for a given $\partial Q/\partial A$. Thus, even with constant marginal costs the risk-evader, for example, who prefers a lower price will tend to advertise less than one linear in risk. This is because with constant $MC$, irrespective of risk preferences, advertising monies are expended to the point at which the next dollar spent is anticipated to bring in but one additional dollar of revenue; and this point is reached at a lower level of expenditure when a lower price is charged. When marginal costs are increasing, or when $\partial Q/\partial A$ is not independent of $Q$, the situation is, once again, not very clear-cut, and we are again forced back to the interesting, if unsatisfying, observation that advertising preferences are likely to differ with risk preferences, but we do not know how. It must further be emphasized that we generally do not know who will actually spend the greatest amount on advertising, since this will depend on price preferences and the second of the first-order conditions. Advertising and price policy will be determined simultaneously.

## 13.6 THE PRICE-QUOTER AND CLASSICAL CONSTRUCTS

Although the model of the price-quoter has the "disadvantage" of permitting individuals to behave as they wish and argues against definitive prescriptions, it has the compensating advantage of making unnecessary the traditional distinctions between various forms of market structure; these are subsumed within $f(P; Q)$, the probability assignments.

Suppose, for example, it is judged that any new price the firm quotes above its current price will result in a loss of *all* customers. That is, the current market price is $P^*$ and $d[\int Qf\,dQ]/dP = \int Qf'\,dQ \rightarrow -\infty$ for $P > P^*$. Further, suppose it is judged that any price reduction will fail to raise demand. That is, $\int Qf'\,dQ \approx 0$ for $P < P^*$. This is the case of the pure competitor's demand curve. In this case, irrespective of risk preferences a price boost above $P^*$ will necessarily eliminate sales, and a price decrease will only reduce profits and $E[V]$. Thus, once all firms recognize the purely competitive nature of their industry (that is, the nature of $f(P; Q)$), as they are certain to do, all will settle on the market price of $P^*$ irrespective of price preferences. Thus the economic theory developed when competition in the economy approached the purely competitive stage did not suffer from its failure to include risk preferences as a factor. The policies followed by the firm are the same in each system.

Similarly, suppose by trial and error the entrepreneur obtains new information and continually revises his probability assignments to the point where he is confident that he knows *with certainty* how much the firm can sell at any quoted price. Then, once again all firms charge the same price irrespective of risk preferences. The price that maximizes $\pi$ is determinate, and the greater is $\pi$ the greater is $V$. Thus, the neoclassical theory that deals with the monopolist who behaves *as if* his world were one of certainty does not require consideration of risk preferences, because the optimal decision is independent of risk preferences. Similar remarks hold for the classical oligopoly models.

Once we move away from these extremes, however, to recognize the presence of uncertainty *both* because the reactions of consumers to various prices need not be deterministic *and* because competitors' prices and related policies are not likely to be known with certainty, the present approach reaps its full advantage. In particular, the interdependence of firms is explicitly detailed directly within $f(P; Q)$. This enters when one must quantify probability judgments with respect to the prices that others may charge, as well as the effects of these prices on the demand for one's own product. In effect, the pricing decision is not as much one of game theory as it is one of *decision* theory. The entrepreneur must consider the options of *all other* firms and their consequences for the demand facing *his* firm. The interdependencies that have traditionally delineated one industry from another, and competitors' possible reactions, are introduced via, the implications of "other" $P_i$ for the density $f(P; Q)$.

The analysis makes clear that it is not the *number* of one's "competitors" that constrains the firm's pricing behavior, nor whether the products produced by the "competitors" are homogeneous with respect to the given firm's product. Rather, the firm is constrained in its actions by the potential behavior of *any* and *all* firms whose policies can affect the demand for its product. Moreover, the effects of these constraints will differ between seemingly like firms, as managements' judgments and attitudes towards risk differ.

By the same token, emphasis is placed on the *information* that each firm has with respect to how competitors are likely to behave, and how this behavior will influence the consumer. If "equilibrium" connotes a situation in which the firm's price is unaltered from one price quote to the next, equilibrium can be assured only if entrepreneurial attitudes *and* judgments are constant. The former demands that risk preferences do not change when income changes; the latter demands that behavior in the system is in accordance with prior expectations in the sense that the posterior probabilities, conditional upon the information generated during the decision period, equal the priors. Furthermore, for equilibrium the entrepreneur must dismiss the option of altering price policy for the express purpose of acquiring sample information that will assist in future decision making.

The present approach therefore lends itself to an analysis of three vital aspects of the modern business community that the traditional theory is not equipped to handle. First, it permits one to undertake a decision-theoretic analysis of the value of information, from which it immediately follows that different entrepreneurs may value information differently. Second, it points up the fact, so clear to antitrust specialists, that equilibrium situations in which prices and quantities are stable from period to period are *abnormal*, and not something towards which firms *necessarily* head—in the absence of collusion or perfect information.[23]

[23] For comment on the roles of information and equilibrium pertinent to the present discussion see the following: F. A. von Hayek, "Economics and Knowledge," *Economica*,

Finally, this analysis makes it abundantly clear that the role chance plays in the success or failure of firms is not to be overlooked. Over the long haul, the entrepreneur with linear risk preferences will be expected to outstrip any of his nonlinear colleagues. He might not do so, but the odds are in his favor. Unhappily, however, it is not guaranteed that every firm will survive short-term misfortunes and endure while the long haul runs its course. The neoclassical firm does not undertake risk and does not enjoy or suffer its consequences; the real-world firm, and the firms considered in this chapter, do both. Given their risk preferences, information, and judgments, their actions are varied if determinable; the consequences of these actions are, and will remain, random.

## 13.7 CONCLUSIONS

The economic theorist is constantly forced to reconcile empirical observation and theoretical dictates. Unfortunately, he has traditionally felt compelled to do so under the guiding beacon of uniformity, and this bill is most ably filled by the neoclassical theory of the firm. Still, even the few models discussed in this chapter have been sufficient to point up the disparate paths that entrepreneurial behavior can take, both because of the potential impact of uncertainty and because of the varied ways in which uncertainty can enter into the picture.

Of the various models discussed, it is our view that the model of the price-quoter provides the most accurate and comprehensive portrayal of the institutional setting within which the modern firm operates. The firm of the real world quotes a price, albeit perhaps the "market" price, and to all intents and purposes waits to observe the buyers' reactions to that price—reactions that are subject to random variation. Yet, this very ingredient of increased realism prevents the model from yielding the sorts of definitive answers that have characterized traditional theory. Unlike the neoclassical microeconomics, forced by empirical observation into intellectual gym-

---

**IV**:13 (1937), 36; Gerhard Tintner, "A Contribution to the Nonstatic Theory of Production," in *Studies in Mathematical Economics and Econometrics* (New York: The Free Press of Glencoe, 1942), pp. 108–109; Oswald Knauth, *Business Practices, Trade Position, and Competition* (New York: Columbia University Press, 1956), p. 118; R. M. Cyert and J. G. March, "Organizational Factors in the Theory of Oligopoly," *Quarterly Journal of Economics*, **LXX**:1 (Feb. 1956), 44–64; Kenneth J. Arrow, "Towards a Theory of Price Adjustment," in *The Allocation of Economic Resources* (Stanford, Calif.: Stanford University Press, 1959), p. 48; G. B. Richardson, "Equilibrium, Expectations and Information," *Economic Journal*, **LXIX**:274 (June 1959), 223–237; and Sherrill Cleland, "A Short Essay on a Managerial Theory of the Firm," in K. E. Boulding and W. Allen Spivey, eds., *Linear Programming and the Theory of the Firm* (New York: The Macmillan Company, 1960), p. 205.

It is of particular interest to consider the suggestion that size itself may yield advantages in the world of uncertainty, both because of the large firm's ability to "spread the risks around" [see, for example, Adolf A. Berle, *The 20th Century Capitalist Revolution* (New York: Harcourt, Brace & World, Inc., 1954), p. 42; T. M. Whitin and M. H. Peston, "Random Variations, Risk, and Returns to Scale," *Quarterly Journal of Economics*, **LXVIII**:4 (Nov. 1954), 603–612] and because "the large firm has a far larger sample than the smaller one. . . [and] would be able to get a far better estimate of the probability distribution than would the small entrepreneur" [Martin Shubik, "Information, Risk, Ignorance and Indeterminacy," *Quarterly Journal of Economics*, **LXVIII**:21 (Nov. 1954), 638].

nastics designed to provide ex post rationales for definite and consistent a priori predictions that have gone awry, the present model is grounded in a philosophy that inherently argues against a priori prediction in the absence of excruciatingly detailed and intimate information; and it is as opposed to uniform prediction as it is sympathetic with the individuality of the decision maker. But, either a priori or ex post, it can rationalize a variety of behavior without ever being forced to go beyond its own boundaries and assumptions.

Whether the product is worth the price is for the customer to decide. One might, however, consider some of the following observations. The neoclassical model has considerable difficulty in explaining such occasionally observed phenomena as price increases following on the heels of both corporate tax increases and increases in fixed costs. If, however, one accepts the premise that corporate managements lean towards risk aversion,[24] and if one further accepts the previous conjectures of the price-quoter model, then these price increases are not only eminently plausible, *they are to be expected.*[25] Similarly, a technological advance that leaves marginal cost unaffected while reducing average cost will not affect the price quoted by the neoclassical firm. Such will, however, tend to lead the price-quoting risk-evader to reduce price, just as similarly we have come to expect the modern firm to "pass along to the consumer" some of the cost savings realized from technological advance.

It is also apparent from the model why prices may tend to be stable upward in the face of deflationary pressures effecting lower profit levels, and thereby lessening the *tendency* of the risk-evader to prefer lower prices.[26] If it is also true, as seems quite plausible, that it is in the younger firms in the newer industries that one is most likely to find the risk-taking managements,[27] then, as the numerical illustration revealed, it should also be in these firms and industries that one observes the greatest variation in price policy. This hypothesis awaits future empirical verification or refutation, but it does provide a clear conflict with the neoclassical model wherein variability is not anticipated, and organization characteristics are of secondary, rather than primary, import.

Profits, though, are likely to be but one of many components to be considered in a risk-preference function, and managements are as unlikely to be consciously seeking a price to optimize *any* risk-preference function as they are to be seeking the price that equates marginal revenue to marginal cost. One suspects that the

[24] One of the clearest explanations for this and the consequences is offered by R. Joseph Monsen, Jr., and Anthony Downs ["A Theory of Large Managerial Firms," *Journal of Political Economy*, **LXXIII**:3 (June 1965), 221–236]: "Middle managers will normally tend to be risk-avoiders in making decisions. A certain degree of advancement can be obtained merely by surviving, doing daily tasks, and not committing any outstanding blunders. . . . Consequently, the firm may pass up many profit-increasing possibilities on the middle-management level which would be taken up by a truly profit-maximizing firm" (p. 234).

[25] For an illustration of how the bounds of the neoclassical model must be stretched to achieve a reconciliation with reality, see K. E. Boulding, "The Incidence of a Profits Tax," *American Economic Review*, **XXXIV**:1 (Sept. 1944), 567–572.

[26] For some comments in a neoclassical setting on microeconomic behavior and cyclical forces, see Moses Abramovitz, "Monopolistic Selling in a Changing Economy," *Quarterly Journal of Economics*, **LII** (Feb. 1938), 191–214; and Carl Kaysen, "A Dynamic Aspect of the Monopoly Problem," *Review of Economics and Statistics*, **XXXI**:2 (May 1949), 109–113.

[27] See Abramovitz, "Monopolistic Selling in a Changing Economy," pp. 210–212.

typical middle manager knows as little about the former as he does about the latter. One also suspects that risk preferences are consistently being altered as wealth and circumstances change. Despite these concessions to practicality, it is also true that in the world of uncertainty the former at least provides a meaningful objective function, whereas the latter does not. And, even without making probability judgments and risk preferences explicit, the decision maker will *necessarily* admit these factors into his decision process, albeit perhaps in a vague, off-the-cuff, and poorly defined fashion. Assuming that what to the decision theorist is a very casual approach to decision making under uncertainty will commonly *point* the decision maker along the general lines that a more sophisticated approach would *prescribe*, without *consistently* leading him to preferred decisions, it does make some sense to speculate about the real world and what we can anticipate observing there.

At the same time, however, it must be acknowledged that individuals continually violate their own preferences because of an unwillingness or inability to take the time and trouble to see that these preferences are satisfied. At best, then, our speculations can only be imperfect predictors. The virtue of the present approach is that it helps to provide a framework within which one can develop a better understanding of the real world and its peccadilloes, as well as creates a foundation upon which more enlightened models of the firm's decision processes will be built.

## EXERCISES

1. Consider a firm facing a demand curve $Q = 10{,}000 - 100P + u$, where $u$ is a normally distributed random variable such that $E[u] = 0$ and $E[u^2] = 400$. The firm's total cost curve is given by $C = 49{,}000 + .04Q^2$.
   (a) If $u \equiv 0$, what is the profit-maximizing price and output?
   (b) If the entrepreneur is linear in risk (in terms of profit) and can instantly adjust production to meet demand, what price should he charge?
   (c) What price will the risk-taker and risk-evader considered in Section 13.4c prefer?
   (d) What do these results suggest?

2. What price *and* output would Mills' firm choose if confronted with the previous demand and cost curves?

3. Suppose a firm is one of many competitors. The firm's total cost curve is given by $C = 150 - 2Q + .01Q^2$. The current market price is $P = 75$. At this price, the entrepreneur judges he can sell $Q = 3850 + u$, where $u$ is a normally distributed random variable such that $E[u] = 0$ and $E[u^2] = 2500$.
   (a) What will output be for Hymans' entrepreneur who is linear in risk?
   (b) What will output be for Hymans' entrepreneur who has a risk-preference function of $V = \pi^{.5}$? What if $V = \pi^{2.5}$?

4. What are the effects on output in each instance in the previous question under the following circumstances: (a) a perfect-loss-offset 10 percent profits tax is imposed? (b) fixed costs increase by 200? (c) price in the market increases to 80?

5. Compare the answers to the previous question with those that would result if $E[u^2] \equiv 0$. What might these results indicate?

6. Can the results of the previous two exercises be generalized and stated as formal propositions? If so, do so; if not, why not?

7. Show that in the Drèze and Gabszewicz model, "competition and free entry with maximization of expected profit lead to an optimal number of firms in the sense of minimum expected total cost for the industry, but expected output for each firm is less than the output for which average cost is minimum" ("Demand Fluctuations, Capacity Utilization, and Prices," p. 127).

8. Reformulate Mills' model so as to include both a value for units held in inventory and a shortage cost. How do these affect the optimum price and output decision under linear risk preferences? How would these factors affect the behavior of Hymans' firm?

9. Determine the price preferences of the firm considered in Section 13.4c if when the demand curve is $P = 50 - .4Q$: (a) a perfect-loss-offset profits tax of 20 percent is imposed; (b) fixed costs increase by 100; (c) fixed costs decrease by 50.

10. Describe *in detail* how the value of sample information would be determined by Mills' and Dhrymes' entrepreneurs. How would this be handled for the price-quoter?

11. Extend Dhrymes' model to the case of the firm producing joint products.

12. Develop each of the models considered in this chapter from the standpoint of an entrepreneur with a quadratic risk-preference function. In doing so, assume that any and all random variables are generated by a normal process.

13. Contrast the behavior of Hymans' firm operating with a quadratic total cost function when the risk-evading entrepreneur shows decreasing versus constant versus increasing risk aversion in Pratt's sense.

14. How would you expect the price policy of the price-quoter to change over time as his wealth changes? Discuss.

# 14

# RECENT DEVELOPMENTS AND THE THEORY OF THE FIRM: Some Empirical Aspects

## 14.1 INTRODUCTION

Chapter 13 demonstrated the ubiquitous effects that uncertainty and attitude towards risk can have on decision making in the neoclassical firm. In view of the disparate modes of behavior that characterize firms of the real world, it was somewhat comforting to observe even staid and coldly calculating neoclassical entrepreneurs disagreeing on appropriate policies to follow, even when they agreed on the essential facts. Two particularly important implications of that analysis merit repetition: first, the analysis called attention to the crucial role that quantification of judgment *can* and *should* play in decision making; second, the analysis supported the argument that random elements will help to determine the degree of success or failure enjoyed by a decision maker, and thus that the path through which a firm is led into the future will be of a stochastic, rather than a deterministic nature.

Most assuredly, the latter suggestions are neither novel nor terribly startling. We have repeatedly remarked upon the subjective interpretation that some neoclassical theorists would not only admit, but indeed would stress, as an appropriate basis for viewing the decision parameters of microeconomic theory. Similarly, the potentially stochastic nature of the industrial process has not gone unnoticed, as evidenced by, for example, the continuing interest in Gibrat's law of proportionate effect, which hypothesizes that the *probability* a firm will achieve a given rate of growth during any specified time period is independent of the firm's size.[1] Neverthe-

[1] R. Gibrat, *Les Inégalités Economiqués* (Paris, 1931). Although the trial is likely to result in a hung jury, the evidence in favor of the law is by no means compelling, and the prosecution has introduced quite interesting data. For some empirical tests of the law, see the following: P. E. Hart and S. J. Prais, "The Analysis of Business Concentration: A Statistical Approach," *Journal of the Royal Statistical Society* (A), **119,** part 2 (1956), pp. 150–181; H. A. Simon and C. P. Bonini, "The Size Distribution of Firms," *American Economic Review,* **XLVIII**:4 (Sept. 1958), 608–617; C. E. Ferguson, "The Relationship of Business Size to Stability: An Empirical Approach," *Journal of Industrial Economics,* **IX**:1 (Nov. 1960), 23–42; P. E. Hart, "The Size and Growth of Firms," *Economica,* **29**:113 (Feb. 1962), 29–39; Edwin Mansfield, "Entry, Gibrat's Law, Innovation, and the

less, it is only recently that such suggestions have been recognized as being of sufficient importance, and as having sufficient validity, to be formalized and provided with a solid and rigorous theoretical underpinning. Now that this has been accomplished, however, certain empirical aspects immediately suggest themselves. In particular, one is encouraged to analyze the nature of the stochastic processes to which firms have historically been bound, and one can attempt to extend the means of quantifying and incorporating prior judgments into the decision-making process.

Each of these subjects is too broad in scope to be adequately discussed in a book such as this, published by a profit-oriented publisher and written by a rapidly aging theorist. It will, however, be feasible and useful to discuss two issues of particular interest and relevance to the preceding analyses. Specifically, we shall introduce the notion of the Markov process as *one* stochastic mechanism that is frequently encountered in descriptions of random processes to which firms and industries are intimately bound.[2] Additionally, we shall consider the possibility of employing prior information directly in the estimation of econometric relationships.

## 14.2 FIRST-ORDER MARKOV PROCESSES[3]

A Markovian view of a system such as the firm sees it as proceeding from a present into a future *stage* in which any one of $n$ possible outcomes or *states* $E_i$ will be attained with a *fixed probability*. If the probability of state $E_i$ $(i = 1, \ldots, n)$ at time $t$ is independent of any and all previous states through which the firm has passed, this represents a zero-order Markov process. Thus any event in which successive trials are independent of one another can be regarded as a zero-order Markov process. In the industrial scheme of things, if the probability that the firm will attain a given rate of growth at time $t$ is independent of growth rates that the firm has enjoyed in the past, its growth will be described by a zero-order Markov process. Clearly, however, the *basic* process to which the firm is tied could be a zero-order Markov process, the *particulars* of which may be alterable by actions taken by the firm. That is, it might well be the case that barring any change in operating procedure, the

---

Growth of Firms," *American Economic Review,* **LII**:5 (Dec. 1962), 1023–1051; Stephen Hymer and Peter Pashigian, "Firm Size and Rate of Growth," *Journal of Political Economy,* **70**:6 (Dec. 1962), 556–569; Ira Horowitz, 'Size, Growth, and Concentration of Investment Funds, 1951–60," *Quarterly Review of Economics and Business,* **3**:3 (Autumn 1963), 78–83; J. M. Samuels, "Size and the Growth of Firms," *Review of Economic Studies,* **XXXII**(2):90 (April 1965), 105–112. Also, see Josef Steindl, *Random Processes and the Growth of Firms,* (New York: Hafner Publishing Company, 1965).

[2] See, for example, S. J. Prais, "Measuring Social Mobility," *Journal of the Royal Statistical Society,* (A), **118,** part 1 (1955), 56–66; P. E. Hart and S. J. Prais, "The Analysis of Business Concentration: A Statistical Approach"; Irma G. Adelman, "A Stochastic Analysis of the Size Distribution of Firms," *Journal of the American Statistical Association,* **53**:284 (Dec. 1958), 893–904; Norman R. Collins and Lee E. Preston, "The Size Structure of the Largest Industrial Firms," *American Economic Review,* **LI**:5 (Dec. 1961), 986–1011; Ann R. Horowitz and Ira Horowitz, "Entropy, Markov Processes, and Competition in the Brewing Industry," *Journal of Industrial Economics,* **XVI**:3 (July 1968), 196–216.

[3] For more detailed and extensive discussions of Markov processes see the following: William Feller, *An Introduction to Probability Theory and Its Applications,* vol. I (New York: John Wiley & Sons, Inc., 1957), chaps. XV and XVI; John G. Kemeny and J. Laurie Snell, *Finite Markov Chains* (Princeton, N.J.: D. Van Nostrand Company, Inc., 1960); D. R. Cox and H. D. Miller, *The Theory of Stochastic Processes* (New York: John Wiley & Sons, Inc., 1965), chaps. 3–5.

probability the firm will achieve a growth rate of $g_i$ is appropriately assessed as $q_i$; but $q_i$ can be altered by a research program or advertising campaign.

One would suspect, however, that as a general rule of economic life successive outcomes are not commonly independent of one another. In the case of the successive rates of growth enjoyed by a firm, it might be speculated that if a "very high" rate of growth is achieved at time $t$, it is less likely than otherwise that a "very low" rate will be suffered at time $t + 1$. In the case of the firm's employees, if the amount of work that each produces can be classified into one of $n$ categories, the probability that a given employee's output at time $t + 1$ will fall into category $E_i$ ($i = 1, \ldots, n$) may be dependent upon his output at time $t$.

Situations such as these would fall into the category of *first-order Markov processes*. In such processes, the fixed probability that state $E_i$ is attained at stage $t + 1$ is *conditional* upon the state in which the system rests at stage $t$—and upon no prior stages. Similarly, one might assume that the states at both stages $t$ and $t - 1$ will influence the probability of attaining stage $E_i$ at time $t + 1$. This would define a second-order Markov process, and so forth for additional higher-order processes. The present discussion will be confined to the first-order Markov process (from here on referred to simply as a Markov process), for this has drawn particular attention, and has been found to be particularly interesting, from the standpoint of firm and industry analysis. It will be assumed throughout that $n$ is finite—that is, the process can enter into only a finite number of states $E_i$ ($i = 1, \ldots, n$).

The fixed *conditional* probability $p_{ij}$ gives the probability that starting from state $E_i$ at any time $t$, the system will enter state $E_j$ at time $t + 1$. This is called a *transition* probability. The entire distribution of transition probabilities is summarized in the *transition probability matrix* $\mathbf{P} = [p_{ij}]$. The following matrix is a transition probability matrix composed of the conditional probabilities with which a consumer who has purchased one of four possible brands ($E_1$, $E_2$, $E_3$, or $E_4$) at time $t$ will purchase each of the brands at time $t + 1$, provided that he does, in fact, purchase the product at every stage $t$:

$$\mathbf{P} = \begin{array}{c} \\ E_1 \\ E_2 \\ E_3 \\ E_4 \end{array}\!\!\begin{array}{c} \begin{array}{cccc} E_1 & E_2 & E_3 & E_4 \end{array} \\ \begin{bmatrix} .8033 & 0 & .1844 & .0123 \\ .1412 & .7547 & 0 & .1041 \\ 0 & .2535 & .7397 & .0068 \\ .2080 & .1232 & 0 & .6688 \end{bmatrix} \end{array}.$$

This particular matrix has been chosen for the illustration, since it contains an actual set of estimates of transition probabilities for purchases of premium beer in the United States. The method by which the matrix was obtained will be discussed in Section 14.6.

Although the matrix is based upon yearly data, for *illustrative* purposes it is convenient to interpret it in the following manner. $p_{32} = .2535$, for example, can be read to imply that about 25 percent of the time the consumer follows purchases of $E_3$ with a purchase of $E_2$; but $p_{23} = 0$ implies that purchases of $E_3$ never *directly* (that is, at the next stage) follow purchases of $E_2$. Note, however, that the consumer might follow purchases of $E_2$ with purchases of $E_1$ ($p_{21} = .1412$), and *then* follow purchases of $E_1$ with purchases of $E_3$ ($p_{13} = .1844$). Thus, one who consumes $E_2$ might consume $E_3$ in the future, but not in the *immediately* following future stage. As discussed below, it will not always be the case that one can reach $E_k$ from $E_i$, even by passing through one or more $E_j$'s. In some situations, once $E_i$ has been entered, $E_k$ can never again be entered. It should also be noted that, in this illustration, the diagonal elements $p_{ii}$ give the conditional probability that the consumer will repurchase his chosen brand over successive stages. As such, the diagonal elements give some insights into consumer brand loyalty.

The matrix $\mathbf{P}$ is called a *stochastic matrix*: it contains only nonnegative elements $p_{ij} \geq 0$, and the row elements necessarily sum to unity, $\sum_{j=1}^{n} p_{ij} = 1$. That is, we do not have negative "probabilities," and from any state at stage $t$ the system *must* enter one of the $n$ possible states at stage $t + 1$. One can always assign the $p_{ij}$ or define the states such that $\mathbf{P}$ will be a square matrix. If the columns as well as the rows sum to unity, the matrix is called *doubly stochastic*.

Suppose, now, that the system is at stage $t = 0$, and has yet to enter into any of the $n$ states $E_i$. Denote by $q_{i0}$ the probability that the first stage entered will be $E_i$. The vector $\mathbf{q}_0' = (q_{10}, \ldots, q_{i0}, \ldots, q_{n0})$ describes the initial distribution over the $E_i$, and will be called an *initial probability vector*. Postmultiplying the initial vector $\mathbf{q}_0'$ by the transition probability matrix $\mathbf{P}$ yields a second vector $\mathbf{q}_0'\mathbf{P} = \mathbf{q}_1'$. Consider the first element of $\mathbf{q}_1'$. The latter will be given by

$$q_{11} = q_{10}p_{11} + q_{20}p_{21} + \cdots + q_{i0}p_{i1} + \cdots + q_{n0}p_{n1}.$$

The computation of $q_{11}$ requires the addition of the probability of being in $E_1$ and returning there to the probability of being in $E_2$ and then going to $E_1$, to the probabilities of being in and then going from all other $E_i$ to $E_1$. Thus $q_{11}$ is the probability that the system will enter state $E_1$ at stage $t = 1$. In general, the vector-matrix product $\mathbf{q}_t'\mathbf{P} = \mathbf{q}_{t+1}'$ yields a vector whose typical element is given by

$$q_{j(t+1)} = \sum_{i=1}^{n} q_{it}p_{ij}.$$

The latter is the probability of being in state $E_j$ at stage $t + 1$. Continuing with the premium beer illustration, suppose the probability the consumer will purchase $E_i$ at stage 0 is contained in the probability vector $\mathbf{q}_0' = (.3757, .2610, .2499, .1134)$. The latter are the 1966 proportions of premium beer purchases held by the four premium brands. Then $\mathbf{q}_0'\mathbf{P} = (.3623, .2743, .2541, .1093) = \mathbf{q}_1'$, where, for example, $q_{21} = .3757(0) + .2610(.7547) + .2499(.2535) + .1134(.1232) = .2743$ is the probability that the consumer will purchase $E_2$ at stage $t = 1$.

Next, let us consider the probability vector $\mathbf{q}_2'$. The latter will be determined from the vector-matrix product $\mathbf{q}_1'\mathbf{P} = \mathbf{q}_2'$. But, $\mathbf{q}_1' = \mathbf{q}_0'\mathbf{P}$. Hence, by direct substitution, $[\mathbf{q}_0'\mathbf{P}]\mathbf{P} = \mathbf{q}_2'$ or $\mathbf{q}_0'\mathbf{P}^2 = \mathbf{q}_2'$; and by induction through successive stages,

$$\mathbf{q}_0'\mathbf{P}^t = \mathbf{q}_t'. \tag{14.1}$$

Thus the probability distribution over the $E_i$ at any stage $t$ is determined solely by the initial vector $\mathbf{q}_0'$, the transition probability matrix $\mathbf{P}$, and the stage $t$ to which we have reference.

To interpret the matrix $\mathbf{P}^t$, note first that the typical element of the matrix $\mathbf{P}^2$ is given by $p_{ij}^{(2)} = \sum_k p_{ik}p_{kj}$. The latter defines the probability of progressing from state $i$ to state $j$ over two successive stages, irrespective of which intermediate state $E_k$ is visited before $E_j$ is entered at $t = 2$. Similarly $p_{ij}^{(t)}$, the typical element in $\mathbf{P}^t$, is given by $\sum_k p_{ik}^{(t-1)} p_{kj}$, and defines the probability of moving from state $i$ to state $j$ over $t$ stages. In the present illustration, we would obtain the following matrices:

$$\mathbf{P}^2 = \begin{array}{c} \\ E_1 \\ E_2 \\ E_3 \\ E_4 \end{array} \begin{array}{c} \begin{array}{cccc} E_1 & E_2 & E_3 & E_4 \end{array} \\ \begin{bmatrix} .6478 & .0483 & .2845 & .0194 \\ .2416 & .5824 & .0260 & .1499 \\ .0372 & .3797 & .5472 & .0360 \\ .3236 & .1754 & .0384 & .4627 \end{bmatrix} \end{array};$$

$$\mathbf{P}^4 = \begin{array}{c} \\ E_1 \\ E_2 \\ E_3 \\ E_4 \end{array} \begin{array}{c} \begin{array}{cccc} E_1 & E_2 & E_3 & E_4 \end{array} \\ \begin{bmatrix} .4482 & .1708 & .3420 & .0390 \\ .3467 & .3870 & .1039 & .1623 \\ .1478 & .4370 & .3213 & .0940 \\ .4032 & .2135 & .1354 & .2480 \end{bmatrix} \end{array};$$

$$\mathbf{P}^8 = \begin{array}{c} \\ E_1 \\ E_2 \\ E_3 \\ E_4 \end{array} \begin{array}{c} \begin{array}{cccc} E_1 & E_2 & E_3 & E_4 \end{array} \\ \begin{bmatrix} .3264 & .3004 & .2862 & .0870 \\ .3704 & .2890 & .2141 & .1263 \\ .3031 & .3548 & .2119 & .1302 \\ .3747 & .2636 & .2372 & .1246 \end{bmatrix} \end{array};$$

$$\mathbf{P}^{16} = \begin{array}{c} \\ E_1 \\ E_2 \\ E_3 \\ E_4 \end{array} \begin{array}{c} \begin{array}{cccc} E_1 & E_2 & E_3 & E_4 \end{array} \\ \begin{bmatrix} .3372 & .3093 & .2390 & .1144 \\ .3402 & .3040 & .2432 & .1123 \\ .3434 & .3031 & .2385 & .1150 \\ .3385 & .3057 & .2434 & .1123 \end{bmatrix} \end{array};$$

and so forth. Thus, we find that $p_{32}^{(16)}$, say, is equal to .3031, or that the probability of the consumer being a brand $E_2$ purchaser sixteen stages after any stage during which he was a brand $E_3$ purchaser is .3031. Again, since it is assumed he will purchase one of the brands, we have

$$\sum_{j=1}^{n} p_{ij}^{(t)} = 1$$

(although the sums above are subject to rounding error in the fourth decimal place).

One might expect that as the number of stages through which the process unfolds increases, and if there is *some* likelihood the consumer will purchase any $E_j$ at a future stage irrespective of his initial purchase, the likelihoods of moving from each of the $E_i$ to a particular $E_j$ should be about the same. The intuitive appeal of this expectation lies in the fact that if $t$ is great enough, then at *some* stage the consumer is, in effect, bound to enter each of the other states. Therefore the state he has initially entered should not really matter, insofar as his probability of being in $E_j$ in "the distant future" is concerned. Indeed, we notice that even in $\mathbf{P}^{16}$ the probabilities of moving from each of the $E_i$ to a given $E_j$ are approximately equal; and, as we let $t \to \infty$, we soon discover that *each row* of $\mathbf{P}^t$ approaches the vector $\mathbf{a}' =$

(.3398, .3058, .2407, .1137), or that

$$\mathbf{P}^t \rightarrow \mathbf{A} = \begin{matrix} & E_1 & E_2 & E_3 & E_4 \\ E_1 & .3398 & .3058 & .2407 & .1137 \\ E_2 & .3398 & .3058 & .2407 & .1137 \\ E_3 & .3398 & .3058 & .2407 & .1137 \\ E_4 & .3398 & .3058 & .2407 & .1137 \end{matrix}, \qquad t \rightarrow \infty.$$

The vector $\mathbf{a}' = (a_1, \ldots, a_n)$ is called the *fixed point vector* of the transition matrix $\mathbf{P}$. The fixed point vector has the property that $\mathbf{a}'\mathbf{P} = \mathbf{a}'$. This is easily verified for the present illustration. As is shown in the Appendix to this chapter, if $\mathbf{P}$ is a transition probability matrix such that at some stage $t$ all $p_{ij}^{(t)} > 0$ (that is, there is a nonzero probability of going from any state $i$ to any state $j$ over $t$ stages) there will be a *unique* fixed point vector $\mathbf{a}'$ associated with $\mathbf{P}$ having the following property: the powers of $\mathbf{P}$ approach a stochastic matrix $\mathbf{A}$, each row of which is the same probability vector $\mathbf{a}'$. Since $\mathbf{a}'\mathbf{P} = \mathbf{a}'$, $[\mathbf{a}']\mathbf{P} = [\mathbf{a}'\mathbf{P}]\mathbf{P} = \mathbf{a}'\mathbf{P}^2$, and by induction $\mathbf{a}'\mathbf{P}^t = \mathbf{a}'$ for all $t$. A transition probability matrix $\mathbf{P}$, having the property that at some stage $t$ after the initial stage all $p_{ij}^{(t)} > 0$, is called a *regular* transition probability matrix. Once a point is reached at which all $p_{ij}^{(t)} > 0$, this will also be the case for all subsequent values of $t$.

To determine each of the $n$ components of $\mathbf{a}'$, we make use of the fact that $\mathbf{a}'\mathbf{P} = \mathbf{a}'$, and that $\Sigma\, a_i = 1$, since $\mathbf{a}'$ is a probability vector. From the former relationship, $\mathbf{a}'[\mathbf{P} - \mathbf{I}] = \mathbf{0}'$, thus yielding a set of $n$ linear *homogeneous* simultaneous equations which, in combination with $\mathbf{a}'\mathbf{i} = 1$, provide us with $n$ independent equations. To determine the above fixed point vector, the following set of equations was solved:

$$\begin{aligned} -.1967a_1 + .1412a_2 \qquad\qquad + .2080a_4 &= 0, \\ -\ .2453a_2 + .2535a_3 + .1232a_4 &= 0, \\ .1844a_1 \qquad\qquad - .2603a_3 \qquad\qquad &= 0, \\ .0123a_1 + .1041a_2 + .0068a_3 - .3312a_4 &= 0, \\ a_1 + a_2 + a_3 + a_4 &= 1, \end{aligned}$$

where the second equation, say, follows from the equation $0a_1 + .7547a_2 + .2535a_3 + .1232a_4 = a_2$.

The fact that fixed point vectors are readily determinable makes regular transition probability matrices particularly nice to have around, and particularly interesting from the firm's and the economist's standpoint. Specifically, if in the general case the matrix $\mathbf{P}$ can be assumed to describe the behavior of *all* customers, then $\mathbf{a}'$ can be interpreted as a vector of market shares to which the industry composed of brands $E_1$ to $E_n$ will gravitate in the long term—provided that $\mathbf{P}$ remains fixed. That is, as one passes through future stages the *probability* that a customer selected at random will be a brand $E_i$ purchaser approaches $a_i$; therefore $a_i$ will be brand $E_i$'s *expected* market share. Of course, it may be a bit too presumptuous to expect $\mathbf{P}$ to remain fixed. Tastes change, populations shift, and products come and go. Moreover, say through price changes or advertising campaigns, the firms themselves may be able to effect changes in the $p_{ij}$. One might expect, for example, that a price cut, or more extensive advertising, or a product improvement on the part of the $j$th firm, will lead to an increase in the $p_{ij}$, perhaps for all $i = 1, \ldots, n$. That is, these policies will make it more likely that customers will shift (or maintain) their next purchases to brand $E_j$. The information provided by the fixed point vector could therefore encourage the adoption of policies specifically designed to enable the firm to *avoid* the fate that allegedly awaits it. One need not adamantly maintain that $\mathbf{P}$ is fixed for all time in order to analyze the implications of *assuming* it fixed, and to glean valuable insights and suggestions from the assumption. In this context, the fixed point vector $\mathbf{a}' = (.3398, .3058, .2407, .1137)$ might be interpreted by firm $E_4$ to imply that, in the absence of change, it can anticipate capturing but 11 percent of the premium market. From the vector $\mathbf{q}_0'$ we note that this was, in fact, the firm's 1966 market share. The analysis would therefore suggest that only by altering the transition probabilities can firm $E_4$ hope to increase its share of the premium market.

There are additional properties of regular matrices that are of considerable interest, and some of these are discussed below. Nonetheless, not all transition probability matrices are regular, and before detailing the properties of regular matrices we should call attention to some other breeds of the species.

## 14.3 CLASSIFICATIONS OF MARKOV CHAINS

Let $E_{it}$ denote the fact that state $E_i$ obtains at stage $t$. Then, if the probability of a given sequence of outcomes from time $0(E_{i0})$ to time $T(E_{kT})$ is given by

$$p(E_{i0} \to E_{j1} \to \cdots \to E_{kT}) = \overbrace{q_{i0}p_{ij}p_{jm}\cdots p_{rk}}^{T}, \tag{14.2}$$

the sequence is called a *Markov chain*. It can easily be shown that (14.2) does in fact describe a probability function. In a Markov *chain*, then, the probability of any sequence of outcomes is given by (14.2). The fact that, except for the initial outcomes, the probability of each later outcome in the sequence depends only on the outcome that precedes it, indicates that the sequence evolves as a result of a first-order Markov *process*.

In the previous illustration it was possible to pass from each state to any other state in no more than two stages (that is, $p_{ij}^{(2)} > 0$ for $i, j = 1, \ldots, 4$). Suppose, however, that the first row of the matrix had been the vector $(1, 0, 0, 0)$. Because $p_{11} = 1$ and $p_{1j} = 0$ $(j = 2, 3, 4)$, once a customer purchases brand $E_1$ he *always* purchases $E_1$ thereafter. In this case, $E_1$ is called an *absorbing* state: there is some probability that a customer will eventually purchase brand $E_1$, and once he does (as he is sure to do), he will never again purchase any other brand. $E_1$ may be said to have "absorbed" him.[4]

In general, a set of states is called *closed* if no state outside the set can be reached from any state within the set. A single state $E_i$ will thus be *absorbing* if by itself it forms a closed set, since then only $E_i$ can be reached from $E_i$. This will occur if and only if $p_{ii} = 1$. Consider, for example, the following matrix:

$$\mathbf{P} = \begin{array}{c} \\ E_1 \\ E_2 \\ E_3 \\ E_4 \end{array} \begin{array}{c} \begin{array}{cccc} E_1 & E_2 & E_3 & E_4 \end{array} \\ \begin{bmatrix} .5 & .5 & 0 & 0 \\ .7 & .3 & 0 & 0 \\ .4 & .2 & .3 & .1 \\ 0 & 0 & 0 & 1 \end{bmatrix} \end{array}.$$

[4] In a manner of speaking, "When you're out of Schlitz, you're out of beer!"

Here, $E_1$ and $E_2$ may be combined to form a closed set $E_{12}$. $E_{12}$ is closed since neither $E_3$ nor $E_4$ can be reached from $E_{12}$. The *set* $E_{12}$ is thus absorbing. Similarly, $E_4$ is a closed set and an absorbing state, since $P_{44} = 1$. $E_3$ is called a *transient* state. The latter terminology implies that the probability is less than 1 that, starting from $E_3$, the process will ever again return to $E_3$. In fact, starting from $E_3$, the probability is $.4 + .2 + .1 = .7$ that $E_3$ will be left permanently at the very next stage. In general, if the probability is one of *returning* to $E_i$, then $E_i$ will be called *persistent* or *recurrent;* otherwise it will be called *transient.* In this illustration, $E_1$, $E_2$, and $E_4$ are persistent, for *once entered* they are certain to be entered again. Note, however, that they will not necessarily be entered.

The above matrix **P** may be rewritten as

$$\mathbf{P}_{12} = \begin{array}{c} E_{12} \\ E_3 \\ E_4 \end{array} \overset{\begin{array}{ccc} E_{12} & E_3 & E_4 \end{array}}{\begin{bmatrix} 1 & 0 & 0 \\ .6 & .3 & .1 \\ 0 & 0 & 1 \end{bmatrix}} \quad \text{or as} \quad \mathbf{P}_{124} = \begin{array}{c} E_{124} \\ \\ E_3 \end{array} \overset{\begin{array}{cc} E_{124} & E_3 \end{array}}{\begin{bmatrix} 1 & 0 \\ & \\ .7 & .3 \end{bmatrix}};$$

that is, we can combine states and pool probabilities. Even in $\mathbf{P}_{124}$, however, there remains a transient state and an absorbing state, and this Markov chain is therefore said to be *absorbing*. If there exists no closed set of states other than the set of all states, the chain is called *irreducible.* The latter occurs only when each state may be reached from every other state. A regular matrix thus describes an irreducible Markov chain; but, as we shall presently see, not all irreducible chains are described by regular matrices.

One can also demonstrate the intuitively appealing facts that in an absorbing Markov chain: (1) the probability is 1 that the process will be absorbed in one of the closed sets; and (2) if we consider a square submatrix of the original transition probability matrix corresponding solely to a closed set of states $C$, then this submatrix will retain all the properties of an irreducible Markov chain.

Suppose, now, that we have the following matrix characterizing an irreducible Markov chain:

$$\mathbf{P} = \begin{array}{c} E_1 \\ E_2 \\ E_3 \\ E_4 \end{array} \overset{\begin{array}{cccc} E_1 & E_2 & E_3 & E_4 \end{array}}{\begin{bmatrix} 0 & .5 & .5 & 0 \\ .3 & 0 & 0 & .7 \\ .2 & 0 & 0 & .8 \\ 0 & .1 & .9 & 0 \end{bmatrix}}.$$

**P** may be rewritten by combining $E_1$ and $E_4$ into $E_{14}$ and $E_2$ and $E_3$ into $E_{23}$, as follows:

$$\mathbf{P}_{14,23} = \begin{array}{c} E_{14} \\ E_{23} \end{array} \overset{\begin{array}{cc} E_{14} & E_{23} \end{array}}{\begin{bmatrix} 0 & 1 \\ 1 & 0 \end{bmatrix}}.$$

In this *cyclic* situation, the states of $E_{14}$ and $E_{23}$ alternate with one another. Each of the $E_i$ is said to be of period 2, because the states can occur only at stages that are two stages apart—for example, at stages 1, 3, 5, . . . or stages 2, 4, 6, . . . . Note that $\mathbf{P}_{14,23}$ is irreducible, but nonregular.[5]

[5] $\mathbf{P}_{14,23}$ is *periodic,* a classification described below.

In general, a state $E_i$ will be said to be of period $T > 1$ if $T$ is the smallest integer such that $p_{ii}^{(t)} = 0$ whenever $t$ is not divisible by $T$. Thus, if a state is periodic of period $T > 1$, a return to it is only possible at times $T, 2T, 3T, \ldots$. If a state is (1) aperiodic but persistent, and (2) the probability is positive that once entered the state will recur before less than an infinite amount of time has passed,[6] the state will be called *ergodic*. Associated with an ergodic Markov process, then, is an irreducible transition probability matrix composed of a set of persistent and aperiodic states $E_i$ $(i = 1, \ldots, n)$ such that $p_{ij}^{(t)} > 0$ for all $i, j$ and for *some* $t$. If, in addition, a $t$ exists such that *all* $p_{ij}^{(t)} > 0$, then the matrix is regular. A regular process is thus an important subclass of an ergodic process. It can be shown that in an irreducible Markov chain *all* states will have the same period $(T \geq 1)$. Thus, if the chain is irreducible and has a single ergodic state, the entire matrix must be ergodic.

Both ergodic and absorbing Markov chains are of special interest for microeconomics. One potential inference drawn from a regular matrix has already been noted. Should the same process have been absorbing, however, say because a consumer never switched *to* brand $E_k$ from any other $E_i$, but did have some positive

TABLE 14.1
Chains and States in a First-Order Markov Process

| Type | Description |
|---|---|
| *Closed set* | No state, other than states included in the set, can be reached from any state within the set. |
| *Absorbing state* | Once entered, the state is never left. |
| *Recurrent state* | Once entered, an eventual return to the state is assured. |
| *Periodic state* | The state can only be entered at times $T$, $2T$, $3T$, $\ldots$, where $T > 1$. |
| *Transient state* | An eventual return to the state is not assured. |
| *Ergodic state* | Once entered, a return to the state is assured within a finite number of stages, but the state is not periodic and may be reentered at *any* $T$. |
| *Irreducible chain* | Each state may be reached from every other state. |
| *Absorbing chain* | The chain contains one or more closed sets and the process will eventually be absorbed in one of the closed sets. |
| *Ergodic chain* | Any state can eventually be reached from any other state, but there are no periodic states. |
| *Regular chain* | Any state can be reached from any other state after no more than $t$ stages. |

[6] If the probability of recurrence at stage $t \to \infty$ is $p_{jj}^{(t)} \to 0$, but $E_j$ is certain to recur, then $p_{ij}^{(t)} \to 0$ and $E_j$ is called a persistent *null* state. We shall ignore such states in the succeeding discussion.

probability of switching *from* $E_k$ to some other $E_i$, then $E_k$ would be transient. Among other things, it would be of interest to know the number of stages that might be expected to pass before $E_k$ is left permanently, and, if there are several absorbing states, in which of these the customer is likely to be absorbed. In the next two sections, we shall therefore establish some of the more important properties of ergodic and absorbing Markov chains.

## 14.4 ERGODIC MARKOV CHAINS[7]

In order to provide a framework for subsequent developments, let us suppose the firm has determined that its customers' purchasing habits are adequately approximated by an ergodic Markov process. Should these conditions continue to prevail, the issue is not *whether* a customer will eventually switch to another product; we can be sure that he will. Rather, the issue is *when* he can be expected to once again purchase from the firm in question, or how much time can be expected to pass until one who is purchasing a rival's product will switch to the product of the firm in question. These are important issues, for their resolution can help the firm to program such future decisions as the timing of new plant construction and the extension of service facilities.

Denote by $f_{ij}$ the number of stages that elapse between the time that the system enters $E_i$ and the very *first* time that it enters $E_j$ thereafter; and it will enter $E_j$ because the process is ergodic; $f_{ij}$ will be a random variable, for $E_j$ can be reached from $E_i$ either in a single step or through a series of steps through other states, and each of these alternatives will occur with a given probability. The mathematical expectation of the random variable will be denoted by $E[f_{ij}] = u_{ij}$; $u_{ij}$ is called *the mean first passage time* from $E_i$ to $E_j$.

In order to determine $u_{ij}$, consider the specific itinerary leading to the first visit to $E_j$ from $E_i$. One can make this first visit in either of two ways: (1) directly in a single step with probability $p_{ij}$; or (2) by taking one step to go from $E_i$ to $E_k$ and then the average of $u_{kj}$ steps that we anticipate the initial sequence from $E_k$ to $E_j$ will require. Since we must first get from $E_i$ to $E_k$, we will take the latter sequence with probability $p_{ik}$ $(k \neq j)$. Thus, the *mean first passage time*, or $u_{ij}$, is given by

$$u_{ij} = p_{ij}(1) + \sum_{k \neq j} p_{ik}(u_{kj} + 1) = p_{ij} + \sum_{k \neq j} p_{ik} + \sum_{k \neq j} p_{ik}u_{kj} = 1 + \sum_{k \neq j} p_{ik}u_{kj}.$$

Denote $\mathbf{S} = [\mathbf{i}, \ldots, \mathbf{i}]$ as a sum matrix, each of whose elements is 1; $\mathbf{u} = [u_{ij}]$; and $\mathbf{u}_d = [u_{ij}\delta_{ij}]$ ($\delta_{ij} = 1$ for $i = j$ and 0 otherwise) as the diagonal matrix with elements $u_{ii}$: then the previous expression may be written in matrix notation as

$$\mathbf{u} = \mathbf{S} + \mathbf{P}[\mathbf{u} - \mathbf{u}_d], \tag{14.3}$$

where $\mathbf{u}_d$ is subtracted from $\mathbf{u}$ because $k \neq j$ in the previous summation.

To determine $\mathbf{u}$, first note that even if $\mathbf{P}$ is not regular we can still derive a fixed point vector $\mathbf{a}'$ such that $\mathbf{a}'\mathbf{P} = \mathbf{a}'$ and $\mathbf{a}'\mathbf{i} = 1$. This is done simply by solving the latter set of equations for the $a_i$. We shall make use of this fact in order to obtain $\mathbf{u}_d$, and shall then derive an expression for $\mathbf{u}$.

[7] The approach followed throughout this and the next section is that of Kemeny and Snell, *Finite Markov Chains*, which may be visited with profit.

Premultiplying both sides of (14.3) by $\mathbf{a}'$,

$$\mathbf{a}'\mathbf{u} = \mathbf{a}'\mathbf{S} + \mathbf{a}'\mathbf{P}[\mathbf{u} - \mathbf{u}_d] = \mathbf{i}' + \mathbf{a}'[\mathbf{u} - \mathbf{u}_d],$$

since $\mathbf{a}'\mathbf{i} = 1$. Canceling $\mathbf{a}'\mathbf{u}$ on both sides of the equation,

$$\mathbf{0}' = \mathbf{i}' - \mathbf{a}'\mathbf{u}_d; \text{ or } \mathbf{a}' = \mathbf{i}'\mathbf{u}_d^{-1}.$$

Written in detail, the latter is

$$(a_1, \ldots, a_i, \ldots, a_n) = \left(\frac{1}{u_{11}}, \ldots, \frac{1}{u_{ii}}, \ldots, \frac{1}{u_{nn}}\right);$$

or $u_{ii} = 1/a_i$ is the *mean recurrence time* (that is, the expected number of stages required to go from $E_i$ back to $E_i$ for the *first* time). For the four-brand illustration of Section 14.2, where $\mathbf{a}' = (.3398, .3058, .2407, .1137)$, the mean recurrence times would be given by (2.9429, 3.2701, 4.1545, 8.7951), and

$$\mathbf{u}_d = \begin{matrix} & E_1 & E_2 & E_3 & E_4 \\ E_1 & 2.9429 & 0 & 0 & 0 \\ E_2 & 0 & 3.2701 & 0 & 0 \\ E_3 & 0 & 0 & 4.1545 & 0 \\ E_4 & 0 & 0 & 0 & 8.7951 \end{matrix}.$$

Even with $\mathbf{S}$, $\mathbf{P}$, and $\mathbf{u}_d$ now known, we cannot directly solve (14.3) for $\mathbf{u}$ simply by moving $\mathbf{Pu}$ to the left and then premultiplying both sides by $(\mathbf{I} - \mathbf{P})^{-1}$. This is because $\mathbf{I} - \mathbf{P}$ is singular, since $\mathbf{P}$ is stochastic and its rows sum to one. Thus $\mathbf{I} - \mathbf{P}$ contains only $n - 1$ independent columns. It will, however, be possible to determine $\mathbf{u}$, as well as convenient for general purposes, if we first define the *fundamental matrix* $\mathbf{Z} = [\mathbf{I} - (\mathbf{P} - \mathbf{A})]^{-1} = [z_{ij}]$, where $\mathbf{A} = (\mathbf{a}, \ldots, \mathbf{a})'$. It is readily shown that such a matrix exists, and that it has the following properties: $\mathbf{P} = \mathbf{ZP}$, $\mathbf{Zi} = \mathbf{i}$, $\mathbf{a}'\mathbf{Z} = \mathbf{a}'$, and $(\mathbf{I} - \mathbf{P})\mathbf{Z} = \mathbf{I} - \mathbf{A}$. Moreover, we shall use $\mathbf{Z}$ to compute $\mathbf{u}$ by showing that

$$\mathbf{u} = (\mathbf{I} - \mathbf{Z} + \mathbf{SZ}_d)\mathbf{u}_d, \tag{14.3'}$$

where $\mathbf{Z}_d$ is the diagonal matrix formed from the diagonal elements of $\mathbf{Z}$.

Subtracting $\mathbf{u}_d$ from both sides of (14.3′) and premultiplying by $\mathbf{P}$, we obtain

$$\mathbf{P}[\mathbf{u} - \mathbf{u}_d] = [-\mathbf{PZ} + \mathbf{PSZ}_d]\mathbf{u}_d = [-\mathbf{PZ} + \mathbf{SZ}_d]\mathbf{u}_d,$$

since $\mathbf{PS} = \mathbf{S}$ because $\mathbf{Pi} = \mathbf{i}$. Adding *and* subtracting $[\mathbf{I} - \mathbf{Z}]$ in the bracketed term on the right,

$$\begin{aligned}[-\mathbf{PZ} + \mathbf{SZ}_d]\mathbf{u}_d &= [(-\mathbf{I} + \mathbf{Z} - \mathbf{PZ}) + (\mathbf{I} - \mathbf{Z} + \mathbf{SZ}_d)]\mathbf{u}_d \\ &= \mathbf{u} + (-\mathbf{I} + \mathbf{Z} - \mathbf{PZ})\mathbf{u}_d\end{aligned}$$

by (14.3′). As we have noted, however, $\mathbf{Z}$ has the property that

$$(\mathbf{I} - \mathbf{P})\mathbf{Z} = \mathbf{I} - \mathbf{A} \quad \text{or} \quad -\mathbf{I} + \mathbf{Z} = -\mathbf{A} + \mathbf{PZ}.$$

With the latter substitution,

$$\mathbf{P}[\mathbf{u} - \mathbf{u}_d] = \mathbf{u} + [-\mathbf{A} + \mathbf{PZ} - \mathbf{PZ}]\mathbf{u}_d = \mathbf{u} - \mathbf{Au}_d.$$

But, the typical *column* of $\mathbf{u}_d$ is $(0, 0, \ldots, 1/a_i, \ldots, 0)'$, and *each row* of $\mathbf{A}$ is given by $(a_1, \ldots, a_i, \ldots, a_n)$. The vector product of any row of $\mathbf{A}$ and any column of $\mathbf{u}_d$

is thus $a_i(1/a_i) = 1$. Hence, $\mathbf{Au}_d = \mathbf{S}$ and $\mathbf{P}[\mathbf{u} - \mathbf{u}_d] = \mathbf{u} - \mathbf{S}$, or $\mathbf{u} = \mathbf{P}[\mathbf{u} - \mathbf{u}_d] + \mathbf{S}$ as in (14.3). Therefore (14.3′) and (14.3) are equivalent, and we may employ (14.3′) to compute $\mathbf{u}$.

In the premium beer illustration, then, we can compute

$$\mathbf{Z} = \begin{array}{c} \\ E_1 \\ E_2 \\ E_3 \\ E_4 \end{array} \begin{array}{c} \begin{array}{cccc} E_1 & E_2 & E_3 & E_4 \end{array} \\ \begin{bmatrix} 2.0413 & -.9936 & .5214 & -.5691 \\ -.1204 & 1.9013 & -1.0100 & .2291 \\ -1.4170 & .6547 & 1.9132 & -.1509 \\ .2113 & -.8402 & -.7750 & 2.4039 \end{bmatrix} \end{array}$$

and then employ (14.3′) to derive

$$\mathbf{u} = \begin{array}{c} \\ E_1 \\ E_2 \\ E_3 \\ E_4 \end{array} \begin{array}{c} \begin{array}{cccc} E_1 & E_2 & E_3 & E_4 \end{array} \\ \begin{bmatrix} 2.9429 & 9.4666 & 5.7822 & 26.1478 \\ 6.3617 & 3.2701 & 12.1444 & 19.1276 \\ 10.1774 & 4.0765 & 4.1545 & 22.4697 \\ 5.3855 & 8.9650 & 11.1681 & 8.7951 \end{bmatrix} \end{array}.$$

Thus, the mean first passage time from, say, $E_2$ to $E_3$ will be given by $u_{23} = 12.14$, or on average the $E_2$ customer will not purchase brand $E_3$ until approximately twelve stages after his purchase of $E_2$.

It must be borne in mind, however, that $u_{ij}$ is only the *mean* of the *distribution* of first passage times $f_{ij}$. The variance of the distribution is given by $E[f_{ij}^2 - E[f_{ij}]^2]$. To compute this variance, we shall first determine $E[f_{ij}^2]$, and then subtract from it $E[f_{ij}]^2$. We do this since $E[f_{ij}^2 - E[f_{ij}]^2] = E[f_{ij}^2] - E[f_{ij}]^2 = E[f_{ij}^2] - u_{ij}^2$, and an expression for $u_{ij}$ has already been found. We shall employ this approach throughout this and the following section.

Duplicating the earlier argument, we first note that

$$\begin{aligned} E[f_{ij}^2] &= p_{ij}E[(1)^2] + \sum_{k \neq j} p_{ik}E[(f_{kj} + 1)^2] \\ &= p_{ij} + \sum_{k \neq j} (p_{ik}E[f_{kj}^2] + 2p_{ik}E[f_{kj}] + p_{ik}E[1^2]) \\ &= \sum_{k \neq j} p_{ik}E[f_{kj}^2] + 2 \sum_{k \neq j} p_{ik}u_{kj} + 1, \end{aligned}$$

since $E[f_{kj}] = u_{kj}$. The entire matrix $\mathbf{W} = [E[f_{ij}^2]] = [w_{ij}]$ is thus given by

$$\mathbf{W} = \mathbf{P}[\mathbf{W} - \mathbf{W}_d] + 2\mathbf{P}[\mathbf{u} - \mathbf{u}_d] + \mathbf{S}, \tag{14.4}$$

where $\mathbf{W}_d$ is the diagonal matrix formed from the diagonal elements of $\mathbf{W}$. The diagonal matrices are subtracted to take care of the $k \neq j$ qualifier in the summation. From (14.3′), however, $\mathbf{u} - \mathbf{u}_d = (-\mathbf{Z} + \mathbf{SZ}_d)\mathbf{u}_d$. Substituting this into (14.4),

$$\mathbf{W} = \mathbf{P}[\mathbf{W} - \mathbf{W}_d] + 2\mathbf{P}[-\mathbf{Z} + \mathbf{SZ}_d]\mathbf{u}_d + \mathbf{S}$$

and

$$\begin{aligned} \mathbf{a}'\mathbf{W} &= \mathbf{a}'\mathbf{P}[\mathbf{W} - \mathbf{W}_d] + 2\mathbf{a}'\mathbf{P}[-\mathbf{Z} + \mathbf{SZ}_d]\mathbf{u}_d + \mathbf{a}'\mathbf{S} \\ &= \mathbf{a}'[\mathbf{W} - \mathbf{W}_d] + 2\mathbf{a}'[-\mathbf{Z} + \mathbf{SZ}_d]\mathbf{u}_d + \mathbf{i}', \end{aligned}$$

since $\mathbf{a'P} = \mathbf{a'}$. But, $\mathbf{a'u}_d = \mathbf{i'}$ and, as a property of $\mathbf{Z}$, $\mathbf{a'Z} = \mathbf{a'}$. Hence to first obtain $\mathbf{W}_d$, note that the expression for $\mathbf{a'W}_d$ will be comparable to that for $\mathbf{a'W}$, except that the $\mathbf{a'}[\mathbf{W} - \mathbf{W}_d]$ term on the right will become a zero vector. Then,

$$\begin{aligned}\mathbf{a'W}_d &= -2\mathbf{a'Zu}_d + 2\mathbf{a'SZ}_d\mathbf{u}_d + \mathbf{i'}\\ &= -2\mathbf{a'u}_d + 2\mathbf{i'Z}_d\mathbf{u}_d + \mathbf{i'} = -\mathbf{i'} + 2\mathbf{i'Z}_d\mathbf{u}_d\end{aligned}$$

since $\mathbf{a'u}_d = \mathbf{i'}$. Written out fully, the equation is

$$\begin{aligned}&(a_1w_{11}, \ldots, a_iw_{ii}, \ldots, a_nw_{nn})\\ &\qquad = (-1 + 2z_{11}u_{11}, \ldots, -1 + 2z_{ii}u_{ii}, \ldots, -1 + 2z_{nn}u_{nn})\end{aligned}$$

or

$$w_{ii} = -\frac{1}{a_i} + \frac{2z_{ii}u_{ii}}{a_i} = -\frac{1}{a_i} + \frac{2z_{ii}}{a_i^2},$$

since $u_{ii} = 1/a_i$. Thus, $\mathbf{W}_d = \mathbf{u}_d[2\mathbf{Z}_d\mathbf{u}_d - \mathbf{I}]$. Since $w_{ii} = E[f_{ii}^2]$, the variances of first recurrence times will be given by

$$\sigma_{ii}^2 = w_{ii} - u_{ii}^2 = -\frac{1}{a_i} + \frac{2z_{ii} - 1}{a_i^2}.$$

In general, the variance matrix for first passage times is $\boldsymbol{\sigma}_f^2 = [\sigma_{ij}^2]$. It is verified, moreover, that

$$\mathbf{W} = \mathbf{u}[2\mathbf{Z}_d\mathbf{u}_d - \mathbf{I}] + 2[\mathbf{Zu} - \mathbf{S}(\mathbf{Zu})_d], \tag{14.4'}$$

by premultiplying (14.4′) by $\mathbf{P}$, substituting for $\mathbf{PW}$ and $\mathbf{PW}_d$ in (14.4), rearranging terms, and noticing from (14.3′) that $\mathbf{Au} = \mathbf{SZ}_d\mathbf{u}_d$. In the present illustration, then, from (14.4′) we determine

$$\mathbf{W} = \begin{matrix} & E_1 & E_2 & E_3 & E_4 \\ E_1 & 32.4152 & 130.1910 & 65.1887 & 1175.3109 \\ E_2 & 71.6078 & 37.3933 & 210.3843 & 828.3993 \\ E_3 & 145.5522 & 30.9320 & 61.8888 & 975.5654 \\ E_4 & 56.1347 & 131.7741 & 183.6182 & 363.1066 \end{matrix},$$

and with $\boldsymbol{\sigma}_f^2 = \mathbf{W} - \mathbf{u}_{SQ}$, where $\mathbf{u}_{SQ} = [u_{ij}^2]$,

$$\boldsymbol{\sigma}_f^2 = \begin{matrix} & E_1 & E_2 & E_3 & E_4 \\ E_1 & 23.7545 & 40.5745 & 31.7549 & 491.6035 \\ E_2 & 31.1366 & 26.6997 & 62.8978 & 462.5342 \\ E_3 & 41.9727 & 14.3141 & 44.6289 & 470.6771 \\ E_4 & 27.1311 & 51.4029 & 58.8917 & 285.7528 \end{matrix}.$$

Thus, to go along with the mean first passage time of $u_{23} = 12.14$, we have a variance of $\sigma_{23}^2 = 62.90$. Note that in the present notation, $\sigma_{ij}^2$ denotes a *variance* and not the square of a covariance.

It might also be noted that given *any* initial probability vector $\mathbf{q}_0'$, the expected number of stages to reach $E_j$ will be given by the sum of the mean number of stages to reach $E_j$ from $E_i$, weighted by the probability of being in $E_i$, or $\sum_{i=1}^{n} q_{i0}u_{ij}$. The vector for the mean stages to $E_j$ will be given by $\mathbf{q}_0'\mathbf{u} = \mathbf{q}_0'[\mathbf{I} - \mathbf{Z} + \mathbf{SZ}_d]\mathbf{u}_d$. As opposed to a second vector $\mathbf{q}_0^{*\prime}$, the difference in mean times to $E_j$ will thus be $\mathbf{q}_0'\mathbf{u} - \mathbf{q}_0^{*\prime}\mathbf{u} = [\mathbf{q}_0' - \mathbf{q}_0^{*\prime}][\mathbf{I} - \mathbf{Z}]\mathbf{u}_d$, since $\mathbf{q}_0'\mathbf{S}\mathbf{Z}_d\mathbf{u}_d = \mathbf{i}'\mathbf{Z}_d\mathbf{u}_d$. In particular, if $\mathbf{q}_0' = \mathbf{a}'$, then $\mathbf{q}_0'\mathbf{u} = \mathbf{a}'\mathbf{u}$ gives the expected number of stages required to reach $E_j$ for the first time when the system has attained equilibrium. In the present illustration, $\mathbf{a}'\mathbf{u} =$ (6.0074, 6.2173, 7.9484, 21.1427), and we would anticipate that on average the consumer will ultimately purchase brand $E_3$, say, once every eight stages. Starting from the previously considered vector of $\mathbf{q}_0^{*\prime} =$ (.3757, .2610, .2499, .1134), the difference in mean times, or $\mathbf{a}'\mathbf{u} - \mathbf{q}_0^{*\prime}\mathbf{u}$, would be (.0873, −.2281, .3017, −.2859). Hence on average the tendency of our random purchaser will be to purchase brand $E_2$, say, with slightly greater frequency (shorter mean time to $E_2$) in the future than is currently the case—unless the firms in question do something to alter the transition probabilities.

## 14.5 ABSORBING MARKOV CHAINS

One of the facts of business life is that new firms appear on, and old firms disappear from, the industrial scene. The particulars of an industry will dictate whether it is in fact meaningful to ascribe to it Markovian tendencies; but suppose they can be so ascribed to the United States brewing industry. Then, let us group the brewers into four categories, $G_1$ through $G_4$, where $G_1$, $G_2$, and $G_3$ are each composed of four of the leading firms in the industry, such that those in each group have similar characteristics, the premium brewers being one such group, and $G_4$ is "everybody else." Assuming that new customers behave in like manner to the old, and that "once a beer drinker, always a beer drinker," the transition probability matrix for these four groups is estimated to be the following:[8]

$$\mathbf{P} = \begin{matrix} & G_1 & G_2 & G_3 & G_4 \\ G_1 & .8923 & .0660 & .0417 & 0 \\ G_2 & .0395 & .9101 & .0504 & 0 \\ G_3 & .2468 & 0 & .7532 & 0 \\ G_4 & .0234 & .0030 & 0 & .9736 \end{matrix}.$$

The most striking feature of this matrix is the string of zeros in the last column, save for the $p_{44}$ element. State $G_4$ is thus a transient state, because while on occasion some of the $G_4$ firms' customers might switch to a $G_1$, $G_2$, or $G_3$ product, there is no possibility of any of the latter firms' customers switching to $G_4$. The result of this phenomenon is that we can anticipate the eventual demise of the $G_4$ firms, with the process being absorbed into the closed set of states $G_1$, $G_2$, and $G_3$. The *latter three* states therefore describe an irreducible Markov chain. With the inclusion of state $G_4$, they combine to depict an absorbing chain. For such a chain, and certainly in the present context, it would be of clear interest to know such things as the proportion of the $G_4$ custom that can be expected to accrue to each of the other groups, and the length of time that can be expected to transpire prior to the disappearance of all $G_4$ firms. In this section, we shall therefore be concerned with deriving general expressions for some of the more pertinent informational gems that can be extracted from absorbing Markov chains.

[8] For a detailed discussion, see Ann Horowitz and Ira Horowitz, "Markov Processes and the Declining Brewing Population," *1967 Proceedings of the Business and Economics Section* (Washington, D.C.: American Statistical Association, 1967), pp. 433–438.

By relabeling or shuffling the states if necessary, we can write any $n \times n$ transition probability matrix with $r$ absorbing states and $s$ nonabsorbing states in so-called *canonical* form, wherein the matrix $\mathbf{P}$ is partitioned into four separate matrices: (1) $\mathbf{I}_r$, an $r \times r$ identity matrix; (2) $\bar{\mathbf{0}}$, an $r \times s$ zero matrix; (3) $\mathbf{R}$, the $s \times r$ matrix of transition probabilities $p_{ij}$ giving the probabilities of moving from a transient state to an absorbing state; and (4) $\mathbf{Q}$, the $s \times s$ matrix of $p_{ij}$'s that give the probabilities of moving from one transient state to another. In the present illustration, combining $G_1$, $G_2$, and $G_3$ into the closed set $G_{123}$, the matrix becomes

$$\mathbf{P}_{123} = \begin{matrix} & G_{123} & G_4 \\ G_{123} & 1 & 0 \\ G_4 & .0264 & .9736 \end{matrix} = \left[\begin{array}{c|c} \mathbf{I}_1 & \bar{\mathbf{0}} \\ \hline \mathbf{R} & \mathbf{Q} \end{array}\right].$$

A matrix with $r = 2$ absorbing and $s = 3$ transient states, such as

$$\mathbf{P} = \begin{matrix} & E_1 & E_2 & E_3 & E_4 & E_5 \\ E_1 & 1 & 0 & 0 & 0 & 0 \\ E_2 & 0 & 1 & 0 & 0 & 0 \\ E_3 & p_{31} & p_{32} & p_{33} & p_{34} & p_{35} \\ E_4 & p_{41} & p_{42} & p_{43} & p_{44} & p_{45} \\ E_5 & p_{51} & p_{52} & p_{53} & p_{54} & p_{55} \end{matrix} = \begin{matrix} & 2 & 3 \\ 2 & \mathbf{I}_2 & \bar{\mathbf{0}} \\ 3 & \mathbf{R} & \mathbf{Q} \end{matrix}.$$

contains as submatrices,

$$\mathbf{I}_2 = \begin{bmatrix} 1 & 0 \\ 0 & 1 \end{bmatrix}, \qquad \bar{\mathbf{0}} = \begin{bmatrix} 0 & 0 & 0 \\ 0 & 0 & 0 \end{bmatrix},$$

$$\mathbf{R} = \begin{bmatrix} p_{31} & p_{32} \\ p_{41} & p_{42} \\ p_{51} & p_{52} \end{bmatrix}, \qquad \mathbf{Q} = \begin{bmatrix} p_{33} & p_{34} & p_{35} \\ p_{43} & p_{44} & p_{45} \\ p_{53} & p_{54} & p_{55} \end{bmatrix}.$$

It follows, then, that

$$\mathbf{P}^2 = \left[\begin{array}{c|c} \mathbf{I}_r & \bar{\mathbf{0}} \\ \hline \mathbf{R} & \mathbf{Q} \end{array}\right]\left[\begin{array}{c|c} \mathbf{I}_r & \bar{\mathbf{0}} \\ \hline \mathbf{R} & \mathbf{Q} \end{array}\right] = \left[\begin{array}{c|c} \mathbf{I}_r & \bar{\mathbf{0}} \\ \hline (\mathbf{I}_s + \mathbf{Q})\mathbf{R} & \mathbf{Q}^2 \end{array}\right],$$

$$\mathbf{P}^4 = \left[\begin{array}{c|c} \mathbf{I}_r & \bar{\mathbf{0}} \\ \hline (\mathbf{I}_s + \mathbf{Q}^2)(\mathbf{I}_s + \mathbf{Q})\mathbf{R} & \mathbf{Q}^4 \end{array}\right], \quad \text{and}$$

$$\mathbf{P}^t = \left[\begin{array}{c|c} \mathbf{I}_r & \bar{\mathbf{0}} \\ \hline \mathbf{R}^* & \mathbf{Q}^t \end{array}\right],$$

where $\mathbf{Q}^t \rightarrow \bar{\mathbf{0}}$ (the $s \times s$ zero matrix) as $t \rightarrow \infty$, by the previously noted theorem that, in an absorbing Markov chain, the probability is one that the process will be absorbed in one of the closed sets. It immediately follows that the probability is zero that after $t \rightarrow \infty$ stages the process will be in a transient state.

Let $s_{ij}$ be the number of times the process enters transient state $j$, starting from transient state $i$, prior to being absorbed. Hence we shall focus on $p_{ij}$ such that $i, j = r + 1, \ldots, n$. $s_{ij}$ is a random variable such that $E[s_{ij}] = n_{ij}$ is the expected number of visits to $E_j$ starting from $E_i$ prior to absorption. Suppose first that $i \neq j$. The probability of going directly from $i$ to $j$ is $p_{ij}$. The probability of being in $E_j$

after two stages is $p_{ij}^{(2)}$; and the probability of being in $E_j$ after exactly $t$ stages is $p_{ij}^{(t)}$. Each time a state is visited, however, it is one single visit. Hence, the expected number of visits to state $j$ is given by $p_{ij}\ (1) + p_{ij}^{(2)}\ (1) + \cdots + p_{ij}^{(t)}\ (1) + \cdots = \sum_t p_{ij}^{(t)} = n_{ij}\ (i \neq j)$. If $i = j$, then the system starts off in state $j = i$, and hence we have an additional visit, the initial one to state $E_j = E_i$, prior to absorption; or the expected number of visits is $1 + \sum_i p_{ii} = n_{ii}$. In matrix notation, remembering that the $p_{ij}$ refer only to transient states and hence are elements of the square matrix $\mathbf{Q}$, $\mathbf{N} = [n_{ij}] = \mathbf{I} + \mathbf{Q} + \mathbf{Q}^2 + \mathbf{Q}^3 + \cdots$. But, with $\mathbf{Q}^t \to \bar{\mathbf{0}}$ as $t \to \infty$, by a well-known property of matrices, $\mathbf{I} + \mathbf{Q} + \mathbf{Q}^2 + \mathbf{Q}^3 + \cdots = (\mathbf{I} - \mathbf{Q})^{-1}$. This is comparable to the numerical result that, for $\alpha < 1$, $1 + \alpha + \alpha^2 + \cdots = 1/(1 - \alpha)$, the latter being a series expansion that was previously employed in developing the single-station queueing model. It therefore follows that

$$\mathbf{N} = (\mathbf{I} - \mathbf{Q})^{-1}. \tag{14.5}$$

The matrix $\mathbf{N}$ is called the *fundamental matrix for the absorbing chain.*

As with the $u_{ij}$'s, $n_{ij}$'s are the means of distributions of $s_{ij}$'s, times spent in state $j$ starting from state $i$ prior to absorption. The variance of this distribution can also be determined as $\sigma_{s_{ij}}^2 = E[s_{ij}^2 - E[s_{ij}]^2]$. This will be determined, as $\sigma_{ij}^2$ was previously derived, by first deriving an expression for $E[s_{ij}^2]$, and then subtracting from this the already determined $E[s_{ij}]^2 = n_{ij}^2$.

First consider $E[s_{ij}^2]$ for $i \neq j$. Then, since $E[s_{kj}]$ is the mean number of times in which $j$ will be visited from $k$, and since the probability of going from $i$ to $k$ is $p_{ik}$, $E[s_{ij}^2] = \sum_{k=r+1}^{s} p_{ik}E[s_{kj}^2]$, $(i \neq j)$. For $i = j$, we must again recognize that initially the system is in state $i$. Hence, we must add one to $s_{kj}$ in the previous computation to allow for the additional initial visit, as well as allow for those times when an absorbing state is immediately entered, or $E[s_{ij}^2] = \sum_{k=r+1}^{s} p_{ik}E[(s_{kj} + 1)^2] + \sum_{k=1}^{r} p_{ik}(1)^2$, $(i = j)$. The first expression takes care of all those times when the process is not immediately absorbed; the second expression takes care of those times when it is. These two formulations may be summarized in the single expression

$$\begin{aligned} E[s_{ij}^2] &= \sum_{k=r+1}^{s} p_{ik}E[(s_{kj} + \delta_{ij})^2] + \sum_{k=1}^{r} p_{ik}\delta_{ij} \\ &= \sum_{k=1}^{s} p_{ik}\delta_{ij}^2 + \sum_{k=r+1}^{s} p_{ik}E[s_{kj}^2] + 2 \sum_{k=r+1}^{s} p_{ik}E[s_{kj}\delta_{ij}]. \end{aligned}$$

When $i = j$, the first term becomes $\sum_{k=1}^{s} p_{ik}(1) = 1$; and when $i \neq j$, the first expression becomes $\sum_{k=1}^{s} p_{ik}(0) = 0$. Thus in a matrix expression $\mathbf{Y} = [E[s_{ij}^2]]$, the first term would be an identity matrix. The second term has the columns of **Y** itself successively multiplied by the rows of **Q**; or this term is **QY**. Similarly, since $E[s_{kj}\delta_{ij}] = E[s_{kj}]\delta_{ij}$, the third term has the rows of **Q** successively multiplying the columns of the matrix formed from **N**, and then $\delta_{ij}$ sets the $i \neq j$ terms equal to zero. Therefore, this term is $2[\mathbf{QN}]_d$. Hence,

$$\mathbf{Y} = \mathbf{I} + \mathbf{QY} + 2[\mathbf{QN}]_d.$$

Rearranging terms,

$$[\mathbf{I} - \mathbf{Q}]\mathbf{Y} = \mathbf{N}^{-1}\mathbf{Y} = \mathbf{I} + 2[\mathbf{QN}]_d,$$

and, premultiplying by **N**,

$$\mathbf{Y} = \mathbf{NI} + 2\mathbf{N}[\mathbf{QN}]_d. \tag{14.6}$$

Note, however, that since $\mathbf{N} = [\mathbf{I} - \mathbf{Q}]^{-1}$, $[\mathbf{I} - \mathbf{Q}]\mathbf{N} = \mathbf{I}$. Therefore it immediately follows that $\mathbf{QN} = \mathbf{N} - \mathbf{I}$, and $[\mathbf{QN}]_d = [\mathbf{N} - \mathbf{I}]_d = \mathbf{N}_d - \mathbf{I}$. Hence

$$\mathbf{Y} = \mathbf{NI} + 2\mathbf{N}[\mathbf{N}_d - \mathbf{I}] = \mathbf{N}[2\mathbf{N}_d - \mathbf{I}]. \tag{14.6'}$$

Denote the variance matrix of $s_{ij}$ by $\boldsymbol{\sigma}_s^2 = [\sigma_{s_{ij}}^2]$, and write $\mathbf{N}_{SQ} = [n_{ij}^2]$. Then,

$$\boldsymbol{\sigma}_s^2 = \mathbf{N}[2\mathbf{N}_d - \mathbf{I}] - \mathbf{N}_{SQ}. \tag{14.7}$$

In the illustration with $G_{123}$ and $G_4$, $\mathbf{I} - \mathbf{Q} = 1 - .9736 = .0264$ and $\mathbf{N} = (\mathbf{I} - \mathbf{Q})^{-1} = 37.8788$. $\boldsymbol{\sigma}_s^2 = \mathbf{N}(2\mathbf{N}_d - \mathbf{I}) - \mathbf{N}^2 = 2831.7282 - (37.8788)^2 = 1396.9247$. Thus, the mean number of stages for the $G_4$ firms to survive, before all consumers are absorbed in $G_{123}$, is 37.9, but with a rather sizable standard deviation of $(1396.9247)^{1/2} = 37.4$. It would seem, therefore, that unless the managements of the lesser lights of the industry take steps to alter the $p_{ij}$, they need not wonder for whom the bell tolls, nor as a group can they expect to accurately forecast when it will sound their demise.

It immediately follows that $m_i = \sum_{j=r+1}^{s} n_{ij}$ is the mean number of stages that, starting from transient state $E_i$, will be spent in *all* transient states prior to absorption, or $\mathbf{m} = (m_{r+1}, \ldots, m_s)' = \mathbf{Ni}$. To compute the variance of the distribution of stages $v_i$ prior to absorption, $E[v_i^2 - E[v_i]^2] = \sigma_{v_i}^2$, we shall again first compute $E[v_i^2]$. In the now hopefully familiar fashion,

$$E[v_i^2] = \sum_{k=1}^{r} p_{ik}(1)^2 + \sum_{k=r+1}^{s} p_{ik}E[(v_k + 1)^2],$$

since we wish to sum the probability-weighted squared values of (1) immediate absorption into any absorbing state following a single period spent in a transient state, and (2) the total number of stages prior to absorption should the process go to another transient state. Rearranging terms,

$$E[v_i^2] = \sum_{k=1}^{s} p_{ik} + \sum_{k=r+1}^{s} p_{ik}E[v_k^2] + 2\sum_{k=r+1}^{s} p_{ik}m_k,$$

since $E[v_k] = m_k$. Translated into vector-matrix notation, the latter expression becomes

$$\mathbf{X} = \mathbf{i} + \mathbf{QX} + 2\mathbf{Qm}, \tag{14.8}$$

where $\mathbf{X} = [E[v_i]]$ is an $s \times 1$ column vector. Rearranging terms,

$$[\mathbf{I} - \mathbf{Q}]\mathbf{X} = \mathbf{N}^{-1}\mathbf{X} = \mathbf{i} + 2\mathbf{Qm}$$

or

$$\mathbf{X} = \mathbf{Ni} + 2\mathbf{NQm}.$$

But we have seen that $\mathbf{Ni} = \mathbf{m}$; and $\mathbf{NQ} = \mathbf{N} - \mathbf{I}$ follows from $\mathbf{N} = (\mathbf{I} - \mathbf{Q})^{-1}$. Hence,

$$\mathbf{X} = \mathbf{m} + 2(\mathbf{N} - \mathbf{I})\mathbf{m} = (2\mathbf{N} - \mathbf{I})\mathbf{m}. \tag{14.8'}$$

Letting $\mathbf{m}'_{SQ} = (m_{r+1}^2, \ldots, m_i^2, \ldots, m_s^2)$,

$$\boldsymbol{\sigma}_v^2 = [\sigma_{v_i}^2] = (2\mathbf{N} - \mathbf{I})\mathbf{m} - \mathbf{m}_{SQ}. \tag{14.8''}$$

In the present illustration with single transient and absorbing states, $\mathbf{m} = \mathbf{N}$ and $\boldsymbol{\sigma}_v^2 = \boldsymbol{\sigma}_s^2 = 1396.9247$.

In the present illustration we also know that the process will be absorbed in $G_{123}$. If, however, there were more than one absorbing state, we might be interested in determining the probability of absorption in each. If, for example, customers of transient brands $E_8$, $E_9$, and $E_{10}$, say, eventually turn permanently to either $E_{11}$, $E_{12}$, or $E_{13}$, the managements of the latter firms will want to know the probability of obtaining the custom of, say, the $E_8$ purchaser.

Let $b_{ia}$ denote the probability of eventual absorption in $E_a$ starting from transient state $E_i$. This probability will be the sum of the probabilities of heading directly into $E_a$ from $E_i$, and the probability of heading back into any transient state $E_j$ and then being absorbed into $E_a$, or

$$b_{ia} = p_{ia} + \sum_{j=r+1}^{s} p_{ij}b_{ja}.$$

In matrix notation, with $\mathbf{B} = [b_{ia}]$, $\mathbf{B} = \mathbf{R} + \mathbf{QB}$, or $[\mathbf{I} - \mathbf{Q}]\mathbf{B} = \mathbf{R}$. Premultiplying by $[\mathbf{I} - \mathbf{Q}]^{-1} = \mathbf{N}$,

$$\mathbf{B} = \mathbf{NR}. \tag{14.9}$$

In the present illustration, with only a single state in which the process can be absorbed, $\mathbf{B} = 37.8788(.0264) = 1$; or, with probability of one the process will be absorbed in $G_{123}$.

It should also be noted that, in the present illustration, the persistent states $G_1$, $G_2$, and $G_3$ themselves form a transition probability matrix representing an irreducible and regular Markov process. The properties of regular matrices carry over to this submatrix:

$$\mathbf{P}_{123} = \begin{matrix} & G_1 & G_2 & G_3 \\ G_1 & .8923 & .0660 & .0417 \\ G_2 & .0395 & .9101 & .0504 \\ G_3 & .2468 & 0 & .7532 \end{matrix}.$$

In particular, the fixed point vector is $\mathbf{a}' = (.4870, .3577, .1553)$. Again interpreting these probabilities as market shares, .3577, say, gives the long-term expected market share of the $G_2$ firms. Similarly, we can compute the means and variances of first passage times as

$$\mathbf{u} = \begin{matrix} & G_1 & G_2 & G_3 \\ G_1 & 2.05 & 17.71 & 22.04 \\ G_2 & 13.40 & 2.80 & 20.45 \\ G_3 & 4.05 & 21.76 & 6.44 \end{matrix},$$

$$\boldsymbol{\sigma}^2 = \begin{matrix} & G_1 & G_2 & G_3 \\ G_1 & 4.48 & 17.79 & 20.97 \\ G_2 & 11.12 & 7.88 & 20.54 \\ G_3 & 2.62 & 18.14 & 14.11 \end{matrix}.$$

As in the earlier illustration, we once again observe considerable brand loyalty, and great variability in the distributions of first passage times.

## 14.6 LEAST SQUARES AND THE TRANSITION PROBABILITY MATRIX

Although with reference to a specific problem one might be convinced that the Markov assumption has sufficient validity, and the prospective inferences to be drawn from the transition probabilities hold sufficient promise to warrant a full-scale Markov analysis, one is likely to be hesitant and somewhat tremulous in *assigning* and *justifying* the transition probabilities. To relieve some of this potential anxiety, certain generally accepted methods for *estimating* the probabilities have evolved. In the case of brand preferences, for example, consumer-panel data could be analyzed in order to determine "the percentage of persons who bought Brand 1 last time and repeated the next time a purchase was made; the percentage of those persons who bought some other brand last time and switched to Brand 1 the following time; the percentage of persons who bought Brand 1 last time and switched to some other brand the following time, and finally the percentage of persons who bought some other brand last time and some other brand the following time."[9] These percentages are then taken as the estimates of the transition probabilities.[10] Similarly, suppose one wishes to analyze corporate mobility, say in terms of the potential for movement from one asset size class to another. Then, "if $a_{ij}$ denotes the number of movements of firms from class $i$ to class $j$ throughout the period under consideration, our transition probabilities $p_{ij}$ become $p_{ij} = a_{ij} \Big/ \sum_j a_{ij}$," with an arbitrary estimate required to deal with "potential entrants."[11]

While the requisite "micromovement" data to facilitate the estimation of the transition probabilities may be available, the economist cannot assume that he will always be accorded this luxury. More realistically, the economist is commonly constrained to working with *macro*economic data. For him, the most pertinent aspect

[9] Richard B. Maffei, "Brand Preferences and Simple Markov Processes," *Operations Research*, **VIII**:2 (March–April 1960), 211.

[10] In particular, if there are a total of $X_j$ shifts to brand $j$ and a total of $x_{ij}$ shifts to brand $j$ from $i$, then the maximum likelihood estimator of $p_{ij}$ is $x_{ij}/X_j$, and the stationarity hypothesis may be subjected, if desired, to statistical testing [T. W. Anderson and L. A. Goodman, "Statistical Inference About Markov Chains," *Annals of Mathematical Statistics*, **28**:1 (March 1957), 89–110].

[11] Adelman, "A Stochastic Analysis of the Size Distribution of Firms," p. 899.

of the estimation issue is whether such macrodata can be utilized to obtain the transition probabilities. In the specific case where data are available only for the sample *proportions* going into state $E_i$ ($i = 1, \ldots, n$) at stages $t = 0, \ldots, T$, it is in fact possible to obtain estimates of the $p_{ij}$ via constrained least squares. Thus the time-series data of market shares for firms in a particular industry, say, will suffice to permit the estimation of the transition probability matrix for "firm-switching."

Earlier we indicated some of the potentially important pieces of information that might be gleaned from a transition probability matrix involving consumer switching patterns between firms. This potential has by no means been lost to economists and statisticians, who have long been interested in the intriguing possibility of estimating the transition probabilities by applying some technique, such as ordinary least squares, to commonly available market-share data.[12] A major step in the resolution of this problem was recently taken by H. Theil and Guido Rey.[13] They first formulate the estimation problem as a quadratic programming problem. Then they suggest a most feasible and attractive procedure for estimating the transition probability matrix by taking advantage of a quadratic programming algorithm *in conjunction with* ordinary least squares. The remainder of this section will be devoted to describing their approach.

Consider a system in which there are $n$ states $E_i$, such that $x_{it}$ is the probability of the $i$th state obtaining in period $t$. It might be helpful to think of $E_i$ as being the $i$th of $n$ firms in an industry, and of $x_{it}$ as being the firm's market share at time $t$. Clearly, if $\mathbf{x}_t' = (x_{1t}, x_{2t}, \ldots, x_{nt})$, then $\mathbf{i}'\mathbf{x}_t = 1$; that is, the sum of the market shares is unity. Denote the transition probability matrix for the industry by $\boldsymbol{\pi} = [\pi_{ij}]$, where $\boldsymbol{\pi}\mathbf{i} = \mathbf{i}$ and $1 \geq \pi_{ij} \geq 0$. We shall ignore the possibility of the new consumer, or the loss to the industry of the former customer. By the Markov assumption,

$$\mathbf{x}_t'\boldsymbol{\pi} = \mathbf{x}_{t+1}'. \tag{14.10}$$

Suppose there are a total of $T + 1$ observations of $\mathbf{x}_t$ and suppose also that $\boldsymbol{\pi}$ will be *estimated* by the matrix $\mathbf{P} = [p_{ij}]$. Again, $\mathbf{Pi} = \mathbf{i}$ and $1 \geq p_{ij} \geq 0$. Then,

$$\mathbf{x}_t'\mathbf{P} = \mathbf{x}_{t+1}' + \mathbf{e}_{t+1}', \tag{14.10$'$}$$

where $\mathbf{e}_{t+1}' = (e_{1(t+1)}, \ldots, e_{i(t+1)}, \ldots, e_{n(t+1)})$ is a vector of residuals, or error terms. One criterion for estimation of $\mathbf{P}$ might simply be to minimize the sum of the squared residuals—as in ordinary least squares—subject to the constraints on the $p_{ij}$. More generally, however, let $\mathbf{D}$ be *any* $n \times n$ symmetric and positive definite matrix. Then we can define the following quadratic programming problem:

$$\text{Minimize} \quad \sum_t \mathbf{e}_{t+1}'\mathbf{D}\mathbf{e}_{t+1} = \sum_t (\mathbf{x}_t'\mathbf{P} - \mathbf{x}_{t+1}')\mathbf{D}(\mathbf{x}_t'\mathbf{P} - \mathbf{x}_{t+1}')' \tag{14.11}$$

$$\text{subject to} \qquad \mathbf{Pi} = \mathbf{i}, \tag{14.11a}$$

$$1 \geq p_{ij} \geq 0, \; i, j = 1, \ldots, n. \tag{14.11b}$$

[12] See, for example, A. Madansky, "Least Squares Estimation in Finite Markov Processes," *Psychometrika*, **24**:2 (June 1959), 137–144; L. G. Telser, "Least-Squares Estimates of Transition Probabilities," in Carl Christ, ed., *Measurement in Economics* (Stanford, Calif.: Stanford University Press, 1963), pp. 272–292; T. C. Lee, G. C. Judge, and T. Takayama, "On Estimating the Transition Probabilities of a Markov Process," *Journal of Farm Economics*, **47**:3 (Aug. 1965), 742–762.

[13] "A Quadratic Programming Approach to the Estimation of Transition Probabilities," *Management Science*, **12**:9 (May 1966), 714–721.

Because $t = 0, \ldots, T$ and there is an $\mathbf{x}_{t+1}$ term, there will be a total of $T$ joint observations for (14.10′). Further, because $\mathbf{Pi} = \mathbf{i}$, given any $n - 1$ estimates in the $i$th row of $\mathbf{P}$ ($i = 1, \ldots, n$), the $n$th will be determinate. Hence, we require a total of $n(n - 1)$ independent estimates of the $n^2$ $p_{ij}$. In effect, given the elements in any $n - 1$ columns of $\mathbf{P}$, the elements in the $n$th column are determinate.

The Kuhn-Tucker conditions apply to yield a *minimum* for (14.11) because $\mathbf{D}$ is positive definite and hence the objective function is convex. To determine this minimum, we shall employ a quadratic programming procedure due to H. Theil and C. Van de Panne.[14] In this procedure, the objective function is first minimized without considering the inequality constraints, here $1 \geq p_{ij} \geq 0$. The rationale is that if the solution so obtained does not violate any of the constraints, it will be the optimal solution; and neglecting these constraints greatly simplifies matters. We will cross the bridge of what to do about violated constraints when we come to it—and we shall.

Ignoring (14.11b), we may write the Lagrange function for (14.11)

$$L = \Sigma\, \mathbf{x}_t'\mathbf{PDP}'\mathbf{x}_t - 2\, \Sigma\, \mathbf{x}_t'\mathbf{PDx}_{t+1} + \Sigma\, \mathbf{x}_{t+1}'\mathbf{Dx}_{t+1} - \boldsymbol{\lambda}'[\mathbf{Pi} - \mathbf{i}], \qquad (14.12)$$

where the summation is over $t = 0, \ldots, T$ and where $\boldsymbol{\lambda}'$ is a row vector of Lagrange multipliers. Note that $L$ is a single *number* derived from the sum of a series of products of vectors and matrices. Note also that while the product of two row or column vectors is not defined, premultiplying a $1 \times n$ *row* vector $\mathbf{x}'$ by an $n \times 1$ *column* vector $\mathbf{x}$ is defined, and will yield an $n \times n$ matrix $\mathbf{X} = [\mathbf{xx}'] = [x_ix_j]$.

With the latter in mind, and since we wish to determine the *matrix* $\mathbf{P}$ that minimizes $L$, differentiate $L$ with respect to $\mathbf{P}$.[15] Setting the resultant *matrix* $\partial L/\partial \mathbf{P} = \bar{\mathbf{0}}$ yields the following:

$$\frac{\partial L}{\partial \mathbf{P}} = 2 \sum \mathbf{x}_t[\mathbf{DP}'\mathbf{x}_t]' - 2 \sum \mathbf{x}_t[\mathbf{Dx}_{t+1}]' - \boldsymbol{\lambda}\mathbf{i}' = \bar{\mathbf{0}}$$

$$= 2\left[\sum \mathbf{x}_t\mathbf{x}_t'\right]\mathbf{PD}' - 2\left[\sum \mathbf{x}_t\mathbf{x}_{t+1}'\right]\mathbf{D}' - \boldsymbol{\lambda}\mathbf{i}' = \bar{\mathbf{0}}. \qquad (14.13)$$

But $\mathbf{D}$ is symmetric, so $\mathbf{D}^{-1} = [\mathbf{D}']^{-1}$. Hence, first postmultiplying (14.13) by $\mathbf{D}^{-1}$,

$$2[\Sigma\, \mathbf{x}_t\mathbf{x}_t']\mathbf{P} - 2\, \Sigma\, [\mathbf{x}_t\mathbf{x}_{t+1}'] - [\boldsymbol{\lambda}\mathbf{i}']\mathbf{D}^{-1} = \bar{\mathbf{0}}; \qquad (14.13')$$

and then postmultiplying by $\mathbf{i}$,

$$2[\Sigma\, \mathbf{x}_t\mathbf{x}_t']\mathbf{i} - 2[\Sigma\, \mathbf{x}_t\mathbf{x}_{t+1}']\mathbf{i} - [\boldsymbol{\lambda}\mathbf{i}']\mathbf{D}^{-1}\mathbf{i} = \mathbf{0}$$

because $\mathbf{Pi} = \mathbf{i}$. But $[\Sigma\, \mathbf{x}_t\mathbf{x}_t']\mathbf{i} = \Sigma\, \mathbf{x}_t[\mathbf{x}_t'\mathbf{i}] = \Sigma\, \mathbf{x}_t = (\Sigma\, x_{1t}, \ldots, \Sigma\, x_{nt})'$ because $\mathbf{x}_t'\mathbf{i} = 1$. Similarly, $[\Sigma\, \mathbf{x}_t\mathbf{x}_{t+1}']\mathbf{i} = \Sigma\, \mathbf{x}_t[\mathbf{x}_{t+1}'\mathbf{i}] = \Sigma\, \mathbf{x}_t$. Therefore,

$$2\, \Sigma\, \mathbf{x}_t - 2\, \Sigma\, \mathbf{x}_t - [\boldsymbol{\lambda}\mathbf{i}']\mathbf{D}^{-1}\mathbf{i} = -\boldsymbol{\lambda}[\mathbf{i}'\mathbf{D}^{-1}\mathbf{i}] = \mathbf{0}, \qquad (14.13'')$$

[14] H. Theil and C. Van de Panne, "Quadratic Programming as an Extension of Classical Quadratic Maximization," *Management Science*, **7**:1 (Oct. 1960), 1–20.

[15] It is readily verified that, given the matrix $\mathbf{P}$ and the vectors $\mathbf{y}_1 = [y_{1j}]$ and $\mathbf{y}_2 = [y_{2i}]$ such that $z = \mathbf{y}_1'\mathbf{Py}_2$ is defined, $\mathbf{y}_1'\mathbf{Py}_2$ is the trace (sum of the diagonal elements) of the matrix product $\mathbf{Py}_2\mathbf{y}_1'$. Then, $\partial\mathbf{y}_1'\mathbf{Py}_2/\partial\mathbf{P} = \partial(\text{trace } \mathbf{Py}_2\mathbf{y}_1')/\partial\mathbf{P} = [\partial\, \Sigma\, p_{ij}y_{2i}y_{1j}/\partial p_{ij}] = [y_{2i}y_{1j}] = \mathbf{y}_1\mathbf{y}_2'$.

by virtue of which $\boldsymbol{\lambda} = \mathbf{0}$ since $\mathbf{i}'\mathbf{D}^{-1}\mathbf{i} \neq 0$. Setting $\boldsymbol{\lambda} = \mathbf{0}$ in (14.13′) and rearranging terms,

$$[\Sigma\, \mathbf{x}_t\mathbf{x}_t']\mathbf{P} = [\Sigma\, \mathbf{x}_t\mathbf{x}_{t+1}']$$

or

$$\hat{\mathbf{P}} = [\Sigma\, \mathbf{x}_t\mathbf{x}_t']^{-1}[\Sigma\, \mathbf{x}_t\mathbf{x}_{t+1}'] = [p_{ij}], \tag{14.14}$$

where the circumflex indicates that all $1 \geq p_{ij} \geq 0$ constraints have been ignored.

There are two especially noteworthy aspects of (14.14), one following directly from the other. We first note that $\hat{\mathbf{P}}$ is independent of *both* $\mathbf{D}$ and $\boldsymbol{\lambda}$. It follows then that (14.14) could be obtained simply by minimizing

$$\Sigma\, \mathbf{e}_{t+1}'\mathbf{I}\mathbf{e}_{t+1} = \Sigma\, (\mathbf{x}_t'\mathbf{P} - \mathbf{x}_{t+1}')\mathbf{I}(\mathbf{x}_t'\mathbf{P} - \mathbf{x}_{t+1}')';$$

that is, $\hat{\mathbf{P}}$ is obtained via ordinary least squares with $\mathbf{x}_{t+1}$ as the dependent variable and $\mathbf{x}_t$ as the independent variable. In particular, the $i$th *column* of $\mathbf{x}_t'\mathbf{P}$ in (14.10′) may be written

$$p_{1i}x_{1t} + \cdots + p_{ii}x_{it} + \cdots + p_{ni}x_{nt} = x_{i(t+1)} + e_{i(t+1)},$$

or, rearranging terms into the more familiar pattern,

$$x_{i(t+1)} = p_{1i}x_{1t} + \cdots + p_{ii}x_{it} + \cdots + p_{ni}x_{nt} - e_{i(t+1)}. \tag{14.10″}$$

The $\hat{p}_{ij}$'s $(j = 1, \ldots, n)$ are then the regression coefficients for (14.10″). Note, however, that since $\sum_{j=1}^{n} x_{jt} = 1$, least squares cannot be applied *directly* to (14.10″) because there is a perfect linear relationship among the exogenous variables. Nevertheless, we can substitute $x_{it} = 1 - \sum_{j\neq i} x_{jt}$ into (14.10)″ and rewrite it as

$$x_{i(t+1)} = p_{ii} + (p_{1i} - p_{ii})x_{1t} + \cdots + (p_{ni} - p_{ii})x_{nt} - e_{i(t+1)}. \tag{14.10‴}$$

The $\hat{p}_{ij}$'s obtained in the latter regression are the $\hat{p}_{ij}$'s obtained through (14.14).

Table 14.2 presents the percent of the four-firm total sales held by the four premium brewers from 1944 to 1964. As discussed in the Appendix to this chapter, based upon these data the matrix $\hat{\mathbf{P}}$ is given by

$$\hat{\mathbf{P}} = \begin{array}{c} \\ E_1 \\ E_2 \\ E_3 \\ E_4 \end{array} \begin{array}{c} \begin{array}{cccc} E_1 & E_2 & E_3 & E_4 \end{array} \\ \begin{bmatrix} .7852 & -.0613 & .3247 & -.0486 \\ .1360 & .6869 & .1410 & .0361 \\ -.0171 & .3298 & .6043 & .0829 \\ .3171 & .3444 & -.5511 & .8896 \end{bmatrix} \end{array}.$$

Now, $\hat{\mathbf{P}}$ is not a stochastic matrix, because the constraint $p_{ij} \geq 0$ is violated in four cases: $p_{12}, p_{14}, p_{31}, p_{43} < 0$. To deal with this situation, we take advantage of the following rule: Let $\mathbf{P}_\omega$ be a feasible solution to (14.11) that satisfies some subset $\omega$ of the $1 \geq p_i \geq 0$ constraints in binding *equational* form. Then, $\mathbf{P}_\omega$ will be the optimal solution if and only if every other solution $\mathbf{P}_{hk}$ violates at least one of the constraints $1 \geq p_{ij} \geq 0$, where $\mathbf{P}_{hk}$ is a solution bound by all constraints of the set $\omega$, except for the $(hk)$th.[16] Thus this rule implies that to obtain the optimal solution to the

[16] Theil and Van de Panne, "Quadratic Programming as an Extension of Classical Quadratic Maximization," p. 8.

TABLE 14.2
Premium Market Shares of U.S. Premium Brewers, 1944–1964

| Year | $E_1$ | $E_2$ | $E_3$ | $E_4$ |
|---|---|---|---|---|
| 1944 | .3813 | .3246 | .2200 | .0741 |
| 1945 | .3621 | .2949 | .2728 | .0702 |
| 1946 | .3230 | .2712 | .3399 | .0659 |
| 1947 | .2973 | .3288 | .3075 | .0664 |
| 1948 | .3033 | .3205 | .3080 | .0682 |
| 1949 | .3103 | .3209 | .2776 | .0912 |
| 1950 | .3153 | .3286 | .2204 | .1357 |
| 1951 | .3086 | .3219 | .2224 | .1471 |
| 1952 | .3101 | .3261 | .2079 | .1559 |
| 1953 | .3656 | .2863 | .2316 | .1165 |
| 1954 | .3464 | .3212 | .2079 | .1245 |
| 1955 | .3331 | .3428 | .1942 | .1299 |
| 1956 | .3416 | .3461 | .1815 | .1308 |
| 1957 | .3584 | .3531 | .1583 | .1302 |
| 1958 | .3611 | .3048 | .2198 | .1143 |
| 1959 | .3879 | .2821 | .2165 | .1135 |
| 1960 | .3982 | .2675 | .2226 | .1117 |
| 1961 | .3833 | .2598 | .2350 | .1219 |
| 1962 | .3680 | .2798 | .2380 | .1142 |
| 1963 | .3515 | .2930 | .2496 | .1059 |
| 1964 | .3502 | .2826 | .2547 | .1125 |

original problem, each of the constraints violated by $\hat{\mathbf{P}}$ should be applied one at a time in *binding* form, the problem resolved, and each of the solutions inspected to see whether it violates any of the constraints.

If *one* of the solutions violates no constraints, the optimum has been found. If one or *more* solutions do not violate a constraint, then the optimum is the one with the smaller sum of squared residuals, weighted in accordance with **D**. If some constraint should still be violated, the problem is then resolved for all cases in which *two* of the violated constraints are held binding at one time. If there is one solution for which no constraint is violated, *and* if the release of *each* of the binding constraints, individually, results in a nonfeasible solution, then the optimum has been found. If constraints persist in being violated, three constraints at a time are set binding, and so forth. It is important to note that putting one constraint in binding form may cause a previously satisfied constraint to be violated. As a precautionary note, it is therefore not advisable to *consider* cutting corners by attempting to omit the gorier details involved in applying the algorithm.

Suppose, then, that at some stage in the operation we elect to set various violated $p_{hk} = \alpha_{hk}$ (= 0 or 1). The Lagrange function of (14.12) thereupon becomes

$$L = \Sigma\, \mathbf{x}_t'\mathbf{PDP}'\mathbf{x}_t - 2\,\Sigma\, \mathbf{x}_t'\mathbf{PD}\mathbf{x}_{t+1} + \Sigma\, \mathbf{x}_{t+1}'\mathbf{D}\mathbf{x}_{t+1} - \boldsymbol{\lambda}'[\mathbf{Pi} - \mathbf{i}] - \Sigma\, \theta_{hk}(\mathbf{e}_h'\mathbf{P}\mathbf{e}_k - \alpha_{hk}), \qquad (14.15)$$

where $\theta_{hk}$ is a Lagrange multiplier, $\mathbf{e}_h$ and $\mathbf{e}_k$ are unit vectors (*not* residuals) with the 1 in the $h$th and $k$th positions, respectively, and the last summation is over all $(hk)$

pairs for violated constraints. Differentiating $L$ with respect to $\mathbf{P}$, and setting $\partial L/\partial \mathbf{P} = \bar{\mathbf{0}}$,

$$\frac{\partial L}{\partial \mathbf{P}} = 2\sum \mathbf{x}_t[\mathbf{D}\mathbf{P}'\mathbf{x}_t]' - 2\sum \mathbf{x}_t[\mathbf{D}\mathbf{x}_{t+1}]' - \lambda\mathbf{i}' - \sum \theta_{hk}\mathbf{e}_h\mathbf{e}_k'$$

$$= 2\left[\sum \mathbf{x}_t\mathbf{x}_t'\right]\mathbf{P}\mathbf{D}' - 2\left[\sum \mathbf{x}_t\mathbf{x}_{t+1}'\right]\mathbf{D}' - \lambda\mathbf{i}' - \sum \theta_{hk}\mathbf{e}_h\mathbf{e}_k' = \bar{\mathbf{0}}. \quad (14.16)$$

As in the earlier machinations, rearrange terms, postmultiply by $\mathbf{D}^{-1}$ and then by $\mathbf{i}$, and arrive at

$$2[\Sigma\, \mathbf{x}_t\mathbf{x}_t']\mathbf{i} - 2[\Sigma\, \mathbf{x}_t\mathbf{x}_{t+1}']\mathbf{i} - \lambda\mathbf{i}'\mathbf{D}^{-1}\mathbf{i} - \Sigma\, \theta_{hk}\mathbf{e}_h\mathbf{e}_k'\mathbf{D}^{-1}\mathbf{i} = \mathbf{0}.$$

As before, the first two terms cancel, whereupon

$$-\lambda\mathbf{i}'\mathbf{D}^{-1}\mathbf{i} - \Sigma\, \theta_{hk}\mathbf{e}_h\mathbf{e}_k'\mathbf{D}^{-1}\mathbf{i} = \mathbf{0}$$

or

$$\lambda = -\frac{\Sigma\, \theta_{hk}\mathbf{e}_h\mathbf{e}_k'\mathbf{D}^{-1}\mathbf{i}}{\mathbf{i}'\mathbf{D}^{-1}\mathbf{i}}, \quad (14.17)$$

since $\mathbf{i}'\mathbf{D}^{-1}\mathbf{i}$ is a scalar, thereby permitting the common everyday garden-variety type of division. Now, substituting this expression for $\lambda$ back into (14.16) in order to solve for $\mathbf{P}$ and $\theta_{hk}$, we get

$$2\left[\sum \mathbf{x}_t\mathbf{x}_t'\right]\mathbf{P}\mathbf{D}' - 2\left[\sum \mathbf{x}_t\mathbf{x}_{t+1}'\right]\mathbf{D}' - \sum \theta_{hk}\mathbf{e}_h\mathbf{e}_k'\left[\mathbf{I} - \frac{\mathbf{D}^{-1}\mathbf{i}\mathbf{i}'}{\mathbf{i}'\mathbf{D}^{-1}\mathbf{i}}\right] = \bar{\mathbf{0}}, \quad (14.16')$$

because

$$\frac{\Sigma\, \theta_{hk}\mathbf{e}_h\mathbf{e}_k'\mathbf{D}^{-1}\mathbf{i}\mathbf{i}'}{\mathbf{i}'\mathbf{D}^{-1}\mathbf{i}} - \sum \theta_{hk}\mathbf{e}_h\mathbf{e}'_k = \sum \theta_{hk}\mathbf{e}_h\mathbf{e}'_k\left[\frac{\mathbf{D}^{-1}\mathbf{i}\mathbf{i}'}{\mathbf{i}'\mathbf{D}^{-1}\mathbf{i}} - \mathbf{I}\right].$$

Premultiplying (14.16′) by $[\Sigma\, \mathbf{x}_t\mathbf{x}_t']^{-1}$,

$$2\mathbf{P}\mathbf{D}' - 2\hat{\mathbf{P}}\mathbf{D}' - \left[\sum \mathbf{x}_t\mathbf{x}_t'\right]^{-1}\sum \theta_{hk}\mathbf{e}_h\mathbf{e}_k'\left[\mathbf{I} - \frac{\mathbf{D}^{-1}\mathbf{i}\mathbf{i}'}{\mathbf{i}'\mathbf{D}^{-1}\mathbf{i}}\right] = \bar{\mathbf{0}}$$

with $\hat{\mathbf{P}}$ given by (14.14). Postmultiplying by $\mathbf{D}^{-1}$,

$$2\mathbf{P} - 2\hat{\mathbf{P}} - \sum \theta_{hk}\left[\sum \mathbf{x}_t\mathbf{x}_t'\right]^{-1}\mathbf{e}_h\mathbf{e}_k'\left[\mathbf{D}^{-1} - \frac{\mathbf{D}^{-1}\mathbf{i}\mathbf{i}'\mathbf{D}^{-1}}{\mathbf{i}'\mathbf{D}^{-1}\mathbf{i}}\right] = \bar{\mathbf{0}}.$$

Denoting $\theta_{hk}^0 = \theta_{hk}/2$ and $\mathbf{G} = \mathbf{D}^{-1} - \mathbf{D}^{-1}\mathbf{i}\mathbf{i}'\mathbf{D}^{-1}/\mathbf{i}'\mathbf{D}^{-1}\mathbf{i}$, and $\mathbf{X} = [\Sigma\, \mathbf{x}_t\mathbf{x}_t']^{-1} = [x_{ij}]$,

$$\mathbf{P}^* = \hat{\mathbf{P}} + \Sigma\, \theta_{hk}^0\mathbf{X}\mathbf{e}_h\mathbf{e}_k'\mathbf{G}. \quad (14.18)$$

Once we are forced to explicitly recognize the $1 \geq p_{ij} \geq 0$ constraints, then, we must also specify a positive definite weighting matrix $\mathbf{D}$ in order to obtain $\mathbf{G} = [g_{ij}]$.

Suppose, now, that $\mathbf{P}^*$ is premultiplied by $\mathbf{e}_i'$ and postmultiplied by $\mathbf{e}_j$, where $i$ and $j$ form an $(hk)$ pair for a now binding constraint. Then $\mathbf{e}_i'\mathbf{P}^*\mathbf{e}_j = p_{ij}^*$, $\mathbf{e}_i'\hat{\mathbf{P}}\mathbf{e}_j = \hat{p}_{ij}$, $\mathbf{e}_i'\mathbf{X}\mathbf{e}_h = x_{ih}$, and $\mathbf{e}_k'\mathbf{G}\mathbf{e}_j = g_{kj}$. We therefore have

$$p_{ij}^* = \hat{p}_{ij} + \sum_{(hk)} \theta_{hk}^0 x_{ih} g_{kj}, \qquad (ij) = (hk). \quad (14.19)$$

In particular, suppose $\mathbf{D} = \mathbf{I}$. In this case all sums of squared errors are given *equal* weight. Then, $\mathbf{G} = [g_{ij}] = \mathbf{I} - \mathbf{I}\mathbf{i}\mathbf{i}'\mathbf{I}/\mathbf{i}'\mathbf{I}\mathbf{i} = \mathbf{I} - \mathbf{S}/n$, where $\mathbf{S} = [1]$. In the present illustration with $n = 4$, $g_{ij} = 1 - \frac{1}{4} = \frac{3}{4}$ for $i = j$, and $g_{ij} = 0 - \frac{1}{4} = -\frac{1}{4}$ otherwise. If we should elect to set, say, $p_{31} = p_{43} = 0$, then from (14.19) we would form the following pair of equations:

$$0 = \hat{p}_{31} + \theta_{31}^0 x_{33} g_{11} + \theta_{43}^0 x_{34} g_{31},$$
$$0 = \hat{p}_{43} + \theta_{31}^0 x_{43} g_{13} + \theta_{43}^0 x_{44} g_{33}.$$

These equations would then be solved for $\theta_{31}^0$ and $\theta_{43}^0$ and all the transition probabilities reestimated from (14.19), with the now known $\theta_{hk}^0$'s. As noted in the Appendix to this chapter, proceeding in this manner the optimal feasible solution to the present problem is determined to be the transition probability matrix **P** of Section 14.2. If, therefore, the Markov assumption is appropriate for United States premium brewers, and *if* the transition probabilities can be assumed fixed over this twenty-year period, those inferences drawn from the properties of a regular matrix would indeed be applicable to these four firms.

It might also be noted that while we have set **D** = **I**, **D** can be *any* positive definite matrix, and alternative **D**'s can lead to quite different solutions to the problem.[17] The choice of **D** will depend upon the weight that one wishes to give to the various residuals.

## 14.7 PRIOR INFORMATION AND REGRESSION ANALYSIS

Prior information is inevitably brought to bear on any regression model. In the previous section, for example, we made use of the knowledge that probabilities cannot be negative, nor can they have values in excess of unity. Similarly, one generally chooses not to include certain variables in a regression, or even to seriously consider their inclusion, simply because one has a dogmatic prior, hopefully based on strong theoretical considerations and empirical observation, asserting that the probability is unity that these variables have coefficients that are, in fact, zero.

In addition to demanding that regression coefficients respect certain sets of relationships or certain sets of dogmatic priors, we can also require that the estimates give weight to one's prior beliefs as reflected in an entire probability distribution. Thus, instead of requiring that, as in one of our earliest formulations, a regression coefficient measuring the price elasticity of demand must not exceed negative one, we might assign an entire probability distribution to reflect prior beliefs about the elasticity of demand. Then, this prior distribution would be revised in light of the sample data, and the regression coefficients estimated accordingly. Although there have been efforts along these lines, they fall beyond the scope of this book.[18] None-

[17] For an illustration, and some logical alternatives to **D** = **I**, see Theil and Rey, "A Quadratic Programming Approach to the Estimation of Transition Probabilities," pp. 720–721. Also see T. C. Lee, G. C. Judge, and A. Zellner, "Maximum Likelihood and Bayesian Estimation of Transition Probabilities," *Journal of the American Statistical Association*, **63**:324 (Dec. 1968), 1162–1179.

[18] See, for example, Howard Raiffa and Robert Schlaifer, *Applied Statistical Decision Theory* (Boston, Mass.: Harvard University, 1961), chap. 13; and Arnold Zellner and V. Karuppan Chetty, "Prediction and Decision Problems in Regression Models from the Bayesian Point of View," *Journal of the American Statistical Association*, **60**:310 (June 1965), 608–616. Also, see J. Drèze, "The Bayesian Approach to Simultaneous Equations Estimation," *O.N.R. Research Memorandum* 67 (Evanston, Ill.: Northwestern University, 1962).

theless, to give some indication of the potential that this broad area holds, we shall discuss an approach that, perhaps not coincidentally, like the procedure discussed in the previous section, is also due to H. Theil.[19]

Let us return to the problem of Chapter 3 in which we wished to estimate an $(n + 1) \times 1$ vector $\boldsymbol{\alpha}$ in the equation

$$\mathbf{Q} = \mathbf{V}\boldsymbol{\alpha} + \boldsymbol{\varepsilon}, \tag{14.20}$$

based upon a set of $N$ joint observations on $\mathbf{Q}$ and $\mathbf{V}$, and subject to the previously stated set of assumptions with respect to $\mathbf{V}$ and $\boldsymbol{\varepsilon}$. The least-squares estimator is given by

$$\mathbf{a} = [\mathbf{V}'\mathbf{V}]^{-1}\mathbf{V}'\mathbf{Q}. \tag{14.21}$$

Suppose, however, that we wish to impose certain prior knowledge about $\boldsymbol{\alpha}$ on our estimator. Specifically, suppose the components of $\boldsymbol{\alpha}$ have been labeled such that the prior information we wish to incorporate is with respect to the first $k$ elements, $\alpha_0, \ldots, \alpha_k$. The beliefs that will be introduced are that $(\alpha_0, \ldots, \alpha_k) = (\beta_0 - \mu_0, \ldots, \beta_k - \mu_k)$, where $\beta_i$ represents the "best prior estimate" of $\alpha_i$, and $\mu_i$ is the error in the prior information. The latter is assumed to be distributed independently of $\boldsymbol{\varepsilon}$. Letting $\boldsymbol{\beta}' = (\beta_0, \ldots, \beta_k)$, $\boldsymbol{\mu}' = (\mu_0, \ldots, \mu_k)$, and $\mathbf{A} = [\mathbf{I}\ \bar{\mathbf{0}}]$, where $\mathbf{I}$ is the $k \times k$ identity matrix and $\bar{\mathbf{0}}$ is the $k \times (n + 1 - k)$ zero matrix, we may then write

$$\boldsymbol{\beta} = \mathbf{A}\boldsymbol{\alpha} + \boldsymbol{\mu}. \tag{14.22}$$

In addition to the prior knowledge on $\boldsymbol{\beta}$, it will also be assumed that associated with the random-error vector $\boldsymbol{\mu}$ is an assigned nonsingular matrix of second-order moments $E[\boldsymbol{\mu}\boldsymbol{\mu}'] = \boldsymbol{\phi}$, where $\boldsymbol{\mu}$ is independent of $\boldsymbol{\varepsilon}$.

For example, suppose that as in the Appendix to Chapter 3 we wish to fit the regression (in logarithms)

$$Q_t = \alpha_0 + \alpha_1 V_{1t} + \alpha_2 V_{2t} + \alpha_3 V_{3t} + \epsilon_t^*$$

to the DURK data of Table 14.3. Specifically, these data are newly discovered observations from the land of GEE, whereas the data employed in the earlier analysis came from the land of WHIZ. These two nations have much in common, and we have formed some prior notions with respect to $\alpha_1$ and $\alpha_2$, seen previously to be the short-run price and income elasticities, respectively, based upon the WHIZ data. In particular, we wish to base $\boldsymbol{\beta}$ and $\boldsymbol{\phi}$ on the earlier estimates of $a_1 = -.06931$ ($s_{a_1}^2 = .02050$), and $a_2 = .06075$ ($s_{a_2}^2 = .00089$; and $s_{a_1a_2} = -.00276$). Rewrite the equation to be estimated as

$$Q_t = \theta_0 V_{1t} + \theta_1 V_{2t} + \theta_2 V_{3t} + \theta_3 + \epsilon_t^*.$$

Then, (14.22) becomes

$$\begin{pmatrix} -.06931 \\ .06075 \end{pmatrix} = \begin{bmatrix} 1 & 0 & 0 & 0 \\ 0 & 1 & 0 & 0 \end{bmatrix} \begin{pmatrix} \theta_0 = \alpha_1 \\ \theta_1 = \alpha_2 \\ \theta_2 = \alpha_3 \\ \theta_3 = \alpha_0 \end{pmatrix} + \begin{pmatrix} \mu_1 \\ \mu_2 \end{pmatrix}$$

and

$$\boldsymbol{\phi} = \begin{bmatrix} .02050 & -.00276 \\ -.00276 & .00089 \end{bmatrix}.$$

[19] H. Theil, "On the Use of Incomplete Prior Information in Regression Analysis," *Journal of the American Statistical Association*, **58**:302 (June 1963), 401–414.

TABLE 14.3

| Year | $Q_t$ | $P_t$ | $I_t$ |
|---|---|---|---|
| 1955 | 5000 | 98 | 150 |
| 1956 | 5000 | 99 | 145 |
| 1957 | 4800 | 100 | 140 |
| 1958 | 4700 | 101 | 140 |
| 1959 | 4750 | 101 | 145 |
| 1960 | 4900 | 101 | 150 |
| 1961 | 5000 | 100 | 160 |
| 1962 | 5100 | 101 | 170 |
| 1963 | 5150 | 101 | 175 |
| 1964 | 5200 | 102 | 175 |
| 1965 | 5200 | 102 | 180 |
| 1966 | 5250 | 103 | 200 |
| 1967 | 5400 | 103 | 220 |
| 1968 | 5500 | 104 | 250 |
| 1969 | 5600 | 105 | 300 |

It is important to recognize that while the prior assignments used here have been based exclusively on previous *estimates*, these may also be subjective *assessments* encompassing one's prior beliefs regarding the coefficients, and in essence one's confidence about these beliefs as reflected in the moment matrix $\boldsymbol{\phi}$.

To estimate $\boldsymbol{\alpha}$ given our prior information, (14.20) and (14.22) are first combined to form the set of equations

$$\begin{bmatrix} \mathbf{Q} \\ \boldsymbol{\beta} \end{bmatrix} = \begin{bmatrix} \mathbf{V} \\ \mathbf{A} \end{bmatrix} \boldsymbol{\alpha} + \begin{bmatrix} \boldsymbol{\varepsilon} \\ \boldsymbol{\mu} \end{bmatrix}. \tag{14.23}$$

The latter may be rewritten as

$$\mathbf{Y} = \mathbf{X}\boldsymbol{\alpha} + \mathbf{v}, \tag{14.23$'$}$$

where the second-order moments of $\mathbf{v}$ are given by

$$E[\mathbf{v}\mathbf{v}'] = E\left[\begin{pmatrix} \boldsymbol{\varepsilon} \\ \boldsymbol{\mu} \end{pmatrix} (\boldsymbol{\varepsilon}', \boldsymbol{\mu}')\right] = \begin{bmatrix} \sigma^2\mathbf{I} & \bar{\mathbf{0}} \\ \bar{\mathbf{0}} & \boldsymbol{\phi} \end{bmatrix} = \boldsymbol{\Omega}.$$

since $\boldsymbol{\varepsilon}$ and $\boldsymbol{\mu}$ have been assumed to be distributed independently of each other.

As a covariance matrix $\boldsymbol{\Omega}$ is positive definite, and so is $\boldsymbol{\Omega}^{-1}$. In this case, a nonsingular matrix $\boldsymbol{\Psi}$ can be found such that $\boldsymbol{\Omega}^{-1} = \boldsymbol{\Psi}'\boldsymbol{\Psi}$. Premultiplying (14.23′) by $\boldsymbol{\Psi}$, we obtain

$$\boldsymbol{\Psi}\mathbf{Y} = \boldsymbol{\Psi}\mathbf{X}\boldsymbol{\alpha} + \boldsymbol{\Psi}\mathbf{v}. \tag{14.23$''$}$$

Note, now, that $E[(\boldsymbol{\Psi}\mathbf{v})(\boldsymbol{\Psi}\mathbf{v})'] = E[\boldsymbol{\Psi}\mathbf{v}\mathbf{v}'\boldsymbol{\Psi}'] = \boldsymbol{\Psi}\boldsymbol{\Omega}\boldsymbol{\Psi}' = \boldsymbol{\Psi}\boldsymbol{\Psi}^{-1}[\boldsymbol{\Psi}']^{-1}\boldsymbol{\Psi}' = \mathbf{I}$. That is, if $\boldsymbol{\Psi}\mathbf{v}$ is now looked upon as a vector of random disturbances, it will be a vector whose covariance matrix has ones on the diagonal and zeros elsewhere. This satisfies the least-squares assumption that the residuals have constant variance (here, equal to 1) and are independent of one another. Further, $E[\boldsymbol{\Psi}\mathbf{v}] = \mathbf{0}$ because

$E[\mathbf{v}] = \mathbf{0}$. Hence, we can estimate $\boldsymbol{\alpha}$ by applying least squares directly to (14.23″).[20] In particular, we seek an estimate of $\boldsymbol{\alpha}$, $\hat{\mathbf{a}}$, such that $(\boldsymbol{\Psi}\mathbf{Y} - \boldsymbol{\Psi}\mathbf{X}\hat{\mathbf{a}})'(\boldsymbol{\Psi}\mathbf{Y} - \boldsymbol{\Psi}\mathbf{X}\hat{\mathbf{a}}) = \mathbf{Y}'\boldsymbol{\Psi}'\boldsymbol{\Psi}\mathbf{Y} - 2\mathbf{Y}'\boldsymbol{\Psi}'\boldsymbol{\Psi}\mathbf{X}\hat{\mathbf{a}} + \hat{\mathbf{a}}'\mathbf{X}'\boldsymbol{\Psi}'\boldsymbol{\Psi}\mathbf{X}\hat{\mathbf{a}}$ is minimized. Differentiating with respect to $\hat{\mathbf{a}}$ and equating the resultant derivative to zero,

$$\mathbf{X}'\boldsymbol{\Psi}'\boldsymbol{\Psi}\mathbf{Y} = \mathbf{X}'\boldsymbol{\Psi}'\boldsymbol{\Psi}\mathbf{X}\hat{\mathbf{a}} \quad \text{or} \quad \hat{\mathbf{a}} = [\mathbf{X}'\boldsymbol{\Psi}'\boldsymbol{\Psi}\mathbf{X}]^{-1}[\mathbf{X}'\boldsymbol{\Psi}'\boldsymbol{\Psi}\mathbf{Y}].$$

But, $\boldsymbol{\Psi}'\boldsymbol{\Psi} = \boldsymbol{\Omega}^{-1}$ by definition. Hence,

$$\hat{\mathbf{a}} = [\mathbf{X}'\boldsymbol{\Omega}^{-1}\mathbf{X}]^{-1}[\mathbf{X}'\boldsymbol{\Omega}^{-1}\mathbf{Y}]. \tag{14.24}$$

If we now write the latter equation out explicitly, substituting for $\mathbf{X}$, $\mathbf{Y}$, and $\boldsymbol{\Omega}$, we obtain

$$\hat{\mathbf{a}} = \left[ [\mathbf{V}'\ \mathbf{A}'] \begin{bmatrix} \sigma^2\mathbf{I} & \bar{\mathbf{0}} \\ \bar{\mathbf{0}} & \boldsymbol{\phi} \end{bmatrix}^{-1} \begin{bmatrix} \mathbf{V} \\ \mathbf{A} \end{bmatrix} \right]^{-1} \left[ [\mathbf{V}'\ \mathbf{A}'] \begin{bmatrix} \sigma^2\mathbf{I} & \bar{\mathbf{0}} \\ \bar{\mathbf{0}} & \boldsymbol{\phi} \end{bmatrix}^{-1} \begin{bmatrix} \mathbf{Q} \\ \boldsymbol{\beta} \end{bmatrix} \right]$$

and

$$\begin{bmatrix} \sigma^2\mathbf{I} & \bar{\mathbf{0}} \\ \bar{\mathbf{0}} & \boldsymbol{\phi} \end{bmatrix}^{-1} = \begin{bmatrix} \mathbf{I}/\sigma^2 & \bar{\mathbf{0}} \\ \bar{\mathbf{0}} & \boldsymbol{\phi}^{-1} \end{bmatrix}.$$

Making the latter substitution and performing the required matrix multiplications,

$$\hat{\mathbf{a}} = \left[ \frac{\mathbf{V}'\mathbf{V}}{\sigma^2} + \mathbf{A}'\boldsymbol{\phi}^{-1}\mathbf{A} \right]^{-1} \left[ \frac{\mathbf{V}'\mathbf{Q}}{\sigma^2} + \mathbf{A}'\boldsymbol{\phi}^{-1}\boldsymbol{\beta} \right]. \tag{14.24'}$$

Comparing (14.24′) with (14.21), the ordinary least-squares estimator, we immediately observe that in the absence of prior commitments $\mathbf{A} = \bar{\mathbf{0}}$ and $\hat{\mathbf{a}} = \mathbf{a}$. Moreover, the greater is $\sigma^2$ the smaller is the role played by the sample information (in the form of $\mathbf{V}'\mathbf{V}$ and $\mathbf{V}'\mathbf{Q}$) in the estimation of $\hat{\mathbf{a}}$; similarly, the greater is $\boldsymbol{\phi}$ the smaller is the role played by the prior information (in the form of $\mathbf{A}'$ and $\boldsymbol{\beta}$) in the estimation of $\hat{\mathbf{a}}$. In essence, the estimator gives less relative weight to sample information the greater is the variance in the unobserved random-error term and the lesser is the potential error in the prior estimate—a reaction evidencing uncommonly good judgment.

Unfortunately, however, (14.24′) requires knowledge of $\sigma^2$, the variance of *unobserved* disturbances. Since a good dogmatic belief would suggest that $\sigma^2$ will not be available, one must also assign it a value. One possibility that immediately pops up is to simply take as an estimate of $\sigma^2$ the variance of the residuals from the ordinary least-squares equation. Unfortunately, too, one's prior beliefs and the sample information are not necessarily going to be compatible. As noted in the Appendix to this chapter, however, Theil has also suggested a procedure for assessing their compatibility.

## 14.8 CONCLUSIONS

In this chapter we have attempted to demonstrate that even though the course charted for a firm may be of a random character, some very definite and informative things can be inferred about that course. Further, and even when on the surface the

[20] For more general details on this, the generalized least-squares approach, see A. C. Aitken, "On Least Squares and Linear Combination of Observations," *Proceedings of the Royal Society of Edinburgh*, **55**(1934–35), 42–48; and H. Theil, *Economic Forecasts and Policy* (Amsterdam: North-Holland Publishing Co., 1961), pp. 220–221.

available data might make it appear otherwise, it may be possible to get a solid grip on what this random process is like, solely on the basis of readily available information. We have also attempted to indicate the practicality of incorporating prior judgments into the estimation of parameters of importance to decision making within the firm.

In the first case, we narrowed our focus to one particular form of random process, the Markov chain. In the second case, we concentrated on one approach to utilizing prior information in least-squares estimation. This particular emphasis should not be allowed to conceal the fact that the possibilities are far more general, and the options are many and varied. Rather, it is hoped that the preceding discussion will provide a continuing stimulus for searching out and expanding upon the specific techniques to suit the specific needs of a particular problem.

# Appendix to Chapter 14

## 14A.1 REGULAR MATRICES AND THE FIXED POINT VECTOR[21]

If $\mathbf{P}$ is a regular transition probability matrix, we shall show that a fixed point vector $\mathbf{a}'$ exists such that: (1) $\mathbf{P}^t \to \mathbf{A}$ as $t \to \infty$, where each row of $\mathbf{A}$ is given by $\mathbf{a}'$; (2) $\mathbf{q}_0'\mathbf{P}^t \to \mathbf{a}'$ as $t \to \infty$ for any probability vector $\mathbf{q}_0' = (q_{10}, \ldots, q_{n0})$; (3) $\mathbf{P}^t\mathbf{c} \to \mathbf{d} = (\bar{d}, \ldots, \bar{d})'$ as $t \to \infty$ for any vector $\mathbf{c}' = (c_1, \ldots, c_n)$, where $\mathbf{d} = f(\mathbf{c})$.

On the one hand, suppose it is indeed the case that $\mathbf{P}^t \to \mathbf{A}$ as $t \to \infty$. Then $\mathbf{q}_0'\mathbf{P}^t \to \mathbf{q}_0'\mathbf{A} = \mathbf{a}'$ as $t \to \infty$ because by the assumption $\sum_i q_{i0}a_{ij} = a_{ij}\sum q_{i0} = a_j$ for all $i$. Similarly, $\mathbf{P}^t\mathbf{c} \to \mathbf{Ac}$ as $t \to \infty$, and $\mathbf{Ac} = \mathbf{d}$ because by the assumption $\sum_j a_{ij}c_j = \bar{d}$ for all $i$.

On the other hand, suppose that $\mathbf{q}_0'\mathbf{P}^t \to \mathbf{a}'$ as $t \to \infty$. Then, the typical term $a_j$ is given by $a_j = \sum_i q_{i0}p_{ij}^{(t)}$ for all $\mathbf{q}_0'$. But if it is true for *all* $\mathbf{q}_0'$, it must be true for $\mathbf{q}_0' = \mathbf{e}'$, where $\mathbf{e}'$ is *any* unit vector. Thus $a_j = \sum_i e_i p_{ij}^{(t)} = p_{ij}^{(t)}$ irrespective of which $e_i = 1$. Hence, $p_{ij}^{(t)} = p_{kj}^{(t)} = a_j$, and each row of $\mathbf{P}^t$ approaches $\mathbf{a}'$. Further, if $\mathbf{P}^t\mathbf{c} \to \mathbf{d}$ as $t \to \infty$ and $\sum_j p_{ij}^{(t)}c_j = \bar{d}$ holds for all $\mathbf{c}$, it also holds for $\mathbf{c} = \mathbf{e}$—any $\mathbf{e}$. Hence, $\sum_j p_{ij}^{(t)}e_j = p_{ij}^{(t)} = \bar{d}_j = a_j$ for all $i$. Again, then, each row of $\mathbf{P}^t$ approaches $\mathbf{a}'$.

It follows, therefore, that any one of the properties implies the others. We shall establish the third property, from which the other two immediately follow.

Let $\mathbf{P}$ be a regular $n \times n$ transition probability matrix, and $c_m$ and $c_M$ be the smallest and largest elements, respectively, in the $n \times 1$ vector $\mathbf{c} = (c_1, \ldots, c_n)'$. Then, $\mathbf{Pc} = \mathbf{d} = (d_1, \ldots, d_n)'$ yields an $n \times 1$ vector whose smallest and largest elements are $d_m$ and $d_M$. But, since the rows of $\mathbf{P}$ are probability vectors, $d_i$ is simply the mean of the $c_j$'s weighted by the $i$th row of probabilities in $\mathbf{P}$. If $p_m > 0$ is the smallest $p_{ij}$, then even if $p_m$ multiplies $c_M$ and all the rest of the probability weight in that row of $\mathbf{P}$ goes to $c_m$,

$$d_m \geq p_m c_M + (1 - p_m)c_m;$$

that is, the average lies somewhere between the extreme values. Similarly,

$$d_M \leq p_m c_m + (1 - p_m)c_M;$$

that is, if the extreme values get the extreme weights—highest the highest and

[21] This development mirrors that of John G. Kemeny, H. Mirkil, J. Laurie Snell, and G. L. Thompson, *Finite Mathematical Structures* (Englewood Cliffs, N.J.: Prentice-Hall, Inc., 1958), pp. 399–401.

lowest and lowest—the resultant average is at least as big as with any other distribution of weights. Multiplying both sides of the first inequality by $-1$ (which changes the direction of the inequality) and adding it to the second,

$$d_M - d_m \leq (1 - 2p_m)(c_M - c_m). \tag{14.25}$$

Now, since $\mathbf{P}$ is regular, at some stage $T$ all $p_{ij}^{(T)} > 0$. Let $p_m^{(T)}$ be the smallest element of $\mathbf{P}^T$. By (14.25) $\mathbf{P}^T\mathbf{c} = \mathbf{d}^T$ is a vector such that

$$d_M^{(T)} - d_m^{(T)} \leq (1 - 2p_m^{(T)})(c_M - c_m).$$

Hence, $\mathbf{P}^{2T}\mathbf{c} = \mathbf{P}^T\mathbf{d}^T = \mathbf{d}^{2T}$ is a vector such that

$$d_M^{(2T)} - d_m^{(2T)} \leq (1 - 2p_m^{(T)})(d_M^{(T)} - d_m^{(T)})$$

and hence

$$d_M^{(2T)} - d_m^{(2T)} \leq (1 - 2p_m^{(T)})^2(c_M - c_m).$$

Because $p_m^{(T)}$ is the smallest element in $\mathbf{P}^T$, $p_m^{(T)} \leq .5$. Proceeding in this way, then,

$$d_M^{(kT)} - d_m^{(kT)} \leq (1 - 2p_m^{(T)})^k(c_M - c_m),$$

where $(1 - 2p_m^{(T)})^k \to 0$ as $k \to \infty$. Hence $d_M^{(kT)} \to d_m^{(kT)}$ as $k \to \infty$, or $\mathbf{P}^T\mathbf{c} \to \mathbf{d} = (\bar{d}, \ldots, \bar{d})$ as $T \to \infty$. Thus the third asserted property of a regular transition probability matrix is seen to hold, so the first two must hold; and since $\mathbf{P}^{t+1} = \mathbf{P}^t\mathbf{P} \to \mathbf{AP} = \mathbf{A}$ as $t \to \infty$, $\mathbf{a}'\mathbf{P} = \mathbf{a}'$; and since the fixed point vectors are determined as the solutions to $n$ linear independent equations, the vector is unique.

## 14A.2 AN ILLUSTRATION OF THE THEIL-REY ALGORITHM

The *first* twenty observations in Table 14.2 are the $x_{it}$'s $(i = 1, \ldots, 4)$, and the *last* twenty observations are the $x_{i(t+1)}$'s $(i = 1, \ldots, 4)$. We calculate the following four regressions from these data:

$$\begin{aligned}
x_{1(t+1)} &= .7852 - .6492x_{2t} - .8023x_{3t} - .4681x_{4t} + e_{1(t+1)} && (R^2 = .7245),\\
x_{2(t+1)} &= .6869 - .7482x_{1t} - .3571x_{3t} - .3425x_{4t} + e_{2(t+1)} && (R^2 = .4827),\\
x_{3(t+1)} &= .6043 - .2796x_{1t} - .4633x_{2t} - 1.1554x_{4t} + e_{3(t+1)} && (R^2 = .6787),\\
x_{4(t+1)} &= .8896 - .9382x_{1t} - .8535x_{2t} - .8067x_{3t} + e_{4(t+1)} && (R^2 = .7024).
\end{aligned}$$

Thus, to obtain, say, the second *column* of $\hat{\mathbf{P}}$, we need only the second of these four equations. The intercept is $\hat{p}_{22} = .6869$; and $-.7482 = \hat{p}_{12} - \hat{p}_{22} = \hat{p}_{12} - .6869$, or $\hat{p}_{12} = -.7482 + .6869 = -.0613$. Similarly, $\hat{p}_{32} = -.3571 + .6869 = .3298$ and $\hat{p}_{42} = -.3425 + .6869 = .3444$. The complete matrix $\hat{\mathbf{P}}$ is given by

$$\hat{\mathbf{P}} = \begin{array}{c} \\ E_1 \\ E_2 \\ E_3 \\ E_4 \end{array}\begin{array}{c} \begin{array}{cccc} E_1 & E_2 & E_3 & E_4 \end{array} \\ \begin{bmatrix} .7852 & -.0613 & .3247 & -.0486 \\ .1360 & .6869 & .1410 & .0361 \\ -.0171 & .3298 & .6043 & .0829 \\ .3171 & .3444 & -.5511 & .8896 \end{bmatrix} \end{array}.$$

$\hat{\mathbf{P}}$ could also be obtained directly from (14.14) after computing

$$[\Sigma\, \mathbf{x}_t\mathbf{x}_t']^{-1} = \begin{bmatrix} 24.65 & -9.08 & -13.13 & -23.34 \\ -9.08 & 39.66 & -19.33 & 40.98 \\ -13.13 & -19.33 & 28.69 & 34.39 \\ -23.34 & -40.98 & 34.39 & 115.43 \end{bmatrix}$$

and

$$[\Sigma\, \mathbf{x}_t\mathbf{x}'_{t+1}] = \begin{bmatrix} 2.3879 & 2.1071 & 1.6440 & .7674 \\ 2.1187 & 1.9016 & 1.4631 & .6905 \\ 1.6106 & 1.4512 & 1.1564 & .5134 \\ .7582 & .6720 & .5027 & .2552 \end{bmatrix}.$$

There are four constraints violated by $\hat{\mathbf{P}}$, and setting the violated constraints binding, one at a time, does not yield a feasible solution. Setting pairs or triads binding does not yield a feasible solution either. For example, setting $p_{31} = 0$ and $p_{43} = 0$, and applying (14.19) by substituting in the appropriate numerical values from the above matrices,

$$0 = -.0171 + \theta^0_{31}(28.69)(\tfrac{3}{4}) + \theta^0_{43}(34.39)(-\tfrac{1}{4}),$$
$$0 = -.5511 + \theta^0_{31}(34.39)(-\tfrac{1}{4}) + \theta^0_{43}(115.43)(\tfrac{3}{4}).$$

Solving this pair of equations, we obtain $\theta^0_{31} = .003473$ and $\theta^0_{43} = .006711$. Given these values, all other $p^*_{ij}$ are determined from (14.19). For example,

$$\begin{aligned} p^*_{32} &= \hat{p}_{32} + \theta^0_{31}x_{33}g_{12} + \theta^0_{43}x_{34}g_{32} \\ &= .3298 - .003473(7.1725) - .006711(8.5975) = .2472 \end{aligned}$$

and

$$\mathbf{P}^* = \begin{array}{c} \\ E_1 \\ E_2 \\ E_3 \\ E_4 \end{array} \begin{array}{c} \begin{array}{cccc} E_1 & E_2 & E_3 & E_4 \end{array} \\ \begin{bmatrix} .7901 & -.0107 & .2186 & .0020 \\ .1544 & .7725 & -.0485 & .1216 \\ 0 & .2472 & .7525 & .0003 \\ .2130 & .1209 & 0 & .6661 \end{bmatrix} \end{array}.$$

We see in this a situation in which not only are two constraints still violated, but one of the violated constraints, $p^*_{23} = -.0485$, had not been violated prior to the addition of the two new restrictions. This points up the fact that even though a particular set of restrictions are violated in the initial unconstrained estimation, the set of constraints that are ultimately set in binding form will not necessarily be a subset of the initially violated constraints.

Moreover, there may be more than one optimal solution. In the present illustration, for example, *either* the transition matrix of Section 14.2 *or* the matrix

$$\mathbf{P} = \begin{array}{c} \\ E_1 \\ E_2 \\ E_3 \\ E_4 \end{array} \begin{array}{c} \begin{array}{cccc} E_1 & E_2 & E_3 & E_4 \end{array} \\ \begin{bmatrix} .8080 & .0058 & .1862 & 0 \\ .1372 & .7534 & 0 & .1094 \\ 0 & .2500 & .7370 & .0130 \\ .2049 & .1162 & 0 & .6789 \end{bmatrix} \end{array}$$

yields an optimum solution (the sums of the squared residuals are equal for each). It is interesting to note that in each case we must set $p_{23} = 0$, although this constraint is not violated in the initial estimation. To show that the above is an optimum, we must resolve the problem four additional times, releasing $p_{14}$, $p_{23}$, $p_{31}$, and $p_{43}$ while holding the other three binding to assure that the solutions thus obtained are nonfeasible. Such is indeed the case. Specifically, where the $ij$ in $\hat{\mathbf{P}}_{ij}$ denotes the released constraint,

$$\hat{\mathbf{P}}_{14} = \begin{array}{c} \\ E_1 \\ E_2 \\ E_3 \\ E_4 \end{array} \begin{array}{c} \begin{array}{cccc} E_1 & E_2 & E_3 & E_4 \end{array} \\ \begin{bmatrix} .8035 & -.0003 & .1844 & .0124 \\ .1411 & .7549 & 0 & .1040 \\ 0 & .2536 & .7396 & .0067 \\ .2079 & .1235 & 0 & .6687 \end{bmatrix} \end{array},$$

$$\hat{\mathbf{P}}_{23} = \begin{array}{c} \\ E_1 \\ E_2 \\ E_3 \\ E_4 \end{array} \begin{array}{c} \begin{array}{cccc} E_1 & E_2 & E_3 & E_4 \end{array} \\ \begin{bmatrix} .7907 & -.0099 & .2192 & 0 \\ .1539 & .7724 & -.0490 & .1226 \\ 0 & .2466 & .7522 & .0012 \\ .2126 & .1198 & 0 & .6676 \end{bmatrix} \end{array},$$

$$\hat{\mathbf{P}}_{31} = \begin{array}{c} \\ E_1 \\ E_2 \\ E_3 \\ E_4 \end{array} \begin{array}{c} \begin{array}{cccc} E_1 & E_2 & E_3 & E_4 \end{array} \\ \begin{bmatrix} .8355 & -.0110 & .1755 & 0 \\ .1828 & .7337 & 0 & .0835 \\ -.0669 & .2800 & .7528 & .0341 \\ .1328 & .1602 & 0 & .7070 \end{bmatrix} \end{array},$$

$$\hat{\mathbf{P}}_{43} = \begin{array}{c} \\ E_1 \\ E_2 \\ E_3 \\ E_4 \end{array} \begin{array}{c} \begin{array}{cccc} E_1 & E_2 & E_3 & E_4 \end{array} \\ \begin{bmatrix} .7400 & -.0867 & .3466 & 0 \\ .1726 & .7527 & 0 & .0746 \\ 0 & .3037 & .6789 & .0174 \\ .3200 & .2956 & -.3863 & .7707 \end{bmatrix} \end{array}.$$

It might also be noted that experience with the procedure suggests that the non-negativity requirement does not have particularly adverse effects on the $R^2$ values for the columns. In the present case, for example, with the matrix above, the four column $R^2$'s are reduced by only .0156, .0320, .0722, and .0291, respectively. This comment is not intended to emphasize the importance of the $R^2$'s in assessing the applicability of the Markov assumption, but to point up that the reduction in $R^2$ is a small price to pay for the extremely useful transition probability matrix that the constrained estimation yields.

## 14A.3 AN ILLUSTRATION OF PRIOR INFORMATION AND LEAST-SQUARES ESTIMATION

The regression equation we are interested in fitting to the data of Table 14.3 is

$$Q_t = \alpha_3 P_t^{\alpha_0} I_t^{\alpha_1} Q_{t-1}^{\alpha_2} \epsilon_t,$$

where the $\alpha_i$'s have been so labeled because prior information is available for $\alpha_0$ and $\alpha_1$. The ordinary least-squares regression is

$$Q_t = 4891.67 P_t^{-.98757} I_t^{.20878} Q_{t-1}^{.41329} e_t \qquad (R^2 = .9472).$$

We wish to make use of the prior information that sets

$$\boldsymbol{\beta} = \begin{pmatrix} -.06931 \\ .06075 \end{pmatrix} \quad \text{and} \quad \boldsymbol{\phi} = \begin{bmatrix} .02050 & -.00276 \\ -.00276 & .00089 \end{bmatrix}.$$

For the present data, ordinary least squares yields $S^2/N_c = .00003$, which we first take as an estimate of $\sigma^2$. We also determine that

$$\mathbf{V'V} = \begin{bmatrix} 60.35967 & 67.53366 & 111.41876 & 30.08957 \\ 67.53366 & 75.67517 & 124.66876 & 33.66161 \\ 111.41876 & 124.66876 & 205.67175 & 55.54268 \\ 30.08957 & 33.66161 & 55.54268 & 15.00000 \end{bmatrix},$$

and $(\mathbf{V'Q})' = (111.55314, 124.82314, 205.91974, 55.60963)$. We additionally require

$$\mathbf{A'\phi^{-1}A} = \begin{bmatrix} 83.74587 & 259.70604 & 0 & 0 \\ 259.70604 & 1928.97604 & 0 & 0 \\ 0 & 0 & 0 & 0 \\ 0 & 0 & 0 & 0 \end{bmatrix},$$

as well as $(\mathbf{A'\phi^{-1}\beta})' = (9.97273, 99.18507, 0, 0)$. Note that the zeros appear in positions associated with variables about whose parameters we are not making prior judgments.

Then, we may compute

$$\left[\frac{\mathbf{V'V}}{.00003} + \mathbf{A'\phi^{-1}A}\right]^{-1} = \begin{bmatrix} .01725360 & -.00197125 & .00330244 & -.04241495 \\ -.00197125 & .00057807 & -.00189599 & .00967758 \\ .00330244 & -.00189599 & .01232548 & -.04800912 \\ -.04241495 & .00967758 & -.04800912 & .24113799 \end{bmatrix},$$

$$\left(\frac{\mathbf{V'Q}}{.00003} + \mathbf{A'\phi^{-1}\beta}\right) = \begin{pmatrix} 3718447.973 \\ 4160870.518 \\ 6863991.333 \\ 1853654.333 \end{pmatrix}.$$

In accordance with (14.24′), we premultiply the second expression by the first to obtain $\hat{\mathbf{a}}' = (-.23836, .11303, .65702, 1.66885)$. The estimated equation is

$$Q_t = 46.65P_t^{-.23836}I_t^{.11303}Q_{t-1}^{.65702}e_t.$$

In similar fashion, if we estimate $\sigma^2$ by .0000175, the variance of the residuals for the regression from Chapter 3 and the land of WHIZ, the estimated equation is

$$Q_t = 87.18P_t^{-.30379}I_t^{.16149}Q_{t-1}^{.56616}e_t.$$

The latter regression is closer to the ordinary least-squares equation than is the former, because the estimate of $\sigma^2$ is smaller and hence the sample information is accorded relatively greater weight in the latter estimation.

In each case the regression parameters, particularly the price elasticity and constant coefficient, are more than slightly removed from the ordinary least-squares estimates. To get some notion of the compatibility of the sample and prior information, we make use of Theil's *compatibility statistic*

$$\gamma = (\boldsymbol{\beta} - \mathbf{A}\hat{\mathbf{a}})'[\sigma^2\mathbf{A}(\mathbf{V'V})^{-1}\mathbf{A}' + \boldsymbol{\phi}]^{-1}(\boldsymbol{\beta} - \mathbf{A}\hat{\mathbf{a}}).$$

The latter is distributed as chi-square with $k$ degrees of freedom.[22] In the present illustration,

$$[\mathbf{V'V}]^{-1} = \begin{bmatrix} 5126.55676 & -370.16132 & 62.56526 & -9684.71365 \\ -370.16132 & 63.94336 & -165.18371 & 1210.68694 \\ 62.56526 & -165.18371 & 866.89627 & -2964.79697 \\ -9684.71365 & 1210.68694 & -2964.79697 & 27688.59779 \end{bmatrix},$$

with $\sigma^2$ set at .00003,

$$(\boldsymbol{\beta} - \mathbf{A}\hat{\mathbf{a}})' = (.16905, -.05228); \qquad [\sigma^2\mathbf{A}(\mathbf{V'V})^{-1}\mathbf{A}' + \boldsymbol{\phi}]^{-1} = \begin{bmatrix} 9.43957 & 46.55960 \\ 46.55960 & 585.52220 \end{bmatrix}.$$

The estimate of $\gamma$ is $\hat{\gamma} = 1.05$. Similarly, with $\sigma^2 = .0000175$, we find $\hat{\gamma} = 5.82$ From tables of the chi-square distribution with $k = 2$ degrees of freedom, the 20 percent significance point is 3.2 and the 5 percent significance point is 6.0. The GEE data and the WHIZ inferences would not appear to be obviously compatible. As noted in Chapter 3, one can easily generate high $R^2$'s when making up one's data, but it would seem that one will not necessarily be a consistent "data constructor."

## EXERCISES

1. Show that (14.2) is a valid probability function.
2. Show that in a Markov chain with a single absorbing state $E_a$, the probability of being absorbed in $E_a = 1$.
3. Show that if $E_t$ is a transient state in a Markov chain, the probability of returning to $E_t$ is less than unity.
4. Show that in an absorbing Markov chain (a) the probability is one that the process will be absorbed in one of the closed sets; and (b) if we consider a square submatrix of the original transition probability matrix corresponding solely to a closed set of states $C$, then this submatrix will retain all the properties of an irreducible Markov chain.
5. Show that in an irreducible Markov chain all states belong to the same class and have the same period, and that every state can be reached from every other state.
6. Show that if $E_i$ is persistent and has period $t$, then $p_{ii}^{(nt)} \to tu_i^{-1}$ as $n \to \infty$.
7. Show that if $\mathbf{P}$ is a stochastic matrix, $(\mathbf{I} - \mathbf{P})^{-1}$ does not exist.
8. Show that the fundamental matrix for a regular Markov chain,

$$\mathbf{Z} = \mathbf{I} + \sum_{n=1}^{\infty} (\mathbf{P}^n - \mathbf{A}).$$

Also show that the four properties ascribed to $\mathbf{Z}$ do in fact hold, and that such a $\mathbf{Z}$ exists.

9. Show that it isn't exactly a coincidence that in the illustration in the text the rows of $\mathbf{Z}$ sum to one.
10. Consider the following transition probability matrix:

$$\mathbf{P} = \begin{array}{c} \\ E_1 \\ E_2 \\ E_3 \\ E_4 \\ E_5 \end{array} \begin{array}{c} \begin{array}{ccccc} E_1 & E_2 & E_3 & E_4 & E_5 \end{array} \\ \begin{bmatrix} .4 & 0 & .1 & .5 & 0 \\ .3 & .2 & .1 & .2 & .2 \\ .1 & .0 & .6 & .3 & 0 \\ .2 & 0 & .1 & .7 & 0 \\ 0 & 1 & 0 & 0 & 0 \end{bmatrix} \end{array}.$$

[22] "On the Use of Incomplete Prior Information in Regression Analysis," pp. 406–407.

(a) Which if any are the persistent and which are the transient states?
(b) Determine the means and variances of times prior to absorption from any transient state to each persistent state.
(c) Determine the expected number of times that each transient state will be entered, prior to absorption, given an initial probability vector $\mathbf{q}_0 = (.1, .6, .1, .1, .1)$. What are the variances?
(d) Determine $p_{11}^{(t)}$, $p_{22}^{(t)}$, $p_{34}^{(t)}$, and $p_{14}^{(t)}$ as $t \to \infty$.

11. What inferences would you draw about the brewing industry from the matrix derived in the Appendix to this chapter?

12. Consider the market-share data in the following table. These are the percent of $G_3$ firm sales held by each of the four firms in the group:

| Year | $E_1$ | $E_2$ | $E_3$ | $E_4$ |
|---|---|---|---|---|
| 1944 | .1925 | .2841 | .2607 | .2627 |
| 1945 | .2027 | .2906 | .2540 | .2527 |
| 1946 | .2069 | .2840 | .2484 | .2607 |
| 1947 | .2326 | .2819 | .2407 | .2448 |
| 1948 | .2715 | .2657 | .2109 | .2519 |
| 1949 | .2936 | .2845 | .2306 | .1913 |
| 1950 | .2673 | .2818 | .2385 | .2124 |
| 1951 | .2511 | .2651 | .2529 | .2309 |
| 1952 | .2587 | .2620 | .2477 | .2316 |
| 1953 | .2475 | .2848 | .2329 | .2348 |
| 1954 | .2576 | .2811 | .2277 | .2336 |
| 1955 | .2764 | .2666 | .2288 | .2282 |
| 1956 | .2684 | .2587 | .2501 | .2228 |
| 1957 | .2666 | .2574 | .2567 | .2193 |
| 1958 | .3018 | .2206 | .2675 | .2101 |
| 1959 | .3302 | .1925 | .2834 | .1939 |
| 1960 | .3546 | .1767 | .2784 | .1903 |
| 1961 | .3683 | .1541 | .2491 | .2285 |
| 1962 | .3943 | .1468 | .2478 | .2111 |
| 1963 | .4101 | .1367 | .2384 | .2147 |
| 1964 | .4163 | .1246 | .2578 | .2013 |

(a) Show that the $\mathbf{D} = \mathbf{I}$ minimum-sum-of-squared-residuals estimator of $\mathbf{P}$ is given by

$$\mathbf{P}^* = \begin{array}{c} \\ E_1 \\ E_2 \\ E_3 \\ E_4 \end{array} \begin{array}{c} \begin{array}{cccc} E_1 & E_2 & E_3 & E_4 \end{array} \\ \begin{bmatrix} .9394 & 0 & .0606 & 0 \\ 0 & .9113 & .0665 & .0222 \\ 0 & 0 & .8615 & .1385 \\ .1256 & .0644 & 0 & .8100 \end{bmatrix} \end{array}.$$

(b) Determine $\mathbf{a}'$ and suggest some of the implications of this fixed point vector.

13. Suppose one's prior belief is that the average cost curve in the brewing industry is U-shaped. In particular, if the general form of the curve is $C_t = \alpha_0 + \alpha_1 Q_t + \alpha_2 Q_t^2 + \epsilon_t$, it is felt that the values of $\alpha_1$ and $\alpha_2$ are $a_1 = -.01$ and $a_2 = .001$, respectively, with standard errors of $\sigma_{a_1} = .01$ and $\sigma_{a_2} = .002$. It is also believed that $\sigma_{a_1 a_2} = -.00001$. Using Theil's approach, reestimate the average cost curve for the data of Table 5.3.

14. Suppose one believes that, in the land of GEE, the adjustment coefficient $\lambda = .9$ ($\sigma_\lambda = .05$). Using Theil's approach, determine the long-run price and income elasticities of demand.

# 15

# MICROECONOMICS AND THE FIRM: A Preliminary, If Parting, Comment

## 15.1 INTRODUCTION

It might seem a reasonable presumption that a plethora of models, matrices, and manipulations centered on decision making and the theory of the firm would provide ample documentation for a series of positive results and definite conclusions. Such a presumption, however, is at least a bit premature.

In this book we have attempted to present a broad and diversified, if necessarily incomplete, description of what microeconomic theory and quantitative methods are able to offer—both to management concerned with decision making in the modern business world and to the economist concerned with the analysis and measurement of microeconomic phenomena. The heterogeneous product of these efforts has been a potpourri of tools and ideas encouraging the following beliefs: (1) Although economic science has a good deal to offer to the modern manager, these offerings will not necessarily ease the latter's decision-making burdens. Over the long haul, however, they should certainly make the results more palatable, and help the manager to stay around long enough to enjoy the sweet and survive the bitter; (2) This selection of offerings is growing by leaps and bounds, not simply in an ad hoc manner, but with a purposiveness that has the real-world *firm's* and *manager's* needs and wants in clear focus as an end to be met; (3) Extrapolating from past trends, what has been accomplished thus far will be dwarfed by new developments in a future that will be upon us all too soon. In this future, progress in computer technology and modern mathematics will combine with an improved understanding of the forces that motivate management in complex organizations to obsolete much of what we currently hold so dear.

It is precisely because we have made only the *initial* strides on what may well be a very arduous path from theory to practice that, in lieu of conclusions, a few brief closing remarks are offered in the vein of a preliminary report.

## 15.2 THE IMPORTANCE OF MICROECONOMIC MODELS

It should now be apparent that "the" economic theory of the firm is not a single package of assumptions and normative prescriptions, despite any strong nostalgic ties that one might have towards the neoclassical model. Instead, "the" theory of the firm is a *conglomeration* of models that are constantly being refined and reevaluated in an effort to have them more accurately depict the milieu in which managerial decision making actually takes place. Nevertheless, all of these models do have a common bond: they attempt to indicate how the levels of those decision variables over which the decision maker may be assumed to exercise control, such as price and output, will be established, and to do so with the end in mind of optimizing a specific criterion function. As such, they are normative models prescribing how a *given* decision maker *should* behave when *he* is placed in a *specific* situation—if he wants to achieve a *particular* goal. They are not descriptive models showing how decision makers *actually do* behave in given situations.

It would be unfortunate for one to be ensnared by the mistaken and misleading belief that the economist expects *all* decision makers, or indeed *any*, to blindly follow the dictates of these models—even when the models have been modified to suit the particulars of an individual decision maker's problem. It would also be unfortunate for one to fail to recognize that the level of abstraction of these models *demands* their modification if they are to be suitable instruments for managerial decision making. It would be equally unfortunate, however, for one to fall victim to the erroneous misconception that the intensive and detailed analysis of a world that never has existed, and never will, has no virtues or rewards. The models of microeconomics have considerable inherent merit that more than justify the theorist's, *as well as* the practitioner's, efforts to refine them and grasp their implications.

First, as *vehicles of analysis* microeconomic models help the economist gain a better understanding of the directions in which the firm, and subsequently the economy, will tend to move in response to changes such as shifts in demand, tax impositions, and technological advances. The economist thus can better analyze the potential impact of policies that will alter the status quo, or the effect of alterations in the decision-making parameters that are part and parcel of a dynamic economic system. At the same time, the models offer the decision maker of the real world a flexible framework within which to construct specialized models for his own purposes.

Second, the models help to condition one in a *method of thinking*, the marginal analysis, so general in nature that its basic philosophy applies to literally all spheres of decision making. Marginal analysis, be it with respect to utility functions, revenue and cost curves, or preference functions, may be built on a foundation of intuitively obvious and geometrically trivial principles, and it may be deceptively simple, but it is no less potent for its simplicity. It clearly demonstrates the importance of assessing the *incremental* benefits and costs of a specific course of action, *in conjunction with* an assessment of the implications of minor variations on the major theme to help assure that a superior choice has not been overlooked. Marginal analysis tells the decision maker what to look for if he wants to reach *better* decisions, and forces him to realize that, in the absence of knowledge of all possible alternatives, the *best* decision will not necessarily be the best of all possible worlds; it can only be the best of the finitely small number of worlds that have come to his attention.

Third, the models of the firm *call attention to some vitally important aspects* of microeconomic decision making. In particular, the models point up those variables and parameters that are of the utmost importance to a particular decision and its outcome. Additionally, they force one into an unavoidable awareness of how crucial the subjective ingredient is and of the influence that it will necessarily exert on these parameters. We see from these models that quantitative precision can never *replace* subjective judgment and experience, nor can objective criteria *replace* individual preferences. Rather, these *all* are important elements to be *blended* into the decision process.

Moreover, these models make it painfully clear that the questions of rationality, uncertainty, and individuality are not to be dismissed and heroically assumed into the background. The representative and rational entrepreneur reaching decisions in a certain world is simply too fictitious a character to command all of the analyst's attention. Chance, irrationality, and personal peccadilloes are omnipresent ingredients that affect and effect individual decisions. We must improve our understanding of these, become more appreciative of the roles they play, and remain tolerant of the need to intimately involve them in our decision processes—for they will be with us whether we like it or not.

## 15.3 THE IMPORTANCE OF QUANTITATIVE METHODS

Fortunately, the emphasis on the personalistic and probabilistic features of decision making is by no means incompatible with the desire to instill in our models the mathematical rigor that permits us to take advantage of a wide range of quantitative tools. Instead, we have seen that we can indeed translate subjective variables into the language of mathematics and incorporate these directly into the models we build and into the decision-making algorithms we develop. Further, we have seen that in order to assign values to the parameters to be employed in the models, there are two particularly interesting and important statistical disciplines that one who is interested in aiding managerial decision making can ill afford to neglect: econometrics and statistical decision theory.

The economist has an important role to play in assisting management in its decision-making chores. To realize his full potential in this role, however, he must not merely look upon himself as, say, a "price theorist," an "econometrician," or an "operations researcher." In a very real sense he must be all of these. The models that he builds to aid in managerial decision making will normally have to reflect the marriage of all of these disciplines in order to reap the full benefits of any one. The "economist" part of the analyst builds the models, the "mathematician" part manipulates the models, and the "statistician" part provides the numbers from which the specific recommendations will follow.[1] Hopefully, his "behaviorist" part will make the models persuasive enough that management will confidently accept and act upon these recommendations as a matter of course—and not regret it. Simultaneously, perhaps the economist will become sufficiently tolerant of management's failure to accept and act upon all his recommendations—and of the vagaries of chance that fail to penalize this obviously cruel, if considered, neglect.

[1] The "entrepreneur" part of him persuades someone to hire a computer programmer to do the honors.

# INDEX